# Great Outdoor Guide

## to Southern California & Baja

Also available:

**Frommer's Great Outdoor Guide to Northern California**

**Frommer's Great Outdoor Guide to New England**

**Frommer's Great Outdoor Guide to the Pacific Northwest**

**Frommer's®**

# Great Outdoor Guide to Southern California & Baja

## by Andrew Rice

MACMILLAN • USA

## MACMILLAN TRAVEL USA

A Pearson Education Macmillan Company
1633 Broadway
New York, NY 10019

Find us online at **www.frommers.com**

Copyright © 1999 by Ahsuog, Inc.
All maps copyright © by Ahsuog, Inc.

ISBN 0-02-861832-7
ISSN 1522-0583

Editors: Neil E. Schlecht and Jeff Soloway
Production Editor: Christina Van Camp
Design by Amy Peppler Adams, designLab
Digital Cartography by John Decamillis,
    Roberta Stockwell, and Raffaele
    DeGennaro
Photo Editor: Richard Fox
Page Creation by Natalie Evans and Linda
    Quigley

Special Sales
Bulk purchases (10+ copies) of Frommer's
and selected Macmillan travel guides are
available to corporations, organizations,
mail-order catalogs, institutions, and
charities at special discounts, and can be
customized to suit individual needs. For
more information write to Special Sales,
Macmillan General Reference, 1633
Broadway, New York, NY 10019.

Manufactured in the United States of America

**Andrew Rice** tries to spend as
little time indoors as possible. When
not on the road for *Outside, Islands,* and
a number of other magazines, he lives
in Santa Monica. He is also the author
of *Frommer's Great Outdoor Guide to
Northern California.*

# Contents

# 3 The Channel Islands: Southern California's Offshore Wilderness . . . . . . . . . . . . . . . . . . . . . . . . . . . . . . . . . . . 63

# 4 Santa Monica Bay & Mountains: Malibu, L.A. County Beaches & the Hollywood Hills . . . . . . . . . . . . . . . . . . . . . . . . 98

# 5 The Angeles & San Bernardino National Forests: L.A.'s Eastern Mountains ...................................128

# List of Maps

**Invitation to the Reader**

In researching this book, we've discovered many wonderful places. We're sure you'll find others. Please tell us about them, so we can share the information with your fellow adventure travelers in upcoming editions. If you were disappointed with a recommendation, we'd love to know that, too. Please write to:

*Frommer's Great Outdoor Guide to Southern California & Baja*
Macmillan Travel
1633 Broadway
New York, NY 10019

**An Additional Note**

Please be advised that travel information is subject to change at any time. Every effort has been made to ensure the accuracy of the information provided in this book, but we suggest that you write or call ahead for confirmation when making your travel plans. The authors, editors, and Publisher cannot be held responsible for the experiences of readers while traveling. Outdoor adventure sports are, by their very nature, potentially hazardous activities. In doing any of the activities described herein, readers assume all risk of injury or loss that may accompany such activities. The Publisher disavows all responsibility for injury, death, loss, or property damage, which may arise from a reader's participation in any of the activities described herein, and the Publisher makes no warranties regarding the competence, safety, and reliability of outfitters, tour companies, or training centers described in this book.

## What the Symbols Mean

| | | |
|---|---|---|
| Backpacking | Golfing | Sailing |
| Biking | Hiking | Scuba Diving |
| Bird Watching | Horseback Riding | Snowboarding |
| Boardsailing | Inns & Lodges | Snowshoeing |
| Camping | Kayaking | Spelunking |
| Canoeing | Mountain Biking | Surfing |
| Coastal & Wetlands Birding | Powerboating | Swimming |
| Cross-Country Skiing | Raptoring & Woodland Birding | Tubing |
| Downhill Skiing | Rock Climbing | Whitewater Rafting |
| Fishing | Rowing | Wildlife Viewing |
| | | Whale Watching |

# THE BASICS

ROWING UP IN NORTHERN CALIFORNIA, I ALWAYS THOUGHT OF the lower half of the state as something of a mystery. My hometown had more in common with Kansas than Los Angeles; still, like everyone else who ever turned on a television, I was regularly bombarded with images of Southern California's glamorous lifestyle. It seemed like everybody there—whether Jim Rockford on *The Rockford Files*, Ponch and John on *CHiPS*, or the Monkees— lived by the beach and carried a surfboard. The Beach Boys harmonized about cute surfer girls and catching a wave. Sitting there chucking rocks at a frog in the canal near my house, I thought to myself: If only I could live there on that beach, now *that* would be the life. To me, like millions before and after, Southern California represented perfection, one of those mythical worlds not unlike Shangri-La or Camelot.

It was only later, sometime after I had moved to Southern California, that reality sunk in: Most of Southern California is not fronted by beach, most Southern Californians are not surfers, vast stretches of desert predominate, and there are huge mountains here. The good news, however, is that the beach lifestyle does exist. There really are guys with names like Wingnut and Tubesteak (even if most surfers are named Dave or Karen). Malibu is an actual place where people really do live in houses right on the sand and check the waves from their bedroom windows. Heck, even I managed to live in a house right on the sand for a few years while I was in college. And, like the Beach Boys promised, anyone who wanted could catch a wave and be sitting on top of the world.

As I began researching this book, several people, all of whom should know better, dismissively asked, "A book about outdoor adventures in Southern California? What outdoors? You mean like hiking down Melrose?" Obviously, they need to read this book. There's a whole lot more to Southern California than movie stars and palm trees. In fact, it's a land of superlatives: Death Valley's 3.6 million acres make it the largest national park in the Lower 48, not to mention the lowest and hottest spot in North America. Joshua Tree, 4 hours east of Los Angeles, is the best wintertime rock climbing in the United States; it draws people from all over the world to its sheer rock faces. Griffith Park, probably most famous for the giant Hollywood sign and Griffith Park Observatory, just happens to be the largest urban park in America with miles of hiking, biking, and horseback riding trails. The San Bernardino and San Gabriel Mountains, which form the L.A. basin's northern boundary, stand over 11,000 feet tall. They receive sufficient snow to be home to a half dozen downhill ski and snowboard areas. You can snowboard in the morning and be back at the beach in time to surf before sunset.

Then there's the matter of the other California, Baja California. By a fluke of geopolitics, Mexico's lovely desert peninsula just missed becoming part of the United States when the treaty of Guadalupe Hidalgo handed Alta California (which we abbreviated as California) to conquering United States forces. Perhaps fortunately for wilderness buffs, it wasn't surrendered, and Baja became to Mexico something like what Alaska is to the U.S.— detached, remote, and inhospitable. Since it's separated from mainland Mexico by the Sea of Cortez, except for a tiny ribbon of land along the U.S. border, and Americans weren't allowed to own property there, the region suffered little development pressure. Until 1973, there wasn't even a paved road down the peninsula.

Still, when my editors asked me to write a book about Southern California *and* Baja, I coughed, "Do you realize you're talking about two entire Mexican states and a land area almost the size of Italy?" They did, but they also had a good argument that a lot of people visiting California go to Baja, too. A compromise was reached: I'd pick and choose my favorite things to do in parts of the peninsula that lay within a reasonable striking distance of the border of one of Baja's commercially accessible airports at Loreto, La Paz, and Los Cabos. For adventurers who decide to make the phenomenal road trip down Mexico 1 from Tijuana to San José del Cabo, I've included lots of advice about how to go about exploring Baja's more remote regions.

Whether you're looking for the perfect wave to practice riding the nose, a 5.12 sandstone overhang, backcountry biking past the roosting spot of the California condor, some of the world's best offshore cruising grounds to explore by bareboat, or just a recommendation for good fish tacos, this book will get you there.

# Getting Started

By my guesstimate, this book covers about 3,000 miles of oceanfront. With that kind of coastline, you can expect a lot of great beaches. Even if you disregard Baja for a second and only count Southern California's 400 miles of beaches plus the Channel Islands, you've still got more great beaches than you can shake a bar of surf wax at. We're also talking about a pretty diverse cross-section: fluffy white-sand beaches, cobblestone beaches, beaches with warm water, freezing cold beaches, nude beaches, locals-only surfing beaches, beaches with cacti, beaches with cows, beaches with in-line skaters and musclemen, and beaches with nuclear power plants.

As a native might say, dude, are you stoked or what?

### FAVORITE BEACHES

◆ Hazard Canyon, Montaña de Oro State Park, The Central Coast (see chapter 2)

◆ Rincon, The Central Coast (see chapter 2)

◆ Malibu Surfrider, Santa Monica Bay (see chapter 4)

◆ Blacks Beach, San Diego (see chapter 9)

◆ Cabo Pulmo, East Cape Baja (see chapter 13)

Between Southern California and the Baja Peninsula, virtually every conceivable type of avian habitat is well represented. There's enough birding opportunity here to expand anyone's life list: from the offshore Channel Islands, which are the most important brown pelican nesting area in the United States; to the desolate desert of Death Valley, where you're likely to see ravens, roadrunners, and other desert birds; to the high peaks of the San Gabriel Mountains, where eagles pluck trout from blue lakes; to the wetland waterfowl habitat of Baja's big lagoons.

Birding in this area is a year-round proposition. While spring and fall migrations are as important here as anywhere else, the varied microclimates and the generally temperate weather allow you to make a birding adventure almost any weekend of the year.

Southern California presents something of a quandary to the enthusiastic boardsailor. The same windless, glassy ocean conditions that cause surfers to drool with delight mean a terrible day at the beach to a boardsailor. For a while in the 1980s, boardsailing was very popular here but it ran into a little problem— it's just not that windy in most of Southern California—and these days you just don't see that many people doing it. There are, however, a few exceptional spots. Jalama Beach in the Central Coast is often called the Hookipa of California. In the wintertime the swells get HUGE here; mast-high breaking waves aren't at all uncommon. And because it juts out on the coast just north of Point Conception, open to nearly any breeze, Jalama is a wind machine.

Baja is a different story—it's one of the most windy places on earth. Baja's most famous boardsailing spot is Los Barriles, a great little town midway between San José del Cabo and La Paz. For 4 months from December to the end of March, howling El Norte winds turn Las Palmas Bay into a perfect high-speed playground. And if you, like me, are still happy just to go out and make a few successful tacks without falling over,

the world is your oyster. Pick a beach, any beach.

## CROSS-COUNTRY SKIING

If you're thinking about getting on a plane and flying to Southern California for the fantastic cross-country skiing, you might want to think again. But if you're here already, give it a whirl. To me, by far the weirdest cross-country skiing experience in the world is at the seemingly oxymoronic Palm Springs Nordic Ski Center. From roughly November to April the Palm Springs Aerial Tramway will pick you up on the desert floor and lift you on a 14-minute, 6,000 vertical-foot ride to Mountain Terminal in San Jacinto State Park, accessible only by tram or by an 11-mile hike. While people back in Palm Springs are playing golf and wearing shorts in 90°F weather, at the Nordic center they'll rent you gear so you can ski around under a lovely forest of lodgepole pines. Tired of snow in your boots? Get back on the tram and be sipping a cocktail poolside in less than half an hour. There is also cross-country skiing in the San Gabriels and San Bernardino Mountains at Lake Arrowhead and Big Bear Lake.

## DOWNHILL SKIING & SNOWBOARDING

The caveats about cross-country skiing apply to downhill skiing as well. If you're considering visiting Southern California for the phenomenal downhill skiing and snowboarding, don't. Yet skiing here isn't as absurd as it sounds. Bear Mountain, Snow Summit, and Mountain High are actually really nice mountains; the problem is that the snow, which is manufactured any time the temperature drops below 28°F (read at night), starts turning to soggy mashed potatoes after lunch. Still, there's something really neat

about driving home from a day at on the slopes and catching an evening surf before the sun sets. And sometimes it's better to ski sloppy snow than sit in a car for 7 hours each way to ski a day at Mammoth.

## FISHING

The wealth of possibilities between Southern California and Baja is enough to make an angler's head spin. Southern California ocean fishing is on a dramatic rebound. Strict efforts to improve water quality in the last 25 years have really paid off. In the summer of 1997, Southern California experienced its best ocean fishing since the 1950s, with more conservative catch limits and regulations forbidding the use of gill nets in state waters playing key roles. The same conscientious management that is bringing back the fishing here also requires anglers to pay attention to the regulations if they don't want to end up on the wrong end of a game warden's ticket book. A standard resident sportfishing license is $26.50 for residents, $71.95 for nonresidents. Ten-day and 1-day licenses are available as well. In addition to a license, you'll want to stay abreast of the annually published regulation book, available free anywhere that sells fishing licenses, and also by contacting the **Department of Fish and Game,** P.O. Box 944209, Sacramento, CA 94244 (tel. 800/ASK-FISH).

Because it lies at the convergence zone between the cold waters north of Point Conception and warmer waters below, the variety of sport species here is remarkable. California halibut, white sea bass, lingcod, calico bass, thresher shark, and rockfish are caught pretty much year-round, with certain seasons (notably spring and summer) bringing the hot "bite." As ocean temperatures change with the currents, other

migrating species such as yellowtail, bonito, barracuda, salmon, and albacore also pass through the area. And every once in a while, when El Niño conditions warm area waters into the 70s, people start reeling in exotic species like marlin and dorado that normally make their homes much farther south in Baja.

Inland fishing in Southern California has a long way to go before it rejoins its former greatness. Before virtually every river in Southern California was dammed for water development, thousands of sea run steelhead trout choked the streambeds on their annual spawning runs. Today, with their numbers down to a couple hundred, the southern steelhead are on the endangered species list and fishing for them is strictly prohibited. Many streams and rivers in the region still have decent trout fishing, and, of course, the same dams that choked out the native steelhead created reservoirs that provide a habitat for introduced largemouth bass and catfish. Many people think that the next world-record largemouth will come out of Lake Castaic just north of Los Angeles.

Then, of course, there's Baja. The first Americans really to take advantage of Baja's vast oceans and wilderness were fishermen. Starting in the 1950s, the Cape region became a famous billfishing destination. Movie stars and industry tycoons flew their private planes down to the strip at La Palmilla and reeled in marlin until they could hardly stand up. With no road and no commercial flights, it was their own little paradise. Well, there's been a road since 1973, and at least 10 flights a day in and out of Los Cabos International Airport, but the fishing in Baja is still amazing. The waters of the Sea of Cortez literally boil with fish sometimes, and it's one of the best places to find world class sportfishing within an easy boat ride. Nothing, in my opinion, compares to the excitement of

watching a 40-pound bull dorado smash your bait when you're fishing from one of the local *panga* fleet—except maybe watching a 200-pound marlin do the same. You can also catch wahoo, tuna, roosterfish, and yellowtail up and down the Sea of Cortez. The Pacific offers great opportunities as well, notably the tuna fishing fleet out of Ensenada, an easy distance from the U.S. border. While there is plenty of room for fishing on your own in Baja, one of the most worthy expenditures you can make is to hire a local *panguero,* the super-knowledgeable sportfishing guides who seem to operate from any beachside community of more than a few people. For between $100 and $150 a day, you and however many of your friends can fit gain access to not only a boat and motor, but an incredible repository of experience. Anyone over the age of 16 fishing in Mexico is supposed to purchase a fishing license, which can be done by contacting the U.S. office of the **Mexican Fisheries Department,** 2550 Fifth Ave., Suite 101, San Diego, CA 92101 (tel. 619/233-6956). In practice, fishing license rules are rarely enforced and game limits and seasons are a bit hazy, another fine reason to hire a local guide.

## FAVORITE FISHING SPOTS

◆ Gaviota Beach, Central Coast (see chapter 2)

◆ Morro Bay, Central Coast (see chapter 2)

◆ Catalina Island, Channel Islands (see chapter 3)

◆ Ensenada, Baja Norte (see chapter 12)

◆ Loreto, Baja Sur (see chapter 13)

## HIKING & BACKPACKING

In most parts, hiking and backpacking are primarily summer sports. Not so here. In fact, it's quite the opposite. Summertime temperatures in all but the tallest inland mountains are much too high for serious hiking. Unless you favor 100°F days and relentless dust, it's better to wait until after the first fall rains have settled the trails and temperatures drop before venturing into the backcountry of Anza Borrego, Los Padres National Forest, Joshua Tree, and, most of all, Death Valley. Spring and fall tend to be the nicest times to visit, though—depending on the elevation— what passes for winter in these parts can be really fine for hiking, too. If you must visit inland Southern California in the summer, look for the high ground. When it's 120°F on the floor of Death Valley, it might be quite cool and pleasant up in the nearby Panamint Mountains. When it's egg-frying hot in Palm Springs, it'll probably be perfectly comfortable up at the top of the Palm Springs Aerial Tramway in San Jacinto Mountain State Park. And if you insist on hiking anywhere when it's up around 100°F and the humidity is down to practically zero (which describes most of the California desert from May to September), remember that it's physically impossible to drink sufficient water. Your body simply can't absorb water as fast as it's losing it. Scale down your plans and avoid the midday sun. What would be an easy hike on a cool day can literally turn deadly on a hot one.

Coastal hiking is a different story. Many parks on the coast contain fantastic trail systems into the nearby hills. In particular, the coastal mountains around Santa Barbara and Malibu lend themselves to exploration any time of the year and undergo subtle changes with each season. One of the greatest pleasures of the California coast is beach hiking. Places like Montaña de Oro, Jalama Beach, and Leo Carrillo State Beach let you combine the pleasures of hiking, tide pooling, and beachgoing.

With regard to Baja, take what I said about inland temperatures in the Southern California desert and multiply it by a couple factors. From roughly May to October you'll want to have nothing to do with inland hiking or backpacking here. The coast again offers some respite from the excruciating heat—but not much. Wintertime is the right time; the payoffs can be fantastic. Baja taught me many valuable lessons about desert hiking, but one of the most useful is this: The animals in the desert are active in the early morning and late evening, so follow their cue and do your hiking then. Not only will you not roast, but you'll get to see all those animals that would be in hiding in the middle of the day. Night can be nice too, but be forewarned that there are a lot of prickly and spiny things in these parts that you don't want to crash into. Another thing I've learned about Baja is that while there are lots of trails, very few of them were made by people.

Range cattle roam everywhere in Baja, and their trails crisscross the entire peninsula. It's almost impossible to get to a particular destination by following a trail description unless it parallels an obvious physical feature, such as the bottom of a canyon or the ocean. There are just too many trails in them thar hills. As a result, my hiking directions for Baja will of necessity assume that you're a capable and self-sufficient route finder.

In this book you'll find both day hikes and backpacking trips listed under this section. The reason one hike was selected as a backpacking trip and another as a day hike is admittedly somewhat arbitrary. Generally, my main criterion for picking a backpacking route is the quality of the destination, whereas my chief criterion for a hike is the caliber of the sights along the route. Many places listed under "Backpacking" are also fine day hikes, and some of the day hikes would make fine overnights. Don't let my need to categorize keep you from following your whim, however. Easy hikes under 3 miles are listed in a different section: "Walks & Natural Roadside Attractions." These are the kind of paths that you'd take a young child on without hesitation—simple, well-marked paths with clear destinations.

While I've tried to give easy-to-follow route descriptions for every hike, these listings are by no means exact descriptions. I make no attempt to detail every fork in the trail or every rock where you should turn right, cross a stream, crawl under three logs, or climb up the hill 300 feet, then descend along a southwest vector. If you don't know how to read a map or follow a trail, this book isn't going to save you. No guidebook can replace good backcountry skills and a map and compass. I'm more concerned with describing the characteristics of a particular hike than with giving a blow-by-blow account of your every footstep.

For day hikes, you generally don't need any sort of permit, except where noted in individual entries. To camp overnight, however, most national parks, state parks, and wilderness areas require backcountry permits. If permits are required, the entry for that location will tell you where to get one.

## HORSEBACK RIDING & PACK TRIPS

If you've got your own horses, you'll find thousands of miles of good riding throughout Southern California, from beach riding to multi-day adventures into the wilderness backcountry. Because of the huge quantity of public land in the region, many people enjoy miles of great riding trails within walking distance of their stable without the burden of managing their own huge ranch.

The rest of us, those without horses, will find lots of places willing to rent and teach us how to ride. While practically every town in Southern California has a stable and riding school, this book is particularly interested in those stables and outfitters whose location allows you to explore wilderness areas.

### FAVORITE STABLES
◆ Circle Bar-B Ranch, Central Coast (see chapter 2)
◆ Griffith Park Stables, Santa Monica Mountains (see chapter 4)

## MOUNTAIN BIKING

The hills and deserts of Southern California are carved with a remarkable legacy of exploration, everything from old Native American footpaths to wagon trails to fire roads. On a knobby-tired bike, all of it can be yours.

The bulk of riding in Southern California takes place on National Forest and BLM land. The national parks allow mountain biking only on dirt roads, no single track, but there are still some memorable rides to be had. A general rule of thumb is that the closer you are to a big city, the less legal mountain biking you'll encounter. Mountain bike enthusiasts have been fighting a losing public relations battle for years. Though bikes have actually been cruising the backroads of California since long before there was such a thing as an official "mountain bike," the exploding popularity of the sport in the 1980s brought a tremendous crackdown. Mountain bikers were seen as Johnny-Come-Lately's to the forests, and when push came to shove, they were seen as invaders usurping the rights of others. To be fair, they often earned the contempt of the public by biking rudely and carelessly. Many of the finest trails in and around the L.A. and San Diego areas are closed to mountain bikers. The situation hasn't reached the levels of absurdity it has in Marin County, where all single-track trails on Mount Tamalpais are closed to bikers and where radar-wielding bike cops will give you a ticket for breaking 15 mph on the fire roads—but it could happen. To keep the situation from getting worse, it's prudent to not blast around blind corners or over blind crests, so you can stop or slow down enough to give hikers and horses their rights of way. A little niceness goes a long way toward diffusing hostility. Whenever I encounter a horse while I'm riding, I make a point of saying, "Nice horse," to the rider as we pass each other. It's hard to hate someone who likes your horse.

The rides in this book take place mostly on fire roads simply because that's what there are more of than anything else in Southern California. Where possible, however, I've included single track as well as combinations of both. Occasionally a ride will require some pedaling on pavement, but I try to limit that.

Something about the Southern California landscape is really suited to exploration by bike. Many times, the "sights" are separated by long distances that would be grueling on foot but are perfect on a bike. The pace at which landscape reveals itself on a bicycle often synchronizes perfectly with the timing of a ride here. Just when you're getting tired or a tiny bit bored, you'll crest a ridge and see a jaw-dropping view, or the dry canyon you've been descending will suddenly reveal a perfect swimming hole. And in a land of such spectacular microclimates, it's possible to hit cactus desert, oak and sycamore woodland, and tall pine forests all in the course of an afternoon ride.

### FAVORITE RIDES

◆ Little Pine Mountain, Los Padres National Forest (see chapter 2)

◆ Bluff Trail, Montaña De Oro State Park (see chapter 2)

◆ Arroyo Seco, Angeles National Forest (see chapter 5)

◆ Arctic Canyon, San Bernardino National Forest (see chapter 5)

◆ Big Sycamore Canyon Fire Road, Point Mugu State Park (see chapter 4)

## ROAD BIKING

Southern California is the sacred church of the automobile. There are more cars per capita here than anywhere in the world. Nobody loves their cars like we do. We drive fast and talk on our cell phones while gripping the wheel with one pinkie and stirring the chocolate sprinkles into our cappuccino with the other. This does not bode well for road cyclists. I see people all the time biking down Highway 1 between Malibu and Santa Monica, up Topanga Canyon Road, along the shoulder of Highway 101 near Rincon, and I can't help but imagine a sign blinking over their heads that says, "Life expectancy 10 minutes."

But with a climate as lovely as Southern California's, it would be a crime to let cars scare you off your bike. Get outside the urban zone a little and there are lots of road rides that'll let you spin off for miles without a care in the world. As a result, rural rides are the mainstay of this book.

### FAVORITE RIDES

◆ Camp Pendleton Coast Trail, San Diego (see chapter 9)

◆ Mount Palomar, Cleveland National Forest (see chapter 10)

◆ El Capitan-Refugio State Beaches Bike Trail (chapter 2)

◆ Badwater and back, Death Valley National Park (see chapter 7)

## ROCK CLIMBING

Some of the great names of American rock climbing actually came up through the Southern California climbing ranks before going on to become legends. Yvon Chouinard, Royal Robbins, and John Bachar literally learned the ropes at local climbing spots here before moving to the big walls of Yosemite and beyond. It used to be that everyone followed that model: Get good and move on to bigger and better things. That's changed recently as Southern California has gained due credit for its excellent climbing. Joshua Tree National Park in particular has become known for the best winter rock climbing in the United States. Other great spots are Gibraltar Rock in Santa Barbara, Tahquitz and Suicide Rocks near Idyllwild, and the Devil's Punchbowl near Palmdale.

## SAILING

It's hard to imagine a more perfect setup than the one enjoyed by sailors in Southern California. The coastal sailing is nice, but it's the offshore islands that make this a world-class yachting destination. From Santa Barbara, Ventura, Marina del Rey, Kings Harbor, Huntington, Newport, and several other harbors, you're within an easy day's sail of one or more of the Channel Islands. The islands are just far enough away that the crossing feels like a real adventure. The real payoff, however, begins when you get out there. Santa Cruz and Santa Catalina are the most popular overnight cruising destinations. Both offer snug harbors and miles of cliff-fringed shoreline, sea caves, diving in the kelp forest, and other great possibilities for exploration. Santa Cruz, in particular, makes you feel like you've fallen back in time a couple hundred years.

Without a doubt, the best way to experience the islands is by chartering a bareboat. Virtually every pleasure harbor has a bareboat charter facility. And if you don't have the sailing skills

needed to rent a bareboat, this is a fine opportunity to learn. In a couple of weekend courses or an intensive resort course, one of the south coast's many sailing schools will turn you into a real sailor and will certify you to rent bareboats—charter boats rented without a captain—anywhere in the world.

If you'd prefer to leave the heavy responsibility to someone else and just enjoy the ride, every charter company on the coast can also rent you one of their boats complete with captain. Depending on the level of service you pay for, this could include full-service cooking, cleaning, and stocking the boat, or it could simply mean that the captain will drive the boat and you'll share galley duties.

You can also charter bareboats or crewed vessels out of La Paz for sailing to the offshore islands in the Sea of Cortez. This region is truly a paradise of warm turquoise water, brisk sailing breezes, and startling topside scenery.

### FAVORITE SAILING SPOTS
◆ Isla Espíritu Santo, La Paz (see chapter 13)
◆ Isla del Carmen, Loreto (see chapter 13)
◆ Catalina Island, Los Angeles County (see chapter 3)
◆ Santa Cruz Island, Channel Islands National Park (see chapter 3)

## SCUBA DIVING & SNORKELING

Diving in California's underwater kelp forests may be the closest you'll ever come to experiencing what a bird feels when it flies through a rain forest. Being suspended in the middle of 70-foot-tall kelp gives you a tremendous feeling of weightlessness. Schools of fish flicker through the "trees" like flocks of birds. The ground below is covered by layer after layer of sea life: nudibranchs, urchins, anemones. Look in a cave and you might see a spiny lobster or a family of shy horn sharks huddling against the invasion of your light.

The best diving, by far, takes place at the Channel Islands, each of which offers a slightly different variation on a theme of kelp, rocks, and sea life. San Miguel is famous for its seals and sea lions, plus the sheer size of its fish. Santa Cruz and Anacapa are famous for their easy accessibility from Santa Barbara or Ventura, and the consistently great visibility. Catalina is the most popular with people from L.A., by simple virtue of proximity.

Shore diving is also great off the Channel Islands, though the added runoff and pollution from the mainland mean dramatically less visibility (though still quite good) and less sea life. The bonus of shore diving, of course, is that you just do it. All up and down the coast are excellent dives reached by just swimming out from the beach.

Baja presents another astonishing palette of choices to the serious or casual diver. By virtue of its remoteness, very few people scuba dive the Pacific Coast. The snorkeling and spearfishing here can be fantastic. I've fed myself easily by just spearing a big fish a day while camping along the Pacific. The real draw for divers south of the border is the southern part of the Sea of Cortez. From Mulege to San Jose del Cabo, the Sea of Cortez is home to some incredible sights. Depending on the season, you might swim with manta rays, play with juvenile sea lions, or hover in a school of circling hammerhead sharks. Snorkelers will find lots of sea life on small coral outcroppings around the cape and at the offshore islands.

## SEA KAYAKING & CANOEING

It seems that every few years a new sport grips the outdoor community by the brain stem and becomes the hot new thing to do. Sea kayaking is currently much in vogue, and it's easy to see why. With so much available coastline it's nice to be able to just go out for a short paddle, get away from shore, and look at life from another perspective. But there's a more serious side to sea kayaking, too: the expedition-style exploration of remote islands, offshore crossings, and narrow sea caves. Whether you choose to paddle around Newport Harbor looking at ducks and boats, venture into the massive and foreboding sea caves of Santa Cruz Island, or spend a week sleeping on white-sand beaches and spearing fish in the Sea of Cortez, Baja and Southern California have plenty to offer.

## SURFING

I was drawn to Southern California by surfing. As a boy, my parents bought me surfing lessons while on a family vacation in Hawaii. It was love at first wave. From that point on it was just a matter of counting down the days until I could live by the beach. Miraculously, the University of California offers not one, but two different universities, UC San Diego and UC Santa Barbara, with surf breaks right on campus. UC Santa Barbara had a better department of political science, which was to be my major. I did just fine in school, but when I look back on it now, I realize that my real major was surfing, scuba diving, sailing, and messing around in the mountains behind town. (Probably in no small measure that's why I find myself writing about adventure travel for a living instead of assuming the role of junior diplomat in Zaire.)

Surfing may have been a Hawaiian invention, but California popularized the sport. In Hawaii it was the sport of kings. Yet the Californian ideal that anyone can grab a board and learn to ride waves has changed forever the way people perceive the ocean. Currently surfing is undergoing another sea change, another chapter in the constant flux that defines the sport. If I had to pick two things that have dramatically changed in the last few years, it would be the return of the longboard and the incredible number of women who've taken up the sport. Both, I think, are good things, and they're interrelated. Longboards make it easier to catch waves, easier to learn the sport. For years the common wisdom was to ride the smallest board you could possibly stand up on; people would argue about the handling difference an inch in board length could make. Guys would say things like, "Dude, I wish I'd brought my 6'1" instead of my 6'2". It's gonna suck riding this big board on these waves."

Now more than 50 percent of the boards sold every year are longer than 9 feet. It's suddenly cool to ride the nose or make a drop-knee cutback. Developments in surfboard design have also enabled longboarders to do things that were impossible before: aerials, radical cutbacks, off-the-lips.

I look at surfing as a quest. It's dependent on so many variables that it's impossible to expect that the conditions in any one place will be great on any given day. The trick is learning to read and anticipate the variables. In every listing of a surf spot I'll try to explain some of the variables. Is it a winter spot? A summer spot? Does it work well on a high tide? Low tide? Is there anything I should watch out for? Where relevant, I've also included places that rent surfboards and give lessons, as well as the best local sources of information.

### BEST PLACES TO CATCH THE WAVES

◆ Jalama County Beach Park, Central Coast (see chapter 2)
◆ Rincon State Beach, Central Coast (see chapter 2)

◆ Swami's, San Diego County (see chapter 9)
◆ Windansea, La Jolla (see chapter 9)
◆ Punta San Pedrito, Todos Santos, Mexico (see chapter 12)

### SWIMMING

Any way you cut it, Southern California and Baja are located in a desert climate. Freshwater is precious, and swimming holes are scarce. That doesn't mean they aren't out there. In fact, some of the most beautiful swimming holes in the world lie hidden in the canyons of this arid land. The secret is finding them. I've listed numerous swimming holes that can be reached by a relatively short hike. There are also a few that can be driven to, though those are generally so overwhelmed with users that they quickly become disgusting. Please remember to treat creeks and rivers with respect by practicing low-impact wilderness habits no matter how close to a road you are. Water is the lifeblood of our communities.

### WALKS & ROADSIDE ATTRACTIONS

A walk, in my estimation, is something you can do with your grandmother or with a young child. Generally it reaches some sort of destination, whether a notable tree, a waterfall, or a lookout. Trails range from paved to dirt but are generally level and gentle. Roadside Attractions is the catchall for things I want to put in the book that don't necessarily fit into the other categories: a surfing museum, a mushroom-shaped rock, the lowest point in North America, that sort of thing.

### WHALE WATCHING

Whales have gone from teetering on extinction to a stunning recovery in a very short time—testimony to how well wildlife can do when humankind gives it a break. Southern California and Baja offer a lot of different options for people wanting to see whales. Explore the calving lagoons of southern Baja, where gray whales are so conditioned to human presence that they'll rub up against an inflatable boat looking to be scratched; it's the experience of a lifetime. When the grays pass Southern California on their way to the Gulf of Alaska, they're making time, but so many go by that it's a great chance to see them up close. Whale-watching boats leave virtually every commercial harbor in the state during the winter migration. In the last decade, blue and humpback whales have begun spending summers in the Santa Barbara Channel feeding on krill. I've seen a lot of different whales in my life, but nothing compares to the time a 100-foot blue lined up right next to the 70-foot boat I was on. It took my breath away.

## WILDLIFE VIEWING

Though it's probably more famous for its wildlife of the Viper Room variety, Southern California is still home to many amazing examples of the natural world at work. Tide pools line the shore of the Central Coast, Palos Verdes Peninsula, and the coast near Laguna. The Channel Islands are home to the world's largest breeding colony of six different varieties of seals and sea lions. Death Valley has ponds and creeks filled with the rarest fish in the world, some species of which exist only in an area the size of a small swimming pool. Whether it's big, dramatic sightings, like watching a desert bighorn come down to drink at a palm oasis or swimming with a giant manta off Baja, that make you happy, or smaller things like observing the color of a Spanish Shawl nudibranch clinging to a rock during a dive, you won't lack for plenty to look at in Southern California and Baja.

# 2

# THE CENTRAL COAST:
## San Simeon to Oxnard

THE CENTRAL COAST IS ONE OF THOSE STRANGE MISNOMERS THAT reflects our collective inability to really grasp geography. California's 1,200 miles of coastline are roughly divided in half at San Francisco Bay. Therefore you'd expect the northern third to be the north coast, the area say 200 miles on either side north and south of the Golden Gate to be the central coast, and everything south of there the south coast. Makes perfect sense, right?

Well, not really. Since the vast majority, something like 90%, of Californians live in the southern half of the state—from the Bay Area to the Mexican border—we consider everything north of the bay to be some other dimension. It seems to barely figure into our thinking. San Francisco Bay, Monterey, and Big Sur, which are all in the southern half of the state, are considered Northern California. Yet by some sort of consensus we've concluded that Southern California proper doesn't begin until somewhere just south of Santa Barbara or Ventura. What that leaves us, between roughly San Simeon and Point Mugu, is the "Central Coast." Never mind that it is found well into the bottom quarter of the state.

Whatever it's called, the Central Coast is one of the most wonderful parts of the state. It combines many of the best attributes of Northern and Southern California. It replicates Southern California's wonderful Mediterranean climate with year-round mild temperatures moderated by the ocean, chaparral-covered hillsides, and oak-shaded canyons. But it has a decidedly more laid-back lifestyle than does Southern California. People here tend to center their lives around the environment rather than reconfigure the environment to suit them, as has been the case in so much of Southern California. Many towns have fought pitched battles to control rampant growth and maintain the beauty of their surroundings as well as the cohesiveness of their community. Quality of life is extremely important to the people who've chosen to live here.

The Central Coast has many things to recommend it, including great towns, theaters, restaurants, and museums, but the main attraction for both visitors and residents is its outdoor activities. That can mean many things. For some, the preferred outdoor activity is lying on one of the area's numerous sandy beaches with a good book. More adventurous climbers are drawn by the chance to test themselves on dramatic sandstone outcroppings pocked with Chumash Indian caves and backed by ocean views. Sailors and divers flock here for the Channel Islands, and fishermen are drawn to excellent salmon, albacore, halibut, and rockfish fishing from Morro Bay, Port San Luis, Santa Barbara, and Ventura. From my former home in Santa Barbara, it was possible to ride my mountain bike a few miles on city streets to the edge of the national forest, then pedal 80 more miles through remote canyons and over 6,000-foot peaks to the

other side of the county without crossing a single paved road. Despite the fact that it is now the least settled part of coastal Southern California, in the early mission and presidio days the Central Coast was a very important area. Back when Los Angeles was just a few adobe huts and corrals, Santa Barbara was an important port, military outpost, ranching community, mission town, and government seat. With adequate fresh water, sheltered coastline, and a pleasant climate, it was superseded only by Monterey in importance. A string of missions connected the two cities, and several remain in Lompoc, in San Luis Obispo, and upward through the Salinas Valley.

Most of the area's population remains clustered along the modern relics of that mission trail, Highway 101 and Highway 1. Away from the sea, the communities are either still largely agricultural or dependent on the oil business for their economy. Small coastal towns like Morro Bay, Cambria, and Pismo Beach depend hugely on tourism, and the larger towns like Santa Barbara, San Luis Obispo, and Ventura subsist on a mix of tourism, academics, high-tech and light industry, and retirement income drawn by the area's pleasant quality of life.

Get away from the major highways, though, and the Central Coast is a look back at an earlier California. Certain large ranches are still held by the families that received the original Spanish land grant. Spanish-speaking *vaqueros* still help brand and herd cattle on the same ranch their great-grandfathers worked. Local vineyards craft some of the state's best merlots and syrahs. And in the backcountry, bears, mountain lions, wild trout, and, yes, California condors still exercise their claim over millions of acres of wilderness.

# The Lay of the Land

By looking at a map you'll see that the most distinctive feature of the Central Coast is where California's coastline turns a big corner. At Point Conception the outline of California's Pacific shore takes a sudden dogleg to the east. This is the source of endless confusion for tourists who will stand on the beach in Santa Barbara and wonder why the sun rises in the south and sets in the north here, since they are certain that the ocean is always to their west—it's called the West Coast, after all.

The coastline isn't the only thing that changes direction here; the mountains do, too. Most mountains in California and, in fact, the entire U.S. run from north to south, but here things are a little different. The backcountry of the Central Coast is where the Coast Range, in the form of the Santa Lucias, ends and the first of the Transverse Ranges begins with the Sierra Madre and the Santa Ynez Mountains. The Transverse Ranges are something of a geological oddity; Southern California's east-to-west trending mountains include the San Gabriel, Santa Monica, and San Bernardino mountains and the offshore Channel Islands. Point Conception is simply the westernmost reach of the Santa Ynez Mountains. The Transverse Ranges are actually much higher than the Coast Range, often pushing over 8,000 feet. I've been snowed on in the Central Coast backcountry as late as May.

The changes here are more than just geological; Point Conception and the Transverse Ranges are the demarcation point between the Northern California ocean environment and the Southern California ocean environment. North of the Point the ocean is colder and stormy, fog is plentiful, and a different community of sea life calls it home. South of Conception the Santa Barbara Channel is sheltered by mountains to the north and by the Channel Islands to the south. The wind, storms, and surf that lash the northern coastline are blunted by this sheltering effect. The ocean water is warmer, and consequently, the species that live here are different. The two separate marine ecosystems meet most dramatically at San Miguel Island, the westernmost of the Channel Islands, more or less due south of Point Conception. Here, 40-some miles off the Santa Barbara coast, San Miguel sits like a sentinel, washed from all sides by the currents. The density of different species is astounding here: eight species of seals and sea lions, white sharks, lobsters, abalone, huge halibut, lingcod, rock fish, garibaldi, gray whales, blue whales, orcas, basking sharks, giant kelp forests, bat rays, you name it. But it's hardly a hospitable place. As the warm southern currents collide with the colder northern waters, San Miguel is often blanketed with fog for days on end. Or else the temperature differential spawns horrendous winds.

In this book, San Simeon marks the northern boundary of California's Central Coast. As with any arbitrary line, it could easily be argued that I've started too far north or too far south, but until California splits into two, Southern California begins wherever you decide it begins. I chose San Simeon. San Simeon, of course, is famous for Hearst Castle, the massively eclectic tribute to William Randolph Hearst's enormous wealth and immeasurable hubris built on a mountain above the town and cove. But San Simeon has been around much longer than Hearst. The Sebastian General Store was opened in 1873 and is still in business. Less well-known than Hearst Castle (which gets more than a million visitors per year) is **San Simeon State Park.** Also part of the Hearst Ranch that was donated to the state (the Hearsts continue to own 86,000 acres in the area) to help absorb the huge tax burden when William Hearst died, the state park has wonderful, rocky beaches. Offshore rocks and deep tide pools accentuate the interaction between land and water. You can camp in one of the 190 campsites, but unfortunately you'll be competing with all those Hearst Castle visitors for space.

Down the coast a bit, **Morro Bay** and **Port San Luis** are hardworking port towns. Morro Bay is particularly important to sailors making the run from Southern California to San Francisco as the last major safe port for more than a hundred miles until Monterey. Plenty of sailors have gasped a sigh of relief at the sight of the town's namesake, the 578-foot-high igneous monolith Morro Rock, marking the entrance to Estero Bay, after a stormy passage down the coast. The Portuguese explorer Juan Cabrillo, who named practically everything in California, also named the rock. Morro means "domed turban," and from a distance the resemblance is apparent, as is the reason for the rock's other nickname, "the Gibraltar of California."

Just south of here is **Montaña de Oro State Park.** Little known or used except by local residents, Montaña de Oro is home to one of the scariest surf breaks on the California coast (Hazard's Reef) and to a fantastic array of mountain biking, hiking, beachcombing, and camping. The park is named for 1,347-foot Valencia Peak, which every spring blooms with such an intense concentration of golden poppies and yellow mustard that it merits the moniker Mountain of Gold. Offshore, seastacks created when erosion gnawed away soft sedimentary rock and left only harder

volcanic rock fight their losing battle with the lashing waves.

At the southwestern boundary of the park begins the **Pecho Coast.** Rugged, wild, and beautiful, dramatic rock cliffs plunge straight into the churning sea below hillsides covered in coastal oaks and springtime profusions of wildflowers. The westernmost point here, **Point Buchon,** is a geological oddity, a rock formation called an ophiolite that was created by volcanic activity in the mid-Pacific ocean and deposited here by plate tectonics. For 10 miles the coast is virtually untouched and little has changed here since the 1800s except for one thing—the construction of Diablo Canyon Nuclear Power Plant, notorious for being built directly on top of an active earthquake fault. As a result of the power plant, and Pacific Gas and Electric's draconian no-trespassing policy, the Pecho Coast was off limits for years. Only recently has it been opened to the public, and then only in the form of docent-guided hikes led by the Nature Conservancy (call 805/541-8735 for updates).

Bookending the other end of the Pecho Coast is **Avila Beach.** Avila is a lovely town that looks like it stepped out of time. You'll wonder, why does it look like nothing's been rebuilt in 20 years? Where's all the development I'm used to? Well, while San Luis Obispo and Santa Barbara struggled with zoning laws, water restrictions, and architectural review boards, Avila stumbled upon the perfect solution to stopping growth: Announce that your entire community sits on top of a toxic plume of gasoline and petroleum from the leaking Unocal oil tanks above town. Since the town sits on top of a toxic site, banks won't make any loans to home or business owners. Without loans, nothing gets built and property is virtually impossible to sell. Couple that with the fact that there's a nuclear power plant sitting on an

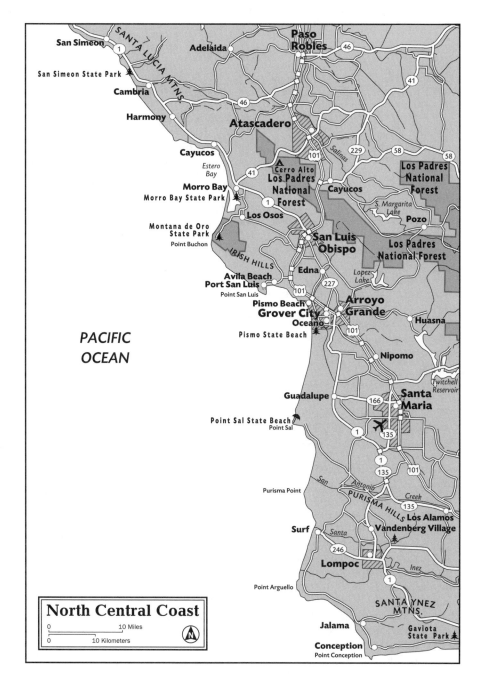

earthquake fault just a couple miles away and, case closed, no growth.

A dramatic change in the landscape occurs at **Pismo Beach,** where the predominantly rocky coastline suddenly gives way to California's largest coastal sand dunes. For miles, the Pismo Dunes and then the Guadalupe Dunes are a tribute to the constant wind that blows here. Grain by grain, beach sand is blown uphill to form continuously changing dunes. While dune buggy drivers and motorcyclists enjoy racing over the off-road vehicle recreation area at Pismo

Beach State Park, nature lovers can experience the dunes without risk of being run over by visiting the Nature Conservancy's Guadalupe Dunes Preserve.

The dunes hide a lot of secrets. Cecil B. Demille filmed *The Ten Commandments* in the Guadalupe Dunes, and relics of the giant "ancient Egypt" set still surface from time to time as the sand shifts. More recently the area doubled for Libya in Demi Moore's action flick *G.I. Jane*. Sadly, the dunes also hide a huge ecological tragedy. From 1950 to 1990, the Unocal oil field at the very western end of the dunes spilled as much as 5 to 10 million gallons of toxic solvents into the sand. The massive underground plume was discovered only when a surfer who worked at the field blew the whistle on the problem after it began leaching into the ocean.

From here to Gaviota, the coast is largely locked up by Vandenberg Air Force Base and several large, private ranches. Public access here is found only at Point Sal State Park on the base's northern edge, Surf Beach just west of Lompoc in the middle of the base, and Jalama Beach County Park on the southern boundary of Vandenberg. The Air Force base is something of a legend among Cold War historians. Since it is America's primary location for launching military satellites and testing new missiles, access is highly restricted. Amtrak trains, however, run right through the middle. When Nikita Khrushchev first visited the United States, he was scheduled to travel by train from Los Angeles to San Francisco. The Air Force panicked at the thought of the Russian leader passing through Vandenberg. How in the world were they to keep the Soviet premier's prying eyes off their secrets? As the story goes, the base commander contacted President Kennedy to demand that Khrushchev be re-routed away from the base. Kennedy assured the commander that everything would be fine and suggested the perfect solution. When Khrushchev passed through Vandenberg, his jaw dropped. Everywhere he looked were huge silos; tall ones, short ones, fat ones, skinny ones— certainly containing mysterious and deadly missiles, a cold warrior's worst nightmares. When the train had safely gone, work crews went out and tore down the plywood facades that had fooled Khrushchev.

Ironically, the base is one of the best-preserved stretches of coastline in California simply because it has been restricted for so long. I once assisted a marine biologist in counting intertidal organisms at a site just below what was to have been the space shuttle's western launching pad. The variety of marinelife was incredible. Abalone clung to rocks right at the waterline. Seals basked on seaside rocks. Tide pools teemed with starfish, scallops, anemones, sculpin, and countless other residents in an abundance unlike any I'd ever seen.

Point Conception lies about 5 miles south of **Jalama Beach Park.** At low tide it's possible to walk to the point, but once there you'll find the Coast Guard lighthouse rather inhospitable and largely inaccessible. Most visitors flock to Jalama for pristine beach camping and some of the best surfing and boardsailing on the coast. East of here (because the coast has turned east-west) are another 15 or so miles of private ranches until Gaviota State Park. From **Gaviota State Park** to Santa Barbara, Highway 101 runs through some beautifully undeveloped coastal ranchlands framed by the Santa Ynez Mountains to one side and the blue Pacific to the other. Three developed state parks, Gaviota, Refugio, and El Capitan, are popular with beach campers, surfers, kayakers, and fishermen.

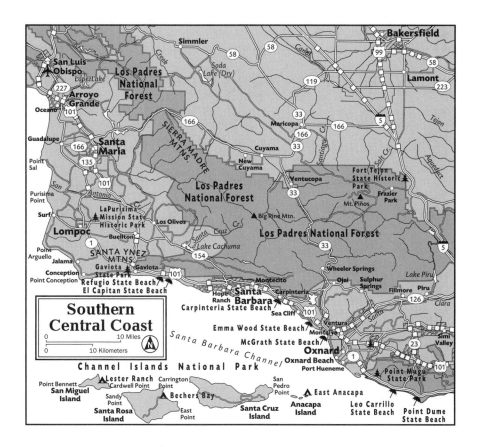

## Southern Central Coast

**Bakersfield**
Simmler
Los Padres National Forest
San Luis Obispo
Lopez Lake
227
Arroyo Grande
Oceano
101
Guadalupe
166
Santa Maria
Point Sal
135
Purisima Point
101
San Antonio
La Purisima Mission State Historic Park
Surf
Lompoc
1
Point Arguello
Jalama
Conception
Point Conception
Refugio State Beach
El Capitan State Beach
Buellton
SANTA YNEZ MTNS
Gaviota State Park
Gaviota
Los Olivos
Lake Cachuma
154
SIERRA MADRE MTNS
Soda Lake (Dry)
58
58
Carla
99
Lamont
223
119
166
Maricopa
33
New Cuyama
Cuyama
166
166
5
Ventucopa
33
Santiago Cr.
Salt Cr.
Tejon
Aqueduct
Fort Tejon State Historic Park
Frazier Park
Mt. Piños
Big Pine Mtn.
Los Padres National Forest
Los Padres National Forest
33
Lake Piru
5
Wheeler Springs
Ojai
Sulphur Springs
Fillmore
Piru
126
Clara
Santa Cruz Cr.
Montecito
Santa Barbara
Carpinteria
Hope Ranch
Carpinteria State Beach
Sea Cliff
101
Ventura
Montalvo
Santa Barbara Channel
Emma Wood State Beach
McGrath State Beach
Oxnard
Oxnard Beach
Port Hueneme
Channel Islands National Park
Simi Valley
23
1
101
Point Mugu State Park
0   10 Miles
0   10 Kilometers
Channel Islands National Park
Point Bennett
San Miguel Island
Lester Ranch
Cardwell Point
Sandy Point
Santa Rosa Island
East Point
Carrington Point
Bechers Bay
San Pedro Point
Santa Cruz Island
East Anacapa
Anacapa Island
Leo Carrillo State Beach
Point Dume State Beach

---

**Santa Barbara** is probably better known for the cheesy soap opera of the same name than for the phenomenal variety of outdoor sports its residents take almost for granted. Tucked into a number of canyons and coastal valleys, Santa Barbara backs up to **Los Padres National Forest** and is fronted by miles of beaches and a fine harbor and wharf. Residents and visitors face but one dilemma: deciding what to do here. Sailing? Surfing? Fishing? Kayaking? Hiking to a beautiful waterfall? Mountain biking into the deepest parts of the backcountry? Hang gliding off a 3,000-foot mountain?

Thirty miles down the coast, **Ventura** has long been perceived as the ugly step-sister to Santa Barbara's red-tiled beauty. Recent years have seen big improvements in Ventura, though, and it's no longer a surprise that an outdoor-minded company like Patagonia would pick it for

their corporate headquarters. Ventura is more isolated from its mountains than is Santa Barbara, but it gets fantastic surf and is just a short boat ride from the eastern end of the Channel Islands. The park headquarters for **Channel Islands National Park** is located here, and all Island Packers boats to the islands leave from Ventura Harbor.

# Parks & Other Hot Spots

## Hearst Castle/San Simeon State Park

42 miles north of San Luis Obispo on Hwy. 1. Tel. 805/927-2068. Open daily year-round. Some areas require fee.

There are few more mythical characters of the early 20th century than William Randolph Hearst. After becoming one of America's richest men by inheriting a huge fortune and making it even bigger through yellow journalism, timber, and ranching, the bombastic tycoon commissioned the construction of a huge castle on one of the many hillsides in the 275,000-acre Hearst Ranch beginning in 1919. Designed by acclaimed Berkeley architect Julia Morgan, the castle took more than 20 years to build. It's one of the more stunningly decadent pieces of architecture in the world, and more than a million visitors come here every year to take a look at the life led by the man immortalized by Orson Welles as "Citizen Kane."

There's much more to the park than the castle, though, including several beautiful beaches and a 1,000-foot pier from which once streamed the glittering stars of the 1920s and 1930s on their way to one of Hearst's parties. Fishing is good, diving is good, and beachcombing along the rocky point is great. Although there are 187 campsites here, they are hard to come by without reservations; thank those million visitors to the castle.

For more information about the little town of San Simeon (pop. 250), contact the **San Simeon Chamber of Commerce,** 9511 Hearst Dr., P.O. Box 1, San Simeon, CA 93452 (tel. 805/927-3500).

## Morro Bay State Park

12 miles north of San Luis Obispo on Hwy. 1. Exit on South Bay Blvd. and turn south. Turn right onto State Park Rd. and follow it into the park. Main St. in Morro Bay also becomes State Park Rd. if you follow it south from downtown.

This state park and the adjacent town with which it shares a name are the bustling center of one of the best wetland lagoons and most sheltered ports between Los Angeles and San Francisco. Rather than marking a clear dividing line between parks that are either "wild" or "man-made," Morro Bay is one of those towns where the two seem to go hand in hand. Seals sun themselves on harbor buoys. Fishermen bring in boatloads of salmon, lingcod, and albacore. The estuary, one of the five largest in the state, feels like the town's backyard, home to breeding shorebirds, waterfowl, and a huge number of juvenile fish. A special sight is the nesting population of great blue herons in a protected grove of eucalyptus trees. Morro Rock towers over the whole scene, an enormous, 800-foot-high igneous monolith that once sat surrounded by ocean and is now connected to the town by a sand and rock causeway.

## Montaña de Oro State Park

12 miles west of San Luis Obispo on Los Osos/Pecho Valley Rd. Tel. 805/528-0513.

This immense, primitive state park covers 8,400 acres and stretches along 3.5 miles of shoreline with terrain ranging from rolling sand dunes to high cliffs, rolling inland hills, and valleys. The park is named after the outrageous wildflower displays that happen every spring when California poppies turn the hillsides gold. The coast here faces right into the brunt of any north Pacific swell, and the surf here is often dangerous. Hazard Reef draws a hardy group of surfers who thrive on the wicked drop and big waves. Numerous hiking trails head along the dunes or into the park hills. On rare calm days, adventurous kayakers and divers enjoy the secluded, rocky shore.

## Pismo State Beach

Between the Santa Barbara–San Luis Obispo county line and Shell Beach, 75 miles north of Santa Barbara, 15 miles south of San Luis Obispo.

This wide, sandy beach backed by dunes is one of the largest coastal dune complexes remaining on the West Coast. The glamour of most other coastal villages has somehow eluded the town of Pismo. It's still known more for its biker bar and trailer parks than for its fantastic seaside location. The main attraction, park-wise, is the dune field that stretches for miles to the south of town. Driving is currently allowed along the beach, and large portions of the dunes are open to off-road vehicles. However, if you continue past the OHV (Off Highway Vehicle) area along the driving beach, there are some nice places to camp on the sand and explore the dune area. The fishing pier in Pismo is a popular way to spend a day, and surfers find peaks up and down the beach. The most famous denizen of Pismo is without a doubt the Pismo clam, known to bivalve connoisseurs as one of the sweetest clams around. Finding the clams involves lots of mucking around in the low-tide sand and requires a fishing license and measuring gauge.

## Jalama County Beach Park

55 miles west of Santa Barbara. Take Hwy. 1 from U.S. 101 and drive north about 10 miles to Jalama Rd. Follow Jalama Rd. 10 miles until it dead-ends at the beach.

Tucked in between two of the most forbidden coastal properties in the state—Vandenberg Air Force Base and the jealously guarded Bixby Ranch—Jalama County Park offers access to a little-visited area. Just a few miles north of Point Conception, the weather and water are noticeably colder than they are in Santa Barbara. Surfers and board-sailors flock here. It's one of the most reliable waves on the south coast. The park itself is small but houses a fine campground, a small store and restaurant, and miles of beautiful beach.

## Gaviota State Park

33 miles west of Santa Barbara. Take U.S. 101 north until you see the left-hand exit for the park. Coming from the north, the turnoff is shortly after the Gaviota rest area.

Gaviota abuts the legendary Hollister Ranch, known in surfing circles for perfect, glassy waves with hardly anyone out. Alas, the ranch is protectively guarded by its property owners and you won't have much luck walking in, which is why the boat-launching hoist on the Gaviota Pier is such a critical asset. Properly executed, you can launch a small boat at Gaviota and be surfing the ranch in about 15 minutes. Kayakers can also paddle up into the ranch, though expect to get hassled if you haul up on the beach. The state park itself is no slouch when it comes to beaches. The main camping area, pier, and beach lie at the mouth of Gaviota Creek, overshadowed by a train trestle. Better beaches lie down the coast, where several marked turnouts off Highway 101 mark San

# Forest Fees Have Users Fired Up

The Adventure Pass, initiated in 1997 as part of a congressional plan to raise revenue throughout America's national forests through a series of fee-based pilot programs, has touched off a flurry of protests and civil disobedience in Southern California. Critics charge that the pass—$5 a day or $30 annually—to use the Angeles, Cleveland, San Bernardino, and Los Padres national forests is just the camel's nose under the tent, a step that will lead to larger fees and greater commercialization of the forests. Many people have taken to hanging spoof "Misadventure Passes" from their car mirrors while they hike or placing protest signs in their car windows. Others simply ignore the law and hope they won't get caught. A car check at several popular trailheads in the San Bernardino and Los Padres national forests reveals that many people there have chosen to ignore the fee, risking a fix-it ticket rather than buying the pass. Since the pilot program is up for renewal in 1999, the Adventure Pass's long-term survival is directly tied to public acceptance and success as a revenue source.

In the Angeles National Forest, directly adjacent to the Los Angeles metropolitan area, people seem less agitated. "For the most part, people say that if they can see the results of their dollars at work, then it's okay," explained public relations point-person Gail Hughes. "They're not really angry with us. They're angry with the entire national budget process that's caused this."

Community activists on the Central Coast, however, have responded by leaning on merchants to cease selling the pass. In the small mountain town of Ojai, all but one business has stopped after customers threatened a boycott. Picketers have targeted the hold-out, the Oakview Shell Station, on recent weekends. "We have encouraged people to be polite, but anger has its place," said Jeff Pine. "The forest is the last thing that's free and we should never let it go."

Onofre and Vista del Mar beaches. Both are secluded and clothing-optional. Inland, 2,700 acres of chaparral and oak savannah open up a wealth of hiking options, and back up to the even larger Los Padres National Forest.

### Refugio State Beach

27 miles west of Santa Barbara off U.S. 101.

A favorite sheltered cove for fishermen, smugglers, pirates, and sailors making their way up and down the coast over the years, Refugio State Beach is also a beautiful setting for a campout or a picnic. The main beach is reminiscent of Hawaii. Date palms and banana trees line the shoreline and the banks of Refugio Creek. Surfing here is hit or miss, a good spot for beginners. Offshore, several reefs make this one of the Central Coast's most popular diving destinations. A gentle entry into the water and a short swim meet with some fantastic underwater scenery. Between here and El Capitan Beach 3 miles south, a bike path and several cove beaches make excellent day trips. A few miles up Refugio Canyon is Circle Bar B Ranch, which offers guided horseback riding.

The Adventure Pass is also under fire on practical grounds that it creates an enforcement problem while actually raising little money for forest maintenance and improvements. Leaked internal Forest Service documents from fiscal year 1997, the first year of the program, reveal that the lion's share of money collected went to pay the salaries of enforcement officers.

"Initially the Forest Service said that 80% of everything collected was going back to the area it came from, and a lot of us supported that," said Alasdair Coyne of the environmental group Keep the Sespe Wild. "But they pulled the wool over our eyes by not clearly stating that most of the dollars raised were going to enforcement staff. What ticks people off is not the money but the principle."

According to Los Padres National Forest Recreation Officer John Bridgwater, the pass has been a big success despite its critics. "There is a tremendous amount of support. It's no mystery that it costs a tremendous amount of money to manage public land. Most people understand that. The question is, should the entire nation pay for a local use, or should the person who uses it pay?"

Opponents counter that pay-per-use sets a dangerous precedent, and they point to heavy lobbying for the program by the American Recreation Coalition, a group of recreational vehicle manufacturers and large corporations including Disney.

"What would have to happen if private enterprise were to take over and make a profit off our forest?" asks Coyne. "First you'd have to get people used to paying a fee. That's what we're seeing now. Then the uniform changes from a forest service to a Disney uniform. In a nutshell, the ARC's agenda is motorized recreation on our privatized public lands with Mickey Mouse giving interpretive tours to visitors for a fee."

## El Capitan State Beach

24 miles west of Santa Barbara on U.S. 101.

This is the first major beach access west of Goleta, and a fine one at that. During west swells the point at El Capitan is a famous surfing wave. Along the other side of the point is a long, sandy beach, popular in summer with families. Camping sites are tucked in several different oak groves overlooking the sea. Spearfishing in the mixed rocky-sandy areas of the point is very productive for halibut. And, of course, the 3 miles of coves and beaches between here and Refugio make for great explorations.

## Los Padres National Forest

Multiple areas in the inland mountains between Morro Bay and Ventura. Headquarters located at 6144 Calle Real, Goleta, CA 93117. Tel. 805/683-6711.

The southern section of Los Padres National Forest stretches unbroken along the mountain spine from Morro Bay to the westernmost edge of Los Angeles County. Two large wilderness areas, hundreds of miles of hiking trails, numerous camping areas, several large creeks, and miles of fire road make this a valuable asset for Southern California outdoorspeople. Peaks range up to almost 9,000 feet, and the terrain, almost universally steep and rugged, is forested in chaparral, oak woodland, and high pine forest. The California condor has been reintroduced to the forest after several years of captive breeding and appears to be doing well.

## Carpinteria State Beach

Located in the town of Carpinteria, 12 miles southeast of Santa Barbara.

Sometimes being on the edge of town is a good thing. With Carpinteria State Beach that's certainly true. While not a wilderness experience, it's one of those great places where the visitors get to live on the beach, albeit in tents, while the permanent residents live farther back. The town itself is a wonderfully laid-back place built on ranching and flower raising. Linden Avenue is the main drag. For a real hit of local culture, stop off at The Palms bar and restaurant any given night. They serve your steak raw here, and you must cook it yourself on the roaring grill. The only downside to Carpinteria State Beach is that it seems like a lot of people "camping" here are really long-term residents living out of their cars. While I can hardly blame anyone without a home for making one here, it sometimes gives the campground a more lived-in feel than you might wish.

## Emma Wood State Beach

3 miles north of Ventura on U.S. 101. Northbound you'll take the State Beaches exit. Southbound, exit at Seacliff and follow the oceanfront road for about 5 miles.

Except for the train tracks and the freeway roaring overhead, this might be a really great park. Unfortunately, the freeway and train tracks are here to stay. Meanwhile, this is the only place to camp in Ventura proper. The beach is rocky and you're more likely to be lulled to sleep by roaring trucks than by waves. As a surfing spot it's known as Ventura Overheads, both for the overpass and for the sometimes sizeable waves that break on an offshore reef.

## McGrath State Beach

Between Ventura and Oxnard off Harbor Blvd. Exit U.S. 101 onto Harbor Blvd. and head south.

At first glance the coastline between Ventura and Oxnard appears completely given over to power plants, working harbors, go-kart race tracks—anything but coastal wilderness. But it's a false impression. McGrath State Beach is a true gem in the middle of some less-than-perfect examples of resource management. McGrath Beach is wide and exposed to virtually every swell direction. While that's a big plus for surfers, swimming here is only for the hardy. Currents and high surf make it inadvisable for casual dips. The campground is laid out in the lee of some nice coastal dunes. South of the campground is a huge electrical generation plant that looms forbodingly over the scene, but north of the camp is the Santa Clara River Estuary Natural Preserve. Birders here rave about the sightings of such rare species as California least terns, Belding's Savannah sparrow, egrets, and great blue herons.

# Point Conception to San Simeon ✦ What to Do & Where to Do It

## BEACHES

It's almost ridiculous to try to choose the best beaches from such a wealth of prospects. Because the Central Coast sits on such a dramatic transition zone, you've got almost every kind of beach known to humankind to choose among. North of Point Conception, fans of dramatic, wave-lashed rocky beaches will love the beaches near San Simeon and Montaña de Oro; sand-dune lovers can lose themselves for hours in the giant coastal dunes of Morro Bay, Guadalupe, or Pismo, where omnipresent winds offer daily lessons in how sand dunes are built. This north- and west-facing part of the Central Coast above Point Conception is generally colder, foggier, and less accommodating for lying on the sand and swimming than are the southern beaches, though certain microclimates do exist where you'll find a bit of sun and warmth. The most notable of these is Avila Beach, in the lee of Avila Harbor. Popular with Cal Poly San Luis Obispo students, this is the closest thing you'll find to the stereotypical Southern California beach-party lifestyle. Avila Beach sits at the end of Avila Beach

Drive, which has its own freeway exit off U.S. 101, 8 miles south of San Luis Obispo. If the collegiate beach scene is overwhelming, Pirate's Cove is just around the corner, a beautiful nude beach hemmed in by 100-foot cliffs. Instead of following Avila Beach Drive all the way to the sea, turn left on Cave Landing Road, and drive to the dead end. From here it's a long climb down to the sand, but the remote, perfect cove is well worth the effort.

Pismo Beach has its fans, but I'm not really one of them. I find wide, flat beaches boring, and Pismo is a wide, flat beach that stretches for miles and miles. It has the distinction of being the only public beach in Southern California where you can drive your car on the sand, which I suppose is an attraction for some. The surf fishing is good, and the sand dunes here, where they're not being torn to ribbons by off-highway vehicles, are really spectacular.

It's below Point Conception that things really start looking up for those of us who like our beaches warm, our surf glassy, and the water tolerably temperate. These beaches are covered in the section "Point Conception to Oxnard ✦ What to Do & Where to Do It," which follows this section.

## BIRD WATCHING

Morro Bay State Park reads like a thesaurus devoted solely to words signifying "birds love to feed and breed here": salt marsh, slough, estuary, tidal basin, eel grass beds, coastal dunes, surf zone, etc. From the park's interpretive center alone you stand a chance of seeing thousands of migratory waterfowl: loons, wigeons, pintails, geese, buffleheads, canvasbacks. The rich tidal areas are a feeding zone for both the California brown pelican and the American white pelican. The latter, much larger than its brown-feathered relative, is rarely sighted on the California coast. In a eucalyptus grove, great blue herons nest in the treetops they share with monarch butterflies. The sandy shoreline and tidal mudflats are almost overwhelmed with populations of shorebirds working hard for their dinner. But the most spectacular resident of the Morro Bay area is the peregrine falcon. Towering Morro Rock is closed to climbing just to protect this endangered raptor. The huge rock is one of the easiest places in the world to spot this bird, since it is surrounded by ocean and sand beach, and sightlines are completely open. Some of the best birding in Morro Bay is done by kayak or canoe. Miles of backwater slough and wetland can be reached by careful paddling. You want to watch your tide tables closely, as certain areas turn into a quagmire of mudflats at low tide. Though the birding will be great as you sit there in your kayak waiting for the tide to refloat you in a couple hours, if you get left high and dry by a dropping tide, it's really not a pleasant experience sitting like a literal stick in the mud.

Just south of Morro Bay State Park, Montaña De Oro State Park offers access to the oceanfront portion of the Morro Bay sand spit. Snowy plovers nest out in the coastal dunes, and numerous raptor species hunt the grassy hillsides for mice and gophers.

## BOARDSAILING

The biggest drawback to boardsailing in Southern California is a lack of predictable ocean breezes. The howlers that make ocean boardsailing such a kick don't show up with much predictability along most of the coast. There are, however, a few worthy exceptions.

Just north of San Simeon is a series of state beaches that are nothing more than pullouts on the ocean side of the road and trails leading down to the sand. Boardsailors find great wind and surfable waves here throughout the year, with the best times being winter and spring. It's advanced turf out there; lots of kelp in the water, strong currents and waves, and big rocks. And the water, of course, is cold. But the beauty of the southern end of the Santa Lucia Mountains rising behind the rolling grazing lands of the Hearst Ranch, while you're ripping along under a 25-knot wind, is not something soon forgotten.

## FISHING

Sit outside Virg's Landing Sportfishing in Morro Bay (tel. 805/772-2216) as the boats are unloading at the end of the day and you're likely to see a lot of fishermen huffing heavy catches up the pier. It's one of the most productive areas of the coast. Depending on the season, the boats will be chasing salmon (March to April), Albacore (September to October), white sea bass (summer), and lingcod and rockfish (year-round). Such phenomenal catches are the results of miles of relatively pristine coastline with light fishing pressure. Depending on the species, your party boat may stop right outside the bay or roam 25 miles.

An excellent alternative to the open ocean fishing grounds is the shallow sandflats of Morro Bay itself. Anyone with a small boat, kayak, or even bellyboat stands a pretty decent chance of bringing home dinner by drifting a live anchovy or casting jigs during the spring and summer months. Port San Luis is the next port down the coast and famous for its excellent bottom fishing. The boats range as far as Point Sal to the south and Point Buchon to the north to wherever the hot fishing is. During the occasional summer albacore runs, Port San Luis comes alive as everyone tries to get into the hot action. For party boat information and charters, call **Paradise Sportfishing** (tel. 805/ 595-7200). And while you're in the area, the San Luis Pier between Port San Luis and Avila Beach is known as the best-producing halibut pier in the state. Summer is the best time, and live anchovies are the proven bait. Pismo pier is almost equally as productive and is a really beautiful setting. Pismo Beach was once famous for the huge numbers of Pismo clams taken here every year. Among clam aficionados, Pismo clams are legendary for their tender, sweet flesh.

Overfishing and pollution from nearby oil spills took their toll, however, and the clam population was decimated. For several years the fishery was closed, but it's open again under much more strictly regulated conditions. You'll want to check the most recent set of California sportfishing regulations before digging.

## HIKING & BACKPACKING

What sets the Central Coast apart from the rest of Southern California is the incredible diversity of wilderness ideal for hiking, all within a stone's throw of the Pacific. Some of the most remote and wonderful destinations are in the backcountry of Santa Barbara County, yet there are also excellent hikes leading right out of downtown Santa Barbara, San Luis Obispo, and Ojai. Many of these are really underutilized by a local population that seems to take what lies in their backyard for granted. With the exception of a few extremely popular hikes, it's usually possible to find solitude within minutes of town.

### Black Mountain Trail, Morro Bay State Park

3 miles round-trip. Easy–moderate. 600-foot elevation gain. Exit Hwy. 1 at Los Osos–Baywood Park exit 12 miles north of San Luis Obispo. Take South Bay Blvd. 0.75 mile south to Morro Bay State Park. Enter the

park and veer left at the fork toward the campground, where you'll find the Exercise Trailhead. Map: Morro Bay Area State Parks Map ($1 from Morro Bay State Park; Tel. 805/528-0513).

Morro Rock is only the most famous of nine volcanic plugs that run in almost a direct north-south line between San Luis Obispo and Morro Bay. Created 15 million years ago as underwater volcanoes, they've since eroded into high, toothy sentinels overlooking the beautiful coast and ranchland of the Central Coast. Black Peak is the second to the farthest north (Morro Rock being the northernmost) and is easily climbed for a fantastic view of the expansive bay and surrounding dunes, mountains, and ocean. From the Exercise Trailhead you'll cross a road and then begin climbing the hill. Approximately a mile from the trailhead comes the first junction, where you want to stick to the left. You'll know you're on the way to the top when you begin to switchback and break out of the coastal scrub that lines much of the trail. The view from the top is extraordinary. From here you're faced with two options; either return the way you came, or follow the summit trail back to the junction where you bore left and follow the other leg. It will take you past the golf course and through a monarch butterfly roosting area. The butterflies are here from about October until March. Look high in the eucalyptus trees for clusters of these beautiful creatures.

### Bluff Trail

4 miles. Easy. Relatively flat. From San Luis Obispo, exit U.S. 101 at Los Osos/Baywood Park and drive 12 miles west on Los Osos Valley Rd. The road changes name to Pecho Valley Rd. and enters Montaña de Oro State Park. About 3 miles into the park, you'll come to park headquarters and a parking

area, where the trail begins. Map: Morro Bay Area State Map ($1 from Morro Bay State Park; Tel. 805/528-0513).

Montaña de Oro State Park is one of the most striking coastal parks in the state. You'll follow the aptly named Bluff Trail south along the top of seaside cliffs and coves. The ocean here teems with life. Keep your eyes peeled for migrating gray whales during the winter months. In spring, you'll want to turn your eyes inland, where the awesome flower blooms that give the park its name (Mountain of Gold, in Spanish) will take your breath away. Along the way you'll pass Spooner's Cove, once a favorite anchorage of rumrunners during Prohibition, and several other coves. The turnaround point is Grotto Rock, where seabirds and seals are often home. Return to the parking area the way you came.

## Valencia Peak Trail

Montaña de Oro State Park. 4 miles. Moderate. 1,300-foot elevation gain. Relatively flat. Drive about 10 miles west on Los Osos Valley Rd. The road changes name to Pecho Valley Rd. and enters Montaña de Oro State Park. About 3 miles into the park you'll come to park headquarters and a parking area, where the trail begins. Map: Morro Bay Area State Parks Map ($1 from Morro Bay State Park; Tel. 805/528-0513).

Valencia Peak is the mountain of gold after which the park is named—but don't start scrounging around for nuggets. So far as I know there is no real gold here. The name stems from the massive displays of California poppies here in the spring. The trail begins as the Rattlesnake Flats Trail but splits quickly at a signed intersection, where you'll stick to the Valencia Peak Trail. Like Morro Rock and Black Peak, Valencia Peak is the remnant of an underwater volcano. The view from the top of this one is a knee-knocker, 90 miles of coastline on a clear day. It's often very windy at the top but well worth the trouble.

## Pecho Coast Trail

Diablo Canyon Nuclear Power Plant. 7 miles. Easy. To enjoy this hike you must be part of the docent-led Nature Conservancy group that makes a limited number of forays behind the high-security gates of PG&E every week. For information, call 805/541-8735. To reach the trailhead you'll exit U.S. 101 at Avilach Dr. and follow the road 4 miles through a lovely canyon to the heavily guarded power plant gate in Avila Beach.

You might think that only Homer Simpson would consider hiking inside the boundaries of a nuclear power plant, particularly one that's famous for being built on an earthquake fault, but if there's ever been a reason to do it, this is the hike. Long before Pacific Gas and Electric got it into their sensitive brains to build a radioactive time bomb on some of the more spectacular coastline you'll ever see, this was a private ranch. The power company bought it all and built their thing. Fortunately, the power plant occupies only a tiny portion of the actual property, the rest of which has been left in pristine condition. After passing through the tense, high-security atmosphere of the gate, you'll quickly decompress when you see the waves crashing on the rocky shore. The most common destination is historic Point San Luis Lighthouse, but along the way you might stop to examine ancient Chumash relics, watch spouting whales and feeding sea otters, or be surprised when a large family of deer leaps out of the brush along the trail. The guided hikes are geared toward a slow pace. Don't expect to racehorse through here and be out in a couple hours. Generally the hike to the lighthouse and back takes all day.

## Point Sal Trail

Point Sal State Park. 7 miles round-trip. Moderate. No serious elevation gain but lots of scrambling and several exposed sections. Access: From Hwy. 1 in Guadalupe, continue south 3 miles to Point Sal Rd. Map: USGS Point Sal.

Though it's technically a state park, there's nothing here but a dirt parking lot and a few fire pits. Oh, and miles and miles of stunningly pristine coastline with not a single building in sight. To the south lies Vandenberg Air Force Base, and hiking into the base is a big no-no that's sure to gain you a visit from some very serious security forces. Save yourself the trouble and venture north instead. The coast is prettier this way and you can see your destination, the massive headland of Point Sal. A small island named Lions Rock sits off the point and is covered with seals. I've heard reports of white shark sightings around the rock, but you're more likely to catch a glimpse of whales passing very close to shore while rounding the point. The trail itself is faint and no place for people with a fear of heights, often clinging to slippery shale hillsides or skirting the tops of eroded cliffs. The best bet is to time your hike with an outgoing tide and try to return before it comes all the way back in, as the going is much easier when you can walk along the beach much of the way. Fog socks this coast in for days at a time, but if you catch Point Sal on one of its glorious sunny days, you'll never forget the place.

### MOUNTAIN BIKING

Maybe it's the lack of population, maybe it's just that people are a little more mellow here, but the Central Coast has

largely avoided the mountain bike vs. hikers and horses wars that have plagued other parts of the state. For a hardcore cyclist, this is phenomenal country. Through the entire area, mountains rise up right next to the sea. This creates the kind of dramatic setting where you can bike up a lushly wooded canyon filled with waterfalls, crest a ridge with 180-degree views of the Pacific, and then ride down into the remote backcountry of the Los Padres National Forest where you're not likely to see another soul.

There is a huge amount of empty land out there behind Central Coast towns like San Luis Obispo, Santa Maria, and Santa Barbara, but it's far from useless. Hundreds of miles of fire road and single track offer rides ranging from a 3-day ride over the high peaks of the Sierra Madre to a short pedal to a deep swimming hole. Enjoy.

## Bluff Trail

Montaña De Oro State Park. 4 miles, round-trip. Easy. Very little elevation change or technical riding. Access: From San Luis Obispo you'll exit U.S. 101 at Los Osos Valley Rd. and continue west 12 miles to the park sign. Los Osos Valley Rd. changes name along the way to Pecho Valley Rd. Map: Montaña de Oro State Park Trail Map.

Bicycle along the wild edge of one of California's most beautiful beachfront parks on this wonderful path. Park at the main headquarters area and catch the trail on the west side of Pecho Valley Road a hundred yards south of the parking lot. The trail heads south, skirting the edge of a dramatic cliff. Below lie the crashing waves of the Pacific. During fall, winter, and spring you're likely to see spouting gray whales passing by on their migration between the feeding grounds of Alaska and their calving lagoons in Baja. Several sheltered coves here were favorites of rumrunners during Prohibition. Now they only occasionally shelter passing fishing boats. Watch your speed on this trail, as it's also one of the park's most popular hiking trails, and everyone seems to pay more attention to the ocean than to where they go. After 1.7 miles of beachfront riding, the road turns up Coon Creek to Pecho Valley Road. Your choice is to either pedal back along the road or to return along the blufftops the way you came.

This is an excellent trail for kids because it's fairly level and there are lots of interesting stops along the way. Nothing makes a better break than sighting whales or seals. The only bad side is that you are riding along the tops of some serious drop-offs, so make sure you steer with a steady hand.

## Islay Creek Loop

Montaña De Oro State Park. 8 miles round-trip. Moderate–difficult. 1,500-foot elevation gain. Some technical sections. Access: From San Luis Obispo you'll exit U.S. 101 at Los Osos Valley Rd. and continue west 12 miles to the park sign. Continue to park headquarters (Tel. 805/528-0513) and park there. Map: Montaña de Oro State Park Trail Map.

Park at the main headquarters area and catch the Islay Creek fire road on the east side of Pecho Valley Road a hundred yards north of the parking lot to explore the high inland hills of Montaña de Oro State Park, with views of the Central Coast. The first 3 miles are easy, passing through beautiful wooded areas and past a waterfall. At the junction with the East Boundary Trail, turn left onto the single track. Almost immediately you start climbing to a ridgeline. There's some easy technical single track riding through here, perfect practice for harder rides. At almost 5 miles you come to a second trail junction, where you'll

choose Ridge Trail, the left fork. It continues climbing to the high point of the ride, Hazard Peak, where you get a tremendous view of the ocean and Morro Bay. From here it's literally all downhill to Pecho Valley Road and your car.

## Upper Hazard Canyon

Montaña De Oro State Park. 4 miles round-trip. Moderate. 800-foot elevation change. Access: From San Luis Obispo you'll exit U.S. 101 at Los Osos Valley Rd. and continue west 12 miles to the park sign. Just inside the park boundary you'll see cars parked where a fire road crosses the main park road. Map: Montaña de Oro State Park Trail Map.

Just after entering Montaña de Oro State Park, look for Hazard Canyon Road. Lower Hazard Canyon is a popular beach and surf break, so there will be cars along the road. You're headed up the fire road away from the ocean, though. For riders intimidated by technical single track, this is an excellent introduction to the riding in this state park. You'll gently climb the bottom Hazard Canyon as it rises up the flanks of Hazard Peak. Beautiful foliage and nice views abound. Watch out for horses, as there is an equestrian camp in the canyon. You'll either get tired and turn around or you'll reach the end of the road near the park boundary. The ride down is a pleasure cruise.

## ROAD BIKING

The Central Coast, relatively undeveloped compared to the rest of coastal Southern California, is a rider's paradise of lonely back routes. You can take your pick from either wine country or beachside rides. And with the moderate climate of this region, the biking is good year-round.

## Cambria to Cayucos

45-mile loop. Difficult. Heavy traffic on Hwy. 1 and strong winds. Access: Take Hwy. 1 north of San Luis Obispo to the small seaside town of Cambria. Park anywhere.

Though you're close to the coast much of the way, this ride is really best for its beautiful ranch country, rather than its proximity to the beach. Beginning in the lovely town of Cambria, pedal south on Highway 1, wind at your back, to Cayucos. (I do this ride counterclockwise because of the wind.) Follow the Old Coast Highway (which also leads to Morro Bay) into Cayucos, and a few miles south of town, make a left on Old Creek Road and start climbing. You'll gain about 1,350 feet before dropping down and crossing Highway 46. Continue north on what's now called Cypress Mountain Road, and it's up to Sky Ranch you go. This is the highest point of the ride. What a view. (To your left is Black Mountain.) It's a snaky descent along Santa Rosa Creek Road and back into Cambria.

## Lake Nacimiento

30 miles out and back. Moderate to difficult. Hills; hot in summer. Access: From U.S.101 in Paso Robles, exit at Nacimiento Lake Rd. Park and ride along the road to the lake and back.

This beautiful road ride through the hills of San Luis Obispo County allows you to top it off with a swim at Lake Nacimiento. It's hilly, with some steep climbing. Paso Robles means "pass of the oaks," and that's exactly what you'll do on your ride through this beautiful countryside. From Nacimiento Lake Drive in Paso Robles, continue west on NLD. Continue straight at the intersection with San Marcos Road, and keep climbing until you get to Lake

Nacimiento. Spring is best for this ride; the wildflowers are beautiful and the lake will still be full enough for a fun swim. After your swim, retrace your path back to your starting point.

## Peachy Canyon Loop

28 miles. Moderate. Rolling hills. Can be hot in summer. Exit U.S. 101 in Paso Robles at Adelaida Rd. Park and begin riding west.

This is a beautiful road ride through hills filled with California live oak in the wine country of San Luis Obispo County. From Adelaida Road in Paso Robles (just west of the 101 freeway), begin pedaling west on Adelaida Road. The rolling hills here are quite beautiful and so peaceful—and there's great wine tasting, too. Soon you'll pass the Adelaida Cellars vineyard. At the first fork stay left, as the road curves around and becomes Vineyard Drive. At Peachy Canyon Road, go left and soon you'll pass the Peachy Canyon winery. When Peachy Canyon Road ends, go left and back to your starting point.

## San Luis Obispo—Morro Bay Loop

36 miles. Difficult. Heavy ocean breezes and potential for bad traffic. Access: Begin at the Madonna Inn off U.S. 101 south of San Luis Obispo.

From the ticky-tacky towers of the Madonna Inn, this loop will take you through the beautiful Los Osos Valley on the way to Morro Bay and then return via Highway 1. To begin, take Madonna Road west about a mile until you reach Los Osos Valley Road. With a nice shoulder and bike lane, you're set for a relaxing warm-up as you pedal through a mixture of tract housing and old farms. Periodic eucalyptus groves scent the air. You'll reach the little village of Los Osos and hang a right on Pecho Valley Road. A nice side trip (which adds 14 miles) is to turn left on Pecho Valley Road and head out to Montaña de Oro State Park. But heading right, you'll zigzag through the residential streets of this bayside town by turning right on Mitchell, left on Pine, right on Ramona, left on Fourth, right on Santa Ysabel, and, finally, left on South Bay Boulevard.

Here you're going to pedal almost 2 miles through Morro Bay State Park between Black Mountain and the shallow estuary of Morro Bay. Several lookouts make for a nice break. Without turning, you'll find yourself on Country Club Drive, which continues into the hardworking port town of Morro Bay.

Your goal here is to simply stay along the waterfront and head for Morro Rock, the towering monolith that marks the north end of the bay. You can ride right up to its base, but climbing is prohibited. A wind- and wave-lashed beach marks the northern edge of the bay. Turning around, you'll want to pedal back into town and follow the signs for Highway 1. It's 10 miles south to San Luis Obispo, but with the prevailing wind blowing at your back it's an easy ride most days. Cross over U.S. 101 on Highway 1 (which becomes Santa Rosa Street in town). Turn right off Santa Rosa onto Higuera, which will take you through downtown San Luis Obispo to the Madonna Road overcrossing and your car.

## ROCK CLIMBING

A couple of years ago, just a few days before Christmas, a couple of my friends from New York City came to visit me in Santa Barbara. They're climbing gym rats but had never climbed on real rock. I took them up to **Gibraltar Rock** (see "Point Conception to Oxnard ♦ What to Do & Where to Do It" for directions), a large area of sandstone outcroppings

that overlooks the Pacific Ocean from high atop the front range of the Santa Ynez Mountains. Their jaws dropped when they saw the warm sandstone face of just one of the climbing spots at Gibraltar. A storm had blown through the day before and left the air clear as glass. From Point Conception and San Miguel Island in the west to Point Mugu in the east, the entire Santa Barbara Channel was sparkling below. There was nobody else around. A red-tailed hawk circled below us.

We rigged a top rope and scurried down a slippery trail to the bottom of the pitch. Stacy went first, racing up the sandstone face like a Lycra-clad spider. At the top she looked around and said, simply, "I can't believe this." Alan went next, picking a tougher line and grunting his way through a couple of tough moves. Then it was my turn. With Stacy as my belay, I cheated my way around the nasty little overhang that you had to surmount just to get on the pitch and started working my way up a wide crack. Knobs and little finger holes presented themselves at perfect intervals. Stopping on a ledge mid-pitch, I stuck my head in a little alcove. There, munching on the only piece of grass for at least 40 vertical feet, was a huge yellow banana slug. This dry, sunny sandstone face seemed the most unlikely place for a slug to live, but he appeared healthy. A couple minutes later I found myself 15 feet from the top of the pitch with what seemed like no holds to follow. I tried to think like the slug, look for tiny little surfaces that would give me purchase. One tiny hold at a time, they appeared, and I was sitting on top of the world.

We each climbed Gibraltar Rock a couple more times before darkness caught us. As I pulled in the rope from the top, the mountains turned purple and the last glow of orange sank into the sea. We motored down the hill to a bottle of red wine and a pasta dinner. We decided that winter in Southern California isn't such a bad thing.

Not every day is that perfect, but the Central Coast presents a surprising amount of good rock climbing. It's almost universally sandstone, the only exception being some volcanic rock at Bishop Peak in San Luis Obispo. The rock quality varies widely, but it's hard to complain in light of the beauty of the surroundings and the climate.

While most Sierra Nevada climbing is shut down by winter, the Central Coast is nice all year. Likewise, when winter meccas like Joshua Tree are roasting under 110°F summer heat, the vast majority of Central Coast climbing spots are comfortably cooled by the ocean influence. It's truly a year-round climbing destination. Though the routes are generally short and the rock not up to the standards of Yosemite or Joshua Tree, you'll find few people complaining.

If you decide to get deeply into Central Coast climbing, you should pick up a copy of *Climbing in Santa Barbara, Ventura, and San Luis Obispo* by Steve Tucker and Kevin Steele (Lorraine Press). With photographs and pitch-by-pitch route descriptions for dozens of climbing spots in the area, it's an indispensable resource.

The northernmost climbing spot in this chapter is **Bishop's Peak.** The peak is one of the Seven Sisters, a series of volcanic plugs that run from San Luis Obispo to Morro Bay and include Morro Rock (which is closed to climbers to protect nesting peregrine falcons). To reach it, take Highway 1 north from U.S. 101 in San Luis Obispo. At Highland Drive, turn left (west) and drive all the way to the dead end under the peak. A gate and well-worn paths lead to the three primary climbing walls: Cracked Wall, P-Wall, and Shadow Wall. A variety of bolted and nonbolted routes range from 5.6 to 5.12a.

San Luis Obispo also has a climbing gym, **Crux Climbing,** at 1150 Laurel Lane (tel. 805/544-2789), which is a good place to hook up with local climbers and cadge information about local secret spots.

## SAILING

North of Point Conception, the Central Coast is the kind of place most sailors like to get through quickly without lingering. It's extremely exposed to both wind and swell, and it lacks any real cruising ground. You're either out on the Pacific in all her glory or you're sitting in port. If you're adamant that you must go sailing here, I suggest you call my friend **Capt. Rob Bollay,** who runs sailing classes and periodic charters out of both Morro Bay and Port San Luis (tel. 805/541-6569).

Below Point Conception is a whole different ball of wax. The **Santa Barbara Channel** is one of the best cruising grounds in the world. Small-boat sailors will enjoy ripping along in the sheltered waters near shore with the dependable afternoon sea breeze, and large-boat sailors are in paradise. You can day-sail out of Santa Barbara Harbor, Ventura Harbor, or Channel Islands Harbor, or make an overnight trip to the Channel Islands from any of those ports. Santa Barbara presents the best approach to the islands—normally it's a 21-mile-plus broad reach to Santa Cruz Island on one tack. Ventura and Onxard are closer to Anacapa and the east end of Santa Cruz, but what you can save in distance you give up by having to sail upwind.

**Santa Barbara Sailing Center** on the Breakwater at Santa Barbara Harbor (tel. 805/962-2826) teaches a full spectrum of American Sailing Association courses and has a rental fleet ranging from dinghies to a 42-foot Catalina with almost anything in between. In Channel Islands Harbor, contact **Offshore Sailing** at 805/

985-3600 for their selection of ASA classes and a description of their Charter Fleet.

## SCUBA DIVING

Central California has the most diverse diving anywhere on the mainland coast of the state. While it is often overshadowed by the world-class boat diving out at the Channel Islands, the near-shore diving between **San Simeon** and **Point Mugu** spans everything from sunken ships to thick kelp beds teaming with life and a warm-water dive in the outlet of a PG&E power plant. While the environments on both sides of Point Conception are similar at first glance, a savvy diver will also notice that the Central Coast is roughly divided into two separate ecosystems. North of Point Conception, certain species, such as spiny lobster, disappear and others, such as abalone and sea otters, become more plentiful. The northern half of the Central Coast is also much more prone to bad visibility and rough surf, while the south-facing coast of Santa Barbara and Ventura counties below Point Conception is more amenable to regular beach diving.

**Virg's Sport Fishing & Scuba Diving** at 1215 Embarcadero, Morro Bay (tel. 805/722-1222), runs eight different boats out of Morro Bay and San Simeon that are mostly used for sportfishing but also run periodic dive trips to the unsullied waters of the southern Big Sur coast or the rarely explored dive sites around Point Buchon and Diablo Canyon. These trips are highly susceptible to bad weather but can be spectacular when the conditions come together. A good dive store in the area is **SLO Ocean Currents** at 3121 S. Higuera in San Luis Obispo (tel. 805/544-7227).

Shore diving sites in this area are so plentiful that describing each and every one of them would take an encyclopedia, not just a section in a book. The following are some of my favorites.

## Morro Rock

Immediately north of Morro Bay at the end of the waterfront Embarcadero. Advanced.

Before a sand and rock causeway was built to connect this towering offshore monolith with the mainland, it was an island. Now getting there is as easy as driving a car. Park in the large lot on the north side of the rock where the giant warm-water outlet from the PG&E electrical generating plant pours into the sea. Stop and check the surf very carefully for at least 15 minutes. If the swell is lying low enough for you to be confident of entering and exiting the water, you're in for a treat.

Gear up and enter the water as close to the warm-water outlet and the shore of Morro Rock as you can. Assuming the plant is in operation, and it almost always is, you'll be carried along in a fast current. Enjoy the smooth transition from this bathtub water to the icy waters that you'll be swimming in soon enough. At first you'll see lots of sand, but this quickly turns to a mixed rock and sea grass structure. Follow the shore of the rock as far as you're comfortable and explore the rocky jumble underwater. Spearfishers have good luck here with rockfish, cabezon, and the occasional lingcod. Watch the surface for sea otters and sea lions.

When it's time to return to shore, stay calm and remember the current that gave you a free ride out. It's obviously working against you now, so you must swim out away from the rock and come back outside the influence of the massive flow. This puts you into a zone of larger surf and a potentially difficult exit. It's best to dive this spot on an incoming tide so you can swim in with-out having to drag your tired body and gear over shallow rocks.

## Fairbank Point, Morro Bay State Park

On State Park Rd. at the south end of Morro Bay. Park south of the Blue Heron Reserve and before you reach the museum. Inter-mediate.

The placid waters inside Morro Bay are a much different dive experience from most of the Central Coast. Visibility is generally poor in this nutrient-rich bay and harbor, but, hey, you don't have to fight for your life to get in and out. From the shore access by the parking lot, you're going to swim out to Fairbank Point in front of the nesting heron re-serve. This is the deepest part of Morro Bay, ranging to about 50 feet. Look for a jumble of rocks that range from shallow to about 50 feet at the bottom of the boat channel. Here you'll likely see some large fish and rays. Remember that you're under a navigable boat channel. Always use a float and be extremely cau-tious when ascending. Dive this spot on a slack tide to avoid struggles with the fast bay currents.

## Shell Beach

Shell Beach Rd. off U.S. 101. Beginner to intermediate.

Several diving opportunities exist in the town of Shell Beach. In particular, the northernmost cove facing Avila Beach and Port San Luis and the southernmost cove facing Pismo Beach present excel-lent nearshore kelp beds and rocky pinnacles covered in invertebrate marinelife. During periods of flat surf, the visibility can get quite good here, up to 35 or 40 feet. Hunters will find a variety of large game fish.

### SEA KAYAKING

In **Morro Bay** you can rent kayaks, ar-range guided tours, and buy gear from **Kayak Horizons,** 551 Embarcadero (tel. 805/772-6444); or from **Kayak's of Morro Bay,** 699 Embarcadero no. 9 (tel. 805/ 772-1119). Both have a fine selection of gear and nearby access to the bay. In Shell Beach, check out Central Coast Kayaks and Shoreline Excursions, 1879 Shell Beach Rd. (tel. 805/733-3500).

## Morro Bay Paddle

1–12 miles. Easy–moderate. Access: From Hwy. 1 take the Morro Bay exit and follow signs to Morro Bay State Park. State Park Rd. eventually reaches the bayside, where there is a nice parking area and shore ac-cess near the museum. Numerous other access points exist near Morro Bay's waterfront street, Embarcadero.

Adjacent to the state park and town with which it shares a name, Morro Bay is one of the best wetland lagoons and most sheltered ports between Los Angeles and San Francisco. Here, seals sun themselves on harbor buoys and fisher-men bring in boatloads of salmon, ling-cod, and albacore. The estuary, one of the five largest in the state, feels like the town's backyard, home to breeding shorebirds, waterfowl, and a huge num-ber of juvenile fish. A special sight is the nesting population of great blue herons in a protected grove of eucalyptus trees. Morro Rock towers over the whole scene, an enormous, 800-foot-high igne-ous monolith that once sat surrounded by ocean and is now connected to the town by a sand and rock causeway.

The shelter of the bay makes this an easy paddle for kids, and the marinelife and waterfowl are amazing. For the most interesting examples of nature, cross the main harbor channel and explore the backwaters of the bay. These shallow regions are inaccessible to larger boats and swarm with birds, fish, rays, and small sharks. Morro Bay State Park also features the Museum of Natural History, with exhibits on geology, oceanography, native plants and animals, and Native American life, so you can get acquainted with the region either before or after your paddle.

## SURFING

With all the turns and corners in the coastline between San Simeon and Oxnard, the coast is literally exposed to every prevailing swell that hits the California coast. Summer finds playful south swells hitting **Cayucos Beach** just north of Morro Bay. A few miles closer to San Luis Obispo, the heavy local spot is **Hazard Canyon** in Montaña de Oro State Park. The locals are tough but it's the wave you should devote your worry to. Coming out of deep water, it hits a shallow rock ledge and pitches in a steep and, some would say, awful takeoff. Getting caught inside here is a study in fear on big winter swells. Pismo Beach on the north side of Pismo Pier is a favorite with surfers of all stripes. Conditions vary from gentle longboarding waves to screaming hollow barrels. The only way to really know is to go look. **Pancho's Surf Shop,** 181 Pomeroy Ave., Pismo Beach, CA (tel. 805/773-7100) is just a few doors up from the Pismo Pier parking lot and has rental surfboards, boogie boards, and wetsuits.

## WALKS & ROADSIDE ATTRACTIONS

### Guadalupe Dunes

1–5 miles. Access: From Hwy. 1, 15 miles south of Pismo Beach, turn west onto Oso Flaco Lake Rd. In 3 miles, you'll come to the entrance of the Nature Conservancy's Guadalupe Dunes Reserve. Pay a small fee and walk into the park.

The Guadalupe Dunes are the most impressive coastal dunes in the state. Towering as high as 400 feet above the crashing surf and a series of small freshwater lakes, they've been used as the backdrop for films ranging from Cecil B. DeMille's *Ten Commandments* to the more recent *G.I. Jane* starring Demi Moore. The real stars of the show, though are the rare wildlife and environment you'll find here. Come in the spring for nice wildflower displays. Coreopsis Hill is the ridge south of Oso Flaco that glows yellow from February to April with the blossoms of wild giant coreopsis, a member of the daisy family that grows up to 8 feet tall.

Keep your eyes open and you'll notice a lot of moving wildlife here. Birds are numerous (more than 200 species), and you might bump into a black-tailed deer or some of the resident coyotes. Walking in the dunes can be strenuous if you get off the beaten path, but there are several well-worn trails that will give you plenty to see.

## WHALE WATCHING

The whale-watching season here is a big deal. Since the coastline takes a huge turn here, it seems to compress the whale migration right up against shore. Whale-watching boats do huge business and give you the best opportunity to observe whales in their natural setting, but it's also quite easy to find a nice clifftop and sit back while the whales go by underneath. Generally, you want to look for a high promontory that sticks farther out to sea than the surrounding coastline. Piers also make nice lookouts.

A favorite spot in the San Luis Obispo area is **Montaña de Oro State Park.** See the listing under "Hiking & Backpacking" in this chapter for directions to the

Bluff Trail. This short hike leads along the top of a coastal bluff perfect for spotting whales as they swim north. The **point at San Simeon** is another excellent lookout. **Virg's Sport Fishing** in Morro Bay (tel. 805/722-1222) and **Avila Beach Sport Fishing** at Port San Luis (tel. 805/595-7200) both take people out on their boats for whale watching during the peak spring and fall migrations.

# Point Conception to Oxnard ◆ What to Do & Where to Do It

**BEACHES**

Because the coast in this area runs from east to west instead of north to south, many fine beaches face directly south, oriented for all-day sun and sheltered from the prevailing north Pacific winds that blow so hard in other parts of the state.

The first three state beaches you'll encounter after reaching the coast at Gaviota on U.S. 101 are each worthy of great acclaim. **Gaviota, Refugio,** and **El Capitan state beaches** are variations on a theme of white sand, wind- and wave-sculpted cliffs, clear blue water, and generally calm conditions. Refugio is particularly pretty, with its overhanging date palms planted right along the beach. El Capitan has the longest sandy stretch and a fine point break during the right swell conditions. Between the three formal state beaches with their parking lots, campgrounds, stores, etc., are numerous other beaches on state property that you can reach by following informal pathways down the bluffs. You'll know them by the cars parked in the pullouts along the highway. Each has its own feature to recommend it.

The downtown beach in Santa Barbara is **East Beach.** It's a wide, sandy beach that's popular with tourists. You already know how I feel about wide, flat, sandy beaches by now so I won't bore you with my opinion, but many people love this beach. During the prime summer tourist season there is very little wave action here, which makes it a great family swimming destination. If you follow the coast west from here you'll come to Ledbetter Point, where summertime waves and a sheltering headland make it one of the more popular beaches with local residents.

South on Highway 101 (really east), the road stays very near the water's edge. Several fine beaches present themselves between Santa Barbara and Ventura. Carpinteria city boosters have saddled their beach with the title "The World's Safest Beach," though it's really no more or less safe than a lot of beaches around here. It is nice and sandy with tame waves and currents; perfect for a family outing.

Just beyond Carpinteria, Highway 101 makes a sweeping curve and begins a descent. The Bates Road exit here will take you to **Rincon Point,** which has a state beach and famous surf break on its east side and a county beach on its west side. For everyone but surfers, the county beach is the ticket. High bluffs drop down to a nice sandy beach. A tall stairway leads to one area of the beach and a trail to another. Dolphins often hang out in the surfline. The beach-break, known to surfers as "backside Rincon," is generally gentle and perfect for beginners or for simply swimming around. At a low tide, the rocky point that indicates the very tip of Rincon Point is a nice spot for tide pooling. Toward the eastern end of Rincon Beach, near the concrete seawall, is a nude beach. While the scene is generally a nice family atmosphere, there have been some problems with voyeurs hanging out on the bluffs.

Between here and Ventura, U.S. 101 is a six-lane expressway largely cut off from the ocean even though it's in sight of the water the whole time. The secret is to exit at Seacliff (or, if you're northbound, State Beaches). This will put you on a nice little two-lane road that follows the shoreline for about 10 miles. Rows of beach houses cut off access for long stretches, but there are plenty of nice spots to stop and get wet. One of the biggest frustrations in this area is that a riprap seawall extends almost the entire way along this coast, resulting in sand-impoverished beaches. At high tide, forget about it. There's simply no place to lay a towel as the waves crash right against the rock wall.

The seawall ends at **Emma Wood State Beach,** but the resulting sand shortage extends until past the Ventura Rivermouth, where **Ventura's Surfrider Point** area has a nice sandy beach and fine surfing. The coast here rapidly curves south, reaching the "normal" north-south alignment for the West Coast until Oxnard. The beaches in this area are largely nondescript, with the exception of McGrath State Beach. In the shadow of a giant power plant, this fine beach offers a glimpse of what all of this area looked like before massive development took place. McGrath has some really nice dunes and is adjacent to the estuary of the Santa Clara River, where numerous endangered birds and animals live. The waves here are often very large, so it's not a great place to plan on taking a relaxing swim. Surfers, however, are often pleased with what they find.

## BIRD WATCHING

Inland of Santa Barbara in the Santa Ynez Valley is **Lake Cachuma.** Located off Highway 154, this 6,600-acre reservoir, the main water supply for Santa Barbara County, is home to one of the most reliable bald eagle nesting sites in Southern California. The Santa Barbara County Parks Department leads regular trips on the *Osprey,* a 48-foot pontoon boat, to see the nesting and feeding eagles. It's not all that uncommon to see the huge eagles stealing trout from osprey that also hunt here. The largest numbers of eagles congregate at Lake Cachuma between November and March, though the nesting pairs stay through the summer. Call **Santa Barbara County Parks and Recreation** (tel. 805/688-4658) for information about or reservations for the eagle cruises on the *Osprey.*

All birders go nuts over rare sightings, and there aren't many birds more rare than the California condor. On the brink of extinction in the late 1980s, the entire remaining wild population of condors was captured and taken to L.A. County Zoo's breeding facility. There, the birds have slowly but surely reversed the trend that had them steering headlong for extinction. At press time almost 20 condors have been reintroduced into the Santa Barbara County backcountry. Since they roam so far (50 miles a day isn't uncommon) and range over the most impenetrable wilderness areas in Southern California, it's hard to find them with any consistency unless you have an inside connection with the biologists of the reintroduction program, who track the birds electronically. The main roosting area, and the wilderness base for the reintroduction program, is at the top of Lion Canyon near Montgomery Potrero in the far eastern corner of Santa Barbara County. You're looking at a long hike or bike ride to reach the spot but it's a lovely site, condors or not.

Finally, **McGrath State Beach** between Ventura and Oxnard (on Harbor

Boulevard) sits right next to the finest remaining rivermouth wetlands in Ventura County. Birders rave about the sightings here of such rare species as California least terns, Belding's Savannah sparrow, egrets, and great blue herons.

## BOARDSAILING

Some boardsailors I know who spend lots of time on Maui refer to **Jalama County Beach Park** in Santa Barbara County as the Hookipa of California. Situated as it is just north of Point Conception, Jalama juts into the path of lots of wind. And it's perfectly situated to pick up almost any swell. Believe me, it's more likely that you'll look at the waves and think they're too big than be disappointed that they're too small. It's easy to get carried away covering lots of ground here. That's a mistake. Remember, Jalama is the only public access for almost 20 miles in either direction. If something breaks or you run out of wind (hah!), you're a long way from help and neither the Air Force nor the Bixby Ranch security guards take kindly to trespassers.

Less gnarly sailing waters can be found at **Arroyo Burro County Beach** Park and at **Ledbetter Beach** in Santa Barbara. Arroyo Burro is a better spot for wave jumping but requires the ability to do a good water start. Ledbetter is perfect for beginners as it sits somewhat sheltered by a high point and has an excellent grassy area for rigging up. Farther out to sea you'll find good steady wind, but immediately inshore it's gentle and generally forgiving.

In Ventura the place to be is **Surfrider Point,** where California Street meets the ocean near the county fairgrounds. There's lots of room for rigging and good conditions for wave jumping and surfing. This is a popular surfing spot, as the name implies, so be on the lookout for people in your path.

## CROSS-COUNTRY SKIING

Surprising as it may sound, there is actually cross-country skiing in the Central Coast, though it's about as far from the coast as you can be and still be within that region. You could just as easily call it Los Angeles, but since this area falls within the Los Padres National Forest and is the closest snow to the Central Coast, I've decided to put it here. Mount Pinos, at 8,831 feet, is the tallest peak for miles around, and it holds a good quantity of snow during most years. In the spring of 1998 people were skiing here until the end of April. A small ski rental operation sits at the end of the road and can outfit you with everything you need.

### Mount Pinos

Access: Los Padres National Forest. Follow I-5 north, take the exit for Frazier Park, and head west.

Mount Pinos has 50 established trails and even more backcountry skiing. Many more trails are available on nearby Frazier Mountain, Tecuya Ridge, and Mount Abel. Snow levels and depths are generally good from late December to mid-March above 6,000 feet. The **Mount Pinos Ranger District** offers a variety of marked Nordic skiing trails within the wilderness of the Los Padres National Forest.

### Mount Pinos Ranger District

The Winter Recreation telephone number is 805/245-3449 for the Forest Service's 24-hour recreation, snow, and road information recording. To reach a real person, call Mount Pinos Ranger Station (tel. 805/

245-3731) during business hours, or visit 34580 Lockwood Valley Rd., Frazier Park, CA 93225.

## FISHING

### FRESHWATER

I've seen pictures of people pulling steelhead trout as thick as my leg from the Santa Ynez River at the beginning of this century. Dams like the ones that plug every Southern California river except the Sespe eliminated runs like that, but created a different fishing opportunity in the lakes they impounded. Santa Barbara County's main water supply is **Lake Cachuma.** Set in the rolling hills of the Santa Ynez Valley, Cachuma is a beautiful setting and a great fishing environment. The lake is stocked with as many as 50,000 trout a year, many of which are immediately scarfed down by the massive largemouth bass that also live here (the lake-record largemouth is 16 pounds, 7 ounces). Catfish are also a popular catch, often up to 20 pounds. Boat fishing is always more productive than shore fishing at Cachuma, and a boat ramp and rentals are available. The county park phone number at Cachuma is 805/688-4658.

Above Cachuma and below Gibraltar reservoir, the **Santa Ynez River** still bears some resemblance to its former self. During spring months, when water is being released from the upstream dam, it's a fantastic mountain stream. Trout fishermen have a ball reeling in limits of stocked trout. By the middle of summer, though, almost all the water can be gone, and with it the trout.

The crown jewel of all Southern California trout fishing is **Sespe Creek.** For 25 miles between Lion Camp off Highway 33 in the mountains above Ojai to Devil's Gate just above the town of Fillmore, the Sespe is a wild trout stream with no equal in the region. The key

here is finding a time when water levels are fishable. Too soon after the winter and spring rains, the Sespe will be a muddy torrent. By the end of summer it can be reduced to a trickle, with the trout hiding in the deepest pools. The best fishing comes as the water level drops to a nice consistent flow, which often happens sometime between April and May. This stretch is a designated catch-and-release area, and only barbless hooks are allowed. Upstream from Lion Camp and along Highway 33 are areas with stocked trout where catch and keep is allowed.

### SALTWATER

Santa Barbara Channel sportfishing is really hit or miss. When it's hitting, it hits big; I recently watched the guy next to me land a 31-pound halibut while a guy in the stern of the boat fought what turned out to be a 35-pound white sea bass. Unfortunately, the rest of us were catching nothing. Other times, the boats come home with limits of small to medium calico bass, and nothing big to show. The best bets from Santa Barbara are the overnight trips to **Santa Rosa** and **San Miguel islands,** where you'd have to be all thumbs not to bring in a big haul. **Sea Landing** is the main dock for all of Santa Barbara's party boats. Call them at 805/963-3564 for current times and prices. Pier fishermen find some of the best pier catches in the area out at little-known **Goleta Pier.** Hidden in beautiful Goleta Beach County Park, this long pier stretches out to deep water and crosses several different habitats. **Stern's Wharf** at the base of State Street in Santa Barbara is also popular with anglers and can generate great action, especially during the summer bonito and mackerel runs.

At the other end of the channel, near Ventura and Oxnard, the spring and summer fishing for halibut, sand bass, and even yellowtail can be sizzling.

Several sportfishing boats frequent the area, with **Cisco's Sportfishing** in Oxnard (Channel Islands Harbor) being the most respected (tel. 805/985-8511). They run trips to the Ventura Flats area, one of the most spectacular spawning areas for large calico bass. During the spring and summer spawn it's not uncommon to see the entire boat limit out on large calicos and then head to another destination to look for some other species.

## HIKING & BACKPACKING

### Jalama to Point Conception

Jalama County Beach Park. 12 miles. Moderate. Beach walking almost the entire way. Access: 35 miles north of Santa Barbara on U.S. 101, exit onto Hwy. 1 north toward Lompoc. In 14 miles, poorly marked Jalama Rd. is on your left. Take it 13 miles to the ocean. $4 entry fee at the county park. Tel. 805/736-3504. No map required.

Before you attempt this hike, make sure you know how to read a tide book correctly, and adjust for local variations. The helpful folks at the camp store will be happy to help you. Heading south along the coast, you are going to walk the narrow margin of public tideland through some of the most jealously guarded private ranchland in the state. Jalama County Park only extends about a half-mile along the beach. After that, you're walking below the Cojo-Bixby Ranch. From Jalama you should be able to see Point Conception in the distance. This strangely shaped headland was sacred land to the Chumash. They called it the Western Gate, and in their mythology it was the portal through which all souls passed on their way to the afterlife. Since the entire way to Point Conception is contained by cliffs on the left and ocean on your right, there's not much to give in the way of trail directions. The quantity of sand on the beaches here varies wildly with wave patterns, so you may find yourself clambering over beach rocks or strolling casually down soft sand. In at least a few places you'll have to walk along the tops of old seawalls. Keep an eye out for rogue waves that can give you a soaking or worse. As you near Point Conception and the lighthouse, you'll encounter a rocky point that stops your southbound progress. Clamber to the top of the coastal bluff and find an axle-busting dirt road leading to the lighthouse. The compound is fenced and the Coast Guard discourages visitors. An older lighthouse sits on a lower marine terrace. It's on Bixby Ranch property and you're trespassing if you go there, but as the well-worn paths indicate, you won't be the first. Return to Jalama the way you came.

### Gaviota Peak Trail

Gaviota State Park. 6 miles. Difficult. 2,000-foot elevation gain. Access: 35 miles north of Santa Barbara on U.S. 101, go past the main entrance to Gaviota State Park and through the tunnel. Exit U.S. 101 at the Hwy. 1 off-ramp to Lompoc but go right instead of left. A short frontage road will lead you back along U.S. 101 to a dead-end parking area. A small day-use fee is charged here by self-registration. Map: USGS Gaviota Peak or Los Padres National Forest Map.

Though it begins in the state park, this trail quickly climbs into the Los Padres National Forest. For the first mile or so the trail is heavily worn since it leads to popular warm springs. The upper one is nicer than the bottom, though both are a little too cool for a proper soak. Save any splashing around for the trip down, and continue past the springs to the high ridges of Gaviota Peak. The single track joins a fire road you'll want to follow to the right. It's steep and rocky but the view is beginning to improve with every step. During the summer this is where you'll pay the piper, as it can be really hot just a mile inland while the beach is cool. Carry on, though; it's worth the sweat. Eventually you'll come to a junction. The right-hand path is the one you want, leading up a steep pitch to the summit of Gaviota Peak, where a cellular phone and microwave tower stands. From here you can see the entire Santa Barbara Channel on a clear day and also look deep into the Santa Ynez Valley. There are a lot of fine vistas of the Santa Barbara area, but this one at the western end of the Santa Ynez Mountains is a fairly unique perspective, as it looks down the length of the range and into the intensely private lands surrounding Point Conception.

## Rattlesnake Canyon

Los Padres National Forest. 5 miles. Moderate. 800-foot elevation gain. Access: From the Santa Barbara Mission take Mission Canyon Rd. to Foothill. Turn right and follow Foothill several miles until Las Canoas Rd., which is marked by a blue water-filtration plant on the left. Follow Las Canoas to Skofield Park. Park at the turnout near the bridge over Rattlesnake Creek. Map: Los Padres National Forest Map.

The hardest part of this hike is finding the trailhead. From the pathway at the upstream side of the lovely sandstone bridge, you'll wander up a lovely canyon of oaks, sycamores, blackberries, and wildflowers. Oh, and lots of poison oak. Because the canyon is very steep, the trail tends to stay high above the creek. Frequent crossings and side trails lend plenty of opportunity to explore for deep swimming holes. I like to take the trail up and then follow the creek down. If you do this, be prepared to scramble and swim a lot. The turnaround point for this hike is Tin Can Meadow. An old

cabin shingled with tin cans once stood here but burned in a long-ago fire. It's a fine place to enjoy a picnic. Bring binoculars and watch the Spiderman antics of climbers on Gibraltar Rock at the head of the canyon and the graceful aerobatics of hang gliders who launch from the mountaintops.

## Seven Falls Via Jesusita Trail

Los Padres National Forest. 5 miles. Moderate to difficult. 500-foot elevation gain. Lots of rock scrambling and high places. Access: From Santa Barbara Mission, follow Mission Canyon Rd. to Foothill. Turn right on Foothill, then left on Mission Canyon Rd. (again) and left onto Tunnel Rd. Park at the end of Tunnel Rd.

This is one of the most popular hikes on the frontside of the Santa Ynez Mountains, and it's obvious why. Your destination is a series of seven perfect waterfalls linked by seven perfect swimming holes pouring through a sandstone gorge. Following the north side of Mission Canyon, the first mile and a half of the route follows a paved but gated road used to access the water tunnel which brings Santa Barbara's drinking water through the mountain. Continue up the paved road until it ends at a three-way intersection. You want the left fork that heads steeply uphill. Within a hundred yards, a sometimes-signed single-track path cuts to the left through oaks. If the sign is standing, it will say Jesusita Trail. If not, just look for the obvious trail and follow it. You'll enter the upper part of Mission Canyon. Spring and early summer are the best times for this hike, as the creek will be filled with water but not roaring. At the creek crossing you want to head upstream. Here you're faced with a choice. A faint trail heads steeply up the left side of the canyon and rejoins the creek several hundred feet above the seven falls—or you can forage your own way up the creekbed and approach the falls from the bottom. I prefer the creekbed. You'll reach several tricky spots where rock-hopping skills are called into use. Eventually you'll reach the bottom of a large (20-foot) waterfall that looks impassable. It's not. Climb up the right side, then cross the falls at the top. Handholds and footholds have been carved into the rock walls above to make it possible to reach the rest of the trail's namesake seven falls and pools that fill this fantastic sandstone narrows. Take your time and the route will reveal itself. On a warm day there's no better swimming hole for miles.

## Reyes Peak Trail

Los Padres National Forest. 3.5 miles. Easy. 300-foot elevation gain. Access: 32 miles north of Ojai. Near the top of Hwy. 33, turn right at the signed turnoff for Pine Mountain Recreation Area. This winding road leads 6 miles to a gate and wide parking area. Trail begins at the gate. Map: USGS Reyes Peak.

As you may have guessed from the name, Pine Mountain is one of the rare pine-forest ecosystems that grace the high country of Southern California. You're above 7,000 feet for the duration of this hike and the setting is much more High Sierra than anything you might expect. From the gate, the trail follows a dirt road for a short distance. Within 200 yards a trail breaks left along the back side of the ridge. This area is the spine of the Pine Mountain Massif, which consists of five or six separate peaks connected by high ridges and is the highest publicly accessible road in the region. Of the several peaks that line this ridge, our destination is Reyes Peak, the highest. Most of the length of this trail lies just below the ridgeline facing the dry ranching area of the Cuyama

Valley and the mountains of the Lockwood Valley area. Periodically you gain a glimpse through the ridge to the entire Sespe Creek Drainage and Ojai Valley below. On clear days you can see the Channel Islands in the far distance. After you've walked 1.75 miles, the trail will begin steeply descending to the left. Cut right and climb to the top of the ridge. Here, you're on the very summit of Reyes Peak, and the sheer face of the mountain drops away directly below. I've sat here listening to the wind blow through the pines for hours while watching hawks coast on the updraft created as the onshore breeze hits this massive mountain. When you've had enough, head back the way you came. The continuing trail leads down to Haddock Camp and the headwaters of Piedra Blanca Creek in another 4 miles. This camp, nestled in a pine forest with the passing creek, is a perfect weekend overnight. Be aware that in winter this area often receives snow that renders the road impassable.

## Santa Paula Canyon

Los Padres National Forest. 6 miles. Moderate. 800-foot elevation gain. Access: From downtown Ojai head east 9 miles on Hwy. 150 to the bridge over Santa Paula Creek. A large parking area is on the right. Trailhead begins across the road at the entrance to Saint Thomas Aquinas College. Map: Los Padres National Forest.

The first mile or so of this hike is enough to turn many away. You pass through a weirdly deserted college campus and then through a field with several oil wells. Don't let the development fool you. You're headed to some of the best swimming holes and waterfalls on the entire Central Coast, and once around the bend, the college and oil rigs will be completely forgotten.

As the trail wanders through the lower reaches of the creekbed, it's often easy to lose, but eventually you'll reach a spot where you must cross the creek and head up a steeply switchbacking fire road. This is the hardest part of the hike and often very sunny and dusty. The creek is far below, teasing you with the sound of occasional waterfalls as you huff up the ridge. The payoff is soon to come, though. You'll know you're almost there when you see Big Cone Camp. This backcountry camp is a fine short backpacking destination and leaves you in prime position to beat the day-hiking crowds to the swimming holes above. At the far end of camp a narrow, sometimes washed-out trail leads to a junction; you want the left fork. Skirting several large falls, the trail leads you into the west fork of Santa Paula Creek. Swimming holes and water slides are plentiful, and the higher you go the more you find. After you've splashed and soaked to your heart's content, it's time to head back down the hill. Luckily, this one always seems shorter going out than coming in. I recommend bringing a pair of sports sandals for the upper part of the hike, as you'll be in and out of the creek several times.

### Lion Camp to Ten Sycamore Flat

Sespe Wilderness, Los Padres National Forest. 20 miles round-trip. Moderate. Relatively level. Access: 20 miles north of Ojai on Hwy. 33, turn right onto Rose Valley Rd., which descends several miles to Lion Camp and dead-ends. The trailhead is at the bottom of Lion Camp. Map: Los Padres National Forest or USGS Lion Camp. Ojai Ranger District (Tel. 805/646-4348) for free Wilderness Permits.

The Sespe is the last free-flowing river in Southern California, and the surrounding Sespe Wilderness is an important habitat for the California condor and other wild animals. This hike explores the upper section of the Sespe as it passes through the wilderness of the same name. From Lion Camp, the trail, once a jeep road, follows a broad river canyon. At the 4-mile mark, Bear Creek joins the flow of the Sespe, and the canyon begins to narrow. This is where things get interesting. The farther you go, the more beautiful this hike becomes. Large sycamores tower over sandy beaches. Trout swim in deep, cool pools. The high peaks of the Topatopa Mountains rise on all sides.

This trail is perfectly suited for families and beginners, but be aware in times of high water. Below Bear Creek the trail crosses the Sespe numerous times and the flow can be deceptive. If you are in the canyon and it starts pouring rain in the spring or winter, you'll want to head out ASAP, as the river can rise rapidly and block your passage. A troop of Boy Scouts once perished when they attempted to cross this river at flood stage and were swept downstream.

### Manzana Schoolhouse

Los Padres National Forest. 18 miles round-trip. Moderate. Access: Take the Hwy. 154 exit to Los Olivos from U.S. 101 about 30 miles north of Santa Barbara. In Los Olivos, turn left onto Figueroa Canyon Rd., which climbs over Figueroa Mountain, and then turn left onto Sunset Valley Rd. (gravel sections) at 21 miles. From here it is only a few miles to the Manzana Creek crossing and the end of the road at Nira Campground, where you leave the car and find the trail. Map: Los Padres National Forest Map.

Tell your kids you're taking them to a new school and then surprise them with this: The Lower Manzana Trail wanders along Manzana Creek through a wonderful canyon of meadows, sandstone narrows, and deep pools. This 18-mile, fairly level round-trip is a perfect 3-day first-time trip for kids. The trail leads to a former pioneer community that existed here from the 1880s until a few years after the turn of the century. The San Rafael Mountains are steep and brushy, with prickly chaparral covering many of the slopes, so most everything to do here centers around the creek and nearby meadows.

Plan on spending one night in the primitive campsites at Potrero Camp (1 mile) or Coldwater Camp (3.5 miles), and at least one at Manzana (9 miles). Trout are numerous along the entire route and not particularly discriminating—no *A River Runs Through It* techniques required (though a California fishing license is). Occasional pools are head-deep and perfect for cold-water plunges to cut the trail dust and sweat. The still-standing Manzana schoolhouse (built in 1895) and the other homestead ruins are real glimpses of hardscrabble pioneer life.

Manzana Creek is heaven in spring, until late June or early July, when deerflies and horseflies will drive you out of your mind; the creek turns into heaven again in the fall after they all die. Watch for poison oak and rattlesnakes.

## Manzana Narrows

San Rafael Wilderness. 14 miles, round-trip. Moderate. Access: Take the Hwy. 154 exit to Los Olivos from U.S. 101 about 30 miles north of Santa Barbara. In Los Olivos, turn left onto Figueroa Canyon Rd., which crosses over Figueroa Mountain; then turn left onto Sunset Valley Rd. (gravel sections) at 21 miles. From here it is only a few miles to the Manzana Creek crossing and the end of the road at Nira Campground, where you leave the car and find the trail. Map: Los Padres National Forest Map.

Manzana Schoolhouse is far from the only interesting destination in the San Rafael Wilderness. The upper Manzana Creek drainage is one of the most popular overnight hikes in the region. From Nira Camp you'll wander up the wide-bottomed creekbed. Look for deer and bears in the alder thickets; there are a lot of both here. Spring and early summer bring tremendous wildflower blooms, and there's always the possibility, however rare, that you might get a flyby from the California condors that have been reintroduced to these mountains. Your overnight destination is the Manzana Narrows, where the gentle nature of this canyon gives way to steep-sided sandstone walls. Pools here are deep enough for swimming year-round, and trout abound. The camp itself is set up out of the creek's flood zone, pleasantly shaded by large trees.

## HORSEBACK RIDING

The Central Coast is extraordinary ranch country, with a long tradition of fine horses and horsemanship. Alas, most of that tradition still takes place privately; you have to know someone with horses or have your own horses to be a part of it.

The **Circle Bar B ranch** in Refugio Canyon is the best way for the rest of us to get a taste of the equestrian good life. Here, on the Gaviota coast 20 miles west of Santa Barbara, the Brown family has owned this land for three generations. With more than a thousand acres, you could ride plenty just on their ranch, but it gets even better than that. The Circle Bar B backs up to Los Padres National Forest, offering literally hundreds of miles of different rides. As dude ranches go, it's pretty low key. The main ranch compound follows something of an Old West motif, but doesn't stray too far into cowboy kitsch. The rooms are nice and the food—all guests are provided with three meals per day—is hearty. Bear in mind, though, that you don't have to be a guest to take part in the ranch's program of trail rides. Many people come here from Santa Barbara just for the day or camp at Refugio State Beach just a few miles down the canyon.

The basic 1.5-hour ride for $25 per person is enough for most greenhorns. Don't worry, you won't be bored. They keep their groups small, and all trips are led by experienced wranglers. Since the ranch is set in a steep-sided canyon, you and your mild-mannered steed will soon be climbing the high ridges against the backdrop of the Pacific Ocean and the Channel Islands. The Reagan Ranch, where the former president and Mrs. Reagan used to retreat to chop firewood, drive jeeps, and otherwise masquerade as real people for the TV cameras, is right up the hill; ask your guide to point it out. Longer rides are available, ranging from several hours to all day. Call the ranch at 805/968-1113 for current prices and schedules.

## MOUNTAIN BIKING

### Red Rock Loop

Los Padres National Forest. 6.5 miles. Moderate. 700-foot elevation gain. A few water crossings and rocky sections. Access: From Santa Barbara take Hwy. 154 over San Marcos Pass to Paradise Rd. Turn right on Paradise Rd. and drive all the way to its dead end in a large dirt parking lot. Fees are collected on Paradise Rd. during summer months. Map: Los Padres National Forest Map. Tel. 805/967-3481 (Paradise Road Ranger Station).

Red Rock is without a doubt the most popular summer destination in the entire southern unit of the Los Padres National Forest, because of its large and deep swimming holes. This ride, however, begins at the fire road that circles behind the Santa Ynez River and up to Gibraltar Dam. It is directly above the

wide dirt parking area and behind the chemical toilets. The first climb is a killer but it gets much better. From this high road you'll be able to see several different sections of river below and know how to dodge any crowds. Once you reach Gibraltar Dam (no swimming in the lake), you can return on the high road, or you can take the more adventurous low road through the canyon. Coming down the road that follows the river more closely, you'll be forced to walk over periodic sections of cobblestone and occasional downed trees. You may also have to carry your bike through some stream crossings if the water is high. It's the price you pay for also being able to get off your bike and take a refreshing plunge. You'll know you're reaching the parking lot when you pass a huge red monolith on the left, the rock from which this area draws its name. People actually jump off the top of this thing into the tiny pool below but I don't recommend it. Several people have died.

### Little Pine Mountain

Los Padres National Forest. 20 miles round-trip. Difficult. 3,400-foot elevation gain. Access: From Santa Barbara take Hwy. 154 over San Marcos Pass to Paradise Rd. Turn right and continue for about 5 miles until the signed spur road to Upper Oso Camp turns to the left. Park at the dead end, where a gate prohibits further travel. The fire road behind the gate is your trail. Map: Los Padres National Forest or USGS Little Pine.

If I had to choose one all-day ride to recommend, one that would show a rider the best the Central Coast has to offer, I would pick Little Pine. From the Upper Oso Campground, the fire road to the top of Little Pine Mountain rises through a spectacular array of Southern California geology and biology. From the bottom it looks daunting beyond belief; the road literally traverses the face of a thousand-foot-tall cliff. But the climb itself is not that difficult if you develop a pace and stick with it. The roadbed follows a steady pitch without any impossible climbs. As you reach the top, the view of the surrounding mountains and the Santa Ynez Valley would be enough to make your knees knock if they weren't knocking already from the effort expended. A short, signed spur road leads to the actual summit of Little Pine, which is covered in a lovely forest and meadow. Early in the season you might find snow here. Later, I'm afraid you'll find swarms of deerflies that will drive you berserk if there's no breeze. Use caution on the descent. After 10 miles of uphill grind it's tempting to haul ass, but the consequences of missing a turn are deadly.

## Murietta Divide

Los Padres National Forest. 18 miles round-trip. Moderately difficult. 1,600-foot elevation gain. Hot in summer. Access: From Santa Barbara take Gibraltar Rd. to the top of the Santa Ynez Mountains and turn right on Camino Cielo. Camino Cielo turns into Pendola Rd. as it drops down the back side of the range. After the first major river crossing (which might be dry), you'll enter Juncal Campground. Park near the locked gate. Map: Los Padres National Forest Map.

Starting at the locked gate near the back of Juncal Campground, this trail climbs gently at first and then very steeply to Murietta Divide, which divides the Santa Ynez drainage from the Matilija Creek drainage. Along the way you pass though rarely visited country filled with deer, eagles, hawks, bears, and, yes, mountain lions. The first 3 miles take you to the edge of Jameson Lake, a Montecito Water District reservoir that's off-limits to the public. The next 2 miles

offer tantalizing glimpses of the lake as you huff along. A worthwhile diversion is to take the short spur road that descends to your right into a thickly wooded canyon about a half-mile after you pass the dam for Jameson Lake. This is Alder Creek Canyon, one of the most reliable water sources in the area and home to the endangered red-legged frog, which means it's unlikely to be dammed or diverted.

This being the north side of the mountain, the canyon is filled with large alder trees and several species of evergreen. Continuing the climb up the main road, you'll reach a distinct saddle and a tremendous view toward the east. A fire road continues down the other side into Matilija Canyon, which makes a fine one-way ride if you have a trustworthy friend waiting on the other side to pick you up. Most of us content ourselves with the view and return the way we came. Be careful on the way down; it's fast. You'll want to carry as much water as possible on this ride. Respect the mountain lions who live here by avoiding rides during dusk, when they are most likely to confuse you for a deer.

## Agua Caliente Canyon

Los Padres National Forest. 10 miles round-trip. Moderate. Access: From Santa Barbara take Gibraltar Rd. to the top of the Santa Ynez Mountains and turn right on Camino Cielo. Camino Cielo turns into Pendola Rd. as it drops down the back side of the range. Continue past Juncal Campground to Pendola Station, where a road signed "Big Caliente" heads to the right. Follow this road to the end. Map: Los Padres National Forest Map.

The main draw to this remote section of Los Padres National Forest is the large hot spring pool at the trailhead, but what is overlooked is the wonderful riding in the canyon above. From the parking area at Big Caliente hot springs, you'll ride past a locked gate and along a single track for a short stretch before crossing the creek and noticing a huge dam in your path. This is Big Caliente Debris Dam, built after a huge fire in 1930 to stop the flow of debris into Gibraltar Dam, at that time Santa Barbara's main water supply. Fill up is what it did; now the uphill side of the dam is a lush sycamore, cottonwood, and alder thicket growing in all the rich sediment that was trapped. A trail leads up the right side of the canyon (people with heights issues will want to walk sections) and then continues up through this lush area. A mile in, you'll come to a trail camp with no water. Beyond here the trail passes through narrow parts of the canyon and wider meadows, eventually reaching a jeep trail where you'll turn around.

## Monte Arido Road to Matilija Canyon

25 miles one-way. Difficult. Though this trail loses 2,600 feet of altitude overall, there are many tough climbs, and some of the descents are very steep. Access: From Ojai take Hwy. 33 north toward Cuyama. To leave your shuttle car at the lower trailhead, keep your eyes peeled for Matilija Rd., which veers left off Hwy. 33 below Wheeler Gorge. Drive to the end of Matilija Rd. and leave your extra car there. Return to 33 and continue up the pass. At the summit of Pine Mountain Pass (milepost 42) you'll see Pine Mountain Rd. to the right and Monte Arido Rd. to the left. Park on the west side of the road near the locked gate blocking vehicle traffic on Monte Arido.

Staying high on the north ridges of Monte Arido, this trail skirts the edge of the off-limits-to-bikers Matilija Wilderness Area and passes through historic ranches. Just the drive to the trailhead should give you a great idea of what's in store. This area of the Ventura/Santa Barbara backcountry is so strikingly remote and beautiful it's hard to imagine you're so close to Los Angeles. This ride is a shuttle, so you'll need two cars or a driver willing to drop you off and pick you up at the lower trailhead. Begin your ride at the locked gate on Monte Arido Road at the very summit of Hwy. 33 between Ojai and Cuyama. Despite an initial steep descent and tough climb, the majority of the first 3 miles are easy until you reach Potrero Seco Camp. You'll pass several side roads and private ranches along the way; stay away from these jealously guarded retreats. From Potrero Seco the ride continues south along Monte Arido Road (6N03 on a Forest Service map) along the boundary of the Dick Smith Wilderness. At almost 7 miles in you'll reach the Three Sisters Rocks, a striking trio of large sandstone outcroppings. Just north of the rocks another road splits off to the right, but stick to 6N03. Though you're losing almost 2,000 feet overall on this ride, the next 13 miles will test your resolve as you go up and down what seems like countless hills. At 13 miles you come to a short spur trail that leads to the actual summit of Monte Arido, but skip it. The view from the top isn't much different from stunning ridge views. Here you really want to watch your speed as you descend the back side of Monte Arido, as you're well beyond the range of easy help if you take a nasty spill, and this is the steepest terrain on the entire ride. Eventually you'll see the blue gem of Jameson Lake far below in the canyon to your right. While you're not going there, this is a good sign; the climbing is almost over. Soon you reach Murietta Divide. The entire drainage of Matilija Creek lies at your feet to the east. Five miles of smoking downhill on Forest Service Road 5N13 brings you to the gate at the end of Matilija Road, where your shuttle car is waiting. A hot spring lies a few miles downcanyon, alongside the creek, perfect for a post-ride soak. Trails and parked cars give its location away.

## Chief Peak Road/Nordhoff Ridge

15 miles out and back. Moderately difficult. Access: From Ojai take Hwy. 33 north about 15 miles, past the Wheeler Gorge ranger station to Rose Valley Rd. (FS 6N31). Follow Rose Valley east about 3 miles to a small lake on your left. This ride begins on Chief Peak Rd. in the Rose Valley Campground.

In the Los Padres National Forest just outside the town of Ojai, this advanced ride takes you on some gravel, on some paved road to Chief Peak, and onto the Nordhoff Ridge with incredible views of the Santa Ynez Mountains and the Pacific Ocean. Beginning at the Rose Valley Campground, you start off on a brutal 2-mile ascent on the paved Chief Peak Road, and you might have to walk your bike for part of it. The road changes to gravel at the intersection with Nordhoff Road, and from this ridge the views of the surrounding land are pretty amazing. Continue straight to Chief Peak and your turnaround point at Sisar Road. The descent on Chief Peak Road is very fast.

## Shelf Road

3.5 miles out and back. Easy. Level dirt road. Access: Hwy. 150 takes you into downtown Ojai, where you can find street parking on Signal St.

A short, easy ride on Ojai's Shelf Road, a gated dirt road at the north edge of town, is perfect for kids, beginners, and mellow riders. From the intersection of Ojai Avenue and Signal Street, follow Signal Street north and uphill. It dead-ends, and on your right, through the gate, is Shelf Road. Stay on the main dirt road to the closing gate, then turn around and head back the way you came. Along the way, you'll have beautiful views of the Ojai Valley. This ride is also used by hikers and walkers, so use caution.

## Sulfur Mountain Road

18 miles out and back. Moderate to difficult. Graded dirt and gravel road. Access: From Hwy. 33, between the San Antonio Creek Bridge and Casitas Springs, turn right (east) onto the paved Sulphur Mountain Rd. Go past the Girl Scout Camp, and at the locked gate, park in the turnout. Begin riding on the gated road.

One of the most popular mountain bike routes in Ojai, Sulphur Mountain Road is a graded dirt and gravel road that connects highways 33 and 150 but is closed to all motor traffic. The terrain is hilly and rugged, and the mountain views are exceptional.

The road turns to dirt just past the gate. Start pedaling uphill. The first mile is steep but you're in a shaded oak forest. After that, the climb is gentle and gradual. Watch out for hikers, horses, and cattle on the road as well as a few more interesting species: tarantulas can often be found on the road in late fall, and coyotes, bobcats, and snakes wouldn't be out of place, either. When you reach Highway 150, return the way you came.

## Monte Arido Road to Potrero Seco

6 miles. Easy. Gentle fire road with a few climbs. Access: From Ojai take Hwy. 33 north toward Cuyama. At the summit of Pine Mountain Pass (milepost 42), you'll see Pine Mountain Rd. to the right and Monte Arido Rd. to the left. Park on the west side of the road near the locked gate blocking vehicle traffic on Monte Arido.

One of the Ojai area's highest rides in altitude that's still suitable for beginners and children, the Potrero Seco trail leads to a beautiful meadow and passes several ranches. This is the baby brother to the Monte Arido/Matiliaja Canyon ride listed above and gives you much of the same beautiful view and terrain without nearly the physical exertion that its big brother demands. Begin your ride at the locked gate on Monte Arido Road at the very summit of Highway 33 between Ojai and Cuyama. Despite an initial steep descent and tough climb, the majority of the ride to Potrero Seco Camp is pretty level. You'll pass several side roads and private ranches along the way; stay away from these jealously guarded retreats. Potrero Seco means "dry meadow" in Spanish, and though it's shaded by lovely pines and trees, you'll find no water here. After a nice lunch and lots of time enjoying the immense views of this route, head back to your car.

## ROAD BIKING

### El Capitan-Refugio State Beaches Bike Trail

4 miles round-trip. Easy. Oceanfront bike path with very little elevation change. Access: North of Santa Barbara on U.S. 101, park at either El Capitan State Beach or Refugio State Beach.

Ask me what is the best ride in the Central Coast for kids or infrequent riders and I'll say, "El Cap to Refugio." This two-lane, asphalt bikeway connects the two beach parks with an easily ridden route along the top of the bluffs. Numerous pocket beaches lie between the main beaches at these two parks, and you'll see them all.

Though a round-trip from one park to the other and back can be done in as little as an hour, my recommendation is to pack for a full day at the beach and make several stops along the way. During the winter whale migration season

you're likely to see the great beast spouting just offshore. Summer brings water warm enough that you won't need a wetsuit to go swimming. There is no need to worry about traffic on the bike path itself, but be careful once you're pedaling around the park roads. Both these parks seem overwhelmed with careless drivers.

### Winery Loop, Foxen & Zaca Canyons

10 miles. Easy–moderate. Little traffic, relatively flat. Access: Park anywhere in the 10-square-block town of Los Olivos off Hwy. 154.

From downtown Los Olivos, pedal west along Highway 154 a hundred yards or so until you come to Foxen Canyon Road. Be careful making the transition from Los Olivos, where you could safely take a nap in the middle of the main drag, to Highway 154, where you could be run down on a moment's notice. At Foxen Canyon you'll veer right, north, and start pedaling through some of the prettiest wine country you could imagine. Foxen Canyon and its neighbor Zaca Canyon are actually valleys and most of the pedaling is flat. Over the last 15 years, there's been a boom going on as the chief agriculture in the Santa Ynez Valley has become wine grapes instead of beef cattle. It's become something of a mini-Napa, and the wineries are spaced conveniently close to each other along this route, many with public tasting rooms. From the top of Foxen Canyon you'll crest a ridge and buzz downhill into Zaca Canyon, where you'll turn left on Zaca Station Road (though turning right offers miles more of beautiful riding if you want to add some mileage to the route). Here you'll quickly pass (or stop at) the Firestone Vineyards and several others. Continue along Zaca Station Road until you reach U.S. 101. Here you're faced with a decision. If you don't mind some traffic, ride along the freeway for 0.3 mile, where you'll find Highway 154 leading back up through a series of hills to Los Olivos. This route is beautiful and has a good shoulder much of the way but is also a high speed corridor. If you, like me, live in fear of being splattered like a bug, I heartily recommend simply reversing your route and returning up Zaca Station Road and back down Foxen Canyon Road.

## Hope Ranch Loop

10 miles. Moderate. Access: Park at La Mesa Park on Meigs Rd. in Santa Barbara. To get there, exit at Carrillo and take that road west about 3 miles until it crosses Cliff Dr. La Mesa Park is on your right in about 200 yards.

This is a road ride from Santa Barbara into the posh Hope Ranch, with a stop at Hendry's Beach. The ride, with some moderate hills, offers great views of Santa Barbara and the Pacific Ocean. From La Mesa Park, located where Meigs Road becomes Shoreline Drive in Santa Barbara, pedal north toward Cliff Drive and make a left (west) on Cliff Drive. It's smooth sailing down to the next major intersection with Las Positas Road and Hendry's Beach; then you begin the mild climb into the opulent Hope Ranch, where it feels like money really does grow on trees. Follow this curvy road through rolling hills filled with California live oaks. You'll come to a flat, undeveloped area, with a great ocean lookout on your right. As you come around the next curve, make a left under the large wrought-iron gate that reads Hope Ranch. Pedaling along Marina Drive, you may get the feeling that you are on some Hollywood movie set: The street is lined with perfectly shaped huge palm trees, the ocean's sparkling, the sky is blue, and hey, here you are. Follow Marina Drive to Las Palmas

Drive and go right. Las Palmas will lead out of Hope Ranch through another wrought-iron gate. Veer right out of the gate, and at the first stop, make a left and a quick right onto the bike path on Modoc Road. Follow the bike path to the intersection with Las Positas Road and turn right. Las Positas is a very scenic road with a bike path, but beware of the traffic. At the light, make a right on Cliff and then a left into Hendry's Beach for a chill-out on the beach. When you've rested, take Cliff Drive east to Meigs Road and turn right, back to La Mesa Park.

From U.S. 101 in Santa Barbara, take the Carillo Street exit and make a right. Carillo becomes Meigs Road after the intersection with Cliff Drive. La Mesa Park (Meigs Road and Shoreline Drive) is on your right, just after Cliff Drive. Parking is available on the street. From here, get on your bike, take the bike path back toward Cliff Drive, and make a left.

## Santa Barbara Waterfront Path

3 miles. Easy. Watch for heavy pedestrian and bike traffic. Access: Exit Hwy. 101 on Garden St. and follow the signs to Stearn's Wharf.

Without a doubt, this is the most popular two-lane bike/in-line skating path in Santa Barbara. Granted, there are lots of tourists, but it's still a beautiful ride along the oceanfront, and anyone can enjoy it, young or old. Pick up the bike path at Stearn's Wharf and pedal along the palm-tree–lined East Beach. When you get to Milpas Street, you'll have to cross Cabrillo Boulevard and pick up the bike path on the other side. Follow it to the Bird Refuge. During certain times of year, this shallow lagoon is swarming with waterfowl. A capybara (essentially a giant guinea pig the size of a real pig) escaped from the nearby Santa Barbara

Zoo once and spent several days mucking happily about in the refuge before he was detained. After you're done, turn around and head back along the bike path to your car.

## Montecito Loop

18 miles. Moderately difficult. Many long climbs. Access: Exit Hwy. 101 at Garden St. in Santa Barbara and follow the signs to Stearn's Wharf. Park on the wharf in the adjacent lot.

This tour of Montecito takes you from Stearn's Wharf in Santa Barbara to the hills of Montecito, along the base of the Santa Ynez Mountains and down along Eucalyptus Hill. You'll find lots of climbing on this ride, although most of it is gentle. Santa Barbara is, really, one of the most perfect places on earth: nestled between the Santa Ynez Mountains and the Pacific Ocean, with an average temperature of 70°F. And next door to Santa Barbara is the wealthier, celebrity-filled picturesque town of Montecito. Both old and new money reside here, but it's the combination of magnificent mansions and amazing natural beauty that make it such a great place to ride.

From Stearn's Wharf in Santa Barbara, follow the bike path along the palm-tree–lined East Beach. When you get to Milpas Street, you'll have to cross Cabrillo Boulevard and pick up the bike path on the other side. Follow it to the Bird Refuge and recross Cabrillo Boulevard. Now follow Channel Drive past the cemetery (an oceanfront cemetery filled with huge mausoleums and a giant pyramid right on the cliff) to the Biltmore/Four Seasons Hotel. Pedal past Butterfly Beach and the hotel, and cross the railroad tracks. Turn right on Danielson and ride through a neighborhood of small houses, each of which sells for about half a million bucks. Turn right on South Jameson Lane to San Ysidro

Road. Go left here and cross over the freeway. Turn right on North Jameson to Sheffield Drive and go left. Sheffield Drive winds around to East Valley Road, where you'll make a left and quick right on Romero Canyon Road. Head up, up, up to Piedras Drive and go left. This curvy road changes names a few times, but just follow it to Buena Vista, which leads you back down to East Valley Road. Pedal along East Valley to San Ysidro and go right. This is probably the toughest climb of the entire ride, up to Mountain Drive. Once you've made it, go left along the base of the Santa Ynez Mountains. Turn left at Ashley Drive (where you'll pass what I think is the most beautiful mansion in the world) and drop down into Sycamore Canyon. At the intersection with Sycamore Canyon Road (Highway 192), turn right and then make a quick left on Eucalyptus Hill. A left on Alston and a right on Hot Springs Road take you back to the Bird Refuge and the bike path to Stearn's Wharf.

## Mission to the Mountains to the Sea Loop

16 miles. Moderately difficult. Traffic and some steep climbs. Access: Follow Mission St. from Hwy. 101 to the Santa Barbara Mission and park there.

This tour of Santa Barbara takes you from the historic Santa Barbara Mission, along the base of the Santa Ynez Mountains on Mountain Drive, into the heart of Montecito's Sycamore Canyon, along East Beach and Stearn's Wharf, and back up to the mission.

This ride begins at the historic Santa Barbara Mission (impress your friends by knowing its full name: Santa Barbara Miaión Virgen y Mártir), founded in 1786. Follow Mission Canyon around the side of the mission up the hill to Mountain Drive and go right. The first few miles up to Sheffield Reservoir are winding and occasionally steep, but after that, most of the climbing is done. This part of the road is lined with beautiful old sandstone walls dating back several centuries. Follow Mountain Drive along the base of the mountains and be sure to stop and take in the spectacular views. You'll pass a cluster of small houses near the intersection with Coyote Road. This is the famous Mountain Drive colony—where it is alleged the redwood hot tub was invented after one of their notorious wine grape–stomping parties. Continue along this winding and often bumpy road. Just past Cold Springs Road is the trailhead for Cold Springs Canyon—something to remember for another time. Descend a long hill and go right to Ashley Drive for a viewing of some magnificent palatial estates. At the intersection with Sycamore Canyon Road, turn left and fly down to Hot Springs Road. Follow the road down to the Bird Refuge and, from here, take the bike path along East Beach to Stearn's Wharf. At the wharf, follow the bike path up State Street to Victoria Street and make a right. At Laguna Street, go left and pedal back up to the mission.

## Figueroa Mountain Circuit

39 miles. Very difficult. Steep, relentless climbs. Rocks, range cattle, and gravel on roadbed. Access: Park in the tiny town of Los Olivos off Hwy. 154 and begin your ride up Figueroa Canyon Rd.

People who love to sweat dream about roads like this. The first 4 miles might lull you into complacency as you pedal through vineyards, ranches, and alfalfa fields, but Figueroa Mountain towering to your northeast should be enough reminder to save some energy. You'll pass a private school on your right and a large, heavily guarded gate on the left. The high-security gate belongs to Michael Jackson, whose legendary Neverland Ranch fronts the road for the next mile or so. You can't really see much from the road, and I hear that they frown heavily on visitors over the age of 13. Soon enough the climbing begins and never really lets up for the next 8 miles. You'll pass through numerous plant communities and microclimates. Unless you're an allergy sufferer, I recommend late spring as the most beautiful time to ride this loop. The upper slopes of the mountain are literally blazing with millions of wildflowers at that time, and the pine forest on the summit smells wonderful.

The paved road falls a little short of the summit, which can be reached by a dirt spur if you've got fat tires. Personally, I don't think it's worth the extra effort, as the view from the paved road is so great. You'll follow the shoulder of the mountain for a nice distance as you pass in and out of the tree line. At several points you can see the entire Santa Ynez Valley, and at other times you catch glimpses of the San Rafael Wilderness. At 16 miles the serious descent begins. Were the road in better condition, this would be the time to let out all the stops and do a Greg LeMond through the turns, but unfortunately that's not a wise option. Sections of this road wash out every year and are replaced with bad patches or entire miles of gravel. Hit one of those coming around a turn at 40 m.p.h. and you're toast.

After a particularly long series of switchbacks, you'll reach Cachuma Saddle and a ranger residence. Turn right onto Happy Canyon Road. This area was badly burned about 5 years ago and is now one of the best wildflower areas in the area. After a few short climbs, the road begins seriously descending along the drainage of Cachuma Creek. During wet years, there are two crossings that merit getting off your bike and carrying it.

Eventually you begin passing more ranch gates and reach Baseline Road at

Mile 31.5. Four more miles will bring you to Edison Street, where a quick left will bring you to Highway 154, and a short downhill to your right brings you back to Los Olivos. I recommend stopping in at the old stagecoach stop bar, Mattie's Tavern, for a cool one after this ride.

## ROCK CLIMBING

Santa Barbara is blessed with more climbing than you feasibly could do in a lifetime. Take a look back at the Santa Ynez Mountains from town sometime and you'll understand what I mean. Huge faces of sandstone jut from the mountain scarp. Many of them are off-trail and may never have seen a climber because getting to them would mean a hideous bushwack through thick chaparral. Others, like Gibraltar, Upper Gibraltar, Lizard's Mouth, Seven Falls, and San Ysidro Canyon, are relatively easy to reach.

**Gibraltar** and **San Ysidro Canyon** are the gems of the area. To reach Gibraltar you need to drive through Mission Canyon on Mountain Drive until you come to Gibraltar Road. Begin the ascent up the road. The ocean views become more spectacular and the hairpin turns become hairier. Eventually you'll come to a huge sandstone cliff to the right above the road and a huge sandstone promontory below, overhanging a deep canyon. Welcome to Gibraltar Rock.

**Gibraltar's Bolt Ladder** (5.10) could actually be belayed out of a car, if the urge struck you. The Ladder (not to be confused with the Bolt Ladder, 5.3–5.5) is the favorite first climb for area beginners. Hundreds of other routes, including **Hazardous Waste** (5.10), **Try Something New** (5.12), and **Death of a Salesman** (5.8+) await you both above and below the road. At 2,900 feet in elevation, this is an excellent place to escape the summer fog layer and also a

nice winter climbing spot, since most of the rock is south facing. Most of Gibraltar is bolted but it can never hurt to have a few assorted protection devices as well as a number of good slings. To reach Upper Gibraltar you begin hiking up a somewhat sketchy trail that leaves from the uphill side of the road near the wide parking pullout.

San Ysidro Canyon is located directly above the world-famous San Ysidro Ranch where John and Jackie Kennedy spent their honeymoon and where Mick Jagger stays whenever he's in town. I don't know if JFK or Mick ever rock climbed, but if they did, they'd have been pleased with what lay a short hike up San Ysidro Canyon. To get there, drive to Montecito and exit on San Ysidro Road. Drive toward the mountains (duh) and at the intersection of East Valley Road turn right. Go through a giant sweeping S-turn and look for Park Lane on your left. Take it and drive until the first left, which is Mountain Drive. About 400 yards down Mountain Drive you'll see a trailhead and parked cars. Follow the trail up the canyon for about 15 minutes. You'll probably see the rock from the trail, but if you don't, watch for a huge prickly pear cactus on the right. If you see it, you've gone too far; turn to your left and you'll see the climbing area across the creek. Backtrack a few yards and there you are.

Unlike the south-facing walls of Gibraltar, San Ysidro faces east and is shady except in the morning. This provides nice shelter on hot days, as do the surrounding oak trees. A nearby creek makes a perfect post-climb swimming hole much of the year. The slab here is short on the left and grows taller to the right. The routes seem to increase in difficulty from left to right too. Many of these routes have brush and trees at the top. Be careful before trusting any of them with your life. Also keep an eye open for poison oak and rattlesnakes. Both are plentiful here.

The best source for climbing gear and advice is the big **Jandd Mountaineering** store at 30 South Salsipuedes (tel. 805/882-1195). The store is difficult to find but worth the trouble. They rent some gear and have a small indoor climbing wall.

In Ventura County the vast majority of climbing occurs in the mountains around and above Ojai. The prize of them all is **Sespe Gorge.** Here, off Highway 33 about 15 miles above Ojai, lie the longest easily accessible routes on the Central Coast. The main face, known as "The Black Wall," reaches heights of 300 feet and lies just across Sespe Creek from the highway. At high water the area may be difficult to access, as most of the routes begin in the creekbed. If the water is flowing too high, don't risk it. No sense drowning to go climbing. In Ventura, your best bet for climbing gear and information is the **Patagonia Great Pacific Ironworks** store and headquarters on 235 W. Santa Clara St. (tel. 805/648-3803). Maybe if you're lucky Yvon Chouinard will come out and tell you some good climbing stories or show you the blacksmith shop where he first started making climbing gear.

## SCUBA DIVING

Santa Barbara is home to the world-renowned **Truth Aquatics** dive fleet at Sea Landing (tel. 805/962-1127; www.truthaquatics.com), but their trips run almost exclusively across the Santa Barbara Channel to dive the islands. I highly recommend any of these trips and the professionalism of the Truth Aquatics crews. For more information on diving the Channel Islands, see chapter 3. For dive shop services I recommend **Anacapa Dive Center** at 22 Anacapa St. (tel. 805/963-8917) in Santa Barbara, or

**Aquatics Dive Locker** at 5708 Hollister, Goleta (tel. 805/967-4456).

Ventura and Channel islands harbors also both have dive boat operations that do most of their business exclusively at the Channel Islands. See chapter 3 on the Channel Islands for more information about dive trips leaving Ventura and Oxnard. **Ventura Dive & Sport** (tel. 805/650-6500) at 1559 Spinnaker no. 108 beside the Ventura Harbor is a nice shop for fills and gear.

### Gaviota State Park

Located where Hwy. 101 first meets the ocean between Buellton and Santa Barbara. Gaviota State Park exit is clearly marked in both directions. Beginner–advanced.

Diving at Gaviota State Park proper is nothing great. A large creek pours into the sea here and visibility usually stinks. But as a gateway into some of the best near-shore kelp beds in Southern California, Gaviota provides a special service. Northwest of here lies the Hollister Ranch, intensely private land that allows no public shore access. As a result the coast is relatively pristine. Visibility can be almost on the same level as the Channel Islands, and the sheer size and frequency of gamefish, abalone, and lobsters is astonishing. You'll need a small boat—either beach or hoist launchable—with a trustworthy motor to explore the ranch. The Gaviota Pier has a hoist for launching small boats. You'll need your own sling and a dolly for your trailer. Once launched, zip up along the inside of the huge ranch kelp beds until you find a likely spot. You won't be disappointed.

### Refugio State Beach

Located off U.S. 101, 25 miles west of Santa Barbara. Beginner–intermediate.

Refugio is a favorite first ocean dive with local dive schools; the reason is immediately apparent when you drive into the park. Sheltered by a high point, the cove in Refugio is out of the prevailing winds and swell. Palm trees line the shore and a large grassy area makes suiting up and gear wrangling a pleasant task. You simply walk down a sandy beach and swim out. The reef at the south-east end of the cove is fantastic for novices. It's heavily dived so you won't see many fish, but the rocks are simply covered with strawberry anemones and other invertebrates. The sand zone in between is filled with sand dollars. Farther offshore is a nice kelp bed. More adventurous divers will want to explore out around the point. A dive kayak or a Zodiak will open a number of fantastic kelp beds and reefs located within a half mile around the point. Tall, rocky ledges form finger reefs and caves here that are plentiful with lobsters and large fish. As you drive Highway 101 both north and south of this park, you may notice pull-outs and trails running to the beach. Many of these lead to semi-secret dive spots that are well worth exploring.

## Arroyo Burro Beach Park

Santa Barbara. Exit U.S. 101 at Las Positas. Travel approximately 2 miles south until Las Positas dead-ends into Cliff Dr. Turn right. Within 200 yards you'll see the park entrance on the left. Beginner–intermediate.

Another favorite with local dive instructors is Arroyo Burro Beach. To be cool and fit in, call it Hendry's Beach, which is what everyone who lives in Santa Barbara calls it. A large parking lot provides easy access to a sandy beach. The best diving is to the east (left as you face the ocean), where a rocky reef system starts that stretches almost a mile. At this writing the kelp beds have been stripped away by huge winter surf and unseasonably warm El Niño water temperatures, but they should be back in full force soon. Look for fat calico bass, sheepshead, and perch in the kelp. The sandy zone is a spawning ground for big halibut in the spring. And all those little nooks and crannies in the rock reef are home to a sizeable number of lobster. Arroyo Burro is more susceptible to winter surf than Refugio and can't be counted on during winter months.

## La Jennelle Park

Take Highway 1 south through Oxnard to Channel Islands Blvd. and turn right. Follow Channel Islands to Victoria and go left. After following the south shore of Channel Islands Harbor, the road will swing left and become Roosevelt. Continue straight and keep going after Roosevelt turns to Island View. Island View will eventually dead-end into Sawtelle, where you take a quick right and drive through a gate to a small parking lot. If you get lost, just remember that you're looking for the southernmost end of Silver Strand Beach. The barbed wire fence of Port Hueneme should be on your left. Novice–advanced.

From this post-modern industrial setting on the edge of a major deepwater port and a Navy Seabee Base, you're about to descend into a wonderful world at the edge of one of California's huge submarine canyons.

From the gentle rock-and-sand entry near the jetty, the bottom drops almost immediately into the Hueneme submarine canyon. Watch your depth, as it's possible to lose track quickly and go too deep. This is especially important on multiple dives. Descend along rocky kelp beds to about 60 to 80 feet, where you stand a good chance of seeing big pelagic fishes that rarely visit other nearshore areas. Use caution when ascending if you get lost underwater. Big ships are cruising through the harbor entrance not too far away and you don't want to accidentally pop up in their way.

The area was named for a passenger liner that ran aground here in a 1970 storm, but you won't find the wreck underwater. Rather than being refloated or salvaged for scrap, it was covered with riprap and turned into the harbor jetty that you walked across to get into the ocean.

## SEA KAYAKING

Santa Barbara has several sea kayak rental concessions that are continually changing names and owners, but the year-after-year standout is **Paddlesports of Santa Barbara,** located a block from Stearn's Wharf at 100 State St. (tel. 805/899-4925). During the summer they usually operate a beach concession somewhere along the Santa Barbara waterfront. My favorite for guided kayak trips in the Santa Barbara area is **Adventours** at 735 Capala St. (tel. 805/963-2248; www.adventours-inc.com). They specialize in guided trips along the Gaviota coast and at the Channel Islands, and they also arrange specialized multi-sport trips combining kayaking with mountain biking, rock climbing, hiking, or anything you can imagine. Also check out **Harbor Watersports Center** at the Santa Barbara Harbor (tel. 805/962-4890) for rental kayaks located conveniently close to the placid waters of the harbor. In Ventura, **O.A.A.R.S. Kayaking** at the Ventura Harbor (tel. 805/642-2912) gives lessons, rents boats for local use, and arranges trips to the Channel Islands.

### Gaviota-Refugio-El Capitan State Parks

Distance 2–15 miles. Easy–advanced. Access: From U.S. 101 north 20 miles west of Goleta you'll encounter El Capitan, Refugio, and Gaviota state parks strung out over approximately 15 miles of coastline. Each park has a clearly marked exit and easy kayak-launching beaches.

This trio of parks on the coast west of Santa Barbara offers an outrageous wealth of opportunities for ocean paddlers. Beginners can simply dabble in the shelter of Refugio Point, getting the feel for their skills. More advanced kayakers will want to journey between two or all three of these parks. A nice intro to point-to-point ocean paddling is the 2- to 3-mile paddle between Refugio and El Capitan. The most ambitious trip involves putting in at Gaviota and paddling downcoast all the way to El Capitan. The wind should be at your back the entire way in normal conditions. Between each of the official state beaches lie dozens of smaller beaches reachable only by boat or by difficult trails. Great diving and fishing can also be found at the large kelp beds you'll encounter en route. Gray whales commonly steer very close to shore here during the spring migration. During big winter swells, kayakers will find good surfable waves at both Refugio and El Capitan.

## SURFING

During the summer, when most people visit, Santa Barbara is generally stuck in the surf doldrums. It's really a fall and winter surfing area, when north and west swells pour down the channel and crash on the beaches here. The closest thing to a year-round sure thing you'll find in Santa Barbara County is **Jalama County Beach Park.** Just north of Point Conception, this remote beach picks up almost every swell, which are often too big in the winter. Where it really shines is in summer south swells that are blocked from the rest of Santa Barbara by the wave shadow of the Channel Islands. In Santa Barbara city proper, **Ledbetter**

**Point** just west of the harbor is a favorite beginners' break. You can rent a soft board at the **Beach House,** 10 State St. (tel. 05/963-1281) and be practicing your bottom turn in minutes. The most famous break in the area is **Rincon,** often listed among the world's best point breaks. To get to Rincon, drive U.S. 101 south past Carpinteria until the Bates Road exit. Turn right and you've got a choice of the state beach on the left and the county beach on the right. The state beach is the famous Rincon Cove but the county beach also gets good waves.

Driving south along the Ventura County Coast below Rincon, you want to take the Seacliff exit and follow this shore road south. Numerous beach, reef, and point breaks line this area and conditions vary widely within a few miles. Favorites are Faria Point, Hobsons Reef, and Emma Wood State Park. Once you reach Ventura the most popular break is the long rocky point known as Surfer's Point. It's also called C-Street (for California Street, which you take to get here), Fairgrounds (for the fairgrounds behind it), and any number of other local nicknames. Finally, as the Ventura County coast curves out to Oxnard, you reach the land of epic summer swells. Here we're finally well out of the island wave shadow. Places like McGrath State Beach and Silver Strand in Oxnard get excellent hollow summer waves while the breaks in Santa Barbara have nada.

### SWIMMING HOLES

There are precious few easily accessible freshwater swimming holes in arid Southern California. The preeminent swimming area on the Central Coast is **Paradise Road,** off Highway 154 between Santa Barbara and Lake Cachuma. During the spring and early summer the Santa Ynez River flows through a beautiful canyon with lots of swimming holes. The most popular lie at the very end of the road. Park in the lot at road's end and follow the well-worn river trail up to Red Rock, where a series of deep pools and jumping rocks can be found. If the lower pools are packed with loud parties, keep hiking a little and you should find solitude.

On the Santa Barbara side of the Santa Ynez Mountains, you have to hike a little more. **Seven Falls** in Mission Canyon is an extraordinary spot, where Mission Creek pours over a series of small falls, including several with small water slides. It generally has water until early June, when the creek ceases flowing. (See the section on hiking and backpacking, above, for exact directions.)

Above Ojai, the Sespe runs year-round, with a number of places where you can access the creek. Below Lion Camp, the pools get deeper and the creek larger. (See "Hiking & Backpacking," above, for exact directions.) But the most popular swimming hole is in **Santa Paula Canyon** between Ojai and Santa Paula. The hike to the first swimming hole will make you rejoice in the cold, deep pool below a large falls. A trail leads above the falls for access to even more swimming holes.

### WALKS & NATURAL ROADSIDE ATTRACTIONS

### Nojoqui Falls

0.6 miles round-trip. Easy. Access: From U.S. 101 just south of Buellton (or just north of Gaviota) you'll see a signed turn-off for Nojoqui Park. Drive 1 mile on Old Coast Hwy., then east on Alisal Rd. another mile to the park entrance. Follow signs to the trailhead.

It's not easy to reach a lot of the striking waterfalls that lace the steep canyons of the Central Coast, but it's hard to imagine anything easier than reaching this one. The walk is level and pleasantly shaded on a wide path. Fifteen minutes tops from car to waterfall.

Once you're at the falls you'll be blown away. It's not that, at 80 feet, Nojoqui (pronounced No-ho-we) is going to give Yosemite Falls or Niagara a run for their money; the delicate beauty of this ribbon of water pouring over a mineral-encrusted sandstone cliff surrounded by lush maidenhair ferns is what makes the site so impressive. Tucked into this lush little grotto, it makes it hard to imagine that most of the surrounding countryside is more suited to cacti than to ferns. Enjoy a picnic or a few minutes of contemplation in this beautiful spot.

## Knapp's Castle

0.75 miles. Easy. Access: From Hwy. 101 in Santa Barbara, take Hwy. 154 to the summit of San Marcos Pass, where you'll turn right on East Camino Cielo. Drive 2.9 miles east on this winding 2-lane until you come to a wide pullout with a locked Forest Service gate on the north side of the road approximately 1 mile after passing the Painted Cave turnoff. Hike down the road, ignoring a trail that forks to the left about a mile down. Stay right and you'll reach the castle shortly.

This is a great short hike to the ruins of a huge sandstone mansion that once stood here on the crest of the Santa Ynez Mountains above Santa Barbara. Built in 1916 by the former chairman of Union Carbide, George Knapp, this mountain lodge had a number of features that set it apart from the average cabin, among them a full-sized pipe organ and an artificial waterworks designed to keep a natural waterfall flowing long beyond its normal season. Knapp went so far as to build observation decks and spotlights so his friends could enjoy "his" waterfall round the clock.

The house burned down in a massive wildfire in 1940 but the sandstone cellar, chimneys, and several large arches still stand and frame a magnificent panorama of the Upper Santa Ynez Valley. Be careful poking around the old house, as there are some unexpected holes and drop-offs.

### WHALE WATCHING

A favorite spot of mine to sit and wait for a passing whale to make herself seen is the top of the point at **Refugio State Beach.** The trail to the point is a little slippery at times, but there are a couple picnic tables here and an expansive view of the surrounding waters. Last time I was here I watched a pod of at least six whales feeding 200 yards offshore.

In Santa Barbara you'll do well to explore Shoreline Park off Shoreline Drive just west of the harbor. Several nice lookouts offer a great place to sit as the whales come near shore. Between Santa Barbara and Ventura, check out **Rincon County Beach Park,** where high bluffs and the point jutting out to sea often make it possible to see the whales clearly.

Santa Barbara has an entire fleet of whale-watching boats. My personal favorite is the *Condor,* owned and operated by Capt. Fred Benko and located at Sea Landing (tel. 805/965-1985). The *Condor* operates year-round, taking advantage of resident blue and humpback whales which come to the Santa Barbara Channel in the summer when the gray whales are up in Alaska. I've seen a lot of whales in my life, but nothing compares to the sight of a 100-foot blue whale and a 70-foot adolescent I once saw in the middle of the channel. The **Santa Barbara Sailing Center** also runs whale watching on their big catamaran the *Double Dolphin,* which is a very pleasant boat. Captain Don's Tours takes people from Stearn's Wharf on their big boat the *Rachel G* (tel. 805/969-5217).

From Ventura and Channel Islands harbors, **Island Packers** runs numerous excursions from December to March (tel. 805/642-1393); and so does **Cisco Sportfishing** (tel. 805/985-8511).

# Campgrounds & Other Accommodations

## CAMPING

Campers face a wide range of choices when deciding where to stay on the south coast. The obvious choice is to camp at the beach, which is what most visitors do, filling up state park and county campgrounds up and down the coast from May to September and on holidays throughout the year. For state park reservations in California you must call **Parknet** at 800/444-PARK. Some Ventura County Beach Parks accept reservations at 805/654-3591. Santa Barbara County's Jalama Beach Park does not accept reservations. Summer isn't necessarily the best time to camp on the beach here. May, June, and early July can be downright gloomy on the coast, while fall and spring are almost unfailingly bright and warm. During those foggy months of early summer I suggest getting away from the coast and enjoying some of the inland camping in **Los Padres National Forest.** Most of the camping in the forest is first-come, first-served, with the exception of a few group campsites on Paradise Road, which can be reserved at 800/280-2267.

### MORRO BAY & SAN LUIS OBISPO AREA

The State Parks present the best opportunity in this region. **San Simeon State Park** (tel. 805/927-2035) is one of the busiest and most popular campgrounds in the state park system, with 132 full-serve campsites and an additional 70 in an overflow area. Most of the people who stay here are more interested in visiting Hearst Castle than in exploring the woods and the beach, so you'll find the outdoor resources here surprisingly underutilized. About 15 miles south of San Simeon, **Morro Bay State Park** (tel. 805/772-2560) is located between the shore of that beautiful bay and a golf course (135 sites, 20 with hookups, year-round) and **Montaña de Oro** (tel. 805/528-0513) has my favorite primitive campground (50 sites, pit-toilets, no water, year-round). By giving up the luxury of flushing, you gain a tremendous amount of wilderness ambience and solitude. You can forget about solitude at **Pismo State Beach** (tel. 805/489-2684; 100 sites, year-round) because this is a very popular stop with the motor home crowd, but if the generators running television sets don't drive you crazy, you'll have a nice time on the beach and giant dunes.

### SANTA YNEZ VALLEY

Tucked behind Santa Barbara lie several mountain ranges and a lot of nice camping. All the campgrounds are in Los Padres National Forest (tel. 805/967-3481) with the exception of the Santa Barbara County Lake Cachuma Campground (500 sites, no reservations; year-round). Of the forest service camps my favorites are Davey Brown and Nira (11 sites, no water, pit toilets, free) on the back side of Figueroa Mountain, and Upper Oso (28 sites, seasonal) and Santa Ynez (34 sites, seasonal) along the Santa Ynez River and Paradise Road.

### COASTAL SANTA BARBARA & VENTURA COUNTY

There's just something special about crawling into your sleeping bag with the sound of crashing waves outside. Between Jalama County Beach Park (100 sites, water, flush toilets, showers, store, cafe) just north of Point Conception, my favorite beach campground, and McGrath State Beach in Oxnard (175 sites, water, showers, flush toilets), you'll find a number of other places to camp right next to the sea.

Among my favorites are Refugio (85 sites, year-round) and El Capitan State Parks (140 sites, year-round). Both are beautifully wooded, wild settings with great beaches. The El Capitan Ranch campground on the other side of the freeway from El Capitan State Park is also very nice and has a freshwater swimming hole and hiking.

Heading down the coast, the campground at Carpinteria State Beach (262 sites, year-round) is very nice but has a large number of seemingly full-time residents living out of makeshift campers. I can hardly blame them, but camping next door to the Grapes of Wrath kind of detracts from the experience. Regardless, the good surfing, surf fishing, and wide, sandy beach make it a worthy stop. The next series of campgrounds down the coast are run by the county of Ventura. Though they're right on the shore, I can hardly recommend them. They're little more than parking lots and are overrun by huge motor homes and, in my experience, have snotty hosts who see their duty in life as making sure no surfers park for even an instant to check the waves without first paying an entry fee. I suggest moving on to McGrath State Beach, where the Santa Clara River meets the Pacific Ocean. This spot has a little something for everyone: great surf fishing, surfing, hiking, and some of the best birding around.

### OJAI & HIGHWAY 33

Highway 33 provides access to extremely remote high country camping complete with pine forests and year-round creeks. It's quite lovely up here

at any time of year, but the camping is best in spring and early summer. All campgrounds here are administered by **Los Padres National Forest Ojai Ranger District** (tel. 805/646-4348). Wheeler Gorge is the biggest (73 sites; year-round) and is only 8 miles outside the lovely town of Ojai on the banks of a burbling creek with fishing and swimming holes. Higher up Highway 33 you'll encounter Lion's Canyon camp at the end of Sespe River Road (22 sites, year-round). This camp is a nice launching spot for explorations into the Sespe Wilderness or up toward Reyes Peak.

### INNS & LODGES

## Sycamore Mineral Springs Resort

1215 Avila Beach Dr., San Luis Obispo, CA 93405. Tel. 805/595-7302. 51 rooms and suites. $125–$250. MC, V.

Located just inland of Avila Beach and Port San Luis, Sycamore Mineral Springs Resort has a long history as a soaking spot for travelers on their way between Los Angeles and San Francisco. It's undergone many permutations in the hundred years since two men drilling for oil found hot sulphur water instead. The rooms are quite fancy and the expensive suites come with their own mineral tubs. While this may seem ideal, I suggest you stay in one of the cheaper rooms without a tub and utilize the resort's secluded redwood hot-spring tubs, which are strewn on a hillside above the hotel. These tubs have much more ambience than the plastic Jacuzzi tub–style ones in the rooms, plus nice views of the stars and canyon. Nearby are several good beaches, sportfishing, and nice country roads to bicycle.

## Best Western Cavalier Inn

9415 Hearst Dr., San Simeon, CA 93542. Tel. 805/927-4688. $71–$125 double. AE, MC, V

I wouldn't mention this inn but for the general lack of suitable lodging in the area. What makes it noteworthy isn't so much what's inside, though the rooms are very nice, as its location. This is the only truly beachfront motel in the area and has almost 1,000 feet of ocean frontage. Since you probably won't want to swim in the sea here, you'll be glad they've got two heated pools, and the rates are a bargain.

## The Madonna Inn

100 Madonna Rd. (off U.S. 101), San Luis Obispo, CA 93405. Tel. 800/543-9666 or 805/543-3000; www.madonnainn.com. Rooms start at $97.

Named after owners Alex and Phyllis Madonna—not the pop diva—this wacky, bright pink hotel in San Luis Obispo features 109 rooms and 25 suites, each decorated in their own individual kitschy way, such as the "Caveman Room," "Love Nest," and "Swiss Alps." The net effect is something like the Flintstones meet Knott's Berry Farm. The inn also offers a full-service restaurant, the flashy Gold Rush dining room, a coffee shop featuring excellent German pastries, and two cocktail lounges. It's worth a visit just to check out the waterfall in the downstairs men's room. Space-age bachelor-pad music not included.

## The Cliff House

6602 Pacific Coast Hwy., Mussel Shoals, CA 93001. Tel. 805/652-1381. Doubles from $95; suites from $165. MC, V.

Thousands of travelers blow past The Cliff House at 80 mph every day and never even notice it tucked on a thin patch of ground between 101 South and the Pacific. But appearances can deceive. Walk though the entrance and you'll find a nice little motel clinging to the rocks above a nice surf break. There's a pool and the rooms look right out on the water. Best of all, the oil piers that have blighted the inn's view for so many years are coming out soon and should be gone by the time you read this. It's a great spot to surf away a day, soak in the pool, and enjoy a great dinner at their restaurant before crashing for a night of sleep.

## Banana Bungalow Hostel

210 E. Ortega, Santa Barbara, CA 93101. Tel. 805/963-0154. $15–$18 for dorm rooms and one $40 private room. Cash only.

Santa Barbara is severely lacking in cheap places to stay, but the Banana Bungalow is a bargain. Tucked a few blocks away from downtown in an old Quonset hut, this hostel hops with travelers from all over the world. It's a good place to hook up with fun-loving folks and to save a few bucks better spent on your outdoor adventures.

# 3

# THE CHANNEL ISLANDS:
## Southern California's
## Offshore Wilderness

**T**HE CHANNEL ISLANDS PROVE THAT LINEAR DISTANCE IS truly elastic. Travel 25 miles by car almost anywhere in Southern California and it's unlikely that the essential character of your surroundings will have changed much; odds are you made it from one suburb to another. Fly or sail the same distance by boat to the Channel Islands, however, and you'll fall back in time, to a world without cars or significant development. You'll fall back, quite honestly, into a remnant of a more peaceful Southern California.

It's really quite magical the way a channel crossing quickly peels away the rough layers of urban existence. Hop aboard a ferry in Long Beach—hardly what anyone would call a center of natural beauty—and less than 2 hours later you're mountain biking a dirt road along the spine of Catalina, with the smog-filled L.A. basin nothing more than a shimmer on the horizon. Get on a dive boat in Oxnard and you can be 60 feet underwater swimming through the kelp forest at Anacapa Island's marine preserve within an hour. Sail a charter boat 4 hours from Santa Barbara to the north side of

Santa Cruz Island, and have your pick of anchorages that are essentially unchanged since the Spanish explorers dropped anchor there 400 years ago. Even on Catalina, the most populated, most visited of the islands, cars are prohibited and things move at a literally pedestrian pace. Why hurry when the island is only 21 miles long, and 86% of it is wilderness preserve?

California actually has eight Channel Islands, but two, San Clemente and San Nicholas, are owned by the military and for most intents and purposes, off-limits. Catalina, the southernmost and most popular of the publicly accessible islands, is located 26 miles from the mainland and is served by commercial ferries from Long Beach, San Pedro, and Newport Harbor. Avalon, the only residential community in the islands, is located on Catalina's northeast shore in a beautiful cove. Most of the rest of the island is owned by the Catalina Island Conservancy, a not-for-profit organization.

The Northern Channel Islands— Santa Barbara, Anacapa, Santa Cruz, Santa Rosa, and San Miguel—and the mile of ocean surrounding each of them were designated Channel Islands National Park in 1980. While hardly as accessible as Catalina—getting to the islands, especially the more interesting ones, requires a substantial investment of planning, time, and money— Channel Islands National Park will reward any effort you expend with experiences and memories like none other. The National Park Service maintains a visitor center in Ventura, at 1901 Spinnaker Dr. on the edge of the Ventura Harbor. Here you'll find exhibits of the geology and biology of the islands and their surrounding ocean. The park concessionaire, Island Packers, which arranges boat transport to and from public areas of the islands, is located in the building next door. Flights by

Channel Islands Aviation can also be arranged to several dirt strips on the larger islands.

Before visiting any of the islands, it's best to know in advance what you're getting into. Anyone, including my grandmother, can have a good time on Catalina. If walking up and down the steep hills is daunting, don't worry, you can rent golf carts to get around Avalon, and passenger buses will take you on a tour of the island. You don't need to be a hiker to get along there, though if you are a hiker (or biker, or kayaker, or diver) you'll have a splendid time. Anyway, you're reading a book called *Frommer's Great Outdoor Guide to Southern California & Baja*. If you're afraid to walk a little, well, perhaps you've picked up the wrong book?

Which brings us to the other islands, the five northern islands that are the combined location of Channel Islands National Park. Visiting any of them certainly qualifies as adventure. They're universally steep, rocky, and windy— hardly the epitome of creature comforts. Just getting to the shore often involves landing a dinghy through rough surf or scrambling up a wet and slippery ladder. If you come by plane, trust me, you'll look down and think, "We're landing on *that?*" when you see any of the island landing strips. And once on terra firma, you're looking at spartan conditions. Campers must come prepared for wind, fog, and possibly rain, particularly on San Miguel. Most of the campgrounds have pit toilets and no running water.

It's easy to get sucked into the whole process of arranging a land visit to the islands, and certainly such a visit is a worthy endeavor, but the vast majority of visitors who come to the islands every year don't even set foot on the land. Remember, a huge portion of the park is the Channel Islands National Marine Sanctuary, the nautical mile of ocean surrounding each of these rocky islands. In many ways the best part of any of these islands is the interplay between land and ocean. Sailors, divers, fishermen, kayakers, and surfers are drawn here by the prospect of such a tremendous amount of unpopulated coastline. The scuba diving here is among the best in the world, drawing visitors from all over to experience the weightless beauty of the underwater kelp forests, which grow taller here than anywhere on earth. Sea kayakers, both expert and novice, revel in miles of rocky coves, deep sea caves, and wonderful offshore rocks. Most make the crossing on a larger boat, then take to the kayaks, but a few times every year advanced kayakers make the channel crossing by themselves. The fishing out here is often dramatically better than on the mainland. As I write this, during the El Niño conditions of 1997, people have been catching marlin, tuna, and dorado off the back side of Santa Cruz Island. And while the breaks on the islands are definitely not for beginners and are heavily localized by the commercial urchin divers who work the islands every day, several surf spots on the islands catch great waves with, as you might imagine, nothing like the crowds of the mainland.

## The Lay of the Land

Because they're so different, and separated by miles of water, I'm going to describe each of the Channel Islands individually. First, though, a bit about their origins and group geography. Like Southern California's other coastal mountains, the Channel Islands are part of the Transverse Ranges. In fact, the four northern islands are actually the western terminus of the Santa Monica Mountains; only their highest ridges and peaks reach out of the sea. Twenty thousand years ago, when sea levels were at least 300 feet lower, the islands were probably connected to land, or at least much closer. As the massive glaciers of the last ice age melted, sea levels rose dramatically. The islands were cut off by the sea. In the meantime, plants and animals trapped on the islands evolved into their own unique species and subspecies. Under the changed evolutionary pressures of an island rather than mainland ecosystem, strange things happened. Over generations the wooly mammoths grew smaller, until they were the size of a pony, as fossilized remains on Santa Rosa show. Bees became extremely docile. The blue jays evolved into a sub-species almost twice the size of their mainland brethren. The islands' cutest evolutionary outcome was certainly the island fox, a species of housecat-sized red fox with a temperament to match. While mainland foxes are extremely elusive, island foxes are fearless of humans, and have even been known to crawl into a human lap. Such species differ among the individual islands as well as from the mainland. An island fox on Santa Cruz is slightly different from one on Santa Rosa and even more different from one on Santa Catalina. Comparison of the evolutionary differences between island and mainland species is a valuable source of research information for evolutionary biologists.

Over the years, of course, humankind has wreaked all sorts of ecological havoc on the islands. The Chumash Indians, the first humans here, seemed to get along fine with a diet of shellfish and acorns. The Spanish explorers, though, released goats and pigs onto the islands, guaranteeing that next time they visited they'd find a supply of fresh meat. Without predators, the pigs and goats reproduced wildly, eating everything in sight. It's impossible to determine how many plant and animal species went extinct in those first decades. Things hardly

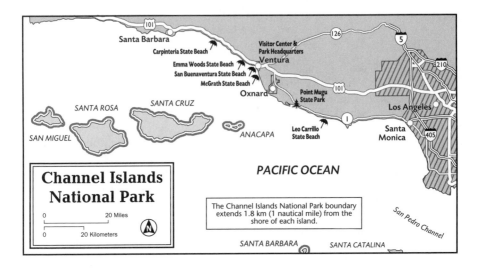

The Channel Islands National Park boundary extends 1.8 km (1 nautical mile) from the shore of each island.

improved with the coming of ranching to the islands. Catalina, Santa Barbara, Santa Cruz, Santa Rosa, and San Miguel were all subjected to intense cattle and sheep grazing, which undoubtedly extinguished even more species. The cattle on Santa Rosa were only removed in 1998 as part of a negotiated settlement intended to protect several endangered plants. But with the creation of the national park in 1980 and the concerted efforts of the Nature Conservancy and the Santa Catalina Island Conservancy, things are looking up for the island ecosystem. The sheep have been removed from most islands. Pig populations are kept under control by regular hunting. And the overgrazing that was once common is a thing of the past. Large portions of fragile island ecosystems are recovering quickly.

Despite the designation of the northern islands as a national park, ownership of the actual land is a hotly debated question. The largest of the islands, **Santa Cruz,** is 90% owned by the Nature Conservancy. Until this year the other 10% was privately owned by the Gherini family. In a move that many cheered and others have decried as virtual theft, the federal government condemned the Gherini land and took it into federal ownership for a sum as yet to be determined.

**Santa Rosa** was owned by the Vail & Vickers cattle ranching operation until they sold out to the National Park Service in 1986. Now it's being developed for visitor use as the cattle have just been phased off the island. Of all the northern islands, this one has the most exciting possibilities for an extended stay.

**Catalina** seems to have worked out its land-use and ownership battles a while ago, while Santa Barbara, Anacapa, and San Miguel are owned in whole by the federal government with no competing claims. Santa Catalina—54 miles of coastline, a Mediterranean climate, isolated beaches, sheer cliffs, 2,000-foot-tall mountains, a seaside village, legendary big game fishing, mountain biking, camping, and some of the state's best skin and scuba diving—is just a short boat ride from Long Beach, San Pedro, or Newport Beach. The island itself is shaped like a lopsided hourglass, pinched in the middle by the narrow isthmus of Two Harbors. From the sea, the connecting land is so low-lying that Catalina is often confused for two distinct islands. Either direction from the isthmus, though, Catalina is characterized by high mountains reaching over 2,000 feet.

Long a hangout for the Gabrielano Indians, then for pirates, explorers, and even gold miners during a short-lived

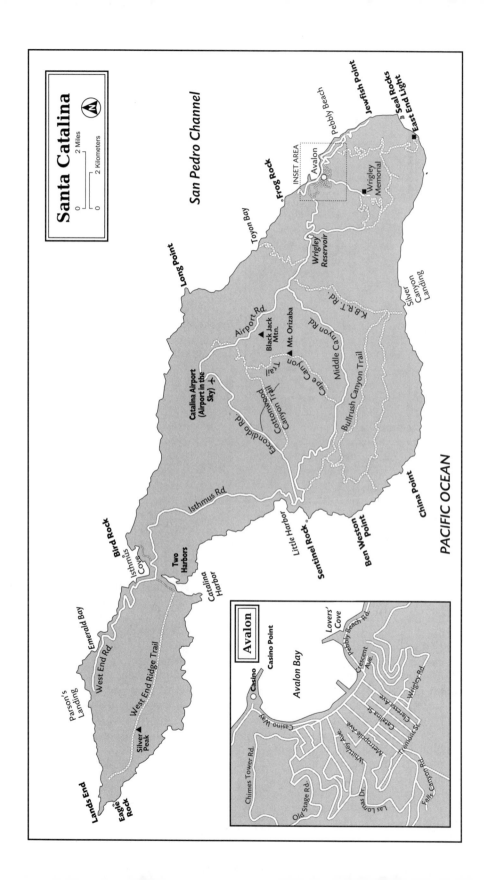

**Santa Barbara Island**

SHAG ROCK

Santa Barbara Island Light

Arch Point

Webster Point

Elephant Seal Cove

Landing Platform

Landing Cove

Museum

North Peak

Canyon View Nature Trail

Arch Point Loop Trail

Cave Canyon

Elephant Seal Cove Trail

Elephant Seal Cove Trail

Signal Peak Loop Trail

Signal Peak

Sea Lion Rookery

SUTIL ISLAND

Cat Canyon

0        .5 Miles

0        .5 Kilometers

△ Campground

🏠 Ranger Station

🚻 Restrooms

gold rush, Catalina came into prominence when William Wrigley Jr. purchased the island in 1919 and developed Avalon as a vacation getaway on the island's northeast end. He constructed the Avalon Casino, which was never a gambling facility but rather a grand ballroom, at the edge of **Avalon Bay.** The setting's romance didn't elude the glamorous crowd of that era, and soon Avalon was awash in big-name entertainment and grand soirees. Zane Grey lived here for a while, and Ernest Hemingway used to visit for the fishing. Pictures of such notables as Winston Churchill posing with his catch hang in the Catalina Tuna Club.

Things have faded a bit since then. It's no longer the hot place to be for the Hollywood crowd, but it's still a favorite place for Los Angeles and Orange County residents to escape the hubbub of mainland life. To explore more than a mile outside of Avalon on Santa Catalina Conservancy land, you need a hiking or biking permit. Daily hiking permits are free. Biking permits are $50 per person or $75 per family and good for a year. Overnight camping permits cost $6.50 per person per night. Get your

permits at the Santa Catalina Conservancy offices at the island airport above Avalon, at the Conservancy office at 213 Catalina St. in Avalon, or at the Two Harbors Visitor Services Office. For information call the **Santa Catalina Island Conservancy** (tel. 310/510-1421).

Catalina is as popular a diving and sailing destination as it is a land-lovers getaway. Commercial dive boats from several Southern California harbors run day trips to the island, and dive boats based in Avalon and Two Harbors run trips to waters around the island as well. **Two Harbors,** at the narrowest part of Catalina, has developed in recent years into an alternative to Avalon, with camping, a store, and some services. Just outside Avalon Harbor, an underwater preserve offers fantastic diving from shore. For sailors, Catalina makes a perfect overnight destination, and numerous coves allow anchoring. At times, the channel between the mainland and Catalina looks like a more picturesque version of an L.A. freeway, as hundreds of vessels converge on the island.

## Santa Barbara Island

At 639 acres, Santa Barbara is the smallest of the Channel Islands and one of the least visited. There's a small campground and interpretive center dedicated to the history of several ill-fated attempts to raise livestock on the island, but other than that it's basically a grassy hill sticking out of the sea, ringed by huge cliffs. The most interesting features of Santa Barbara are the **diving,** which is among the best in the park, and the **bird and marine mammal viewing,** which are largely accomplished from boats, not from land.

## Anacapa Island

Anacapa is actually three linked islets, totaling 639 acres—only one of which you're allowed to visit (the others are

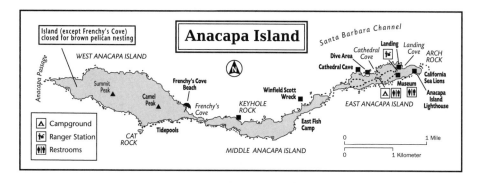

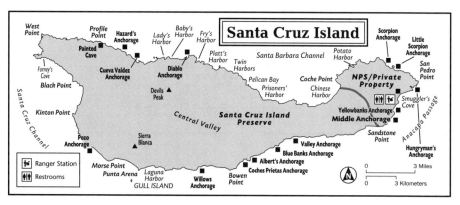

important seabird rookeries). Anacapa is basically a large mesa sticking from the sea. It's ringed by cliffs; to reach the top you must first climb a ladder and then a long staircase. Since it's only 14 miles from the National Park Service visitor center in Ventura, Anacapa is the most visited of the islands. **Diving** here is tremendous, as is the **bird watching.** The campground and visitor area share east Anacapa with a lighthouse and foghorn. If you chose to camp here, do yourself a favor and bring good earplugs.

## Santa Cruz Island

Without a doubt the most beautiful of the entire chain, extremely mountainous Santa Cruz has an area of 60,645 acres and a long central valley dividing two mountain ranges. With peaks ranging over 2,000 feet, the diversity of microclimates and ecosystems here is startling. Sadly for visitors, 90% of the island is owned by the Nature Conservancy and is off-limits to public

visitation. The eastern 10% of the island was recently acquired by the National Park Service, and plans for visitor use are being developed. Currently you're allowed to camp, hike, and adventure around the new addition to the park, and lodgings in the old ranch facilities may be available soon. Seagoers love Santa Cruz. Its got the best harbors of any of the islands and is an easy day's sail from either Santa Barbara or Ventura. Numerous **dive-boat** operators visit the island, with trips ranging from single day to several days. The coast is largely high cliffs, but there are numerous sand **beaches.** Also, Santa Cruz is cut by a number of large sea caves begging to be explored by **sea kayakers.**

## Santa Rosa

Santa Rosa is the second-largest island after its neighbor Santa Cruz, but the topography of the islands is considerably different. Santa Rosa is more rolling and grassy. Perfect terrain for cattle

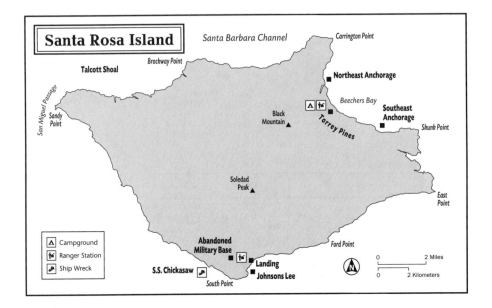

## Santa Rosa Island

Santa Barbara Channel

Carrington Point

Talcott Shoal

Brockway Point

San Miguel Passage

Northeast Anchorage

Sandy Point

Beechers Bay

Black Mountain ▲

Torrey Pines

Southeast Anchorage

Skunk Point

Soledad Peak ▲

East Point

△ Campground
†⚤† Ranger Station
⚓ Ship Wreck

Abandoned Military Base

Ford Point

0        2 Miles
0        2 Kilometers

S.S. Chickasaw

Landing
Johnsons Lee

South Point

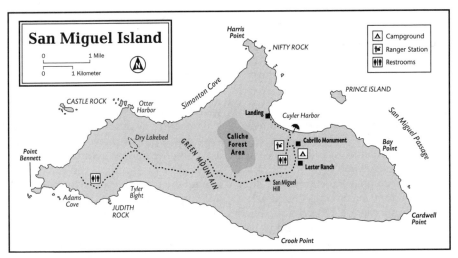

## San Miguel Island

0        1 Mile
0        1 Kilometer

Harris Point

NIFTY ROCK

△ Campground
†⚤† Ranger Station
†⚤† Restrooms

Simonton Cove

PRINCE ISLAND

CASTLE ROCK

Otter Harbor

Landing

Cuyler Harbor

San Miguel Passage

Dry Lakebed

GREEN MOUNTAIN

Caliche Forest Area

Cabrillo Monument

Bay Point

Point Bennett

Lester Ranch

San Miguel Hill

Tyler Bight

Adams Cove

JUDITH ROCK

Cardwell Point

Crook Point

ranching, which is what it's been used for the last 100 years. The old **Vail and Vickers Ranch** headquarters is an interesting look at history in motion. The ranching techniques used here haven't changed much in the last 100 years. Cowboys still make their own saddles, train their own horses, and work the cattle much like their grandfathers did. The island is much worse for the wear after years of cattle grazing, though, and several lawsuits have been filed to force the removal of cattle from the island prior to the 2011 end date of the ranching lease.

**Campers** at Santa Rosa are fortunate because the main visitor area is located just above a wonderful sandy beach that stretches for miles. Since this is the single biggest land area (52,794 acres) accessible to visitors in the park, rangers at Santa Rosa often offer transportation to other areas of the island. For **diving, sailing, and kayaking,** Santa Rosa is a bit of an exotic destination. Less visited than Santa Cruz or Anacapa, Santa

Rosa has several shipwrecks, larger fish, and more rugged sea conditions than those islands.

## San Miguel Island

Foggy, windy San Miguel is without a doubt the wildest spot in the Channel Islands. Anchoring the western end of the chain, 9,325-acre San Miguel sits at the intersection of the Northern California and the Southern California ocean ecosystems. As a result of a continuous upwelling of nutrients as major currents come together, you'll find an incredible diversity of marinelife. Divers emerge slack-jawed from the sea, marveling at the size of the fish they see here, as well as the wildness of the sea. It's possible to **dive** with young sea lions here, and the possibility that a white shark could be nearby never quite escapes your mind. **Point Bennett,** the western tip of San Miguel, is one of the most amazing **wildlife** sights anywhere. More pinniped species (California sea lion, Stellar sea lion, northern fur seal, Guadalupe fur seal, northern elephant seal, and harbor seal) hang out here than anywhere on earth. At times as many as 10,000 come together all at once. The noises and smells they produce must be experienced to be believed. **Campers** on San Miguel are restricted to the area of the island around Cuyler Harbor and must be accompanied by a ranger on hikes through the island's fragile natural wonders.

# Catalina ◆ What to Do & Where to Do It

### BEACHES

Like all the Channel Islands, Santa Catalina is largely ringed by rocky cliffs. While the island does have its share of beautiful beaches, don't expect to find Venice Beach here. Island geography lends itself more to the intimate cove beach. In Avalon proper, take your pick of **Crescent Beach,** a thin line of sand below Crescent Avenue inside Avalon harbor; **Pebbly Beach,** a mile south of Avalon on Pebbly Beach Road; or **Descanso Beach,** a privately owned beach club next to the Catalina casino. For $1.50 per person, Descanso Beach is definitely the nicest patch of sand in the Avalon area and offers showers, bathrooms, and cabanas as well.

The really nice beaches on Catalina, however, don't lie in Avalon. To reach them you've got to either take a boat or start hiking. Without a doubt, the nicest strand on the island is **Little Harbor Beach** on Catalina's south shore, 17 miles from Avalon or 6.8 miles from Two Harbors. Not one, but three separate beaches in their own individual coves, the Little Harbor area is a spectacular natural setting. Peaks reaching 2,000 feet rise behind palm-shaded sand and turquoise water. There's a 17-site primitive campground here, with running water, showers, and chemical toilets. Snorkeling is great in the offshore kelp, and adjacent Shark Harbor often gets enough swell for bodysurfing or boogie boarding. **Two Harbors Visitor Services** (tel. 310/510-2800) also offers periodic shuttles from Two Harbors to Little Harbor and can arrange for kayaking or snorkeling gear rental.

### BIRD WATCHING

All of the Channel Islands are hot spots for seabirds and shorebirds like Cassin's auklets, Brandt's cormorants, pigeon guillemots, sandpipers, California brown pelicans, and several species of gulls and terns. **Catalina,** however, is also well known among birders for its raptors. Since 1979, a program to reintroduce the bald eagle to the island has met with some success. They nest on inaccessible cliffs overlooking the sea, but are most often spotted soaring over the inland canyons and reservoirs. A number of peregrine falcons have also been reintroduced to the island.

## FISHING

It wasn't by accident that Zane Grey ended up in Avalon. His old house, now an inn, stands overlooking Avalon, and way back, literary bad boys like Grey and Hemingway would sit around drinking whisky and comparing notes on the day's fishing there. Like any old-timer will tell you, the fishing just isn't as good as it was in the old days, but during the summer months off **Catalina,** excellent billfishing for striped marlin and broadbill swordfish can still be found. Blue fin tuna are also regularly taken during summer months. Those of us who don't have the patience or pocketbooks for chasing billfish and tuna can content ourselves with chasing California halibut, calico bass, yellowtail, and white sea bass around the kelp beds of the island. Divers also take a lot of fish here by spearfishing the kelp beds and floating offshore kelp patties. And come the beginning of October, Catalina is always warm with lobster divers out looking for their limit of the tender-fleshed crustaceans.

As on the California mainland, you must have a fishing license to take anything here, and regulations are strictly enforced. You can get your license, daily or annually, at **High Tide Traders** near the base of Avalon's green pleasure pier (tel. 310/510-1612). They sell tackle as well. Prefer to rent some gear for the day? Stop by the **Avalon Boat Stand** on the pleasure pier itself. If you're hanging out in Two Harbors, don't hike 17 miles to buy a fishing license or a couple lures; you can just stroll down to the Two

Harbors General store and buy whatever you need there.

Since most of the island is ringed with inaccessible cliffs, fishing generally means getting out in a boat. Avalon and Two Harbors both have just about every type of watercraft available for rent, from sit-on-top kayaks to skiffs to sailboats to pedal boats to get you to where you can dip a line. Try **Joe's Rent-A-Boat** at the Green Pleasure Pier for serious skiffs with outboards. If you're willing to fish from a kayak, and many people have great luck doing so, try **Descanso Beach Ocean Sports** near the casino (tel. 310/510-1226) or **Wet Spot Rentals in Avalon** (tel. 310/510-9588). Anytime you fish out of Avalon, be aware of the boundaries of the Avalon Underwater Park, where fishing is very, very, heavily frowned upon and subject to hefty fines. In Two Harbors, hit up the Catalina West End Dive Center for a kayak rental.

Finding your own way is nice, but without a doubt the best way to experience Catalina fishing is to charter a boat and captain. It's more expensive, sure, but if you really want to catch fish and see the ocean from the perspective of someone who is on it every day, it's hard to beat a chartered trip. They generally provide everything (tackle, bait, snacks, beverages, and lunch) that you'll need to have a happy trip, and they'll generally clean your catch for you too. Or if you're lucky enough to hook into a big marlin, they'll handle the tricky part of catch and release when amateurs sometimes find themselves on the wrong end of a long, pointy fish bill. **Captain Dave's Catalina Boat Charter Company** (tel. 310/510-2720) in Avalon offers half-day (5-hour) trips for $300 for two people and $50 each additional person. Full-day (8-hour) trips run $450 for the first two passengers and just $50 for any extras. Eight hours on the water can be a little trying if you're not a fishing maniac, but on the other hand it gives you the added range that's sometimes necessary to reach wherever the tuna or marlin are biting at the moment. From the west end's Two Harbors, the 38-foot twin diesel sportfisher *Sea Bass* is available for private charter with complete packages ranging from half-day to multi-day trips including cross-channel transport, lodging, and several days of fishing (tel. 800/ 785-8425).

## HIKING & BACKPACKING

### HIKING

**Catalina** is a hiker's dream. Whether you come ashore at Avalon or Two Harbors, the most self-evident fact of seagoing life is that you disembark at sea level. The island, though, is anything but level. Most of the hiking involves scrambling up through the 2,000-foot plus mountains of the interior. Go up and down those suckers a few times and it's easy to rack up some serious vertical in a day. Don't fool yourself with visions of barefoot strolls down a long sandy beach—this is a place for real hiking boots and a hardy composition. But while 22 miles away in Long Beach the teaming millions are choking on smog and melting down in mass episodes of road rage, anyone in reasonably good shape can happily ramble through the virtually uninhabited canyons and ridges of Catalina. With serpentine ridges, switchback climbs, and an unlimited lifetime supply of spectacular views, it's hard to go wrong here. Add to that the curiosity factor of island wildlife and a herd of 400 bison descended from 14 bison brought out for the filming of *The Vanishing American* in 1924, and you've bought yourself a winner. Catalina has something else you should be aware of, which you won't find on any of the other islands: rattlesnakes. They're protected by law from you and you're not protected from them, so watch where you

put your hands and feet. Also be aware that the island is home to vastly different microclimates. Layers are the best way to dress. It's often as much as 20° warmer inland than on the coast.

Backpackers can have a really great time here, too. Backcountry **camping** opportunities range from improved sites with water and toilets to sheltered beaches offering nothing but a place to lay your bed in the sand campsites. You can catch the ferry to Avalon, spend a couple days covering the distance to Two Harbors, and then return to the mainland from there. Whatever you do, remember that water is scarce on the island. There are no potable sources of water in the interior other than the ones in developed campgrounds, so carry plenty of containers and stock up whenever presented with the opportunity.

The first matter of business wherever you step onto the island is to get your free **hiking permit** from the Catalina Conservancy offices (listed under "The Lay of the Land," above). Backpackers will also want to secure their overnight **camping permits** at $6.50 per person per night. A quirk of Catalina transportation that smells like a boondoggle to me is the ferry companies' and island airlines' unanimous prohibitions (due to Coast Guard regulations, though no other passenger ferry I've been on has mentioned these regs) against carrying stove fuel onboard. Consequently, you either have to smuggle your stove fuel and risk the captain's wrath (something you really don't want to encounter judging by the ship's captains I know) or you bite the bullet and buy stove fuel at inflated island prices. What I wonder is if, it's prohibited to bring fuel on the ferries and airplanes, how do they bring over the fuel they're selling in the store?

So buy your fuel, get your permits, fill up the old canteen, and get ready for some fun. A lot of people on the island cheat the steep climb out of Avalon by catching the early morning **airport van** for the 10-mile ride to the airport at 1,600 feet. The one-way trip is $5 per person and lets you choose a number of downhill routes back or gives you a big head start on your excursion toward the other side of the island. You must make reservations the day prior to your trip. Call 310/510-0143 between 8am and 7pm.

## Wrigley Memorial-Avalon Canyon

6.5 miles. Moderate. 1,000-foot elevation gain. From anywhere in Avalon, walk up Catalina St. until it joins Avalon Canyon Rd. From here climb on the road for 1.5 miles to the Botanical Garden.

As we know it today, Catalina and Avalon are something of an homage to the economics of chewing gum. Suck on a slice of Juicy Fruit, lace up the wafflestompers, and enjoy this look at the Wrigley family's contribution to the island. Walking up Avalon Canyon road, you'll pass Bird Park on your right. Now a campground, Bird Park at one time was home to a huge aviary filled with hundreds of exotic birds brought here by the Wrigleys. Just a little farther on the left is the former spring training camp for the Chicago Cubs, another Wrigley family enterprise. I don't know where the Cubs train now, but I find it hard to imagine a better place to get away from it all and play some hardball than Catalina. The road ends at the Botanical Garden. This great exhibit was initially the brainchild of Wrigley's wife, Ada, who began planting cacti and succulents here shortly after the family purchased the island in 1919. For years it served as a memorial to Mr. Wrigley, and then in 1969 the Wrigley Memorial Garden Foundation instituted an ambitious plan to turn it into a showcase of island botany. Today it's one of the best places in the world to learn about the plants of the Channel Islands, and admission is only a buck.

Take the time to explore the garden and study such rarities as the Catalina mahogany, Catalina live forever, and Catalina ironwood, which occur only on this island.

Follow the dirt path to the Wrigley Memorial. For many years, Mr. Wrigley's corpse was entombed here, but it's since been moved to the mainland. The imposing 130-foot tower was constructed largely from native stone and materials. The view from the top is great, but then again so is the view farther up the trail. Find the unlocked gate to the right of the memorial and make your way up the hill on Memorial Road. It's steep, but each turn reveals new and interesting perspectives of the harbor below. Use your newfound plant knowledge on the roadside growth. After a good mile you'll reach a divide and a fork in the road. Bear right along the top of ridge. From this point you can see both sides of the island and if the weather is right, you can see the mountains of the mainland. Take a good look at the island stretched out below you. Pull out another piece of Juicy Fruit and think, chewing gum bought this island. Then put the gum away. The ridge here is covered in pulpy and delicious prickly pear cactus. Picking and eating them is a dicey proposition for the uninformed. My favorite technique is to gingerly grab one between two sticks (or with a leather glove) and use a pocketknife to peel off the outer skin and spines (they're small and furry but pack a punch). Then I slice the pear in half and slurp out the colorful seedy pulp. It's kind of like a kiwifruit crossed with a pomegranate and you'll have a purple kisser when you're finished, I guarantee. In about 0.75 mile, you need to catch the unmarked Hermit Gulch Trail, which bears right off the ridge. It's steep and, as the name implies, follows a gulch. Enjoy the hike down this scenic canyon and eventually you'll intersect with Avalon Canyon

Road, just below the memorial and garden. From here I'm sure you can figure out the way back to town.

## Two Harbors to Little Harbor

7 miles one-way. Difficult. Trailhead begins at the southeast edge of Two Harbors, following rugged Banning House road out of the small settlement.

Hollywood film makers brought a herd of 14 bison to Catalina in 1924 as backdrop for the Zane Grey western *The Vanishing American*. The movie company got their shots, then left the bison behind. They've been anything but vanishing ever since. This hike will bring you through the heart of Catalina's buffalo country, where today about 400 of the shaggy beasts roam. You're crossing from the channel side to the Pacific side of the island, and will pass through several rugged canyons along the way. Banning House Road is a little-used and rugged track that shortcuts the longer, but more-reasonable-for-vehicles-route followed by Little Harbor Road. It's steep going for the first couple miles, but eventually you'll crest the ridge and gain outrageous views back toward Two Harbors and the entire central island. Descend the steep canyon below until you reach the grasslands of Little Springs Canyon, which is cut by Little Harbor Road. You'll bear right at the intersection with Little Harbor Road (left would take you about 3.5 miles back to Two Harbors) and descend toward Little Harbor through a visual oxymoron, the great symbol of the plains states grazing both sides of the canyon on a small Pacific island. Take pictures and gaze at the bison, but keep in mind that they may be shaggy, but they're really not huggable or nice. Eventually, the road spills you out into Little Harbor, the most popular campground and anchorage on the south side of the island. This spot was home

to a large Indian village, and archaeological digs here have revealed much of what we know about the earliest Catalina inhabitants. Open to the brunt of the entire Pacific, Shark Harbor, the larger of the two coves here, is often an exciting bodysurfing break. From here, periodic shuttle buses will take you back to either Avalon or Two Harbors, or you can make the hike into a 14-mile round-trip.

## Blackjack Trail

8 miles. Moderate. 1,500-foot elevation loss. From Avalon take either the airport shuttle or the Catalina interior shuttle (fee for both) and ask to be dropped off at Blackjack Junction.

Over the years, Catalina has seen many strange enterprises, not the least of which was a brief mining boom that extracted lead and silver from the central peak of the island at the Black Jack Mine. Following a rough fire road, you'll climb through an arid cactus forest, ignoring tempting trails which lead to the two highest peaks on the island, Orizaba (2,097 feet) and Black Jack (2,006 feet). Instead, bear ahead on the Cottonwood/ Black Jack Trail, which descends toward the southwest. Throughout this hike, keep your eyes peeled for wildlife. You'll be passing through some of the wildest portions of the island frequented by wild boar, bison, goats, and deer. None of these critters is native to the island, but seeing them can be quite a thrill. Eventually you'll come to several sets of gates. This is Rancho Escondido, Catalina's horse breeding ranch, still owned by the Wrigley family. Please shut the gates behind you so the horses don't get out. Catalina Arabians are famous worldwide for their stamina and dispositions. Reaching the main road from Airport in the Sky to Little Harbor, bear left and enjoy the 3.5 miles of downhill hiking to the beaches and campground of Little

Harbor. From here you can catch the inland shuttle back to Avalon or Two Harbors.

## BACKPACKING

Catalina is the only one of California's offshore islands to allow backpacking. It's a wonderful place to lose yourself in island time for a few days. Catalina has many subtleties—microclimates, plant communities, animals—that reveal themselves best after a few days spent in the open air. But don't think you're going to have a solitary experience. Even if you hike to the most remote beach on the island, somebody, and probably several somebodies, will most likely already have gotten there by boat. On busy holiday weekends it's not at all uncommon to find 200 people camped at the popular oceanfront camps. The inland campgrounds are less popular, but you'll still be camping in a campground. The Catalina Conservancy frowns heavily on people who just pitch a tent in some isolated canyon. The island bears a tremendous amount of human pressure, and the ecology of the island is best protected by people confining their camping to designated spots. When planning a trip, it's best to map out a rough itinerary and reserve your campsites (tel. 310/510-0303 for reservations). My personal bias leans toward hiking to one spot with all my gear, staying there a couple days, and leaving open my options to hike or hang out on the beach each day. In contrast, many people like to cover the entire island, camping in different spots each night. The following trips are simply suggestions that have worked for many before. String them together. Cut them in half. Pick the parts you like and discard the rest. Catalina backpacking lends itself to customization.

## Two Harbors to Parsons Landing

7 miles. Easy. Access: Ferry to Two Harbors or Catalina Interior Shuttle to Two Harbors from Avalon.

Seven miles west of Two Harbors on the least developed and visited side of the island, Parson's Landing is a great destination for a family hike. The trail, actually a fire road, is fairly level, something of an oddity on this jaggedly formed island. You'll follow the coastline, passing several private youth camps, and be treated to wonderful ocean views almost the entire way. Both Emerald Bay and Cabrillo Bay on the way to Parson's Landing have primitive beach camping—nothing more than a place to pitch a tent or lay your sleeping bag—but at only 7 miles, Parson's Landing is an easy enough hike for most folk. The campground itself is adjacent to the beach and faces the mainland. There are no assigned sites, but enough fire rings, barbecues, latrines, and limited running water for about 150 campers. During the high season a shore boat runs from Two Harbors to here, so don't expect everyone else to be backpackers. This is the best camping spot from which to explore the remote western end of the island. The trail that brought you here continues west, offering more and more spectacular views, though most of the coastline is far below and inaccessible because of steep cliffs. Boushey Road and the Silver Peak Trail will take you to the highest peak on the West End, 1802-foot Silver Peak. At about 13 miles round-trip, it's a hard day's hike.

## Three-Day Catalina Circuit

15 miles round-trip. Moderate. Access: If you fly to Catalina, this hike begins at the

airport. If you took the ferry, take the airport shuttle to Catalina's Airport-In-the-Sky.

From the airport, hike back down the Avalon-Airport Road to Blackjack Junction (about 3 miles). Turn right here and ascend along the flanks of Mount Blackjack, the second highest peak on the island. You'll crest a ridge and descend down to Blackjack Camp, which is tucked in a pine-shaded hollow on the side of Mount Blackjack. If you're lucky, the 75-camper capacity of the campground will only be a hypothetical number. Before throwing down your gear, assess the situation: If it's windy, look for shelter. If not, wander around and go for a campsite with a view. A couple of spots are situated just perfectly for a nighttime showing of the mainland lights. Depending on how tired you are from your travel to the island and the short hike here, you might consider climbing the summit of Black Jack Peak or Mount Orizaba, the highest spot on the island.

The next morning your goal is to reach Little Harbor. Follow the directions of the Blackjack Trail Hike (see above). You'll pass through Rancho Escondido and some of Catalina's best wildlife areas. Keep an eye peeled for goats and wild boar, both of which are quite common in this area. Your 5.5-mile descent to Little Harbor also brings you through several different plant zones. Depending on your orientation, you may be walking through pine forest, prickly pear cactus, or a lovely chaparral of island mahogany, sage, and scrub oak.

Your destination, Little Harbor, is one of the best beaches (actually three different beaches) on the entire island. During Prohibition, this was a favorite staging area for rumrunners preparing for nighttime runs into Los Angeles. Well

before that, its crescent coves were a favorite anchorage for pirates and explorers. Now it's just a fine spot to camp, and a popular anchorage with yachters from all over. It's advisable to leave Black Jack Camp early enough to give yourself plenty of warm afternoon sun in which to enjoy swimming at Little Harbor's fine sand beaches.

Day 3 is the day to suffer. You'll backtrack up Rancho Escondido Road toward the airport, a 1,600-foot elevation change. The trail is shadeless and often dusty. But there will be plenty to distract you. This is the heart of Catalina's buffalo zone. Anywhere along this stretch you might encounter the shaggy descendents of 1924 movie bison. While it's unlikely that one will surprise you and even less likely that you'll surprise one of them, do keep in mind that these are very wild animals. Give them plenty of respect and space. It's a long trudge up the hill, but eventually you'll see the airport, and from there you either catch a ride home on a plane or back to Avalon.

## HORSEBACK RIDING

**Catalina Stables** is located at 600 Avalon Canyon Rd. just outside town on the edge of the golf course (tel. 310/510-0478). With guided rides ranging from $25 to $100 and from 1 to 5 hours, the equestrian center here has a little of something for everyone. Beginners will enjoy the 1-hour ride that explores the hills surrounding the golf course without getting out into the rough backcountry. It's a nice introduction to horseback riding that won't leave you too saddle sore. More experienced riders will want to sign up for the longer rides. The most involved is a 5-hour ride that penetrates deep into the island backcountry, where you might have the pleasure of riding alongside wild buffalo or sighting the wild deer, pigs, or goats that live here. The stable accepts only cash or traveler's check, no credit cards. Reservations for shorter rides must be made in person. For the 5-hour ride, call in advance of your visit.

## MOUNTAIN BIKING

I love steep, winding climbs, out-of-the-saddle grinds where you just keep going up and up. But I have one requirement—they must pay off with a spectacular view. There are plenty of spectacular views where I live, but nothing beats the 360-degree neck-twisters that an island offers. With all of its dirt roads and incredible variety of geographic tricks up its sleeve, Catalina is perfect mountain biking turf. Distances that are too long for a casual hike, Avalon to Two Harbors and back for example, are easily doable by a fit cyclist.

There's a catch, though. To mountain bike anywhere outside of the immediate township of Avalon, you must purchase an annual **bicycle permit** good from May 1 to April 30. No day passes are available, and the annual permit costs $50 per person or $75 per family. While that's no biggie if you spend every weekend on the island, it certainly makes going for a little bike ride on your one visit to the island a very pricey proposition. Bear in mind that the permit is for the person riding the bike, not the bike itself, so even renting a mountain bike from the bike shop in Avalon won't save you from having to cough it up. As much as I admire the Catalina Conservancy's good work, this permit policy is clearly intended to discourage the use of bikes to get around the island and to foster dependence on the fossil-fuel-burning (and revenue-earning) interior shuttles and tour buses. I really wish they'd formulate a more reasonable plan that encouraged responsible bike

riding, because this island is tailor made for bike exploration.

Each of the ferry companies charges a slightly different price for bringing your bike over, but it's generally minimal, from $3 to $3.50. If you're flying in or don't have your own bike, **Brown's Bikes** near the boat landing in Avalon rents everything from cruisers and tandems to 21-speed mountain bikes. Only the latter are allowed out of Avalon.

For a great exploration of mountain and beach, the ride from Avalon to Little Harbor takes you through the heart of the Catalina backcountry. The first 2 miles out of Avalon on Stage Road will get your heart going; it's 1,500 feet to the top. From here you've got several great choices. The main road between Avalon and Two Harbors is surfaced and carries a lot of traffic, especially big semi-truck-pulled tour buses. Since bicycles are only permitted on the roads, you'll always have to be alert to what's around the next corner. The buses don't go very fast; the big worry is coming around a blind corner too fast and slamming into them.

The most popular route is Middle Canyon Road from Middle Ranch Junction to Little Harbor. From here you can loop back up Cottonwood Canyon Road to Airport in the Sky, and then back to Avalon. Or simply return via Middle Canyon. You may also take Little Harbor Road all the way to Two Harbors and back. It's easy to lose yourself on some of these long downhills and forget that you've got to go back up and over them to get back to Avalon.

## ROAD BIKING

If you're going to leave the confines of Avalon, you'll be doing it on a mountain bike. But if you just want to putter around town, **Brown's Bikes** (see above) adjacent to the boat landing has everything from beach cruisers to bicycles built for two.

## SAILING

The most popular overnight sailing destination in all of California, Catalina's harbors range from the bustle of Avalon to tiny pocket anchorages with only enough room for one or two boats. The San Pedro Channel crossing is just enough distance to lend a sense of real adventure to a trip, yet it doesn't demand too much of your crew. On a nice breeze you'll make landfall at one of the leeward side ports within 4 or 5 hours of the mainland. The more remote backside of the island is best as a destination for a 3- or 4-day trip. Both Avalon and Two Harbors offer full amenities: year-round fuel and water, mechanics, mooring buoys, shoreboat service, and on-shore restaurants and stores. For the Catalina Island Boaters Guide, which lists all anchorages and local protocols, call the **Catalina Island Harbor Department** at 310/510-COVE. When arriving by sea, contact them on VHF Channel 9.

A number of charter boat operations on the mainland will either outfit you for a bareboat trip to the island if you're qualified, or arrange for a skippered charter.

## SCUBA DIVING

Catalina is sometimes called "The Checkout Island," because it's the mother of all spots for Southern California divers doing their first open-ocean dive. The implication, of course, is that it's just a spot for beginners, and serious divers go elsewhere. Nothing could be more misleading.

Catalina, in fact, is such a fantastic diving destination it was ranked the no. 1 dive destination in North America by *Rodale's Scuba Diving* magazine's

Reader's Choice Awards in 1997. The visibility is nothing short of amazing for a temperate dive spot, ranging from 40 to 100-plus feet depending on season, and below the waters of this one small island you'll find sea caves, wrecks, hydrocorals, ledges covered with invertebrate tube anemones, nudibranchs and strawberry amemones, shark diving, lobster hunting, protected game reserves, and much much more. Nor do you have to be a scuba diver to enjoy the underwater world. Snorkelers can't go as deep, but they move through the water with a grace and quiet that bubble-blowing tank divers can only dream of. Consequently they often see bigger fish and have close encounters with underwater wildlife. **Lover's Cove Marine Preserve** is just outside Avalon Harbor past the boat landing (opposite the casino) and is the best snorkeling spot near town. For rental gear, go to **Descanso Beach Ocean Sports** near the casino (tel. 310/510-1226) or **Wet Spot Rentals** in Avalon (tel. 310/510-9588).

Summer water temperatures range from 65° to 70°F and winter temperatures from 55° to 63°F. Full suits are used year-round for scuba, but snorkelers can often get by quite happily with just a spring suit during summer months.

Catalina is also probably the safest place in the world to get the bends; there's a hyperbaric chamber at Two Harbors that is a center of diving medicine research. Nobody, of course, wants to get bent no matter what, but it's somehow reassuring to know that they medivac injured divers from the mainland to Catalina for treatment more often than the other way around. Nowhere on the island are you more than a 30-minute boat ride from help.

Avalon and Two Harbors both offer dive charters that will take you to spots around the island, and dive boats from the mainland make the 2-hour trip from San Pedro and Long Beach almost every day. Without a doubt the most popular dive spot in the entire Channel Islands is **Avalon's Underwater Park.** Located directly off the casino in Avalon Bay, this area has a little of everything. During the summer the shore will be crowded with divers sunning themselves and gearing up. Winter, the best season for visibility, often finds the beach empty. Several wrecks have been placed within park boundaries, and the kelp forests here are as fine as any on the island. Since it's been a protected game reserve since 1965, this is a great spot to see big and fearless fish. Somehow they know the boundaries of the reserve too, and fish inside and outside the protected zone act completely different. Protection of the park isn't limited to fish. Don't take anything but photographs from here. More adventurous divers will find depths to 100 feet off the harbor breakwater. A favorite dive is to the wreck of the *Sue Jack,* a 65-foot sailboat that lies in 90 feet of water near the breakwater. During busy times, **Catalina Diver's Supply** operates an air truck right from the beach, so you can get as many fills as you want. The underwater park is roped off to boat traffic, but be very aware of where you are before surfacing. Snorkelers, also, want to be very aware of their location at all times. Since this spot lies just outside the busy harbor channel, coming up on the wrong side of the boundary ropes is a very bad idea.

A recent craze at Catalina is shark diving and snorkeling. Both **Argo Diving Services** and **Catalina Charter Boat Company** offer special shark dives here. Running out of Avalon, you'll motor several miles into the open San Pedro Channel. Here, your captain will lower the shark cage and start laying out a line of chopped mackerel chum. Often within minutes the blue sharks will begin to gather. Divers slip into the cage and watch as the 4- to 8-foot blues devour

mackerel. Occasionally a larger mako shark will arrive, looking like a finned, toothy torpedo. Of course, some days no sharks respond to the call; other days you'll see as many as 40 at once.

Without a doubt the most difficult to find and most subtly gorgeous dive in the Catalina area is the **Farnsworth Bank.** Two miles off the back side of Catalina, the Bank is a series of several rock pinnacles which rise from a sandy bottom in hundreds of feet of water to reach within 60 feet of the surface. An average dive here reaches 100 feet deep and it's easy to accidentally go deeper, so proper dive planning and buoyancy control are vital. But the danger and difficulty are well worth it. Here you'll descend through deep blue water where it's not at all uncommon to find 100-foot visibility. As you follow the anchor line down, the bottom will suddenly take shape. Past 100 feet deep, purple hydrocorals branch off the rock substrata almost everywhere you look. This purple coral was once collected for jewelry, but it's now protected and taking even a small piece is forbidden. The open ocean waters are rich with plankton that support an outrageous showing of anemones. It's not uncommon to find 10 different colors and species on a single rock. The fish are large here, too. Look for white sea bass, yellowtail, barracuda, and even the occasional giant sea bass.

Many different mainland dive operators visit Catalina. For the purposes of this chapter I've listed only the dive shops and boats that operate from Avalon or Two Harbors. Boats from mainland ports that regularly visit Catalina will be listed with their home port. Virtually every Southern California charter boat visits Catalina at some point or the other, but the regular take-off spots for a day trip to the island are San Pedro and Long Beach harbors.

## DIVE CHARTERS

### Argo Diving Services

A small, 6-pack diving operation based in Avalon, Argo was one of the pioneers of shark diving on the island. The small size of their boat allows them a lot of flexibility in planning your itinerary (tel. 310/510-2208).

### Catalina Charter Boat Company

Another 6-pack boat, Catalina Charter's 30-foot *Island Diver* offers 2-tank ($75) and 3-tank ($95) dives to spots around the island. The price includes 80-cubic-foot tanks, weights, snacks, and beverages. They also offer introductory dives for first-timers and full certification. On request they'll arrange shark cage diving. P.O. Box 203, Avalon, CA 90704 (tel. 310/510-2720).

### Catalina Divers Supply

Catalina Divers Supply's 42-foot *Cat Dive* is an ideal diving platform. The twin hulls offer great stability and a wide deck. Big enough for up to 15 divers. Catalina Divers Supply is also a full service dive center at no. 7, Avalon Pleasure Pier (tel. 800/626-0720 or 310/510-0330).

### Catalina Scuba Luv

A well-known live-aboard dive boat that's earned a 5-star rating from PADI, the *Scuba Luv* is often booked for charter groups. Call 310/510-2350 or write P.O. Box 2009 for a schedule of trips.

### Catalina Ocean Rafting

One of the best ways to become intimately acquainted with the shoreline of Catalina, these adventure rafting trips are done in 24-foot rigid, inflatable boats, basically the same craft used for Coast Guard rescue teams. Their small size, high speed, and stability let the Catalina Ocean Rafting captains pull into sea caves, tuck into the smallest anchorages, and race right alongside the breaking waves. Snorkeling (no scuba) is an element of all their trips, which range from a $32, 2-hour snorkeling trip to 1-day ($130) and 2-day ($270) circumnavigations of the island that concentrate on wildlife viewing and exploration. All equipment and meals are provided. P.O. Box 2075, Avalon, CA 90704 (tel. 310/510-0211).

### Catalina West End Diving Center

In addition to being a full-service dive shop, the West End Dive Center offers boat dives on their boats the *Garibaldi* and *Sea Bass*. All tanks and weights are provided. Their location at Two Harbors makes for a short run to some of the island's more spectacular and remote sites. 1 Banning House Rd., Two Harbors (tel. 310/510-0303).

### Snorkeling Catalina

A hit with the beginners, Snorkeling Catalina offers 1-hour, 45-minute guided snorkeling trips to Lover's Cove or Willow Cove based from Joe's Rent-a-Boat on the Green Pleasure Pier. Including mask, fins, snorkel, and basic instruction, the trips run $32 for adults and $22 for kids under 12. For an extra $3 they'll throw in a wetsuit (tel. 310/510-0455).

## SEA KAYAKING

With so many pocket coves and beaches, miles of rocky coastline, and enough nooks and crannies to spend a month exploring, Catalina is well-suited to kayak-based exploration. Getting your own kayak to the island is difficult. The passenger ferries aren't particularly accommodating when you show up with a couple of boats of your own. Unless you're prepared to paddle the whole distance yourself, be sure and arrange for your kayak's safe passage with your ferry company in advance, and be prepared to pay extra for the space you take up.

You'll never want for a place to rent sit-on-top kayaks by the hour or day here. **Descanso Beach Ocean Sports** (tel. 310/510-1226), **Wet Spot Rentals** (tel. 310/510-2229), and **Catalina Island Expeditions** (tel. 310/510-1226) can set you up from Avalon. **Catalina West End Dive Center** in Two Harbors (tel. 310/510-0303) is a good place to rent a boat for exploring the west end of the island. All of the above offer guided tours of varying lengths along the rocky coastline. A typical half-day trip from Avalon would take you a couple miles to a snorkeling stop at Willow Cove or Seal Rock, allow you to eat lunch, and return, and would cost around $65. Single and double kayaks are available from most dealers, and at the West End Dive Center and Descanso Beach Ocean Sports a limited number of traditional (decked) touring kayaks are available for experienced ocean kayakers who like the added performance of a boat they can sit inside. Both can also arrange overnight kayak camping expeditions to a variety of locations on the island.

Self-supported kayakers can take advantage of the several beachside campgrounds scattered around the island to make a multi-day voyage. While some of the campgrounds are reachable by hikers and people riding the island buses, others can only be reached by sea. The most remote and beautiful of these is **Starlight Cove,** only 1 mile short of the Land's End at the westernmost part of the island. Here you'll find great diving and camping. It's a hard day's paddle

up the coast from Two Harbors, but the return trip is usually aided by a tailwind.

## WHALE WATCHING

**Catalina Ocean Rafting** (tel. 310/510-0211), which specializes in exploration of the island by inflatable boats, is also a great whale-watching option. Their deftly maneuverable craft are perfect for sneaking up on migrating whales. The peak season is winter from January through April. During this time Catalina Ocean Rafting runs 2-hour whale-watching trips Tuesday, Saturday, and Sunday from noon. Cost is $30 adults and $20 for kids.

## WILDLIFE VIEWING

The landmass of Catalina is almost a freak show of strange wildlife. Besides the endemic foxes, migrating whales, and hordes of seabirds, you've got a herd of 400 bison, feral pigs, goats, and deer. The bison, of course, are the most dramatic inhabitants of the island. They tend to congregate in the same areas, and, well, the island just isn't so big that 400 bison can hide out. The goats are a little more difficult to spot, but anyone who goes for a few long hikes in the island backcountry will probably run into them. Descended from goats set ashore by the Spaniards, these island goats are wild looking creatures—shaggy, sure-footed, and often toting 2- to 3-foot tall sets of horns. While it's better in my opinion to just go hiking and hope to see some interesting wildlife (you will), there are numerous tour options that will also give you surefire results.

The Santa Catalina Conservancy Jeep Tours are probably the most low-key of the many commercial tours offered. Unlike the large semi-truck buses of the larger tour companies, these trips are done in open-topped jeeps bouncing along the remote backroads of the conservancy land. A trained naturalist will help you find everything from the bison to the island fox to the island rattlesnake, and will tell you all about each animal and plant community you pass through. The variety of the island is startling. Sometimes a group will see everything from a bald eagle to a gray whale on the same trip. Two-hour trips run $65 per person, and longer trips can be arranged. Call for reservations at 310/510-2595 ext. 0.

For much less than half that cost, you can hop on one of the inland wildlife tours run by **Discovery Tours** (tel. 310/510-TOUR) or **Catalina Adventure Tours** (tel. 310/510-2888). Bear in mind that these trips are done in huge buses that must stick to the main road, and you'll be with 50 other people, so you won't encounter Catalina with the same subtlety as the smaller jeep trips. The ride up out of Avalon is so switchbacked and narrow, though, that the very act of riding in one of the tourist coaches (they're giant trailers pulled by semi-trucks) rivals the thrill of many roller coasters. You could easily forget to look at the scenery and wildlife and still have a good time.

To me, though, the most interesting wildlife isn't what's on land, but what's in the water. The interplay between land and sea at any of the Channel Islands is one of the most spectacular wildlife zones on earth, and Catalina is no exception. Obviously, diving, snorkeling, and kayaking are great ways to meet the local wild things, but so are some of the commercial tours.

Glass-bottomed boats have been big business in Avalon for as long as there's been a tourist industry here. As turn-of-the-century visitors arrived in port, an entire fleet of glass-bottomed boats would encircle their steamer, each vying for business. Tourists would step directly into the boats and get a underwater tour on the way to shore. Run night and day, now, glass-bottomed boat trips are still a great quickie way to see what it looks like down there. More recently, semi-submersible tour boats have become a big hit. Designed to look like a submarine, these craft are really just big boats designed so the passengers sit below waterline and can see out through large Plexiglass windows. Kids love them, though, because they look like a real submarine, and as you brush through the kelp forest, calico bass, garibaldi and opaleye perch swish around the craft. At night, glass-bottomed and semi-submersible trips shine bright lights into the sea for a glimpse of nocturnal lobsters, moray eels, and possibly even sharks. Both **Discovery Tours** and **Catalina Adventure Tours** can provide reservations for all the glass-bottomed and semi-submersibles. They also arrange trips to the sea lion rookery at Seal Rocks on the east end, where barking and basking are a way of life. During summer months the huge bulls guard their harems on guano-covered rocks. Juveniles vie for sunning space, and the losers content themselves with hanging out in the water below.

One of the best ways to become intimately acquainted with the shoreline and wildlife of Catalina is **Catalina Ocean Rafting's** trips. The small size, high speed, and stability of their 24-foot inflatables let the Catalina Ocean Rafting captains pull into sea caves, tuck into the smallest anchorages, and race right alongside porpoises. Snorkeling (no scuba) is an element of all their trips, which range from a $32, 2-hour snorkeling trip to 1-day ($130) and 2-day ($270) circumnavigations of the island that concentrate on wildlife viewing and exploration. All equipment and meals are provided. Write P.O. Box 2075, Avalon, CA 90704 (tel. 310/510-0211).

# Channel Islands National Park ◆ What to Do & Where to Do It

## BEACHES

At first glance, the shoreline of the Channel Islands can be a bit of a disappointment. If you're like me, the word "island" conjures up fantasies of South Seas beaches fringed with gently waving palm trees. Much to the contrary, the majority of shoreline on these islands is cliff: rocky, crumbling, overhanging, wave-lashed cliff. Both Anacapa and Santa Barbara are so rocky that you have to climb a tall ladder just to set foot on shore. The three larger islands, however, do have their share of lovely beaches, some of which are even relatively easy to reach.

The main visitor area on the newly acquired east end of Santa Cruz is **Scorpion Ranch.** To come ashore here, you'll land on a nice but rocky beach. Just to the south is **Smuggler's Cove,** which has a nice sandy beach. The better beaches on the island necessitate your own boat. Along the south shore, **Coches Prietos** anchorage is my favorite sandy beach on the island, a horseshoe cove framed by rocky cliffs and a dramatic canyon. The Nature Conservancy owns this western nine-tenths of the island and requires landing permits to come ashore (which can be purchased by writing Nature Conservancy Santa Cruz Island Project, 213 Stearns Wharf, Santa Barbara, CA 93101; tel. 805/962-9111). Many other beaches line the west end, though anchoring here is often dangerous, and the leeward side of the island holds some real gems: tiny cove beaches with freshwater creeks that make delicious places to rinse off on a hot day.

**Santa Rosa** is more beach-friendly that Santa Cruz. The National Park Campground at **Beecher's Bay** sits right above a white-sand beach that stretches for miles to the east point of the island. All you need to do is start walking until you find a piece of sand that suits your fancy. The vigorous winds of the Santa Barbara Channel hit Santa Rosa headlong, and continually rearrange the wind lines and dunes of Beecher's Bay. The wharf in the middle of **Beecher's** was used to load and unload Hereford cattle from the island ranching operation.

**Cuyler Harbor** on San Miguel is, in my opinion, one of the most beautiful beaches anywhere. The perfect blue water contrasts with two huge sand slides, and a bright white-sand beach rings about half the cove. Prince Island, a towering pinnacle of rock, rises from the center of the bay. Fortunately for visitors here, Cuyler Harbor is where you'll come ashore, and it's one of the few places on the island you're not required to visit with a docent. The downside is that it can be darn windy and cold on San Miguel any time of year.

## BIRD WATCHING

Some of the most important seabird and shorebird nesting habitats in the country are located on these five islands. Much of Anacapa is given over to the birds; more than 50% of the island land mass is dedicated to the endangered California brown pelicans who nest here. Nearly driven to extinction by DDT poisoning, the primitive-looking pelicans are now a common sight up and down the California coast. Most of them were born on Anacapa. Anacapa was also made famous by the discovery of "lesbian seagulls" there several decades ago, where during a shortage of male gulls the females paired off and raised their broods cooperatively.

Santa Barbara Island is the most seaward of the park islands, and consequently enjoys the distinction of being the largest colony of Xantus' murrelets and black storm petrels in the United States. Normally these birds are seen only far out to sea and they only return to land once a year to nest.

Santa Cruz has achieved a bit of birder fame recently, as the Santa Cruz island jay was recognized as an entirely separate species rather than the subspecies of the scrub jay it was previously considered to be. As a result, both the Nature Conservancy and National Park Service areas of the island have seen a marked increase in people flocking to the island to add this very rare (it only occurs on this island) bird to their life lists. You may also spot some of the 14 breeding pairs of peregrine falcons that have recently begun reproducing on the island.

Both Santa Rosa and San Miguel are important bird nesting zones as well. One of the most endangered and most charming shorebirds in California is the snowy plover, which likes to nest right on the beach. For obvious reasons this nesting strategy hasn't worked too well for the plovers as mainland beaches became more populated, but the desolate dunes and sand beaches of these two westernmost Channel Islands have been something of a saving grace to the species.

## FISHING

Old-timers tell tales of when the fishing was so good out at Anacapa and Santa Cruz that they'd catch giant sea bass using wine kegs and a cable with a baited hook. The huge black sea bass were good to eat and none too smart, so the fishermen would simply wait for them to bite, then toss the keg overboard. Eventually the big fish would tire of pulling the giant wine barrel along and stop. But in the meantime the fishermen would go on hooking other giant sea bass and throwing more wine kegs overboard. By the end of the day they'd pull up half a dozen or more 500-pound fish. Needless to say, there aren't many giant sea bass around the islands any more.

Compared to the mainland, though, the fishing at the islands is quite extraordinary. Depending on the season, it's not uncommon to haul in a 30-pound halibut or a big mako shark, or to catch your limit of calico bass. The number of game species fished at the islands is fittingly diverse for an archipelago located at the convergence of two very rich marine ecosystems. Depending on the season, people might be pulling up salmon, which are cold-water fish, or they might be pulling up warm-water species such as dorado and striped marlin.

The reason the fishing is so much better here than on the mainland, of course, is the islands' remoteness. A day on a party boat at the islands can be a long haul. The shortest crossing is the day trips out of Oxnard and Ventura to fish around Anacapa, but to reach the really rich fishing grounds of Santa Rosa, back side Santa Cruz, or San Miguel involves a serious expenditure of time and fuel. If you're serious about catching big fish, though, there's not much that can beat it. The following places offer open boats and charters to fish the waters of Channel Islands National Park.

◆ Cisco Sportfishing, 4151 S. Victoria Ave., Channel Islands Harbor, Tel. 805/965-8511.
◆ Sea Landing Sportfishing, Santa Barbara Harbor, Sea Landing, Cabrillo Blvd. at the end of Bath St., Tel. 805/963-3564.
◆ Wavewalker Charters, Santa Barbara Harbor, Custom 6-pack charter. Capt. David Bacon. Tel. 805/964-2046.

## HIKING

### Anacapa Loop Trail

1–2 miles. Moderate. Access: via Island Packers boat from Ventura Harbor.

In 1980, when Congress designated Channel Islands National Park as such, the work of protecting the islands and developing some sort of system for people to visit them had only just begun. The first island to be developed for public use is Anacapa, which is so tiny that to call what you do there hiking is somewhat of an overstatement. The most strenuous walking you'll do on a visit here is the 154-step climb up a rusty iron stairway from the boat landing. The loop trail on the flat mesa of East Anacapa is actually a figure eight—but who's going to quibble. If you hike every single foot of trail on East Anacapa, you'll have covered almost 2 miles. What's attractive, though, is the dramatic setting. A pamphlet available at the island will give you a nice overview of the natural history and human history of this fragile place. Since you'll have brought all your own food because nothing is available on the island, pack a picnic and have a nice lunch away from the bustle of the landing area and campground. During spring, the island blooms bright yellow as the giant coreopsis burst into flower. This time of year is also excellent for spotting gray whales as they migrate between their summer feeding ground off Alaska and their calving grounds in the shallow lagoons of Baja.

## SANTA CRUZ EAST END HIKES

The eastern tenth of Santa Cruz has only recently been incorporated into the park. Because of that, very little formal development has happened, which is something of a blessing. Visitor use of Santa Cruz has skyrocketed, though, since the opening of the east end as a park hugely expands the horizons of visitors making a day trip out of Ventura. You'll land at Scorpion anchorage if you're coming to the park via the Island Packers service (which is the only way other than private boat to visit the park). From here, in a lovely oak-shaded valley, trails run up along the clifftops in

both directions, and it's possible to follow old ranch roads for miles inland. While the Nature Conservancy, owners of the other 90% of the island, have eliminated feral sheep and done much to control the wild pigs on their part of the island, this end is still pretty hammered by overgrazing. That, too, will change as the park service removes the animals.

From the campground at Scorpion Ranch, several fine hikes are possible.

### Cavern Point Overlook

2 miles round-trip. Moderate.

Cavern Point is a high overlook above the Santa Barbara Channel that offers a nice perspective of the north shore of the island. This is one of the better spots in the park for whale watching during the winter months, as the large grays round the point very close to land, and your high perspective gives you the chance to actually see the whales underwater, not just their spouts. Follow the road 100 feet past the ranch buildings up the canyon and take the trail to the right. You'll scramble up a rocky climb and then follow the blufftop for about a mile. Stay back from the cliff edges here, as the rock is highly eroded and unstable.

### Potato Harbor Overlook

4 miles round-trip. Moderate.

Potato Harbor Overlook also grants you a fine view of the channel and north coast of the island, but this trail is a little longer. Follow the road up to the northwest edge of the airstrip. Watch for landing planes as you're walking across the dirt field that passes as a runway. You'll find a trail continuing northwest that will take you all the way to Potato Harbor, an interestingly shaped notch in the island coastline. There's no way down to the sea here, but the view is splendid.

## Smugglers Cove Hike

7 miles round-trip. Difficult.

This last hike isn't recommended if you're visiting Santa Cruz for the day on the Island Packers boat unless you're a fast walker. People have missed the return trip home by overestimating their ability. At the same intersection where you'd turn right to go to Cavern Point, you're going to go left and follow Smuggler's Road up and out of Scorpion Canyon. The 3.5 miles to Smugglers are an interesting mix of grasslands, steep canyons, and occasional ocean views. When you descend into Smugglers Cove, you'll find a wonderful, sandy, south-facing beach and a ranger station. During summer south swells, this is a great place to bodysurf the shore break.

## SANTA CRUZ ISLAND NATURE CONSERVANCY PRESERVE

Almost every weekend from April to November special trips run from the **Island Packers** (tel. 805/642-1393) dock in Ventura to Prisoners' Harbor on Santa Cruz. Here, you'll be met by a Nature Conservancy naturalist. Two specific hikes are offered.

## Prisoners' Harbor to Pelican Bay

5 miles round-trip. Strenuous.

From Prisoners' Harbor you'll quickly climb the ridge and follow the island shore west. You're entering some of the steepest country on the island. Past Pelican Bay the shoreline becomes virtually impassable. Your guide will point out such unique residents as the island scrub-jay, a species of blue jay that is found nowhere but this island. You may also encounter wild boars. Your effort will be rewarded with phenomenal views of the waters surrounding the island. Watch for migrating whales, seals, and dolphins. Your turnaround is Pelican Bay, once developed as a resort and the site of numerous location shoots for Hollywood adventure films; it is now marked only by a few old foundations and one of the most picturesque anchorages on the island. On busy weekends 50 or more yachts will swing at anchor here. A trail to the water is a great chance for a swim before heading back.

## Central Valley Hike

6 miles round-trip. Moderate.

A large creek drains into the sea at Prisoners' Harbor. Following it upstream, you'll pass under the shade of huge oaks and sycamores. Unlike any of the other Channel Islands, Santa Cruz contains a large central valley. The creek canyon opens up into a scene reminiscent of the 19th century. The historic Main Ranch compound is a wealth of old ranching and vineyard equipment and currently houses Nature Conservancy caretakers. Here, away from the immediate coastal influence, the smells and sounds are dramatically different from those of the shore. Wild turkey often gobble on the hillsides and horses graze around the fenced pastures.

## SANTA ROSA HIKING

1–5 miles. Easy–strenuous. All hikes begin at Beecher's Bay (water canyon) campground.

Since it's at least a 3-hour boat trip to Santa Rosa, most day visitors confine themselves to short hikes around the landing area. Fortunately there are several interesting choices. Just up the hill behind the main ranch is a grove of Torrey pines, which occur naturally only here and in Torrey Pines State Reserve near La Jolla. The trail to the trees continues out to East Point, where there is a large freshwater wetland, home to numerous wild birds. More strenuous hikes lead into Lobo Canyon (5 miles), where the shell middens of an old Chumash Indian village indicate many years of successful feasts; the hikes then take you out to some nice tide pools, very likely some of the same ones where the Chumash found their abalone. Another trail leads up Cherry Canyon into the island interior, where you'll see grazing cattle and perhaps some of the wild elk and deer that were introduced here for hunting. Rangers lead hikes from the Beecher's Bay ranch compound almost every day. Contact the park service (tel. 805/568-5711) for schedules.

### SAN MIGUEL HIKING

Because of the fragile ecology of San Miguel, all hikers here must accompany a ranger. Luckily for you, the ranger will be busy explaining all the interesting things that make San Miguel such a unique place. The most popular hike on the island, an 8-mile round-trip from Cuyler Harbor to Point Bennett, is a nature-crazy kid's dream. This sandy point on the island's northwest end is famous as the only place in the world you can see six different pinniped (seal and sea lion) species at once. As many as 20,000 Northern elephant seals, harbor seals, Stellar sea lions, California sea lions, and Guadalupe fur seals all gather here at one time. You'll probably get close to the seals, but bring binoculars because it always seems they're doing something really interesting at the other end of the beach. On the hike back to camp from Point

Bennett, ask your ranger to stop and show you the unique caliche forest, a miniature petrified forest left behind when calcium carbonate present in blowing soil reacted with ancient plants' organic acid, leaving behind these eerie casts of their long-gone trunks and branches.

### SANTA BARBARA HIKING

Santa Barbara is the smallest of the entire island chain, essentially a grassy hill sticking up in the middle of the sea. It's just 1 square mile of land, but it contains 5.5 miles of hiking trails. You can easily walk every step in an afternoon, since the island is not very steep. For starters I'd recommend the Canyon View Self-Guided Nature Trail. The brochure that makes this a self-guided hike is found right at the Quonset hut that's the only real structure on the island. Another trail leads to the tip of 635-foot Signal Peak. On a very clear day you can see every Channel Island except for San Miguel (which is blocked by Santa Rosa) from this point.

### MOUNTAIN BIKING

Mountain biking is forbidden on all the publicly owned property in Channel Islands National Park.

### SAILING

On summer weekends the anchorages of **Santa Cruz** and **Santa Rosa** are filled with hundreds of happy sailors, and with good reason; this is some of the finest cruising anywhere. Boats leaving Santa Barbara Harbor are looking at about a 4-hour crossing to reach the popular coves of Pelican Harbor, Lady's Harbor, Fry's, and other northside destinations. People who set sail from Channel Islands Harbor in Ventura have less distance to cover to reach Anacapa or the East End of Santa Cruz, but they're facing an upwind sail most of the time. Either way, the crossing is not one for beginners. You must cross both a busy shipping lane (look both ways before crossing, then beat it) and the infamous Windy Lane, where winds funneling around Point Conception and down the channel can suddenly jump by 15 or 20 knots without warning. Don't underestimate the ability of the Santa Barbara Channel to dish up trouble. There are plenty of boats sitting on the bottom that can attest to that.

People who are looking to charter a bareboat should contact the **Santa Barbara Sailing Center** (tel. 805/962-2826; www.sbsailcentr.com) located adjacent to the harbor launch ramp, or the **Offshore Islands Sailing Club** at 3150 S. Harbor Blvd., Channel Islands Harbor (tel. 805/985-3600). Expect to pay around $400 for a 30- to 36-foot boat for the weekend. Both can also arrange for a qualified skipper for an additional fee.

A special treat for anyone who enjoys classic wooden sailing ships (and who doesn't?) is an island trip on the *Spike Africa*, a 70-foot gaff-rigged schooner that makes its home in Santa Barbara. She's a startlingly beautiful craft that has been featured on the cover of Wooden Boat Magazine and starred in the movie *Joe Versus the Volcano* alongside Tom Hanks and Meg Ryan. Generally you'll sail to Santa Barbara, cruise the coastline, and drop anchor in any number of beautiful spots. Then they'll send you out snorkeling, swimming, or just lounging around. When you come back to the boat, prepare to be stuffed with plenty of fine food before the sail home. Trips run on an irregular schedule and prices vary with specific details, ranging from $100 to $250. Call **Sea Landing** (tel. 805/963-3564) to make reservations.

## SCUBA DIVING & SNORKELING

If I had to name one reason why anyone should visit the Channel Islands National Park, I'd say the diving. Diving the kelp forests is the closest you'll ever come to experiencing what a bird must feel flying through a tropical rain forest. Giant kelp *(Macrocystis pyrifera)* is the fastest growing plant on earth, and at any of the four northern Channel Islands— Anacapa, Santa Cruz, Santa Rosa, and San Miguel—you'll swim through 100-foot-high underwater cathedrals formed by the towering stems.

Kelp fronds laid over on the surface form a ceiling penetrated by dramatic beams of light; schools of large calico bass and bright orange garibaldi patrol the middle of the water column. Red and purple urchins litter the bottom between jumbled boulder piles holding abalone, spiny lobsters, and horned sharks. Look around on the sandy bottom and you'll find angel sharks, halibut, or even the California electric ray, which looks like a garbage can lid with fins and packs a cattle-prod-like punch if tormented. And every free surface of every rock is covered with beautiful gardens of strawberry anemones, purple nudibranchs, and almost any permutation of starfish imaginable. On San Miguel, the westernmost and wildest island, you might dive with a colony of young sea lions, rowdy punks who blow bubbles in your face and like to head-butt and nip visitors. Better them than the white sharks that also call San Miguel home.

There are no dive facilities on the islands. The channel crossing to the islands is its own adventure. In the summer, dive boats regularly encounter feeding blue whales on their trip across the channel. Other seasons you can catch up with migrating gray whales, basking sharks, and the year-round contingents of porpoises numbering in the hundreds. Any time of year it can be a queasy trip, but once on-site the captain will usually find a smooth anchorage. Trips run all year and are only cancelled in the event of extremely bad weather. If you're out at the islands on your own boat and don't have a compressor, the commercial dive boats will usually refill your tanks for a small fee. Since they come and go rapidly, it's often wise to get on the VHS and ask them before rowing over with a dinghy full of tanks.

**Snorkelers** will enjoy the landing cove at Anacapa or Santa Barbara, and the cove at Scorpion Ranch is also a home to some great kelp beds and rock piles. Water here is cold enough year-round to require a wetsuit. Truth Aquatics of Santa Barbara is the unrivaled expert at Channel Islands trips. Their three boats, *Truth, Vision,* and *Conception,* boast comfortable sleeping berths for overnight trips, dual onboard compressors, heated wetsuit drying rooms, hot showers, circulating mask rinsers, clothes dryers, tasty onboard food, and highly skilled and knowledgeable crews. Open-boat single-day trips are $71 per person. Three-day overnights are $377 plus meals. Contact **Truth Aquatics** (tel. 805/962-1127) at Sea Landing Breakwater, Santa Barbara, CA 93109.

Three well-equipped dive boats also service the Channel Islands from Ventura Harbor: the *Liberty* (tel. 805/ 642-6655), the *Spectre* (tel. 805/483-6612), and the *Peace* (tel. 805/658-8286).

## SEA KAYAKING

The Chumash were the most ocean-going of California's native inhabitants. Paddling wooden-planked tomals, a type of giant open-topped canoe, they'd journey from the mainland to the islands and from island to island. After spend-

ing some time paddling around the islands yourself, you'll come to realize the magnitude of their undertaking. Every year people cross the channel (usually from Ventura to Anacapa where it's narrowest) in modern ocean kayaks, but it's not something to undertake lightly. The Santa Barbara Channel can turn from glass to raging chop in minutes.

Most kayakers at the islands do it the easy way: They hop a boat from Ventura or Santa Barbara and leave the driving to someone else. Then, once the dirty work is over they hop overboard and enjoy the tremendous kayaking along the island shore.

Paddling through crystal clear water at the base of Santa Cruz's or Anacapa's shoreline cliffs is breathtaking. Faulting in the island rock has created numerous arches and sea caves. The largest sea cave in the world, **Santa Cruz's Painted Cave,** is a favorite stopping point when conditions allow. Stretching a quarter-mile back into the island, this cave is filled with barking sea lions and frescoed with algae and lichen. You'll need a strong flashlight or headlamp to enjoy it, since the ceiling is 50 feet high and much of the cave is in total darkness. Hundreds of other caves await on more protected shores if the swell won't allow you to enter Painted Cave. Always be super aware of your headroom, the tide, and the swell conditions before entering any cave. You don't want to get stuffed in a dark crack by a monster set.

Snorkeling off a sit-on-top kayak is another great pleasure out here. The freedom to poke into little coves or to explore areas that larger boats can't safely anchor lets you see tons of underwater life.

The opening of **Santa Cruz's East End** as a public park has opened up a world of opportunity for self-supported kayakers. You're not allowed to camp anywhere but the main park campground, but the coastline in either direction from Scorpion Landing is a wonderful day trip. Expect sea caves, lots of marinelife (including whales), and isolated beaches. This end of the island is the most sheltered from the predominant northwest weather, so it's great for learners.

**Santa Rosa** is more for the hardy, but the payoff is that you're allowed to camp from your kayak on numerous island beaches. Depending on wildlife breeding and birthing seasons, certain areas of the island are closed; so before heading out to the island, you'll want to call the park service at 805/658-5730 and ask them to send you the latest sea kayaking and beach camping site bulletins. Compared to Santa Cruz, Santa Rosa ocean conditions can be much less forgiving. You should be comfortable paddling, launching, and landing in heavy winds and waves before planning a trip here. Though you may set out from **Beecher's Bay** in what seems like gentle conditions, things change rapidly as you round Carrington Point to the north or Skunk Point to the south. Beyond Carrington there is no safe landing point for several miles until you reach Lobo Canyon. At Skunk Point to the south you may encounter difficulty coming back around the point because of rushing currents between Santa Rosa and Santa Cruz.

One of the most respected companies running kayak trips to the park is **Adventours,** based in Santa Barbara (tel. 805/963-2248; www.adventours-inc.com). They run day trips to Santa Cruz concentrating on the East End, and special overnight trips to Santa Cruz that allow time to cruise up the island to Painted Cave.

## SURFING

The Northern Channel Islands are home to several excellent surf breaks. You'll need your own oceangoing vessel to visit them, though, since there are no commercial trips. The most famous are **Yellowbanks** and **More Meadows** on the southeast end and **Chinese Harbor** on the north side. Yellowbanks and More Meadows are summertime spots that only break on a substantial south swell. Chinese Harbor on the northeast side catches wintertime west swells and is a ledging left reef wave. The inside is a pile of barnacle-covered rocks, no pleasure swim if you break a leash, take my word for it. Each of these spots involves anchoring and paddling to the break. Choosing where to anchor is something of an art: You don't want to be too far away from the break in case you lose a board and have to swim back to the boat, but on the other hand you definitely want your boat to be securely out of harm's way. Newcomers should be aware that though there clearly should be no "locals" on an island with no inhabitants, the urchin divers who work here are sometimes surly about "outsiders" surfing their breaks. Try not to incite their wrath, because anyone who spends 12 hours a day raking spiny urchins off the sea bottom is probably a lot tougher than you.

## WHALE WATCHING

Any time you visit the islands, there's a good chance you'll see whales on the channel crossing. Prime viewing season is December through April. During the summer, Sea Landing in Santa Barbara runs day-long whale-watching trips to island waters aboard *The Condor* to view the blue whales that feed in the channel. Otherwise, it's simply too far for most whale-watching cruises to bother with special trips to the islands during the winter season, when there are as many whales along the mainland coast as out there. If you're planning a special camping trip to the island with whale watching in mind, the **East End of Santa Cruz** or **Anacapa** are probably your best

# Santa Cruz Island's Painted Cave

From the sea, the northwest shore of Santa Cruz looks like a mariner's nightmare: a lee shore with tiny anchorages and unpredictable conditions, hemmed in by 200-foot-tall sea cliffs for miles at a time. Hardly anyone's idea of an island paradise. But we're not here to work on our tans—there's almost no light where we're headed. As we close the last few miles to the island from Santa Barbara, we're excited to find perfect conditions. Just a light wind, and virtually zero swell.

Our vessel is the *Spike Africa*, an 80-foot gaff-rigged schooner. She's a beauty of a boat: teak rails, brass portholes, varnished spars, jutting bowsprit, a web of rope ladders and lines ascending her two masts. Stacked on her cargo deck are a dozen open-topped kayaks belonging to Adventours, the Santa Barbara adventure travel company that has put together this trip for a mixed group of journalists, some of the vessel's owners, and friends. The plastic kayaks look rather like bathtub toys in comparison to *Spike*'s sweeping wood hull, but they can reach places *Spike* will never see.

We hove-to about a quarter mile offshore. Chief Adventours guide Eric Little gives us a safety pep talk and then we quickly offload the kayaks. If a wave surges up and smashes you into the cave ceiling, he tells us, roll out of your boat and let your kayak take the beating. Otherwise, he explains, the surging kayak meets the immovable rock, and all the protoplasm in between—you—gets squished out the side. With that on our minds, we grab helmets and paddles striking a course for the gothic-looking stone archway that marks the entrance to Painted Cave.

Painted Cave looks like a classic fairy tale cave, where you might find a fire-breathing dragon or a Viking princess. Basaltic cliffs crumble into the sea, hung with scraggly ferns and lichen. A huge archway narrows down to an entrance maybe 10 feet high. You can hear sea lions barking far in the distance, echoes reverberating around what must be an enormous inner chamber.

Inside, the entrance passageway extends back several hundred feet, so symmetrically finished that it could easily be a railway tunnel or a gold mine. Abruptly, the room opens up into an enormous grotto. I can't see all the dimensions because my eyes haven't adjusted to the sudden darkness, but from the sound of things it must be the size of a basketball gymnasium. Using a dive light, Adventours owner Joe Coito shows me the dripping, multicolored mineral deposits that give Painted Cave its name. Nice, I say, but I'm more interested in a narrow passageway I can see that leads several hundred feet farther back.

Joe and I make a move to explore that way, but first we stop to size up a rather large bull sea lion, who's puffing himself up on a rock right in our path. We give him as wide a berth as possible in a 10-foot wide chamber, but even as I scramble past I can smell his fish breath as he barks in my face.

We bounce over a few shallow rocks, back another 60 feet, and then we're at a dead end, a tiny gravel beach that never sees the light of day. It occurs to me that if ozone depletion is really as bad as some say, this beach might be the only safe place to lay out.

The rest of the group has since followed us back, and because we're at a dead end in total darkness, there's a lot of crashing and bumping of boats as we try to get turned around. Then, as if on cue, I see a small swell rolling down the passageway, not a huge one, but enough to get your pulse going when in a low-ceilinged cave. Stuck in back of everyone else, Joe and I start encouraging people to move out. More swells roll in, crashing with a booming sound into the back of the cave. A couple times my helmet bumps overhanging rocks. We start really encouraging the people in front of us to get the heck out of here. The ensuing chaos adds a bit of excitement to the paddle back to the central grotto, and makes me suddenly very in tune with why you're never supposed to go in these caves during a heavy swell. It'd be easy to get stuffed in some tiny chamber or conked into an overhanging rock by the rising water.

On our way back out, my eyes have completely adjusted to the light and the central chamber seems bright as day. I can see the main room is as big as a good-sized airplane hangar, and off to the same end where the sea lions are, a surge tube periodically gushes with a spray of saltwater. I wonder about these sea lions: do they live most of their lives back in this darkness? In the pale light they look almost white, not the rich chocolate brown of most sea lions, and I imagine a separate race of cave-dwelling seals, white like Moby Dick, lurkers in the underground tunnels of Santa Cruz. Caves do weird things to your imagination, and when I finally paddle out of Painted Cave it's into a new world of color; deep blue ocean, bright blue sky, jet black rocks, white foam on the ocean. The sun warms me, lifting the clammy dampness.

We paddle down the island. Painted Cave is only the first of many caves on this stretch of coast. None is as big, but they're all interesting in their own way.

Some are occupied by seals and sea lions. Others, empty, are just big water-filled rooms. A few go back several hundred feet. Eric finds a blowhole outside one cave and shows us a trick. During a lull, he backs his kayak down into the mouth of the blowhole. Suddenly, a swell rolls by, and with a gurgle, then a rushing roar, Eric gets blasted by a fire hose-sized jet of spray. I'm overheating, so I try the same thing; the blowhole is like the world's greatest squirt gun, a horizontal shower of atomized ocean water. I sit there getting hosed again and again until Joe comes back to get me.

We paddle down coast another mile to where *Spike Africa* is waiting. After a huge lunch, a naturalist-led hike on the Nature Conservancy's Santa Cruz Island Preserve, and diving out of Spike's rigging, arching 25 feet down into the sea, we set sail for Santa Barbara. With the sun going down I ask Captain Bill Irvine Jr. if I can take the helm. Surprisingly, he says yes. We make good time across the channel. When we finally reach the harbor I give the helm back to the good captain. What seemed like such a graceful vessel on the open sea seems huge and clumsy in the tight harbor, and I'm glad it's not me that has to back her into a tiny slip. That night I rock to sleep on ghost waves, dreaming of albino seals, secret passageways, and having a tall ship and a star to steer her by.

◆ **Spike Africa Bookings.** Tel. 805/ 963-3564. Full-day trip to the Islands. $73 per person or $2,200 per day for the entire boat (up to 35 people).

◆ **Adventours.** Tel. 805/963-2248. www.adventours-inc.com. One-day kayaking trips to the islands, including passage, lunch, snacks, drinks, gear, and guides, $159.

bets. The combination of high bluffs, calm, sheltered water, and constriction of the channel to its narrowest point here makes these ideal places to see lots of whales.

**WILDLIFE VIEWING**

All the Channel Islands have their own unique flora and fauna. Point Bennet on **San Miguel** is one of the most exhilarating spots in the world to see as many as 10,000 seals and sea lions gathered on a single beach at once. This spot is famous as the only place in the world where six species of pinnipeds (California sea lion, harbor seal, northern elephant seal, Guadalupe fur seal, Stellar sea lion, and northern fur seal) haul out at the same time. The noise is deafening and the stink is remarkable, but quite simply it's one of the greatest shows on earth. Getting there involves a long hike, and details are spelled out in the hiking section above.

**Santa Cruz** and **Santa Rosa** are both home to the charming little island fox, a diminutive red fox about the size of a small housecat. Having evolved on an island with no predators, these tiny canines are virtually tame. One of the funny things about the foxes is that it's hard to find them, but they'll come to you. In fact, they're something of pests at the park service campgrounds, where they break into your food and make a feast. Santa Rosa is also home to a large population of deer and elk, which were introduced to provide hunting opportunities for mainlanders. Rumor was that the island guides always knew where the elk and deer would be, since there are only so many places a herd of large animals can hide on the island; thus they'd have to guide their clients away from the herd until enough suspense had been built up. Then, when the client was feeling a bit tired of traipsing around a steep, windblown island, they'd crest a rise and lo and behold, a trophy elk or deer would be standing there. Blammo, another happy customer.

# Campgrounds & Other Accommodations

**CAMPING**

Reservations for all the public campgrounds on Catalina are handled through the **Catalina Camping** offices, located in either Two Harbors or Avalon (tel. 888/510-7979 or 310/510-0303). The exception is Hermit Gulch Campground 1 mile from Avalon. For reservations there you must call between 9am and 5pm Monday to Saturday at 310/510-8368. All the camping sites on the five islands encompassed by Channel Islands National Park can be reserved when you arrange your boat transportation with the park concessionaire, **Island Packers** (tel. 805/642-1393). You can also arrive at Santa Cruz or Santa Rosa by one of **Channel Islands Aviation's** charter flights for anything between $100 to $200 per person round-trip (tel. 805/987-1301). Alternately, if you choose to arrive at the islands by private vessel, you'll need to obtain a **camping permit** from the park directly by calling 805/658-5700 or writing to **Channel Islands National Park,** 1901 Spinnaker Dr., Ventura, CA 93001. Camping permits on all the islands are free, though Island Packers charges more for you to be dropped off 1 day and picked up on another than they do for single-day trips.

**CATALINA**

The only campground within easy walking distance of Avalon, **Hermit Gulch** is a busy place with 75 campsites, teepees, special group sites, and six-person wall tents. It's hardly roughing it, with such amenities as microwaves, security lockers, showers, and a camp store, but compared to even the cheapest hotel in Avalon, it's a real steal. They'll also rent you just about everything you could possibly need for camping. The camp is located off Avalon Canyon Road on the way to the Wrigley Memorial Garden. Fees are per person, $7.50 per night October 1 to April 30. The rest of the year the price steps up to $8.50. There is an hourly shuttle to the campground from the boat landing. Site reservations are recommended year-round and required during the summer. Call 888/510-TENT, Monday to Saturday between 9 and 5. Call **Catalina Camping Services** for reservations at all the following campgrounds (tel. 888/510-7979 or 310/510-0303).

**Two Harbors** campground is located less than a quarter mile from its namesake village at Catalina's isthmus, which has become something of a center for outdoorspeople and overlooks Little Fisherman's Cove, a wonderful snorkeling and swimming spot. Private, semiprivate, and shared campsites are available, though the reality is that 250 people essentially share the entire area. Don't count on a lot of privacy if you're here in the high season; in addition to a general store, Two Harbors campground even has its own bar. Little Harbor is a spectacular cove on the seaward side of the island, a 7-mile hike from Two Harbors. With room for 150 people, Little Harbor is one of the most popular camps on the island. Palm trees and clear blue water make it look like something out of a South Pacific fantasy. An excellent feature is that the camp has two beaches; one is sheltered, the other gets surf, something for everyone. You can either hike the 7 miles from Two Harbors or take an interior shuttle. **Blackjack Camp** sits between the island's two highest peaks, Blackjack and Orizaba, at an elevation of 1,600 feet. Nestled in a pine grove, this 75-person camp is a great way to get away from the beachside bustle. Several of the sites have nice ocean views, though. Located 1.3 miles from the nearest shuttle bus stop at Blackjack junction, you'll want to pack light for this camp. **Parson's Landing,** 7 miles west of Two Harbors on the most remote part of Catalina, is a 50-person campground that's accessible by trail only. You can hike the entire 7 miles, or during the summer you can take a shore boat to Emerald Bay and hike the remaining 1.5 miles to Parson's Landing. Either way, you'll want to pack light. This is a great camp for sea kayakers and those wishing to explore the least-visited part of the island. **Coastal Cove Camping** has 10 sheltered coves accessible only by private boat on the leeward shore of Catalina open to camping. No facilities are provided and campers are required to practice no-trace camping. That includes use of Porta-Pottis and hauling out all human waste.

### SANTA BARBARA ISLAND

Windy, 1-square-mile Santa Barbara has eight primitive tent sites with pit toilets and tables. The camp is located overlooking the landing cove and directly adjacent to the island's only building, a Quonset hut that now functions as the island museum. You must bring all your own water and supplies to the island and carry them up a ladder, several flights of stairs, and a steep trail to the camp. Fires are forbidden.

### ANACAPA ISLAND

Anacapa's six primitive sites share a flat blufftop with the island's foghorn. Pray that it's not foggy when you're trying to sleep here, but it often is. As with Santa Barbara, there is no water on the island and no fires are permitted. Pack light because you'll be clambering up a slippery ladder and then more than 100 stairs with everything you bring.

### SANTA CRUZ ISLAND

Compared to the last two listings, life on Santa Cruz is the lap of luxury. Fifty primitive sites are tucked into **Scorpion Canyon** above Scorpion Ranch on the island's East End. As with the other islands, you must bring everything, including water, but the pleasant, sheltered location of this camp in a large eucalyptus grove is fantastic. Fires are permitted only in the provided fire rings. Because tents and backpacks have been destroyed by the island's wild pigs, mice, and foxes, the park service requires that you either hang your food in the trees or bring animal-proof containers.

### SANTA ROSA ISLAND

Fifteen primitive sites are located a mile and a half from the Beecher's Bay landing on Santa Rosa. There's not a lot of cover in this canyon, but each site comes with its own windbreak and picnic table. The campground is fenced to keep cattle out, but island foxes have been known to raid campers' food, so bring an appropriate fox-proof container. Unlike the other campgrounds in the park, on Santa Rosa you don't have to bring your own water.

### SAN MIGUEL ISLAND

San Miguel's nine primitive sites come with windbreaks, tables, and chemical toilets. You must bring all your own supplies, including water. The weather here is generally colder and windier than on the other islands, so a good tent and sleeping bags are worth their weight in gold. No fires are permitted, and it's a steep climb from the landing cove to the campground with all your gear.

## INNS & LODGES

## CATALINA

Avalon is the epicenter of the Catalina lodging industry, and a dollar doesn't exactly go a long way here; you're paying for location, location, and location. There are numerous places where you can drop $100 a night for little more than that location, but a few places stand out of the crowd.

### The Inn on Mount Ada

398 Wrigley Rd. (P.O. Box 2560), Avalon, CA 90704. Tel. 310/510-2030. 6 rms, 2 suites. Weekends and June–Oct, $320–$490 double, $490–$590 suite. Mon–Thurs and Nov–May, $230–$370 double, $370–$470 suite. All rates include 3 meals per day. MC, V.

Okay, so it's the most expensive place to stay on the island, but it's a chance to live like a millionaire for a lot less than a million dollars. This ornate mansion overlooking Avalon was the home built by William Wrigley, Jr. as his home after he purchased the island in 1921. Little seems to have changed since then. Wood paneling, deep rugs, a formal library, several sitting rooms, and a wicker-furnished sunroom round out the island lifestyle. The only flaw associated with staying here is that with this kind of luxury and the high ticket price, you may want to spend all day lounging around instead of having outdoor adventures.

### Zane Grey Pueblo Hotel

Off Chimes Tower Rd. (P.O. Box 216), Avalon, CA 90704. Tel. 310/510-0966. 17 rooms. June–Sept, $75–$125 double. Nov–March $55 double. Rest of the year

$65–$85 double. Rates include continental breakfast. AE, MC, V.

High on the hill overlooking town, Zane Grey's old island retreat has the best view of any hotel on the island. Some of the 17 rooms are awkwardly carved out of what must have been much larger rooms in Grey's house, but others are quite lovely. The original living room is filled with Grey memorabilia, and the hotel has a pool and sundeck. A courtesy shuttle runs to town and back.

## Pavillion Lodge

513 Crescent Ave (P.O. Box 737), Avalon, CA 90704. Tel. 310/510-2550 or 800/343-4491. 20 rooms. $75–$240 per night. MC, V.

Located just across the street from Crescent Beach in Avalon, the Pavillion Lodge is laid out around a center courtyard, creating a peaceful shelter from the bustle of Crescent Avenue. You're a short walk from Lover's Cove, the boat landing, and the Green Pleasure Pier.

## Banning House Lodge

Two Harbors. Tel. 310/510-2800. 11 rooms. $65–$92 double. MC, V.

Before Wrigley bought the island, this unpretentious 11-room house at Two Harbors was the summer home of the pioneering Banning brothers. Now an inn, the Banning House is decked out in Victorian style but doesn't overdo it. The location overlooking the ocean at Two Harbors leaves you poised for kayaking, diving, or hiking in the morning.

## CHANNEL ISLANDS NATIONAL PARK

There are no hotels or inns anywhere in the national park.

# 4

# SANTA MONICA BAY & MOUNTAINS: Malibu, L.A. County Beaches & the Hollywood Hills

I T SEEMS PARTICULARLY IRONIC THAT LOS ANGELES, THE MOUNT Olympus of 20th-century car culture, should have a wilderness mountain range running right through its middle. Everyone knows the legendary stories about Los Angeles's wild edge: coyotes snatching poodles behind movie star mansions; epic landslides, fires and floods, often one right after another; mountain lions camping out under somebody's redwood deck in Malibu. Well, they're true, and I like to think of all of them as the Santa Monica Mountains fighting back, the wilderness struggling to exert its last shred of influence over the 16 million people who pack the Los Angeles Basin. And considering that they're surrounded by millions of people, the Santa Monicas are still a remarkable wilderness, rendered even more remarkable when you look down from their peaks and see the packed-in civilization below.

Like the other major mountains in Southern California, the Santa Monicas are a transverse range, trending from east to west instead of the more typical north to south of most other North American ranges. Stretching from Point Mugu (pronounced like Mr. Magoo) in the west over 50 miles to

Griffith Park in the east, the Santa Monicas include everything from hidden Chumash rock art to the manicured lawns and tennis courts of that famous wilderness, Beverly Hills; from the landmark Hollywood sign and observatory in 4,500-acre Griffith Park to the original nudist resort, Elysium Fields, in Topanga.

Though not particularly tall—only a little over 3,000 feet at their highest—the Santa Monicas could win some awards for steepness. It's a rarity to find more than a few hundred yards of level trail. In this land of little rain, huge canyons like Topanga, Big Sycamore, and Malibu cut down through the sedimentary layers, providing shade and water for the oaks, sycamores, poison oak, and even ferns that grow in the riparian zone. The hillsides are another story; more than 50% of the range is covered in impenetrable chaparral, a diverse but prickly plant community, while the remainder is grassland and oak woodland.

Of course a lot more than plants live here. Mountain lions, deer, rattlesnakes, bobcats, coyotes, hawks, woodpeckers, and countless other species call the mountains home, as well as a lot of human beings, including Marlon Brando, Jack Nicholson, Joni Mitchell, and thousands of other famous and not-so-famous (but fortunate) people who can afford houses in places like Coldwater Canyon, Mullholland Drive, and Laurel Canyon. Their poodles may get eaten, and their houses are prone to fire, but what a view!

It's impossible to talk about the Santa Monicas without talking about Santa Monica Bay and the Pacific Ocean. The ocean has a heavy influence over the land here, as well as the mountains, affecting the way we encounter the sea. Perhaps the most famous and illuminating example of this symbiosis is the 29-mile stretch of coast through Malibu. On the western end, Mugu Rock presents a

dramatic entrance to the winding coastline, towering over Highway 1 like a blackened stone sentinel. The old road went on the ocean side of Mugu Rock; now it's half-fallen into the Pacific. Like all of California, Malibu is falling into the sea, only here it's happening a little faster. Towering cliffs and hillsides rise on the inland side of the road, while the Pacific splashes against offshore rocks, curving cove beaches, cobblestone points, and dramatic headlands. Near the water's edge, the marine layer provides moisture in the form of drizzling fog, supporting giant coreopsis, coastal sage, palms, and exotic eucalyptus, but as you climb higher away from the sea, the climate turns more arid, supporting yuccas, chaparral, and prickly pear. Originally a Spanish land grant *rancho* called Rancho Topanga Malibu Sequit, most of Malibu was purchased by Frederick and May Rindge in 1887. Soon afterward, the state government cast its eye on Malibu as the route of State Highway 1. The Rindges fought back, hiring thugs to run off trespassers and dynamiting attempts at road construction. After Frederick died, May Rindge exhausted the last of her fortune in a series of failed court battles. In 1929, the highway opened and development of Malibu as an exclusive colony for the rich and famous began soon after. The Rindge family made a second fortune leasing and selling off their land, now worth millions.

Parts of the coastline near Malibu look nearly as pristine as during the Chumash era. Seals sun on offshore rocks. Thick kelp beds wave over beautiful rocky bottoms. Whales spout just offshore, and dolphins regularly play in the surf lineup below towering bluffs. You could easily fool yourself into believing you were deep in Baja California. Farther south into the bay, however, things change quickly. From Sunset

Boulevard south the bayshore is largely a single, broad, sandy beach hemmed in by houses or highway until Marina Del Rey. The names change—Will Rogers, Santa Monica, Venice, Marina Del Rey—but it's effectively the same beach for miles on end. It is wide, heavily used, and patrolled by yellow L.A. County lifeguard trucks; only the piers and the changing character of each beachside neighborhood reveal practically invisible dividing lines. At Marina Del Rey, the continuous beach is broken briefly by the mouth of the world's largest man-made pleasure-craft harbor. Dredged out of one of Southern California's largest wetlands in 1960 and opened in 1962, Marina Del Rey covered 405 acres of water and a nearly equivalent area of land, providing home to literally thousands of recreational boats.

What remains of the huge wetland that was once a rich breeding ground and shelter for marine and avian life here is the terribly degraded Ballona Wetlands on the south side of Marina Del Rey and the channelized Ballona Creek bed. A restoration is being attempted on one part of the wetlands, but development, including the SKG Dreamworks mega movie studio, threaten other parts.

From here you're into what locals call the South Bay, the crescent moon–shaped coastline leading to the rocky Palos Verdes Peninsula through the towns of Manhattan Beach, Hermosa Beach, Redondo Beach, and Torrance. This area was once a huge 36-square-mile dune field. Now only a few hundred acres of sand dunes remain, compliments of Los Angeles International Airport. The site was once a tract home neighborhood much like neighboring Playa Del Rey, but in the 1970s the city of Los Angeles, concerned with the liability dangers of a jet falling out of the sky and ruining the American dream, bought up all the homes under the flight path. The homes were removed but the streets, sidewalks, and fire hydrants remain. In the meantime, remnant endangered species like the El Segundo blue butterfly, the Pacific pocket mouse, and the pholisma herb that had been hanging on in a tiny 40-acre undeveloped parcel have now recolonized much of the native dune ecosystem, along with numerous other birds and animals.

Below the bluffs is Dockweiler State Beach, a lovely strand almost identical to Venice or Santa Monica, except that it's virtually uninhabited. Wait 20 seconds at most and you'll understand why—jets from LAX shriek overhead with ear-splitting regularity. But the most significant meeting place of urban Los Angeles with the Pacific Ocean lies just south of the airport takeoff zone and the Chevron Refinery—the Hyperion Wastewater Treatment Plant. You really have to see it to believe it. Hyperion looks like a mad Escher painting of a plumber's nightmare. Miles and miles of pipes, huge separating ponds, wires, domes, conduits, generators, chrome, concrete, heavy machinery. Considering that it processes the effluvia of the entire Los Angeles Basin, the stench you'd expect is noticeably absent.

Hyperion is an icon of one of Southern California's largest environmental disasters, and likewise emblematic of what can be done to reverse such disasters. In the 1930s, L.A.'s heavy industry began dumping their toxic effluent into the city sewers, which empty into the bay. What was once a rich fishery collapsed. It wasn't until the 1960s that people began tracing this toxic soup back to the chemical plants, refineries, and factories where it came from. But by then it was almost too late. There were hardly any fish left in the bay, and those that were left had DDT concentrations so high that they often qualified as toxic waste. The brown pelican, which ate the fish in the bay and concentrated DDT in their bodies, was nearly extinct. Seals and sea lions beat a retreat to more palatable waters.

Though gradual improvements occurred as toxic dumpers were forced to stop, it wasn't really until the 1980s that Los Angeles implemented EPA standards on their Hyperion outfall contents. Since then the level of waste dumped into the bay has shrunk to a fifth of its previous level and the number of toxic metals going into the bay by 90%. Still, huge problems remain. Winter storms overwhelm the treatment facility, and raw sewage gets flushed into the sea, rendering the bay a literal cesspool for days afterward. Huge concentrations of DDT cover an area the size of Santa Monica just off the coast of Palos Verdes, and non-point source pollution—the grease, paint, oil, and waste that wash from the streets to the sea after every rain—still pose a significant problem. But Hyperion, at least, has cleaned up its act, and the wildlife in the bay is coming back.

Framing the south end of Santa Monica Bay is the Palos Verdes Peninsula. Once, long ago, Palos Verdes was an offshore island, much like Catalina. Marine terraces up and down the hillsides attest to this, and the rocky coastline of the peninsula is more reminiscent of Santa Cruz Island than neighboring Redondo Beach. Unlike the Channel Islands, however, Palos Verdes is built up, a wealthy wonderland of Spanish-style mansions. Several excellent coastal nature preserves along this coast are open for tide pooling, diving, kayaking, and surfing. During the spring and fall migrations of the California gray whale, the coastal bluffs here are fine whale-watching hot spots.

# The Lay of the Land

There are basically two ways to approach the western end of the Santa Monicas: You either come from the south, along **Pacific Coast Highway 1,** the most popular access route to Malibu parks and beaches, or you approach from the **San Fernando Valley,** coming from Highway 101. Several winding mountain passes connect the two highways, most notably Malibu Canyon Road and Topanga Canyon Road. Running along the spine of the Santa Monicas between 101 and 1 is one of L.A.'s more famous streets, **Mulholland Drive,** named after the famous water commissioner William Mulholland who brought Owens Valley water to the L.A. Basin and was the inspiration for Roman Polanski's movie *Chinatown,* starring Jack Nicholson. Mulholland is a great destination for a day-long drive through the hills, but for getting from point A to point B it's excruciatingly slow going.

It's important to remember here that though the highway signs might say north and south, the overwhelming trend of the coastline is east to west. Particularly in the northern stretches of Santa Monica Bay, this confuses the uninitiated, who refuse to believe that the ocean can be to their south if they're standing on the West Coast. Then, come sunset, they go crazy wondering how the sun could possibly set in the "north."

For beachgoers interested in the Santa Monica–to–Palos Verdes stretch, your main thoroughfare is Highway 1. Unfortunately, this stretch hardly lives up to its official name, Pacific Coast Highway. Instead, it swoops inland through miles of minimalls and auto

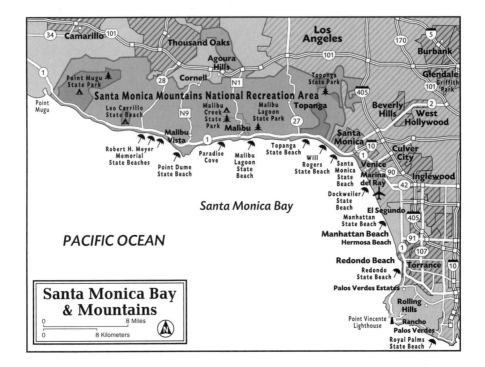

**Santa Monica Bay & Mountains**

0        8 Miles

0        8 Kilometers

dealers. Bluffs separate it from any ocean view, and it swerves way inland to get around LAX. There is a beachfront route that continually changes street names: Ocean Park, Pacific Avenue, Vista Del Mar, Hermosa Avenue, Catalina Avenue. It is fairly easy to navigate along the beachfront by feel, though; just keep following the coast and steer inland to avoid dead ends. As nice as it is to cruise the beachfront on a sunny day, on weekends this area gets gridlocked, and it's usually better to take Highway 1 until you're parallel with your beach destination, then cut over.

The **Hollywood Hills,** though still part of the Santa Monicas, are separated from the western part of the range by the 405 (San Diego) freeway and Highway 101 (Hollywood Freeway). Between the two freeways are Beverly Hills, Bel Air, and other wealthy enclaves. The largest public portion of the eastern Santa Monicas lies east of the Hollywood Freeway, 4,500-acre-plus Griffith Park, which has numerous local access points. This section of the Santa Monica range is distant from the Pacific's cooling influence and consequently gets much hotter and dryer in the summer than the already hot and dry western extension.

## MALIBU

Historians say that Malibu is a Chumash word meaning "where the mountains meet the sea." If so, there's no better name for it, unless the Chumash had a word for "where the movie stars meet the sea." Though Malibu incorporated as a city in the last 5 years or so, it's really not so much a town as it is a state of mind—how many towns do you know that are 27 miles long and one street wide? Downtown Malibu, as it is, reaches from the intersection of Malibu Canyon Road east along Highway 1 for a couple miles, with Malibu Point and Pier pretty much the center of town. In this stretch you can find anything you need—gas stations, surf shops, kayak rentals, drugstores, fine dining, fast food, groceries, a movie theater. If you're going north and need something, stock up here because pickings are slim on the other end of "town."

## TOPANGA CANYON

The intersection of Topanga Canyon Boulevard and Pacific Coast Highway looks like just another fast food and gas station zone. Turn up the road, though, and you'll quickly leave urban Los Angeles behind. Topanga Creek has carved a narrow gorge through sedimentary layers here, filled with sycamores and oaks. After about 5 miles of winding, you'll enter the little town of Topanga. Despite its location, literally on the edge of a huge metropolis, Topanga has more in common with Santa Cruz or Woodstock than Los Angeles. The markets sell hippie food and herbal remedies. The world's most famous nudist resort is right up the street—Elysium Fields. Kids ride horses, and the finest dining in town is at a restaurant called, no kidding, The Inn of the Seventh Ray, where the menus extol the virtues of purple light. But most of all, Topanga remains this way because it's virtually surrounded by wilderness: Topanga State Park and 9,000 acres of wild mountain terrain (see "Parks & Other Hot Spots").

## PACIFIC COAST HIGHWAY (CALIFORNIA HIGHWAY 1)

PCH, as it's known to locals, runs the entire length of the Los Angeles County coast and well into Orange County before reuniting with Highway 5. Your coastal experience will vary, though, depending on what part of PCH you choose to drive. The northern stretch between Oxnard, Malibu, and Santa Monica is lovely by anyone's definition. The ocean is in sight almost the whole way, and much of the coastline is still semiwild. Once you get into Santa Monica, Venice, and the south bay, the whole character of PCH changes. It's really just another ugly four- to six-lane L.A. roadway flanked by donut shops, car dealers, and burrito stands. You could as easily be in Phoenix for all the ocean influence. What PCH is good for in this part of the county, is getting near enough to your destination beach that you can cut over on local surface streets and find a place to park. But don't think it's going to be a beautiful drive.

# Parks & Other Hot Spots

## Point Mugu State Park

30 miles north of Santa Monica, 4 miles south of Point Mugu Naval Air Station on Hwy. 1. Tel. 805/488-5223. Open daily year-round, dawn to dusk. Fee and nonfee areas.

Far and away the largest state park in the Santa Monica Mountains, at 15,000 acres, Point Mugu is a rare gem, combining an isolated and relatively undeveloped coastline with some of the best wilderness in the whole area. You can surf, climb a giant sand dune, scuba dive, mountain bike, nature watch, or backpack to remote mountain peaks and the wildlands of the Boney Mountain Wilderness. And the park has 80 beach campsites and 50 canyon sites, so you don't necessarily have to do it all in 1 day.

## Leo Carrillo State Beach

24 miles north of Santa Monica. 36000 block of Pacific Coast Hwy. Tel. 805/488-5223. Open year-round.

# The Mystery of Wind Caves

If I were to pick one geologic feature that epitomizes Southern California to me, it would be the wind cave. In the same way that granite domes and spires spell Sierra Nevada in the language of my senses, lying on one's back on the gritty sand floor of a wind cave makes for an essential moment. Some are tiny, barely big enough to squeeze into. Others are so big that I've shared them with 5 or 6 friends, camping or taking shelter in them during surprise rainstorms in the Sierra Madre, Santa Ynez, and Santa Monica Mountains.

On several magical occasions I've stared at a wall, only to see the faded remnant of an ancient Chumash pictograph suddenly gel into focus—condors, sundials, amoebas, and figures that look remarkably like giant bipedal salamanders. Another time, during the height of the Hanta virus scare, I climbed a cliff face to reach an attractive-looking cave. The sand in the bottom of the cave looked a little strange, speckled with, no, wait, completely consisting of mouse turds, the exact same thing that spreads the Hanta virus. I left that cave to the mice.

Wind caves are by no means limited to California, but the conditions that create them are in abundance here. The basic recipe, repeated thousands of times throughout the southern part of the state, has four basic ingredients: the type of rock (mostly sandstone), the stone's water permeability, mineral and crystalline structures within the rock, and the wind's force and angle of attack. With your basic sandstone outcropping on a coastal mountain somewhere in the mountains above Santa Barbara, the prevailing ocean breeze will begin to play with its weaknesses. Rain works away at a crack in the rock. Soon, the wind finds a coarse vein of igneous crystals that breaks down faster than the finely grained sandstone. Now give it a few thousand years. Grain by grain and crystal by crystal, the cave will form, a negative image of the wind's patient labor. Wind caves take all sorts of forms, twisty tunnels, open-ceilinged grottos, houselike series of chambers with flat sandy floors. But, consistent with the means of their creation, they're light and airy places, places where you can feel and see the power of dynamic nature.

It's no accident that the ancient shamans had their visions in these caves, no mystery that you'd seek one out in a gully-washer, and no secret that those cliff-dwelling mice had found a really nice place to live. Windcaves are intimate little worlds worth getting to know.

Many people think the namesake of Leo Carrillo State Park was a famous Spanish explorer who must have anchored here in the lee of Sequit Point during an epic voyage of discovery. But that is Cabrillo, Juan Rodriguez Cabrillo. This being Malibu, Leo Carrillo, was of course a famous actor, born in California and the son of a prominent ranching family. He's most famous for his role as the Cisco Kid's sidekick Pancho, but I think his best legacy is this beautiful beach park.

It's hard to miss Leo Carrillo State Beach. Whether you're coming from the north or the south, PCH makes a long sweeping descent into a creek bottom. You'll see a large blue lifeguard dispatch station—tower two—perched on a high rock. If there's any surf at all, you'll see a crowd, drawn by the perfection of Sequit Point, AKA Secos. There's much more to the park than what you can see here. The beach stretches north for almost a mile, broken up into pocket beaches by occasional rock outcrops. Inland of the highway are 134 campsites for tents or vehicles. If you've got a self-contained camper that's less than 8 feet tall, the beachside campground has 32 sites overlooking the water.

From November until May this is a prime whale-watching area. And it's popular for diving, tide pooling, surfing, swimming, and hiking year-round. There's a day use fee if you park inside the park, but it's often just as easy to park on the shoulder of PCH and walk in, especially when there's a line waiting to enter the park.

## Nicholas Canyon County Beach

1 mile south of Leo Carrillo State Beach. Tel. 310/457-7247. Pit toilets. Self-registration fee area.

There's really only one reason to stop here, the surf. It's a beautiful beach, sure, but Nicholas Canyon is better known among surfers as the location of Zeros, one of the few left-point breaks on the southern coast. If you're a goofyfoot craving some frontside action in a land of many rights, this is your spot.

## Robert H. Meyer Memorial State Beaches

Three beaches spaced evenly between Leo Carrrillo and Zuma. Tel. 818/880-0350 or 805/488-5223. Blufftop picnic areas and pit toilets. Stairways to beach. Parking fee.

These three public beaches give the rest of us access into a cliff-ringed seacoast that would otherwise be available only to oceanfront residents. It's a scramble down to any of these three beaches, but worth the effort. A little walk in either direction will often earn you your very own stretch of beach, though be respectful of any residents you might encounter; everything above the high tide line is technically the private property of the homeowner above. Diving is often fantastic, and the surfing, while not as good as Secos or Malibu Point, is often uncrowded. El Matador has a neat collection of off-shore sea stacks fluted with tunnels and caves. The beaches are located as follows.

♦ El Pescador State Beach. 32900 Pacific Coast Hwy., Malibu.

♦ Piedra State Beach. 39700 Pacific Coast Hwy., Malibu.

♦ El Matador State Beach. 32350 Pacific Coast Hwy., Malibu.

## Zuma County Beach Park

20 miles north of Santa Monica. 30000 block of PCH. Tel. 310/457-9891. Outdoor showers, playground, dressing rooms, rest rooms, volleyball courts, lifeguards. Parking fee.

People seem to love or hate Zuma. I happen to fall into the latter category, but feel obligated to tell you about Zuma because so many people do love it. If you like big, wide, sandy beaches packed with people with lifeguard towers every few hundred feet, this is your place. Every high school in the San Fernando Valley has their own tower by which they gather. If you know the map, you can tell where someone comes from just by where they lay their towel. One thing you can almost bet is that they don't come from Malibu.

Perhaps Zuma's only saving grace in my estimation is its incredible body-surfing potential. During a big south swell it can get positively hairy here. When it gets like that, "the real *Baywatch* lifeguards" park their rescue boat just outside the surf and pluck wayward swimmers from the rip. Boogie boarders and surfers sometimes catch it going off too, but much of the time Zuma gets blown out early. Mostly, it's a high school cruising scene, and you either like that or you don't.

## Point Dume State Park

South end of Westward Beach Rd. just south of Zuma. Tel. 310/457-9891. Rest rooms and parking. Fee required.

There is no more beautiful beach in the Southern California state park system—and none with as bad of a public access issue as Point Dume. The main park entrance is off Westward Beach Road at Westward Beach, which is really the westward extension of Zuma. The majority of the park and its finest beach, however, is about a mile away and largely cut off from the parking area by difficult cliffs. You can drive to the other side of the park, but you can't park. The wealthy residents of this neighborhood (among them Cher) have succeeded in having the entire roadway declared a no-parking zone for miles around; never mind the huge shoulders and plentiful spaces. So basically, we've got a wonderful state park that's largely reserved for the use of its wealthy neighbors.

If you do hike into the Point Dume Headlands and Point Dume Cove,

which I encourage you to do, you'll find a beautiful 215-foot-high bluff, which marks the northern boundary of Santa Monica Bay, covered in a wonderful coastal sage community. In spring, huge bushes of wild giant coreopsis bloom here. Point Dume is the highest promontory on this part of the coast, and migrating whales pass very close by. The Point Dume Cove beach below has great diving when it's calm, and fantastic surf when it's breaking. The beach is clothing optional, so don't visit if you're offended by nudity.

## Paradise Cove

28128 Pacific Coast Hwy., Malibu. Tel. 310/457-2511. Pier, restaurant, rest rooms, showers. $15 per car fee.

Anybody still remember the TV show *The Rockford Files*, in which private investigator Jim Rockford lived in that cool mobile home overlooking a beautiful beach? Well, this is the spot, and there are, in fact, people living in mobile homes with million-dollar views here.

Jim Rockford got anywhere he wanted just by acting tough. The rest of us have to pay $15 per car to use Paradise Cove, which is kind of a rip-off compared to the wonderful state beaches a few miles in either direction that are either free or $5. But a lot of people come here anyway, and the beach itself lives up to its name. Don't expect to go surfing, though; they won't even let you in the parking lot with surfboards on your car. Fishing in the surf isn't allowed either. Scuba diving, picnicking, swimming, and sunbathing were still okay last time I checked.

## Malibu Creek State Park

28754 Mulholland Dr. (between Malibu Canyon Rd. and Kanan Dume Rd). Tel. 818/880-0350 or 805/488-5223. 60 tent campsites, picnic areas, visitors center, rest rooms, showers. Fee.

If, when you look around, you're struck by an eerie feeling that you've been here before, don't worry. For years this land was a 20th Century Fox movie ranch, and most famously, the home of television's 4077th M*A*S*H unit. Every time the choppers brought in a new load of wounded, those hills in the background were the Santa Monica Mountains, not South Korea. Not much of the movie days remains besides the rusting hulk of one of the series's army jeeps. Another part of the park was once owned by Ronald Reagan, back when he was an actor. And a section of the rocky Malibu Gorge was the location for *Planet of the Apes.*

But even more wonderful than this slice of showbiz history is the incredible nature found in this 5,000-acre park. The centerpiece of the park is Malibu Creek and its riparian corridor, which provides haven for an incredible diversity of creatures and plants: big-leaf maple, California bay laurel, black cottonwood, stream orchids, giant ferns, arroyo chub, Pacific lamprey, steelhead trout, frogs, king snakes, garter snakes, horned lizards, golden eagles, turkey vultures, deer, bobcats, coyotes, and even mountain lions. Many excellent hikes follow the park's perennial streams and enter the chaparral highlands. Rock climbers find excellent routes in the gorge area.

## Malibu Lagoon State Beach

23200 Block of Pacific Coast Hwy., Malibu. Tel. 310/457-8185 or 818/880-0350. Rest rooms, outdoor showers, picnic tables, museum, interpretive trails. Fee. Some free parking on PCH.

When surfers talk about Malibu, this is the spot they mean: the point break made famous by Mickey Dora, by the Gidget movies, by the Beach Boys. Catch it on a good day and you'll see what the hype is about. It really is one of the world's best waves. Sadly, it's also among the most crowded. On a summer weekend they say you can walk across the cove just by stepping from surfboard to surfboard, and it's almost true.

You don't have to be a surfer to enjoy yourself here. It's a classic Southern California beach experience just to sit and watch. There are also volleyball courts on the sand and plenty of room to lay out a towel. Several nearby businesses rent surfboards, kayaks, and boogie boards if you want to get into the water yourself. This is also the mouth of Malibu Creek, which creates a huge brackish lagoon that's popular with local and migrating waterfowl. Informal trails follow the contours of the constantly changing lagoon. Current information on nature tours led by a park naturalist can be had by calling 310/457-8142. The Adamson House, an Andalusian-style beach house built on the site of a former Chumash village in 1928 for Frederick Rindge's daughter and son-in-law, is now a State Historical Landmark and museum. It's also a popular site for weddings, television commercials, and movie shoots. For a great glimpse of the early, opulent Malibu days, wander around the self-guided exterior tour, or take a docent-led tour of the interior. The house is most famous for its incredible ceramic tilework created by Malibu Potteries. No two tiles are the same. Lead glass windows, teak railings, and numerous murals add to its beauty. Adamson House is open Wednesday through Saturday. For information call 310/456-8432.

## Topanga County Beach

Topanga Canyon Blvd. and Pacific Coast Hwy., Malibu. Tel. 310/305-9546. Rest rooms. Parking fee.

Until a few years ago, this beach was managed by Topanga State Park, but recently the county has taken over management. Mostly well-known as a surf spot, the rocky intertidal zone is less accommodating to swimmers. Still, it's a really nice beach for sunbathing and very popular. A picnic area at the north end of the park sits on a bluff overlooking the sea.

## Topanga State Park

20825 Entrada Rd., Topanga (off Topanga Canyon Blvd.). Tel. 310/455-2465. Open 8am to sunset. Picnic areas, visitor center, rest rooms. Fee.

The community of Topanga owes its isolation from the rest of L.A. to this enormous state park. Nine thousand acres of chaparral, sycamore-shaded canyons, oak woodland, and rocky peaks create an abrupt break from the urbanization of Pacific Palisades and Santa Monica.

Come here for great hiking with dramatic ocean and valley views; the park sits right on the crest of the range. Longer trails and fire roads connect Topanga with nearby Will Rogers State Historic Park and the beach.

## Will Rogers State Historic Park

14235 Sunset Blvd., Pacific Palisades. Tel. 310/454-8212 or 818/880-0350. Open 8am–5pm. Picnic area, rest rooms, historic ranch estate, store, polo field.

Will Rogers—trick roper, newspaper columnist, radio announcer, cowboy philosopher, and film star—left this 187-acre ranch to his family when he died in a plane crash in Alaska. They, in turn, gave it to the state in 1944. Nothing much has been altered since. The two-story ranch house is filled with memorabilia from Rogers' showbiz career, and a polo field still hosts matches. Trails lead from here into the wilds of Topanga State Park. Though there are stables here, they are for the polo ponies. No rental horses are available.

## Santa Monica Mountains National Recreation Area

Headquarters and information center at 22900 Ventura Blvd., Woodland Hills. Tel. 818/888-3770.

The SMMNRA is a park administration in search of a park. Though the Santa Monicas were considered important enough to be designated part of the national parks system, they weren't so important that sufficient monies were appropriated to purchase all the available land outright. As such, the park administration works to develop partnerships with private landowners and to oversee the cohesive planning of the 65,000 acres currently in the public domain as state, county, and national park land. Currently the park service manages four small recreation areas (Rocky Oaks, Paramount Ranch, Castro Crest, and Circle X Ranch) and is constructing the Backbone Trail, which when finished will run the entire 55-mile length of the range.

## Rocky Oaks

Corner of Mulholland and Kanan Dume Rd. between Malibu and Agoura. Tel. 818/888-3770. Rest rooms. No fee.

On the upper reaches of Zuma Creek, this park is famous for, you guessed it, rocks and oaks. A picnic area and small pond make a perfect place to spend an afternoon, and short hikes will lead you to interesting formations of pillow basalt, formed when lava hits cold ocean water and cools. Rangers lead nature hikes on some weekends.

## Paramount Ranch

Cornell Rd. at Mulholland Hwy. Tel. 818/888-3770. Rest rooms, picnicking.

Once Paramount Studio's 4,000-acre movie ranch, Paramount Ranch is now a small (336-acre) but beautiful remnant of its former self. It's one of the closer parks to the San Fernando Valley, and great for hiking and horseback riding.

## Griffith Park

4,107 acres situated between the Hollywood Freeway on the west, Golden State Freeway to the east, and Ventura Freeway to the north. Multiple entrances. Tel. 213/485-4825.

New York's Central Park and San Francisco's Golden Gate Park may be more famous, but Griffith Park is the largest municipal park in the United States. About 70% of the park remains wild—rugged, steep, sometimes desolate mountain terrain. In the folds of these steep hills lie many surprises, including fern-filled canyons, oak and sycamore forests, and, yes, the famous Bat Cave of Batman and Robin fame.

The majority of the park was donated to the City of Los Angeles by Colonel Griffith Jenkins Griffith, a gold mining and real estate millionaire, in 1896. Later, after serving 2 years in jail for the attempted murder of his wife, Jenkins made the city another generous offer, $100,000 to build an observatory. Not wanting to sully their hands with what was seen as his guilt money, the city refused his gift, waiting until after his death to accept. The resulting Griffith Park Observatory is among the most famous L.A. landmarks, and a great place to take in a sweeping view of the L.A. Basin.

Despite its wild side, Griffith Park is inseparable from Hollywood in the public mind. The famous Hollywood sign is located on the flanks of a Griffith Park hillside, many films have been and continue to be shot in the park, and the toyon berries after which the town draws its name grow in profusion here.

## Will Rogers State Beach, Santa Monica Beach, Venice Beach; Dockweiler, Manhattan & Redondo State Beaches

Access: Stretching 15 miles from Pacific Palisades to Redondo Beach, the entire bayfront can be reached from Hwy. 1 and local surface streets. Will Rogers begins near the intersection of Hwy. 1 and Temescal Canyon Rd. in Pacific Palisades, stretching to the Santa Monica Pier; Santa Monica Beach is the entire beachfront within the city of Santa Monica; Venice is a continuation reached from Pacific Ave. Dockweiler is on the other side of Marina Del Rey from Santa Monica, reached via Imperial Hwy. and Vista Del Mar; Manhattan is the beachfront community of Manhattan Beach, west of Hwy. 1 to Highland Ave., and Redondo is west of Hwy. 1 at the extreme south end of Santa Monica Bay. Facilities: Picnic areas, volleyball courts, rest rooms, showers, lifeguards.

When people in the heartland imagine the California dream, this is what it looks like. In-line skaters, *Baywatch*-handsome lifeguards, tall muscular volleyball players, bicyclers along the beach, surfers, sailboats, houses right on the sand, weight lifters, tiny bikinis, jugglers, you name it. Other than Dockweiler, where there's an RV campground and some backing dunes, these are all very urban beaches. Venice, perhaps the most famous beach in this whole stretch, brings the carnival nature of Southern California to its apex. Along Ocean Front Walk, vendors hawk everything from tattoos to your name written on a grain of rice. Santa Monica Beach is a little more subdued, but Santa Monica Pier is a whole different story.

South of Marina Del Rey, the towns become more like bedroom communities, set on bluffs overlooking the ocean.

Again, the beaches are wide and sandy, with highly developed infrastructures. Dockweiler is backed by undeveloped dunes but constantly strafed by the deafening sounds of jet traffic leaving LAX. The beach at El Porto, just north of Manhattan Beach, has an offshore marine canyon that consistently funnels the best surf in the south bay ashore. Manhattan Beach is famous around the world as the Wimbledon of beach volleyball. Redondo is well known as a sportfishing harbor. Connecting them all is the wonderful paved bicycle path that was built over the tracks of the defunct Pacific Electric Railway. Paid parking is available at all beaches and fills up quickly.

## Santa Monica Pier

Colorado and Ocean Ave., Santa Monica. Amusement park, shops, in-line skating, rest rooms. Tel. 310/458-8689.

First built to off-load tar from the La Brea Tar Pits that was being shipped to San Francisco to pave the streets there, Santa Monica Pier has been built up and torn down several times, changing its face along the way. Its current incarnation is a fun one, that of a 1920s amusement pier. A roller coaster and Ferris wheel offer thrills. Jazz and blues clubs line the walkway, while restaurants dish up fine food. And you can still drop a line off the end of the pier to catch halibut, mackerel, bonito, or whatever happens to be running.

## Venice Fishing Pier

Ocean Front Walk and Washington St., Venice.

Built in 1965 specifically as a recreation fishing pier, Venice Pier has been closed for renovation for several years. It's now open again and provides a great place to cast a line or to simply get a little perspective on the Santa Monica Bay coast.

## Manhattan Beach Municipal Pier

Foot of Manhattan Beach Blvd., Manhattan Beach.

Another recreational fishing pier, Manhattan Pier is of special interest to nature lovers because it houses the Roundhouse Marine Studies Lab, which offers classes in marine biology and oceanography for school groups.

## Hermosa Beach Municipal Pier

Foot of Pier Ave. Hermosa Beach. Rest rooms, parking, bait shop.

In many ways the center of Hermosa Beach's oceanfront, this pier is great for watching surfers or dipping a line. A tackle and bait shop will sell you whatever you need and give you advice.

## King Harbor

West of Harbor Dr., Redondo Beach. Tel. (harbormaster) 310/372-1175.

King Harbor is more manageable than Marina Del Rey in size. It provides slips for numerous pleasure boats, as well as dry docks, fuel, boat charters, kayak rentals, fishing trips, parking, rest rooms,

and whale-watching charters. A unique treat for little kids is the Seaside Lagoon, a sandy-bottomed, warm-water saltwater lagoon open to swimming in the summer where they don't have to worry about waves. You can also fish within the harbor from the Redondo Beach Municipal Pier.

# What to Do & Where to Do It

### BIRD WATCHING

The peaks and deep canyons of **Topanga State Park** are filled with such birds as western screech owls, turkey vultures, Cooper's hawks, and California quail. In the wetter sycamore forests of **Santa Ynez Canyon** you'll spot Swainson's thrushes, canyon wrens, Hutton's vireos, and a number of woodpecker species.

More than 200 species frequent the lagoons where Malibu Creek reaches the sea at Malibu Surfrider Point, in **Malibu Lagoon State Park.** Wading birds such as great blue herons and snowy egrets are here almost year-round. Migrating waterfowl like Canada geese, buffle-heads, ring-necked ducks, and mallards are common in fall and winter. You're also likely to spot hawks patrolling the estuary, and the beach itself is popular with plovers and other shorebirds.

Divided by Marina del Rey, which was carved from the heart of an extensive wetland, **Ballona Lagoon,** on the north side, and **Ballona Wetlands and Del Rey Lagoon,** on the south, are some of the last remaining wetlands in the Los Angeles area. When you see them, you'll laugh or perhaps cry. From looking at them you'd never know that this was home to numerous endangered species—Belding's Savannah sparrow, the California least tern—and numerous migrating waterfowl. Along Ballona Lagoon and Del Rey Lagoon, homes are built right to the edge of the tidal estuary. The Ballona wetlands, south of channelized Ballona Creek, are the target of plans to restore certain areas and develop others, including a huge proposal to house the Dreamworks SKG Movie Studio.

## BOARDSAILING

Like almost all of Southern California, Santa Monica Bay lacks the constant wind to make it a real boardsailors' paradise. The favorite spot on the Malibu Coast is **Leo Carrillo State Beach,** with its large sandy beach for rigging and semipredictable afternoon winds. Wave jumping is a real possibility here, but the main peak in the cove is closed to boardsailors most of the day. The lifeguard dispatch tower sits right on the bluff overlooking this peak, and the bay watchers will write tickets for violating the buoy marking the "surfers only" area. After they go home at 5 pm, though, anything goes, and the waves are all yours. Another popular spot in Malibu is **County Line,** a surf spot several miles farther up the coast from Leo Carrillo, across the street from Neptune's Net restaurant. It's one of the easiest places to access the beach in the whole area.

## FISHING

As I'm writing this, **Santa Monica Bay** is in the throes of its best fishing season since the 1950s. This is partially attributable to the El Niño condition that has brought numerous warm-water species like albacore, dorado, and even marlin into the bay, but it's also to a large degree a credit to efforts to clean up Santa Monica Bay and the success of California's ban on indiscriminate gill netting. Twenty years ago, if you'd told people you were going fishing in Santa Monica Bay, you might as well have told them you were angling in the sewer. But

L.A. has vastly improved the level of water treatment at Hyperion Wastewater Treatment Facility as well as gone after industrial polluters.

The most common catches here aren't marlin and dorado, I'm afraid, but calico bass, halibut, sheepshead, corbina, and, if you're very fortunate, white sea bass. All the way in Santa Monica, Venice, Manhattan Beach, Hermosa Beach, and Redondo public fishing piers make it possible to dip a line for very little investment.

**Marina Del Rey** and **Redondo Beach** are where you'll want to head for day trips on party boats. **Captain Frenchy's Sportfishing,** 13759 Fiji Way, Marina Del Rey, CA 90292, has three boats, *Del Mar, Spitfire,* and *Betty-O.* Half-day trips are $20 per person including all bait; three-quarter-day trips allow a little more flexibility to reach the hot spots and cost $25. Gear rentals are available. For reservations call 310/822-3625.

**Redondo Sport Fishing** charges $31 for their three-quarter-day trip and $22 for a half day. They also maintain an offshore fishing barge, which is available for $17 per day. All trips leave from the Redondo Pier. For information call 310/372-2111.

If you insist on doing it on your own, **Marina Boat Rentals** in Marina Del Rey, at 13719 Fiji, rents individual fishing boats ranging from a 15-foot skiff with a 15-horse outboard for $90 per day to a 19-foot 115-horsepower center console fishing boat for $400 a day.

## HIKES, BUSHWACKS & BACKPACK TRIPS

### DAY HIKES

### Santa Ynez Trail, Topanga State Park

6 miles round-trip. Moderate but steep. Access from Topanga State Park main

entrance. End of Entrada Rd., Topanga. Map: USGS Topanga topo.

Perhaps the most wild-feeling canyon in the city limits of Los Angeles, Santa Ynez is wonderful year-round, but especially in winter or spring when rains boost the creek and make the canyon's 15-foot waterfall roar. In summer months the creek flows largely underground, even as huge groves of oaks and sycamores attest to the plentiful groundwater. Remember that this hike descends first, and that the hard work is the 1,000-foot elevation gain on the way out. From the Topanga parking lot, follow the signed nature trail until it intersects with a large fire road in about a quarter mile. Turn left on the fire road and make a short climb. The view to the Pacific Ocean and down the canyon is fantastic, stretching all the way to Catalina Island on a clear day. At the sign for the Santa Ynez trail, turn right and begin your descent. You'll wind around a long sloping ridgeline until just before the canyon bottom, where you'll pass a large sandstone outcropping shaped like a dinosaur's back. Here the trail switchbacks into the lush riparian woodland below. Ferns and, unfortunately, poison oak grow under the shade of hundred-foot tall trees. The trail loosely follows the creekbed—prepare to get wet feet if it's flowing—until another signed intersection. Here, a side trail points you back up another side canyon 0.75 mile to the base of the waterfall. Enjoy, and return the way you came.

## Nicholas Flat Trail, Leo Carrillo State Beach

7 miles round-trip. Difficult (1,600 ft. elevation change). Map: USGS Truinfo Pass topo.

A hike with a view if there ever was one. What's special about this trail is the way it connects the seaside environment of Leo Carrillo with the higher mountains above, unhindered by development once you're past the campground. After a moderate first mile, the Nicholas Flat Trail unrelentingly follows the course of a steep ridge on its way to the trail's namesake: a beautiful meadow and pond. Bring lots of water, good shoes, and binoculars. You'll be stopping for several rest breaks on the way up, so you might as well take the time to scope out migrating gray whales in the ocean below, or soaring raptors hunting the hillsides. On a clear day you'll be able to see some of the more remote Channel Islands, Santa Barbara, and San Nicholas, as well as more frequently sighted Anacapa and Catalina. After cresting the top of a rocky outcrop, you'll see Nicholas Flat and the pond below. Once used to water cattle during ranch days, it's now a good spot for sighting wildlife. After a spell here, return the way you came.

## Sycamore Canyon Trail, Point Mugu State Park

4 miles. Easy. Access: Drive Hwy. 1 through Malibu until you come to Sycamore Cove Beach and campground. Park and begin walking up the canyon.

Nobody would ever tell you to travel to California for its fall colors; everyone knows it's the land of the endless summer. But even Southern California gets its seasonal changes, and Big Sycamore Canyon in Point Mugu State Park is the best place to see them. The most obvious ingredient in bringing about fall colors here is the changing of the giant sycamore leaves. These enormous trees are a wonder to behold: graceful, towering, creaky in the wind, and home to everything from bee hives to owls, who nest in the holes left when a side limb falls from the main trunk. This canyon is also home to a large monarch butterfly roosting area, and fluttering monarchs are a fine addition to your fall foliage tour.

The hike is nearly level. From the Big Sycamore Canyon campground, simply follow the trail of the same name along the creek. Depending on the time of year, the creek can be a rushing torrent or invisible. Even when it's visually empty, there's a lot of water flowing underground, which is what allows the sycamores to grow so tall and keeps the surrounding foliage green through the summer and fall. Our destination for this hike is a picnic area about 2 miles in. Several longer routes allow further exploration of the canyon and surrounding hillsides.

A fine, much longer variant of this hike is to follow Big Sycamore Trail until it passes Wood Canyon Trail on your right. Soon, Big Sycamore will become the Overlook Trail, ascending the ridge between Big Sycamore Canyon and its sister canyon to the west, La Jolla Valley. The trail crosses this ridge several times with wonderful views of the canyons below and the Pacific Ocean. Eventually you'll encounter a fire road about 0.5 mile from your original trailhead. This loop adds approximately 6 miles to the length of the hike and substantially more difficulty. Regardless of which loop you choose, when you're finished, simply cross the road for a swim or rest on one of the Malibu coast's most intimate beaches, Sycamore Cove.

## The Malibu Creek—M*A*S*H Trail, Malibu Creek State Park

5 miles round-trip. Easy. From Hwy. 1 in "downtown" Malibu, take Malibu Canyon Rd. to the state park.

This little hike covers more real show business history than the entire Universal Studios Tour. From the main parking area at Malibu Creek State Park,

descend and cross a bridge over Las Virgenes Creek. In a quarter mile, Crags Road crosses another bridge over Malibu Creek to the left. Follow it, and continue up through a grassy open area. Within half a mile you'll see the park visitor center; check in to learn more about park history, or continue past it to see it for yourself. Continuing on, you'll cross the creek again. Almost immediately, you're faced with the choice of the Gorge Trail to the left. Take this detour. Malibu Gorge, a striking canyon cut through skyscraper-sized cliffs, awaits within a couple hundred yards. Rock climbers often gather here and draw a crowd of onlookers. The creek cascades through a series of pools. The most famous of these, Rock Pool, was the swimming hole used in *The Swiss Family Robinson* and several of the Tarzan movies. *Planet of the Apes* was shot nearby, too. After a swim or just a look, descend back to the main trail (Crags Road), and continue your trip up over a slight rise and back down to Century Lake. Created by wealthy sportsmen at the turn of the century, and periodically dredged when this was the 20th Century Fox movie ranch, the lake is now quickly silting in and will soon be just another meadow. Within a mile things begin to look really familiar, at least if you ever watched the hit television series M*A*S*H. The towering Korean peaks that served as the opening shot of every M*A*S*H episode weren't in Korea after all. They were the beautiful Goat Buttes that loom over the empty field where the M*A*S*H set once stood. All that remains of the 4077th now is the rusting hulk of an army jeep, and that will soon be gone. The trail continues for miles into the wild backcountry of the Santa Monicas, but this hike turns around here, returning via Crags Road to the parking lot.

## Ferndell to Mount Hollywood Summit, Griffith Park

5 miles round-trip. Moderate. Access: Ferndell Dr. off Los Feliz. Park at Ferndell picnic area.

A bubbling brook in the middle of L.A.? Redwood trees? Ferns? You've got to be kidding! Nope, they're there all right. Just don't get too attached to the idea that this year-round stream is some sort of pristine relic from the last Ice Age. Quite the contrary, Mococahuenga Canyon was once a dry, scrubby canyon like any other in Griffith Park. Then they built the observatory, which used a lot of water in its cooling system. Not wanting to let all that water go to waste, the builders recycled it by letting it trickle down Mococahuenga (pronounced Ferndell) Canyon and it fostered an eco-system unlike any other in L.A. Imported redwoods and eucalyptus tower alongside native sycamores. Ferns cling to the damp north slopes. Following what's officially called the Lower West Observatory Trail, look out for wildlife. Coyotes often stop off here for a drink the morning after a hard night of eating cats and poodles in the neighborhood below. Deer, squirrels, and a zillion birds also hang out here. Three-quarters of a mile up the trail you'll reach a junction, where you bear right. At 1 mile is another junction; bear left. Soon, you'll come out of the canyon to the grassy lawn of Griffith Park Observatory. Continue across its parking lot (this might be a good time to get a cool drink at the snack bar) and look for the clearly marked trailhead. From here it's easy to follow the signs and the hordes of other hikers to the summit of Mount Hollywood. If you've been waiting all your life to climb up those fantastic white Hollywood letters like some lovelorn actress . . . oops, you've climbed the wrong mountain. The Hollywood sign is actually on a neighboring peak, but you can see it clearly from here. In fact, assuming that the smog isn't too bad, you should be able to see the entire L.A. Basin clearly from the San Gabriels to the Pacific.

L.A. for me is always a difficult city to visualize; it doesn't have a clearly defined center or boundaries like New York or San Francisco, but sitting here on top of 1,625-foot-high Mount Hollywood with my AAA road map, granted, I have at least some understanding of where things lie relative to each other. From the peak, descend the alternate fire road to Dante's View, a 2-acre grove of trees and succulents. Below here, the trail reconnects with the observatory. From there, return to Ferndell the way you came.

## Palos Verdes Coast Hike

10 miles one-way. Difficult. Access: From Hwy. 1 turn right on Palos Verdes Dr. Before Malaga Cove Plaza, turn right on Via Corta, then right again onto Via Arroyo. Park in the lot beside Malaga Cove School. Trailhead is toward the beach.

The Palos Verdes coast is the closest thing to the Channel Islands you can find on the mainland of Southern California. That's because at one point the high peninsula was an island just like Catalina. These days, however, it's a favorite residential neighborhood for wealthy Angelenos. Spanish-style mansions cling to steep hillsides. Winding streets climb the marine-terraced shore. Your hike will take you around the best part of this coast from Malaga Cove to Point Vicente, where a lighthouse marks your destination. The pathway follows the shoreline through coves filled with thousands of tide pools and several nice beaches. In many places the going is rocky and potentially wet, especially during high tides and heavy surf. Since the hike will take you about 5 or 6 hours, you'll do well to consult a tidebook. Leave Malaga Cove about 2.5 to 3 hours before the next low tide to take advantage of the easiest passage and optimal tide pooling.

### OVERNIGHT HIKES

There are numerous wonderful places to spend the night in the Santa Monica Mountains. Unfortunately, most of them are highly discouraged if not explicitly forbidden. I'll be the last to dissuade anyone from discreetly bedding down in the remote regions of the Santa Monicas, but you're on your own. The main reason backcountry camping is discouraged here is the incredibly high wildfire danger much of the year and the high user pressure on virtually every square mile of this mountain range. So if you do decide to have a secret little campout, don't call attention to yourself, and whatever you do, don't build a fire. This is a perfect place to use that camp stove, enjoy the stars, and leave sitting around the campfire for another time and place.

Just before this book was finished, the federal government announced that it was appropriating $5.5 million to buy the remaining 400 acres needed to finish construction of the 70-mile-long **Backbone Trail.** Long stalled by lack of funding, the trail is suddenly back on track, no pun intended. By the time you read this, the trail, which reaches from Pacific Pallisades to Thornhill Broome State Beach near Point Mugu, should be completed and open to hikers as well as providing a valuable corridor for wildlife migration. Along with providing hikers with a route the entire length of the Santa Monica Range, the Backbone Trail is slated to include as many as eight different backcountry camping areas, a

wonderful boon for hikers. For current information on the status of the trail, contact the Santa Monica Mountains National Recreation Area (tel. 818/888-3770) or any of the state parks in the area.

### HORSEBACK RIDING

As often as the Santa Monica Mountains have played the Wild West in movies, it's inevitable that you should be able to go riding here. The greatest network of equestrian trails in any major American city laces **Griffith Park,** where four, count them, four separate stables rent horses for individual and guided rides on the park's 45 miles of horse-friendly trail. Three of the four are located on the Burbank side of the park: **Griffith Park Livery,** 480 Riverside Dr., Burbank, CA 91506 (tel. 818/840-8401); **J.P. Stables,** 914 S. Mariposa St., Burbank, CA 91506 (tel. 818/843-9890); and **Bar S Stables,** 1850 Riverside Dr., Glendale, CA 91201 (tel. 818/242-8443). The fourth, **Sunset Ranch,** is located in a hidden canyon above the historic Hollywoodland neighborhood and below the white Hollywood sign: 3400 N. Beachwood, Hollywood, CA 90068 (tel. 213/464-9612).

The Burbank-side stables offer access to the northeast side of the park and trails to the summit of the highest peak in the park, 1,625-foot tall Mount Hollywood. You can ride along the edge of Forest Lawn Memorial Park, where glittering stars such as Clark Gable, Nat "King" Cole, W.C. Fields, Karen Carpenter, Humphrey Bogart, and Walt Disney were laid to rest, or past the Gene Autry Western Heritage Museum, where the ex-movie cowboy's collection of Western memorabilia is on display.

For a special experience, Griffith Park Livery Stable arranges 2-hour moonlight rides up the winding ridgelines of the park, from which you can see the glittering lights of the San Fernando Valley below. Prices set by the three stables are approximately $13 per hour, decreasing with additional hours to $11 or $12.

Sunset Ranch on the Hollywood side is the only equestrian access from the southwest side of the park, where the famous Griffith Park Observatory and the HOLLYWOOD sign overlook the city. It's a pleasure to sit in the saddle and look at the automotive madness spreading for miles below. For a few hours, at least, you're free of it. Without a doubt, the most unique trail ride for miles around is the Friday night moonlight ride. Leaving the stables at 6pm, you'll be led through the backcountry of Griffith Park all the way to the other side. There, in Burbank, you dismount and enjoy a fine Mexican dinner at Viva's Restaurant while your horse waits outside. Freshly fueled, you'll get back on your trusty steed and head for the barn. No reservations are accepted for the Friday ride and the line often starts as early as 4 pm. If you've got a large group (15 or more), the stable will arrange a moonlight ride any night of the week. Day riding at Sunset Ranch costs $15 per hour and the Friday-night ride is a flat $30 plus whatever tab you run up at the restaurant.

Away from the city, in the hills above Malibu, is **Red Barn Stables.** Located near the corner of Mullholland Highway and Kanan Dume Road, almost adjacent to the National Park Service's Rocky Oaks Park, this stable is situated in the heart of some of Santa Monicas' finest riding. The popular 2-hour guided ride here will take you up through Rocky Oaks to a stunning 360-degree view of the Pacific to your south and the San Fernando Valley to your north. Special rides are scheduled to coincide with sunset, as well as full-moon rides. Longer all-day rides take a backcountry route to

Malibu Creek State Park, where you'll ride through the valley that housed the old *M\*A\*S\*H* set. Red Barn will also provide all-inclusive backcountry overnights into Point Mugu State Park, given enough advance notification to get camping permits (this can mean several months to a year for high season). The most unique ride option, however, is reserved for 1 day a month, when the stable brings several of their mounts down to a private beach in Malibu and makes them available for running on the sand and into the surf. You must have advance reservations, as the location changes regularly to avoid conflicts with local residents.

Trail rides are $40 for 2 hours, $90 half day, and $180 full day. The monthly beach rides cost $40 for 1 hour. For additional information, contact Red Barn Stables at Mullholland Highway, Malibu, CA 90265 (tel. 818/707-9395).

## MOUNTAIN BIKING

The Santa Monica Mountains should be a paradise for mountain bikers, but the intense pressure created by their proximity to a huge urban center has closed many possible rides to two-wheeled travel. If there was ever a place to demonstrate your best bicycle manners, it's here, because the sport is under intense scrutiny; bikers are finding more areas off-limits every year. But pockets of good riding remain, mostly in Topanga, Malibu, and Point Mugu state parks. In other places, free-rambling cyclists can find plenty of good trails and fire roads, but private property often stands in your way.

As mentioned several times in this chapter, the Santa Monicas are steep—very steep. As such, it's inevitable that if you ride more than a couple miles you wind up climbing a big hill. Get used to it and charge ahead. The payoffs are great. Like anywhere else in Southern California, it can be deadly hot on a summer day here. On rides that start near the ocean, it's easy to let the cooling marine layer fool you into thinking that it's a cool day. It might be foggy and 60°F at the beach in June, but a few miles inland it'll be pushing 95°F. Keep that in mind when deciding how much water to carry, how far you're going, and what time you ride.

## Big Sycamore Canyon Fire Rd., Point Mugu State Park

Distance: 16 miles. Easy. Graded fire road and paved road. A 1,000-foot elevation gain makes this one just enough work without being a killer. Be careful on descents; there are a lot of blind corners and pedestrians. Access: Park on PCH at Sycamore Cove in Point Mugu State Park. Map: Point Mugu State Park.

Splendid at any time of year, this area is sublime in the spring and fall. In spring, the fresh greenery and bright wildflower displays are mind boggling. Giant coreopsis, a wild native sunflower, blooms along the coastal bluffs. Farther inland, California poppies and lupine paint the hillside. When fall comes around it's a different display. This time, the sycamores that give the canyon its name shimmer with what is certainly one of the finest displays of fall color in the southern part of the state. Monarch butterflies that roost here add to the finery.

Catch the trail, which is a wide fire road, at the far end of the Big Sycamore Campground away from the ocean. The directions from here are easy. At every fork on your way out, veer right (with the exception of the short paved spur road to the Danielson multiuse area at mile 5, which you'll bypass by going left). Coming back, do the opposite. The

first several miles are almost flat, curving along the bottom of the canyon under towering sycamores and oaks. If you're riding with kids, this section alone might be a great introduction. Soon, you begin climbing a few short hills, but nothing debilitating. The only steep haul comes around mile 7, where you'll climb up a steep hill to a water tower and then descend to the Satwiwa Nature Center and the Newbury Park exit. If you ride all the way to Satwiwa, you can honestly say you've crossed the Santa Monicas on a mountain bike. If bragging rights don't impress you, feel free to turn around at the water tower and enjoy coasting back down to the coast.

## Overlook Trail Loop, Point Mugu

10 miles. Moderate. Mostly fire roads with one steep hill and a short section on nontechnical single track. Wonderful ocean views. Access: Park on PCH at Sycamore Cove in Point Mugu State Park. Map: Point Mugu State Park.

Begin at the same place as the previous ride. The first 4 miles are the same beautiful cruise under oaks and sycamores. At the Wood Canyon View Trail, veer left. Ride up this trail approximately 2 miles until you hit the Overlook Trail. Here you're going to go left and descend back to the ocean along a series of ridges and finally Big Sycamore Canyon. There are several options to make this ride more challenging. A favorite is to overshoot the Wood Canyon View Trail and instead ascend left via Wood Canyon Road (which is about 200 yards farther up Big Sycamore Canyon) to Deer Junction, then ascend the aptly named Hell Hill. The elevation gain is exactly the same as if you'd climbed the view trail, but this route saves it for one brutal burst at the end. You can also extend the ride with an out-and-back up the north Overlook Trail. Instead of turning left on Overlook, turn right. It'll take you another mile and a half over the mountain crest to the park boundary, where you'll reverse course and descend the Overlook Trail to the sea.

## Killer Topanga Loop, Topanga State Park

20 miles. Very difficult. Steep, hot, hot and steep—you get the picture. Mostly fire road with a brief section of urban paved road. Access: Trippet Ranch Parking area, Entrada Rd., Topanga State Park.

My first reaction on looking down from Topanga State Park was: Man, this place is really up here. Look way down there at the ocean. If you're not physically ready to drop almost all the way back to the ocean and then climb a fire road back up, think seriously about choosing a different ride. This is a dramatic loop that allows you nearly continuous vistas of the Pacific, the city, and several different canyons.

From the main park entrance at Trippet Ranch, ride up the fire road to a T and veer left. You'll follow the ride for about a mile until a three-way fork presents you with a choice. You want to stay right. The trail will descend slightly to Eagle Springs and then climb back up to the Temescal Canyon Fire Road. Veer right, toward the ocean. Be on the alert for several closed gates, which may require you to dismount. Continue down until a closed gate marks the park boundary and paved Michael Drive. Here you're going to do some fancy navigating. A left on Vereda de la Montura for half a block will take you to Palisades Drive. Descend to Sunset Boulevard and turn right. You'll only be on Sunset for a few hundred yards until Paseo Miramar, where you turn right again. You're now a little more than halfway as

far as distance goes, but the best is still ahead. Drop into climbing mode and grind. The paved road lasts about 2 miles until the park boundary. Then it's fire road again for the next four. All but the most gonzo hill climbers will be thankful for their granny gear on this one.

## ROAD BIKING

Los Angeles is America's monument to the automobile. The freeway system is the most elaborate in the world, and just like Steve Martin in *L.A. Stories*, it seems like people must get in their cars to visit the next-door neighbor. In my opinion anyone who voluntarily rides a bike on the major surface streets of L.A. can count their life expectancy in a matter of hours—people here simply don't see bicycles—but there are numerous nice rides to be had that take advantage of some of the city's 300 miles of bikeways and less busy streets.

## Mineral Wells Loop

7.7 miles. Difficult. Several steep climbs. Griffith Park. Exit I-5 at Los Feliz. Go west and turn right on Crystal Springs Dr. into Griffith Park. At the visitor center, turn left and park by the merry-go-round. At the end of the parking lot a gate blocks the road to automobiles.

Though you start on a closed bit of road, you'll quickly join Griffith Park Drive. There is traffic here but it's park traffic, none of the commuter madness of the city below. As you leave the irrigated lower reaches of Griffith Park, the landscape will reveal its natural dry self, a forest of chaparral and occasional pines. You're riding over the very eastern nose of the Santa Monica Mountains, known hereabouts as the Hollywood Hills. Climb steadily past the golf course and up to the Mineral Wells picnic ground.

This is the high point of the ride, about 600 feet. You'll begin a zooming descent to the intersection with Zoo Drive, where a marked bike route will take you right toward the zoo. The street changes names to Crystal Springs Drive at the zoo, but you'll keep going straight until you reach the visitor center. Turn right, the way you came in, and climb back up to your car. People looking for a good workout can do a few consecutive loops.

## South Bay Bike Trail

19.1 miles. Easy. From Santa Monica Beach to Redondo Beach.

The South Bay Bike Trail is without equal anywhere in Los Angeles. While parking and dead-end streets make it difficult to follow Santa Monica Bay's shoreline by car, this fantastic bike path makes it a snap on a bike. Even though it's flat, the entire 19.1 miles can be a tiring day's ride, since it's likely that you'll be dodging strollers, tourist surreys, errant Frisbees, and the carnival that is the Santa Monica/Venice beachfront scene. Beachfront parking can be expensive or even impossible to find on busy weekends—which is why you brought a bike. I often forage inland into nearby residential neighborhoods looking for free parking. After all, what's an extra mile when you're on a bike? Officially, the trail begins a third of a mile north of the Santa Monica Pier, where California Street hits the coast. Feel free to catch it anywhere south of here. Bring a lock and a few bucks along, as you're likely to get drawn into some of the trailside attractions. Santa Monica Pier was restored recently and has great jazz clubs, restaurants, and a couple of roller coasters. Two miles south, you'll cross the invisible line into Venice. The trail actually wanders across the sand here,

and the combination of blowing drifts and some sudden curves can make it a little dicey. You'll notice quite a lot of commotion to the landward side of things. This is the famous Venice Board-walk, which isn't made of boards at all. You can get your name written on a grain of rice, get your nose pierced, buy a counterfeit Rolex, and, rider beware, get your bike ripped off while you're not paying attention. As you reach the Venice pier, the path veers inland up Washington Boulevard. The next 4 miles are a necessary detour around Marina Del Rey, unless you can swim and carry your bike at the same time. The path is marked, but in case the signs are missing, you ride Washington to Admiralty to Fiji, keeping the marina on your right at all times. At the loop marking the end of Fiji, you'll find a bike path leading to the end of the south harbor jetty. The 12 miles from Playa Del Rey (south side of Marina Del Rey) to Redondo Beach are a piece of cake and a lovely ride. The next couple miles are the most desolate of the entire stretch. There is virtually nobody here because there's no public parking and the L.A. airport takeoff path goes directly overhead. Strangely post-apocalyptic, the dunes and beach here are probably the closest you can come to seeing what L.A. looked like before it was L.A.

Once you pass the monstrous Hyperion sewage plant and the giant power plant at El Segundo, you enter Manhattan Beach. With the exception of a short detour around King Harbor in Redondo Beach, the path follows the beach the entire way. It's worth noting before you plan a ride that the predominant breeze in the area runs from Santa Monica toward the south bay. Therefore, if you plan a round-trip ride beginning in Santa Monica, factor in the increased difficulty of the return leg into a headwind.

## Sepulveda Basin Bike Trails

3–8 miles. Easy. Exit Hwy. 101 onto Balboa Blvd. in Encino. Go north to free parking for Sepulveda Basin.

Everyone's first thought on seeing Sepulveda Basin is "What the heck is all this country doing in the middle of the San Fernando Valley?" It seems odd—grassy fields, a few small farms, golf courses, trails—everything, it seems, except the houses, mini-malls, and streets that carpet the rest of the valley. The reason is flood control. Sepulveda Basin is the sacrificial lamb of the L.A. flood control strategy. When massive runoff turns the L.A. River into a torrent, it's the job of this bowl-shaped valley within a valley to take the peak off the flood crest, thereby saving the city downstream. Consequently, nothing that can't safely be flooded has been built here. Several great trails wind around the basin and along the L.A. River as it cuts through the park. On a clear evening it's almost possible to forget you're in the heart of a big city. Gazing at the Santa Monica Mountains to the south and the Santa Susanas to the north, it's easy to imagine why early settlers thought this valley was heaven on earth.

## ROCK CLIMBING

The gorge cut by Malibu Creek through the Santa Monicas contains some fine routes. The most visited and famous area is **Planet of the Apes Wall.** Like seemingly every other location in Malibu Creek State Park, this rocky wall was once a movie set. I can only imagine some pioneering 1970s climber coming here to unwind and finding the beautiful area filled with a location shoot, the director yelling at extras in ape suits, "No, no, leap up and down and grunt like this!"

The wall is easily top-roped and no bolts other than the ones in place are allowed. The surface is a fine sandstone, and much of it is overhanging. Routes tend toward the harder end of the spectrum, 5.11s and 5.12s. A little farther along the stream is a second climbing area called The Ghetto, where you'll find some easier climbs plus 5.13a Maximum Ghetto, one of the hairiest climbs in the park. While the creek can often make it difficult to reach the Ghetto during high water, it's such a bonus to have a nice swimming hole near your climbing area that the trade-off is a good one.

Across the San Fernando Valley from Topanga Canyon is **Stoney Point,** the oldest climbing zone in Los Angeles. Owned as a city park since the 1980s, this rambling series of canyons and rock formations was the early proving ground of many famous climbers, including John Bachar, Royal Robbins, and Yvon Chouinard. To get there you'll take Topanga Canyon Road north of 101 (not south, as you would to reach Topanga State Park) about 10 miles. The park entrance is located just off the road. While no routes here are taller than 50 feet (all can be easily top-roped), the variety and sheer number of climbs are phenomenal. Expect a crowd on any given weekend, and be aware that it can be unbearably hot here in the middle of summer.

The last spot, I hesitate to even mention because I've only seen people climbing there a couple times: **Point Dume.** The huge, rocky headland has some big empty faces. The rock quality looks bad: Salt air and rock climbing just don't seem to go together that well. But if you like greasy holds, rotten rock, and the Pacific crashing below while you climb, well, take a chance on it.

## SAILING

Santa Monica Bay is home to the largest pleasure craft harbor in the United States: **Marina Del Rey,** where you'll find just about everything that floats, from 100-foot mega-yachts to dilapidated old dinghies. Several charter and sailing schools here teach it all, from what is a jib to offshore navigation. You can also charter bareboats or skippered boats for the day or for an overnight to Catalina. The largest sailing school in the marina is **California Sailing Academy,** at 14025 Panay Way (tel. 310/821-3433), with boats from 14 to 40 feet and the full spectrum of instruction. They teach intensive weekend and longer resort courses during which students live on the boats. **Bluewater Sailing** at 13505 Bali Way (tel. 310/823-5545) also offers a full slate of classes and charters to 36 feet. **Rent-A-Sail** boat rentals at 13719 Fiji Way has smaller boats like Hobie Cats and Capri 14's for people who want to sail inside the harbor (tel. 310/822-1868).

At Redondo Harbor, **Marina Sailing** offers 15 different charter boats and a full spectrum of American Sailing Association classes. It's at 819 N. Harbor Dr. (tel. 310/318-2772).

## SCUBA DIVING

Those wide sand beaches of central and southern Santa Monica Bay are an indication of what you'd see below the water as well: not much. But along the Malibu coast and also off the rocky shores of Palos Verdes, scuba divers find fantastic visibility (by mainland standards), beautiful underwater rock formations, and surprisingly healthy populations of fish. The rule of remoteness (the harder you have to work to get there, the better the diving will be) applies even more here. There are plenty of spots where you can suit up right next

to the road and go for a really nice dive an easy swim away. But it'll be even better if you put a little distance between you and the next guy.

The numerous kelp beds and rock formations off **Leo Carrillo State Beach** get a lot of diver traffic, but remain fantastic dives. I can attest firsthand that there are a lot of gamefish out here, especially big halibut. Up the coast a little ways, where Deer Creek Road intersects with Highway 1, there is a nice access to the beach and what is often one of the clearest areas in Malibu.

In keeping with the rule of remoteness, one of the better strategies for diving Malibu is to free dive from a sea kayak. Malibu, after all, is synonymous with "exclusive," and exclusive means that there's a lot of coastline that regular folks are excluded from. A kayak, however, gives you mobility and access to even the most exclusive private beaches in the area.

While people do dive spots like the Marina Del Rey breakwater, the Hyperion Sewage Outfall (I'm not kidding), and such, my advice is to leave that to the loonies and dive either **Malibu** or spots on the **Palos Verdes Peninsula.** Palos Verdes once upon a time was probably the richest and most diverse diving on the coast. I've seen pictures of guys pulling in 20-pound lobsters while they were out surfing—no mask, no tanks, no game bag. Abalone used to cling to practically every rock. But Palos Verdes, more than anywhere, bore the brunt of L.A. and Orange County pollution problems in the 1950s, '60s, and '70s. It's coming back, now that outfall controls are much stricter, but has a long way to go. Both scuba and free divers will find plenty of fine underwater scenery in Malaga Cove, Lunada Bay, and Portugese Bend Cove.

**Malibu Divers,** at 21231 Pacific Coast Hwy. (tel. 310/456-2396) are very helpful and will recommend destinations based on the most current conditions. And, of course, they'll happily sell or rent you a pile of gear. **Dive-n-Surf** at 504 North Broadway in Redondo Beach (tel. 310/372-8423) is one of the oldest dive shops in the state, and is a great source of knowledge about Palos Verdes conditions and destinations.

## SEA KAYAKING

Beginners will enjoy bobbing around in the still waters of Marina Del Rey (but watch out for boat traffic!). Because it's the largest pleasure boat basin in the United States, you could spend hours poking around the many marinas and docks looking at boats. **Boat Rentals of America,** at 13719 Fiji Way (tel. 310/574-2821), charges $10 an hour for singles and $15 for double kayaks.

More adventurous paddlers can rent boats at Redondo Harbor and explore the open sea toward Palos Verdes or along the Redondo Breakwater. Seals, sea lions, and dolphins are quite common in this corner of the bay and will often approach kayakers. **The Kayak Store** at 1312 Aviations Blvd. no. 102 (tel. 310/318-1717) in South Redondo sells and rents a diverse line of touring kayaks. Right on the water in the Redondo Beach Marina, **G'day Charters** rents kayaks for $15 the first hour and $10 subsequent hours. They also offer basic lessons. Find them at 161 N. Harbor Dr. (tel. 310/798-1310).

Right across the highway from Surfrider Point, **Malibu Ocean Sports** rents several different types of sit-on-top kayaks by the day ($35) and by the hour ($15). Look for the big white truck with all the kayaks on it right next to the pier. Contact them at 310/456-6302. Many people rent kayaks here, put in across the street, and decide that by golly, they're going to go out and catch some waves at the point. Stop. Do not, I repeat, do not, go out and start dropping

in on surfers at the point. Besides being extremely bad form, this is one place where I'd honestly fear for the life of someone who did that. Instead, paddle under the pier, around the point, and up the coast into the exclusive Malibu Colony. If a more glitteringly famous beach community exists anywhere in the world, I don't know about it. When you've had your share of peering into windows trying to see Madonna or Richard Gere, there are a couple offshore rocks that often draw lots of interesting birds and seals. Malibu Ocean Sports also arranges full moon paddles in Marina Del Rey and does guided Malibu coastline tours every Saturday and Sunday.

People with their own kayaks or willing to rent one and drive with it can do some more hardcore exploring. The paddle down from Point Dume State Park around Big Dume Point and down to Little Dume is one of the prettiest stretches of coast in Malibu. All told, you'll cover about 6 miles there and back. Bring a mask in case the snorkeling looks good. Point Dume also is a real hot spot for seeing whales. In addition, either direction up and down the coast from Leo Carrillo State Beach is a sure winner.

## SURFING

Summer is the best time for surf through much of Santa Monica Bay, since the coastline is largely south-facing. South swells line up on the point breaks and beach breaks of Malibu like nobody's business; some have described the wave at Malibu Point as the perfect wave, bar none. While I'd be inclined to agree that **Malibu Point,** or **Surfrider Point,** as it's also known, is one of the finest waves I've ridden, I also feel that it's way too crowded for its own good. On a busy day you could literally step from surfboard to surfboard the entire length of the point. I leave Surfrider Point to all the tourists and to the surly locals who hate the tourists, and head elsewhere. **Secos,** the point break at Leo Carrillo State Beach, is another fine point, and also gets fairly crowded. Nicholas Canyon County Park, just south of Leo Carrillo, is home of something of an oddity for Southern California, a left-hand point break called **Zeros.** I'm regular-foot, so I'd just as soon surf elsewhere, but for a goofy-foot it's a great treat to rip a racing point wave frontside.

The south bay from Santa Monica to Redondo is a more or less unbroken sandy beach, with hundreds of individual beachbreaks. As you head south along the bayshore, the coastline curves and begins to face more west. What that means is that in winter, when most swells come from the north and west, this area receives a lot of surf. The most famous breaks in this area are **El Porto,** just at the northern edge of Manhattan Beach, where a submarine canyon comes close to shore and generates waves about twice the size of the surrounding beach, and the **Redondo Breakwater,** which can get absolutely huge in the winter. The most notorious break in this neck of the woods is **Lunada Bay,** long famous for the most surly locals on the coast, where harassment has been raised to such a level that one out-of-town surfer actually had to get a restraining order against several people who beat him up. It's a beautiful wave, and I hate to let jerks like that win, but is it ever really worth going to war to catch a few waves?

**Malibu Ocean Sports** (see above) rents longboards and shortboards by the day for $25. A 2-hour surfing lesson is $74 per person, or $55 per hour for private lessons with a 2-hour minimum. The **Stewart Surfboard Shop** at 18820 Pacific Coast Hwy., near Topanga Point (tel. 310/317-8688), rents boards for $35

a day and offers lessons for $25 per hour, not including board rental. In Redondo, **Dive-n-Surf** at 504 N. Broadway in Redondo Beach (tel. 310/372-8423) is owned by the same people who make Body-Glove wetsuits and rents a full line of surfing gear.

## SWIMMING

Unique on the West Coast, **Seaside Lagoon** is a smash hit with both little kids and not-so-little kids who don't like cold water. Water is heated in the Edison Electric plant across Harbor Drive and piped into the sandy lagoon, creating a warm, shallow swimming hole. It's basically a miniature version of a real beach, heated up and sized down to make it manageable for little tykes. Admission is very inexpensive. The lagoon is open from 10am to 5:45pm every summer day. It's located just off Harbor Drive in Redondo Beach.

## WALKS & RAMBLES

### Santa Monica Pier

All the piers on this coast are great short walks, but the Santa Monica Pier is the most interesting, with a mixture of action-packed roller coasters, jazz clubs, restaurants, street musicians, and a zillion other things going on at once, plus the natural beauty of walking out over the sea. The end of the pier is popular with fishermen, who often pull bonito, mackerel, and perch from the depths. Pelicans and gulls rest on the railings and buildings.

### Estuary Trails, Malibu Lagoon State Beach.

Here at the most seaward point of Malibu Creek, you can easily watch the wildlife attracted to the freshwater lagoon formed when the beach dams up the creek. Constantly changing, the lagoon is home to migrating waterfowl, endangered pelicans and terns, and hundreds of western gulls; plus, this creek is home to the southernmost run of Pacific steelhead trout. If you tire of all that, follow the boardwalk trail out to the beach and walk in either direction. Left will take you into Malibu Cove. Right, you'll run into a barrier erected to keep people out of Malibu Colony. If it's low tide, walk right around the barrier and stay on the wet sand. It's public property below the high tide line.

## Venice Canals

Venice was designed by eccentric tobacco millionaire Abbot Kinney as a sister city to its Italian namesake. A network of canals was fashioned from 160 acres of wetland. A city was built around them. For a while it was a big success. Visitors flocked to partake of the gondoliers, roller coaster, and carousel, plus concerts and theater in a large auditorium. But after Kinney died in 1920, things began to unravel. The canal system had been designed without adequate circulation and often became quite stinky and stagnant. Tired of the stench and potential for disease, in 1929 the city of L.A. filled in most of the canals. The four canals that remain are still crossed by Venetian-style bridges and home to a constantly quacking population of ducks and geese. The homes along the canals, once considered blight, are now prime real estate. Park on Venice Avenue in the first or second block inland from Pacific Avenue. The Canal neighborhood is to the south. Take some time to poke around and explore the backwaters of Venice, and imagine what it must have been like when the whole town was paved with water.

WHALE WATCHING

The best whale watching always seems to occur in places where a jutting point, headland, or island creates an obstacle for the migration. As they round such promontories, the whales swim closer to shore than usual, and their location is more predictable than when you're just poking around on the open sea looking for spouts.

**Point Dume State Park** in Malibu is without a doubt the best place on this stretch of coast for observing gray whales as they head up and down the coast. The high headland drops straight into the sea, marking the northernmost boundary of Santa Monica Bay. The parking is at beach level, but a stairway and trail lead to the top of the point. Even if you strike out on whales, the beauty of this place is a sure winner.

The southern boundary of Santa Monica Bay is marked by the **Palos Verdes Peninsula.** Again, high rocky bluffs and headlands make a fine vantage point for scanning the sea. The Point Vicente Lighthouse at the farthest reach of the peninsula is a popular spot to watch from, but just about any high bluff in this area will do.

Both Marina Del Rey and Redondo Beach harbors offer whale-watching cruises. If I had to pick one over the other, I'd go with **Redondo Sportfishing,** 181 N. Harbor Dr., Redondo Beach, CA 90277 (tel. 310/374-3481), simply because Redondo is that much closer to the whale-rich waters off Palos Verdes. In Marina Del Rey, the two main whale-watch operations are **Charter Connections,** 5015 Pacific Ave., Marina Del Rey, CA 90292 (tel. 310/827-4105); and **Del Mar Sportfishing,** 13759 Fiji Way (tel. 310/372-2712). The peak of the 14,000 whale-strong annual migration passes by this area between Christmas and the end of April, which is when tours are run regularly. Occasional summer trips will be made if there are blue whales or other mammals in the area.

A unique mural on the Southern California Edison Plant on Harbor Drive in Redondo Beach shows a complete underwater scene of several California gray whales and other sea creatures. The length of two football fields, this huge artwork was crafted by world-famous painter Wyland, who specializes in depictions of sea life, although generally on a smaller scale.

# Campgrounds & Other Accommodations

**CAMPING**

Like most visitors, you're probably coming to the Santa Monica Mountains with a mixed agenda: you'd like to visit the beach, surf, dive, or kayak, but you're anxious to get in some hiking or mountain biking too. **Point Mugu State Park** has 80 campsites right on the sand at Thornhill Broome Beach. The downside to these sites is that you're backed by the Pacific Coast Highway and there's no privacy between the sites. During the night, traffic on the road is sparse and probably won't keep you up, but in the day it can seem like you're parked on a freeway. The upside, of course, is the rare pleasure of sleeping right on the beach, a rarity anywhere in California. My preference at Point Mugu is to forgo the ocean view for the more sheltered campground across Highway 1 in **Sycamore Canyon.** You're still only a stone's throw from the water, but the surroundings are much more sheltered and peaceful (54 sites). The other fine beach camping option on the Malibu

coast is **Leo Carrillo State Beach,** where 138 campsites are spread in several loops on the inland side of Highway 1, though they're connected to the beach by an undercrossing. People with self-contained campers under 8 feet high are really in luck, as there are 32 beachside campsites secluded from both the main campground and the noise of the highway by high coastal bluffs. For reservations for all the campsites above, call 800/444-PARK. The cost ranges from $12 to $20 a night.

Though the 60 campsites at **Malibu Creek State Park** are miles from the beach, they are perfectly situated for rock climbing or hiking in the backcountry. Likewise, the National Park Service campground at Circle-X Ranch is a fine place to base yourself for hiking the more remote peaks and canyons of the range.

Right on the urban edge of Los Angeles, **Topanga State Park** has a small hike-in campground reached off Sunset Boulevard in Pacific Palisades.

All these campgrounds fill up quickly. Reservations are always a good idea and a necessity during summer months. State park campgrounds are managed through **Destinet** at 800/444-7275. To reserve the group site at the National Park Service's **Circle-X Ranch,** call 818/597-91929, ext. 333. The individual campground at Circle-X is first-come, first-served.

**INNS & LODGES**

### Santa Monica American Youth Hostel

1436 Second St., Santa Monica, CA 90405. Tel. 310/393-9913. $15 per person per night. $2 sheet rental. AYH card required from June to September, available on the premises. Laundry, kitchen, storage, pool table. No credit cards.

Situated midway between Santa Monica's hopping Boardwalk and even more hopping 3rd Street Promenade, with the venerable Pussycat Adult Theater as its next-door neighbor, it's hard to imagine a more ideal location for a youth hostel. The beach is just down the block, and the nightlife is some of the most happening outside of Hollywood. It's hardly a rustic backwoods hunting lodge, but even the most die-hard outdoorsman will find a good time here. The only major drawback is that parking in the neighborhood will cost you about as much for the day as a bed does.

## Cadillac Hotel

401 Ocean Front Walk, Venice, CA 90291. Tel. 310/399-8876. 9 dorm rooms ($15 bed). 30 private rooms ($49 double or single). Laundry, gym, sundeck. MC, V.

Half hotel, half hostel, this fun and funky art deco establishment sits just a block from the heart of Venice's wacky beach scene. If you're traveling alone, it's a great place to meet others. If you're traveling with friends, it's just a good location for a great price.

## Casa Malibu

22752 Pacific Coast Hwy. (just south of Malibu Pier), Malibu, CA 90265. Tel. 310/ 456-2219 or 800/831-0858. 21 rms. $90–$110 double with garden view. Ocean-view double $130. Oceanfront rooms $145–$155.

Right on the sand in the heart of Malibu, this fine little hotel is perfectly poised for surfing the point or kayaking into the Malibu Colony. Nearby are Malibu Lagoon and Malibu Creek State Park. At high tide the beach here disappears, actually intruding under some of the oceanfront rooms. When the surf is big the sound can make it hard to sleep, but that can be its own pleasure.

# 5

# THE ANGELES & SAN BERNARDINO NATIONAL FORESTS: L.A.'s Eastern Mountains

**W**ITHOUT THE SAN GABRIEL AND SAN BERNARDINO MOUN-tains there would be no Los Angeles Basin—rather, just an endless plain. Yet people lead their entire lives in the city without any awareness that, only 45 miles from L.A.'s skyscrapers and the clogged traffic arteries of the I-10 freeway, there are enormous 10,000- and 11,000-foot mountains.

How could that be? The answer, of course, is smog. The basin's prevailing sea breezes blow all the air pollution in the region up against the stupendous wall of its northern and eastern mountains. Most days of the year you can stand in Pasadena, Glendora, Fontana, Riverside, or Redlands, literally at the foot of the range, and look up to see nothing but scrubby foothills ascending into a giant cloud of brown haze. Almost every year there's a front-page *Los Angeles Times* photo of downtown with a backdrop of snow-covered peaks after a particularly fierce storm blows through and washes the sky clean for a day or two. It's news when you can see the mountains.

It wasn't always that way. I own a 1930s tourist book that promoted the Los Angeles Basin. In virtually every photo you can see the mountains. But

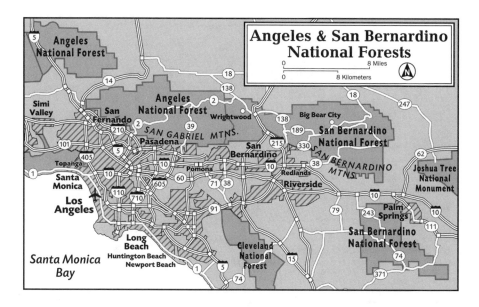

the advent of the automobile that gave us such rapid mobility also robbed us of the beautiful presence of these towering peaks.

The San Gabriels and the San Bernardinos owe their existence to the San Andreas Fault. Twisting and tortured, the San Gabriels are the most geologically fractured of any range in California. As the fault snakes beneath the range, it creates a great jumble of granite rock so steep that many places are much steeper than can be naturally maintained. As a result, landslides and debris flows are the norm rather than the exception, and any attempt at permanent construction in the hills faces great challenges.

Even just getting into the mountains was a brutal challenge for the early explorers. Arroyos quickly turned into impassable box canyons. The hillsides were covered in loose and slippery rocks. And where it wasn't too steep or slippery to walk, the slopes were covered (and still are) with a thick chaparral community of thorny, scraggly plants that grabbed at every loose thread and had a special propensity for poking sticks in your eyes. Once you reached the high, alpine areas, the going got easier, but the first miles were a killer. It wasn't until

around the end of the 19th century that explorer William Sturtevant blazed the first official north-to-south trail through the San Gabriels. Until then people had simply gone the long way around, or dabbled around the edges of this great wilderness. Soon, though, California was gripped with a "Golden Age of Hiking"; linked backcountry lodges played hosts to hundreds of guests. You could leave one side of the ranges and hike for days, stopping each night for the camaraderie of other hikers and the convenience of a soft bed and a hot meal.

The Great Flood of 1938 scoured many of these camps and resorts from the canyons that were their natural location. Trails were devastated too. And the construction of the Angeles Crest Highway and the Rim of the World Drive fell as the final blow to the great hiking era. Why hike for days to reach your favorite spot when you could drive there in a few hours?

Today, the Angeles and San Bernardino National Forests are the most heavily used in the entire country. The Angeles alone counts more than 15 million visitors per year, most of them between April and October. Because it's the outlet for so many urban dwellers, the problems of the city are bound to

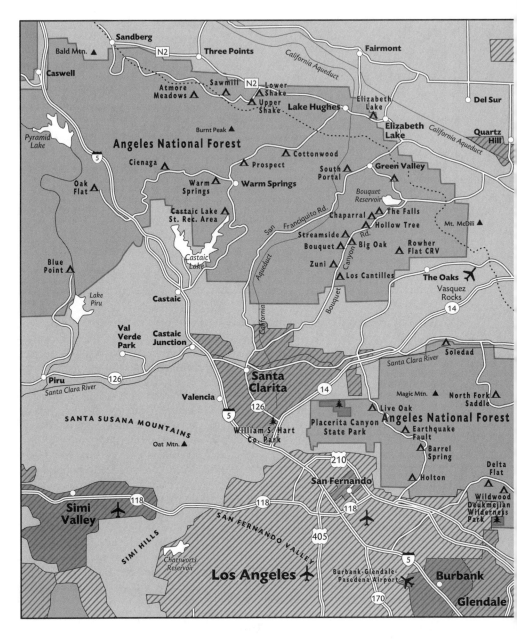

make their way into the forest. In a July 1997 feature story, *Outside Magazine* declared the Angeles "the most dangerous forest in America" and painted a portrait of a wilderness of Satanists, meth cookers, psycho killers, arsonists, survivalists, and run-of-the-mill loonies. That assessment, in my opinion, was a bit on the alarmist side. Sure, out of 15 million people who visit every year, you're bound to have every type, but for the majority of people who visit the forest it's a place of peace and happiness—otherwise people wouldn't keep coming back. That said, it's wise to keep your wits about you here. Lock your car. Don't leave valuables in your car. Don't cop an attitude when a bunch of guys

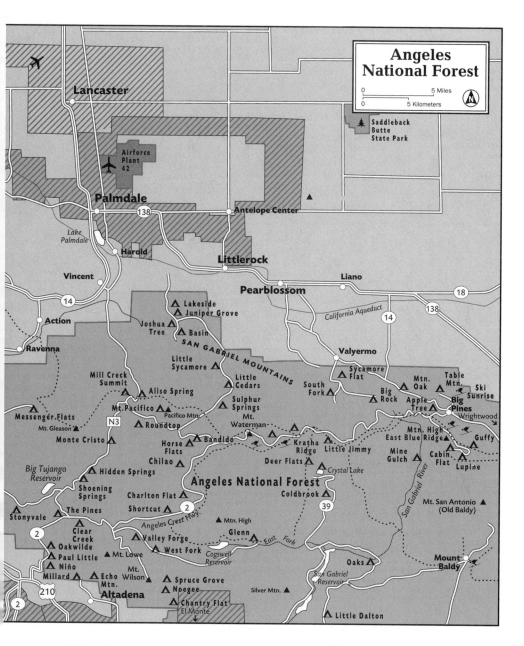

with beards and big tattoos decides to rev their Harleys next to your "private" fishing hole. And if you're a young gangbanger with a can of spray paint just itching to tag some rocks and stake out some new turf for the homies while you're up on a relaxing camping trip with Mom and Dad, do the rest of us a favor and stay home, okay?

## The Lay of the Land

People from out of state are always surprised when I tell them there are 11,000-foot peaks within a stone's throw of the Los Angeles Basin. For some reason Southern California's "endless summer" public image doesn't gibe with snow-capped peaks and evergreen forests. But

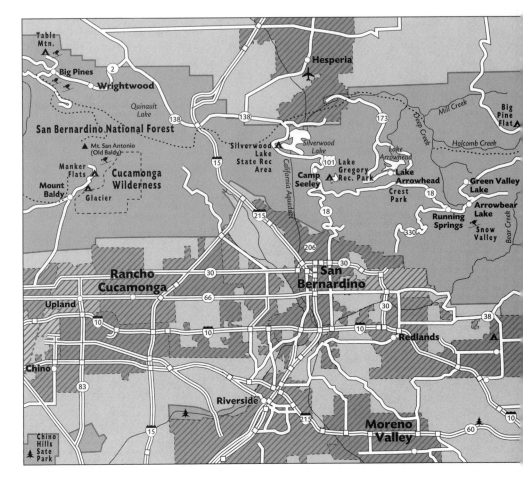

the San Gabriels and San Bernardinos are mountains with a capital M. A simple glance at a map reveals something peculiar about these mountains. They run on an east-west axis, rather than north to south like the Sierra Nevada, the Cascades, the Rockies, and virtually every other mountain range over 10,000 feet in the Lower 48. As such they are the largest of Southern California's transverse ranges.

At some point in distant geological history these two ranges were one. Eventually, however, a large earthquake fault cut them in two and created the gap that's now the path of Interstate 15 through Cajon Pass. The **San Gabriels** went on to be even more fractured and tortured by the San Andreas Fault, which runs directly through the range.

In some areas the mountains are so shattered they look like they've been clobbered with a cosmic sledgehammer.

The **San Bernardinos** have fared more gently at the hands of time. They're more gentle and rolling, less topsy-turvy than their larger (but shorter) neighbors. As a result it's possible to hike and bike farther in the San Bernardinos without logging a million vertical feet, and the rounded basins between the mountain peaks were big enough to form several large natural lakes—something you won't find in the San Gabriels.

Both ranges and forests have peaks that break the 10,000-foot mark. The highest point in the Angeles National Forest is **Mount San Antonio,** better known to many as "Old Baldy." Nearby

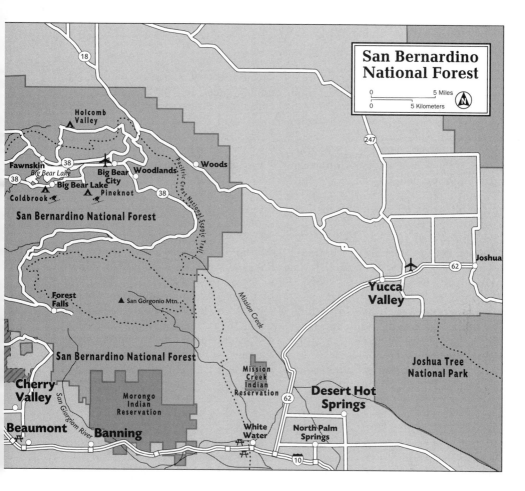

San Bernardino
National Forest

0       5 Miles

0       5 Kilometers

Holcomb Valley

Fawnskin

Big Bear Lake

Big Bear City

Woodlands

Woods

Big Bear Lake

Pineknot

Coldbrook

San Bernardino National Forest

Pacific Crest National Scenic Trail

Forest Falls

San Gorgonio Mtn.

Mission Creek

Joshua

Yucca Valley

San Bernardino National Forest

Joshua Tree National Park

Mission Creek Indian Reservation

Cherry Valley

Morongo Indian Reservation

Desert Hot Springs

Beaumont

San Gorgonio River

Banning

White Water

North Palm Springs

are numerous mountains over 9,000 feet, including **Mount Baden-Powell** and **Throop Peak.**

The San Bernardino Range tops out at the dramatic summit of **Mount San Gorgonio,** at 11,499 feet. From the summit of this gorgeous peak, the Coachella Valley and much of the inland desert seem to lie at your feet. It's hard to believe that within less than 150 miles as the crow flies, entire towns lie below sea level in the Imperial Valley.

There are numerous routes into both these national forests. The urban edge of the Angeles is fronted by communities like Pasadena, Sunland, and Glendora, where trailheads leave residential neighborhoods for the nearby forest. Other visitors penetrate the forest on the network of paved roads that opened up so much of the range to vehicle traffic. The two main routes are the **Angeles Crest Highway,** a winding ribbon of concrete that twists along the spine of the mountains, from the affluent communities of La Canada to the tiny ski town of Wrightwood, before descending to **Highway 138** near Phelan. Along this route are many of the best campgrounds, lush pine forests, wildlife viewing areas, numerous lookouts, picnic stops, and trailheads. It's not a road for people in a hurry, but it's perfect for a leisurely mountain drive.

The biggest area of the forest that has undergone the greatest impact has to be the **San Gabriel River Canyon,** reached via Highway 39. During the summer, hot days drive thousands up from the smoggy, sweltering city to cool off in the pools of the San Gabriel. Often there are more people than water, and by the time September rolls around it's shocking to see what passes for a swimming hole. But during the off-season and even mid-week you can get a glimpse of what this corner of the woods was like during the great hiking era, when sportsmen would fill their creels with hundreds of wild trout and cars weren't double parked because there was no road.

Visitation to the **San Bernardino National Forest** is heavily concentrated around the Big Bear Lake and Lake Arrowhead. Big Bear touts itself as "Southern California's only year-round mountain resort" and while I can think of a lot of places that would argue that point, it is certainly popular around the entire calendar.

To get there, visitors generally come one of three ways. The most direct from Los Angeles is to hop on the I-10 to Redlands, where you'll catch Calif. Highway 330 up to Running Springs where it meets Calif. Highway 18, the "Rim of the World Drive." Smog often obscures the world, but rest assured, on a clear day you'd see that this road is really on the rim of it.

The other major route starts in Redlands too, but loops east and just under the watchful presence of Mount San Gorgonio before veering north into Big Bear. Finally, those of us coming from the northern part of the state do well to follow Calif. Highway 18 up the back side of the San Bernardinos from the Mojave. This is one of the most dramatic roads in the state, rising from parched cactus desert to a lushly forested mountain lake in just a few steep miles.

Despite being the most visited national forest in the nation, the **Angeles** is virtually uninhabited. It was set aside as a forest reserve very early, way back in 1892, by President Harrison. Consequently, it has few private inholdings and only one real town, Wrightwood,

within its borders. San Bernardino National Forest, on the other hand, is a virtual boomtown. All along the Rim of the World Road are little towns like Crestline, Lake Arrowhead, Running Springs, Arrowbear, Fawnskin, and Big Bear City. As you might gather, Big Bear City is the Big City in these parts. With every fast-food restaurant, grocery chain, drugstore, and gas station known to humankind, it's a far cry from *The Sound of Music*, but it's doing a good job of maintaining its own local dives, haunts, and hot spots too. The chief attraction here is, of course, Big Bear Lake, a striking blue gem covering 3,000 acres and surrounded by high mountain peaks. The whole setting is so alpine that it seems really out of place this far south. During the summer the lake draws flocks of water-skiers, fishermen, swimmers, and others who just want to camp along its shore and hike or mountain bike the surrounding hills. Winter brings a different, snow-loving crowd. Two large ski areas, **Bear Mountain** and **Snow Summit,** rise directly out of Big Bear City. When the snow is great, the skiing is great. Unfortunately, it's all too rare for the snow here to be great, even with substantial snowmaking capacity.

# Parks & Other Hot Spots
## Angeles National Forest

Access: I-5, Hwy. 126, and N2 for the Saugus District. I-210, Hwy. 2 (a.k.a. the Angeles Crest Hwy.), N3, and Hwy. 39 for all others. Information Office: 701 N. Santa Anita Ave., Arcadia, CA 91006. Tel. 626/574-5200 or 626/574-1613. Web site: www.fs.fed.us/recreation.

The Angeles National Forest is nature's cinematic backdrop to the city of Los Angeles. Stretching across the entire northern edge of L.A. County, the forest spans 694,187 acres and includes almost the entire San Gabriel mountain range, which separates the Los Angles Basin from the Mojave Desert, as well as a section of the Tehachapi Mountains to the north. The San Gabriel River runs through it (as do many of its forks). The forest also includes a few lakes (the largest of which is Castaic Lake) and over 500 miles of hiking, mountain biking, and equestrian trails, ranging from easy and paved to rugged and desolate. Wintertime brings lots of snow—and skiers—to the developed downhill and cross-country areas, all located along the eastern end of Hwy. 2. The topography varies from the peaks of Mount San Antonio (10,064 ft.) and Mount Wilson (5,710 ft.) to canyon floors just 1,000 feet above sea level. The higher elevations are blanketed in pine and fir, while the foothills are shaded by riparian growth and chaparral. Small towns like Lake Hughes, Green Valley, and Wrightwood dot the northern edge of the forest, with Tujunga, Altadena, and Glendora on the southern edge, but once you start climbing up into the mountains, there's not much but wilderness. The San Gabriel and Sheep Mountain Wilderness cover over 125 square miles, and the Cucamonga Wilderness, which lies on the border of Angeles and San Bernardino national forests, covers 13,000 acres.

### Castaic Lake

Access: I-5 to the Lake Hughes Rd. exit. Tel. 805/257-4050.

Operated by the Los Angeles County Department of Parks and Recreation,

Castaic Lake is known for its fishing: largemouth bass, bluegill, trout, crappie, and catfish, to be precise. Motor boats are permitted on the lake itself, while only engineless crafts are allowed on the small lagoon. The lake also features two launching ramps and allows overnight camping.

### Pyramid Lake

Access: 20 miles north of Santa Clarita. From the I-5 exit at Smokey Bear Rd., go left on the Old Hwy. 99 section to Emigrant Landing. Tel. 805/296-9710. Vista del Lago Visitors Center, tel. 805/294-0219.

Named for the pyramid-shaped rock formation that highway engineers carved out of the mountain (you can see the rock near the dam), Pyramid Lake is extremely popular with boaters, waterskiers, and people who love to fish for striped bass and rainbow trout. Because it is shaped like a hand with all five fingers outstretched (well, sort of), all the little inlets make the lake bearable when the crowds descend.

### Lake Hughes/Elizabeth Lake

Access: I-5 to Lake Hughes Rd. and head northeast. Turn right on Elizabeth Lake Rd. It's 3 miles to Lake Hughes; Elizabeth follows. From Palmdale, follow Elizabeth Lake Rd northwest. Tel. 805/724-2206.

The towns of Lake Hughes (once home to Roy Rogers before he was anybody) and Lake Elizabeth are nestled in the Angeles Forest hills at 3,200 feet. The eastern half of Elizabeth is private and can only be accessed by guests who are

staying at the lake's fancy resort, while the western half is open to the public, and swimming is allowed. Fishing for trout and bass is popular, and there's lots of great mountain biking in the area, too. Both lakes are totally dependent on rainfall and can be quite low during summer months, although permanent water may already be on its way as of this writing.

## Placerita Canyon State and County Park

Access: From I-5 and Hwy. 14, head northeast on 14. Exit Placerita Canyon Rd. and turn right. Continue to the park entrance. Tel. 805/259-7721. Historic sites, nature center.

A full 7 years before gold was discovered at Sutter's Mill and the 49ers rushed in, gold was found here in Placerita Canyon. Today, a beautiful, hollow-footed live oak tree marks the spot of this premier discovery and is called the Oak of the Golden Dream. Placerita Canyon offers several easy trails (valuable for both their historic and natural elements) and a waterfall, as well as a fine nature exhibit where you can see red-tailed hawks, snakes, a tarantula, all sorts of neat-looking beetles, lizards, and more.

## Vasquez Rocks County Park

Access: Hwy. 14, near Agua Dulce. Exit Agua Dulce Canyon Rd. and head north to West Escondido Canyon Rd. Follow the signs to the park entrance. Tel. 805/268-0840.

While Vasquez Rocks is technically not in the Angeles National Forest, I'm not

going to let a tiny detail like that get in the way of mentioning this awesome spot. The spectacular rock formations here look at once prehistoric, otherworldly, and decidedly Western—which is why they've been used as a location for countless movie and TV shows from *Star Trek* to *Bonanza* to *The Flintstones*. They were also the secret hideout of 1870s bandito Tiburcio Vasquez, who made a name for himself throughout this region robbing gringo stagecoaches, stealing gringo cattle, and otherwise making life hell for gringos in the backcountry.

## William S. Hart County Park & Museum

Access: From Hwy. 14 in Newhall, exit San Fernando Rd. Continue straight to the park entrance. Tel. 805/254-4584. Picnicking, museum, zoo.

This 246-acre park sits in a beautiful canyon just over the northern ridge of the San Fernando Valley. The land was purchased in the 1920s by William S. Hart, a veritable John Wayne of the silent screen, and on it he built the Hart Mansion, an elaborate 22-room hacienda. When Hart died in 1949, he willed the ranch "to the people." Today you can hike around, visit the museum filled with cool old cowboy memorabilia, and check out the old Saugus Train Station and the small zoo, too.

## Wrightwood

Access: Angeles Crest Hwy. (Hwy. 2) just west of Hwy. 138. Tel. 619/249-4320.

The mountain town of Wrightwood is a great place to stop (well, it's also one of the only places to stop around these parts) and refuel during your great mountain adventure. You'll find groceries, gas, restaurants, lodging, and several places to get liquored up, and it's close to the slopes, too.

## San Bernardino National Forest

Access: Hwy. 18 in the northern section, and Hwys. 243 and 74 in the southern section. Supervisor's Main Office: 1824 South Commercenter Circle, San Bernardino, CA 92408. Tel. 909/383-5588. Web site: www.fs.fed.us/recreation.

On the eastern edge of the urban sprawl known as the Inland Empire, the San Bernardino National Forest encompasses 633,000 acres of open space. It extends into both San Bernardino and Riverside counties, and is divided in two sections. The northern half includes a bit of the San Gabriel Mountains, the San Bernardino Mountains, the Silverwood Lake State Recreation Area, and the bustling resort communities of Lake Arrowhead (very exclusive) and Big Bear Lake (very down-home) as well as several other tiny mountain towns. San Gorgonio (11,499 ft.), the highest peak in Southern California, is also part of this forest. The southern section of the forest includes the San Jacinto Mountains; Mount San Jacinto State Park; the towns of Idyllwild, Pine Cove, and Pinyon Pines; and Lake Hemet. The forest also offers four designated wilderness areas: San Gorgonio, San Jacinto, Santa Rosa, and Cucamonga. A Wilderness Visitor Permit, available at certain ranger locations and through the mail, may be required. The geography varies from rolling hills and cool alpine forests to sun-scorched rocky peaks dotted with thorny chaparral. All told, there

are 538 miles of hiking trails, 193 of which are part of the Pacific Crest Trail, a trail system extending from Mexico to Canada. In the summertime, the forest is hopping with swimmers, boaters, and hikers; and in the wintertime, the area is home to several downhill, cross-country ski areas, as well as one snowboarders-only fun park.

## Silverwood Lake State Recreation Area

Access: From I-15 heading toward Victorville, exit Hwy. 138 and head east for 12 miles. Tel. 760/389-2303.

Situated on the northern face of the San Bernardinos, this hourglass-shaped reservoir offers 13 miles of shoreline. Surrounded by steep slopes, the lake is rather quiet on the southern end, while water- and jet-skiers hoot it up on the northern end. Designated swimming areas (which are all on the southern end) are Sawpit Canyon, Cleghorn Cove, and the hike-in/bike-to Serrano Beach. A section of the Pacific Crest Trail overlooks the lake.

## Lake Gregory Regional Park

Access: Hwy. 138 to Crestline; follow the Old Mill Rd. cutoff to the lake. Tel. 909/338-2233.

Just outside the tiny mountain town of Crestline and a few miles southeast of Silverwood Lake, Lake Gregory offers summertime fun. In fact, since Lake Arrowhead (see below) is privately owned, campers and visitors staying in the Arrowhead district usually come to

Lake Gregory to boat, fish, or swim. Various watercraft are available for rent, and there's a 300-foot water slide that's pretty fun.

## Lake Arrowhead

Access: Hwy. 18 north/east from the city of San Bernardino. Hwy. 138 off I-15; head east to Hwy. 18. Tel. 909/337-3715. Web site: www.lakearrowhead.net.

Since Lake Arrowhead is privately owned, there are only two ways an outsider can enjoy its beauty. One, tour the lake on the *Arrowhead Queen* (tel. 909/336-6992), which operates year-round. Two, rent one of the private homes or stay at one of the pricey and rare lodges, both of which include lake access. Camping is also available in the Arrowhead District and reservations can be made by calling the Arrowhead Ranger District at 909/337-2444. The last stretch of road leading toward Lake Arrowhead is known as Rim of the World Highway, which reportedly offers a stunning panoramic view of the valley below. Unfortunately, I drove this road in white-out blizzard conditions, so I had to use my imagination.

## Green Valley Lake

Access: Hwy. 18 east to Green Valley Lake cutoff. Tel. 909/867-2009. Picnic area, volleyball, playground.

Green Valley Lake is a great place to stop and cool off, especially if you're mountain biking from the town of Fawnskin to Green Valley Lake along Snow Slide Road (see "Mountain Biking" below) or

involved in any number of bike/hike/ walks or drives around the area.

## Big Bear Lake

Access: From Redlands, take Hwy. 330 to Hwy. 18 and head east, or take the more scenic route, Hwy. 38. From Victorville, take Hwy. 18 southeast. Tel. 800/4BIGBEAR or 909/866-7000. Web site: www.bigbearinfo.com.

About 100 miles northeast of Los Angeles you'll find Big Bear Lake, the last and largest in our little chain of lakes, nestled high in the San Bernardino National Forest. Once an exclusive getaway for Hollywood stars in the 1930s (it's where Clark Gable took Carole Lombard for their honeymoon), this Baby Lake Tahoe-of-the-South is now a year-round resort loaded with outdoor activities, from skiing and snowboarding in the winter to water sports in the summer.

## Mount San Jacinto State Park

Access: By trails from Idyllwild (26 miles south of I-10 on Hwy. 243) or by tram from Palm Springs. Tel. 909/659-2607. Palm Springs Aerial Tramway 760/325-1391.

While Mount San Jacinto is technically in the San Bernardino National Forest, I've included its details in chapter 8, "Joshua Tree & Palm Springs/Coachella Valley."

## Lake Perris State Recreation Area

Access: 11 miles southeast of the city or Riverside. From Hwy. 60, exit Moreno Beach

# Outdoor Resources

**USDA Forest Service Recreation Home Page**
http://www.fs.fed.us/recreation
National Parks Homepage
http://www.nps.gov/parks.html

**Angeles National Forest Ranger Districts**
Supervisor's Office
701 N. Santa Anita Ave.
Arcadia, CA 91006
626/574-1613

**Los Angeles River District**
Oak Grove Park
Flintridge, CA 91011
818/790-1151

**Little Tujunga Work Center**
12371 N. Little Tujunga Canyon Rd.
San Fernando, CA 91342
818/896-6727

**San Gabriel River District**
110 N. Wabash Ave.
Glendora, CA 91741
626/914-3790

**Santa Clara/Mojave Rivers District**
30800 Bouquet Canyon Rd.
Saugus, CA 91350
805/296-9710

**Mojave Work Center**
P.O. Box 15
29835 Valyermo Rd.
Valyermo, CA 93563
805/944-2187

**San Bernardino National Forest Ranger Districts**
Supervisor's Office
1824 South Commercenter Circle
San Bernardino, CA 92408
909/383-5588

**Arrowhead Ranger District**
28104 Hwy. 18
Skyforest, CA 92385
909/337-2444

**Big Bear Ranger District**
P.O. Box 290
Fawnskin, CA 92333
909/866-3437, 3438, 3439

**Cajon Ranger District**
1209 Lytle Creek Rd.
Lytle Creek, CA 92358
909/887-2576

**San Gorgonio Ranger District**
34701 Mill Creek Rd.
Mentone, CA 92359
909/794-1123

**San Jacinto Ranger District**
P.O. Box 518
Idyllwild, CA 92549
909/659-2117

**Southland Ski Server**
http://www.skisocal.org
Provides a comprehensive list of alpine, Nordic ski, and snowboard areas in Southern California, as well as ski information.

**Southern California Mountain Bike.Com**
http://www.socalmtb.com
This page is a great resource for all sorts of mountain bike info. There are hundreds of mountain bike shops grouped by county and listed alphabetically, too.

---

Dr. Tel. 909/657-0676. Picnicking, regional Indian museum, water slide.

Lake Perris is powerboat-yahoo central, but I've listed it here because of Big Rock, a year-round rock climbing spot that's located right next to the lake. There's also the rarely traveled hike up to Terri Peak from the parking area. I suggested visiting this place in the off-season and after a good rain, so the smog's not a problem.

# Angeles National Forest ◆ What to Do & Where to Do It

## BIRD WATCHING

Just outside the western edge of the Angeles National Forest near the town of South El Monte, you'll find the **Whittier Narrows Nature Center** (tel. 818/575-5523). Situated along the bank of the San Gabriel River, this urban sanctuary is home to nearly 275 species of birds, from orange-crowned warblers to Cooper's hawks to ospreys. Birds can be viewed along the nature trail or from the observation blind. Just inside the western edge of the forest, a few miles from Pasadena, lies the **Eaton Canyon Natural Area** (tel. 818/398-5420). This riparian canyon offers excellent birding in April and May, with over 150 species. Eaton Canyon is also where you pick up the trail to Henninger Flat and Mount Wilson (see "Hiking" below.) Twenty-seven miles up the Angeles Crest Highway, the **Chilao Visitor Center** (tel. 818/796-5541) also offers excellent year-round birding. This pine forest is home to over 100 species of birds, and viewing (especially of the mountain quail) is easy from the observation deck.

## DOWNHILL SKIING & SNOWBOARDING

### Snowcrest at Kratka Ridge

Access: 36 miles northeast of I-210 in La Cañada on the Angeles Crest Hwy. Tel. 626/440-9749. Snow report: 626/583-9477. Web site: www.aminews.com/snowcrest. 850 vertical feet, 2 lifts, snowboard terrain park. Adult lift ticket $25, child $10 or free with paying adult.

This small resort in L.A.'s backyard offers great mid-week deals ($15 all day) as well as low-priced packaged deals for both beginning skiers and snowboarders. They also host amateur snowboarding contests.

### Mount Waterman

Access: 34 miles northeast of I-210 in La Cañada on the Angeles Crest Hwy. Tel. 818/440-1041. Ski Report: 818/790-2002. Web site: www.aminews.com/waterman. 1030 vertical feet, 3 lifts, snowboard terrain park. Adult lift ticket $25, child $10.

Only 55 minutes from downtown Los Angeles, Mount Waterman is the big city's closest place to ski. Larger and steeper than Snowcrest (60% of their terrain is considered advanced), this resort attracts shredders. That said, they do have a recently expanded beginner area, and the warming hut located at the top of Chair One is cozy.

### Mountain High

Access: On the Angeles Crest Hwy., 3 miles west of Wrightwood. Tel. 760/249-5808. Web site: www.mthigh.com. 1600 vertical feet, 11 lifts (including 1 express quad). Night skiing hours. Adult lift ticket $39. Kids 10 and under ski free.

One good thing about Mountain High is that it's just 15 minutes off I-15, and there's not a lot of winding mountain driving involved to get there. It's also one of the largest ski resorts in the southland, with a fairly even mix of beginner, intermediate, and advanced runs. Another good thing is that the resort stays open until 10pm daily, and you can ski under the stars.

## Ski Sunrise

Access: 4 miles west of Wrightwood on Table Mountain Rd. Follow the Angeles Crest Hwy. to Big Pines and head north on Table Mountain Rd. Tel. 760/249-6150. Web site: www.skisunrise.com. 816 vertical feet; 3 tows, 1 quad. Adult lift ticket $30, child $20.

Billing itself as the "friendly little fun place just past the big crowded place," Ski Sunrise is a perfect place for families with small kids or for adults who've never skied before and feel a bit intimidated. The beginner area is set apart from the more advanced runs, so you won't have big shots whooshing past you as you try to figure out how to snowplow, and the instructors are very, very patient.

## Mount Baldy

Access: I-10 east to Mountain Ave. Head north and follow the signs. Tel. 909/982-0800. Ski, road, and weather report: 909/981-3344. Web site: www. mtbaldy. com. 2,100 vertical feet, 4 lifts. Adult lift ticket $40, child $25. Year-round scenic chair rides $10.

The Mount Baldy Ski Lifts opened in 1952 and have attracted skiers and sightseers ever since. Mount Baldy Peak (a.k.a. Mount San Antonio) is, at 10,064 feet, the highest, craggiest peak in the Angeles National Forest. Skiing here is not for the timid. There are beginner and intermediate runs, but the majority fall into the black and double-black diamond category with names like Nightmare and Psychout. Chair 4 takes you to Baldy's back side, which is hairy, indeed. If you don't ski or snowboard,

you can still enjoy the spectacular panoramic views of the ocean and desert by taking the scenic chair ride all the way to the top any time of year.

### FISHING

Not too long ago the Angeles was a true fisherman's paradise. The forks of the San Gabriel River flowed year-round and supported tremendous numbers of wild trout. Other creeks, like Big Tujunga, Arroyo Seco, and Bouquet also supported lots of fish. A thirsty city grew up next door, however, and sucked up much of that water. Consequently, the fishing is now more seasonal and depends heavily on overflow from upstream water district reservoirs.

**Big Tujunga** is still one of the best spots around, though you must catch it in the spring while the water is still up. From opening day until about June, Big Tujunga is stocked with rainbow trout. Come summer the creek goes dry, and we all know what happens to fish out of water.

The epicenter of Angeles National Forest fishing, however, is the **San Gabriel River.** Considering that it's fronted by busy Highway 39 for much of its length, this can hardly be a surprise. The road follows the East Fork, where you can park your car and be casting before the dust settles on your windshield. If you had something more secluded in mind, drive a little farther to the North Fork, or stop at the mouth of the West Fork near Rincon Guard Station and hike in to the Wild Trout Section. A paved, gated road offers good access to this steep canyon, but the gate keeps vehicle-addicted people at bay. You'll be surprised what a difference that makes. Between the confluence and the second bridge upstream is put and take fishing for stocked rainbows. Above the second bridge is the wild trout section, which reaches the next 4.5 miles to Cogswell Reservoir. This stretch is strictly catch and release.

## Sturtevant Falls

3 miles round-trip. Easy. Best season: December–July. Access: From the I-210 in Pasadena, head east toward Arcadia. Exit at Santa Anita Ave. and head north 6 miles to the end of the road at Chantry Flat. The trail starts across the road from the parking area.

In the Angeles National Forest, there are quite a few waterfalls—Cooper Canyon Falls, Devil's Canyon Falls, Millard Canyon Falls (see below), Eaton Canyon Falls—the list goes on and on. Sturtevant Falls in Big Santa Anita Canyon is easily accessible, perhaps the most stunning and undoubtedly the most popular. From the parking lot, head down the paved Gabrieliño Trail for about a half mile. At the bottom of the canyon, veer right on the wide dirt path toward Sturtevant Falls, named after William Sturtevant, who bushwhacked many of trails in this mountain range. Along the way you'll pass what's left of Roberts Camp, a popular weekend resort from 1912 to 1936. Continue straight toward the falls at the next junction, which suddenly appears as you round a curve, with water spilling 60 feet down into a clear pool. It's hard to believe such a wild place exists just a few miles off the Pasadena Freeway.

## Millard Falls & Millard Canyon to Dawn Mine

1 mile round-trip. Best season: December–June. To the falls: easy. To Dawn Mine: moderate, with stream crossings and boulder hopping. 5.5 miles round-trip. Access: I-210 in Pasadena, exit at Lake Ave. Head north 4 miles where the road veers left and becomes Loma Alta Dr. At Chaney Trail, turn right and go 1 mile to the junction at Sunset Ridge. If you're going to the falls, stay left here and follow the signs down to Millard Campground. Park in the lot and walk along the fire road that leads into the campground. If you're going to Dawn Mine, stay right at the junction and park outside the gate at Sunset Ridge Fire Rd.

If you want to get away from it all but don't have the time or energy to go too far, lush Millard Canyon Falls is a good bet. One of the more secluded spots in the front range of the San Gabriels, this canyon is shaded by oak and sycamore, and city views are conveniently blocked by Sunset Ridge. The hike to the falls is easy if wet—be sure to wear shoes you don't mind getting wet—since you'll probably be picking your way up the creekbed rather than staying on the trail. From the Millard Campground, follow the trail to your right, passing a few cabins as you head upstream to the falls.

The hike to Dawn Mine, where gold was extracted from 1895 to the 1950s, is a bit more intense. From the Sunset Ridge parking area, head up the fire road to the marked Sunset Ridge Trail, which takes you down into Millard Canyon and rewards you with a great view of the falls. Near the canyon bottom, veer left on the trail that takes you past a cabin and down to the canyon floor. (This junction is easy to miss on the way back, so make a good mental note of it.) You'll hike along the canyon floor, following what's left of an old trail, crossing streams and boulder hopping, passing the rusted remains of old mining tools. As you hike up-canyon, things start to veer north. From this turn, it's about a mile to the closed Dawn Mine. Return the way you came.

## Switzer's Camp/Switzer Falls/Oakwilde

2–9 miles. Easy–moderate. Access: From I-210 in La Cañada/Flintridge, head north on the Angeles Crest Hwy. for 11 miles to the turnoff for Switzer's Picnic Area and descend to the parking lot.

The Arroyo Seco Canyon is one of the most beautiful and most famous of all the canyons in the San Gabriels. Rugged and filled with live oak, alder, and spruce, it's cut by a stream that pours over granite boulders and collects in deep pools. At the turn of the century, Perry "Commodore" Switzer (so nicknamed for his gonzo mountaineering ability) built one of the first resorts in the San Gabriel Mountains in Arroyo Seco Canyon and named it Switzerland. From the parking lot, it's an easy 1 mile to Switzer Trail Camp, where Switzerland once stood, perched on top of 50-foot Switzer Falls. It's another mile for a view of the falls from below. Cross the stream and follow the trail on the west slope. At the first signed junction, stay left and hike down into the gorge of the Arroyo Seco. At the creek, head upstream about 0.25 miles to the falls. If you're headed to Oakwilde Trail Camp (an excellent place for an overnight), stay right at the signed junction, following the Gabrielino Trail, high above the canyon. The last mile to Oakwilde Trail Camp follows the creekbed, and if you're here in the spring, the wildflowers are something. Oakwilde Resort, yet another retreat built during the Great Hiking Era, was demolished in the flood of 1938. Today you can still see some of the ruins at the trail camp, as you rest and get ready to hike back the way you came.

## Mount Lowe Railway Tour

11 miles round-trip. Moderately easy. Access: I-210 in Pasadena, exit Lake Ave. Head north 4 miles where the road veers left and becomes Loma Alta Dr. At Chaney Trail, turn right and proceed 1 mile to the junction at Sunset Ridge. Go right to the Sunset Ridge parking area. Trail begins at the locked gate.

This hike traces the grade of the old Mount Lowe Railway that brought visitors from the big city by trolley to Echo Mountain and the Mount Lowe Tavern from the turn of the century to the 1930s. Passengers from Pasadena took a trolley up Rubio Canyon, then switched to the hair-raisingly steep incline railway that carted them up 3,000 feet to the Echo Mountain Resort, also known as White City. From here, the brave could continue to the Mount Lowe Tavern at the end of the line. Initially, the end of the line was planned for Inspiration Point, but financial trouble intervened and was followed by a devastating fire that shut things down for good in 1936.

From the gate at the Sunset Ridge parking lot, start walking on the paved fire road. Now, you can either take the paved road all the way to Echo Mountain Trail, or take this more scenic detour: 0.25 mile up the paved road, take the Sunset Ridge Trail, which appears on your left, into Millard Canyon. Near the canyon bottom, the trail divides. Stay right and climb back up Sunset Ridge Fire Road, following it along to the intersection with Echo Mountain. Veer right on Echo Mountain Trail. Soon you'll see the ruins of White City, named so because the white buildings of the mountain getaway were lit at night by the resort's searchlight. Back on the Sunset Ridge Fire Road, stay right. The road turns to dirt near the sign that says CAPE OF GOOD HOPE, as you follow the old grade, passing Granite Gate, Horseshoe Curve, and the remains of the Circular Bridge, on your way to the site of Mount Lowe Tavern. Nothing much is left of the old joint, but there are water and rest rooms. From here, it's a half-mile to Inspiration Point, where vintage sighting tubes are still aimed at local points of interest down below. Return the way you came.

## Mount Wilson Toll Road

6 miles round-trip from Altadena to Henninger Flats. Moderate. (Strenuous if you hike the 18 miles round-trip from Altadena to the summit.) Access: I-210 in Pasadena, exit Lake Ave. Head north to Altadena Dr. and turn right, then left on Pinecrest Dr. The trailhead is located in the 2200 block of Pinecrest.

It is the Mount Wilson Toll Road that's often credited with ushering in the Great Hiking Era, which lasted from 1891 to 1938. It was also via this road that the first telescope was placed at the Mount Wilson Observatory. But with the advent of the automobile and the Angeles Crest Highway, the road was abandoned. The toll road connects with the Mount Wilson Trail, the very first trail to the summit blazed by Benjamin Wilson. And while the hike to the summit is well worth the overnight trip, a shorter trip to Henninger Flats ain't so bad.

From the gate on Pinecrest Drive, hike down the fire road to Eaton Canyon and then up the chaparral-covered slopes. When you reach the flats, you'll be greeted not only by water, shade, and two campgrounds, but by an experimental tree nursery founded over a century ago. Today the nursery is run by the Los Angeles County foresters, and its primary activity is sending seedlings to fire- and flood-damaged areas all over Southern California.

## Fish Canyon Falls

9 miles round-trip. Moderately strenuous. Access: I-210 in Duarte, exit Irwindale Ave. Head north on Irwindale to Huntington Dr. and make a left. Turn right on Encanto Pkwy. and continue to the trailhead.

For years this badly eroded trail was inaccessible because of the rock quarry operations at the foot of the canyon. But in 1998, the trail got a face-lift and was reopened. (Unfortunately, the nearby gun club is also open and the noisy blasts can harshen your wilderness experience.) From the Encanto Parkway the trail, which is at times very steep and very narrow, winds upcanyon for about 4.5 miles. But if you can do it, the waterfall at the end is quite spectacular, plunging about 80 feet total over several granite plateaus. Return the way you came.

## West Fork of the San Gabriel River

13 miles round-trip. Moderate. Access: From I-10 or I-210, exit Azusa Ave. (Hwy. 39) and head north. Azusa eventually becomes San Gabriel Canyon Rd. as you pass Morris and San Gabriel Reservoirs. After you pass the Rincon Ranger Station, park near the West Fork National Scenic Trail trailhead.

If you're looking for trout in the backcountry, this one's for you. The paved road to Cogswell Reservoir is closed to private vehicles, but the road is in great shape and you can cut down on the travel time by biking in to your destination, Glenn Camp. The first mile or so is often crowded, but once you pass the Bear Creek junction, things start to quiet down. Along this route, you'll pass the ruins of several old fishing camps and hear the psychic splash of all the big ones that got away. Return the way you came. *Note:* Be sure to check with the forest service to see if any sections of the West Fork are currently considered wild trout preserves.

## East Fork Trail

12 miles round-trip. Strenuous. Access: From I-10 or I-210, exit Azusa Ave. (Hwy.

39) and head north. Azusa eventually becomes San Gabriel Canyon Rd. as you pass Morris and San Gabriel reservoirs. Turn right on East Fork Rd. and drive 8 miles to the East Fork Ranger Station. Follow the service road to Heaton Flat. Parking and Wilderness permits required.

This (rather wet) hike takes you along a section of the east fork of the San Gabriel River, which cuts through the Sheep Mountain Wilderness, to The Narrows, the steepest river gorge in Southern California. From the Heaton Flats Campground, follow the trail down the canyon floor and get ready to make lots of wet river crossings. As you head north, you'll hike up the remains of East Fork Road and eventually reach the bizarre Bridge to Nowhere. In the 1930s, developers started building a highway that would connect the San Gabriel Valley with Wrightwood, but the flood of 1938 put the kibosh on their plans. The bridge is still standing, even though the road on either side has vanished. Just on the other side of the bridge lies The Narrows, with a rough trail leading about a mile or so through the gorge to Iron Fork, your turnaround point.

## Mount Baldy Summit

7 miles round-trip (13 miles if you hike up to Baldy Notch). Strenuous. Access: From I-10, exit Mountain Ave. and head north 12 miles to the road's end just past Manker Campground. Park in the ski area lot. Tel. 909/982-0800.

Its official name is Mount San Antonio, but everyone just calls it Mount Baldy, which makes much more sense when you look up at its big, bare summit. At 10,064 feet, Mount Baldy is the highest peak in the San Gabriels. And now you are going to hike to the top. But first, you must get to Baldy Notch. To do this

you can either buy a chairlift ticket from the Mount Baldy Ski Resort (open weekends and holidays year-round) or walk up the fire road, which adds 3 miles and 1,300 feet in elevation each way. Once at Baldy Notch, follow the wide gravel path up to another chairlift. From here the trail leads you onto a steep ridge called the Devil's Backbone and, yes, things start to get a bit hellish as you switchback your way up the steep summit. It's quite cold and windy at the top, and the expansive views are very cool, too. Return the way you came.

## MOUNTAIN BIKING

### Saugus District, Burnt Peak

12 miles out and back. Moderately difficult. Access: From L.A., head north on I-5 to the Hwy. 138/Quail Lake/Lancaster exit. Follow Hwy. 138 east about 4 miles. Here, 138 branches off to the left and you continue straight on what's now called Pine Canyon Road/N2. Continue straight toward Lake Hughes and Elizabeth Lake. When you see the sign that says UPPER SHAKE 3 MILES, the beginning of FS 7N23 will be on your right. Park in the turnout.

This ride uphill to Burnt Peak is a workout for strong cyclists. From the intersection of Pine Canyon Road and FS 7N23, start pedaling uphill on 7N23 past the sign to Upper Shake Campground. Follow the road for 2 miles and at the junction, go right on 7N23A and continue past the sign that says BURNT PEAK 3 MILES. This section is tortuously steep but it levels out a bit after a mile. Things go up and down in moderation for a while, and then the final ascent to the peak is a killer. When you reach the summit at 5,788 feet, you'll have some wonderful views of the Tehachapi Mountains and Antelope Valley. Return the way you came.

## Grassy Mountain

13-mile loop. Moderate. Access: From L.A., head north on I-5 to the exit for Six Flags/ Magic Mountain. Head east on Magic Mountain Rd. about 2.5 miles and turn left on Bouquet Canyon Rd. Go north about 18 miles and turn left on Spunky Canyon Rd. At the intersection with San Francisquito Rd., go right and follow it along to the top of the hill where a sign says GRASS MOUNTAIN, SOUTH PORTAL, TULE RIDGE. Park along San Francisquito Rd. near the junction with FS 6N04.

This is a dirt/paved road ride to the peak of Grassy Mountain with a loop through South Portal Canyon. The summit of Grassy Mountain (4,605 ft.) offers great views stretching from the nearby Lake Hughes and Lake Elizabeth, to the Tehachapi Mountains and Antelope Valley. From the intersection of San Francisquito Road and FS 6N04, start pedaling west on 6N04 past the sign to Grass Mountain. Stay straight, go through a gate; at 1.5 miles, take the left, unmarked fork that goes to the summit of Grass Mountain. It's a moderately steep climb to the top, but nothing un-manageable. From here, head back downhill, and at the junction, go left on the unmarked FS 6N04. You'll go through another gate. Stay left at the several upcoming junctions, and soon the downhill road through South Portal Canyon (FS 7N02) will be obvious. Stay on the main fire road as you loop through the canyon. At the San Francisquito Road, go left and pedal along this paved road past the Green Valley Fire Station and back to your car.

## Liebre Mountain

14 miles out and back. Moderately diffi-cult. Access: I-5 to the Hwy. 138/Quail Lake/Lancaster exit. Follow Hwy. 138 east

about 4 miles. Here, 138 branches off to the left and you continue straight on what's now called Pine Canyon Rd./N2. At Old Ridge Route Rd., turn right. Go through the tiny town of Sandberg, and FS 7N23 will be on your left. It's marked by a sign indicat-ing mileage to Castaic, Bear, and Sawmill campgrounds. Park in the turnout.

The ride up Liebre Mountain is a great workout and provides some expansive views to the north, south, and east. From the intersection of Old Ridge Route Road and FS 7N23 (just south of Sandberg; it's marked by a sign indicat-ing mileage to Castaic, Bear, and Saw-mill campgrounds) pedal east on 7N23. Stay left and uphill at the very first fork. (There are lots of side roads but don't detour. From here on out, the main road is obvious; just stay on it.) Don't be dis-couraged by the first mile: It's the steep-est mile of the entire trip. After this, things actually get easy. And, well, then back to moderately difficult on the final rocky ascent to the top. When you've rested, it's a great descent back to your car.

## Sandberg to Reservoir Summit

17 miles out and back. Moderate. Access: I-5 to the Hwy. 138/Quail Lake/Lancaster exit. Follow Hwy. 138 east about 4 miles. Here, 138 branches off to the left and you continue straight on what's now called Pine Canyon Rd./N2. At Old Ridge Route Rd., turn right and head toward Sandberg.

Even though it's paved (though not well-maintained), the Old Ridge Route Road is a favorite with mountain bikers. This section is generally quite remote, and you'll pass lots of urban ruins and get some terrific views. Also known as the Grapevine, this section of road through the Angeles National Forest was once the main auto artery in these parts before Highway 99 was built. Hotels, inns, and other rest stops sprang up along the Ridge Route, but the route soon proved to be too treacherous for traffic. Steep grades, narrow lanes, and sharp curves sent quite a few drivers speeding off the cliffs to their death. And so the road was abandoned.

As you pedal on the broken asphalt from Sandberg to the Reservoir Summit, the crumbling foundations are mostly what's left of places like The Sandberg Hotel and Motor Inn and the Halfway Inn. The road takes you downhill first, then up to the summit. From here, you can see Liebre, Red Rock, and Warm Springs mountains. Return the way you came.

## Pelona Ridge

9.5 miles out and back. Moderate. Access: I-5 to the exit for Six Flags/Magic Mountain. Head east on Magic Mountain Rd. about 2.5 miles and turn left on Bouquet Canyon Rd. Go north about 17 miles to the Bouquet Reservoir. Watch for FS 6N08 on your right. (If you reach Spunky Canyon Rd., you've gone too far.) Turn right on 6N08 and at the intersection, park off-road. Continue along 6N08 on your bike.

The best part of this ride is the fun, fast downhill. But the Sierra Pelona ridge offers views of the Sierra Pelona Valley, Soledad Canyon, and Magic Mountain, too. From the parking area near the intersection of Bouquet Canyon Road and FS 6N08, just east of the Bouquet Reservoir, start pedaling south on 6N08, downhill at first and then uphill as the trail cuts hard to the right. Stay straight at the Artesian Spring Trail when it appears first on your left and then on your right. Two miles after the spring, go left at the junction. From here, you're almost at the crest. Return the way you came. Whee!

## Upper Shake Campground

6 miles out and back. Easy. Access: I-5 to the Hwy. 138/Quail Lake/Lancaster exit. Follow Hwy. 138 east about 4 miles. Here, 138 branches off to the left and you continue straight on what's now called Pine Canyon Rd./N2. Continue straight toward Lake Hughes and Elizabeth Lake. When you see the sign that says UPPER SHAKE 3 MILES, the beginning of FS 7N23 will be on your right. Park in the turnout and begin your ride.

This uphill ride to Upper Shake gives beginners a great chance to hone their skills in a beautiful wilderness setting. From the intersection of Pine Canyon Road and FS 7N23, start pedaling uphill on 7N23 past the sign to Upper Shake. Follow along for 2 miles, and at the junction, go left on 7N23B and descend to the campground. It's shaded and cool in the summer, making it a great spot to rest. When you're done, return the way you came.

## San Gabriel Mountains, Arroyo Seco

7.5 miles. Moderately easy. Access: Take I-210 east. Exit Arroyo Blvd. and turn left on Windsor Ave. There's a parking lot on the left, just across from the Jet Propulsion Lab. Park here and begin pedaling north on Windsor.

This relatively easy and exceptionally beautiful ride takes you through the Lower Arroyo Seco Canyon, on one of the most popular roads in the San Gabriels. In the late 19th century, Perry "Commodore" Switzer built one of the first resorts in the San Gabriel Mountains in Arroyo Seco Canyon and named it Switzerland. It remained a popular getaway, along with other resorts that soon dotted the canyon, until the flood of 1938 destroyed most of the paved roads and buildings in its path.

From the intersection of Windsor and Ventura avenues in West Altadena, pedal north up Windsor to a sharp curve where the road splits—you want the middle road that goes around a gate, following a sign that tells you you're in the Gabrieliño National Recreation Area. Soon you'll cross the first of 10 bridges that pass over the lovely Arroyo Seco Creek. Near the third wooden bridge there's a drinking fountain and a picnic area. It was once the site of Teddy's Outpost, a roadside rest stop popular in the 1920s. Pedal past Gould Mesa Campground (the terrain starts to get a bit tricky here) and the Nino Picnic Area, crossing more bridges and splashing through some streams. The Paul Little Picnic Area is your turnaround point. If you want more of a challenge, try this: When you reach the Paul Little Picnic Area, take the detour on your left, through Paul Little to a nice waterfall coming from the Brown Canyon debris dam. It's a great place for a picnic or rest along the way.

Back on the main trail, you'll have to push your bike up the steep, sandy section along the dam. Then you drop down into some great single track, which takes you all the way to Oakwilde. In 1911, another resort was built here, which also lasted until the flood of 1938. Return the way you came.

## Inspiration Point

13.7 miles. Difficult. Access: Take I-210 east through Pasadena. Exit at Lincoln Ave. and head north through Altadena. Turn right on Loma Alta Dr. and left (north) on Chaney Trail. Stay left at the Y with Alzada Dr. and go 1 mile to another intersection marked Brown Mountain Rd. Stay right and park in the pullout on the right near the locked gate.

This route traces the grade of the Mount Lowe Railway, which brought visitors from Los Angeles by trolley almost to Inspiration Point from the turn of the century to the 1930s. In the 1890s, engineer David Macpherson and investor "Professor" Thaddeus Lowe teamed up to build the Mount Lowe Railway to bring visitors from Los Angeles to Inspiration Point in the San Gabriels. Although they never completed the line to Inspiration Point—financial trouble stopped them—this area once boasted four hotels and was known as White City. All that's left today are the ruins, stretches of the original track, and of course, the incredible mountains.

At the intersection of Brown Mountain Road and Chaney Trail, pass around the gate and start climbing on the FS 2N50. It's paved, but still a very steep climb. Stay right at the fork to Echo Mountain Trail, where you can see Echo Mountain to your right, and 2N50 turns to dirt. You'll pass a rock formation known as the Cape of Good Hope and near it is a photo of a section of track from the original Mount Lowe Railway. Next, you'll pass the site of Dawn Mine (an old gold mine), a treacherous bit of road called Devil's Slide, and the remains of the Circular Bridge built to help the trolleys up the steep incline. At 5 miles, you'll pass the Mount Lowe Campground at Crystal Springs. This was once the site of Ye Alpine Tavern, one of Lowe's hotels, and it's where the railway actually ended. Turn right at the sign for Inspiration Point. At the point are some vintage sighting tubes aimed at local points of interest down below. (Don't be surprised if you can't see Catalina Island through the smog; most people couldn't see it during the railway's heyday either.) Continue on 1 mile to Panorama Point at the water tank. Return the way you came. From the Circular Bridge, the downhill is excellent.

## Echo Mountain

7 miles. Moderate. Access: Take I-210 east through Pasadena. Exit at Lincoln Ave. and head north through Altadena. Turn right on Loma Alta Dr. and left (north) on Chaney Trail. Stay left at the Y with Alzada Dr. and go 1 mile to another intersection marked Brown Mountain Rd. Stay right and park in the pullout on the right near the locked gate.

This paved/dirt road takes you to Echo Mountain and White City, an area that once boasted two hotels, a zoo, a museum, and an observatory. At the intersection of Brown Mountain Road and Chaney Trail, pass around the gate and start climbing on the FS 2N50. It's paved but still a very steep climb. Go right at the fork to Echo Mountain Trail, where you'll see Echo Mountain below you to your right. Now the trail turns to dirt and it brings you down to the ruins of White City. Return the way you came. (On the way back, you'll see the Sam Merrill Trail forking off to your right. If you're feeling rugged, you can climb this rough single track to Inspiration Point.)

## Rincon Road/Shortcut Canyon

24 miles. Moderately difficult. Access: About 14 miles northeast of La Cañada/Flintridge on the Angeles Crest Hwy. Park at the Red Box Station parking lot on the south side of the highway.

This is a pretty intense dirt/paved road ride along the West Fork of the San Gabriel River, with an unrelenting ascent up Shortcut Canyon and a return along the paved, two-lane Angeles Crest Highway. Beginning at the Red Box Station parking lot, start pedaling along Rincon Road. At 1 mile, turn left, following the signs to Valley Forge and West Fork campgrounds. If you're wondering what those ruins are, they're the remains of the 1920s Valley Forge Lodge, advertised as "The Gateway to the Wild" until it was destroyed in the flood of 1938. The road continues to drop as you approach the West Fork Campground. Continue straight, past the water tank and the trail to Newcomb Saddle on your right. Turn left on Shortcut Fire Road. It's a fast drop on Shortcut Fire Road—loose, rocky, not the best conditions—that gets you started on a 6-mile-plus climb up Shortcut Canyon to the Angeles Crest Highway. Make a left at the highway. There's little shoulder and some traffic. The final left turn back to Red Box Station is dangerous: It's on a blind curve. You might want to walk your bike across carefully.

## West Red Box Loop

5 miles. Moderately easy. Access: About 12 miles northeast of La Cañada/Flintridge on the Angeles Crest Hwy. Watch for the sign that says 4,000 FEET. Park off-road. You begin riding on the Gabrielino Trail, which is on the right side of the road just before the sign.

This loop takes you along a shady section of the Gabrieliño Trail to Red Box Station, with a fun downhill return along the paved, two-lane Angeles Crest Highway. Beginning at the dirt road on the right (south) side of the Angeles Crest Highway (about 12 miles from La Cañada), pedal along the easy grade toward Red Box Station. Along the way, you'll pass through oak groves and have some good views of Strawberry and Josephine peaks. Stay left where the old trail is closed, go around the chain-link fence, and pedal to Red Box Station, where you can get a drink of water. Return on the Angeles Crest Highway. It's a fun downhill but be cautious of traffic.

## West Fork-Rincon Roads

30-mile loop. Easy. Access: Take I-210 east and exit at Azusa Ave./Hwy. 39. Follow Hwy. 39 north through the town of Azusa and into the San Gabriel Recreation Area, where the road becomes San Gabriel Canyon Rd. West Fork Rd. begins near mile marker 27. There's a parking lot on your left near the trailhead.

This excellent long ride starts out easy on the paved West Fork Road through the San Gabriel Canyon Recreation Area and gets more challenging on the return along Rincon Road. It ends with a great 8-mile descent. Beginning at the intersection of West Fork Road and San Gabriel Canyon Road, pedal west along West Fork. West Fork is closed to traffic and quite pleasant. You'll cross the bridge over Bear Creek and parallel the west fork of the San Gabriel River. If you're here in the spring, the canyon walls will be lined with wildflowers and you'll pass several small waterfalls. At Glenn Trail Camp, the pace picks up as the road rises sharply and the pavement ends. Follow West Fork past Cogswell Dam and Cogswell Reservoir. At 13.2 miles, turn left at the gate and onto Red Box Rincon Road, which you'll follow for 16 miles, back to San Gabriel Canyon Road. Go left here and head back to your car.
    *Note:* There are a lot of side roads leading off the main trail once you pass Glenn Trail Camp, so stay aware.

## West Fork Road

3 miles out and back. Easy. Access: Take I-210 east and exit at Azusa Ave./Hwy. 39. Follow Hwy. 39 north through the town of Azusa and into the San Gabriel Recreation Area, where the road becomes San Gabriel Canyon Rd. West Fork Rd. begins near mile marker 27. There's a parking lot on your left near the trailhead.

This is a beautiful and easy ride on West Fork Road through the San Gabriel Canyon Recreation Area. In the spring, you'll be graced with tons of wildflowers and several waterfalls as you pedal along this closed-to-traffic paved road. Beginning at the intersection of West Fork Road and San Gabriel Canyon Road, pedal west along West Fork. You'll cross the bridge over Bear Creek and parallel the west fork of the San Gabriel River. At Glenn Trail Camp, you can rest in the shade. Return the way you came.

### ROAD BIKING

## Mount Baldy Loop

42 miles. Moderately difficult. Access: From the L.A. suburb of Glendora ( just east of Pasadena along the 210 freeway), drive to the corner of Sierra Madre Ave. and Glendora Mountain Rd. and park your car. The ride begins on Glendora Mountain Rd.

From the intersection of Sierra Madre Avenue and Glendora Mountain Road in the L.A. suburb of Glendora, start pedaling up Glendora Mountain Road. Pass the ranger station and continue on up for, oh, about 22 miles. Near the summit you'll find Baldy Village, with its small restaurant and store. Mount Baldy Road takes you all the way down into the town of Claremont. From here, the minutiae are as follows: Baseline to Foothill Boulevard to Valley Center Road, jog right, and then go straight on Sierra Madre and back to your car.

### ROCK CLIMBING

There's only one place to rock climb in the Angeles National Forest and it's **Williamson Rock.** (Devil's Punchbowl is also in the Angeles, but it's reached from near Palmdale, so I've included it with the Mojave Desert in chapter 6.) There are over 100 routes at Williamson, ranging from easy to difficult, with an average of 70 feet in length. Most are located on the popular and generally crowded London Wall. To get to Williamson Rock, take the Angeles Crest Highway approximately 38 miles up the mountain. Two miles after you pass the Snowcrest at Kratka Ridge Ski Resort, watch for a parking area on the side of the road. From here, follow the short, steep trail that leads down into the streambed and to the base of the rock.

## WALKS & NATURAL ATTRACTIONS

### Placerita Canyon Trails

0.5–5.5 miles. Easy. Access: The Nature Center in Placerita Canyon State Park.

Placerita Canyon offers several easy hikes for the whole family. Starting at the Nature Center (which is a fun stop all in itself), pick up the Heritage Trail, a short half-miler that runs from the historic Walker Cabin to the Oak of the Golden Dream, where gold was first discovered in California in 1842. Also from this starting point, you can access the short Hillside Nature Trail (0.3 miles), or, if you're feeling more adventurous, walk over to Placerita Creek Falls (5.5 miles round-trip). Follow the Canyon Trail, which crosses Placerita Creek, to Walker Ranch. Walk all the way through the Walker Ranch picnic area and watch for the sign that says WATERFALL TRAIL. The falls drop 25 feet in a narrow stream, and the best time to visit is December through May. If you'd like to see the falls but don't feel like hiking 5 miles, you can simply drive to the Walker Ranch gate, and from there, the waterfall is only 2.4 miles round-trip.

One spectacular natural attraction not to be missed is the Vasquez Rocks in **Vasquez Rocks County Park.** As I mentioned in "Parks & Other Hot Spots," above, the giant rock formations here look at once prehistoric, other-worldly, and decidedly Western—which is why they've been used as a location for countless TV shows and movies from *Star Trek* to *Bonanza* to *The Flintstones*. They were also the secret hideout of 1870s bandito Tiburcio Vasquez, who made a name for himself throughout this region robbing gringo stagecoaches, stealing gringo cattle, and otherwise making life hard for gringos in the backcountry. There are no marked trails per se, but from the main picnic area you can wander around for several miles and be amazed.

### Mount Wilson Observatory

Access: Follow the Angeles Crest Hwy. out of La Cañada/Flintridge 14 miles to Red Box Rd. Turn right, and go another 5 miles to the observatory gate. Parking is available in the large main lot. Hours: weekends 10am–4pm, weather permitting. Web site: www.mtwilson.edu.

In 1864, Benjamin Wilson built a trail leading to the top of a high peak in the San Gabriel Mountains to do some logging. (Down below, a small settlement known as the Indiana Colony was becoming the city of Pasadena.) But a visionary astronomer named George Hale saw the mountaintop as more than a money-making forest or a beautiful view, and in 1904 the first telescope was hauled up the mountain and the Mount Wilson Observatory was officially founded. For many years the Mount Wilson Observatory housed the world's largest solar telescope, the 100-inch Hooker reflector, an instrument that revolutionized our scientific concepts about the stars. Today, the actual telescopes aren't open to the public but the Mount Wilson Observatory Association (MWOA) does host "star parties" on-site, where public viewing is done through telescopes brought to the mountain by dedicated amateurs.

### WILDLIFE VIEWING

Twenty-seven miles up the Angeles Crest Highway from La Cañada, the **Chilao Visitor Center** (tel. 818/796-5541) offers excellent year-round birding. This pine forest is home to over 100 species of birds, and viewing (especially of the mountain quail) is easy from the observation deck. In the dry season (May to September) many animals drink from the center's watering pan, and chances are you'll see mule deer, chipmunks, lizards, and even a coyote or two. Farther along Highway 2, close to the town of Wrightwood, you'll find the **Jarvi Bighorn Sheep Vista** (tel. 818/790-1151). The expansive views of San Gabriel Canyon are terrific, but it takes patience to spot the rare, elusive bighorns. Although they may only be 100 yards from the highway pullout, they blend in well with the scenery. Binoculars are a must.

# San Bernardino National Forest ◆ What to Do & Where to Do It

### BIRD WATCHING

Over 130 bird species, as well as bears, bobcats, and other mammals, inhabit the shores of **Silverwood Lake State Recreation Area** (tel. 760/389-2303). Ospreys and Canada geese winter here, and bald eagles can often be seen on the seasonal guided boat tours offered by the park. Great blue herons roost in South Miller Canyon, with juncos, mountain chickadees, and Steller's jays higher up in the pines.

### CROSS-COUNTRY SKIING

## Rim Nordic

Access: 5 miles east of Running Springs on Hwy. 18, across from Snow Valley. Tel. 909/867-2600. 20 km of trails. Trail Pass: Adult $8, children 10 and under free. Rentals (includes skis, poles, and boots) adult $13, child $10.

Located across the street from Snow Valley, Rim Nordic added several new trails in '98. They offer both skiing and telemark lessons, and they also rent snowshoes. In warmer months the trails turn into 25 miles of single track—the favorite terrain of mountain bikers. Package deals with local hotels are available, too.

### DOWNHILL SKIING & SNOWBOARDING

## Bear Mountain Resort

Access: I-10 to Hwy. 38 or Hwy. 30/330 to Hwy. 18 or Hwy. 18 through Lucerne Valley. 43101 Goldmine Dr., Big Bear Lake. Tel. 909/585-2519. SnowPhone: 800/BEAR-MTN. Web site: www.bearmtn.com. 1665 vertical feet, 12 lifts (including 1 high-speed quad), and snowboard terrain park. Adult lift ticket $42, young adult $32, child $10.

Of the two ski resorts in Big Bear Lake, Bear Mountain is the one with the snowboard park called The Zone. From the spacious outdoor deck at the base of the mountain, you can watch boarders do the most amazing aerial stunts—if you're not doing them yourself. Half of the runs are intermediate, and views from the top include Big Bear Lake and San Gorgonio Mountain.

## Snow Summit

Access: I-10 to Hwy. 38 or Hwy. 30/330 to Hwy. 18 or Hwy. 18 through Lucerne Valley.

880 Summit Blvd., Big Bear Lake. Tel. 909/ 866-5766. Web site: www.snowsummit. com. 1,200 vertical feet, 12 lifts (2 express quads). Night skiing hours. Adult lift ticket $32, child $10.

The larger of the two resorts in Big Bear Lake, Snow Summit has more intermediate runs than Bear Mountain. A special mountaintop section called Family Ski Park offers easy terrain and is off-limits to snowboarders on busy days. (To be fair, they also have a half-pipe for boarders only.) The views are great, too. In the summer, Chair 1 takes sightseers and mountain bikers to the peak.

## Snow Valley Ski Resort

Access: 5 miles east of Running Springs on Hwy. 18. Tel. 909/867-2751. Snow-Phone: 800/680-SNOW. Web site: www.snow-valley.com. 1141 vertical feet, 13 lifts, 1 tow, 2 terrain parks. Night skiing hours. Adult lift ticket $34, child $5.

Promoting itself as "the alternative experience," Snow Valley is value-priced, offers two terrain parks (one big, one small), and has a 20,000-square-foot skateboard park out front called The Lot. Most of the runs, however, are advanced and intermediate, which makes it hard to ski here with people of different skill levels. Snow Valley also offers mountain biking during the summer and hosts outdoor concerts.

## Big Air Snowboard Park

Access: Just north of Hwy. 18 on Green Valley Lake Rd. in Green Valley Lake. Tel. 909/867-2338. 40 acres, 470 vertical feet, 3 lifts. Adult lift ticket $27, child $18.

Big Air is a snowboarders-only resort. Full of both natural hits and low-level terrain, it's great place to learn how to snowboard. Instruction and package deals are available.

## FISHING

There's something fishy going on at **Lake Arrowhead,** and it's not my line twitching with a big strike. Despite the fact that the lake is essentially the private fiefdom of homeowners and the guests of a few expensive lodges around the lake, it still receives thousands of publicly funded trout every year. The only way most of us are ever going to hook into one of those trout is if we fork out for one of the few rental boats at the Arrowhead marina. Don't show up with your own boat, no matter if it's a rubber duckie or the *Queen Mary*—it's not going in that lake. And don't even think about standing in someone's front yard and shore casting.

**Big Bear** is much more egalitarian and a great fishery. Set at 6,700 feet, the 3,000-acre lake stays cool all year long and holds some whopper trout. Fish & Game stocks the lake every year with more than 200,000 rainbows. Many of these go right into the gullet of holdovers from years before—trout have no compunctions about eating their young. Trolling in the early morning before the water-skiers and jet-skiers whip the lake to a froth is the best bet, but morning and evening shore fishing can produce, too. Spring, before the water is warm enough to appeal to recreational boaters, is the best time, when limits of chunky rainbows are not at all uncommon.

There are numerous marinas around the lake that will launch your private boat or rent you one of theirs. Call **Big Bear Marina** (tel. 909/866-3218) or **Pleasure Point Landing** (tel. 909/866-2455) to reserve a boat in advance.

## HIKING

### Heart Rock Falls

2 miles round-trip. Easy. Best season: Jan–June. Access: From the town of Crestline,

turn north on Hwy. 138 and drive 2.5 miles to Camp Seeley; turn left. Cross the creek and park across from the main lot for the campground.

Also known as Seeley Creek Trail, this hike takes you to an extraordinary waterfall whose most distinguishing characteristic is Heart Rock, a perfectly formed valentine-shaped missing chunk of granite. It's as if the gods took a cookie-cutter to the rock, it's that exact. Follow the trail opposite Seeley Camp 1 mile to the end, veer right, and climb the granite steps to get the best view of the 25-foot fall cascading to the right of the heart.

## Champion Joshua Tree

2 miles round-trip. Easy. Access: Hwy. 18, east of Big Bear City, to Baldwin Lake. Turn right (southeast) on Smarts Ranch Rd. and continue 5.5 miles up the valley, just past Arrastre Creek. Watch for off-road jeep tracks, and park your car.

While Joshua Tree National Park is famous for its collection of J-trees, this stand is alleged to include the largest Joshua tree in the world. Its goofy title, "Champion," is a knockoff of the champion lodgepole pine also found in these parts. The tree in question is huge, for a yucca plant: 33 feet tall and 15 feet in diameter at last measurement. And you can find it by following the jeep tracks into the smaller Joshuas, pinyon pines, and junipers by the roadside. The trees grow larger the farther in you go, and, finally, in the shadow of Granite Peak, you'll see the "monsta tree." Marvel, then return the way you came.

## Deep Creek Hot Springs

3–12 miles round-trip, depending on route. Moderate. Access: I-15 exit at Hwy. 138 east to Hwy. 173 north. See below for detailed directions, depending on route.

The only hot spring in the San Bernardinos, the pools at Deep Creek range from warm to hot and are enclosed by rocks along the edge of the creek itself. Upstream, the creek spills over huge boulders and collects in giant pools filled with rainbow trout. Downstream, the creek, which is actually a branch of the Mojave River, disappears into the sand. Now, to get to the hot spring you can go the long way or the short way. The long way involves hiking along a well-maintained, 6-mile stretch of the Pacific Coast Trail. For this trailhead, take Highway 173 north until it ends and you see the trailhead sign for the PCT. Follow the trail across the creek and over the top of the dam to the spillway, where the trail condition improves. Ascend the north canyon wall, staying high up for about 2 miles, then dropping down to Deep Creek and crossing it on an arched bridge. Another mile and you'll cross McKinley Creek onto the section of Deep Creek where the hot spring is. Aaahhhh. Nature's hot tub at last. On the other hand, you could go the short way, taking what locals call the Goat Trail. To do this, take Highway 173 north to Rock Springs Road and turn right. Veer right (east) again on Roundup Way, following it to Bowen Road, and turn right (south). At the fork, stay right toward the Bowen Ranch house, where you pay a toll. The Goat Trail begins where the road ends. The only drawback to this short route is that you have to cross the creek, which can be difficult during the spring or any time the water is high. You might want to check with the Arrowhead Ranger District on the latest creek/trail information.

## Castle Rock

2 miles round-trip. Moderately easy. Access: 1 mile east of Big Bear Dam or 3 miles west of Big Bear Lake Village on Hwy. 18.

On the south shore of Big Bear Lake are a number of knobby granite towers, the most magnificent of which is Castle Rock. Legend has it that a despondent Indian princess spent long, lonely hours on the rock, wailing for her lost husband, and that if you listen closely, you can still hear her cries. To reach the rock, follow the trail uphill, which begins alongside Highway 18 near a clearing, to the base of the rock. Climbing the rock is a bit of a scramble, but the views of the lake are wonderful, especially when it's surrounded by fall colors.

## Cougar Crest to Bertha Peak

6 miles round-trip. Moderate–strenuous. Access: North shore of Big Bear Lake, along Hwy. 38. Just west of the Big Bear Ranger Station, you'll see the sign for the Cougar Crest Trailhead and a parking area.

The Cougar Crest Trail traverses the Cougar Crest, the ridge that separates the lake from Holcomb Valley. The dirt trail starts out wide but narrows and switchbacks as you ascend. This is an uphill hike, so when you're stopping to catch your breath, remember to look over your shoulder at the world spread out beneath you. When you reach the junction with the Pacific Crest Trail, go right and then right again on the trail up to Bertha Peak. Retrace your path on the return.

## Historic Holcomb Valley

11 miles. Moderately easy. Access: Just east of the Stanfield Cutoff as you head toward Big Bear City on Hwy. 38, you'll see a sign for Van Dusen Canyon and Holcomb Valley. Turn left (north) here and drive to where the paved road ends. Park in the turnout.

This dirt road hike leads up to the historic—and possibly haunted— Holcomb Valley Settlement on the north shore of Big Bear Lake. Start walking where Van Dusen Canyon Road turns to dirt, right on up to the Holcomb Valley Campground. Legend has it that the historic Holcomb Valley is haunted by the ghosts of dead, angry miners. Don't say I didn't warn you. During the 1860s, this place was a boomtown set off by the discovery of gold by one Billy Holcomb. Much like Jed Clampett, he was out one day shooting at some food (bear, actually) and up from the ground come a-bubbling, er, gold. Wander through the camp and examine the remains of the settlement: Two Gun Saloon, the Quarts Mill, and Hangman's Tree. A short spur to the east of camp takes you to the Original Diggings and the old log cabin. There's a nice campground here with 19 sites, so you could make this trip into an overnight. There's no piped water, however, so bring plenty.

## South Fork Trail: Mount San Gorgonio Peak & Wilderness

21 miles round-trip. Strenuous. 4,600 ft. elevation gain. Access: I-10 in Redlands to Hwy. 38. 19 miles past the ranger station to Jenks Lake Rd., turn right. From here it's 3 miles to the South Fork trailhead.

If you're looking at San Gorgonio—at 11,499 feet it's the highest peak in Southern California—and you're wondering how the hell you climb to the top, wonder no more. From the parking area, cross Jenks Lake Road and follow an unsigned trail, crossing Poopout Hill Road, which is now closed to traffic, and veering right at the following intersection with the old Poopout Hill Trail. (Poopout? Hah! Okay, enough.) Make your way to Lower South Fork Meadows Trail Camp. From here, the trail splits, and while either direction will ultimately bring you to the summit of San G., I've chosen the right-hand path toward Dollar Lake Forks to the summit and the left path for the return. A short spur to the left of the main will take you right to the lake, which is said to shine like a silver dollar and is quite a popular spot for an overnight—popular for the San Gorgonio Wilderness, that is. Back on the main trail, you'll reach a three-way junction at Dollar Lake Saddle. Go left and onto Dry Lake View Camp. Eventually you'll pass the Vivian Creek Trail; stay left. (Vivian Creek is another lovely way to the summit, beginning southwest of the peak at Big Falls Picnic Area.) And stay left at Sky High Trail, too. Finally, the moment of truth: the tippy top. From up here, you can see the Santa Ana River Valley to the north, the smog of L.A. to the west, the Mojave Desert to the east, and south to the border of Mexico. On the way down, take the Sky High Trail. Stay left and the trail takes you past Trial Flat, on to Dry Lake, and eventually back to the South Fork Meadows and civilization.

## HORSEBACK RIDING

**Baldwin Lake Stables,** just southeast of Big Bear City on the edge of Baldwin Lake (tel. 909/585-6482), offers guided hour-long trail rides and full-day and overnight pack trips year-round. **Magic Mountain Stables** in the city of Big Bear Lake (tel. 909/878-4677) also offers guided trail rides. **North American Hiking and Packing** out of Big Bear Lake (tel. 909/585-1226) offers 3- to 5-day llama pack trips into the San Bernardino wilderness, as well as guided day hikes without a llama.

## MOUNTAIN BIKING

### Big Bear Lake, Arctic Canyon

19.5 mile loop. Difficult. Access: Head east on I-10 to Redlands. Exit at Orange St. and head north to Lugonia Ave., or Hwy. 38. Turn right (east) and follow Hwy. 38 about 60 miles to Big Bear Lake. Take the Stanfield Cutoff to the north side of the lake and turn right (east) to Big Bear City. Soon you'll see a sign for Van Dusen Canyon and Holcomb Valley. Turn left (north) here and drive to where the paved road ends. Park in the turnout and begin riding.

Here's a challenging climb up to the amazing Arctic Canyon Overlook on the north shore of Big Bear Lake. *Be warned:* This is a rough, rolling ride on unmarked Forest Service roads that requires solid route-finding and handling skills. Begin riding where Van Dusen Canyon Road turns to dirt on the way to Holcomb Valley Campground. (Legend has it that the historic Holcomb Valley is haunted by ghosts of dead miners.)

Turn left at the camp and then make a right on FS 3N07 at the sign for Wilbur's Grave and Arctic Canyon Overlook. Veer left at FS 3N43 and follow it up, up, up on a rocky, rutted road to the overlook. From here, you can see the vast Mojave Desert, and if you get off your bike and clamber up the rocks, you'll get some incredible views of the Lucerne Valley and Arctic Canyon. Continue past the overlook about a mile and stay left at the fork. Just after the fork, you'll see a sign that says, GREENHORN CLAIM, so you'll know you're headed the right way. At the next T, make a right on FS 3N32. At the next junction, turn left (by the sign marked NO GREEN STICKER VEHICLES) and continue on FS 3N32 1.5 miles, then turn right on FS 3N02. Follow it to FS 3N16 and go right, which takes you back to the Holcomb Valley Campground. (Scary!) Make a left on Van Dusen Canyon Road and head back to your car.

### Butler Peak

13.7 miles out and back. Strenuous. Access: Rim of the World Dr. and Hwy. 38 in Fawnskin.

This strenuous but rewarding ride from the town of Fawnskin, on the north shore of Big Bear Lake, takes you up to Butler Peak, where you'll get outstanding views from the fire lookout. From the intersection of Highway 38 and Rim of the World Drive, pedal north up the Drive. The pavement soon ends and becomes FS 3N14. At the next junction, stay right, heading toward YMCA Camp Whittle. Immediately after the turnoff to the camp, make a left on FS 2N13 or Snow Slide Road, and continue through an open gate. Lots of little roads veer off left and right, but you want to stay on 2N13 until you're 4 miles into the ride and the road cuts sharply to the left. This is 2N13C—take it. Go through an open gate and begin the long, rocky climb up to Butler Peak. Around one curve, you'll be greeted with a view of the Inland Empire, or at least the smog covering it. (Doesn't it feel good to be looking at it rather than trapped in it?) Around the next bend: the fire lookout tower built almost 65 years ago. Continue toward the monolith. It's a short hike up to the actual tower, and let me say, it's not for those with a fear of heights. When you've soaked up the outstanding view, head down the footpath and return the way you came.

## Champion Lodgepole

10.5 miles. Moderately difficult. Access: Follow Hwy. 18 around to the south side of Big Bear Lake and make a left (south) on Mill Creek Rd. Park in the lot.

This ride takes you on fire roads, single track, and some pavement to one of the largest stands of lodgepole pines anywhere. You'll also see some amazing rock formations along the way. From the Aspen Glen Picnic Area on Mill Creek Road, ride south on Mill Creek, pick up FS 2N10, and start climbing. This part of the road is paved but turns to dirt at about 1 mile. Here you'll pass through a

gate. There are lots of roads branching off to your left and right, but stay on 2N10. (It really helps to bring a map with you and have your route-finding skills honed.) The steepest sections are at the beginning, up to about 3 miles or so. When you see a sign announcing distances to the YMCA Bluff Lake Camp and Lodgepole Pine and pointing to the left, go right on 2N86 and go between some larger boulders. The rock formations here are really cool. At 2N86A veer left and then right at an unmarked Y. At about 4 miles, look for a sign pointing you to the Bluff Mesa Trail and Champion Lodgepole Pine and turn left there, onto Trail 1W16. Now you'll have fun on some great single track. Cross a small wooden bridge, turn right, and there you are at the pines, in a beautiful meadow. You can't miss the World Champion Lodgepole—it's the tallest one. Return the way you came.

## Delamar Mountain

10.5-mile loop. Moderately easy. Access: Rim of the World Dr. in Fawnskin.

This is a beautiful dirt/paved road ride along the base of Delamar Mountain and the north shore of Big Bear Lake. From the intersection of Highway 38 and Rim of the World Drive, pedal north up the Drive. The pavement soon ends and becomes FS 3N14. At 2 miles, turn right on FS N12 and make another quick right onto FS 2N71. This takes you along the southern base of Delamar Mountain. From here, you'll get some terrific views of Big Bear Lake, the San Gorgonio Wilderness, and the San Gabriel Mountains. At the junction with FS 2N09, turn right and head downhill. This leads you back to Highway 38, where you'll go right and follow the highway back to Fawnskin.

## Snow Slide to Green Valley Lake

30.4 miles out and back. Moderately easy. Access: Rim of the World Dr. and Hwy. 38 in Fawnskin.

It's a strenuous but very rewarding ride from the town of Fawnskin to Green Valley Lake along Snow Slide Road. From the intersection of Highway 38 and Rim of the World Drive, pedal north up the Drive. The pavement soon ends and becomes FS 3N14. At the next junction, stay right, heading toward the YMCA Camp Whittle. Immediately after the turnoff to the camp, make a left on FS 2N13 or Snow Slide Road, and continue through an open gate. Lots of little roads veer off left and right, but you want to stay on 2N13. At 5.5 miles, you'll crest Snow Slide summit and get nice views of Mount Baldy in the San Gabriels. From here, you'll start dropping down toward Green Lake Valley— no piece of cake. It's up down UP DOWN for the next 5 miles or so. When you encounter the trailheads for several cross-country ski trails, go right, and continue on FS 2N13 until you hit pavement and roll into the town of Green Valley Lake. Take some time to explore this mountain town or take a cold plunge in the lake itself, and when you're ready, head back the way you came.

## Holcomb Valley

11.8 miles. Moderately easy. Access: Just east of the Stanfield Cutoff as you head toward Big Bear City, you'll see a sign for Van Dusen Canyon and Holcomb Valley. Turn left (north) here and drive to where the paved road ends. Park in the turnout.

This is a nontechnical climb on paved/dirt roads up to the historic—and haunted?—Holcomb Valley Settlement on the north shore of Big Bear Lake. Begin riding where Van Dusen Canyon

Road turns to dirt on the way to Holcomb Valley Campground. Turn left at the junction with FS 3N16, pass the Holcomb Valley Campground, and then make a right on FS 3N05, marked by a pick axe and shovel sign, and begin cruising through the old settlement. Legend has it that the historic Holcomb Valley is haunted by ghosts of dead, angry miners. Don't say I didn't warn you. During the 1860s, this place was a boomtown set off by the discovery of gold by one Billy Holcomb. Much like Jed Clampett, he was out one day shooting at some food (bear, actually) and up from the ground come a-bubbling crude—gold, that is. Be sure to check out what remains of the settlement: Two Gun Saloon, the Quarts Mill, and Hangman's Tree. When you've looped back around to FS 3N16, go left (east) and check out the Original Diggings and the old log cabin. You'll have to get off your bike to do some exploring. When you're done, head west on FS 3N16 back to Van Dusen Canyon Road and your car.

## Skyline Drive

9 miles. Moderate. Access: Follow Hwy. 18 around to the south side of Big Bear Lake and make a left (south) on Summit Blvd. to the Snow Summit Parking Lot. A one-way ride to the mountaintop with your bike on the Snow Summit chairlift is $7, an all-day pass is $19.

Team Big Bear Mountain Shop is a separate business located at the base of the hill. They rent a complete line of bikes starting at $6.50/hour. Their new Demo Center allows the serious downhill rider to try the newest, top quality bikes. This is a great summer ride for beginners and those who of us who sometimes just don't feel like hauling our lazy butts uphill. First, get your lift ticket from Team Big Bear Mountain Bike Center at the base of Snow Summit. You and your bike ride separately to the top of the ridge. (If you didn't bring your bike, you can rent one along with a helmet.) There's a lot of possibilities when you exit the lift, but here's a fairly easy one: Follow the bike trail when you exit the lift and take it to Skyline Drive (FS 2N10). Go right. Follow the road past Grandview Point and the terrific views of San Gorgonio, the highest mountain in Southern California. Go right at the junction with FS 2N08 and start heading downhill. As you descend, watch for a trail that squeezes between two giant boulders—take it. This is Town Trail and it takes you back to the lift. (If you miss it, you'll end up on paved Knickerbocker Road. Go right and you'll get back to the lift.) Ready to go again?

*Note:* If you don't want to fork out for the chairlift and you desire a climb, other fire roads in the area will get you to Skyline Drive, but it's a tough one.

## ROAD BIKING

### Silverwood Lake Bike Path

12.5 miles out and back. Easy. Access: I-15 north of San Bernardino to Hwy. 138 east to the Silverwood Lake park entrance.

Unfortunately, this paved two-lane path doesn't go all the way around the lake; rather, it makes a giant U shape at the southern end. Still, it's a very nice ride. Pick up the path just behind the main lot, behind the rest room. From here you can pedal east and back to the lot, then head west and back to the lot. (At the end of the westerly paved path, there's also some single track for more experienced riders.)

### Big Bear Lake Circuit

18 miles. Easy. Access: Park in or near the Vons lot at the east end of Big Bear Lake on Hwy. 18.

Here's a great way to survey the Big Bear Lake scene, without being trapped in your car. Starting at the east end of the south shore in the Vons parking lot, head west on Big Bear Boulevard and continue straight on Lakeview Drive at the third stop light. Getting through this residential section involves the following: left on Edgemoor, right on Big Bear Boulevard, left on Cienega. Next, make your way through a neighborhood called Boulder Bay and soon you'll be riding on Highway 18. At the western edge of the lake, turn right on Highway 38 and head up to the north shore town of Fawnskin. Just after Fawnskin, turn right on North Shore Drive and head toward the observatory. On your left you'll see the paved bike path. The path ends near the Stanfield Cutoff, where you go right, crossing to the south side of the lake. Go right on Big Bear Boulevard and head back to your car.

## ROCK CLIMBING

Located 1 mile east of Running Springs just off Highway 18 on Keller Peak Road, **Keller Peak** offers about 20 warm-weather climbs on overhanging granite, ranging from 5.8 to 5.12d, all of which can be top-roped. High up in the San Bernardino Mountains, it's a good summer spot, since the crag is in the shade during the afternoon. Snow closes the peak in the winter. Year-round climbing can be found at **Big Rock,** next to the Lake Perris State Recreation Area (tel. 909/657-0676), and at Mount Rubidoux, in the city of Riverside. Big Rock is popular with beginners and intermediates, with most routes in the 5.4 to 5.10 category; there are a few 5.11s. Most of the climbs are low-angle face climbs with bolt protection, although some routes will require nuts or anchors. With picnic tables and the lake across the street, it's a good place to go if not everyone in your party is a climber. *Beware:*

the crag gets sun all afternoon in the summer and the air quality is often poor. To get there, drive through the entrance to Lake Perris and turn left on Bernasconi Road. Park and walk along the paved road to the base of the rock.

Easily recognizable by the large white cross at its top, **Mount Rubidoux** offers 35 granite climbs. Many can be top-roped, with a few lead climbs thrown in. The biggest drawback is the smog, which is often poisonous during the summer. Mount Rubidoux is located in Mount Rubidoux Park. To get there from Riverside, follow 9th Street to Rubidoux Road and take the one-way Up Road to the peak. The Up Road is only open to traffic at odd hours, so you may have to park along San Andreas and hike up.

## SNOWPLAY

### Magic Mountain

Access: Hwy. 18 in the heart of Big Bear Lake. Tel. 909/866-4626. Alpine Slide $3 per ride, water slide $1 per ride, tubing $10 per day including the tube and rope tow.

Magic Mountain is the hokey kind of place five-year-olds dream about. There's an Alpine Slide that's open year-round (it's like a sled on wheels that follows a cement chute), a water slide during summer months, and a snowy bunny hill for tubing during the winter. My wife, who's 34, insisted that we check this place out since she'd never ever been tubing. "My childhood was a rip-off! I never got to go anywhere," she pointed out. If you feel the same way, Magic Mountain is your spot.

## SWIMMING

When it comes to swimming, Big Bear Lake has few spots, actually. Most of the activity on the lake involves fun with some kind of powercraft: waterskiing, jet skiing, fishing from boats. But there is one swimming beach on the south shore of the lake at Meadow Park, at the intersection of Park and Knight avenues. The general public can also swim at Lake Gregory, Green Valley Lake, and Silverwood Lake.

## WALKS & NATURAL ATTRACTIONS

### Heap's Peak Trail

0.75-mile loop. Easy. Access: Heap's Peak Arboretum. Hwy. 18 between Lake Arrowhead and Running Springs, 4 miles west of the junction of Hwys. 18 and 330.

This easy, self-guided nature trail is one of the best hands-on ways to learn about the diverse ecology of the San Bernardino range, which ranges, by the way, from chaparral to alpine to Joshua tree. The arboretum grows trees and shrubs that represent all parts of the forest, and in the spring, the trail is covered with wildflowers. It's also a great place to spot a variety of songbirds, as well as gray foxes and dark-eyed juncos.

### Walk to the Champion Lodgepole

1 mile round-trip. Easy. Access: Hwy. 18 to the west end of Big Bear Lake village; turn south on Tulip Lane. Turn right on FS 2N11 and follow the signs to the trailhead.

It's a short walk to the world's largest champion lodgepole pine tree. Follow the trail lined with Indian paintbrush (those red flowers) across the creek and into the pines. You can't miss the world champion—110 feet tall, 75 inches in diameter, and about 400 years old. Generally speaking, lodgepole pines—also known as tamarack pines—are found in higher elevations, measuring 12 to 24 inches around. You can identify lodgepole pines by the fact that they have only two needles per bundle.

## Trail of the Phoenix

1 mile round-trip. Easy. Wheelchair facilities. Specially designed to accommodate the visually and physically disabled. Access: Entrance to the National Children's Forest on Keller Peak Rd., just outside Running Springs.

This paved nature trail near the 8,000-foot summit of Keller Peak was specifically designed for those with physical or visual disabilities. The trail is an easy 5% grade, and the interpretive signs are printed in both large type and Braille. A dirt road (open during summer months) leads up to the actual summit, where the views are even more amazing.

## Big Bear Lake Stroll

1.3 miles round-trip. Easy. Access: Hwy. 38 to North Shore Rd. Runs from the Stanfield Cutoff to Serrano Campground. You'll see the paved bike/walking path running along the lake shore.

The easy, pleasant path takes you right along the shore of Big Bear Lake. During the spring and summer, just off the paved trail closer to the lake, people are set up under the trees with their lawn chairs and fishing poles, trying to snag the big one. The path ends near the Stanfield Cutoff, at which point you return the way you came.

### WILDLIFE VIEWING

All along the **Rim of the World Scenic Byway,** wildlife abounds. Start your driving tour at Mormon Rocks on Highway 138 (2 miles west of I-15) for a sighting of coastal horned lizards and birds of prey. Follow 138 east to Silverwood Lake (see "Bird Watching,"

above) and Highway 18, where pullouts on this windy road make it possible to stop and spot golden eagles and red-shouldered hawks. Continuing east, you'll pass Heap's Peak Arboretum (see "Walks & Natural Attractions," above) where songbirds, wildflowers, coyotes, and foxes can be glimpsed from the nature trail. Of course, you may get lucky and see coyotes or mule deer simply crossing the road. At Big Bear Lake, follow Highway 38 along the north shore and then south to Onyx Summit, where you'll catch glimpses of various forest birds, squirrels, and other small mammals. Drop down through the Santa Ana watershed, where riparian species from Pacific tree frogs to orioles to black bears live. Aside from the generous wildlife, the drive itself is unbelievably spectacular—except when there's smog. Be sure to check the air quality before you head out.

The San Bernardinos support the largest wintering bald eagle population in Southern California. Each year from December to March, volunteers assist the forest service in counting the bald eagle nests and observing eagle activity. For times and dates, contact the Big Bear Ranger Station at 909/866-3437.

# Campgrounds & Other Accommodations

### CAMPING

## THE ANGELES NATIONAL FOREST

So this is the skinny on camping in the Angeles. It's the world's busiest forest, but they don't take camping reservations. That creates a situation something like musical chairs on a Friday evening, when too many people race to throw down their ice chests, stoves, and tents in too few campsites. Get there early. Obviously, not everyone can do that.

The other way around the lack of reservations is to exploit the one loophole in the system. While individual sites are not available by reservation, group sites are. Get together a few of your friends and reserve the group sites at **Lightning Point, Bandido, Sulphur Springs, Coulter, Deer Flat, South Fork,** or **Jackson Flat.** Not only will you leave home with the peace of mind that you've actually got a site for the night, you'll also probably sleep better than you would in the sometimes noisy and crowded individual campgrounds. For all of these group sites, which are located along the Angeles Crest Highway and Highway 39, you must call the special **Angeles National Forest Concession** at 818/449-1749 as far in advance as possible.

Of the numerous other individual campgrounds in the forest, which charge $5 to $10 per site, my favorites are **Chilao,** a 110-site campground with pit toilets, running water, fire pits, and picnic tables for all the sites, located next to the Pacific Crest Trail in a forest of large trees; and **Buckhorn,** near Kratka Ridge in another well-forested area on the flanks of Mount Waterman. Nearby hiking and wildlife viewing are plentiful at both these campgrounds.

### SAN BERNARDINO NATIONAL FOREST

The same difficulties that apply to camping in the Angeles apply here, though to a somewhat lesser degree. Because there are so many hotels and private homes inside the forest here, the pressure on campgrounds is slightly, mind you, only slightly less than along the Angeles Crest and Highway 39. The biggest difference is that you can call the **San Bernardino National Forest** at 800/280-CAMP) and reserve your favorite site well in advance. Then take your

time and enjoy the ride up instead of worrying about beating the other campers at the latest round of musical campsites.

Big Bear Lake is surrounded by great group and individual campgrounds. Among my favorites are **Coldbrook** (25 sites), which sits on Metcalf Creek near the south shore of Big Bear Lake; **Pine Knot,** which is off Summit Boulevard right next to the ski mountain and walking distance from downtown Big Bear City; and **Serrano** (132 sites), a modern campground with all the amenities right next to the lake. Farther afield I like the **Holcomb Valley** campground 3 miles out of Big Bear on Van Dusen Canyon Road and far away enough to lose the crowds; or **Big Pine Flats** 7 miles outside of Fawnskin on Forest Road 3N14. Fees for these sites range from free to $21.

### INNS & LODGES

Lodging is an easy decision within the Angeles National Forest—there is none. The San Bernardino forest, on the other hand, is a gold mine of attractive options.

### LAKE ARROWHEAD

Like they say, if you can't beat them, join them, and the easiest way to beat the access restrictions on exclusive Lake Arrowhead is to stay at an inn with lake frontage. The two main options are as follows:

### Chateau du Lac

911 Hospital Rd. (near Calif. 173), Lake Arrowhead, CA 92532. Tel. 909/337-6488. 5 rooms. $135–$240 including breakfast and afternoon tea. AE, DISC, MC, V.

As the name implies, Chateau du Lac is a big house sitting right on the shore.

Though it's only got 5 rooms, the house has more than 100 windows. With views like that you might not want to go outside, but please do.

## Lake Arrowhead Resort

27984 Hwy. 189, Lake Arrowhead, CA 92352. Tel. 800/800-6782 or 909/336-1511. Fax 909/336-1378. 177 rooms. $119–$229 double, $299–$399 suite. AE, CB, DC, DISC, MC, V.

Normally I don't like to list big corporate hotels like this 177-room former Hilton, but in light of the limited number of hotels on the lake and the excellent location of this one, I must. The hotel has its own beach, docks, and full recreational facilities, including pools, racquetball courts, and Jacuzzis. It's overbuilt compared to the surrounding community but, hey, it's a place to stay and it gets you on the lake.

### BIG BEAR LAKE

There are numerous chain hotels and mom-and-pop motels in Big Bear City. For complete listings call the Big Bear Lake Resort Association at 909/866-8700. They can also help you line up a condo or cabin. But as far as actual inns and lodges, there are two places in Big Bear I recommend.

## Gold Mountain Manor Inn

Anita Rd., Big Bear Lake, CA 92315. Tel. 909/585-6997 or 800/509-2604. 6 rooms, $130–$190. Includes breakfast and snacks. MC, V.

At the height of the roaring '20s, the movie magnate Alexander Buchanan Berret built a stunning nine-bedroom, eight-fireplace, three-story-tall log mansion in the woods near Big Bear Lake— Southern California's answer to Lake Tahoe, as a retreat for his family and friends, including Clark Gable, who brought Carol Lombard here for their honeymoon. The Depression hit Berret hard, and Gold Mountain Manor gradually slid into disrepair until new owners Bob Angilella and Jose Tapia restored the place to its original grandeur last year. Unlike so many bed and breakfasts, which err on the side of Victorian stuffiness, Gold Mountain Manor is comfortable, like a well-worn pair of moccasins. It's no coincidence that this spot is a favorite location for film and commercial crews seeking the ultimate log cabin atmosphere. One room is a converted donkey stable filled with bent willow furniture, Indian art, and a Jacuzzi. Other rooms have claw-foot tubs, unique furniture, and even a fireplace made from fossil-encrusted rocks.

Guests mingle near the woodstoves and swap tales over the pool table. Every morning, Bob and Jose stuff their guests with wonderful breakfasts (peach pancakes one day, omelettes the next) before sending them out into Big Bear's endless opportunities for adventure.

## Windy Point Inn

39015 North Shore Dr., Fawnskin, CA 92333. Tel. 909/866-2746. 5 rooms. $125–$225. Includes breakfast. MC, V.

There are numerous B&Bs around Big Bear, but this is the only small inn located right on the shore. And, like the Gold Mountain Manor, the Windy Point Inn is appointed with good taste, free of the overwhelming Victorian knick-knacks and frills that cloak so many inns. Here, the main attraction is the beautiful lake view and the chance to swim right outside your door. Nearby hiking and mountain biking are just up the ridge behind town.

# 6

# THE MOJAVE DESERT

UMAN PRESENCE IN THE MOJAVE IS ANCIENT. IT'S NOT AT ALL uncommon to find rocks covered in 10,000-year-old petroglyphs, or to climb into a precariously perched wind cave to discover some relic of a long-ago resident—a bead, a pot sherd, maybe even a complete basket. The dry desert air preserves these things well, protecting them from the moisture-induced erosion that dooms so many other archaeological sites. But it wasn't always this dry here.

When the first known people settled in areas of the East Mojave almost 10,000 years ago, the Pleistocene was in full swing. The Paleoindian tribes wandered through a lush region of rivers, tall grasslands, forests, and rich marshes flocked with wildlife. Today, the marks of this wetter climate live on in some of the desert's more distinctive features. Barren salt and sand *playas* were once the bottoms of deep lakes. Marine terraces mark the flanks of high mountains, where ancient waves carved away at the stone. Large canyons remain where rivers once ran, now only occasionally filled with water.

The Paleoindians lived well until things began drying out. Yet, rather than a single continuous trend from wet to dry, archaeologists and geologists have determined that the entire California desert has swung from wet to dry and back several times. The exact motions of this pendulum are less important than the fact that for the last 200 years it's been getting consistently dryer, not wetter. Today, the Mojave is much more a desert than it was even when the 49ers first crossed it on their way to the gold field. Springs and rivers that gushed 50 years ago hardly hold a trickle.

Of course, our technology for exploring the desert has improved over time, so our explorations are less dictated by physical constraints of water and limits of distance than ever before. That's good, because there's a heck of a lot to see and do in this allegedly empty land.

Still, it takes conviction to deal with this region. Many people are turned away simply by the weather. Combine that with a lack of tourist infrastructure and the general remoteness of so many of the fine places out in the Mojave, and you've effectively filtered out most people. Those who are determined to discover the Mojave, however, will find a complex and continually evolving place.

In my opinion the best way to explore the desert is on foot. Mountain bikes and a good trusty 4-wheel drive can also open up a lot of territory. To reach many of the best places in the Mojave, you'll want to drive off the paved highways, and throughout the desert there are networks of old mining roads that lend themselves quite well to exploring by bike. But simply hiking, putting one foot in front of the other, has revealed more of the desert to me than any other mode of travel.

# The Lay of the Land

When most people think of the desert, they picture a vast, fairly flat expanse of sand, horizon to horizon dryness, easy to define. You'll have no such luck categorizing the Mojave. Its very nature is change and diversity. Among deserts, the Mojave is what's known as a transitional desert, connecting the high-altitude Great Basin Desert that covers most of Nevada with the low-lying Colorado Desert, also known as the Sonoran Desert. Since it's a desert sandwiched between two other deserts, it's sometimes hard to tell where one begins and the other ends. For example, some experts will tell you that Death Valley is part of the Great Basin; others say it's the northernmost reach of the Mojave. And some will describe the Mojave as reaching across Nevada into Arizona and Utah, while others describe it as a uniquely Californian phenomenon.

For simplicity's sake, the Mojave Desert is best defined by the presence of one species, the **Joshua tree,** a weird and some would say repulsive member of the yucca family. A transitional desert such as the Mojave is defined by indicator species more than by geographic confines, and the spiky Joshua tree is indicator species number one—even though you can find a few Joshua trees in areas outside the Mojave and though there are many areas of the Mojave in which you won't see them. Personally, I find the trees beautiful. At a distance they look like cacti, but on closer examination they're, in fact, trees. Spiky fronds cap knobby branches that jut at awkward angles. The trunk looks silvery and soft, but it's not really a tree you'd want to hug. There are no spines, but plenty of dried leaves make a prickly surface.

To describe the area in geographic boundaries, it's mostly high desert, ranging from 2,000 to 4,000 feet, roughly 54,000 square miles. Occasional peaks exceed this altitude, creating what are known as nondesert islands, small ecosystems of pinyon pine, juniper, and white pine forest that are extremely isolated and home to numerous rare and endangered species. Within this region you'll find some of the most fantastic desert landscape in the American West. While the western end of the Mojave is beginning to groan under development pressure spilling over from the Los Angeles Basin, this huge tract of land is largely unpopulated. Particularly in the eastern half, it's easy to lose yourself for days in a land of steep canyons, mountainous sand dunes, monzogranite peaks, and mirage-shrouded desert playas without seeing more than a couple of people.

Antelope Valley at the base of the Tehachapi Mountains is the westernmost extension of the Mojave. It was once a boomtown region based on the aerospace and military projects centered in Palmdale, Lancaster, and Edwards Air Force Base, but the economy here has fallen onto hard times. While it's not the kind of gold many people here would prefer to see, just outside Lancaster the Antelope Valley Poppy Reserve is justly famous as one of the best displays of springtime wildflowers, particularly the state flower, the California poppy. Much of the desert in the Antelope Valley has been degraded by tract housing and general urban sprawl. You'll have to travel a little farther to get into the wide open spaces. One exception, however, is Saddleback Butte State Park, where 3,000 acres of pristine high-desert Joshua tree forest and rocky peaks have been preserved. A small campground and network of trails make this a fine intro to the Mojave.

On Calif. Highway 14 north of Lancaster, the geological boundary of the Mojave occurs at spectacular **Red Rock Canyon State Park.** Here, you're at the intersection of several different bioregions: the Sierra Nevada, the Great Basin, and the Mojave Desert. Rock walls over 600 feet high rise from

sandy-floored washes; a geologist will note that there's a real jumble of different layers and formations here. The reason is underfoot. You're also standing at the intersection of three major faults: the Garlock, El Paso, and Sierra Front faults. Like the highway that passes through it, Red Rock Canyon was a major passageway for trade between coastal Indians and the tribes of the Great Basin for thousands of years.

The major east-west thoroughfare across this part of the Mojave is Calif. 58, which skirts the northern edge of Edwards Air Force Base's massive dry lake bed. The Pearblossom highway, Calif. 18, also runs across the southern Antelope Valley to Victorville. It's east of **Victorville** that things start to get really exciting. In contrast to the western Mojave, which is largely flat, the east Mojave is most accurately described as a desert of mountains. Once you cross the Mojave River (usually dry) on U.S. 15, the terrain changes dramatically. You'll journey through numerous mountain passes and down into valleys cut by north-south trending faults. The rugged topography has created a widely varied mix of landscapes and environments.

Rainbow Basin National Landmark is just one of those places: so bizarrely colored you'd swear it's a fake. It's not. The seemingly handpainted hillsides are created by decomposing iron in the soil. At various concentrations it paints the hills green, brown, and red. Encased within the sedimentary deposits here, though, is a virtual Jurassic Park of fossils. Saber-toothed cats, camels, and three-toed horses are only some of the remains pulled from the earth here.

A more controversial fossil record can be observed at **Calico Early Man site,** 15 miles northeast of Barstow off I-15. Here, on what once were the shores of Lake Mannix, archaeologists continue to pull evidence that human beings may

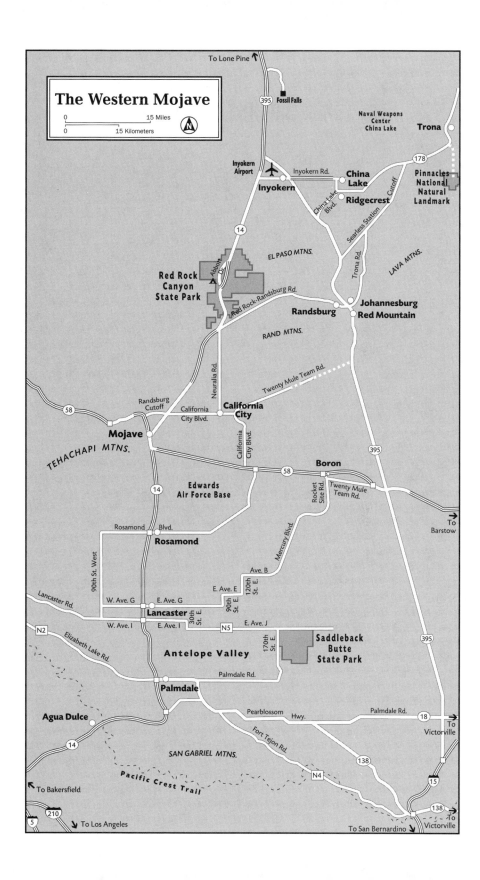

# The California Desert Protection Act

The desert has long been seen as a wasteland, empty of anything worthy of respect or protection. We've used it for a dump. We've bombed it. We've mined it for minerals. We've driven tanks and motorcycles and dune buggies over it. Maybe this attitude stems from the European ancestry of our country's original settlers; to them, the ideal landscape was lush and green, not rocky and dry. Or maybe our belief that it's evil is owed to the Biblical interpretation of the desert as the place where Jesus went and encountered the devil. Whatever the cause, the desert has long suffered from a lack of respect in the realm of public opinion, but that has taken a dramatic turn for the better in the last decade.

After years of political turmoil, President Clinton signed the California Desert Protection Act on Halloween of 1994. With a single signature he set aside 3.57 million acres of land, in 69 different areas, for wilderness protection. The bill also increased the size and level of protection of Joshua Tree and Death Valley National monuments, transforming them both into national parks and expanding their boundaries to encompass the area of natural bioregions that had previously extended outside park protection. Death Valley National Park is now the largest park in the lower 48 states, at 3.3 million acres (Yosemite, to give a little perspective, is a little less than 1 million acres).

The act was hardly what you'd call uncontroversial. In the first year after the act, the newly elected Republican Congress blocked funding to manage the new lands, leaving them national parks in name only. Furthermore, the act was presented by certain lobbying groups such as the Sahara Club, an off-road vehicle advocate, as elitist and exclusionary. According to their logic, if they can't drive their truck anywhere they damn well please, well, they're being excluded.

But for the most part things are going well. Most important is the designation of areas as wilderness, which prevents further destruction. The desert heals slowly, and the scars of our past trespasses will be with us for lifetimes, but for now the desert has won a major victory.

have lived here as much as 200,000 years ago. No bones have been found, but an on-site museum will show you tools that some observers, including the late Dr. Louis Leaky, believe offer evidence of the human occupation of North America well before commonly accepted dates.

At **Barstow,** I-15 continues northeast to Las Vegas, while I-40 cuts straight west to Needles and the Arizona border. The area between them is often referred to as the Lonely Triangle, as it's some of the least-visited desert in the state. The only real town between Barstow and the Nevada line is Baker. Besides being home to the wonderfully eclectic Mad Greek Restaurant, **Baker** is where you want to stop for information about the East Mojave National Preserve.

In what looks like a former Denny's, the Desert Information Center is the building with the huge neon thermometer towering over it along Baker's one main street. The thermometer is 134 feet tall, and registers temperatures as high as 134°F, the highest temperature ever recorded in nearby Death Valley. A helpful Park Service information

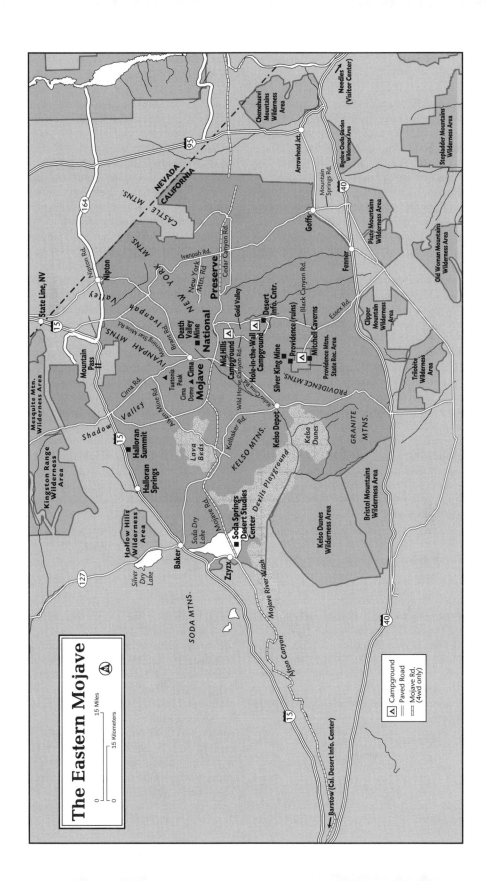

# The Eastern Mojave

0       15 Miles

0       15 Kilometers

Ⓐ

**Legend:**
- ⚐ Campground
- Paved Road
- Mojave Rd. (4wd only)

NEVADA / CALIFORNIA

State Line, NV

Needles (Visitor Center)

Chemehuevi Mountains Wilderness Area

Bigelow Cholla Garden Wilderness Area

Stepladder Mountains Wilderness Area

Arrowhead Jct.

Mountain Springs Rd.

Goffs

Fenner

Piute Mountains Wilderness Area

Old Woman Mountain Wilderness Area

Cedar Canyon Rd.

Ivanpah Rd.

New York Mtn. Rd.

Black Canyon Rd.

Essex Rd.

Clipper Mountain Wilderness Area

Gold Valley

Desert Info. Cntr.

Providence (ruins)

Mitchell Caverns

Providence Mtns. State Rec. Area

Trilobite Wilderness Area

CASTLE MTNS.

NEW YORK MTNS.

YORK MTNS.

Death Valley Mine

Mid Hills Campground

Hole-in-the-Wall Campground

Silver King Mine

PROVIDENCE MTNS.

Ivanpah Valley

Nipton Rd.

Nipton

IVANPAH MTNS.

Morning Star Mine Rd.

Cima Peak

Cima Dome

Tuetonia

Cima

Mojave

Cima Rd.

Alkali Mine Rd.

Shadow Valley

Lava Beds

Mountain Pass

Mesquite Mtn. Wilderness Area

Kingston Range Wilderness Area

Halloran Summit

Halloran Springs

Hollow Hills Wilderness Area

Silver Dry Lake

Baker

Zzyzx

SODA MTNS.

Soda Dry Lake

Mojave Rd.

Soda Springs Desert Studies Center

Mojave River Wash

Afton Canyon

KELSO MTNS.

Wild Horse Canyon Rd.

Kelbaker Rd.

Kelso Cima Rd.

Kelso Depot

Kelso Dunes

Devil's Playground

GRANITE MTNS.

Kelso Dunes Wilderness Area

Bristol Mountains Wilderness Area

National Preserve

Barstow (Cal. Desert Info. Center)

specialist explained the difference between a national park and a national preserve. "In a word," she said, "hunting." You can hunt in a national preserve; you can't in a national park. Other than that, they're the same. Since it was deer season, she advised me to wear bright clothes and make lots of noise while I was hiking. I had a hard time imagining deer living in this sun-blasted desert, but when we drove off I-15 and into the East Mojave, my jaw dropped. It's filled with huge mountains, pinyon pine forests, even a few small creeks. I did, indeed, see deer, and if there were any hunters around, they saw me and didn't shoot.

South of I-40, most of the desert is occupied by the Marine Corps' 29 Palms Training Center. Whatever is out there, forget about it, since it's under near-constant bombardment by Marine aircraft and land troops. You'll only want to pass this way to skirt the base on your way to the very southern Mojave, where Joshua Tree National Park straddles the transition zone between the Mojave and Colorado deserts. Because it's such a huge attraction, Joshua Tree has been given its own chapter.

# Parks & Other Hot Spots

## East Mojave National Preserve

Between I-15 and I-40. Approximately 70 miles east of Barstow to the Nevada border. For information call the Mojave National Preserve (tel. 760/255-8801), the California Desert Information Center in Barstow (tel. 760/255-8760), or the Desert Information Center in Baker (tel. 760/733-4040).

Little-visited East Mojave National Preserve is an enigma to the millions of

travelers who breeze past it on their way to Las Vegas. From the main highway it looks like nothing special, but follow the network of skinny roads that leads to its heart and you'll find a rich mosaic of desert features. Mountains in the park soar as high as 8,000 feet. Ancient cinder cones rise out of a landscape called the Devil's Playground. Giant dunes turn muted colors with every change in the light. Old ranches and mines dot the landscape, and the world's most healthy Joshua tree forest spreads for miles. Rivaling its better-known brethren, Joshua Tree and Death Valley national parks, for sheer unspoiled desert beauty, the 1.4 million-acre East Mojave receives only a fraction of the visitors. There are only two campgrounds in the park, and both are usually empty. A few sites cost $4 per night, but most are free. Someday this may be a popular park, with ranger walks, tourist hotels, and a million signs telling you which way to look; but I, for one, hope that never happens. It's cool the way it is.

## Providence Mountains State Recreation Area

From I-40 take the Mitchell Caverns exit and follow signs north 15 miles to the visitor center. For information call 760/389-2281.

This tiny state park centers around its namesake, two large limestone caverns named Tecopa and El Pakiva. The caves are highly developed, with concrete walkways and lighting throughout. An air lock connects the two through an underground passageway so you go in one and out the other. Though no longer a "living" cave, these caverns display some remarkable features: flowstone, stalactites, stalagmites, cave shields, coral pipesbell canopies, cave popcorn, and, of course, a bottomless pit. Above ground, the Mary Beale Trail is an excellent nature trail devoted to desert flora, and a longer trail leads to a remote spring where sometimes bighorn sheep are sighted. Visit the park as a side trip on your way in or out of the adjacent East Mojave National Preserve. Camping here costs $12 to $14 per night.

### Red Rock Canyon State Park

Calif. 14, 25 miles north of Mojave. For information call 805/942-0662.

Though cut through by a busy freeway, the red rock palisades of this desert badland are some of the most striking in the state. You've seen this backdrop in countless Westerns and sci-fi classics, since its easy accessibility and remarkably varied terrain make it a favorite with Hollywood scouts. The photography here is excellent. While I wouldn't recommend spending more than a few days in this park, it's a great stopping point on the way to Death Valley or up the eastern front of the Sierra Nevada.

### Antelope Valley California Poppy State Preserve

13.2 miles west of Lancaster on Avenue I. For information call 805/942-0662. Visitor center.

From March through May, this is the home to California's best display of its state flower. In addition, you'll see huge expanses of lupine, tidy-tip, monkeyflower, and numerous other wildflower species. Seven miles of hiking trails lead to several different viewpoints. The timing of the bloom varies from year to year

with rainfall. The best years have a lot of rainfall early in the season to start the germination that leads to a springtime explosion.

# West Mojave ◆ What to Do & Where to Do It

## BIRD WATCHING

The harshness of the desert ecosystem is in many ways a boon to birders. All creatures living on such thin margins tend to follow predictable patterns. While you'll find certain species throughout even the most desolate parts of the Mojave, avian life tends to cluster in certain areas that provide the water, forage, and cover that birds need. Anywhere with water quickly becomes a bonanza of different species and interesting interactions.

One of the finer birding spots in the northern Mojave is **Butterbredt Canyon,** reached by taking Calif. 14 20 miles north of the town of Mojave to Jawbone Canyon Road, where you'll turn west. Six miles into Jawbone Canyon, turn north onto a dirt road through Hoffman Canyon for another 6 miles. You'll shortly come to a turnoff with a sign designating **Butterbredt Spring** a wildlife sanctuary. The sanctuary is owned by the National Audubon Society and is considered one of the most important flyways for species migrating between the Sierra Nevada and the California deserts. With a vastly varied community of plants ranging from the Joshua tree and cacti to willows and cottonwoods, you might see just about anything from desert standbys like roadrunners, desert quail, and cactus wrens to Scott's orioles, ladder-backed woodpeckers, and black-chinned sparrows. Also resident are golden eagles and long-eared, great horned and barn owls.

The name of **Harper Dry Lake** is misleading, as this oasis spot is probably the single best spot in the Mojave to see wading birds and waterfowl. Located 6 miles north of Highway 58, 18 miles west of Barstow, the marshes and lakes here draw huge flocks of American white pelicans, teal, mallards, pintails, snowy plovers, killdeer, Wilson's phalaropes, and sandpipers. And like all sources of water in the desert, this wet spot is the source of life for numerous small critters that may in turn draw abundant numbers of birds of prey. Look for prairie falcons, golden eagles, northern harriers, and the adorable little burrowing owls.

## FISHING

You laugh now, but there are actually people who come to the desert to go fishing. As you might imagine, it's hardly *A River Runs Through It* out here. But people adamant about dipping a line actually do quite well sometimes fishing the banks of the **California Aqueduct,** which cuts across the entire southern boundary of the western Mojave. I can think of a million better things to do than sitting on a gravel road by a concrete canal waiting for a displaced striped bass or catfish to come along and chomp on my bait, but anything is possible.

## HIKING & BACKPACKING

### Saddleback Butte Trail, Saddleback Butte State Park

4 miles round-trip. Easy–moderate. 1,000-foot elevation gain. Trailhead: Saddleback Butte Campground, 18 miles east of Lancaster on Avenue J.

Reaching the summit of the most prominent outcropping in the Antelope Valley at 3,651 feet, this short hike begins as a wide, sandy trail under a forest of large Joshua trees. Without wavering, it's almost a beeline course up the flanks of the peak. After a little more than a mile of fairly level walking, you'll hit a nasty series of switchbacks that take you up to the rocky summit. On a hot day this is a tough climb, but those who persevere are rewarded with a grand vista of the entire valley. Once, this valley was home to massive herds of pronghorn antelope who migrated back and forth across its floor following seasonal food and water sources. With the arrival of the railroad the antelope were suddenly precluded from making their necessary migrations. It seems they were psychologically unable to cross the shiny metal tracks, even though no real physical barrier stood in their way. Unable to find food or water, they died by the thousands.

### Antelope Loop, California Poppy Reserve

2.5 miles. Easy. Access: From Hwy. 14 in Lancaster, exit at Ave. I and take it west for 15 miles to the park entrance. (Ave. I becomes Lancaster Rd., but make no turn.)

The desert is beautiful at any time, but to see this spot put on its finery you must time your visit to coincide with the spring wildflower bloom. March through May is the best time to visit, but the bloom varies from year to year. It's best to call ahead (tel. 805/724-1180) before planning a trip. The Antelope Loop is a nice winding trail that takes you away from the parking area, which will be swarming with visitors during the flower season. It's nice to get out away from the snapping of endless photos and the noise of cars coming and going to get a feel for this extraordinary desert event.

### Punchbowl Trail

6 miles. Moderate. Access: From the Pearblossom Hwy. (Hwy. 138) in Pearblossom, turn south on Longview Rd. and

then left onto Fort Tejon Rd. In less than a mile, you'll see the entrance of Devil's Punchbowl County Park on the left. Turn in and drive to the trailhead at the south end of the lot.

California has a lot of geological oddities, and this one ranks right near the top. Most people spend a lot of time worrying about avoiding earthquakes, but we're going to venture on a 6-mile hike through the middle of the San Andreas Fault. Here the fault runs smack into the mountains of the Angeles Crest and cuts a tripped-out canyon of teetering rocks that look like they've been tossed around by some sort of crazed demon—hence the name. The hike's eventual destination is the Devil's Chair, where the fault has thrust a huge white monolith out over the abyss of the punchbowl. It's 3 miles from the parking area to the Devil's Chair, and you'll not want for things to look at the entire way. Return the way you came.

### Butterbredt Canyon

1–10 miles. Easy–difficult. Access: take Calif. 14 20 miles north of the town of Mojave to Jawbone Canyon Rd., where you'll turn west. 6 miles into Jawbone Canyon, turn north onto a dirt road through Hoffman Canyon for another 6 miles. Shortly you'll come to a turnoff with a sign designating Butterbredt Spring a wildlife sanctuary.

This important wildlife oasis is also crossed by numerous trails. Most hikers will want to explore the shorter trails that lead you around the wildlife sanctuary, but gung-ho trail stompers can get on the Pacific Crest Trail and head as far as they like. This is the very southern edge of what many would argue are the foothills of the Sierra Nevada.

Binoculars are good to bring here to help you spot always-wary desert wildlife. Butterbredt Canyon is famous among birders, but lots of other critters live here as well, including lots of rattlesnakes, so watch your step.

### MOUNTAIN BIKING

Mountain biking finds itself in a strange state of limbo in much of the Mojave. There are, of course, zillions of miles of old trails ranging from wagon tracks to current mining roads, but very little exploration of their biking potential has been done. Until very recently most of the desert was wide open to motorcycles and dune buggies, which are generally the last things a bicyclist wants to share his or her wilderness experience with, but the Desert Protection Act changed that. Much potential remains to be explored, and a body of well thought-out rides needs to be developed.

### Red Rock Canyon

Various rides. Easy–strenuous. Access: Drive north of Mojave 25 miles on U.S. 14. The main park road forks off to the left but there are numerous side roads. Map: USGS Saltdale.

This 4,000-acre park straddles the busy highway, but don't think that you've seen it all from driving through it on the main road. To really see the ridiculously convoluted geology of Red Rock Canyon, you need to get out and explore the park's extensive network of dirt roads. A car, of course, isolates you from your surroundings. Traveling on foot is simply too slow to cover lots of ground. A bike, on the other hand, is your perfect mode of transport.

Get the park map of its dirt roads. Any and all of these are suitable for biking, though you do need to be aware that cars travel these roads too. Particularly worth visiting are the Red Cliff Road, which ventures along the base of an escarpment of beautiful organ-pipe formations jutting from a huge cliff, and the dirt road through Hagen Canyon, which is one of the park's nature preserves. Always carry twice as much water as you think you'll need and everything you'll need to fix a flat or a broken chain.

### Red Rock Canyon

Access: Drive north of Mojave 25 miles on U.S. 14. The main park road forks off to the left but there are numerous side roads.

Red Rock Canyon is one of the easiest places in the west Mojave to really get up close and personal with striking desert geology. Here, at the meeting place of three earthquake faults, the ground has been lifted, cracked, and torqued to expose brilliant layers of red rock. Over the years various strata have eroded into a wonderland of different formations. You can literally see them from the highway, but it's best to pull off at the Red Cliffs parking area or drive into the main park visitor center.

A nice short nature trail near the White House Cliffs campground explains a lot of local geology and biology.

## WILDLIFE VIEWING

### Antelope Valley California Poppy Reserve

2.5 miles. Easy. Access: From Hwy. 14 in Lancaster, exit at Ave. I and take it west for 15 miles to the park entrance. (Ave. I becomes Lancaster Rd. but you make no turn.)

The desert is beautiful at any time, but to see this spot put on its finery, you must time your visit to coincide with the spring wildflower bloom. When it's in full swing, this is the spot where the golden poppies bloom thickest. Once-muted desert colors change to a riot of golds, blues, purples, and reds. Then, come summer, the poppies dry up and

disappear. March to May is the best time to visit, but the bloom varies from year to year. It's best to call ahead (tel. 805/724-1180) before planning a trip.

# East Mojave ◆ What to Do & Where to Do It

## BIRD WATCHING

**Afton Canyon** is one of the rare spots where the Mojave River flows aboveground in the East Mojave. Here, midway between Baker and Barstow and 3 miles southeast of I-15, the river surfaces and flows for 8 miles through what is hyperbolically called the Grand Canyon of the Mojave. It's no grand canyon, but under these pretty, 600-foot-tall rock walls and their side canyons is a phenomenal place for spotting all forms of desert wildlife drawn to the life-giving water. Numerous raptors, including golden eagles, are drawn by the high concentrations of tasty mice and gophers as well as by the numerous nesting and roosting areas the inaccessible rock walls provide.

Songbirds flit through riparian areas lush with willows, cottonwoods, and wild grapes. Look for vermilion flycatchers, yellow-breasted chats, yellow warblers, and summer tanagers. Within the waters of the slow-moving river, fishing birds like egrets and great blue herons earn their precarious living.

Much more remote **Hole-in-the-Wall** lies in the very heart of the East Mojave National Reserve. To get here you'll drive through one of the most beautiful Joshua tree forests in the world, then through a forest of pinyon pine and back down into cactus desert. The big attraction at Hole-in-the-Wall is **Banshee Canyon.** Nobody can say for sure, but my guess is that this wonderful box canyon was named for the shrieking of the huge numbers of owls, golden eagles, and endangered Swainson's hawks that nest in the shelter of its towering rock walls. In some areas the canyon is littered with the skeletal remains of gophers and mice that met their end on the wrong end of a raptor's beak.

## HIKING & BACKPACKING

### Teutonia Peak Trail

4 miles round-trip. Easy–moderate. Access: From I-15 east of Baker, exit and head south on Cima Rd. In 9 miles, you'll come to a signed trailhead on the right.

Cima Dome is the most symmetrical rock dome in the United States. It's so symmetrical, in fact, that lots of people look for it and can't find it. That's because we've been programmed to equate "dome" with steep-sided Sierra Nevada granite—striking landmarks like Half-Dome. But Cima Dome is considerably more subtle and best seen from a distance. Though it rises more than a thousand feet above the surrounding desert, it does so over the course of 75 square miles. Think of a small globe mostly imbedded in the surface of a huge one and watch to your south as you approach the Cima Road exit on I-15. At some point a huge, gently sloping dome covered with giant Joshua trees will come into focus.

The Teutonia Peak Trail is going to take you for a nice walk through this extraordinary Joshua tree forest to a monzogranite outcropping, something of a pimple on the otherwise perfectly symmetrical face of Cima Dome. The trees here are almost as big as the biggest ones in Joshua Tree National Park, and the forest as a whole seems much healthier than what you find in Joshua Tree National Park.

The trail officially ends at the base of Teutonia Peak, but anyone with good scrambling skills can make the last several hundred feet to the top of this outcropping for an excellent view of the surrounding desert.

### Mid Hills to Hole-in-the-Wall Trail

8 miles one-way. Moderate. 1,000 foot-elevation loss. Access: From I-40 about an hour and a half east of Barstow, you'll exit onto Essex Rd. and drive 9.5 miles north to Black Canyon Rd. Turn right here. In 8 miles, you'll see Wild Horse Road. You can either leave a car here or drive another 0.5 miles to Hole-in-the-Wall Campground and leave one there. Continue up Black Canyon Rd. another 9 miles and turn left on the signed road to Mid Hills Camp. Park across the dirt road from the campground at the trailhead, which heads south from here.

This is my favorite hike in the East Mojave. The immense diversity of plant and animal life in the desert is revealed over a relatively short journey. Beginning at Mid Hills, you're in a relatively lush and sweet-smelling juniper and pinyon pine forest. After driving through such desolation to reach the east Mojave, these trees seem like a lush rain forest in comparison. Look around, though, and you'll notice that there's also a healthy population of many different kinds of cacti growing right among the pine trees.

Heading south, you climb quickly to a small, high point with nice views. From here the hike is mostly downhill, and the pinyon forest quickly gives way to more arid plant communities. You'll descend through a sandy wash and past several watering holes where it's possible to see desert bighorn sheep and deer, not to mention the range cattle that are still allowed to run here as part of the compromise that created the park.

All along this trail you've been passing beneath giant black rock mesas, but suddenly a towering white cliff signals that you're reaching the halfway mark. These are the Opalite Cliffs, and your guess is as good as mine if there are actually opals there. In the wash below the Opalite Cliffs are a couple beautiful campsites that would make this a great overnight spot.

You'll ascend a rocky stretch of trail and pass through a gate. The next 4 miles take you through some of the healthiest cactus country in the area. Giant barrel cacti, several species of cholla, and various ocotillo and beavertail cacti line the trail. Watch out for their spiny limbs, especially the chollas. As the trail levels, you'll see a fork in the path. The left one heads through Banshee Canyon and up to the Hole-in-the-Wall Campground. If you left your car at the Wildhorse Road trailhead, forge ahead.

## Kelso Dunes

2–5 miles. Moderate. Access: From I-40 about 85 miles east of Barstow, turn north on Kelbaker Rd. and head north about 5 miles to the signed dirt road, which leads 3 miles west to a designated parking area.

The Kelso Dunes are among the tallest sand dunes in California and certainly some of the most spectacular. Rising out of a relatively flat plateau to the northwest, they're truly something out of *Lawrence of Arabia*. No fixed trails lead into the sand dunes for the simple reason that they're always shifting and changing. It's pretty easy to navigate them, though, as long as you maintain a sense of direction. The worst thing that could happen would be that you have to climb to the top of the highest one and look for your car.

Come here in the early morning or at sunset. Besides the fact that it's cooler at those times, the low-angle light also reveals the voluptuous lines of the dune field better than the noonday sun. Ideally I'd visit the dunes at sunset with a rising full moon and spend some time there after dark, too.

## Caruthers Canyon

3.5 miles. Moderate. Access: From I-40 115 miles east of Barstow, exit on Mount Springs Rd. and head north. You'll pass through the tiny town of Goffs (store) and head north on Ivanpah Rd. for 28 miles. Look for a few ranch buildings marked as the OX ranch and turn left on New York Mountains Rd. almost immediately. Reset your odometer and drive 5.5 miles to an unsigned dirt road that heads north (right). 2 miles of driving will take you to a lush and woody camping area. Park here and continue hiking up the road.

As the Mojave became a desert, the lush environments that once covered the entire area retreated until they became islands. Existing only where there's still adequate moisture to support their plants and animals, these biological islands occur in the Mojave wherever the mountains stick up enough to grab a little extra moisture.

Caruthers Canyon is a lovely community of white fir and pinyon pines on the flanks of the New York Mountains. More than 300 different plant species occur here, including a number normally found only in coastal areas: yerba santa, ceanothus, manzanita, and, of course, the large pines. New York Peak towers over the entire setting. At 7,532 feet, it's the tallest peak for quite a ways, and hikers willing to scramble off-trail can make its summit within a half-day of hiking. Wear tough shoes and bring lots of water if you decide to go that way.

Our hike simply continues up the dirt road you came in on. Beyond the unofficial camping area, the road becomes almost impassable to vehicles and is better utilized as a foot path. The old road wanders back and forth through a wash that sometimes carries water. Look for pockets of water and you might surprise one of the elusive desert creatures who come here to drink. Don't stake out waterholes, though, as you'll generally just end up driving away animals and making their lives difficult.

The road leads to an abandoned mine from an old gold strike. I don't know what kind of luck they had with the gold, but you'd be hard pressed to find a nicer spot to live in the Mojave while you were mining. As always, be careful around old mine shafts and decaying buildings.

## Crystal Springs Trail

2 miles. Moderate. Access: From I-40 about an hour and a half east of Barstow, you'll exit onto Essex Rd. and drive northwest until you reach the signs for Mitchell Caverns-Providence Mountains State Recreation Area. Follow the park road for several miles to the hillside visitor center.

Virtually everyone who visits this great state park comes for the cave tour and then leaves, casting hardly a second glance at the soaring mountain peaks above. But it's worthwhile to schedule a little extra time to hike up into the canyon above the visitor center to Crystal Springs.

A small oasis lies tucked into a steep-walled canyon. Rangers say it's one of the best places in the entire Mojave to see desert bighorns. Even if you don't see a bighorn, you'll enjoy this pleasant canyon and the beautiful birds, flowers, and plants that surround you.

## MOUNTAIN BIKING

## Mojave Road

Various lengths. Easy–strenuous. Access: Runs east-west through the East Mojave south of I-15 and north of I-40. Best reached from secondary roads running north to south between the two freeways.

The Mojave Road was originally called Old Government Road, an old wagon track that tied together a series of forts stretching 130 miles between Needles and Barstow. Better roads had long rendered most of the track obsolete until an ex-marine named Denis Casebier noticed the old road on government topos and began to explore it in the 1970s. He and other desert rats pieced a route back together, calling it the Mojave Road.

Mostly a one-lane, rugged dirt track suitable only for real four-wheel-drive vehicles, the Mojave road is heaven on earth for self-sufficient mountain bikers. I'm sure somebody has pedaled the entire stretch, but I haven't—yet. The road passes through virtually every variation of the east Mojave, from cinder fields to pine forests. Obviously you don't have to ride the entire thing. The first section I'd recommend is the one between Cima Road and Ivanpah Road. Running through the highest part of the east Mojave, this 20-mile section is marked on maps as Cedar Canyon Road until Cedar Canyon Road forks south off the Mojave Road. Pedaling west to east, you'll pass through pinyon forests and monzogranite outcroppings that might look more at home in New Mexico or southern Colorado than in the middle of the Mojave. The road is smooth going, and, though it goes up and over several climbs, none of them is too harsh.

A totally different stretch that's worth at least a short pedal is the Mojave Road, as it crosses Soda Lake near Zzyzx Road near the western boundary of the East Mojave Preserve. Pedaling across the bed of a desert playa gives you that cartoon, lost-in-the-desert feel. Plan your timing carefully. Summer is simply too hot to be out on a sun-blasted dry lake. Winter rains can turn the normally dry surface into an impassable quagmire. Shoot for something in between: dry ground and reasonable temperatures.

The best book for anyone interested in series explorations of the Mojave Road is *Mojave Road Guide*, written by Dennis Casebier and the Friends of the Mojave. It's sold at the Desert Information Center in Baker. The book is a mile-by-mile description of the various ruts, paths, and roadways that make up the Mojave Road and, though designed for four-wheelers, it's also useful for planning bike routes.

## Wildhorse Canyon Road

11–19 miles. Moderate. Access: From I-40 about an hour and a half east of Barstow, you'll exit onto Essex Rd. and drive 9.5 miles north to Black Canyon Rd. Turn right here. In 8 miles, you'll see Wild Horse Rd., but keep going up Black Canyon Rd. another 9 miles and turn left on the signed road to Mid Hills Camp. Park across the dirt road from the campground at the trailhead by the Windmill.

Many people are tempted to ride the Mid Hills to Hole-in-the-Wall Trail, but they'll be disappointed. Not only is it illegal to ride single tracks in the East Mojave Preserve, but even if you were a scofflaw, you'd soon be carrying your bike over long rock gardens and plucking cholla cacti out of your legs. Don't do it.

Instead, take advantage of one of the most scenic and underutilized roads in the park. The trip from Mid Hills to Hole-in-the-Wall on Wildhorse Canyon Road is about 2 miles longer than on Black Canyon Road, and rougher, so all the car traffic flocks to Black Canyon Road, leaving the more scenic route to those of us on bikes.

Leave Mid Hills and head southwest on the road. You'll climb gently for the first couple miles, passing through high pinyon pine country (it's about 5,000 feet here). The road turns south and east and begins descending quite quickly. Take your time and enjoy the view. Wildhorse Mesa is off to your right. Macedonia Canyon beckons with its own jeep trail for additional exploration. And all along the route you'll see gradual change from the pinyon forest to the serious cactus desert toward the bottom of Wild Horse Canyon.

Eventually you'll run into Black Canyon Road. Here you have a choice. You can return to Mid Hills by pedaling up Black Canyon Road. You can return the way you came by pedaling up Wild Horse Road. Or, if you've shown great foresight, you'll have a friend meet you at Hole-in-the-Wall with cold beer and a campsite ready. It's your pick.

## ROAD BIKING

There's very little middle ground between high-speed freeways and nice, paved two-lane out here in the desert. Frankly, I think anyone who brings a road bike out here is nuts. It's mountain bike country and limiting yourself to pavement is just silly; you'll miss too much.

But if you're a hardcore roadie or you've misplaced your mountain bike and must find somewhere to spin, these are the roads I recommend.

**Kelbaker Road,** a.k.a. Hellbaker Road, leads out of the small town of Baker and across a literal moonscape of cinder fields and lava beds. There's not a speck of shade big enough to hide anything larger than a mouse this entire route, and no services. It's about 30 miles from Baker to **Kelso Dunes.** A round trip to Kelso and back is enough for most. Get going early before the sun gets scorching.

**Cima Road** is a less daunting landscape. Here, heading south off I-15, you'll pedal through one of the world's most magnificent Joshua tree forests, growing on top of Cima Dome. As you descend the back side of Cima Dome and down into the "town" of Cima (there's a post office, store, and one house), at approximately mile 14 the views of the Mid Hills and New York Mountains are stunning. Another 17 miles of riding through dryer desert will bring you to Kelso Depot, where an old passenger depot lies abandoned along the Union Pacific tracks.

## ROCK CLIMBING

A little-known fact about the East Mojave Preserve is that it's studded with monzogranite outcroppings much like the ones that make Joshua Tree such a famous climbing site. There are, to my knowledge, no climbing guidebooks or route maps to the East Mojave—but it's only a matter of time. Within sight of Mid Hills Campground is a towering spire of monzogranite a couple hundred feet high. It's a bushwhack to get there, but a short one.

Another place that merits exploration is the Granite Mountains. With a name like that it's a wonder they're not already overrun. I've only superficially hiked

this region and done no climbing, but there are huge walls of monzogranite everywhere you look.

## SPELUNKING

### Mitchell Caverns

1.5 miles. Easy. Access: From I-40 about an hour and a half east of Barstow, you'll exit onto Essex Road; drive northwest until you reach the signs for Mitchell Caverns-Providence Mountains State Recreation Area. Follow the park road for several miles to the hillside visitor center. Guided tours daily Sept 16–June 15 and on weekends during the summer. Adult $6, child $3.

Mitchell Caverns was developed as a tourist resort in the 1930s by Jack and Ida Mitchell, L.A. real-estate millionaires. Indians had utilized the caverns here for thousands of years, but the Mitchells were the first to see that money could be made taking tourists on thrill-and-chill heavy trips underground. Business was good—word got out about the two elaborate limestone caves on the Mitchell property, and George Mitchell exhibited a showman's knack for making the geological seem like a Hollywood adventure epic—but it was never the bonanza they'd hoped for. When Mitchell died, the State of California bought the caves and opened a visitor center.

It's always a delicate dance to balance the desire to open caves to the public with preserving their remote and forbidden nature. In my opinion the state park service has largely degraded the cave experience with the construction of huge concrete pathways and elaborate lighting systems that make seeing this cave as easy as shopping at the local mall.

By removing any difficulties, they've also removed much of the sense of adventure, but the cave formations here are still quite spectacular and merit a visit anyway. Rarities like cave shields, coral pipes, and cave popcorn make this a priceless cave.

Actually, it's two caves: **Tecopa** and **El Pakiva.** You enter through one and exit through the other. The two are connected by a 30-foot, man-made tunnel that was blasted through the rock and is sealed with a double airlock door, courtesy of the state park, to shorten the path and make it possible to shuffle groups through without them having to backtrack and cross paths.

Hardcore spelunkers can make arrangements to explore the third cave at Mitchell Caverns, **Winding Stair Cave,** which requires a special entry permit and technical knowledge, since it involves a 320-foot drop just to get started. After that there are several more 100-foot-plus descents. It's clearly for people who know what they're doing. For information about visiting the Winding Stair Cave or to make reservations for the tour of El Pakiva and Tecopa, call the state park at 619/928-2586.

## Lava Tubes

Moderate–difficult. Access: From I-15, exit at Kelbaker Rd. and drive southeast about 15 miles to Aikens Mine Rd. Turn northeast on this dirt road for about 4 miles on the road to Aikens Mine. The lava tube is poorly marked after a short hike in the cinder cone field to the north. It's best to ask for specific and current directions from the Desert Information Center in Baker before trying to locate this spot.

In addition to Mitchell Caverns' limestone chambers, the East Mojave is home to another kind of cave. In the cinder cone area of the preserve off Aiken's Road there is a decent-sized lava tube. Formed when the outer surface of a lava

flow cooled and the hotter inner magma kept flowing, this lava tube is a neat spot in which to retreat from the heat of the desert. Getting into it involves descending via a rickety ladder. Flashlights are extremely useful for exploring the back corners of this cave and checking out the bats that live here. The climb into the cave is not for people who are afraid of tight spaces and heights.

## WALKS & NATURAL ROADSIDE ATTRACTIONS

### Hole-in-the-Wall

0.25–1 mile. Easy–moderate. Access: From I-40 about an hour and a half east of Barstow, you'll exit onto Essex Rd.; drive 9.5 miles north to Black Canyon Rd. Turn right here. In 8.5 miles you'll come to Hole-in-the-Wall Campground and Visitor Center.

Around Hole-in-the-Wall swirl numerous legends; it is variously described as the hideout of bandits, Indians, and any number of other desert characters. But what's important isn't its mythology. As you descend into Banshee Canyon from Hole-in-the-Wall through a series of tight slot canyons, you'll have to climb down a series of iron rings mounted in the stone. Anyone who can climb a ladder should have no problem. You'll come out in the bottom of Banshee Canyon, where Swiss-cheese volcanic walls play home to numerous raptor nests (their screams gave the canyon its name). This small alcove canyon off the north edge of wide-open Wildhorse Canyon is otherworldly. Enjoy the bizarre rock formations, the cool shade, and the beautiful wildlife.

People who can't climb down the iron rings can enjoy Banshee Canyon by peering from a dramatic overlook near the visitor center or driving around to Wild Horse Mesa Road and hiking up into the canyon—rather than down from Hole-in-the-Wall.

## Afton Canyon

0.3–2 miles. Easy. Access: From I-15 east of Barstow, exit at Afton Canyon Rd. and drive 3 miles to the camping area.

Afton Canyon is the Grand Canyon of the Mojave, testimony to a time when lots of water flowed through this now-docile river. For most of its length the Mojave River flows underground now, but here at Afton Canyon it comes to the surface year-round. As a result the canyon is alive with birds, plants, and animals.

The gorge, with walls as high as 600 feet, is 8 miles long and has lots of nice side canyons. You needn't walk far, though, to experience this wilderness oasis in the middle of the desert.

## Mary Beal Nature Study Trail

0.75 miles. Easy. Access: From I-40, about an hour and a half east of Barstow, you'll exit onto Essex Rd.; drive northwest until you reach the signs for Mitchell Caverns-Providence Mountains State Recreation Area. Follow the park road for several miles to the hillside visitor center.

Named after a former librarian-turned-desert botanist who classified hundreds of California desert plants, the Mary Beal Trail is one of the best interpretive plant trails I've ever seen. The desert flora is so thick with different species here that every 30 feet there's a new thing to see. I learned a lot about what was what in the Mojave after walking this path. Simple descriptions and distinguishing characteristics help separate out the vast supply of prickly things into individual plants and species.

## Cinder Cones

Easy. Access: From I-15, exit at Kelbaker Rd. and drive southeast about 15 miles to Aikens Mine Rd. Turn northeast on this dirt road for about 6 miles to Aikens Mine.

This area of the East Mojave stands in stark contrast to just about any earthly landscape. It's about the closest thing you'll find to the moon without having to fly in a space ship; 25,600 acres have been designated a National Natural Landmark, where 32 separate volcanic cones create a lunar landscape of black and red cinders.

Aikens Mine was exempted from this designation and continues to mine cinders, the same ones you may very well have bought at the local garden store. Take a look around and enjoy a short walk through this unique setting.

# Campgrounds & Other Accommodations

### CAMPING

#### WEST MOJAVE

Opportunities to camp are relatively scarce in the West Mojave, a land of many trailer parks and few real campgrounds. **Red Rock Canyon** (50 sites, year-round) and **Saddleback Butte** (50 sites, year-round) are excellent options if you must camp in this part of the desert. Red Rock is certainly more away-from-it-all, as Saddleback Butte is now coming under the influence of Palmdale's suburban sprawl. Otherwise I recommend camping in the small **Angeles National Forest** campgrounds that lie just outside the region covered in this chapter; the canyons of the Angeles Forest are much nicer for camping than the desert floor. Three campgrounds: Basin (15 sites, year-round), Lakeside (6 sites, year-round), and Juniper Grove (7 sites, year-round) lie near Little Rock Lake about 15 miles from Palmdale off Cheesebro Road. Another excellent spot to escape the dust, heat, and urban sprawl of the West Mojave is up on the slopes of the Tehachapi Pass. Here, at 7,000 feet, **Tehachapi Mountain Park** has 65 sites that are a cool refuge from the desert below. To get there, drive up Highway 202 from Mojave to Tehachapi, where you'll turn left on Water Canyon Road and drive 8 miles to the park.

### EAST MOJAVE

Excellent camping can be found in the East Mojave, particularly inside the **National Preserve.** Just north of Barstow, the Owl Canyon campground is a desolate but functional BLM camp (31 sites, year-round). The campground is in Rainbow National Natural Landmark; the beauty is in the setting, not the immediate surroundings of your campsite. Use it as a base to explore Owl Canyon and the peaks of this spectacular display of mineral-stained soil and stone.

**Calico Ghost Town Regional Park,** 7 miles east of Barstow on I-15, has 114 campsites, but my impression is that they're mostly used by motor homes. Wilderness buffs would be better off pressing on another 33 miles to **Afton Canyon,** where a BLM campground (22 sites, year-round) sits in the luxurious setting of the only year-round section of the Mojave River. Trees, shade, and lots of wildlife plus a stunning canyon make this a great place for exploring the Barstow Area.

Once you reach the **East Mojave Preserve,** there are only three official campgrounds, but self-supported camping is allowed anywhere within reason. The three official campgrounds are Mid Hills (25 sites, year-round), Hole-in-the-Wall (45 sites, year-round), and Providence

Mountains State Recreation Area (6 sites, year-round). Mid Hills is a pleasant setting in a fragrant juniper and pinyon pine forest. The view of Cima Dome from here is incredible, and it's often the coolest place for miles. Hole-in-the-Wall is lower and more dramatic, located in Black Canyon and within a short walk of Banshee and Wild Horse canyons. It's an excellent place when the weather isn't too hot, but it sorely lacks shade. The tiny campground in **Providence Mountains State Recreation Area** has little to recommend it other than a nice sunrise view. By 10am, you'll be scorching in the sun in this shadeless spot. My advice is to camp at either Mid Hills or Hole-in-the-Wall and drive to Providence Mountains State Reserve to spend some time seeing Mitchell Caverns, but don't spend the night.

Undeveloped but well-worn roadside camping areas are located near Kelso Dunes, Caruthers Canyon, and opposite the trailhead for Teutonia Peak on Cima Road.

### INNS & LODGES

Palmdale, Lancaster, Victorville, Barstow, and Baker are awash with cheap hotels and motels, none of which merits special mention. Needless to say, you can easily find a Motel 6 or the charmingly named Bun Boy Motel if you really need to. The only really unique inn in the area covered by this chapter is the tiny Hotel Nipton.

### Hotel Nipton

10 miles south on Nipton Rd., off I-15 just west of the Nevada Border, Nipton, CA. Tel. 760/856-2335. $54 double including breakfast. 4 rooms.

Built in 1904, the Hotel Nipton is stuck in a time warp, still boasting signs bragging about its electric lights. Nobody comes here for the lights anymore but rather for the darkness. At night the sky is a twinkling starscape. Two hot tubs let you soak away your worries under this spectacle. The four rooms share two bathrooms, but this is hardly the busiest hotel in the world, so you're likely to have one to yourself.

# 7

# DEATH VALLEY & VICINITY

**I** OFTEN WONDER WHAT WOULD HAVE HAPPENED HAD DEATH VALLEY been christened differently. This fantastic place makes our minds grasp for words—which is understandable enough, but without fail travelers here come up with cheesy clichés to describe what they see. For almost a century and a half, adjectives like lifeless, hellish, alien, God-forsaken, forlorn, and desolate have been matched with place names like Dante's View, Devil's Racetrack, Devil's Golf Course, and Badwater to conjure up an image of a place nobody in their right mind would want to go. Yet they do, and they keep coming back. Over a million people visit every year, and the numbers just keep increasing.

The reason we're drawn here, quite frankly, is that Death Valley is anything but lifeless, hellish, alien, God-forsaken, Satanic, or forlorn. I will grant that it's desolate. And like all deserts, it is unforgiving to the overconfident and the unprepared, but historically it's been a lot less deadly than many other regions of the state. The 3.4 million acres that constitute Death Valley National Park are home to many of the richest and most unique wilderness experiences available anywhere. Nowhere I've been, including the Grand Canyon, is the earth laid more bare for our perusal than here. Freed from the cloaks of topsoil and vegetation that cover so much

American landscape, the basin and range topography of the park stretches past the horizon in a continually changing Rorschach print of geology: layered mountains that look like tiramisu and Neapolitan ice cream; volcanic craters, salt flats, alluvial fans, bajadas, playas, arroyos, jagged peaks, and slot canyons; yellow, purple, pink, black, green, blue, red, and white hills; miles-long dune fields that look straight out of *Lawrence of Arabia*. This look beneath what we usually consider the surface of our world is beautiful, stunning even. The name confuses people who assume that the land here is lifeless, inert. But the only constant in Death Valley is change; you can literally watch as the mountains crumble and the sand dunes shift and grow. With every changing hour the landscape looks different.

People have been coming here for more than 10,000 years, and through those millennia the climate has swung from lush, when the valley was home to a 600-foot-deep lake, to parched and scorching, to lush again when the Desert Shoshone first settled here 2,000 years ago. Slowly it has returned to the dry and hot place it is today. Adapting to the changing climate, the Shoshone have stayed here ever since and continue to live in the valley. Mexicans explored Death Valley long before it was known by that name and encountered few hardships outside the normal difficulties imposed by the desert on those who attempt to settle or mine it. It wasn't until a party of American settlers, drawn to California by the Gold Rush of 1849, found themselves stuck in the valley that it acquired its fierce name and reputation. Following the lead of Captain Orson K. Smith, who had a map showing a shortcut to the gold fields heading west through the mountains instead of south along the Spanish Trail to San Bernardino, 27 wagons carrying 100 people broke away from the established trail and struck off on their own. Blindly, they stumbled into the driest of deserts only to discover a wall of 11,000-foot tall mountains, the Panamints—which weren't on any map—blocking their progress west. After months of trying, the 49ers eventually made it out of the valley through rugged mountain passes on foot, but only one of the 27 wagons actually made it out. Only one person is know to have died during their stay. But on the whole the story of the 49ers in Death Valley is one with a happy ending; they got away with their lives intact.

If they'd been here in summer it would have been a different story. But there are much worse places to get stuck in the winter. While the Death Valley 49ers were lamenting their bad fate, a few hundred miles to the north the members of the Donner Party were dropping like flies and eating each other for lunch while they froze on the banks of Donner Lake. Yet it was Death Valley that got saddled with the sinister name.

Ironically, the Spanish Trail, off which the 49ers turned back in Utah, passes through the southern end of Death Valley. If, instead of taking their "shortcut," they had continued on the main path, they might have become rich. The group they broke away from discovered gold along the trail less than 50 miles south of where the 49ers desperately struggled to escape the valley.

Tourism, in the modern sense of the word, didn't begin in earnest here until the 1920s. Strangely, it was Hollywood's first all-color feature film, Zane Grey's smash hit *Wanderer in the Wasteland*, that gave the American public their first real glimpse of the valley. By the 1920s, the last of Death Valley's many mining booms was tapering down. The Pacific Coast Borax company could read the writing on the wall and realized it was time to mine something else, tourist dollars, to keep their infrastructure alive. They built the Furnace Creek Inn on a terraced hillside below Furnace Creek Wash. With a spectacular view of the valley and wonderful architecture and service, the inn has stayed in business to this day. With the advent of automotive travel in the 1930s and the naming of the area as a National Monument on Herbert Hoover's last day in office, tourist visits to the park slowly but surely began to increase, from 9,000 in 1933 to 60,000 visitors in 1939. One of the most popular radio shows of the 1930s was "Death Valley Days," later turned into a television show by the same name, hosted by none other than Ronald Reagan.

For the modern visitor, Death Valley and its vicinity present a rare opportunity to experience a place that's actually less populated now than it was a hundred years ago. While the main attractions of the park—Badwater, Scotty's Castle, the Artist's Palette, and the main Furnace Creek visitor area—become crowded during Thanksgiving and Christmas holidays, outside those areas lie literally millions of acres of outrageous landscape just begging for you to explore it. Most people, unfortunately for them and fortunately for us, experience Death Valley by automobile or tour bus. It doesn't take a lot of work to escape the Death Valley tourist circuit and experience the desert on its own terms.

Common wisdom holds that you should only visit Death Valley from about October 15 to the beginning of May, since temperatures on the valley floor can soar well over 100°F any time in between. Since the area was declared a national park, however, its popularity with European tourists has skyrocketed, and now July and August are among the park's busiest months. Regardless of what the Europeans are doing, I still would never recommend coming here during the summer, except to visit the

high country around Wildrose and Telescope Peak, which can be quite pleasant when the temperature at Furnace Creek is unbearable. And why go to hot Death Valley when the rest of the country is hot too? Better to wait until the possibility of a 85° or 90°F winter day sounds like a real treat, a break from the monotony of winter's grip elsewhere. Then head for the park. Regardless of what time of year you come, underestimate your tolerance for heat when planning activities and carry about three times as much water as you think you'll need. It's so dry here even when it's not hot that you can just chug water all day.

In my opinion the best way to explore Death Valley is with a trusty vehicle that you're not afraid to take on rugged dirt roads. Four-wheel-drive is preferable but not necessary. With a vehicle you're confident will get you back, it's easy to take risks, to poke around the remote corners of the park where few people go. But whether you're driving a 1986 Yugo and aren't sure if it'll get you from the gas station to your motel, or an expedition-ready Land Rover that you'd drive across the Sahara, the most important thing you can do is stop and walk. Walk into the desert, into the dunes, up a rocky cinder cone. The intimate Death Valley reveals itself when you're on foot. The smells and sounds and the million tiny pockets of life in this desert that you'd never notice near the road wash over your senses. The immensity of the desert seems to grow, too, the farther you venture from the lifeline that is your automobile.

When you begin to deal with the desert on its own terms, a million unexpected pleasures await. What looks barren and lifeless at 60 miles per hour turns out to be rich with life and color. What looked like just another black rock turns out to contain petroglyphs thousands of years old. A tan rock on the hillside moves and suddenly shows itself to be one of the park's elusive desert bighorn sheep.

# The Lay of the Land

In 1994, President Clinton signed the California Desert Protection Act, which changed the designation of Death Valley from national monument to national park and added more than a million acres to its area. As it stands, Death Valley, at 3.4 million acres, is the largest national park outside Alaska. You could spend a lifetime getting to know the different folds of this crumpled topography. The valley floor is what makes it famous, but within the park are a tremendous assortment of mountains: the Panamints, the Funeral Mountains, the Greenwaters, the Grapevine mountains, the Cottonwoods, and the Last Chance Range (my favorite mountain moniker). It's a land of extremes. The lowest place in the western hemisphere is here, **Badwater,** at 282 feet below sea level. But only a few miles away **Telescope Peak** exceeds 11,000 feet and is covered with snow much of the winter. The highest air temperature ever recorded in the United States was recorded at **Furnace Creek,** 134°F, and summertime temperatures regularly exceed 120°F with ground temperatures that reach 200°F—literally hot enough to fry an egg. In the winter, winds exceeding 70 miles per hour are not uncommon, howling so fiercely that they actually blow boulders around the muddy surface of **Racetrack Playa,** a dry lake in the northwest part of the park.

Technically speaking, the park lies at the transition zone between the Great Basin Desert and the Mojave. A geologist would call it part of the basin and range area that marks the southwest boundary of the Great Basin; a zoologist or botanist would tell you that the plant and animal communities here are typical of the Mojave. Both

would be right. At more than 140 miles long and 60 miles wide, though, there's little need to categorize Death Valley. It very much occupies its own place in the sun.

Most of the park receives very little precipitation. The highest peaks in the Lower 48, Mount Whitney and its surrounding mountains, lie about a hundred miles to the northwest and wring most of the moisture out of Pacific storms before they reach here. What water does fall as rain or snow flows into the 100-mile long basin that we call Death Valley, or nearby Saline Valley or Panamint Valley, and is trapped. Not a single drop of it flows to the sea. In a wetter climate, these huge basins would be lakes, filling until their waters spilled over the lowest mountain passes as a river; as it stands, they serve as giant evaporation pans. On the floor—the playa—of Death Valley, the accumulated salt and sediments of the millennia lie 9,000 feet deep.

Geologists say that due to the action of an earthquake fault along the eastern floor of Death Valley, the valley floor is still sinking and the Panamint Mountains rising. As this happens, erosion does its part to keep up, stripping sediments off the steep slopes and depositing them on the valley floor. From just about anywhere in the valley you can see the traces of this process. At the base of even the smallest mountain canyon you'll find an alluvial fan, the detritus of many flash floods. Farther downslope, these alluvial fans merge together, with the resulting structure called a bajada. As erosion flushes sediment out of the canyons, the largest pieces settle out first. Look at the top of any alluvial fan and you'll find large, heavy rocks. Downslope the pieces get smaller until at the very base of a baja you'll find small gravel and sand. With all this upheaval and erosion, rarely seen layers of geology are brought to the surface. Some of the oldest rocks in the world are found here: 1.8 billion years old.

The geographical and tourist focus of the park revolves around its namesake, the actual 100-mile long basin called Death Valley—but there's much more to the park than that. The Desert Protection Act of 1994 added a million and a half acres to the park to include **Saline Valley,** a remarkable valley to the west of Death Valley; part of the **Panamint Valley;** and several smaller basins, mountains, and the **Eureka Dunes** to the north. The commercial heart of Death Valley is the **Furnace Creek Area,** which lies along the edge of the salt flats below Furnace Creek Wash and Echo Canyon, where a massive spring provides water for this 4-square-mile patch of civilization. There's a certain amount of tourist kitsch and hullabaloo (Anybody want a plastic tomahawk? How about fake gold nuggets?) that turns off the wilderness purist here, but after a few days in the park you'll come to appreciate the fact that there's at least one place within a 100-mile drive where you can fill up on gas ($1.95 a gallon last I checked) and buy cold beer and ice. This is also home to the park post office, visitor center, and most of the park's lodgings, which range from drab to deluxe, with prices ranging from expensive to extravagant. There's even a golf course here, the audacity of which I find hard to comprehend in one of the driest places on earth.

Because of the hotels, the restaurants, and the other infrastructure, this is the Death Valley that most people see. And within a half-hour drive lie Badwater, Dante's View, 20 Mule Team Canyon, the old Borax works, and the Artist's Palette—an incredible diversity of really cool things to see and do. Quite honestly, you could do much worse than the average tourist vacation to Death Valley.

**Stovepipe Wells Village** is the alternate tourist center of the park. Here, 24 miles north and west of Furnace Creek, where Highway 190 first touches the valley floor after crossing the Panamint range, you'll find another visitor center, more hotel rooms, restaurant, gas, RV park, and virtually the same exact store as in Furnace Creek (in case you missed out on the rubber tomahawk the first stop). Just a mile to the east, though, are the most easily accessible and splendidly beautiful sand dunes in the park. Any time of day the light plays tricks with shadows and color on these enormous sand mountains. Also nearby is **Mosaic Canyon,** famous for its colorful marble and breccia walls, which have been polished to a shine by roaring flash floods.

The Northern part of the park contains some wonderful gems. **Ubehebe Crater** is an ancient cinder cone that blew a 500-foot deep, half-mile-wide crater out of the hillside about 3,000 years ago. What it left, besides one hell of a hole in the ground, is a several-square-mile moonscape of cinders and other smaller craters. Near here is the beginning of the 28-mile dirt road to **Racetrack Playa,** famous for its moving rocks. The tracks left by the moving rocks are mysterious, but the real beauty of this place lies in the remoteness of its setting. Mirages waver over the cracked mud surface of the playa and reflect shimmers of the surrounding mountains. From the middle of the playa rises **"The Grandstand,"** an outcropping of black rocks that looks like an island.

Tucked away in the far northern corner of the park are California's most stupendous dunes. Measuring in the neighborhood of 700 feet tall and covering 4,300 acres, the **Eureka Sand Dunes** are an area of abundant plant and animal life. Unlike the dunes at Stovepipe Wells, no mountain casts its rain shadow over the Eureka Dunes. Consequently, this is one of the wettest regions of the park (although still dry by any standard) and home to a remarkable species of

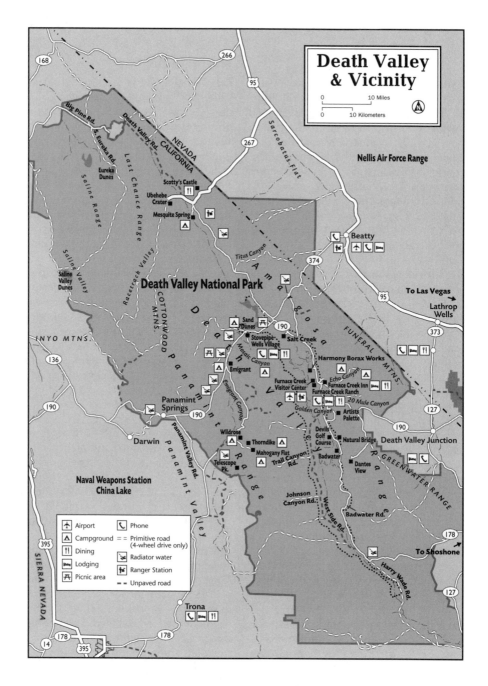

**Death Valley & Vicinity**

0    10 Miles
0    10 Kilometers

Nellis Air Force Range

NEVADA
CALIFORNIA

Big Pine Rd.
Eureka Rd.
Death Valley Rd.

Eureka
Dunes

Scotty's Castle

Ubehebe
Crater

Mesquite Spring

Beatty

Titus Canyon

374

Saline
Range

Last Chance Range

Racetrack Valley

Saline
Valley

Saline
Valley
Dunes

**Death Valley National Park**

To Las Vegas

95

Lathrop
Wells

373

INYO MTNS.

COTTONWOOD MTNS.

136

Sand
Dunes

190

Stovepipe
Wells Village

Salt Creek

Harmony Borax Works

Mosaic Canyon

Echo Canyon

Furnace Creek
Visitor Center

Furnace Creek Inn
Furnace Creek Ranch

Emigrant

Emigrant Canyon

Golden Canyon

20 Mule Canyon

190

Artists
Palette

127

Panamint
Springs

Devils
Golf
Course

Natural Bridge

Death Valley Junction

Darwin

Wildrose

Thorndike

Mahogany Flat

Telescope
Pk.

Trail Canyon
Rd.

Badwater

Dantes
View

GREENWATER RANGE

190

**Naval Weapons Station
China Lake**

Panamint Valley Rd.

Panamint Range

Johnson
Canyon Rd.

West Side Rd.

Badwater Rd.

178

To Shoshone

395

Harry Wade Rd.

127

SIERRA NEVADA

Trona

14    178    395    178

| | Airport | | Phone |
|---|---|---|---|
| | Campground | === | Primitive road (4-wheel drive only) |
| | Dining | | Radiator water |
| | Lodging | | Ranger Station |
| | Picnic area | - - | Unpaved road |

FUNERAL MTNS.

Amargosa

plants, like the Eureka dune grass that is found only here. The dunes are also singing or booming dunes that emit noises ranging from the sound of a string bass to deep sub-sonic woofs. Forty miles of dirt road separate this corner of the park from the rest.

One of Death Valley's most famous characters, Death Valley Scotty (Walter Scott), built a remarkable Moorish-Spanish style castle now known as **Scotty's Castle** near a spring in Grapevine Canyon. A true miner of men, Scotty was a former Buffalo Bill's

Wild West Show rider and prospector who found his mother lode in the form of Albert Johnson, a wealthy insurance magnate from Chicago who bankrolled the $2 million construction of this outpost, at what was truly the edge of the world during the time of its construction between 1922 and 1930. Allegedly Johnson thought he was financing a secret gold mine, but one look at the place tells you that Johnson was either thick in the head or realized that he was what Scotty was mining. Known officially as **Death Valley Ranch,** this huge pleasure palace, with a 270-foot swimming pool, stables, 1,100 pipe theater organ, and several guest houses, played host to numerous high jinks during visits by numerous movie stars and cultural icons like Betty Grable and Will Rogers.

Just south of Furnace Creek you get into the southern end of Death Valley. This is the truly deadly part of the park. Miles of salt field stretch out in an unrelenting plain. Near the lowest point in the hemisphere, 282 feet below sea level, **Badwater** is a several-square-mile section of salt flat so fractured and jumbled by geological pressures that it's earned the name Devil's Golf Course. To walk or ride a horse through here would be a near impossibility, but it's a wonderful place to visit. Badwater itself is the location of a spring seeping water that's almost the chemical equivalent of ocean water. Within these tiny pools have developed ecosystems of algae, brine flies, and tiny pupfish, proving that life will spring forth even in the harshest section of the valley named after death. The salt flats stretch for many miles south of Badwater, and then the basin floor begins to rise. Before too long you're above sea level again. The desert here becomes less startling. Vegetation fills in and after miles of salt flat, the setting looks downright lush. About 28 miles south of Furnace Creek, interpretive signs show the fossil shoreline of

**Lake Manley,** the lake that filled Death Valley at the end of the last ice age and slowly evaporated away. Wave-cut marine terraces here prove that there really was a lake in this dry land.

Most visitors to the park either come from Los Angeles via highways 14 and 395 to Highway 190, or from Las Vegas via highways 170 and 190. Most of the Vegas-to-Death Valley route lies outside the purview of this book, but along the Los Angeles-to-Death Valley route are several different parks and sights worthy of their own mention. The trip up through **Antelope Valley** at the western edge of the Mojave quickly gives way from the suburban sprawl of Palmdale and Lancaster to a starkly beautiful landscape of Joshua trees and dry lakes. In winter the **Tehachapi Mountains** provide a snow-covered backdrop. More or less halfway between Los Angeles and Death Valley is **Red Rock Canyon State Park.** This small (relative to Death Valley) park straddles the highway with striking red sandstone and breccia cliffs very reminiscent of the canyonlands of southeast Utah. Three major earthquake faults intersect here: the Garlock, the El Paso, and the Sierra Frontal Faults. Where they meet, the earth goes crazy in displaying cliff faces eroded into organ pipes, hoodoos, weathered faces, and areas that look like underground flowstone, only you're aboveground. Red Rock Canyon is a perfect location to stop for a short hike before grinding on down the road to Death Valley, or it's worthy of a visit in its own right. Another fine distraction from the drive is a short side trip to the **Trona Pinnacles.** Soaring out of Searles Dry Lake on the back road between Ridgecrest and Death Valley, these 100-foot tall tufa towers look like something from another world. So much so, in fact, that sci-fi movie fans will recognize this site as the backdrop for a lot of different films, including several Star Trek scenes. Created when the lake was full of calcium carbonate, these tufa spires now stand high and dry. If you've ever wanted to know what Mono Lake would look like if the L.A. Department of Water and Power hadn't been forced to stop diverting all inflow into the lake, go to Trona and take a look around.

Besides the main tourist corridor between Stovepipe Wells and Furnace Creek, adventurous visitors will want to spend plenty of time poking around the less visited but no less striking parts of the park. Without a doubt, the least-visited region of Death Valley National Park is one of its recent inclusions: Saline Valley. North and east of Death Valley Proper, **Saline Valley** is a similar basin with spectacular geology, hot springs, and one of the only year-round wetlands in the park.

# What to Do & Where to Do It

## BEACHES

Death Valley has the greatest beaches in the world—now it just needs an ocean. It's not the same, certainly, but for the ultimate desert beach party, take a sunset walk into the **Stovepipe Wells sand dunes.** With scenery like this you'll forgive the lack of water.

## BIRD WATCHING

As you might expect, Death Valley is hardly the point zero for bird watching. With the exception of ravens, which are ubiquitous in almost every parking lot and picnic area, the bird life of this harsh desert climate tends to be out from dusk to dawn, with very few birds flying around in the midday heat. Keep your eyes peeled, though, for the Greater Roadrunner. Without fail you can never find one when you're actively looking, but if you just stay alert, one will pop out of the roadside scrub, often running with a dead lizard or mouse in its bill. If you're an early riser, a sunrise hike will reveal all sorts of migrating songbirds, white-throated swifts, Wilson's Warblers, and plenty of California quail. Evening tends to be best for spotting the great horned owls and short-eared owls that prowl all night long. Perhaps the best spot in the park for birding is hard-to-reach **Saline Valley Marsh,** where year-round wetlands draw such migrating waterfowl and shorebirds as the long-billed dowitcher, northern pintail, teal, least sandpiper, white pelican, snowy plover, and Virginia rail. The rich marsh ecosystem also means plenty of prey for the numerous raptor species of the area.

## HIKING & BACKPACKING

The classic cliché of Death Valley hiking is some poor soul crawling across desert sands pitifully dragging an empty canteen. Don't let it happen to you. Carry at least 2 liters of water for a short hike and at least 4 per person for a day-long hike. It's best to rethink your ideas of distance when planning hikes here, and also your thoughts on when is the best time to go. For me, the best times to be out in the desert, any desert, and Death Valley's hot spots in particular, are the first couple of hours after sunrise and the late afternoon and dusk. Full moons also offer a great chance to experience the desert at its most alive. And don't forget that even when it's unbearably hot at *any* time of day in the low-lying parts of the park, it will be totally manageable in the high country around Wildrose and Telescope Peak.

### Stovepipe Wells Sand Dunes

Variable distance. Allow at least 1 hour, preferably more. Easy–moderate. Numerous pullouts along Hwy. 190 east of Stovepipe Wells Village lead to the dunes. A photocopied guide to the dunes is usually available in boxes at the parking area. Note: The sand here is remarkably soft. Anything dropped (especially car keys) tends to disappear forever. Zip your keys and important items into a sealed pocket before somersaulting down the dunes.

The most accessible of the large dunes in Death Valley, the Stovepipe Wells dune field is one of the most spectacular landscapes in the world. Come here at sunrise or sunset when the light will be soft and the shadows deep. The voluptuous lines and curves of these 100-foot-tall waves of sand will pull you deeper and deeper. While it seems like you could get lost in the dunes, the high peaks of the Panamint range offer fantastic landmarks that make routefinding a cinch. Though seemingly sterile on first glance, a walk through them will reveal all sorts of animal tracks and signs. If you're lucky you may even glimpse the shy sidewinder rattlesnake, which lives off the thousands of mice and kangaroo rats that make their homes near the base of the shrubs and bunchgrasses. A full moon is another excellent time to visit the dunes, when their flanks come alive with the nocturnal activity of the desert fauna.

## Golden Canyon Trail

3 miles round-trip. Easy. Trailhead 3 miles south of Furnace Creek Visitors Center off Badwater Rd. (Hwy. 178). Interpretive guide and map available at parking area.

The otherworldly landscape of Golden Canyon is one of the many sites chosen by the film director George Lucas as a location for his *Star Wars* trilogy. The winding trail, which was a road until a flash flood tore it to bits in the 1970s, leads upward through a yellowish array of ridges and washes. High palisades soar on all sides. The views only get better as you climb higher. From the head of the canyon the 400-foot-tall Red Cathedral stands blood red from leaching iron oxide. The contrasting colors of land and sky, plus the views back into the valley, make for endless photographic and contemplative possibilities.

## Ubehebe Crater Trail

1–2 miles. Moderate. 56 miles north of Furnace Creek via Hwy. 190 and Scotty's Castle Rd. Overlook and trailhead are well signed.

You'll know you're getting near Ubehebe Crater when the road passes through a blackened pumice moonscape. About 3,000 years ago—a blink of an eye in geological time—a rising dome of volcanic magma bubbling toward the surface met up with millions of gallons of groundwater (Death Valley was much wetter then) that were percolating downward. The net effect was a massive pressure cooker effect, and as the water instantly boiled into steam a humungous explosion blew this 500-foot deep, half-mile-wide crater in the ground. From the rim of the crater you can see where all that volcanic cinder went; it was cast north and west for several square miles, creating the moonscape you drove through to reach here. Several hikes are possible. The most popular heads up and to the south along the rim to Little Hebe Crater, a miniature version of Ubehebe. It's harder going than it looks. I made the hike in sandals, which I don't recommend for anyone. The constant sharp cinders in my shoe annoyed me to no end. You may also do a complete circuit around the crater by simply following the trail past Little Hebe and along the rim. Be careful because the slopes along the back wall of the crater are vertical and very slippery. The final option is the trail to the bottom of the crater. You can get down in about 15 minutes, but it's a whole different story coming back up the 30 degree cinder slope. Save some energy and time for the climb out.

## Eureka Sand Dunes

Distances vary. Allow several hours. Located 100 miles north of Furnace Creek via Hwy. 190, Scotty's Castle Rd., Big Pine-Death Valley Rd., and South Eureka Rd. Be aware of the fact that almost half this distance is on rough dirt roads.

This is one of the most isolated corners of the park and well worth the trouble it takes to get here. The prime attraction is the 4,000-plus acres of the Eureka Dunes. Many times larger in magnitude than the Stovepipe Wells dunes, these enormous waves of sand tower to a main peak standing 600 to 700 feet above the floor of the surrounding Eureka Valley. And since the Eureka dunes don't lie in the direct rain shadow of the surrounding mountains, they receive much more rain and snow than other parts of the park. You'll find more than 50 different plants living on the dunes, including three that live only here. Make your way into the dunes in the early morning or evening when the light is best. Sometimes you may hear deep bass notes booming out of the hills, somewhat like an earthly pipe organ. These "singing" dunes have been explained by any number of variables, including changes in moisture content, shifting grains, and the heat-induced expansion and contraction of the sand; but whatever the real cause, standing on top of a windblown sand mountain in the middle of nowhere listening to it groan is quite a unique thrill.

## Mosaic Canyon

2–6 miles round-trip. Easy–moderate. Just west of Stovepipe Wells Village, a spur road

leads 2.5 miles to a parking area at the canyon bottom.

From the parking area on the alluvial fan below Mosaic Canyon, you'll quickly enter a narrow-walled land of polished breccia sparkling in white, black, gray, and blue chunks. Numerous floods have scoured and polished the same featureless brown rock that makes up many mountains in the park into a shining mosaic of jagged shapes. The floods carry so much sediment as they rush through that they have very much the same effect as a rock tumbler, polishing away the drab outer layers to reveal the beauty held within the rock. You can easily hit and run here, but the canyon actually continues upward for 9 miles. At least the first 3 of those are easily hiked without any serious bushwhacking or climbing.

## Wildrose Peak Trail

8.4 miles round-trip. Moderate–difficult. From Stovepipe Wells Village, take Emigrant Canyon Rd. 16 miles to the Wildrose Charcoal Kilns. Trail begins at the north end of the parking area.

During hot summer months this is the best day hike in the park. You're starting at 6,894 feet and ascending to the 9,064 summit of Wildrose Peak, where you'll get a drop-dead view of sweltering Death Valley to the east and Panamint Valley to your west. The altitude here ensures that it will be dramatically cooler than the frying-pan temperatures below. During the hottest part of summer, shimmering heat haze distorts the valley below into a shifting mirage. The hardest part of the trail is the last mile to the summit. Switchbacks just keep coming, and, while the view is getting better with every step, the shock of coming from below sea level to

# Death Valley: What's in a Name Anyway?

Of all the sinister place names in the American West—Hangtown, Dead Man's Gulch, Massacre Creek—none evokes quite the same amount of dread as Death Valley. It's a biblical landscape, the kind of wilderness where you could wander 40 days and surely meet the devil, if you lived at all. But what's interesting is that when it was named, the moniker Death Valley was based more on myth than fact.

It's considered common wisdom that Death Valley received its name after gold-seeking 49ers, lured by the mother lode, mistakenly sought a southern shortcut and met their end here, dying like flies baking on the frying-pan bottom of the valley. It's true that 49ers did come through the valley; the Bennett-Arcane Party, the Brier Family, the Jayhawkers, and several others found themselves in a terrible predicament, running out of food and unable to blaze a route over the 11,000-foot Panamint Mountains to Death Valley's west. Fortunately for the immigrants, however, they arrived in winter, when Death Valley is actually livable. Considering that a few hundred miles to the north the Donner Party was having their notorious run-in with a hard Sierra winter, the parties crossing Death Valley actually had a pretty easy go of it. In the initial 1849–50 gold rush crossing of Death Valley, historians agree that only one person died: Captain Rober Culverwell, who became separated from his party and died of starvation. Surely, though, their tales of privation and the fearful landscape of Death Valley lived on.

It wasn't until later, during the mineral mining booms of the late 19th and early 20th century, that Death Valley really began to earn its name. During this era of intensive exploration, literally hundreds died. In the summer of 1880, a pack train of seven miners left the tapped-out mines of high-altitude Panamint City and struck out for Arizona, where they'd heard the mining was picking up. As they descended the mountains into Death Valley, they were hit by a wall of heat. Rather than turn around, though, the young men continued on, confident they could make the crossing.

They were wrong, dead wrong. With their canteens swinging empty and the ultra-dry atmosphere wicking their sweat away, they became crazed with desperation. In a final, cinematic act of desperation, the miners slashed the throats of their mules and drank the spurting blood. Two members of the party headed for an Indian camp, where they found water. When they returned bearing canteens full of water, they found three of their compadres dead and two barely hanging on.

The mining era of Death Valley is full of tales like this. Men crawling across the desert on their hands and knees. Mummified corpses found by the side of the trail. Suicides of people gone crazy with the heat. Murder, treachery, and greed facilitated by such an unforgiving environment.

Even today, in an era of air-conditioned cars, visitor centers, rangers, swimming pools, and plentiful traffic in the valley, Death Valley continues to claim an unfortunate few. As the saying goes, a chain is only as strong as its weakest link, and many people continue to travel through the desert with one or more weak links—a rickety car, no water, no planning. As tough as the elements are, Death Valley is hardly full of surprises. You know it's going to be scorching from May to September, and potentially unforgiving the rest of year. You'd be wise to plan for it.

9,000 feet-plus can make for a wheezy climb.

## Telescope Peak Trail

14 miles round-trip. Difficult. Follow road directions to Charcoal Kilns/Wildrose Peak trailhead and then continue another 1.8 miles to Mahogany Flat parking area.

Your chief destination is the highest point in the park, 11,049-foot-tall Telescope Peak. Along the way you'll pass through a number of different ecosystems, including a green meadow and a forest of bristlecone pines, the oldest trees in existence. As you wind up the ridges of Telescope Peak, you begin to get some sense of how it earned such a name: The views are stunning. From the top you can see the highest and lowest spots in the Lower 48 with just the turn of your head. The steep escarpment of the eastern side of Telescope Peak drops seemingly straight down to Badwater, 282 feet below sea level.

Since this hike takes 6 to 8 hours just to reach the summit along the steeply pitched trail, it's best to pack the necessary gear for a light overnight. By striking out in the afternoon and camping along the route, you'll have the pleasure of watching the sun set and rise from this spectacular spot. Remember that it can be freezing at night here, regardless of how hot it can be below.

### HORSEBACK RIDING

Mules, donkeys, and horses played an important part in the exploration of this desolate corner of the state. Without them the logistics of hauling gear in and ore out would have been impossible. Take a gander at the 20-mule team wagon on display at Harmony Borax Works for some idea how hard it was to be a working mule in those days.

Modern-day wranglers can get a sense of what the pioneers experienced riding through this desert by joining the professional guides at Furnace Creek Stables for a number of guided trail rides. One-hour rides ($20 per person) stay close to the valley floor by necessity. Better to take the 2-hour ($35) ride that ranges rather afield into the side canyons and foothills of the Funeral Mountains. And without a doubt the most fun is the $30 moonlight rides that take place each month during the peak of the full moon. Since you can't really see the ground in front of you, you'll have to put your trust in Trigger, or whatever your horse is named, and sit back to enjoy the dramatic shapes and shadows of nighttime Death Valley. For reservations call 760/786-2345, ext. 230.

### HOT SPRINGS

After several hot and dusty days camping in the northern part of Death Valley, my wife and I checked into the very fancy Furnace Creek Inn for a night of luxury. Nothing sounded better than a refreshing swim in a cold pool, and I'd noticed that the inn had a beautiful one. As I set my towel down on a chaise lounge I thought it strange that a lovely hotel like this one didn't also have a Jacuzzi. Then the thought hit me: Death Valley, duh! Who wants to sit in boiling water in the hottest place on earth? I stepped up to the edge of the nearly Olympic-sized pool and dove in. Ugh. Gross. The pool was at least 95°F. Instead of cooling off I was actually sweating in the pool. Disgusted, I went back to the room and took a cold shower. I found out later that the pool is heated by a huge hot spring located just up the canyon.

It's a cruel irony that such a hot place with so little water would actually have a large supply of hot mineral springs. The best by far are Upper and Lower

Warm Springs in **Saline Valley.** Only the most dedicated hot springers will make it here, since the drive in involves hours of washboard road. The pools, reached by Saline Valley Road and then a 7.5 mile side spur that cuts east just north of the Saline Valley sand dunes, are surrounded by palm trees and connected by hand-laid rock trails. Though incredibly remote, the springs are well known and draw a semi-permanent population of hot springs aficionados who camp, run around naked, socialize, and generally have a fun time.

Outside the park to the southeast, the tiny town of **Tecopa** is little more than a hot spring with a neighboring trailer park. Just off Highway 127, 57 miles north of Baker, Tecopa maintains two separate-sex bathhouses where for free you can soak your worries away in really nice hot water. It's a popular place with retired folks in their trailers and motor homes who flock here to get away from northern winters and to soak in this strangely isolated fountain of youth. I wouldn't recommend camping here, but it can make a great break from the relentless distances of desert driving.

## MOUNTAIN BIKING

Like all national parks, Death Valley prohibits off-road biking and restricts cycles to paved and dirt roads. Unlike all other national parks, however, Death Valley has an enormous number of miles of dirt roads that are perfect for mountain biking. While none of the riding terrain here is what you'd call world-class, the setting and surroundings are unbeatable. The biggest benefit of getting out of your car and onto a bike saddle is that you get to experience the magnitude of this spot without any of the isolation brought by the "comforts" of automotive transport. It's so easy to get lulled into driving through Death

Valley with the windows up, air conditioning on, and the stereo blaring, looking at the world outside like it's a TV show. On a bike, for better and sometimes for worse, you experience the complete package, smells, sounds, heat, cold, etc.

Given the huge distances and unforgiving conditions here, preparation is of the essence. Break down 10 miles from help and you're in big trouble. Always pack not just enough water for the ride you plan but also some extra for the hours you might spend cursing the cholla cactus that just ripped your tube to ribbons and waiting for a jeep to come by or trying to pound a tacoed rim back into shape with a rock. This is the land that Camelbacks and other giant backpack hydration systems were made for. Bring as much water as you can possibly lash to your bike and body; you won't regret it. Also, consider tucking a space blanket into your pack. If you break down, you can use it to create shade, which will save you lots of grief and possibly your life. You'll also want extra tubes, spokes, chain links, chain puller, duct tape, and any other tools or wrenches specific to your trusty steed. There are no bike shops in the valley or for at least 100 miles in any direction, so you must bring what you'll need.

Rather than recommend specific rides here, I'm going to suggest that you go to certain areas of the park and explore on your own. Without a doubt, the single best place to explore by mountain bike in the park is **Saline Valley.** Within 10 miles of the main camping area at the hot springs you'll find old mines, sand dunes, a large salt marsh, and tons of interesting sights. Since it's all dirt roads out here, and lots of them, you're limited mostly by endurance and your imagination. And after a long, hot day of riding, what could be better than unwinding in the numerous hot spring pools?

The road from Ubehebe Crater to Racetrack Playa is another fine (though long) route through some of the prettiest terrain the park can offer. Ranging from cactus desert to Joshua tree forest and the flat dry lake surface of Racetrack Playa, this 26-mile route makes a great one-way ride. Of course, making it a one-way ride means that somebody will have to drive a vehicle in, but it's a nice drive too. Please don't ride your bikes on the surface of Racetrack Playa, which is famous for its sliding rocks and the trails they leave behind. Bike tracks destroy the subtle effect of the Racetrack rocks entirely.

Closer to Furnace Creek and the main Death Valley tourist region, **20 Mule Team Canyon** is a wonderful short ride along a smooth dirt road through the most surreal landscape I've ever seen. From the Furnace Creek area it's up Highway 190 4 miles to the signed turn-off. You can park a car here at the edge of the paved road and start riding. It's also a fine huff up the hill from Furnace Creek if you want the extra miles, though the road is quite busy. The road is one-way, dusty, and mostly uphill, but worth every pedal stroke. The yellow-brown hills are deeply scarred and seemingly barren of any plant life whatsoever. This badlands area is filled with old mining tunnels, as it was once rich with borax. Eventually you'll crest a rise out of the yellow hills and pass through a region of coal-blackness before coming out on Highway 190 again. From here it's a short ride back to the beginning of 20 Mule Team Canyon where you left your car, or a fast coast back down-canyon to Furnace Creek.

Another fine option, if you're looking for a way to ride through the lowest part of Death Valley on dirt, is the **West Side Road.** This 45-mile gravel road parallels the much busier Badwater Road (paved) on the opposite side of the park starting about 7 miles south of Furnace Creek. The first couple miles cross the pancake-flat floor of the valley and give an extraordinary sense of the way early prospectors must have felt crossing the valley before it was civilized by hotels, gas stations, and a golf course. The Westside Road is also where you want to head to find several excellent jeep trails into the rugged canyons on the east face of the Panamint Mountains (including Telescope Peak). They are, from north to south, 10.4-mile-long **Trail Canyon Road,** which passes several old mining sites and a lush oasis at the site of Old Dependable Mine; 42-mile **Butte Valley Road,** which passes many interesting geological features; and 9.8-mile **Johnson Canyon Road,** home to many of Death Valley's most reliable springs and accompanying plant and wildlife. All these roads are steep and often rocky. Flash floods can make them alternately sandy and soft or covered in brutal rocks and debris.

## ROAD BIKING

During the fall and winter months, Death Valley actually attracts a large number of road-cycling visitors. Most come with supported trips and stay in hotels. Certainly it's a fine way to see the park, unmediated by the glass and air-conditioning that isolates so many car-driving visitors from the surroundings. But don't think you need to have a sag wagon following you to explore Death Valley by bike. Using Furnace Creek as your starting point, there are several great tours that will satisfy everyone from a casual cruiser to a hardcore climber.

### Badwater and Back

36 miles round-trip. Easy–moderate. 300-foot elevation gain. Beginning at Furnace Creek, take Hwy. 190 less than a mile to

the Badwater Rd. turnoff just below the Furnace Creek Inn.

This nicely paved road remains fairly level as it descends along the east side of Death Valley to the lowest point in the western hemisphere, 282 feet below sea level. Along the way you'll pass through an outrageous chemical desert landscape of crystallized salt flats, alluvial flood deposits, multi-hued mineral formations, and towering mountains. Coming around a long curve, you'll spot the final destination, a shallow pool of spring-fed water at the edge of a 200-square-mile salt flat. The flats are all that remain from a shallow lake that evaporated about 2,000 years ago, leaving a massive accumulation of salt. The tiny pools at Badwater are similar in composition to sea water and are home to a population of desert pupfish, uniquely evolved to the harsh realities of this existence. A sign at the edge of the pools gives the elevation, and if you look back toward the sheer wall of the Black Mountains towering over Badwater, you'll spot a sign 25 stories high on the wall above you. Its two words convey a tremendous sense of where you are as you crane your neck to read it: SEA LEVEL.

## Artist's Palette Loop

22 miles. Moderate–difficult. Head south out of Furnace Creek and immediately turn right (south) on Badwater Road. 9.5 miles later you'll come to the left-hand turn for Artist Dr., a one-way, 9.5-mile loop through the hills above. It rejoins Badwater Rd. a few miles back north toward Furnace Creek.

As you're riding south along Badwater Road, the multi-hued blues, reds, yellows, and whites of the mineral-laden Black Mountains catch your eye. But little can prepare you for the intensity of the colors up close. This loop road winds up through rugged arroyos and over massive alluvial fans created as flash flooding scours debris out of the quickly eroding mountains above. The road is paved, but you may have to cross periodic drifts of sand, especially when passing through some of the large dry (hopefully) washes on the route. A visitor handout designed for a driving tour explains the geological features at play and can make for interesting reading if you don't mind stopping periodically.

You'll reach a short turnout, 4.5 miles into the loop, that leads to the namesake feature of the area. The Artist's Palette is a steep hillside mottled with a profusion of naturally occurring mineral colors that look like they were dabbed there by a working artist. You can walk up into the deposits of manganese, mica, limonite, and hematite if you want, but my impression is that the Palette is more impressive from a distance. From here it's mostly a downhill ride back to the Badwater Road, which you'll ride back north to Furnace Creek.

## Dante's View Hill Challenge

50 miles round-trip. Extremely difficult. 5,475-foot vertical rise. From Furnace Creek take Hwy. 190 south 12.5 miles to Dante's View Rd. Follow Dante's View Rd. right another 12.5 miles. The last half mile before the 5,475-foot vista point parking area is one of the steepest climbs around.

If I had to chose one vista that best describes Death Valley, it would be the one from Dante's View. Here, a mile above the lowest point in the western hemisphere, you can look straight down at the desolate salt flats that define the lower regions of Death Valley. Directly across the valley is 11,049-foot Telescope Peak, rising from the valley floor. Slightly to the right of Telescope Peak you can often see the summit of Mount Whitney, the highest place in the Lower 48 States at 14,495 feet. All the contrasts and extremes of Death Valley are laid out at your feet.

To achieve this view by bicycle, though, is a brutal challenge. The 25-mile climb from Furnace Creek to the top is virtually unrelenting. The last 5 or 6 miles will especially knock the socks off even the toughest rider. Stick with it and you'll eventually get there. When you see the pullout for parking trailers on your left, the top is almost in sight. Hammer up through a few brutally steep switchbacks and suddenly the entire valley opens up below. The worst is behind you now. Enjoy the view and have a nice fast ride home. Remember when planning for this ride that the top can be really cold when the valley floor is roasting.

## SWIMMING

Especially in summer, there's nothing like a plunge in a swimming pool to cut through the heat-induced haze that will overtake you here. All three major hotels have swimming pools: Stovepipe Wells Village, Furnace Creek Inn, and Furnace Creek Ranch. The pool at Furnace Creek Inn, the most posh lodging in the park, is unfortunately too warm to be refreshing (it's fed by a hot spring). The other pools vary. Generally you're supposed to be a registered guest to use any of these pools, but enforcement is lax.

## WALKS & ROADSIDE ATTRACTIONS

The massive scale of Death Valley makes it particularly well suited to exploring by car. While I'm generally loathe to encourage people to spend any more time in cars than necessary, for many the Death Valley experience *is* all about motorized exploration. There's a transcendent beauty to watching the desert world whiz by that appeals even

to an automotive cynic like me. The following roadside attractions and short walks are what make the difference between literally seeing Death Valley through the windows of your car at 70 mph and experiencing it face to face, however limited.

## Zabriskie Point

0.25 miles. Easy. 100-foot elevation gain. 4.5 miles south of Furnace Creek on Hwy. 190.

One of the finest spots in all of Death Valley for watching the sunset, Zabriskie Point is a nice view any time of day. For visitors who don't want to make the 25-mile drive to Dante's View, this is a great substitute. From the top of the yellow mudstone hill that is Zabriskie Point, you look down into a maze of rippling canyons and hills and across the valley to the Panamint range. It's unlikely you'll be alone here, since this is a big stop with the tour bus and motor home crowd, but it's a lovely view all the same.

## Dante's View

No walking required. Vista Point. At the end of Dante's View Rd. 25 miles from Furnace Creek. Take Hwy. 190 12.5 miles south to Dante's View Rd. and then another 12.5 miles to the dead-end viewpoint.

Early in the tourist history of Death Valley, a bunch of local promoters went searching for the best view in Death Valley. The winning spot was Dante's View, a remote peak in the Black Mountains. The road was improved and eventually a vista point and interpretive signs were installed. Here, a mile above the valley floor below, you can see the most dramatic features of Death Valley's geology. The salt desert of Badwater, Devil's Golf Course, and the Amargosa River drainage lie below. The 11,049-

foot Telescope Peak lies straight ahead, rising abruptly out of the valley floor in a single steep face. Far beyond that you can just see the top of Mount Whitney, the highest point in the lower 48 states, at 14,495 feet. Colors and shadows shift constantly, and as an added bonus it's often as much as 25° to 30° cooler here than in the valley below. And don't forget to look east, away from the valley. A whole lineup of Great Basin mountains stretch out toward Las Vegas.

### Death Valley Borax Museum

Adjacent to the visitor center in Furnace Creek.

Though it's called the Borax Museum, this fine little interpretive museum's collection spans everything from Shoshone baskets to mineral collections to a 60-ton locomotive, which once hauled borate from Death Valley to market. While much of the museum's displays are about mining, you'll get a great sense of the people and culture of this hardscrabble place.

### Devil's Golf Course

No walking required. 13 miles south of Furnace Creek on Hwy. 178.

A rutted 1-mile dirt road leads out to the middle of this incredible salt formation. The ground here consists almost exclusively of sodium chloride crystals, known to most of us as table salt. As the crystals form they thrust upward, creating a jagged, spiky landscape of jumbled ruts, lumps, and chunks. This salt field covers 200 square miles, the remains of a shallow lake that dried up 2,000 years ago. Ground water continues to dry out, and the crystals are actively forming.

Take a short walk a few hundred yards into the golf course and try to imagine having to cross it on foot or horse. Though the ground is often brown and stained, a taste of any part will prove to you that this is the world's largest salt shaker.

### Harmony Borax

0.25-mile walk. Easy. 1.5 miles north of Furnace Creek on Hwy. 190.

While it was gold and silver that were the glamorous objects of miners' affections during the many mineral rushes to pass though Death Valley, neither was as profitable as the mining of borate, which was used to manufacture soaps, fertilizer, and any number of industrial products. Harmony Borax Works was one of the most successful borate mines. Chinese laborers mined the actual deposits out on the salt flats to the west. The structures left standing here at Harmony Borax are the boiler and settling tanks uses to crystallize the borax, after which it was loaded onto a huge 20-mule-team wagon like the one on display and hauled 165 miles through the harsh desert in California to a railhead in Mojave. The wagons hauled not only 20 tons of borate, but also a 1,200-gallon water tank and all the food needed for their long journey.

### Titus Canyon

One-way, 26.4-mile dirt road through one of the park's most interesting canyons. Check with rangers before going. Can be closed due to weather or to protect wildlife. To reach the beginning of Titus Canyon Rd., exit the park on Daylight Pass Rd. toward Beatty, Nevada. Just outside the park boundary, Titus Canyon Rd. begins on your left.

This wonderful journey takes you through ghost towns and sheer rocky canyons, over a mountain pass, and through a prehistoric Native American site. Pick up a Titus Canyon visitor booklet at any of the park visitor centers before making the trip. Highlights of the trip include The Narrows, where the rock walls pinch in until it seems like your car will barely fit through; the old town site of Lead Field, which was built as a stock promoting scam in the 1920s; and Klare Spring, where you stand the best chance of seeing an elusive desert bighorn sheep in the park. Just east of the beginning of Titus Road is the old gold-mining town of Rhyolite, one of the greatest standing ghost towns in the area.

## Scotty's Castle

53 miles north of Furnace Creek on Hwy. 190 and Scotty's Castle Rd.

This 1930s-era landmark is one of the strangest monuments to the symbiotic relationship between rich people looking for excitement and exciting people looking for riches you'll ever see. Albert Johnson, a wealthy insurance tycoon from Chicago, was approached by a charismatic prospector named Walter Scott, more commonly known as Death Valley Scotty. Convinced that Scotty knew his stuff, Johnson began bankrolling his mining efforts beginning in 1904. Under enormous secrecy, Scotty began mining, so secret in fact that he'd show no one his mine, including Johnson. Eventually Johnson figured out that it was his wallet that was being mined, not the earth, but by now he and Scotty had become fast friends, and his love for the desert was solidified. Johnson and his wife Bessie set out to build a palatial vacation home in this lush canyon.

> This is the chemical desert and in a few days a living thing out there would be embalmed like a salt cod—preserved forever and thoroughly dead.
>
> —"Growing Up Dry," a sign at Dante's View in Death Valley explaining life in various regions of the park.

Scotty was hired on as the resident manager and supervisor, and two million dollars in construction later stood this fanciful Moorish castle. From the 270-foot swimming pool to the pipe organ in the music room and the visits by early silent film and radio stars, it was a glamorous place to see and be seen. Park service employees lead living history tours for groups of visitors most days from 9am to 5pm. Adult $8, child $4.

## Trona Towers, AKA Pinnacles National Landmark

About 30 miles southwest of the park boundary on Calif. 178, you'll pass through the hardscrabble town of Trona, essentially a company town for the Kerr-McGee mineral mining operation that utilizes the leftovers of Searles Dry Lake. To give you some idea of how inhospitable the environment is, some of the houses built during the first big mineral boom were constructed with asbestos shingle exteriors to repel the heat. You'll continue through this charming town to a singed dirt road heading south across the dry lake. Shortly you'll see a landscape from another planet appear on the horizon. Earthen towers, like giant termite mounds, jut toward the sky. At first you'll think they're small, maybe

15 or 20 feet tall, but then you realize they're miles away. Keep following the dirt road (there are many tracks across the dry lake, but the current "best" one is usually obvious) for 13 miles. Eventually you'll arrive at California's finest example of tufa towers, some of which reach 140 feet tall. Like the more famous but less spectacular tufa towers at Mono Lake, these mineral spires were formed underwater when Searles Lake filled this basin. Blue-green algae living in hot springs underwater combined with calcium from the springs and carbonate from the lake water. The result was tons of calcium carbonate that formed around the edges of each spring and left behind these spectacular spires.

Be very careful climbing on the towers because the calcium carbonate rock is soft and unreliable. It's also very abrasive on hands and any bare skin that has the misfortune to scrape it. While they're fun to poke around, to me the towers are best enjoyed from a slight distance; they make a wonderful fantasy backdrop. Their other worldliness has earned them roles in several of the *Star Trek* films and other sci-fi adventures.

## WILDLIFE VIEWING

The thread of life runs thin in such an unforgiving environment. While you might think that Death Valley is barren, that nothing could live here, closer examination reveals that the desert is filled with life. You simply have to learn to find it. The first thing to realize is that most desert wildlife is nocturnal. Your best bets to see things are during the dawn and dusk hours. You can hike around all day looking for wildlife under the blazing sun and not see so much as a mouse. But come out during the first rays of light or under a full moon and you'll find the desert bustling with activity. Listen for the yapping of coyotes, which stay fat and healthy from the large resident population of mice and kangaroo rats. The most spectacular and elusive of the large mammals in the region is the desert bighorn sheep. Titus Canyon is a good spot to see them, especially climbing on the rock walls of The Narrows.

Waterholes are the foundation of almost every animal's existence here. While it's tempting to stake out a spring and see who comes to drink in the evening, just remember that many of the desert animals will simply stay away and go thirsty if they smell you there. It's for this reason that camping near waterholes is prohibited everywhere in the park. Existing on such thin margins, one night without drinking can be enough to weaken and possibly kill a desert bighorn.

Of all the different ecosystems that exist in the desert, none are as isolated and alien as the aquatic ones. Believe it or not, there are fish that live here— several different species and subspecies of pupfish, which look a lot like fat guppies. Though rattlesnakes, vultures, and coyotes have a bigger reputation, I think the all-around award for toughest animal in the park has to go to these fish. See the largest populations of them at **Salt Creek,** 14 miles north of Furnace Creek at the end of a mile-long gravel road. A winding boardwalk will take you on a tour of this strange, salty wetland, where pickleweed bunches line the banks of a saltwater creek, the temperature of which ranges from almost freezing to almost boiling over the course of the year. A similar but much more extensive environment can be found at the **Saline Valley Salt Marsh,** which is large enough to attract numerous migrating waterfowl and shorebirds.

# Campgrounds & Other Accommodations

Two words of advice to people camping here, no matter what time of year: BRING SHADE. As you might expect from a place with very few trees, the campgrounds are very exposed.

Park camping reservations can be made up to 5 months in advance for sites at the **Furnace Creek Campground** by calling 800/365-2267. The other eight campgrounds are first-come, first-served.

Depending on the time of year you visit, some campgrounds are more desirable than others. In the heat of summer, the high-country camps of **Wildrose, Thorndike,** and **Mahogany Flat** are by far the most comfortable. It's estimated that the temperature drops 5°F for every 1,000 feet you climb in Death Valley, and when it's 120°F in Furnace Creek, you'll sure appreciate the difference when you're sitting around 8,133-foot Mahogany Flat. Winter finds the situation exactly reversed. During this season the lower camps are nice and toasty, while it might be snowing up in the mountains. Camping is also allowed in the undeveloped areas of the park subject to the following limitations: Overnight sites must be 1 mile from the nearest paved road and at least a quarter mile from any water source (to protect wildlife and water quality). You must not practice trace camping wherever you go.

The nine official campgrounds in the park are as follows:

## Furnace Creek

Located directly behind the main visitor area in the park at the junction of highways 178 and 190. 136 sites. Flush toilets, running water, tables, fire pits, and lots of nearby services. Wheelchair accessible. Pets okay on leash. This is the only campground in the park that takes reservations (tel. 800/365-265). Open year-round. $16 per night.

The good news is that Furnace Creek campground is one of the only places in the park with tree-shaded sites. The bad news is that they're not all shady, and it's damn hot here most of the year and unbearable in summer. For people looking for a really civilized camping option in the park, though, this is it. You can walk to stores, restaurants, even a golf course, as well as museums and a full spectrum of ranger programs.

## Sunset Camp

Across the highway from Furnace Creek. 1,000 sites. Water, flush toilets, picnic tables, dump station, and ranger programs. Pets okay on leash. Open year-round. $10 per night.

This is the only place I've ever seen the number of campsites reach into four figures—that isn't an extra zero on the number of sites above. Sunset is where those unfortunate enough to not have a reservation for Furnace Creek wind up. It's got all the ambience of a parking lot, which is effectively what it is. Good luck.

## Texas Spring

0.5 mile east of the Furnace Creek Inn on Hwy. 190. 93 individual sites plus two group sites that each accommodate up to 70 people. Group sites are available by reservation. Water, flush toilets, fireplaces, picnic tables, dump, and ranger programs. Pets okay on leash. Open Nov–April. $10 per night.

Texas Spring is easy striking distance from the main Death Valley attractions in the lowest part of the valley and the services of Furnace Creek, but it's tucked slightly up a side canyon and is much more attractive than Sunset. Try here first before giving in to camping in that parking lot.

## Stovepipe Wells

Hwy. 190 adjacent to the Stovepipe Wells dunes. 200 sites. Water, some fireplaces, flush toilets, and ranger programs. Pets okay on leash. Open Nov–April. $10 per night.

The camping here is nothing special, but the location is wonderful for its access to the rolling dunes of Stovepipe Wells. Nearby are a hotel, camp store, gas station, and, last but not least, a pool.

## Emigrant

Hwy. 190, 9 miles west of Stovepipe Wells. 10 sites. Flush toilets, running water, fireplaces, and picnic tables. Open May–Oct. Free.

Little more than a gravel field with separate sites, Emigrant's most attractive feature is its price and the fact that at 2,000 feet in elevation it's out of the most forbidding heat. Also, the small size is nice, but noise from the nearby road will make up for the lack of loud neighbors.

## Wildrose

Located on Wildrose Rd. on the very western edge of the park between Hwy. 190 and Panamint Valley Rd. 30 sites. Piped water (except winter), pit toilets, fireplaces, and tables. Open year-round. Free.

Wildrose is a perfect base for exploring the high country of the Panamint Mountains. At 4,100 feet, it's pleasant even in summer. During the depth of winter it can be cold and snowy. The nearby Wildrose ranger station is a good resource for planning your backcountry adventures.

## Mahogany Flat

9 miles east of Wildrose in Wildrose Canyon. Difficult access. 10 sites. No running water. Pit toilets, picnic tables, fire pits. Open April–Oct. Free.

The highest campground in the park, Mahogany Flat is also near the trailhead to Telescope Peak, the highest point in the park. Head here when it's too hot in the valley below. These 10 sites, though difficult to reach without a sturdy, high-clearance vehicle, fill up quickly during the summer months.

## Thorndike

8 miles east of Wildrose on Wildrose Canyon Rd. Difficult access. 8 sites. No running water. Pit toilets, picnic tables, fire pits. Open March–Oct. Free.

Another great hot-weather hangout. The nearby Charcoal Kilns were built by Chinese laborers to provide fuel for ore smelters in surrounding mines. The scrubby pinyon pines here in the Panamints were the only significant source of fuel wood for miles.

## Mesquite Springs

Located in the north-central part of the park on Hwy. 178, 4 miles south of Scotty's Castle. 30 sites. Water, flush toilets, tables, fire pits, ranger programs. Open year-round. $10 per night.

This campground is one of my favorites. It's at an elevation of almost 2,000 feet, so it's cooler than the Furnace Creek area, but it gives a great sense of the barren geology of Death Valley. A large spring waters the namesake grove of mesquite trees near the entrance, plus several other species of trees, including cottonwoods.

## INNS & LODGES

### Stovepipe Wells Village

Hwy. 190 and Cottonwood Canyon Rd. Tel. 760/786-2387. 88 rooms. $90–$130. AE, DC, DISC, MC, V.

The best thing you can say about the motel at Stovepipe Wells is it's got air-conditioning and there's a swimming pool. Other than that, it's just your basic national park concession hotel, average in every way. Lots of fun things to do are nearby, though, so you won't be spending much time indoors.

### Furnace Creek Ranch

Hwy. 190 near the main park visitor center. 224 rooms and cabins. $90–$130. AE, DC, DISC, MC, V.

Located in the middle of downtown Death Valley under the shade of towering date palms, the old cabins here are pretty charming in their own way. Swamp coolers rattle through the night trying to keep up with the heat and it's hardly luxury, but it's the most popular and economical lodging in the park. The newer motel units are nicer but less charming. You're walking distance from everything you could possibly need: golf course, bar, two restaurants, museum, pool, horseback rides, date farm. Now the challenge is to actually get out and see the park.

### Furnace Creek Inn

Intersection of Hwy. 190 and Hwy. 178 just south of Furnace Creek. 66 rooms. $245–$345. AE, DC, DISC, MC, V.

When huge deposits of borates were discovered near Boron, California, in 1926—hundreds of miles closer to market than Death Valley—the owners of mines here realized that they'd better look for a new way to earn money. The Pacific Coast Borax Company, with the encouragement of the Tonopah and Tidewater Railroad, commissioned Los Angeles architect Albert Martin to design a luxury hotel at the mouth of Furnace Creek Wash. A year later this fantasy of a hotel was complete. This is the place to see and be seen in Death Valley; the list of famous and fabulous people who've slept here is a mile long, including presidents, movie starlets, and mobsters. The rooms are nice but not spectacular. What you're really paying for is the timelessness of the stonework, the phenomenal view, and the feeling that you've just dropped back into a more glamorous era. When I stayed here I was stunned to discover that the restaurant—which is easily the best in Death Valley—actually requires men to wear a sport jacket to dinner, a nice touch, but one that I wasn't prepared for on what was mostly a camping trip. There's also a beautiful pool, which, unfortunately, is fed by a hot spring. Any other place but Death Valley I'd find that refreshing, but 95°F water isn't what I want after a hot day of hiking.

# 8

# JOSHUA TREE & PALM SPRINGS/ COACHELLA VALLEY

O F THE CALIFORNIA DESERT'S THREE LARGE NATIONAL PARKS, Joshua Tree lies closest to the L.A. metropolis and is thus incredibly popular. Thousands come here every year to camp under the jumbo rocks, hear the coyotes sing, and wander through a desert garden of cactus, Joshua trees, and rare palm oases. Even more come to test their climbing skills on the endless monzogranite outcroppings that have made Joshua Tree into North America's most famous winter climbing spot. The climber's camp in Hidden Valley feels like Yosemite's Camp Seven once did; racks of climbing gear hang from every truck, four-season expedition tents look out of place pitched in the California sun, and scruffy, sunburned men and women with biceps of steel sit around their camp stove espresso makers swapping tales of their latest exploits. And there are routes galore. Just the published guidebook routes could take you a lifetime to explore, and they only scratch the surface. Away from the easy road access there are hundreds of square miles of rock that have hardly been climbed.

Despite its overwhelming popularity, Joshua Tree remains low-key. Much to the credit of the park administration, Joshua Tree National Park still maintains an outback feel, with none of the kitsch so prevalent in popular national parks. Camping is free and first-come, first-served. Visitor centers are small and on the fringes of the park. There are no stores, motels, or gas stations within the park. In short, it's a place for people who like to be outdoors rather than merely look at the outdoors.

People have flocked to Palm Springs and lesser-known Coachella Valley towns like Palm Desert, Rancho Mirage, and Desert Hot Springs to escape the grip of winter since Bob Hope and Frank Sinatra were up-and-coming youngsters. The brat pack and conservative celebrities like Charlton Heston and Ronald Reagan flocked here for golf and gala parties in rambling ranch homes replete with swimming pools and waterfalls. The area amounted to a beach town without that troubling reality of beach life—fog and cool weather. The sun shines almost every day of the year here. Summers are hot and dry and winters are shirt-sleeve warm without fail.

The main crowd in Palm Springs is still retirement age, but retirement is no longer the only game in town. Having fun is no longer just a choice between golf, the Indian casino, and martinis by the pool. People also come here to hike, rock climb, mountain bike, camp, bird watch, and, yes, cross-country ski. Long-closed canyons on the Indian reservation are being reopened to public hiking, an air-conditioned climbing gym sits under a giant canopy, and mountain bikes are almost as common as golf carts.

## The Lay of the Land

Though the **Coachella Valley** lies near sea level, huge mountains rise on almost every side. Joshua Tree National Park's **Little San Bernardino Mountains** hold down the northeast, the **San Jacintos** lie to the southwest, and towering **Mount San Gorgonio,** at 11,499 feet the tallest mountain in Southern California, sits to the north. Only to the southeast does the land drop away, where the Coachella Valley slopes gradually to 228 feet below sea level at the Salton Sea.

Geographically speaking, this region is the major transition zone between the high desert of the Mojave and the low-lying Colorado Desert. Driving south through Joshua Tree on El Dorado Mine Road, you can actually watch the change occur. The Joshua trees become smaller and less healthy, and creosote bush becomes the predominant vegetation. The cactus population increases, too, with significant stands of ocotillo and jumping cholla lining the road. The difference between the two deserts is soft-spoken and often too subtle for those of us accustomed to the overstated antics of more temperate climates to see clearly, but desert aficionados are unanimous that this is one of the best places to see the demarcation between the two zones.

The high peaks of **San Jacinto State Park** and the San Gorgonio Wilderness in **San Bernardino National Forest** are something else entirely, islands of pine forest having more in common with the Sierra Nevada than with the desert only 5 miles away. Perhaps the most dramatic way to experience this abrupt transition is the Palm Springs Aerial Tramway. Step on the tramway just outside Palm Springs in the heat of the Colorado Desert and within 15 minutes you'll step off at the altitude of 8,516 feet in an alpine forest of lodgepole and limber pines, grassy meadows, granite outcroppings, and, during the winter, several feet of snow. With a little ambition you can hike a 10-mile round-trip to the 10,804 summit of Mount San Jacinto, where you've got 360-degree views of everything from the Pacific Ocean to the Salton Sea and beyond.

In between these extremes lie many points of natural and historic interest. The **Santa Rosa Mountains** are a lesser extension of the San Jacintos, less lofty but equally beautiful. Pinyon forests, juniper, manzanita, prickly pear, and yucca bring to mind the mountain forests of New Mexico and Arizona, narrowly separated from the desert by the luxury of a few extra inches of annual rainfall.

The **Colorado Desert** is quite a place to visit, too. Within an hour's drive of Palm Springs are several grand desert oases, where plentiful spring water comes to the surface, allowing plants to capitalize on the generous energy of the desert sun without withering away. With water and plants come animals, and these desert oases are the best places to see elusive desert dwellers like mule deer, coyotes, mountain lions, and bighorn sheep. The most striking exhibition of this is at the Coachella Valley Preserve, where the San Andreas Fault allows subterranean water to seep upward, providing sustenance for 1,200 California fan palms that grow in this 13,000-acre park. Another excellent oasis is **Big Morongo Canyon Park and Preserve,** where several springs contribute to a wetland that by appearances has more in common with the Sacramento River Delta than the desert just half a mile away. Numerous other sources of water, both large and small, make the most interesting hiking and nature viewing destinations.

Though this region is wild, it's hard to classify it as wilderness in the same sense as Death Valley and the East Mojave. More than 300,000 people live in the immediate area, and 12 million more are just a short drive away. Interstate 10, which connects Southern California with Phoenix and Albuquerque, runs right through the Coachella Valley. Highway 62, which leads northeast along the northern boundary of Joshua Tree, is a more or less continuous strip of tract homes, trailer parks, and strip malls from Whitewater to 29 Palms, which in addition to being the gateway to Joshua Tree is home to the enormous 29 Palms Marine Corps Combat Training Center. Some days you can sit on the rocks in Joshua Tree and watch the rising dust clouds as Marines make mock-combat in every form of war machine imaginable.

Despite the region's proximity to so many people, solitude is quite easy to come by. A little effort and preparation pay off with every footstep you take away from parking lots and air-conditioning. Most people simply pass through this desert on the way to somewhere else, or come to lounge poolside in the dry heat. But the desert has always rewarded those who approach it on its own terms with a deep and rich, if sometimes uncomfortable, experience.

# Parks & Other Hot Spots

## Joshua Tree National Park

100 miles east of Los Angeles on I-10 and Hwy. 62 to the town of Twentynine Palms, where an access road leads into the center of the park. The visitor center is at 74485 National Park Dr., Twentynine Palms, CA 92277. Tel. 619/367-7511.

Although the park was obviously named for the striking Joshua trees that sprout in some areas, these yuccalike members of the lily family are hardly the most distinguishing characteristic of this nearly million-acre preserve. In fact, the park lies right at the southern edge of the Joshua tree's range, and there are far

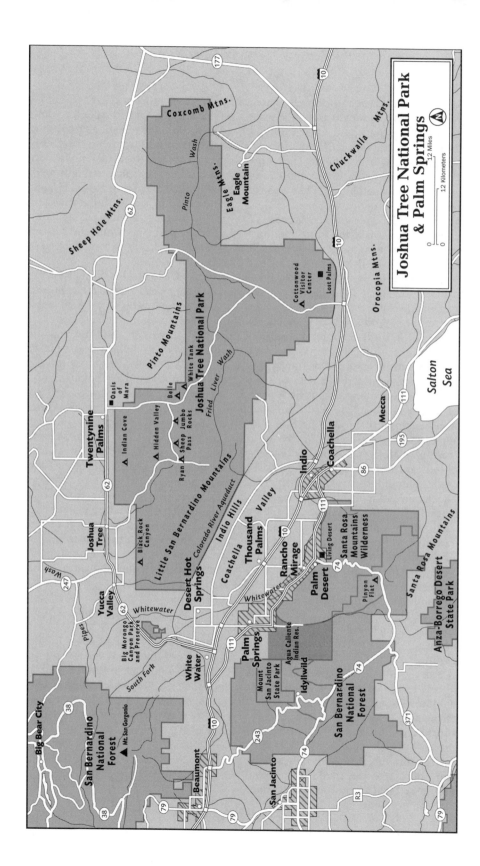

Joshua Tree National Park
& Palm Springs

12 Miles

12 Kilometers

**Coxcomb Mtns.**

Pinto Wash

**Eagle Mtns.**
Eagle Mountain

**Chuckwalla Mtns.**

77

10

10

**Sheep Hole Mtns.**

62

Cottonwood
Visitor Center

Lost Palms

**Orocopia Mtns.**

White Tank
Belle

**Pinto Mountains**

Oasis
of Mara

Fried Liver Wash

**Salton
Sea**

**Joshua Tree National Park**

Indian Cove
Hidden Valley
Jumbo
Rocks
Ryan Sheep
Pass

Mecca

111

**Twentynine
Palms**

62

**Indio**

**Coachella**

86

195

Joshua
Tree

Black Rock
Canyon

**Little San Bernardino Mountains**

Colorado River Aqueduct

**Indio Hills**

**Coachella
Valley**

**Thousand
Palms**

Living Desert

**Santa Rosa
Mountains
Wilderness**

247

Wash

Pipes

**Yucca
Valley**

62

Whitewater

Big Morongo
Canyon Park
and Preserve

South Fork

**Desert Hot
Springs**

**Rancho
Mirage**

10

111

**Palm
Desert**

74

Pinyon
Flat

**Santa Rosa Mountains**

**Anza-Borrego Desert
State Park**

**White
Water**

111

Whitewater

**Palm
Springs**

Agua Caliente
Indian Res.

**Big Bear City**

38

**San Bernardino
National
Forest**

Mt. San Gorgonio

10

243

Mount
San Jacinto
State Park

Idyllwild

74

**San Bernardino
National Forest**

74

371

**Beaumont**

79

**San Jacinto**

74

R3

79

better examples of the tree elsewhere in the Mojave. If they'd asked me what to name the park, I'd have called it Jumbo Rocks National Park, for the wondrous geology here is like now here I've ever seen. Huge jumbles of rounded monzogranite boulders tower over large parts of the park. One section, the Wonderland of Rocks, is literally 12 square miles consisting of nothing but canyon after canyon of gigantic rock faces that are like a never ending Rorschach test. Some look like skulls, others like animals, and one even looks just like the squaw on the Land-o-Lakes butter box. And they shelter secret water holes, Indian rock art, and desert wildlife.

The most visited part of the park is along the Loop Road that connects the West Entrance Station in the little town of Joshua Tree with the Main Entrance in Twentynine Palms. Along this awesome route you'll climb quickly up to the high plateau that is the centerpiece of the park and see the Jumbo Rocks, a really splendid display of reddish granite; Queen Valley, where the best Joshua trees in the park grow; the Geology Road, an 18-mile dirt-road tour that visits Indian petroglyphs and explains the forces at work on the landscape; Hidden Valley, where much of the climbing in the park is centered; and the Wonderland of Rocks. Scattered throughout the park are the remains of old gold mines and desert ranches that eked a living out of running cattle over this hardscrabble ground.

Another fine thing to see are Joshua Tree's lovely palm oases. Vital to the wildlife of the desert, these natural watering holes stand in striking contrast to the harsh landscape that surrounds them. Birds flutter and chirp, the wind rustles through palm fans, frogs peep and croak, and the shade is cool and heavenly. The Cottonwood Oasis sits at the park's southern entrance off I-10 where there's a visitor center, campground, and ranger station. You can get to 49 Palms Oasis from a trailhead at the end of Canyon Road off Highway 62. And the Oases of Mara sits right on the outskirts of Twentynine Palms. Groundwater pumping and suburban encroachment have a negative impact on this one, but it's worth a look while you're at the visitor center, if only to compare it to the others.

Indian Cove and Black Rock Canyon are two park areas that are not connected by road to the center of the park and lie at a lower elevation. Both are popular in the dead of winter when the high altitude areas can be chilly and even get snow. Indian Cove, in particular, is a popular climbing area. Black Rock Canyon is a nice example of a classic desert wash that drains a large area of the Little San Bernardino Mountains. The park has very little in the way of services. With the exception of Black Rock Canyon and Indian Cove, none of the seven other campgrounds in the park has water. Camping is first-come, first-served, and fills up quickly on winter weekends. There are no stores, gas stations, or motels in the park, but all those services are available a short drive away in the cities of Twentynine Palms or Joshua Tree.

## San Jacinto State Park

Reached via Palm Springs Aerial Tramway at the end of Tramway Road 3.7 miles off Calif. 111, or through the town of Idyllwild, approximately 20 miles west and 26 miles south of Palm Springs via I-10 and Hwy. 243. For tram information call 619/ 325-1449. Park information is 909/ 659-2607.

San Jacinto State Park is unique in that most visitors arrive via aerial tramway. It's pretty weird to step aboard the tramway (exactly the same as many ski area trams) in the heat of the Colorado Desert and step off in a cool piney forest or, in winter, step out into a snowy wonderland.

Many people just ride the tram, take in the view, and leave, but those who explore the high country of this park find a lot to recommend it. Granite peaks, flowing streams, and grassy meadows offer respite from the endless summer down below. And the views up here are mind-blowing. From the summit of Mount San Jacinto, roughly a 10-mile round-trip from the tramway, you can see from Nevada to the Pacific Ocean and all the way to Mexico.

The alternate route to visiting the park is to drive to the charming little mountain town of Idyllwild. This side is popular with climbers who come to enjoy the long, multi-pitch routes on Tahquitz and Suicide Rocks.

### Santa Rosa Mountains Wilderness

From Palm Desert turn south from Hwy. 111 onto Hwy. 74, which you will take up into the mountains for 16 miles to the Sugarloaf Cafe. Several trailheads are marked off Hwy. 74 in this area.

This is another island of high mountain wilderness within a short drive of the Palm Desert area. The Santa Rosa Mountains are lower than the neighboring San Jacintos and more arid. Much of the region is covered in a desert chaparral combining plants like manzanita, yucca, juniper, prickly pear, and agave. The highest peaks in the wilderness are

Santa Rosa (8,000 ft.) and Toro Peak (8,716 ft.).

### Mecca Hills Recreation Area

Located between I-10, Hwy. 111, and Box Canyon Rd., this BLM and county recreation is reached by a variety of rugged dirt roads. Call the BLM in Palm Springs for road information (Tel. 619/251-4800). Hiking, spelunking.

The Mecca Hills is an eerily eroded badland of slot canyons, mineral-stained hillsides, and secret oases. It's one of the hottest places in the state, but if you time your visit for the cool season, you'll be rewarded with some fantastic desert experiences.

### The Living Desert Museum & Wildlife Park

From I-10 exit onto Bob Hope Dr. and go south 5.5 miles to Calif. 111. Turn left (east) onto Calif. 111 for 3 miles to Portola Ave. Turn right (south) on Portola for 1.5 miles to 47–900 Portola Ave., where you'll see the entrance to the reserve. Adult $7, child $3.50. Daily 9am–5pm. Closed June 16–Aug 31 and on Christmas. Lectures, museum.

This 1,200-acre nonprofit facility is the best single concentration of desert information and displays in the state, if not the whole world. It's hard to describe the place in just a few words. Part research facility, part school, part museum, and part wildlife park, the Living Desert has gardens representing many different desert ecosystems, from the Joshua trees of the Mojave to the saguaro cactus forest of the Sonoran Desert.

What will thrill the kids, though, are the animal inhabitants of the park. Displays range from desert bighorn sheep, coyotes, and foxes to such things as sidewinder rattlesnakes, a bat exhibit, and a pond filled with desert pupfish.

### Indian Canyons

S. Palm Canyon Dr., Palm Springs. Tel. 619/325-5673. Adult $5, student $3.50. Open daily 8am–6pm. Closed June–Sept.

Long before movie stars and golfers had descended on Palm Springs, the Native Americans knew a good thing when they found it. Several beautiful canyons lie on the Agua Caliente Indian Reservation just minutes from downtown Palm Springs. They're kind enough to allow visitors to hike through these palm-filled oases beside rushing creeks. It's a totally different world in these canyons and would be a bargain at twice the price.

### Big Morongo Canyon Preserve

From Calif. 62 about 9.5 miles north of the intersection with I-10, look for a sign for Big Morongo Canyon Preserve. Open 7:30am–sunset.

This 3,900-acre reserve is one of the most famous birding spots in the desert. As Morongo Creek flows underground from the San Gorgonio Mountains, it hits a layer of nonporous rock here that forces its flow to the surface. As a result, trees, plants, and wildlife flourish. Several great hikes begin in this area, a nice spot for a picnic.

### Coachella Valley Preserve

10 miles east of Palm Springs near Thousand Palms, just off I-10. Tel. 619/343-1234.

The San Andreas Fault creates a surplus of groundwater here. As a result, thousands of California fan palms grow in the series of gently sloping canyons. The Valley Preserve is a nice, mellow place to gain an introduction to the desert. Stay away during the summer, however, when temperatures rise into the unbearable range.

# What to Do & Where to Do It

## BIRD WATCHING

As in every desert environment, the limiting factor here is water. Find water and you'll find a plentitude of species. Away from water, the number of birds becomes limited to those specialized enough to exist on thin margins of moisture.

**Big Morongo Canyon Preserve** is the finest concentrated birding spot in the area. This narrow canyon sustains five different plant communities ranging from cottonwood and willow wetlands to cactus forest. The best viewing is in the spring, when as many as 72 species nest here. Annual bird counts generally find around 250 species, including vermilion flycatchers, Costa's hummingbirds, marsh wrens, and several birds of prey.

The bristling branches of the namesake trees in **Joshua Tree National Park** are a draw for cactus wrens, ladder-backed woodpeckers, and Scott's orioles. Prime time for these species is spring, when the popcorn-white blossoms of the

Joshua trees are in bloom. The park also is home to five palm oases, all of which provide water and shade for numerous species, including mourning doves, finches, and quail.

For a total change in scenery, ride the Palm Springs Aerial Tramway to the granite peaks and tall pine forests of **Mount San Jacinto State Park.** Species more common to the Sierra Nevada like Clark's nutcrackers, Steller's jays, and western bluebirds call this biological island home.

## CROSS-COUNTRY SKIING & SNOWSHOEING

The very thought of snow sports near Palm Springs seems preposterous, but it's true. The enormous vertical contrast between the valley floor and the surrounding peaks means it's truly possible to lounge poolside all morning and then, after just a 14-minute tram ride, cross-country ski through a beautiful evergreen forest. One fine benefit is that you'll never have to put on chains to get here; all driving is done well below snowline.

It'll never put Tahoe out of business, and the very name seems like an oxymoron, but the **Palm Springs Nordic Ski Center** in Mount San Jacinto State Park is a unique place well worth the visit. Generally open from November 15 to April 15, snow permitting, the Nordic center has a few packed groomed trails and rental equipment averaging $18 per day for ski packages and $15 for snowshoes. For current snow conditions call 760/327-6002. You may also bring your own gear to the park and ski the extensive network of backcountry trails for free. Everyone, however, must pay the $17.65 round-trip tram fare ($11.65 children 5 to 12). For tram information call 760/325-1391.

## HIKING & BACKPACKING

You'll find more diverse hiking in this area than anywhere in the state. Within an hour's drive you can find everything from narrow slot canyons and secret swimming holes, to baking hot desert arroyos, to palm oases, to granite-capped peaks and pine forests. There's an enviable surplus of choices, where the biggest struggle is deciding which of many attractive options to choose.

Keep in mind that weather and season mean the difference between a great excursion and disaster. Summer can be hot everywhere in the chapter and incredibly, dangerously hot in the low-lying areas like **Mecca Hills** and **Coachella Valley Preserve.** No matter where you are, don't fool yourself into attempting a tough hike when the temperatures are roasting. Always carry more water than you think you'll need, and plan your trips so you'll be out of the heat during the middle of the day.

### Barker Dam Loop, Joshua Tree

1.25 miles. Easy. Access: From Hidden Valley Campground, a signed dirt road leads 2 miles to Barker Dam Trailhead.

This is a fun and easy hike that will take you into the fringes of the Wonderland of Rocks to a hidden lake. Cowboys built a series of dams here, the most recent built in the 1950s, to expand a naturally occurring water hole. The resulting lake covers several acres and provides a vital source of water for wildlife. You may also notice huge numbers of freshwater shrimp in the murky water as well as tadpoles and adult frogs.

From the trailhead, follow the sandy trail through an arroyo between towering granite rocks. Shortly, it opens up into a wide valley, which is filled by Barker Lake. The trail just skirts the southern edge of the lake, but more intrepid explorers can easily rock-hop around the entire perimeter. The air is always noticeably cooler here on the shore of the lake; during the early morning and evening hours birds flit through the air.

Continue following the trail in a counterclockwise loop that will pass through a sandy area of Joshua trees and numerous cacti. Eventually you'll come to a low line of cliffs. A little exploring in either direction will reveal Indian petroglyphs. The most obvious set was badly desecrated by a Hollywood movie crew, which painted over them in bright colors to make them more visible on film. Many others remain in the area and are not marked to avoid such destruction. Obviously you should treat any petroglyphs you find with the same respect you'd treat any other invaluable thousand-year-old art form. Beyond here the trail quickly returns to the parking area.

### Lost Horse Mine Trail, Joshua Tree

3.5 miles. Moderate. 400-foot gain. Access: From the main loop road through central Joshua Tree, turn south at Caprock Junction onto Keys View Rd. In 2.5 miles, you'll come to a dirt road marked "Lost Horse Mine" on the left. Follow it to a parking area.

Long after the gold rush of the Sierra Nevada had dried up, prospectors were making important strikes in the Mojave. Johnny Lang's Lost Horse Mine was the most lucrative strike in this corner of the desert, producing more than 9,000 ounces of gold between 1896 and 1899.

Lang's career as a miner was checkered with glory and ignominy. A display at the trailhead chronicles his rise and fall; his life culminated in his emaciated and desiccated body being found by the side of the road you drove in on.

The hike follows an old mine road from the parking area through a desert wash and up to the site of the Lost Horse's 10-stamp mill and several old mine shafts. While the park service has gated many of these old mines, there's always the chance of stepping somewhere you really don't want to step. Keep one eye open when stomping around off the trail.

Besides its mineral wealth, the Lost Horse was also wealthy in views, something that was probably lost on the miners but not to you. A short scramble to the top of the nearest hill will pay off in great vistas of the park.

### Lost Palms Oasis, Joshua Tree

8 miles round-trip. Moderate–difficult. 300-foot elevation gain. Access: From I-10 east of Indio, drive into the park's south entrance and 8 miles to the visitor center and Cottonwood Spring Campground.

Lying in the lower section of Joshua Tree, this hike takes you through an excellent array of Colorado desert plant communities to visit two oases.

The first you'll come to is Cottonwood Spring Oasis, only a half-mile from the trailhead. Here, prospectors and other explorers planted trees to create shade. The resulting cottonwood oasis is a nice break from the unrelenting heat of the Colorado Desert sun. Continue on through a series of sandy washes with some very vague intersections that are fortunately marked by the park. You'll crest a final rise and see what seems like a miracle below: At least a hundred tall California fan palms nestled into a narrow canyon of dark rock.

Once upon a time there was standing water here, but except for the wettest of years it's all underground now. The trees provide shade, food, and shelter for a variety of desert birds and animals. Enjoy yourself in the shade and return the way you came.

## Palm Canyon Trail, Indian Canyons

3–6 miles. Moderate. 200–400 foot elevation gain. Access: From Palm Springs take South Palm Canyon Dr. to the Agua Caliente Indian reservation tollgate. Pay the $6 per person entrance fee and drive to the trailhead at Hermit's Bench.

It wasn't without reason that Palm Springs gained its name. Above the groomed golf courses and strip malls of the town lie several stunning canyons where perennial streams flow beneath thousands of palm trees. This is the greatest concentration of native California fan palms in the world.

From the slightly ticky-tacky Indian trading post, this trail descends into Palm Canyon for several miles. Groves of palms and deep pools appear along the way. During winter the water in the creek is frigid snowmelt, but later in the spring and fall it's nice for swimming. Go as far as you like and then turn around and return the way you came. Remember that the reservation is closed to outsiders at 5pm—and they're serious about that. It's also closed entirely from late June to early September.

## Tahquitz Canyon

3 miles round-trip. Easy. From South Palm Canyon Dr., take Tahquitz Canyon Dr. west to the gated trailhead. Pay a $6 admission fee to the Agua Caliente Indians and begin hiking.

Only blocks from downtown Palm Springs, this lovely canyon has long been off-limits to outsiders—since a 1969 Canned Heat concert ended in thousands of partygoers stampeding into the canyon for days of debauched fun that trashed the place and left the Agua Caliente tribe with a bad taste in their mouths. They fenced and posted the canyon after that and are only just now reopening it to the public 19 years later.

The trail leads 1.5 miles to a 70-foot waterfall. While the canyon continues for miles upstream, the tribe has chosen to keep that area closed because of dangerous waterfalls and the difficulty of rescuing people who are hurt in the upper reaches. For now enjoy this lovely spot with palms and a roaring waterfall just minutes from downtown Palm Springs, and remember that if you packed it in you can—must—pack it out too.

## Big Morongo Canyon Trail

6 miles, one-way. Moderate. Access: From Hwy. 68 10 miles north of I-10, turn at the signed Big Morongo Wildlife Preserve. For the pickup or shuttle at the bottom of Big Morongo Canyon, exit Hwy. 68 at Indian Ave. Drive exactly 1 mile east, where a dirt road turns off to the left. Park here near the chain-link fence.

This area is an important transition zone from the high desert to the low desert. Used by both human inhabitants and wildlife for thousands of years as a migration route, Big Morongo Canyon is widely known as a fantastic wildlife viewing spot.

This hike leads one-way downhill through the canyon with a 1,900-foot elevation loss. You can also do it as a round-trip, but that's a long, hard 12 miles. Shorter paths and hikes lace the upper part of the canyon where the best birding and wildlife viewing are. From the parking lot you'll want to pick your way through the upper preserve's maze of trail to the Canyon Trail. For the first 3 miles the creek is almost always above ground and the proliferation of birds, lush plantlife, and larger animal tracks reflects this wealth of water. Lower in the canyon the creek descends into the ever-widening sandy wash and disappears.

Stay to the right as the streambed widens and you'll reach the chain-link fence at the edge of the preserve where you left your shuttle car.

### Living Desert Jaeger Nature Trail

2-mile loop. Easy. Access: From Hwy. 111 in Palm Desert, turn south onto Portola Ave. and follow it 1.5 miles to the entrance of Living Desert Wildlife and Botanical Park. Pay the entrance fee (adult $7.50, child $3.50) and enter the park.

The 2-mile **Jaeger Nature Trail** in the Living Desert Wildlife and Botanical Park loop (see "Parks & Other Hot Spots," above) has a corresponding interpretive booklet that will help you understand many of the complex relationships among desert inhabitants and give names to many of the formations and plants you see. I highly recommend that anyone new to the desert come here before heading out to do some real hiking on his or her own.

A popular hike that departs from Living Desert is the 6-mile **Eisenhower Peak Loop,** which begins at the quail guzzler on the Jaeger Trail. This hardscrabble hike gains 700 feet on the way to the summit of its namesake peak. Bring lots of water and wear sturdy shoes.

### Coachella Valley Preserve Trails

0.5–5 miles. Easy–moderate. Access: From I-10 just west of Indio, exit onto Washington St. Drive north 5 miles and turn right at Thousand Palms Rd. In 2 miles, you'll see a lush palm oasis and a park entrance on your left.

Come here any time but summer for a gentle exploration of one of the most immense native palm groves in the state. This 13,000-acre preserve wasn't set aside strictly to preserve the palm groves. In fact, the species that inspired humankind to save this great area from the development that's taken much of the rest of the Coachella Valley isn't a tree at all, but a lizard.

If you're lucky, you might spot one of the Coachella Valley fringe-toed lizards, an 8-inch long critter known for "swimming" through sand dunes using its spade-shaped head and scaley toes. And if you don't, you'll surely enjoy the desert wildlife that flocks to this spot. Credit for the incredible lushness of the area is due to the San Andreas Fault, which created all the springs that water this area.

Several trails leave from the dirt lot where you've parked. A favorite is the 1.5-mile **McCallum Trail,** a nature trail that explains the workings of this environment. For a deeper experience I recommend the **Wash Trail,** which explores the rocky, northern edge of the preserve.

### Palm Springs Cactus to Clouds Hike

22 miles one-way. Very difficult. 10,400 foot elevation gain. Access: Drive to the end of Ramon Rd. off I-10 in Palm Springs and park.

Only the truly demented need consider this hike. While most people who want to reach the high alpine forests of Mount San Jacinto State Park do it the easy way—taking the Palm Springs Aerial Tramway—there's always a cadre of gnarly folks who would rather hike than ride. For those hardcore devotionalists, I present the Palm Springs Cactus to Clouds Hike.

Begin by hiking the Lykken Trail at the end of Ramon Road. It will switchback for almost 1.5 miles as Palm Springs starts to shrink in the valley below. Take it easy because there's a long way to go. At 1.5 miles you'll reach a sign, a painted rock, actually, that says TO LONG VALLEY 8 MILES and indicates the left fork. Take this fork and get in that switchback rhythm. The next 8 miles are totally unrelenting as you climb out of the Coachella Valley.

The tramway operators brag that the ascent from the valley floor to the Long Valley Station encompasses the floral and faunal changes equivalent to driving from Sonora, Mexico, to the Arctic Circle. If you're not too busy wiping sweat off your brow and cursing yourself for attempting this trip on foot, you might notice that you are passing through a continuously changing natural community.

After the first 11 miles you'll reach Long Valley and the ranger station only a short walk from the tramway. Water is available here. The temperature should be 20° to 40° cooler than it was on the valley floor. If you're pooped, this is the time to bail out by hopping a tram ride down to the Valley Station, because the next 11 miles are difficult going too. Do it proudly because even this first 11 miles are one hell of a difficult hike.

Those gonzo hikers who are game to keep going need to get a Wilderness Permit from the ranger station and follow the clearly marked trail for the next 5.5 miles to the summit of Mount San Jacinto. Though most of the big elevation gain is behind you, this hike is still a tough one (read the following hike for more detail). From the summit you can see from the Pacific to Nevada, and down into Mexico. Return to Long Valley and the tram station the way you came, where you'll definitely want to take the easy way down, in the company of all the tourists who took the easy way up.

## Tramway to Mount San Jacinto Summit Hike

11 miles. Strenuous. 2,300 foot elevation gain. Access: From Hwy. 111 take Tramway Rd. 3.5 miles to Valley Station. Buy a ticket and ride the tram to Mountain Station.

From the tram landing at Mountain Station, walk the quarter-mile path to the state park ranger station. Here you can pick up a Wilderness Permit and a map.

The first 2 miles follow Long Valley Creek through meadows of wildflowers and a lovely forest of firs and pines. You'll know you've reached Round Valley when you come to the backcountry ranger station and camp in a forest of lodgepole pines. Here's where the going gets tough. Find the trail to Wellman Divide and follow it to the divide, where the view reveals many of the surrounding high peaks. Continue on the trail 2.7 more miles to the stone hut just below the summit. The formal trail doesn't actually reach the peak, but a short spur boulder hops to the top. Here you're blessed by one of the widest ranging views on earth. Below you can see the Pacific, the Los Angeles Basin, the Coachella Valley, the Salton Sea, and San Gorgonio Mountain, the highest in Southern California. After you've had enough, backtrack to Mountain Station the way you came and ride the tram down.

This trip can be split into a 2- or even 3-day trip by backpacking into the Round Valley backcountry camp. Doing so makes what is normally a very strenuous 1-day hike into a pleasant camping trip. Overnight camping anywhere in the state park requires a free special permit, which can be obtained either at the ranger station or as much as 56 days in advance by writing **Mount San Jacinto State Wilderness,** P.O. Box 308, Idyllwild, CA 92349 (tel. 909/659-2607).

## HORSEBACK RIDING

**Smoke Tree Stables** in Palm Springs can help equestrians tap into the feeling that must have greeted early travelers here when they first explored the palm-filled Indian canyons. All rides are guided and cost $25 per hour. Reserve by calling 760/327-1372.

A hit with the kids and senior citizens is the 25-minute nature tour of **Long Valley** at the top of the Palm Springs Aerial Tramway. Sturdy-footed mules carry their passengers on a short loop while their guide explains the flora and fauna of Mount San Jacinto State Park. The ride is $7 per person and operates spring, summer, and fall beginning at 11am weekdays and 10am weekends until dusk.

## HOT SPRINGS

There are no wild hot springs in the Joshua Tree and Palm Springs area, but the region has a long history as a hot-spring resort. The Agua Caliente band of the Cahuilla Indians were already partaking of the healthful aspects of naturally heated mineral water when the first white settlers came to Palm Springs. What was once just a natural pool has grown into a ridiculously overblown and tacky Spa Hotel and Casino, still owned by the Agua Caliente Band, at 100 N. Indian Canyon Dr. I can't recommend that anyone visit it unless a miniature Las Vegas is what you crave.

More in keeping with the natural beauty of the area is **Two Bunch Palms** at 67425 Two Bunch Palms Trail, Desert Hot Springs (tel. 619/329-8791). You have to be a guest to use the steaming pools of flawless, odorless hot water, but as legions of famous people, from Al Capone to current movie stars, and even more numerous normal people know, Two Bunch is the ultimate discreet place to unwind.

## MOUNTAIN BIKING IN & AROUND PALM SPRINGS

### Live Oak Canyon

21 miles one-way. Difficult. Access: Hwy. 74 and Penrod Canyon Rd. Car shuttle required. From Palm Desert, drive 19 miles southwest along Hwy. 74 to the parking area for the Palm Canyon Trail. In car no. 2, continue southwest on Hwy. 74 about 7 miles to Penrod Canyon Rd. Park along the highway.

Just south and west of Palm Springs lies some of the best mountain biking in the U.S. Here, low desert meets alpine forests. The views, the weather, the lack of crowds, and fine single track make the Coachella Valley a mountain-biking heaven. This one-way ride through Live Oak Canyon in the Santa Rosa Mountains is very difficult, both technically and in terms of route-finding—it requires a car shuttle—but the wild beauty and solitude make it all worthwhile.

Begin riding north on Penrod Road along a white fence, and go left at the fork and then through a gate. At about 5 miles, you'll reach Gold Shot Mine. Go right through the gate on **Trail 4E03,** which takes you across the Pacific Crest Trail and on a rough descent to Live Oak Spring. From here, it's a grueling trip to the **Palm Canyon Trail**—it's a difficult downhill and is easy to get lost. Make a right on the Palm Canyon Trail and climb up, switchbacking it about 5 miles to a fence, and continue up the hillside to the Palm Canyon trailhead and your car.

Remember, mountain biking access in these parts is always shifting. As of this writing, you'll need to contact the **Forest Service** (tel. 909/659-2117) for access status into Live Oak Canyon via Penrod Road, as it crosses private property.

## Pinyon Flats

4- to 12-mile loops. Easy. Access: Hwy. 74 and Palm Canyon Dr. From Palm Desert, drive 17 miles southwest along Hwy. 74 and turn right (north) on Palm Canyon Dr.

The small town of Pinyon Pines in the Santa Rosa Mountains offers lots of flat dirt roads, which comprise great beginner mountain biking and great views of Mount San Jacinto. The Santa Rosa range is full of challenging terrain, but this ride through the Pinyon Flats is easy, and there's a lot of loop possibilities. Start cycling on Palm Canyon Drive and have fun!

## Pinyon-Palm Canyon Loop

13 miles. Moderate–difficult. Access: Hwy. 74 and Palm Canyon Dr. From Palm Desert, drive 17 miles southwest along Hwy. 74 and turn right (north) on Palm Canyon Dr.

If Pinyon Flats was too easy for you, check out this amazing ride through Palm Canyon in the Santa Rosa Mountains on dirt roads, single track, and pavement. Beginning at Palm Canyon Drive in the town of Pinyon Pines, ride north on Palm Canyon, and at 3.3 miles, turn left (west) on an unmarked road just after Chalet Drive. Watch carefully and take the second dirt road on your right, then go left. Watch on your left for an unmarked single track that follows a fence line. Follow this single track though some sharp turns, over a ridge, and for the drop (very steep!) into Palm Canyon. At the bottom, cross Omstot Creek and pick up the trail on the other side, heading uphill. Now you're on the Palm Canyon Trail, switchbacking to the top of the ridge. Pedal along the ridge until you pass though a cattle gate (leaving it open or closed, depending on how you found it). It's down and then up to Hwy. 74, where you'll turn left on Palm Canyon Drive and head back to your car. Again, mountain biking access in these parts is always in flux, so call the **Forest Service** (tel. 909/659-2117) for current status.

## Thomas Mountain Loop

14-mile loop. Moderate. Access: Hwy. 74 and Thomas Mountain Rd. From Palm Desert, drive 25 miles southwest along Hwy. 74 and turn left (west) on Thomas Mountain Rd. Park along the road.

This is one of the most popular rides in the San Jacinto Mountains, with over 5 miles of great downhill single track as you pedal along Thomas Mountain Road. Start pedaling on the paved Thomas Mountain Road and turn left on Hop Springs Patch. Soon the road turns to dirt, and it's a short but steep climb up to a summit where you can overlook the town of Anza. Now the road continues north, climbing steadily through chaparral. At 5 miles, turn right at Tool Box Springs Camp (there's drinking water here) and follow it to its end and the beginning of the Ramona Trail, which is not marked.

Switchbacking through the pines never felt so good! This is quality single track. This trail brings you back to Highway 74, where you'll make a right and head back to your car.

### MOUNTAIN BIKING IN JOSHUA TREE

## Barker Dam/Queen Valley Bike & Hike

5 miles round-trip. Easy. Access: From the main paved park road, drive to Jumbo Rocks campground and park in the day use area.

Here's a fun and easy paved/dirt road ride from Jumbo Rocks campground to Barker Dam. This section of the park is called the **Queen Valley** and is crisscrossed with many dirt roads suitable for biking and exploring. There are also several bike racks in the area so you can safely lock up while you hike. From the **Jumbo Rocks Campground,** pedal west along the paved road, heading toward Barker Dam. After you pass the turnoff for the Geology Tour Road, make a right on the next dirt road on your right, and stay left as the trail splits. Follow it to the parking area and trailhead. Lock up your bike in the rack and hike the short loop trail that explores Barker Dam, which was built to water cattle during Joshua Tree's ranching days.

This tiny hike is an epicurean sampler of everything Joshua Tree has to offer. Within its mile-plus course you can find abundant wildlife, including rare bighorn sheep drawn to the water of the dam, migratory waterfowl, plus the possibility of deer, coyote, and any other desert dwellers. Barker Dam lies in the middle of one of the most interesting and daunting parts of the park, **Joshua Tree's Wonderland of Rocks**—12 square miles of jumbled granite spires and boulders.

## Eureka Peak

7.5 miles out and back. Moderate. Access: Yucca Trail and La Contenta Rd., just north and west of the West Entrance Station.

On this dirt road right out along the Covington Flats, you'll see some of the largest Joshua trees in all the park as you head out to Eureka Peak and back. Beginning at the intersection of Yucca Trail and La Contenta Road, pedal south on La Contenta. As you cross the boundary of the national park, you'll be in the section known as **Lower Covington Flats,** one of the lushest areas in the park. Here, you'll be surrounded not only by some of the largest Joshua trees

in the park but also by junipers and pinyon pine. Turn left on the dirt road heading to **Eureka Point** (5,516 ft.) just before the Covington Flats picnic area. From here it's almost 4 miles to the peak, with some very steep sections near the end. When you reach the top—and you'll need to take a short hike to get to the actual peak—you'll be rewarded with views of Palm Springs and the Morongo Basin.

Head back the way you came, or if you're feeling adventurous, make a right on the first dirt spur as you head down the peak. This will take you to Upper Covington Flats and eventually to the **California Riding and Hiking Trail**—riding for horses, that is. Bikes are prohibited on that trail.

## Geology Tour Road

20 miles round-trip. Moderate. Access: Geology Tour Rd. near Jumbo Rocks Campground.

While most people drive this self-guided geology tour, it also makes a great bike ride. Generally speaking, it's a pretty desolate road, although it's bumpy and often sandy. From the **Jumbo Rocks Campground,** pedal west along the paved road, heading toward Barker Dam. Turn south on the dirt Geology Tour Road. Be sure to pick up a free guide to the tour at the roadside box, so you'll know which geological wonders are which. Among the alluvial fans, monolithic boulders, and desert washes, you'll see Squaw Tank, an ancient Indian campsite turned rancher's dam; petroglyphs; old mine ruins; and, at the end, a spectacular vista as you circle **Pleasant Valley.** From there it's a long, uphill huff on the same road that brought you in, or you can have someone meet you with a car.

## Black Eagle Mine Road

18 miles out and back. Moderate. Access: Black Eagle Mine Rd. begins 6 miles north of the Cottonwood visitors center.

This dirt road out and back on Black Eagle Mine Road takes you through the foothills of the Eagle Mountains and into abandoned mine country. Black Eagle Mine Road begins 6 miles north of the **Cottonwood visitor center.** From here, pedal east on the dirt road. With the Pinto Basin on your left and the Eagle Mountains on your right, you'll pedal across several dry washes and wind through some beautiful canyons. Watch for old mine shafts and prospect holes. At 9 miles, the road leaves the park boundary and enters the world of the Bureau of Land Management. Just beyond here are several side roads that lead to old mines. Use extreme caution around these old mines, as the structures are potentially dangerous. As the park service will tell you: Stay Out and Stay Alive.

## Old Dale Road

23 miles one-way. Moderate. Access: Old Dale Rd. begins 6 miles north of the Cottonwood visitor center. This ride requires a car shuttle. Park the first car along Hwy. 62, about 10 miles east of the Oasis visitor center, near Gold Crown Rd. In the second car, head back to the park. From the North Entrance Station drive south, past Ocotillo Patch along Pinto Basin to the intersection with Black Eagle Mine Rd. and Old Dale Rd.

This dirt road ride takes you through the Old Dale Mining District in Joshua Tree. Old Dale Road begins 6 miles north of the **Cottonwood visitor center.** From here, pedal north on the dirt road across the Pinto Basin, a flat, sandy, dry lake bed, for the first 11 miles. All the way, you're surrounded by mountains: Pintos to the north, Hexies to the west, Eagle and Coxcombs to the east, and Cottonwoods to the south. As you leave the basin, you'll be entering what's called the Transition Zone—where the Colorado Desert meets the Mojave—and you'll notice the subtle but distinct change as the larger plants of the Mojave give way to the smaller cacti of the Colorado. You'll also begin climbing up into the Pintos and leaving the park. Along the way, several side roads lead to old mines and residences. Use extreme caution around these old mines; the structures are potentially dangerous. The road eventually becomes Gold Crown Road as you approach Highway 62.

You can pedal back along the paved park roads, but I'd opt for the car shuttle.

## Pinkham Canyon Road

25-mile loop. Moderate–difficult. Access: Cottonwood visitor center. Car shuttle recommended.

This challenging dirt road ride takes you through the lovely Pinkham Canyon. From the **Cottonwood visitor center,** begin pedaling west (it's the only way you can go) on Pinkham Canyon Road. You'll travel along Smoke Tree Wash and then down into Pinkham Canyon. On your right, you'll see Monument Mountain, and to your left, the Cottonwood range. The road here is tricky: rocky flood plains, soft sand, ups and downs. The road eventually crosses the park boundary and connects to a service road that runs into **Interstate 10.** From here, you can pedal along the highway for about 8 miles back to the visitor center or, if you're like me and hate traffic, you'll want to have one car waiting here to take you back.

## ROCK CLIMBING

In the last 10 to 15 years Joshua Tree has become the premier winter climbing destination in the U.S. While Yosemite, Smith Rock, and the Gunks shiver under ice and snow, the climate in the southern Mojave is just perfect for climbing. People climb here year-round, but the main season is from about the end of September to May. During summer it's just too darn hot here for most of us. Winter can bring occasional snows, but overall the weather is good.

More than 4,000 established routes form a climber's spider web over the monzogranite domes and spires of the park. The rock is rough, coarser than Sierra Nevada granite, but generally high quality. Currently there's a debate raging about bolting routes between the park management and climbers' access groups. The park superintendent wants to ban bolting of new routes and replacement of old bolts on established routes, eventually returning the park to pure placement climbing. The climbers' access groups argue that not only is this totally unnecessary and arbitrary, but it's a recipe for disaster as old bolts age and can't be replaced, eventually leading to failure while somebody's life is in the lurch. By the time this book reaches you, some resolution of this conflict may have been reached. Be sure to check at the park visitor center for the latest in climbing regulations.

Obviously 4,000 established and countless other potential routes are far beyond the grasp of this book. If you're making a serious pilgrimage to Joshua Tree, I recommend Randy Vogel's excellent routebook to Joshua Tree (Chockstone Press) or his equally useful *SoCal Select* (Chockstone Press) guide to major climbing areas of Southern California.

An excellent way to get acquainted with the best local climbing is to book a lesson or a guided climb with **Joshua Tree Rock Climbing School** (tel. 800/366-4745). Located just outside the park in the town of Joshua Tree, the school teaches everything from how to tie on a pair of climbing shoes to advanced lead climbing techniques. It's just a hop, skip, and a jump from their office to the park's best climbing.

Climbers looking for a quick fix while in Palm Springs should drop by the air-conditioned but outdoor artificial crag at **Uprising Climbing Center,** located at 1500 S. Gene Autry Trail (tel. 619/320-6630 or 888/CLIMB-ON). Covered, lighted, and misted, the gym is quite impressive.

Finally, Tahquitz and Suicide rocks are huge granite crags that because of their high altitude (8,000 and 7,500 feet) are often much cooler than Joshua Tree during the summer months. They're approximately 20 miles west and 26 miles south of Palm Springs via I-10 and Highway 243 near the town of Idyllwild. Park in Humber Park (at the end of North Circle Drive) and follow the well-worn trails. Expect a 20- to 30-minute approach to both Tahquitz and Suicide. Bring lots of traditional protection, as there are very few bolts and some of the down climbs are also quite technical.

## SPELUNKING

### Box Canyon's Grottos

5 miles. 300-foot elevation gain. Flashlights needed. Information Tel. 619/251-4800. Access: From Hwy. 111 in Mecca, exit on Hwy. 195 and head east. After you cross the Coachella Canal, check your odometer. In 5.25 miles you should see a red painted rock on the right shoulder marking a jeep road. Follow it for 100 yards to the Sheep Hole Oasis Trailhead.

The destination of this hike is an interesting cave system formed when geological upheaval on this shaky ground caused a series of slot canyons to close at the top, leaving a half-mile-long series of grottos. There are several entrance and exit points. Because these are sandstone tunnels rather than limestone caverns, you won't find any stalagmites or stalactites, but the dark and jumbled course through these formations is great fun to explore. Wear sturdy shoes and watch your head. There are lots of low-hanging rocks.

From the trailhead, follow the main trail to the grottos. Along the way you'll pass by a man-made water hole that provides sustenance for the desert bighorns who live in this area.

## SWIMMING

The extent of swimming possibilities in this desolate desert region can be summed up in two words: Indian Canyons. The spring-fed creeks in the **Agua Caliente Indians Park** offer the best places to get wet and cool down in a natural setting. Follow the directions in the Palm Canyon or Tahquitz canyon hikes to reach great swimming areas. Unfortunately the Indian Canyons are closed during summer, which is when they're most attractive for a dip. If you find yourself in the area during those sad months, my only advice is that there are a lot of nice hotel pools around.

## WALKS & NATURAL ROADSIDE ATTRACTIONS

### Geology Tour Road

20-mile round-trip drive. High-clearance vehicle recommended. Access: Geology Tour Rd. near Jumbo Rocks campground. Pick up the numbered brochure from the box at the turnoff.

Heading south on the dirt Geology Tour Road, you'll pass through a gradually changing desert as you descend from the park's high-plateau Joshua tree forest to a lower altitude, where you'll see grasslands and a boulder field of petroglyphs. The brochure leads you to periodic stops. Among the alluvial fans, monolithic boulders, and desert washes that the guide points out, you'll also see Squaw Tank (an ancient Indian campsite turned rancher's dam), old mine ruins, and, at the end, a spectacular vista as you circle Pleasant Valley. Plan at least 2 or more hours for this trip.

### Desert Queen Ranch

Even within the scope of man's recent memory, this area of the Mojave has seen dramatic climatic change. When the Desert Queen Ranch was first settled in 1880, this canyon—now dry and desolate—received about 10 inches of rain per year. Grass was lush, reaching over the top of a cowboy's boot. This wealth of forage and the area's remote location made it popular with two brothers, Jim and Bill McHaney, who weren't exactly known for acquiring their herd through legal means. Many a stolen heifer or steer wound up growing fat on Joshua Tree's grasslands before being shipped off to slaughter.

The tour of the Desert Queen Ranch is an interesting look at this era and the mining era that came later. Trails lead to a variety of displays.

The ranch is only open on certain days. Call the **park service** at 760/367-7511 for current schedules.

### Oasis of Mara

Of all of the park's oases, the Oasis of Mara is the easiest to find. It sits right behind the park visitor center in Twentynine Palms. A concrete path and numbered interpretive signs introduce visitors to some of the novel inhabitants that appear when water graces the desert. The Oasis of Mara was once much larger but groundwater pumping in the nearby town has reduced its flow. It's still worth taking a 15-minute walk through on your way to or from the park.

### Coachella Valley Preserve

10 miles east of Palm Springs near Thousand Palms just off I-10. Tel. 619/343-1234.

It's a nice, mellow place to gain an introduction to the desert. Several excellent short hikes, including the quarter-mile Smoke Tree Ranch Trail, help you understand the initially intimidating desert. Another fine nature trail is the McCallum Trail. At 1.5 miles it's a little long to be called a walk, but too short for a hike. Whatever you want to call it, I think it's great. Pick up the numbered interpretive pamphlet at the beginning of the trail. Stay away from this low-lying preserve during the summer, when temperatures become unbearable.

# Campgrounds & Other Accommodations

**CAMPING**

Considering the tremendous visitor pressure on Joshua Tree, camping there is actually really easy and pleasant. I wish more park administrators would mimic the Joshua Tree system. Instead of creating a cumbersome and expensive reservation system and a massive bureaucracy, Joshua Tree makes it simple. Sites at nine of the park campgrounds are first-come, first-served, and even better, they're free. All these sites are without running water or showers but have nice pit toilets. The two

campgrounds closest to civilization (Black Rock and Indian Cove) are available by reservation at 800/365-2267 for a fee of $10 per night and $25 for group sites. They have running water and flush toilets.

As far as the individual campgrounds go, they're all pretty good. **Hidden Valley** is located nearest the prime climbing areas; in fact, you can literally rock climb out of many of the sites. Its 39 sites fill up early. **Ryan** is the next campground over and is also located next to great climbing (31 sites). **Jumbo Rocks** is the park's biggest campground, with 125 sites and seemingly endless loops running through fields of absolutely giant boulders. The sites are varied but there are some amazing ones tucked into the nooks and crannies of the namesake Jumbo Rocks. When the weather is colder you might want to head for **Cottonwood** (62 sites), **Black Rock** (100 sites), or **Indian Cove** (101 sites) to take advantage of their more sheltered location. The reverse, of course, is true during the summer heat, when you'll want to head for the higher ground of Hidden Valley, Jumbo Rocks, and Ryan.

Pickings get slim as you head toward Palm Springs. Basically it's motor home city. One RV park has 1,300 sites, a golf course, several pools, tennis courts, a health club, and shuffleboard. If that sounds like the kind of place you'd like to camp, well, you're reading the wrong book.

To find camping around Palm Springs and the Coachella Valley, you need to head for high ground. Take I-10 about 20 miles west of Palm Springs and turn south on Calif. 243. Here you'll find a mother lode of camping. **Boulder Basin** is 9 miles north of Idyllwild at the end of dirt Forest Road 4S01 (33 sites, water, open May–Oct) and makes an excellent location for exploring the backcountry of Mount San Jacinto State Park. **Dark Canyon Campground** lies on the next forest road south, 4S02

(22 sites, water, May–Oct). For information about either of these camps call **San Bernardino National Forest** (tel. 909/659-2117).

The Mount Jacinto State Park also operates several campgrounds in the area: **Stone Creek Camp** (50 sites, water, open year-round) is located 6 miles north of Idyllwild on Calif. 243. **Idyllwild Camp** is off Calif. 243 on the northern edge of the town of the same name (33 sites, water, year-round). Sites can be reserved at both camps by calling 800/444-PARK. Finally, **Idyllwild County Park** has 90 sites, flush toilets, and showers located on Riverside Country Playground Road at the edge of town. To reserve sites call 800/243-PARK or contact Riverside County directly at 909/659-2656 for more information. Both campgrounds in town are very popular with hikers going into the state park and climbers heading out to scale Tahquitz and Suicide rocks.

## INNS & LODGES

### 29 Palms Inn

73950 Inn Ave., Twentynine Palms, CA 92243. Tel. 760/367-4425. Fax: 760/367-4425. 17 rooms. $62–$260. AE, DISC, MC, V.

Within the boundaries of Joshua Tree, the lodging choices are simple: You can camp, or you can camp. To find a hotel you must head to Twentynine Palms. The town is also home to a marine base, and, consequently, also home to plenty of cheap motels. But for truly classy lodgings, I suggest the 29 Palms Inn, which is practically next door to the main park visitor center.

This inn is a grand oasis from the desert heat. A spring-fed pond is home to a flock of ducks and geese. Fruit grows on well-watered trees. The lovely rooms are set in adobe cottages and cabins that date back 70 years. There's also a pool

and the best restaurant in Twentynine Palms, with really reasonable prices for excellent food. From here you're within walking distance from the park boundary and about a 20-minute drive from the heart of the park.

### Korakia Pensione

257 S. Patencio Rd., Palm Springs, CA 92262. Tel. 760/864-6411. 20 rooms. $109–$239. 1 house for 2 people, $365. No credit cards.

In Palm Springs, things are much more centered to the golf and tennis crowd than to hikers, bikers, and nature lovers. For a taste of bohemianism in this land of plaid pants and tasseled loafers, make yourself a reservation at the Korakia Pensione, which dates from the 1920s. This Greek-Moroccan oasis is worlds removed from the hustle and bustle of Canyon Drive, which is actually only a few blocks away. Some of the rooms have kitchens and fireplaces. All are done in very tasteful decor and have views into beautiful gardens.

### Two Bunch Palms

67425 Two Bunch Palms Trail, Desert Hot Springs, CA 92240. Tel. 800/472-4334. 45 rooms. $175–$595. AE, V, MC.

Desert Hot Springs has a long way to go before it gives Calistoga a run for its money as a town, but Two Bunch Palms, once the desert hideout of Al Capone, is one of the most famous spas in the world. Capitalizing on a beautiful setting of discreet bungalows, pretty gardens, and zillions of gallons of geothermally heated spring water, this place is one of the favorite weekend escapes of Hollywood big wigs. It's also great for the rest of us little wigs, though the prices are a bit harder on us.

# 9

# SAN DIEGO & ORANGE COUNTY COASTS

I REMEMBER A TRIP TO SOUTHERN CALIFORNIA AS A SMALL BOY. WE visited an aunt and uncle in Seal Beach, at the very northern edge of Orange County, and then drove south to explore Lion Country Safari, a now-defunct African game park way down by Laguna Beach. We drove through a patchwork of tract homes, strip malls, and citrus orchards. As town gave way to country, the sweet smell of blooming oranges hung over everything, lending a certain sensuality to driving through the morning light. We drove through Lion Country Safari and continued down to San Diego, which in my memory was a small city clustered around Mission Bay and the ocean. Strawberry fields still grew close to downtown, and our host went for a dive and pried abalone off the Point Loma rocks for dinner.

Sometime between then and now the sprawl won. The miles of orange groves that gave Orange County its name are little more than a memory, if even that, plowed under into a continuous stretch of suburban development. The Irvine Ranch, once the biggest working cattle ranch in the nation, has metastasized into ritzy shopping plazas and miles of red-tile-roofed condos. San Diego now reaches far into the desert from its seaside foothold. What little wild land remains is increasingly fragmented. In the county parks around Irvine, mountain lion sightings and periodic attacks have risen as the large predators find themselves squeezed on all sides. One woman reportedly encountered a mountain lion in a park rest room, where it had come to drink from a toilet.

Coastal wetlands once covered a large area of this coast, from the marshes of Bolsa Chica to the lagoons of San Diego Bay. Most have now been developed, either filled and covered with houses or dredged and turned into harbors. Those that remain are a natural treasure, a breeding ground for fish, birds, and other wildlife. It's somehow disorienting to look at Bolsa Chica wetlands just north of Huntington Beach with its oil rigs and surf shops and realize that there are not only several endangered species that depend entirely on this wetland for their existence but also that there are archaeological sites dating back to 2500 B.C. here from the original inhabitants of this land.

There are still huge amounts of beauty and opportunity along this southern coast. Nowhere in the entire country is blessed with better weather. The sun shines almost constantly, yet the moderating effect of the cool Pacific keeps the heat from becoming stifling. As the afternoons heat up, they automatically trigger cooling onshore breezes, the sort of natural air-conditioning system that other places only dream about. To go with all that sun, of course, it's nice to know that there are plenty of beaches and water that's warm enough in the summer to swim without a wetsuit. It's not at all abnormal for water temperatures to reach into the 70s, which, for the West Coast, is quite warm.

The beach communities, which developed first and have the oldest history (mind you, purely by West Coast standards), have preserved much of their charm. Though old-timers rail about new money in Newport, the zoolike

conditions in the water at Huntington, the nuclear power plant at San Onofre, the fake New England architecture of Dana Point, and the inflated home prices everywhere, the fact is that visitors and many others find it entertaining and downright lovely. The days of surfing alone at Trestles and then prying a couple abalone off the rocks for supper before tumbling into the back of your Woody for the night are long gone, but the wonderful traditions of the California beach lifestyle remain.

Between the Mexican border and Long Beach is an incredible diversity of places to go and things to do. Huntington Beach will always be surf city. Newport Harbor will always be a sailors' mecca. Catalina is still just a short sail away. Laguna Beach, no matter how many mudslides and brush fires sweep through it, will always be beautiful. San Onofre's gentle, Waikiki-style waves will continue to be a hit with young and old surfers alike, who camp in the shadow of the twin nuclear containment vessels. Hang gliders will soar off Torrey Pines State Reserve, while nudists sun on Black's Beach below and surfers drop in on hollow tubes. La Jolla continues to be a great scuba diving destination, especially within the protected marine reserve, and San Diego itself offers everything from offshore big-game fishing trips into Mexican waters to world class sailing and the best zoo in the United States.

## The Lay of the Land

The southern coastline of California begins a long and gradual curve from a southwest-facing beach to a west-facing alignment here, beyond the purely south-facing beaches of **San Pedro** and **Long Beach.** Orange County begins at the mouth of the San Gabriel River and the southeastern end of Long Beach with the bedroom community of Seal Beach. **Seal Beach** is typical of the Orange County coastline. Once built as a resort getaway for Los Angeles, it has matured into a full-fledged city.

**Highway 1,** also known as the Pacific Coast Highway, is your key to accessing this region. Though it rarely follows the exact edge of the coast, it generally remains within a few blocks of the beach and allows you to make much better time than if you were to try following the maze of residential streets that hug the beach.

This northern part of Orange County lies geographically in the southern end of the Los Angeles Basin. Though both Orange County and Los Angeles residents are quick to distance themselves from each other, to an outsider there is little obvious difference between the two. **Huntington Beach,** quite frankly, looks a lot like Manhattan Beach or Venice, and the ocean is the ocean in either place. Long sandy strands, local fishing piers, and occasional yacht harbors break up the coastline. Along much of the coast, pedestrian and bike paths offer excellent opportunities to cruise along the water's edge.

The low-lying coast continues until you reach **Newport Beach.** Newport Bay is a fossil relic of a river that once drained the very southern edge of the L.A. Basin during the Pleistocene. That river dried up long ago, but the naturally protected bay and wetlands it created remain. Lower Newport Bay was developed as a huge yacht and pleasure boat harbor. It's one of the most important sailing centers in California. Races run from here to Ensenada (in Baja California) every May, and hundreds of local competitions occur every year. The harbor is separated from the Pacific by a narrow sand spit. Houses sit right on the beach, and it's quite a surfing scene.

Perhaps the most famous aquatic attraction in Newport is **The Wedge,** a bizarre and terrifying wave created as incoming south swells refract off the Newport Harbor Jetty and jack up to phenomenal sizes. For years it was only a bodysurfing and boogie-boarding wave, but recently surfers have taken to dropping in on this crunching left. It's not a place to take lightly—people are rescued here on a seemingly daily basis, and more than a few misguided souls have broken their necks in the pounding shore break.

Beyond Newport Harbor is the end of the Los Angeles Basin, marked by the rolling San Joaquin Hills and the pretty blufftop town of **Corona del Mar.** The **San Joaquin Hills** are just the leading edge of the larger peninsular ranges that reach inland for miles. To the south they stretch as far as Dana Point. Inland the mountains stretch all the way into the Cleveland National Forest and encompass several state and regional parks. While it's generally temperate on the coast, these inland wilderness parks are hot and dry during the summer and make for excellent spring and fall visits.

From Newport to Dana Point is among the best coastline in Southern California. In contrast to the flat and sandy shore of northern Orange County, this is a wonderland of rocky points, sandy pocket beaches, steep canyons, and dramatic hills. Underwater it's spectacular too. The diving here can be quite extraordinary, especially in light of the dense population.

Laguna Beach still carries somewhat of a reputation as a bohemian, artsy town. Real estate inflation has driven many of the artists and counterculture figures out, as showbiz and stockmarket money discovered what a wonderful piece of coast this is. New mansions sprout next to old cottages, and Rolls-Royces park next to hippie buses. In the end, they're all brought together by the fires, landslides, and floods that

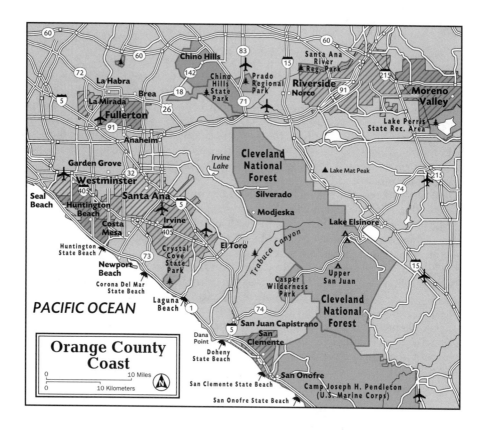

**Orange County Coast**

PACIFIC OCEAN

0 — 10 Miles
0 — 10 Kilometers

(Map labels:)
Chino Hills, La Habra, Brea, La Mirada, Fullerton, Anaheim, Garden Grove, Westminster, Santa Ana, Seal Beach, Huntington Beach, Costa Mesa, Irvine, Huntington State Beach, Newport Beach, Corona Del Mar State Beach, Laguna Beach, El Toro, Crystal Cove State Park, Dana Point, Doheny State Beach, San Clemente State Beach, San Clemente, San Juan Capistrano, San Onofre, San Onofre State Beach, Camp Joseph H. Pendleton (U.S. Marine Corps), Chino Hills State Park, Prado Regional Park, Riverside, Norco, Moreno Valley, Lake Perris State Rec. Area, Cleveland National Forest, Irvine Lake, Silverado, Modjeska, Lake Mat Peak, Lake Elsinore, Trabuca Canyon, Casper Wilderness Park, Upper San Juan, Santa Ana River Reg. Park

seem to sweep through this lovely town as regularly as clockwork.

**Dana Point** sits just south of Laguna Beach on a giant, rocky headland. The lee of the point was a historic anchorage where schooners and tall ships would anchor while trading with the Mission San Juan Capistrano. Richard Henry Dana, after whom the town is named, wrote in *Two Years Before the Mast* of stopping here to trade manufactured goods from New England for cow hides and tallow from the mission ranches. At that time, the 1830s, ranching was so important to the California economy that cow hides were called "California banknotes." It wasn't until the late 1800s that people permanently settled and farmed above the harbor, and it took until the 1960s before residential growth really took off. Dana wouldn't recognize the place at all now. In lieu of *vaqueros* and mission roofs he'd see a fake New England motif that might strike him as

surprising after sailing all the way around the horn from New England. And where Dana once bobbed at anchor in the *Pilgrim* is a huge pleasure boat harbor, the construction of which destroyed a famous 1950s surf break, Killer Dana's. You can visit a replica of Dana's ship in the harbor, or use it as your launching point to fish, dive, or sail.

South of the looming headland of Dana Point the terrain flattens out again and Highway 1 stretches through the towns of **Capistrano Beach** and San Clemente. **San Clemente** is world famous as the site of Richard Nixon's western White House, which sits on the beach at Cotton's Point. Surfers used to hate when the president was in residence because a coast guard cutter was stationed offshore and guards patrolled the beach, keeping surfers from their waves. Nixon, of course, is ancient history here and there's not a lot to mark his stay.

More recently, San Clemente has become ground zero for the surf publishing industry. Magazines like *Surfing, Surfer, Surfer's Journal* and an ever-rotating camp of pretenders to the throne are all clustered in offices within a stone's throw of each other. It's a tremendously incestuous scene. They all know each other and what each other is up to, which might explain why there's so little original thought or writing in most of these magazines. The possibility of being captured on the cover of *Surfer* or *Surfing* also draws world class surfers to San Clemente far out of proportion to the quality of its waves (which are good, but not *that* good).

San Clemente is also home base to the Surfrider Foundation, an environmental group that strives to be to surfing what the Sierra Club has been to hiking. Centering around a platform of clean water and unrestricted coastal access, the Surfrider Foundation has had great success garnering celebrity support and national attention.

Just south of San Clemente, Highway 1 merges with Interstate 5 for the next 20 or so miles. Beach access here is severely restricted, as you're passing through **Camp Pendleton Marine Corps Base.** This huge base extends inland for miles, over the mountain ranges in the backdrop. Allegedly, herds of bison and other large mammals are found back there, coexisting along with the war games of a few good men. From the highway you'll be lucky to see anyone at all. It's actually a nice break from the roadside development of the rest of the area.

The only major exception to the off-limits beaches of Camp Pendleton is the state beach at **San Onofre.** Lying in the shadow of a nuclear power plant that can only be fairly described as looking like a giant pair of breasts erected on the sand, San Onofre is a lovely, gentle surf spot and a wide sandy beach below sandstone bluffs. A campground lies to the south of the big nuke plant and is popular, in spite of the giant warning signs that remind you to flee immediately if the sirens go off because somebody's pulled a Three Mile Island.

For the purposes of this chapter, all activities are divided into two separate regions, Orange County and San Diego County. San Diego follows Orange in the "What to Do & Where to Do It" section.

**Oceanside** is the first town to the south of Pendleton and the first real dose of San Diego County you'll get. It's a nice town with a big harbor, a 900-foot pleasure pier, and wide sandy beaches. Nature lovers will also enjoy the several salt marshes and rivermouths that empty into the sea here: **San Luis Rey River, Loma Alta Marsh,** and **Buena Vista Lagoon.** All are a great glimpse of what the extensive wetlands that once lined the California coast must have been like. Blue herons hunt spawning fish while migrating waterfowl take shelter from their long journeys. In the shoreline scrub, foxes, coyotes, and even deer make their homes.

As you pass through this part of northern San Diego County, you'll want to follow Old Highway 101. It changes names at virtually every city limit, but it's easy to follow and offers a perspective on beach life that you'd miss entirely whizzing by on Interstate 5 just a few miles inland. **Carlsbad** lies just south of Oceanside. **Leucadia** follows and soon after you'll reach **Encinitas.** They're all nice residential communities that seem light-years removed from the big city life of San Diego. Numerous state and county beaches offer access to the sea, some of which allow camping. Surf shops seem to appear on every corner, and on weekends the area is packed with beachgoers. This stretch has become

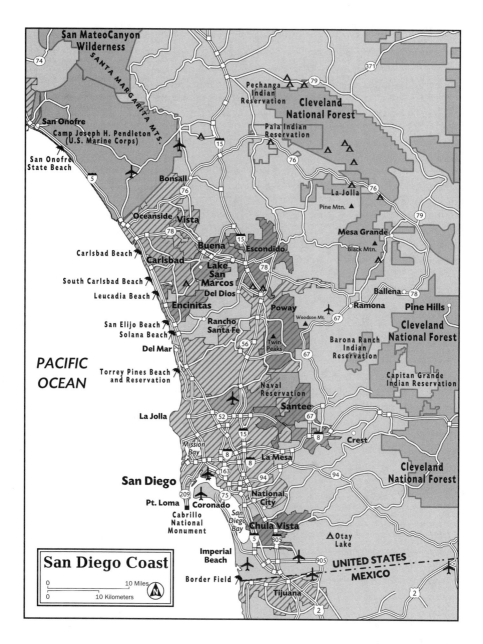

famous in the last decade or so as the home training grounds of many world class triathletes, many of whom moved here because it offers great year-round weather to practice all three of their disciplines. It's also home to a different, though certainly not mutually exclusive, kind of discipline. The Self-Realization Fellowship Ashram Center in Encinitas is one of the oldest yoga centers in the United States. With 1,000 feet of beach frontage, meditation areas, housing, and a cafeteria, the Ashram has been getting people in touch with their prana since 1937. Directly in front of the Ashram is a famous surf break called "Swami's."

The gentle hills and bluffs of the north county suddenly give way to steep, sheer-sided slopes after you pass through Cardiff, Solana Beach, and Del Mar. Here, the coast road suddenly winds up in the **Torrey Pines State Reserve,** one of only two places in the state (the other being in the Channel Islands) where Torrey pines grow naturally. This 1,000-acre clifftop nature preserve is a wonderful spot to hike and gaze at the ocean below. Hang gliders sometimes launch here and fly along the bluffs. Far below, reachable by a winding trail, is **Black's Beach,** a famous surfing and nude beach. The two different cultures, nudists and surfers, seem to get along just fine, and it's always good to know you can surf naked if the urge strikes without anyone frowning at you.

**La Jolla** is justly famous as one of California's most expensive communities. Mansions crawl up towering slopes that cradle a small downtown village below. The coastline is broken by Point La Jolla here, and the marine topography gets really interesting. A marine canyon leads right into La Jolla Bay, and a protected marine preserve marks its edge. Divers love this spot for its clear water and plentiful fish. The nearby marine canyon means you might see pelagic species that otherwise would never come this close to shore. A series of sea caves here were once used by bootleggers to hide their smuggled Mexican liquor after it was brought in by boat.

Just around Point La Jolla is **Children's Pool Beach,** a favorite swimming spot that's partially enclosed by a breakwater. A little farther down the coast is a different kind of play spot, **Windansea Beach;** Tom Wolfe made it famous in his New Journalism classic *The Pump House Gang,* which chronicled the zany 1960s surf scene at this remarkable beach. The surf is as good as ever, and the locals as disdainful of outsiders as they were in Wolfe's day. Surfing is king on this patch of coastline, so much so

that at Tourmaline Surf Park at the very southern end of La Jolla, no swimming is permitted. You must either surf or get out.

**False Point** marks the end of the high hills of La Jolla and the beginning of San Diego proper, beginning with the Mission Beach and Mission Bay area. San Diego is a huge and bustling port city with two great bays, Mission Bay and San Diego Bay. It's long been the largest naval center on the West Coast, and for many years it was thought of as little more than a border town and military garrison. Times have really changed. A towering and modern downtown sits poised between the two bays, skyscrapers filled with international businesses and streets below crawling with life. Suburbs, unfortunately, stretch for miles in all directions, and though the city does have a few great parks, notably **Balboa Park** and the wilderness of **Mission Trails Regional Park,** it seems like the ocean shore is the main outlet for the masses trying to get away from it all. And along the San Diego City shoreline you'll find tremendous diversity of both people and topography.

**Mission Beach** is a studied contrast to the Riviera-like beauty of the north county. Here, tiny beach houses are crammed right up against each other on a narrow sand spit. The Pacific rules one side with crashing waves while gentle and warm Mission Bay sits just a few blocks in the other direction. Roller skaters, sunbathers, jugglers, surfers, and pier fishermen all vie for their own little patch of turf.

**Mission Bay** is actually a linked series of bays and coves—Sail Bay, Mariners Basin, Ventura Cove, Enchanted Cove—that make up a huge aquatic playground. Boardsailors and catamaran sailors whiz over the shallows on brisk breezes. Other areas cater to water-skiers and power boats. And some of the back bays and islands have been set aside as nature preserves where birds still nest in rare marshland habitat. **Seaworld,** the famous aquatic park that is home to killer whales, dolphins, seals, and a penguin habitat, also sits on the edge of Mission Bay.

Ocean Beach, Sunset Cliffs, and Point Loma sit south of the mouth of Mission Bay. The coast here is again high and rocky, with lots of small pocket beaches for diving and surfing. The Navy owns the southern half of Point Loma; allegedly a secret submarine base under the point is reached by an underwater tunnel. But the public is allowed onto the point to visit Cabrillo National Monument, a favorite whale-watching spot and nature preserve; the Point Loma Ecological Preserve; and the Point Loma Lighthouse. Inside the protection of the point is Commercial Basin, home to more than 600 small craft, including sportfishing, diving, and whale-watching boats.

**San Diego Bay** stretches back for miles between Point Loma and Coronado Island, which isn't really an island but a peninsula. It's considered one of the best natural harbors in the world, a 17-mile-long deepwater port big enough to drive an aircraft carrier in. Huge navy ships loom over docks, and the skyscrapers of downtown seem to rise almost straight out of the bay. Thousands of smaller powerboats and yachts also call it home. On a busy day, which is almost every day, San Diego Bay is not a place for the faint of heart. If you venture out there, bear in mind that not only are those big ships not going to stop or change course for you, they simply can't. Stay out of their way.

From Coronado to the Mexican border, the Silver Strand Beach is a long, straight, white sand expanse. It isn't until you reach **Imperial Beach** and the **Tijuana River National Estuarine Sanctuary** that things get really interesting again. This huge marsh preserve is home

to 245 species of birds and countless rare plants. Fish like anchovy, white croaker, and halibut come to the shallows to spawn. It's a bird watcher's paradise but is beset by pollution problems since the Tijuana River drains countless million gallons of untreated effluent over the border from its namesake city. This pollution keeps the beach in Imperial Beach and Border Field State Park closed much of the year and presents problems to the natural inhabitants of the marsh. Currently, projects are underway to treat growing Tijuana's sewage, but there is a long way yet to go.

The Mexico–U.S. border is an interesting place. The main crossing is at **San Ysidro,** where the hustle and bustle is continuous. My favorite place to just look at the border, however, is **Border Field State Park.** It's a noteworthy visit just because you can walk down the beach to where a fence says you must turn back. The Tijuana Bullring towers on the other side, just a few hundred feet and an entire country away, but it's on the SAME beach. Makes you realize how arbitrary borders are. Many people have waded around the fence as a way of getting from one country to the other, but border authorities from both sides keep a pretty close eye on this spot.

# Parks & Other Hot Spots

## ORANGE COUNTY

### Seal Beach & Pier

Access: In the town of Seal Beach, at Main St. and the Seal Beach Pier. Lifeguards, rest rooms, showers. For beach information, contact the Seal Beach Lifeguard Station at 562/430-2613.

Located just south of the Los Angeles County line and the San Gabriel River, the town of Seal Beach is where Highway 1 (Pacific Coast Highway) picks up again after the crazy maze of L.A. freeways. Populated by surfers (although good surf is erratic), sunbathers, and swimmers, the beach itself is split in two by a concrete jetty, with most of the sand lying south of the divide. The currents here can be dangerous at times, so beware. The pier runs from Main Street, where there's a grassy park, to the sea.

## Bolsa Chica State Beach & Ecological Reserve

Access: In Huntington Beach, along PCH from Main St. to Warner Ave. Lifeguards, rest rooms, showers, picnic areas, fire pits. Tel. 714/846-3460. Bolsa Chica Conservancy: 714/846-1114.

Bolsa Chica is just one of the beautiful beaches that comprise the 8-mile sandy stretch of shoreline to the north and south of the town of Huntington Beach. Blufftop Park, located near the southern end of Bolsa Chica, has picnic tables and great views. Nearby is the Ecological Reserve, a 300-acre wetland that's home to several endangered bird species and many not-so-endangered ones. There's also a paved bike path that runs south to the Santa Ana River Trail and back. The beach disappears at high tide.

## Chino Hills State Park

Access: From the junction of Hwy. 71 and Hwy. 60, head south on 71 about 6 miles and turn right on Pomona-Rincon Rd. Then turn left at Soquel Canyon Dr., and left at Elinvar Dr. Elinvar becomes a dirt road as you head up into the hills and the park entrance. Tel. 909/780-6222.

On the northeastern edge of Orange County is where you'll find the 12,000-acre slice of wilderness called Chino Hills State Park. The park headquarters is the old Rolling M main ranch house. Other historical ranch buildings, like the barn for instance, have also been converted for park use. It's a beautiful chunk of land—rolling oak hills, broad valley bottoms—that's also home to the largest remaining stands of native Southern California black walnut trees. And it would seem like paradise if it weren't affected by the sickening smog from the L.A. Basin. Hiking or biking here is totally dependent on the air quality.

## Huntington Pier, City Beach & State Beach

Access: Pier: Main St. and PCH. Tel. 714/536-5281. City Beach: From Main St. to Beach Blvd. Lifeguards, rest rooms, showers, fire pits, picnic tables. State Beach: From Beach Blvd. to the Santa Ana River. Tel. 714/536-1454.

Built in 1914, this 1,800-foot pier was destroyed by storms in the mid 1980s. Since then it's been newly rebuilt and a restaurant has been added to its end. You can fish from the pier, but the most popular activity is watching the surfers. Huntington Beach is "Surf City" and just south of the pier is Huntington City Beach, home of the famous OP Pro surfing competition as well as many other international surfing contests. The beach is loaded with fast-food joints and plenty of places to rent water gear. Farther south still is Huntington State Beach, a 2-mile sandy stretch that looks a lot like the City Beach, except it's more wheelchair accessible and is closer to the

5-acre nature preserve along the Santa Ana River that protects a nesting area for California terns.

## Newport Pier, Municipal Beach & Harbor

Access: In Newport Beach, along Ocean Front at Newport Pier. Lifeguards, rest rooms, showers, picnic tables, and fire pits. For beach information, contact the Newport Beach Marine Department at 714/644-3044. For Harbor info: 714/729-4400.

Newport Pier and Municipal Beach are part of the Balboa Peninsula, a narrow strip of land separated from the mainland just south of the Santa Ana River, that protects the Newport Harbor. Every morning the dory fleet leaves the pier—as they've been doing for over 100 years—and return by 9am or so to sell their catch on the beach. (Close to the pier is the Crab Cooker, a must-try, no-frills, incredible seafood joint that's been around for almost 50 years.) The exquisite sandy beach, which is studded with some popular surfing spots, stretches from the Newport Pier to the Balboa Pier. The paved Ocean Front Promenade runs nearly the entire length of the peninsula, which you can walk or bike. Behind the peninsula lies the Newport Harbor, one of the largest yachting harbors in the country. The town of Newport Beach has a reputation for being filthy rich, and you'll definitely find those who light their cigars with $100 bills, but you'll also find plenty of eccentric bohos, beach bums, and down-to-earth types.

## Balboa Beach, Pier & Pavilion

Access: In Balboa, at the pier and along Balboa Blvd. Lifeguards, rest rooms, show-

ers, BBQ pits. For beach information, contact the Newport Beach Marine Department at 714/644-3044. For Pavilion info, call 714/673-5245.

Balboa Beach stretches from Balboa Pier to the end of the Balboa Peninsula. (At the southern end is where you'll also find West Jetty View Park, a.k.a. The Wedge, the place to watch bodysurfers and boogie boarders ride big waves.) The beach is soft and sandy, with plenty of concessionaires selling food and renting beach and bike gear along the Promenade. Directly east of the pier, on the harbor side of the peninsula, is the Victorian-styled Balboa Pavilion. Since 1905, the Pavilion has been the center of activity. From here, you can take a ferry to Catalina Island, go on a harbor cruise, go whale watching, charter a fishing boat, and more. Ferries to Balboa Island, a small community of cottages in the middle of Newport Bay, also leave from the Pavilion. Close by is the Fun Zone, a small amusement park built in 1936, that features an old-fashioned Ferris wheel, a few more modern rides, and an arcade.

## Corona del Mar State Beach

Access: In Corona del Mar, at Ocean Blvd. and Marguerite Ave. Lifeguards, rest rooms, showers, volleyball, picnic tables, fire pits. For beach information, contact the Newport Beach Marine Department at 714/644-3044.

This popular, gorgeous, sandy beach lies just south of the eastern jetty to Newport Harbor. From here you can hike around to several other beaches, including Little Corona del Mar Beach, a wonderful cove just south of Corona at Poppy Avenue known for its tide pooling, snorkeling, and diving. Rocky Point, north of the state beach at Ocean Boulevard and Harbor Channel, was once called Pirates Cove for its many small sea caves. China Cove, at Ocean Boulevard and Fernleaf, is farther up the harbor channel. Each of these beaches can be also accessed by paths or stairs leading down from Lookout Point and Inspiration Point, two grassy blufftop overlooks, or other pedestrian walkways.

## Crystal Cove State Park

Access: 4 miles south of Corona del Mar on the Pacific Coast Highway. Rest rooms, lifeguards. Tel. 714/494-3539.

This gorgeous, 3-mile sandy beach surrounded by wooded hills is one of the last remaining undeveloped areas of Orange County. If you've ever wondered what Southern California looked like before Disneyland, then go to Crystal Cove State Park. This 2,800-acre park stretches from the ocean up into the San Joaquin Hills, which offers nice hiking and mountain biking. There are three coastal access points: Pelican Point, Los Trancos, and Reef Point. The beach, which is popular with swimmers, surfers, sunbathers, and divers, has been designated the Irvine Coast Marine Life Refuge. In the 1920s, 46 small resort cottages were built on the bluffs above the beach and although the resort is closed, the cottages have remained intact and are now on the National Register of Historic Places. Excellent for wildlife viewing.

## Cleveland National Forest/Trabuco District

1147 E. 6th St., Corona, CA 91720. Tel. 714/736-1811.

The Cleveland National Forest is made up of three sections, the northernmost of which is the Trabuco District. This district encompasses much of the Santa Ana Mountain Range, which includes Santiago, Modjeska, and Los Piños Peaks, and also contains the San Mateo Wilderness: 40,000 acres of rugged Southern California chaparral wildland and steep canyons. Completely separate from the other two districts, Trabuco is located southeast of Los Angeles, roughly bordered by Interstate 15, which runs along the eastern side of the range, and Interstate 5, which runs through the western foothills and from Highway 91 to Camp Pendleton.

## O'Neill Regional Park

Access: In Trabuco Canyon. From I-5 in El Toro, exit El Toro Rd. and head east 7.5 miles to Santiago Canyon Rd. (S-18). Turn right and go 3 miles to the park entrance. Tel. 714/858-9366.

This park is a breath of Santa Ana mountain wilderness in Orange County. On the edge of the Cleveland National Forest, it offers 1,700 acres of wooded hills, as well as Trabuco Canyon and the nearby Live Oak Canyon. There are several nice hikes along the fire roads, a picnic site, and campsites, too.

## Caspers Wilderness Park

Access: From I-5 in San Juan Capistrano, exit Hwy. 74 and head inland 8 miles to the park entrance. Tel. 714/728-0235 or 831-2174.

This 7,600-acre park in the Santa Ana Mountains east of San Juan Capistrano was in the news some years ago because of two mountain lion attacks involving kids. As result, the park only allows adults (18 or over) in groups of two or more to hike in, and a wilderness pass is required. While the chances of seeing a mountain lion are incredibly rare, you will spot over 30 miles of trails covering grassy valleys and chaparral-covered ridges. There are also several native stands of live oak and sycamore. Overnight camping is available.

## Laguna Beach

Access, main beach: Laguna Canyon Rd. and the Pacific Coast Hwy. Lifeguards, rest rooms, showers, volleyball, basketball courts, picnic tables. For beach information contact the South Beaches Operation Office of Orange County Harbors, Beaches and Parks at 714/661-7013 or 714/497-9229.

Although it's well-connected to the California coast, residents of the wealthy town of Laguna Beach like to think of it as an island. And it comes close in several ways. Unlike most of coastal Orange County, it's bordered on three sides by hills and canyons; and unlike most of

politically conservative, Republican Orange County, it's an oasis for artists and other iconoclastic creative types. At least, it used to attract those types before things got so incredibly expensive. Still, the town is loaded with high-priced galleries and very proud of its heritage as the birthplace of California Impressionism. (The Pageant of the Masters—live re-creations of famous paintings—is not to be missed. See "Walks & Attractions" below for details.) Main Beach, as its name implies, is the biggest and the sandiest, and the center of beach activity in the town of Laguna Beach. But all along PCH to the north and south of Main Beach are 30 or so truly breathtaking pocket beaches: small individual coves tucked below cliffs. Almost all have stairways or paths leading down to them. 1,000 Steps, Divers Cove, and Shaw's Cove (diving); West Street Beach (boogie boarding); Brooks Beach (surfing); and Victoria Beach (beauty and privacy) are just a few of them. (Last time I checked, all of them were uptight about enforcing the 10pm curfew, so beware.) The undeveloped hills above are known as the Laguna Greenbelt: 15,000 acres of coastal wilderness. The "belt" is comprised of four sections: Aliso & Wood Canyons Regional Park (tel. 714/831-2790), Crystal Cove State Park (tel. 714/494-3539), The Irvine Open Space Reserve (tel. 714/832-7478), and the Laguna Coast Wilderness Park (tel. 714/854-7108).

## Dana Point Harbor

Access: In Dana Point, along the Pacific Coast Hwy., just south of South Laguna Beach. From PCH, turn left onto Dana Harbor Dr. Tel. 714/496-1555 or 800/290-DANA.

Dana Point, named after writer and seaman Richard Henry Dana, was once a rugged chunk of the California coastline. In 1969, it became a man-made yacht harbor and harborside community, complete with jetty flanked by motels, gift shops, and fancy restaurants. Still, if you're in the neighborhood and want to fish or sail, this is the place. A small saving grace is the Orange County Marine Institute (tel. 714/496-2274) at the west end of the harbor. They're studying marinelife in their new 70-foot research ship, the *Sea Explorer.*

### Doheny State Beach

Access: South of Dana Point, along Dana Pt. Harbor Dr. and PCH. 120 indoor/outdoor showers, rest rooms, volleyball, picnic areas, visitor center. Tel. 714/496-6172.

This mile-long sandy beach is divided by the San Juan Creek where, if you're lucky, you can glimpse an egret or heron. The San Juan Creek Bike Trail runs along the west bank and links to a trail that heads north to Bolsa Chica. Set back from the beach is a wide lawn shaded by palm and eucalyptus trees—excellent for napping. The campsites aren't very private, but the ones in the first row offer great ocean views and hey, you can't beat that. The beach itself is in the lee of a Dana Point Harbor jetty, so the water's usually nice and calm for swimming.

### Capistrano Beach & San Juan Capistrano

Access: Pacific Coast Hwy. and Palisades Dr. Lifeguards, showers, rest room, and picnic tables. For beach info contact the South Beaches Operation Office of Orange County Harbors, Beaches and Parks at 714/661-7013. San Juan Capistrano: From I-5, exit at Ortega Hwy./Hwy. 74. Tel. 714/493-4700.

Welcome to the town of Capistrano Beach and its main attraction, Capistrano Beach Park. This unbroken, sandy plateau connects with Doheny State Beach to the north and is known in geographic terms as the Capistrano Bight. The beach comes with ample parking and is generally not too crowded. Farther south is Poche Beach, another sandy gem popular with surfers. Heading inland, you'll reach the town of San Juan Capistrano, famous for the swallows that arrive every year on March 19 and depart on October 23. While the town goes cuckoo with parades and bell-ringing for the little birds, the birds themselves have become increasingly scarce over the years. Could this be because the once-wild countryside is now overdeveloped?

### San Clemente City Beach & Pier

Access: In San Clemente, on Avenida del Mar at Avenida Victoria. Lifeguards, showers, rest room, and picnic tables. For beach info, contact the San Clemente Dept. of Marine Safety at 714/361-8219.

Just about where San Clemente begins, the Pacific Coast Highway turns inland and soon merges with Interstate 5. Former President Nixon built his home-away-from-the-White-House here in 1969 and put this upscale seaside town on the map. Access to the San Clemente City Beach and pier involves crossing the railroad tracks, which run parallel to the ocean here, but pedestrian overpasses and stairways make that quite easy. It's a wide, well-tended municipal beach with the usual selection of beach amenities. The pier is open for fishing every day from 4am to midnight, and includes a restaurant, fish-cleaning sinks, and bait shops.

## San Clemente State Beach

Access: In San Clemente, at Avenida del Presidente. Lifeguards, showers, rest rooms, picnic tables, fire pits. Tel. 714/492-3156.

San Clemente State Beach offers camping atop a striking sandstone bluff overlooking the ocean. It's a great view, but you have to hike down the precipitous trail to the water and cross the railroad tracks. It's not the best place to swim, due to the occasional rip tides and steep berm, but the natural beauty makes up for it.

## SAN DIEGO COUNTY

## San Onofre State Beach

Access: Just south of San Clemente. I-5, exit Basilone Rd. Lifeguards, rest rooms, showers, picnic tables, fire pits. Tel. 714/492-4872.

San Onofre Beach is a longboarder's paradise—slow, gentle, rolling waves reminiscent of Waikiki. Unfortunately, it's on the largest military base in the U.S. (Camp Pendleton) and in the shadow of a nuclear power plant. There

are five parts to San Onofre State Beach: the Bluffs, a 3.5-mile stretch of amazing beach, backed by steep cliffs with a campground on top; Surf Beach, just north of the Bluffs; the San Mateo Creek Natural Preserve and San Mateo Campground, which lie inland; and Trestles Beach. Both Surf Beach and Trestles are world-famous surfing breaks—Surf Beach for smaller, gentle waves and Trestles for its great point break. Not to mention it's a great place to swim (there's a clothing-optional section for all you naturists) and there's a paved bike path that runs south through Camp Pendleton to Oceanside.

## Oceanside Harbor, City Beach & Pier

Access: City Beach: In Oceanside, along Pacific St., between Witherby St. and the San Luis River. Lifeguards, rest rooms, showers, picnic tables, and barbecue grills. For beach information, contact the Oceanside Department of Harbors and Beaches at 760/966-4535.

With Camp Pendleton in its backyard, the city of Oceanside is, basically, a military town. Since the building of the harbor in the 1960s, the profiles of the beaches here have changed dramatically. Once a wide and uninterrupted stretch of soft golden sand, they became virtually sandless as the natural currents were blocked by the slick, new marina. Today, constant dredging and a high-tech sand bypass operation are helping to restore the shoreline. Fishing takes place off the 1,942-foot pier; whale-watching trips and Catalina Island cruises can be arranged through the harbor. Farther south of City Beach is Linear Park, where a blufftop walkway offers a nice view of the ocean; South Oceanside

Beach; and the Buena Vista Ecological Reserve, a wetland with a self-guided trail. Call the Buena Vista Audubon Nature Center (tel. 760/439-2473) for more information.

## Carlsbad State Beaches

Access: Carlsbad State: In Carlsbad, along Carlsbad Blvd. at Tamarack Ave. Lifeguards, rest rooms, and picnic tables. Tel. 760/438-3143. South Carlsbad: 4 miles south of Carlsbad, along Carlsbad Blvd. at Poinsettia Lane. Lifeguards, rest rooms, showers, picnic tables, and fire pits. Tel. 760/438-3143.

The seaside town of Carlsbad is one of the few places along the southern coast that doesn't have much Latin influence. It was settled by a German named Gerhard Schutte who, after discovering mineral water just like that of the Old World, modeled the town after a Bohemian spa village named Karlsbad. Carlsbad State Beach is a sandy/rocky place backed by bluffs, with overlooks and picnic areas above and a paved walkway below that runs along the seawall. As you move south along Carlsbad Boulevard, you'll encounter the western basin of the Agua Hedionda Lagoon. Farther inland, the lagoon draws swimmers, fishers, water-skiers, and boaters. Sales and rentals are available through the Snug Harbor Marina (tel. 619/434-3089). Next comes the Overlook, a blufftop scenic view, followed by South Carlsbad State Beach, which offers overnight camping, and the Batiquitos Lagoon Ecological Reserve, an important waterbird habitat.

## Swami's

Access: In Encinitas, at First St. below Seacliff Roadside Park. Lifeguards, rest

rooms, showers, picnic tables, BBQ grills. For beach info contact Encinitas Community Services at 619/633-2880.

Located just below a small blufftop park is Swami's, a small beach with one of the most popular surf breaks in Encinitas. If this location is too high-energy for you, try the nearby Self-Realization Fellowship Retreat, Gardens and Hermitage (tel. 619/753-1811), where you can meditate in the lovely garden overlooking the sea. Marked by three lotus towers, you can't miss this 17-acre spiritual landscape. Also worth a visit is the Quail Botanical Gardens, where you'll find over 3,000 varieties of flowers, trees, and plants. (See "Walks & Natural Roadside Attractions" below for details.)

## San Elijo State Beach

Access: On the north side of Cardiff-by-the-Sea, along Old Hwy. 101 at Chesterfield Dr. Lifeguards, rest rooms, showers, and picnic tables. Tel. 619/793-5091.

San Elijo is the southernmost developed campground in the State Beach Park system. The campground is located on top of a large bluff overlooking the ocean, and a generous wooden stairway leads down to the cobblestone beach. The campground is stocked: grocery store, Laundromat, blue ocean, orange sunsets. An offshore reef attracts divers and snorkelers, but due to the cobbles and cant of the beach, most walking is done on the cliffs above.

## Cardiff State Beach

Access: In Cardiff-by-the-Sea, along Old Hwy. 101 at San Elijo Lagoon. Lifeguards and rest rooms. Tel. 760/753-5091.

Just west of the San Elijo Lagoon and across Old Highway 101 is Cardiff State Beach, a wide, sandy beach catering to swimmers, surfers, and the occasional surf fisher. The north end of the beach has a carry-on boat launch, and the south end has some very nice tide pools.

## Torrey Pines State Reserve

Access: A few miles north of La Jolla on N. Torrey Pines Rd. From I-5, exit at Carmel Valley Rd. Head west for 1.5 miles and turn south, following N. Torrey Pines Rd. Visitor center, interpretive programs, rest rooms. Tel. 619/755-1275. For beach information, call 619/755-2063.

Sitting on the blufftop just above the Scripps Institute of Oceanography and Pier (see "Walks & Natural Roadside Attractions" below) is the 2,000-acre Torrey Pines State Reserve. Named after the rare Torrey pine tree that grows only here and on Santa Rosa Island, the park and the beach below (Torrey Pines State Beach) remain one of the wildest stretches of land on the Southern California coast, loaded with indigenous chaparral, Torrey pines, miles of unspoiled beaches, and the Los Peñasquitos Lagoon that is vital to migrating seabirds. At the southern end of the Torrey Pines Scenic Drive, you'll find Torrey Pines City Park, where there's ample parking and two stairways leading down to Black's Beach.

## Black's Beach

Access: In La Jolla, take the service road at the junction of La Jolla Farms Rd. and Blackgold Rd. No facilities. For beach information call the San Diego Coastline Parks Division at 619/221-8900.

Black's Beach (officially named Torrey Pines City Beach) is famous for its big, hollow surf and nude sunbathers. It is, perhaps, one of the most famous nude beaches in all of California, in part because of all the local attempts over the years to ban nudity there. You can most easily access the beach from the pedestrian-only service road directly above, or walk down one of the stairways at Torrey Pines State Beach or the city park, and head south down the sand. There are other paths but they are quite steep and the 1998 rains have seriously damaged them.

## La Jolla Cove

Access: In La Jolla, at Coast Blvd. and Girard Ave. Lifeguards and rest rooms. For beach information call the San Diego Coastline Parks Division at 619/221-8900.

La Jolla is a misspelling of La Joya, or "the jewel" in Spanish, and it's hardly a misnomer. Despite the town's hoity-toity affluence, the coastline here is some of the most magnificent in all of Southern California. At the southern end of the La Jolla Bay, just down from the flat expanse of La Jolla Shores Beach, you'll find this breathtaking cove. Granted, beauty often attracts crowds, but a trip here is well worth it, especially if you're a diver, snorkeler, or swimmer. The calm, protected warm waters in the cove kiss a sandy beach that lies beneath the cliffs. An underwater park stretches from here to the northern tip of Torrey Pines State Beach, and features a kelp forest, artificial reefs, two submarine canyons, and tide pools.

## Windansea Beach

Access: In La Jolla at Neptune Place and Bonair St. No facilities. For beach information call the San Diego Coastline Parks Division at 619/221-8900.

This is one of the most legendary surfing spots on the Southern California coast. The waves and the lifestyle surfers who rode them were immortalized in Tom Wolfe's '60s classic, *The Pump House Gang,* and it was in these pages that America was introduced to a quintessential Southern California word: bitchin'.

## Mission Trails Regional Park

Access: 1 Father Junipero Serra Trail, just a few miles from downtown San Diego. From I-8 east, exit at Mission Gorge Rd. Turn right at the T intersection and continue to the park entrance. Tel. 619/528-7000. Web site: 206.31.38.177/foundation/foundation.html.

On 5,760 acres of mostly unspoiled open space, you'll find two lakes; nearly 3 miles of the San Diego River, which runs through Mission Gorge; and five mountain peaks, including Cowles Mountain, the highest peak in the city at 1,591 feet. Aside from the Old Mission Dam and the visitor center, the place looks pretty much like it did when Cabrillo landed near here in 1542. The park is well known for its 50 miles of hiking and mountain-biking trails.

## Los Peñasquitos Preserve

Access: 24 miles north of San Diego proper. I-15 north to Mira Mesa Blvd. Tel. 619/694-3049.

Los Peñasquitos Canyon Preserve is part of Los Peñasquitos County Park. The canyon itself is 6 miles long and shaded by sycamore, willows, and live oak. On both ends of the preserve trail lie historic adobes: Ruiz-Alvardo on the west and Johnson-Taylor on the east, which is San Diego's oldest rancho.

## Pacific Beach/Mission Beach

Access: In Pacific Beach, along Ocean Blvd. from Thomas Ave. to Diamond St., and in Mission Beach along Mission Blvd. between Pacific Beach Dr. and Mission Bay Channel. Lifeguards and rest rooms. For beach info call the San Diego Coastline Parks Division at 619/221-8900.

Pacific Beach is both the name of the small beach town between La Jolla and San Diego, and the northernmost end of the Ocean Front Walk, a paved 3-mile promenade that runs down through Mission Beach, a peninsula just west of San Diego. The beaches are flat and sandy, and the Walk is generally jammed with bikers, in-line skaters, joggers, and the college kids who live in many of the oceanfront shacks. (Okay, they're steps above shacks, but there's still a laid-back, no-frills beach bum aura about this part of town.) Be sure to take a ride on the 70-year-old Giant Dipper Roller Coaster, located in the nearby Belmont Park (tel. 619/491-2988), a restored amusement park that still retains much of its old charm. To the west of Mission Beach are Mission Bay and Mission Bay Park (tel. 619/236-1212) where you can swim, fish, sail, powerboat, and go to Sea World (tel. 619/226-3901). Families with small children often gravitate to the bay side because of the warmer, calmer waters. There are some campsites in this 4,200-acre "aquatic park," alongside the fancy hotels and condos, and restored natural areas that offer year-round wildlife viewing.

## Balboa Park

Access: Laurel St. and Balboa Dr. in San Diego. Tel. 619/239-0512.

Balboa Park is a mother lode of fun. It's filled with gardens, walkways, pavilions, grassy knolls, theaters, and tons of museums, which are centered around the Pan-American Plaza and the Pedestrian Mall. The most famous attraction is the San Diego Zoo, located on the park's northern edge. (See "Walks & Natural Roadside Attractions" below for zoo information.) You could spend days here and not see it all.

## Ocean Beach Park, Pier & City Beach

Access: Park: In Ocean Beach between Voltaire St. and Niagara Ave. Pier: At the end of Niagara Ave. City Beach: Between Niagara and Pescadero Aves. Lifeguards and rest rooms. For beach information contact the San Diego Coastline Parks Division at 619/221-8900.

Ocean Beach Park, just south of the San Diego River, was once a fairly rough

neighbor of San Diego, but it has cleaned up in recent years. The litter is gone and the pier has been refurbished, yet the ambience is, luckily, still far from nouveau riche. The beach park features a paved promenade, grassy area for picnicking, and a northern section (past Voltaire St.) known as Dog Beach, where doggies can be legally off-leash. Surfers hang below the huge T-shaped Municipal Pier waiting for waves, while anglers cast from above. South of the pier, the city beach is a series of small pocket beaches, good for sunbathing or surfers. The rip tides here are very strong; swimming is not recommended.

## Sunset Cliffs Park

Access: In Ocean Beach, off Sunset Cliffs Blvd., from Pt. Loma Ave. to Ladera St.

While the landscape is rather flat around Mission Beach, it picks up again as you head south toward Ocean Beach and Point Loma. Perched on sandstone bluffs rising high above the ocean, Sunset Cliffs is, as the name implies, a lovely place to watch the sun go down. There are several parking areas along the boulevard, some trails wandering atop the cliffs, and several steep trails leading down to the pocket beach, frequented by divers and surfers. A stairway at Ladera Street will also get you down on the sand.

## Cabrillo National Monument

Access: I-5 or I-8 to Rosecrans St. (Hwy. 209). Follow Catalina Blvd. to Point Loma. Tel. 619/557-5450. Open daily 9am–5pm. $4 per vehicle, $2 walk-ins.

This monument—dedicated to Juan Rodriguez Cabrillo, the Spaniard who "discovered" San Diego Bay—is located near the tip of the Point Loma peninsula. The views of Coronado Island and the bay are pretty fantastic, as is the old Point Loma Lighthouse that kept ships safe from 1855 to 1891. The 1.5-mile Bayside Trail offers interpretive displays, while oceanside trails will take you to some excellent tide pools and views of California gray whales in the winter. (See "Wildlife Viewing" for more info.)

### Coronado Island

Access: From San Diego, drive across the 2.1-mile Coronado Bridge to the island. Tel. 619/437-8788. Web site: www. coronado.ca.us. Public bus transportation is also available from downtown San Diego, or you can take the San Diego Ferry—both allow you to bring your bicycle. For ferry information, call 619/234-4111.

This 5.3-square-mile island just west of metropolitan San Diego offers beaches, fishing, boating, golfing, and biking. It's most famous for the Hotel del Coronado, which is now a National Historic Landmark. Built in 1888, this red-and-white Victorian masterpiece looks like something out of a fairy tale. It's pricey and usually booked solid, but cocktails are always an option.

### Silver Strand State Beach

Access: Between Imperial Beach and Coronado, along Silver Strand Blvd. (Hwy. 75). Lifeguards, rest rooms, showers, picnic area, fire pits. Tel. 619/435-5184.

Silver Strand Beach is located on the tiny strip of land that connects Coronado Island with Imperial Beach. Its main attraction is its oceanfront RV park. Across the bay lies the Sweetwater Marsh National Refuge (tel. 619/422-2482), the largest remaining salt marsh in the area. Over 215 species of birds, several of them endangered, can be viewed only through walks conducted by the Chula Vista Nature Interpretive Center. Just south of here, near the southern edge of San Diego Bay, is the South Bay Marine Biological Study Area, another local spot for bird watching. A paved bike trail and nature trail cut through the area.

### Imperial Beach & Pier

Access: In Imperial Beach, along Seacoast Dr. from Palm to Encanto aves. Lifeguards, rest room, showers. Tel. 619/23-8328.

You can see Tijuana from this border beach town and feel its cultural impact. Unfortunately, you may also experience its pollution, as untreated sewage from the Tijuana River almost constantly contaminates the beach. On the bright side, though, this wide sandy beach hosts the U.S. Open Sandcastle Competition every July. South of the beach is the Tijuana River National Estuarine Reserve (tel. 619/575-3613), where the last few miles of the Tijuana River flow into San Diego County and out to sea. Great for birding and the occasional coyote sighting.

### Border Field State Park

Access: I-5, exit Dairy Mart Rd. Follow signs to the end of Monument Rd. Rest rooms, picnic tables, fire pits. Tel. 619/428-3034.

Located on the U.S. border with Mexico, this park sounds great: 2 miles of sandy beach, grassy picnic spots, equestrian trails. In reality, it's separated from Tijuana, Mexico, by a giant ugly fence; honchos from Immigration are always busting undocumented aliens; and the garbage and vandalism ain't a pretty sight either. If you're into social anthropology rather than recreation, however, this place has its plusses.

# Orange County ◆ What to Do & Where to Do It

## BIRD WATCHING

The **Bolsa Chica Ecological Reserve** (tel. 714/846-1114) is a restored urban salt marsh home to over 200 bird species, including the well-camouflaged Belding's Savannah sparrow and great blue heron. From the boardwalk, you can use binoculars to watch the nesting islands for the endangered California least terns and the Black Skimmers. The **Upper Newport Bay Ecological Reserve and Regional Park** (tel. 714/640-1751), a shallow estuary bordered by bluffs, was saved from development by concerned citizens, I'm happy to report. Over 30,000 birds take shelter here from August to April, including the black-necked stilt and American avocet. Both sites offer nature trails around the reserves.

## BOARDSAILING

It's getting harder and harder to find a spot to go boardsailing in Orange County. The beaches are simply so crowded and heavily patrolled that it's often actually illegal to launch anything harder than a rubber ducky from the beach (this is the hated "blackball" period of the day when many beaches are designated "swimmers only").

Use caution and pick your spots wisely. The **Water Planet** at 5932 Bolsa Ave., no. 107, in Huntington Beach is something of a mecca for local boardsailors. Not only do they have all the gear you could possibly want, but they'll be happy to point you to the most happening spot of the day. Happy sailing!

## FISHING

Ocean sportfishing is big business in these parts. You're far enough south that even in non-El Niño years it's still common to catch the occasional tuna or dorado. Opportunities range from casting for surf perch (and if you're lucky, a halibut) off the **Huntington Pier** or the rocks in **Laguna Beach,** to signing on for a 3-day, long-range sportfishing trip deep into the waters of Baja.

Much depends on what season you visit. While there are plenty of fish native to the area, like calico bass, cabezon, and others, it's when the migrating schools of albacore, white sea bass, bonito, and yellowtail make themselves known in spring and summer that the fishing really heats up. Few trips beat the action of catching fat, torpedo-shaped albacore as they school around your boat. A few hours of reeling in these muscular 25 pounders will make you sleep like a baby when you get home.

Deep-sea fishing trips leave from every commercial harbor along the coast. One good source of information is the *Los Angeles Times* fish count. You'll have to search, because it's hidden way back in the sports page with things like golf scores, horse handicaps, and so on, but it gives yesterday's fish count for every

# Outdoor Resources

**Huntington Beach Chamber of Commerce**
101 Main Street, Suite 2A (corner of Main and PCH)
Huntington Beach, CA 92648
Tel. 714/969-3492 or 800/SAY-OCEAN
http://www.hbvisit.com

**Newport Beach Visitors Bureau**
3300 West Coast Highway, Newport Beach, CA 92663
Tel. 949/722-1611 or 800/942-6278
http://newportbeach.com

**Newport Harbor Chamber of Commerce**
Tel. 714/729-4400

**Laguna Beach Visitors Bureau**
252 Broadway, Laguna Beach, CA 92651
Tel. 714/497-9229 or 800/877-1115
http://www.laguanbeachinfo.org

**Dana Point Chamber of Commerce**
24681 La Plaza, Suite 115, Dana Point, CA 92629-1802
Tel. 714/496-1555 or 800/290-DANA
http://www.danapoint-ca.com

**San Juan Capistrano Chamber of Commerce**
31931 Camino Capistrano, Suite D, SJC, CA
Tel. 714/493-4700
http://www.sanjuancaptistrano.com

**Oceanside Visitors Information**
I-5 and Route 76, Oceanside, CA 92054
Tel. 619/721-1101

**Carlsbad Chamber of Commerce**
5411 Avenida Encinas #100, Carlsbad, CA 92008
Tel. 619/931-8400

**La Jolla Town Council**
1055 Wall Street #110,
La Jolla, CA 92037
Tel. 619/454-1444

**San Diego Visitor Information Center**
I-5 at the Clairemont Drive exit.
Open daily 9am to dusk
2688 East Mission Bay Drive,
San Diego, CA 92109
Tel. 619/276-8200
http://www.infosandiego.com

**San Diego County Park Reservations**
Tel. 619/565-3600;
Park Information 619/694-3049

**Southern California Mountain Bike.Com**
http://www.socalmtb.com
This page is a great resource for all sorts of mountain bike info. There are hundreds of mountain bike shops grouped by county and listed alphabetically, too.

**mOthEr rOck: Southern California's Climbing Magazine**
http://members.aol.com/motherrock
This page offers some of the most up-to-date climbing information for the southland.

**The WWW Guide to Southern California Beaches**
http://www.califmall.com/beacj/BchSou.html
This comprehensive site offers maps, descriptions, and useful phone numbers for all the beaches in SoCal.

**San Diego County Surf Report**
Tel. 619/221-8884

harbor from San Luis Obispo to the Mexican border. It's amazing to see how different the fishing can be between places just a few miles away. It's also a lesson in being in the right place at the right time: Watch the fish count over a few days and see how things shift up and down the coast. Within the region of

Orange and San Diego counties, the following are most, but not all, of the well-known operations, most of which run several different kinds of trips on several different boats every day.

♦ Newport Harbor: Newport Landing, 5 boats, 714/675-0550; Davey's Locker, 7 boats, 714/673-1434.

♦ Dana Point: Dana Wharf Sportfishing, 8 boats, 714/496-5794.

But you don't need to head far out to sea to have a good time. This stretch of coast has more piers per mile than any other part of the state. While the action is nothing like that on the offshore sportfishing boats, pier casters regularly do really well at Huntington Pier, Newport Pier (which sits close to the deep waters at the mouth of the Newport submarine canyon and is consequently one of the hottest fishing piers in the state), San Clemente Pier, Oceanside Pier (periodic barracuda), Shelter Island Pier (in San Diego Bay), Crystal Beach Pier, and Ocean Beach Pier. While you can pier fish year-round, summer is the right time to find fast action.

Many people are surprised to find out that there's also a world-class freshwater fishery in this area. In fact, there are several. **Irvine Lake** is home to everything from bluegills to largemouth bass, but it's especially well-known for trophy-sized rainbow trout. Ten-pounders and up are not uncommon. Fishing pressure is less than you'd expect because there's a $10 fishing fee. That money is put back into the lake in the form of stocks of big, fat trout.

## HIKING

### Hills for the People Trail

4–15 miles round-trip, depending on turnaround. Moderate. Access: Trailhead parking lot in Chino Hills State Park. When the road forks just past the main park entrance, stay to your left. You'll see the trailhead parking at the end of the road.

Start hiking on the signed Hills-for-People trail. You'll drop down to a small creek and then follow it upcanyon, passing a number of old livestock ponds and other elements of old ranching history. Especially of interest are the semi-rare California walnut trees. It's 2 miles to McDermont Spring, a fine turnaround. If you keep going, the trail joins the Telegraph Canyon Trail and drops gently down in the canyon through more oak and walnut trees. The trail ends at Carbon Canyon Road, where you can either: 1) turn left onto the road and hike over to Carbon Canyon Regional Park (which also has some nice trails); or 2) turn around and head back the way you came. *Note:* Plan this hike for a cool spring or fall day; the summer heat and smog are unbearable.

### Moro Canyon

7 miles round-trip. Moderate. Access: Moro Canyon parking lot at Crystal Cove State Park.

This section of the San Joaquin Hills above Crystal Cove State Beach is filled with several trails to hike. For this one, begin at the Moro Canyon parking lot, walk along the road marked "Official Vehicles Only," and drop down past a trailer park and to the Moro Canyon Trail. At the canyon bottom, head left and up. Stay in the canyon, ignoring other fire roads and heading to the ridgetop. Now's the time to eat your lunch and marvel at the view of Catalina Island. To return, you can hike to your left and pick up another fire road that loops back around to the main canyon trail, or simply head back down the way you came. Use caution, as mountain bikers also use this trail.

## Corona del Mar to Abalone Point

2–7 miles round-trip depending on turn-around. Easy. Access: Marguerite Ave. and Corona del Mar Beach.

Before you start out on this beach hike, be sure to consult a tide table. Low tide is the only way you'll be able to check out tide pools, walk out to Arch Rock, and ensure your return. Beginning at the east jetty of Newport Beach, walk south along the sand to Little Corona del Mar, a beautiful, sandy cove. About 1 mile from the jetty, you'll see Arch Rock, which is just offshore. Continuing south, you'll pass through Crystal Cove State Beach, Reef Point, and El Moro Beach. From here you can see Abalone Point, a rock outcropping composed of eroded lava and other volcanic stuff. It's capped by a grass-covered dome that rises 200 feet out of the water. Along this stretch, you'll find some incredible tide pools filled with crabs, starfish, anemones, urchins, and more. Return the way you came or, when passing through Crystal Cove, take a trail up to the blufftop and hike along the ridge for a while.

## Bell Canyon Trail

4-mile loop. Easy. Access: Caspers Wilderness Park. From the park entrance, follow the park road to its end. Pick up the trail at the signed Nature Trail Loop.

The oak-lined Bell Canyon is the heart of the Caspers Wilderness Park, and the trail that loops around it is one of the nicest here, although there are many others. Follow the Nature Trail north to the Oak Trail, which follows the west wall of Bell Canyon and west bank of Bell Creek. Follow along to Star Rise, which joins Bell Canyon Trail. A wide dirt road, Bell Canyon Trail travels along the canyon floor and then turns south, through an oak meadow and back to the

parking lot. Remember, this park is only open to adult hikers who travel in groups of two or more, and a wilderness permit must be obtained from the visitor center before you head out.

## Trabuco Canyon to Ocean Vista Point

3 miles round-trip. Moderately easy. Access: Begin at the entry station to O'Neill Regional Park.

Start hiking north along a service road that parallels Live Oak Canyon Road, which leads toward some water tanks. A dirt road branches off to your right and ascends along a ridge. From here you can see red-tailed hawks circling over rural ranchland country in one direction, and suburban sprawl in the other. Continue up to the 1,492-foot summit and you'll be at Ocean Vista Point, where on a clear day you can see all the way out to Catalina Island. (You'll know you're at Ocean Vista when you see all the cell-phone communications hardware. Some people call this spot Cellular Hill.) Return the way you came or, about 200 yards into your descent, make a left at the first fork. This route takes you through an old Youth Camp and eventually back to the service road and your starting point.

## Harding Trail

3 miles round-trip. Moderate. Access: Cleveland National Forest. Santiago Canyon Rd. to Modjeska Grade Rd. and veer right. Go 1 mile, turn right, and follow Modjeska Canyon Rd. to its end at the Tucker Wildlife Sanctuary. Park in the gravel lot by a tiny observatory. The trail, Forest Road 5S08, begins at a locked gate on the north side of the road.

The Tucker Wildlife Sanctuary is the trailhead for the Harding Trail, which goes up the western slopes of the Santa

Ana Mountains and all the way to Old Saddleback, a dip formed by Modjeska and Santiago peaks. (The entire journey would be 20 miles round-trip, but this hike takes you the first 1.5 miles to Goat Shed Overlook.) Over 200 bird species have been spotted in the sanctuary, but best known are the hummingbirds. As you head up through the chaparral and oak-covered hills, you'll soon reach the remains of what locals call the Goat Shed and a great place to soak up the view. If you're up for more adventure, you can hike 3.5 more miles to Laurel Spring, where there's a very fragrant bay laurel oasis and terrific views of Harding and Santiago canyons. Return the way you came.

## MOUNTAIN BIKING

### Moro Canyon Trail

9.3-mile loop. Moderately difficult. Access: Moro Canyon parking lot at Crystal Cove State Beach. This ride takes you out on Moro Canyon Trail and back on Rattlesnake Trail, and you'll get your share of very steep sections with loose rocks and sand.

From the Moro Canyon parking lot, pedal along the road marked "Official Vehicles Only," and drop down past a trailer park to the Moro Canyon Trail. Start climbing this fairly bumpy, washboard road. At 3 miles, turn left on West Loop Trail and continue up to a gate at the single-track Fenceline Trail. Turn left on Fenceline and follow it to the T with Red-Tail Ridge and go left again. Red-Tail narrows and becomes the fabulous single-track Rattlesnake Trail as you head down the canyon. At the electrical tower, Rattlesnake cuts hard to the right and widens to a fire road. At West Cut-Across, you'll do just that—go left and cut across back to Moro Canyon Trail. Make a right and return to the parking lot.

### Moro Ridge Trail

6-mile loop. Moderately difficult. Access: Moro Canyon parking lot at Crystal Cove State Beach.

On this ride, you head out on Moro Ridge Trail and return on Moro Canyon Trail. The direction begins just like the ride listed above, only at 1 mile from the trailer park, turn right on a connector trail that brings you to the Moro Ridge Trail and some great single track riding. Just before you reach the top of the ridge (about 200 yards), you'll want to cut across to the Moro Canyon Trail—no small feat. Go through a wire fence, onto a foot trail that takes you up, then down a hill and to a fence line. Here the bike trail continues for about 1 mile; it's a technical one: sharp turns, rocks, roots, cactus. Finally, when you reach Moro Canyon Trail, go left and it's all downhill back to the trailer park and onto the parking lot.

### Aliso Valley

8 miles. Easy. Access: From Anaheim, take Hwy. 91 east to Hwy. 71. Head north on Hwy. 71 about 6 miles to Pomona-Rincon Rd. and turn left. At Soquel Canyon Dr., go left to Elinvar Dr. and turn left again. Elinvar becomes a dirt road as you head up into the hills and the park entrance. Enter the park and drive through Bane Valley to the park headquarters and parking area.

This easy out and back along the Aliso Valley Trail in Chino Hills State Park is the closest thing to wilderness in Orange County. Of course, a feel-good ride here is totally dependent on the air quality. Smog is the enemy of the people. From the park headquarters, pedal south on the paved road to the entrance to Aliso Valley Trail, marked by a campground and a metal gate. Go through the gate and start biking though the canyon valley. Stay on the main road, avoiding all the little side trails to keep this an easy ride. (Of course, if you're looking for a challenging ride, then many of those little side trails are for you.) The trail ends just south of Scully Hill Trail at a metal gate. Retrace your path back to the park headquarters from here.

## Telegraph Canyon Trail to Main Divide

11 miles. Moderately easy. Access: From Anaheim, take Hwy. 57 north and exit at Lambert. Follow Lambert east until it becomes Brea Canyon Dr. In 2 miles, you'll see the entrance to Carbon Canyon Park on your right.

While this trail explores Chino Hills, the best way to access the trail is to enter at the west end, through Carbon Canyon Regional Park. From the main entrance of Canyon Park, turn right outside the park and ride past an orchard and a metal gate, down into a creekbed and up the other side through a fence. Take the dirt road on your right and then it's a quick left onto the Telegraph Canyon Trail. Stay on the Telegraph Canyon Trail to keep this an easy ride. (There are lots of other trails you can take out of Telegraph Valley and some are quite challenging. Consult a park map for these rides.) The 1,000-foot climb from here up to the Main Divide is so gradual you hardly notice it. From the Main Divide, you'll reach a north-south ridge that separates east and west Chino Hills, turn around and retrace your path back to your car.

## Modjeska Peak

13 miles. Moderate. Access: From Anaheim, take Hwy. 91 east to Hwy. 55 and head south. Exit at Chapman and head east. Chapman becomes Santiago Canyon Rd. after 5 miles. Follow Santiago Canyon Rd. about 9 miles, past Modjeska Canyon Rd., and make a left on Modjeska Grade Road. Park on the blacktop and pedal up the road and through a gate, which puts you on the Santiago Truck Trail.

This ride cuts through the Modjeska Canyon located at the western edge of the Cleveland National Forest in the shadow of the Santa Ana Mountains, and takes you up to Modjeska Peak. Both peak and canyon are named after the Polish-born actress Helena Modjeska, who purchased hundreds of acres here and built an estate called Arden. From the beginning of the Santiago Truck Trail, start pedaling uphill. At 6.5 miles, you'll come to Joplin Road—but don't take it. It dumps you downhill and then dead-ends. Instead, continue 1 mile past the road and take the left fork that descends to a small valley ending at Old Camp and Modjeska Peak. Retrace your path on the return.

## Silverado Canyon to Maple Spring Trail

16 miles. Moderately easy. Access: From Anaheim, take Hwy. 91 east to Hwy. 55 and head south. Exit at Chapman and head east. Chapman becomes Santiago Canyon Rd. after 5 miles. In another 5 miles, turn left on Silverado Canyon Rd. You can park near the Water District facilities.

This town, located at the western edge of the Cleveland National Forest in the shadow of the Santa Ana Mountains, was booming in the late 19th century, after silver was discovered here; hence the name, Silverado Canyon. Pedal along the paved Silverado Canyon, through a residential neighborhood lined with tiny, old homes. The pavement ends at a gate, and here the road turns to dirt. Now the canyon narrows as it follows the Silverado Creek, and oak trees are everywhere. When you cross the creek, it's time to turn back and return the way you came—the trail gets quite challenging from here on out, which is always an option if you're feeling ambitious. See the ride below for details.

## Silverado Canyon to Santiago Peak

22 miles. Moderately difficult. Access: Same as above.

Follow the directions above to the creek. When you cross the creek, things start to toughen up. Head up the Maple Spring Trail to the Main Divide Truck Trail and make a right. Follow Main Divide up to Santiago Peak via a short spur. From here, the views are spectacular and on a clear day you can see Catalina Island. Retracing your path back to your car, be sure to take the left fork (FS 3S04) as you head down from the peak and turn left on the Maple Spring Trail.

## ROCK CLIMBING

The Beach (also called Pirates' Cove), by the east jetty to Newport Beach Harbor, is one of the only places to climb outdoors in Orange County. The soft sandstone of The Beach offers excellent bouldering, and all problems (which tend to be difficult) are done almost exclusively without a rope. There's plenty of overhangs and some routes are as high as 45 feet. Good thing for the sandy beach landing. Climbing here is dependent on the crowds and weather. During the summer, there's no climbing until after 5pm, and when it's foggy, the rock soaks up moisture like a sponge. Climb when the air is dry. Indoors, Rockreation Sport Climbing Center in Costa Mesa (tel. 714/556-ROCK) is one of the largest climbing gyms in the country. It's close to The Beach and offers foot-lead and top-rope routes, extensive bouldering, and weight equipment. Rental gear is available.

## SAILING

Orange County, and Newport Beach in particular, is one of the most sailing-crazy parts of the state. Newport Harbor is packed with literally thousands of yachts ranging from dilapidated tubs to elegant maxi-racers. So many sailors congregate here that there's not just one Newport yacht club but six, not to mention numerous more casual congregations of sailors in local bars and beaches.

It's 26 miles as the crow flies from the mouth of Newport Harbor to Catalina. Closer to home, you can cruise down the coast of Crystal Cove State Park or into Laguna Beach for a nice day sail or overnight. There are a number of places to rent boats in Newport Beach. Newport Sailing Club and Academy of Sailing is a complete instructional and charter sailing operation with boats from dinghies to 55-foot-long ones (tel. 949/675-7100). Marina Sailing of Newport Beach is an American Sailing Association certified school and charter operation that can teach you your first tack or set you up with a fully loaded yacht for a trip to Catalina (tel. 714/673-7763). The Balboa Boat Rentals facility at Balboa Landing has lots of smaller boats that are perfect for ranging around the harbor (tel. 949/673-7200).

Like most harbors with active racing fleets up and down the coast, Newport is a good place to bum rides on the night of their weekly "beer can races," when everyone turns out just to race for glory. Take a clue from the name and show up with a 12-pack. You'll get a place on a boat.

## SCUBA DIVING

Orange County goes from diving famine to feast as you travel north to south. From Seal Beach and Huntington to the mouth of Newport Harbor, there's not a lot to see. While people do dive

Huntington Beach, the Newport Pier, and the breakwaters on both sides of Newport Harbor, if you want to go diving in Orange County I suggest you head south.

Once you cross Newport Harbor and hit the suddenly mountainous coastline of Corona Del Mar, Laguna Beach, and Dana Point, you've entered a shore diver's dreamland. One look at the shoreline reveals what you can expect underwater: rocky reefs, steep drop-offs, and lots of life. It's an area with clean, clear water and more sea life than you'd ever imagine living in such close proximity to a megalopolis: spiny lobsters, sheepshead, barracuda, urchins, kelp forests, eels, lush beds of sea grass, all make this a wonderful diving destination.

Virtually every square foot of the ocean between the Big Corona Breakwater and Camp Pendleton is somebody's dive spot and has a name. Don't feel that you have to stick with the suggested spots at all; there's a million places to see, and discovering your own spot is lots of fun. I chose the following locations because they are easily found and have good access.

### Big Corona Breakwater, Corona Del Mar

Beginner–intermediate. Snorkeling okay. Access: Via Ocean Blvd. and Iris Ave. in Corona Del Mar. Parking fee.

This is a peculiar dive spot; it certainly doesn't seem like it would be any good. It is, after all, inside one of the busiest harbors in California. You'd expect it to be nothing but mud and garbage. However, this sheltered spot is an excellent place for beginning scuba divers and all levels of scuba divers to check out. Even when big swells are pounding most of the coast, it's calm inside the breakwater. Rocky reefs are home to lobsters,

garibaldi, perch, and lots of small invertebrates on the rocks. Do stay aware of the fact that there is a nearby boat channel when you're surfacing. The swimming area is clearly marked from the surface but not so easy to remain aware of when you're underwater. And nobody wants to pop up right in front of a fast-moving yacht.

### Crystal Cove State Park: Pelican Point, Scotchman's Cove & Reef Point

Intermediate–advanced. Snorkeling okay. Parking fee. Access: Several different lots off Hwy. 1 between Corona Del Mar and Laguna Beach.

There are many different dive sites in the 3-mile coastline of Crystal Cove State Park. All will offer you access to long rocky reefs, tremendous quantities of fish, beautiful kelp forests, and the possibility of spotting larger pelagic species like white sea bass and yellowtail. The three spots listed above are accessible from nearby parking lots. If you desire more solitude, simply walk down the shore a ways or bring a dive kayak. The entire area is a marine preserve but spearfishing is allowed and lobster can be taken by hand. No taking of artifacts or other marinelife is allowed.

### Shaw's Cove, Laguna Beach

Beginner–intermediate. Snorkeling excellent. Access: Park at the intersection of Cliff Dr. and Fairview and carry your gear down a stairway to the beach.

Though you have to carry your gear down (and up) a stairway, well-protected Shaw's Cove is one of the most popular spots in Laguna Beach for beach diving. Even during south swells it's rarely too surf-lashed to dive. On any given weekend there might be 40 divers here, so don't expect too many game fish and too much solitude, but the reefs are covered with beautiful nudibranchs and anemones, and the kelp and sea grass beds are lovely.

## Diver's Cove, Laguna Beach

Beginner–intermediate. Access: Cliff Dr. passes right by this spot. All parking is metered so bring lots of quarters.

This is the single most popular spot on all of Orange County for divers; every morning on weekends it's packed with checkout classes. But if you time things right, you can have a nice dive here without too much company. Laguna Beach has restricted all commercially operated dive classes to before 10am on city beaches. That means that by mid-morning as many as a hundred divers suddenly pack up and leave. Be there to take their parking spots and hit the water. Granted, the fish and other wildlife have probably been scared starkers by the sound of all those heavy-breathing beginners, but it's a nice dive and the access is about as easy as it comes.

## Wood's Cove, Laguna Beach

Intermediate–advanced. Access: Intersection of Ocean Way and Diamond St. Metered parking, bring change.

Wood's Cove is an interesting jumble of underwater boulders. With the rocks comes a profusion of sea life. The fish get larger and more abundant on the outer rock reefs, and the visibility here is sometimes spectacular, which means 45 or 50 feet. The only catch to Wood's Cove is that it's slightly more difficult to access than the more popular spots, and it's exposed to more swell. During big south swells it may not be diveable.

## San Juan Rocks, Dana Point

Intermediate–advanced. No snorkeling. Access: Park at Dana Harbor lot near the *Pilgrim* sailing ship exhibit.

The San Juan Rocks are a collection of spires sticking out of the water below the striking headland here in Dana Point. While they're notoriously fickle as far as visibility goes, on a good day this spot can bring big surprises, really big surprises. Dana Point sticks far out to sea, and migrating gray whales round it very closely. It's not unheard of for divers to spot the giant mammals as they make their way north. That's a long shot, but the possibility is enough to keep you thrilled while you enjoy the schools of calico bass, garibaldi, and several different kinds of perch that hover around this rocky area.

Recommended dive shop:

◆ Beach Cities Scuba Mania, 19036 Brookhurst St., Huntington Beach. Tel. 714/378-2612.

## SEA KAYAKING

So much ocean and so little time! That's the problem confronting even the most avid kayaker here. While the northern stretch of beach from Huntington to Newport is largely kayaker-unfriendly unless you are adept at paddling in and out through relatively powerful surf, **Newport Bay** is a wonderful place to learn to kayak or to explore the back reaches of Upper Newport Bay. Remember that boat traffic is very busy in the lower bay, and try to stay out of the main channels. Attractions range from gawking at multimillion-dollar houses on Lido Isle and Balboa Island to paddling through the remaining wild sections of the upper bay looking at birds, stingrays, and fish. An ever-changing cast of concessionaires rents sit-on-top kayaks here. **Southwind Kayak Center** at 2801 Pacific Coast Hwy. (tel. 714/261-0200) is an old standby that rents kayaks by the hour and teaches basic kayaking lessons. For a neat glimpse of some of the few remaining natural wetlands in this area, sign on for one of their nature tours of the Upper Newport Bay. At **Corona Del Mar** and **Laguna Beach,** the coastline becomes rocky and high, with scalloped coves and sandy beaches in between. It's a dream to paddle along, poking from one cove to the next. Laguna is a diver's dream and it's worth tossing a mask into your kayak so you can stop and snorkel. Places where it's possible to launch your own kayak easily are **Crystal Cove State Park, Main Beach** in the heart of downtown Laguna, and **Aliso Beach County Park** in South Laguna. Paddling either direction from these beaches will take you to more remote and less crowded spots, and they're close enough together that you could do a 1-day tour of the entire Laguna coast by putting in at Crystal Cove and taking out at Aliso. Check with **Hobie Sports** at 294 Forest Ave. (tel. 714/497-3304) about kayak rentals and gear.

The huge pleasure harbor at **Dana Point** is large enough to entertain a lot of paddlers. Those who seek more adventure should paddle out of the harbor and explore the offshore bird rocks and the stunning Dana Point headland just about a half mile north of the harbor mouth.

## SURFING

When Jan and Dean sang their number one 1963 smash hit "Surf City," they weren't just talking about an imaginary place. Since the first one in 1928, Huntington Beach has hosted hundreds of surf competitions and, more importantly, thousands of surfers have caught literally millions of waves here, earning the sobriquet "Surf City" long before Jan and Dean. With 8 miles of sandy beach, this northern edge of Orange County is a California archetype. Boys and girls with bushy, bushy blond hairdos still sun on the beach while surfers (now almost as many female as male) carve the almost constant summer waves. **Huntington's Surf Museum,** with a wealth of memorabilia and paraphernalia dedicated to the history of the sport, is a favorite pilgrimage at 411 Olive St. (tel. 714/960-3483). There's also a surfing walk of fame, which begins at the corner of Main and Highway 1. And this is only the beginning of a wealth of both literal and cultural surfing potential as you head south.

Though not as consistently exposed to big winter swells as the northern and central California coasts, the **Orange and San Diego counties coastline** to the Mexican border is almost entirely wide open to south swells driven up from the southern hemisphere winter and summertime hurricanes off Mexico. As a result, day after day of sunny, playful surf is broken only by short flat spells and periodic days when it's just HUGE. It's only natural, then, that an enormous culture has grown up around this sport of kings. Following the coast, there are simply too many surf shops to count. New ones open every season, and old ones close. A few trusty legends hang on year after year. Surf clothing, an industry centered largely in Newport Beach and surrounding Orange County towns, is a billion-dollar-a-year industry, selling most of their wares to kids in the heartland who can only dream about getting deeply tubed at the Wedge. And, as mentioned before, the surfing press is almost entirely centered in San Clemente, giving the local scene an influence far beyond its home turf.

And finally, not everyone is born knowing how to rip. Surfing is hard to learn. In fact, it's one of the hardest sports to master, simply because there are so many foreign elements. You've got this strange board, waves are crashing on you, and there are people all around you getting every wave. What's a wannabe surfer to do? I recommend surf camp. Surf camps have really taken off in the last few years. Ranging from weeklong camps where you eat, sleep, and dream surfing to short weekend clinics to special Baja expedition camps, there's nothing to get you up and riding like several days of professional instruction. **Summer Fun Surf Camp** (tel. 714/361-9526) and **Groundswell Surf Camp** (tel. 949/ 364-2262; www.surfcamp.com) are both established favorites based in San Clemente with a long history of satisfied customers.

So the question isn't "Where's the surf?" There's surf everywhere. The real question is "What kind of surf do I want?" Whatever your answer, there's one thing you can be sure of: There will be a lot of other people who had the same thought. Crowds are an inevitable fact of life in this overpopulated stretch of coast. Every spot has its locals, its old-timers, and its outsiders, which in this case means you.

Being cool goes a long way toward being accepted in the water. I don't mean cool like paddling out to the biggest guy in the water and saying "Ya, bro, check out my new board. Isn't it cool?" Rather, I mean being confident but non-confrontational. It also helps a lot if you can really rip, but in general just remember that we're all visitors here and it's really not worth getting into a fight when there are miles of beach in either direction.

Since there are so many fine surf spots in Orange County and San Diego County, I'm not going to even attempt to list them all. That alone would take an entire book, and since my editors are barking at me to finish this book I think I'll keep this brief by simply mentioning my favorite picks, a nice variety of everything from the completely white-knuckle to nice, gentle waves perfect for learning.

From north to south, within Orange County, my favorites are:

### The Huntington Pier

On both sides of this concrete pier at the base of Main Street, you'll find great and punchy waves. It takes a lot of guts to surf under the pier for your first time and lots of surfboards have met their demise when their rider chickened out halfway through, but shooting the pier is something of a tradition with the locals. You don't need to do it yourself to appreciate it. This is something of an arena for high performance surfing because the pier offers such a great audience of spectators. If you're a little shy, there are plenty of peaks in either direction. Huntington is also nice in that the pier lights are bright enough to encourage night surfing.

### The Wedge (a.k.a. West Jetty View Park)

At the end of Channel Rd. in Balboa. For surf report call 714/673-3771.

So often mankind screws things up when building jetties, but here is an example of something done quite right. When the jetty on the western edge of Newport Harbor went up, I don't think anyone could have imagined the monster wave it would spawn. South swells pour straight into the jetty and compress, doubling and tripling in size until they are just terrifying to behold. Summer surf frequently dishes out 20-foot faces on a grinding, tubular peak. For years it was unheard of to surf the Wedge, and it was known solely as a hardcore bodyboard and bodysurfing spot. Recent years have seen an influx of board surfers, but it's still pushing the outer limits of board surfing just to make the drop. On smaller days it's a blast to bodysurf. Be careful if you decide to go out. Do not, whatever you do, take off straight over the falls. People break their necks quite frequently doing that. A good angle to the left is what will make all the difference between getting slammed and the ride of your life.

## Crystal Cove State Park

On Hwy. 1 between Corona Del Mar and Laguna Beach. Tel. 714/494-3539.

The name is a little misleading—there is no cove here—but this 3-mile long beach park is simply beautiful. In a region where almost every square foot of beachfront property is developed, it's startling to encounter this park. Not only is the shoreline relatively pristine, but the hills on either side of the Pacific Coast Highway remain much the same as the entire county once was. More than 3,000 acres of hiking trails and wild space give you plenty to do if the waves don't deliver. But with 3 miles of beach, you'll find someplace that's breaking well enough to beckon you into the water.

## Salt Creek

In Dana Point. Off Ritz-Carlton Dr.

There are a lot of things that piss me off about Dana Point, notably the fake New England seaport architecture and the fact that rampant development has made beach access something of a bear here. But Salt Creek is one of the finest hollow beach breaks in the state and well worth taking the effort to surf. Park at the metered lot and follow a stairway and trails to the sand. From there you've got access to a long beach with numerous peaks. Have at it.

## San Onofre State Beach (Trestles & Surf Beach)

Take the Basilone Rd. exit off I-5 3 miles south of San Clemente.

Ah, San Onofre, wind-sculpted sandstone bluffs, long gentle waves, camping on the shore, and, a gigantic nuclear power plant. Nuclear power plant!?!? Yep, that's right. On one of the state's most lovely beaches is where PG&E and the state of California thought it was a good idea to build a huge, two-reactor, nuclear power plant. They say it's safe, but signs around the park telling you to evacuate if you hear an alarm tend to indicate otherwise. So it speaks to the quality of the surf here that people practically line up to get into San Onofre. Surf Beach at the northern edge of the state park is rightly famous as the Waikiki of California, with wonderful beginner waves that will build confidence in anyone. They break gently and go forever. More hardcore surfers make the 1.5-mile trek from the San Mateo Campground to Trestles, one of the best points in the area. Despite the hike, you won't be alone. Surfrider is currently fighting the military over plans to build staff housing right on the point here at what is currently a lovely nature preserve. If you see houses there now, well, it once was a lovely nature preserve.

## WALKS & ATTRACTIONS

## Surfing Walk of Fame

0.25 mile. Easy. Access: The corner of Main St. and Pacific Coast Hwy. in Huntington Beach.

Starting at Jack's Surfboards, this easy jaunt up Main Street takes you past 12 stone monuments dedicated to surfers who've been inducted for various outstanding achievements. And don't forget to visit the Huntington Beach International Surfing Museum, 411 Olive Ave., Huntington Beach, CA 92648. Tel. 714/960-3483; www.surfingmuseum.org. Summer, noon to 5pm daily; winter, noon to 5pm Wednesday to Sunday. Admission $2. Since Huntington Beach is also known as "Surf City," it's fitting that it hosts one of the best surfing museums in the world. Here, you can discover the history of surfing through photos, various exhibits, and memorabilia collections.

## The Pageant of the Masters

Each year, Laguna Beach hosts the **Festival of Arts** during July and August. The indisputable highlight is **Pageant of the Masters,** which re-creates famous classic and contemporary paintings using real people. The amazing stage production looks at once two-dimensional and eerily 3-D at the same time, and a narrator describes the history of each "painting." The pageant takes place nightly in a huge outdoor amphitheater, and tickets run $15 to $50. Call 714/497-6582 or 800/487-3378 for details. Or check out their Web site: www.foapom.com.

## WILDLIFE VIEWING

**Crystal Cove State Park** (tel. 714/494-3539) features 3 miles of bluff-bordered beach opening up into riparian woodland. Down near the water, shorebirds are everywhere and the tide pools are full of life. From December to February, watch for gray whales migrating. Dolphins, harbor seals, and sea lions can be seen all year long. The hills are home to many songbirds, as well as to coyotes and bobcats—although you'd be one lucky person to sight a bobcat.

# San Diego County ◆ What to Do & Where to Do It

## BIRD WATCHING

The Buena Vista Lagoon Ecological Reserve (tel. 619/439-2473), just outside San Clemente, is Southern California's only freshwater lagoon. It's the main pit stop for birds navigating the Pacific Flyway, and a breeding ground for the light-footed clapper rail and a few other endangered species. Viewing is good year-round but excellent during the spring and fall migrations. Near La Jolla, the rugged sandstone bluffs laced with the rare Torrey pines in Torrey Pines State Reserve/Los Peñaquitos Marsh (tel. 619/755-1275) are the place to look for western scrub-jays and California quail. Closer to the marsh, the pickleweed hides Belding's Savannah sparrows and the light-footed clapper rail. In San Diego, Mission Bay Park has two wildlife preserves that are a mix of mudflats, tidal channels, and salt marshes. The preserves offer excellent year-round waterfowl viewing, with an especially high number of waterbirds in the winter. At Cabrillo National Monument (tel. 619/557-5450) on the Point Loma peninsula, you'll find prairie falcons and great-horned owls as well as shorebirds such as the wandering tattler and marbled godwit. All in all there are over 375 bird species, plus some of the best viewing of marine and ocean mammal life on the West Coast. Sweetwater Marsh National Wildlife Refuge is the largest remaining salt marsh in San Diego Bay. Here, you can check out over 215 species of shorebirds, waterfowl, and wading birds on the mudflats and wetland, from the observation decks around the Chula Vista Nature Center. Rare sightings of little blue herons and black skimmers can happen to you! Guided walks are conducted by the Chula Vista Nature Interpretive Center (tel. 619/422-2482) and you'll need to catch the shuttle bus there, since no vehicles are allowed on the refuge. Call the Nature Center for details. Finally, the Tijuana Slough National Estuarine Research Reserve (tel. 619/575-3613) is host to over 400 bird species; at least six endangered ones nest here, including the least Bell's vireos. With its mix of tidal sloughs, beaches, riparian canyons, and hills, you can also sight birds of prey and other small mammals.

**BOARDSAILING**

Southern California is a big sailing area, but among the sailing world it's known for light and fluky air. For learning how to ride a sailboard it's great, but once you reach the level where you really want to rip on small boards, you'll find the lack of wind a little annoying. There are plenty of boardsailors around, but most of them live for trips down into Baja or up to Jalama where the wind really blows.

The heavily populated and restricted beach scene in this part of the state doesn't exactly make it easy, either. Many beaches are blackballed (which means they're designated swimming only) through the prime afternoon hours when the wind is likely to blow. So don't go looking for the next big boardsailing paradise here in San Diego County.

The best bet is to head to popular surfing beaches like **Encinitas, Swami's,** and **Tourmaline Surf Park** when the afternoon winds blow conditions out for surfers and leave it just right for boardsailors. Keep a close eye on local closures at any of the San Diego beaches, since there are zillions of weird rules and regulations about what kind of fun you can have in what place at what time. Once you're past the shore break, of

course, the whole world is your oyster; just be careful where you enter and exit the water.

**Mission Bay** is the most popular flat water spot. The wind is about the same as on the open Pacific here, but since Mission Beach cuts the bay off, the waves are really small or, more accurately, nonexistent. This is wonderful for learning how to start, stand, tack, gybe, and all the other basics. **Windsport** at 844 West Mission Bay Dr. (tel. 619/488-4642) has a complete line of gear and teaches lessons at all levels. It's conveniently located near the popular sailing areas of Sail Bay and Hilton Point.

Farther inland, **Lake Hodges** in Escondido is a great freshwater spot. Open from the beginning of May until the end of October, the lake gets some of the most consistent wind in the area, 10 to 20 knots much of the time. The **Lake Hodges Aquatic Center** rents gear and offers lessons. Their phone number is 619/272-3275.

In the north county, **North County Windsurfing** is the place to stop for advice. They're at 1940 Freeman St. in Oceanside.

**FISHING**

Ocean sportfishing is big business in these parts. You're far enough south that even in non–El Niño years it's still common to catch the occasional tuna or dorado. Opportunities range from casting for surf perch (and, if you're lucky, halibut) off the **Huntington Pier** or the rocks in **Laguna Beach,** to signing on for a 3-day long-range sportfishing trip deep into the waters of Baja.

Much depends on what season you visit. While there are plenty of fish native to the area, like calico bass, cabezon, and others, it's when the migrating schools of albacore, white sea bass, bonito, and yellowtail make themselves known in spring and summer that the fishing really heats up. Few trips beat the action of catching fat, torpedo-shaped albacore as they school around your boat. A few hours of reeling in these muscular 25 pounders will make you sleep like a baby when you get home.

Deep-sea fishing trips leave from every commercial harbor along the coast. One good source of information is the *Los Angeles Times* fish count. You'll have to search, because it's hidden way back in the sports page with things like golf scores, horse handicaps, and so on, but it gives yesterday's fish count for every harbor from San Luis Obispo to the Mexican border. You'll note how different the fishing can be between places just a few miles away; try to watch the fish count over a few days and see how things shift up and down the coast. That way you can be in the right place at the right time.

Within the Orange and San Diego counties region the following are most, but not all, of the well-known operations, most of which run several different kinds of trips on several different boats every day.

### OCEANSIDE

◆ Helgren's Sportfishing (Specializing in trips to San Clemente Island), 9 boats, 619/722-2133.
◆ Mission Bay: Seaforth Sportfishing, 6 boats, 619/224-3383.
◆ Islandia Sportfishing, 4 boats, 619/581-4200.

### SAN DIEGO

◆ Polaris Supreme, 1 boat, specializing in long-range trips to Baja, 619/670-8902.
◆ H&M Landing, 21 boats, 619/222-1144.
◆ Fishermen's Landing, 3 boats, 619/222-0391.
◆ Point Loma Sportfishing, 16 boats, 619/223-1627.

◆ LoPreste Sportsfishing, 2 boats, 619/226-8030.

But you don't need to head far out to sea to have a good time. This stretch of coast has more piers per mile than any other part of the state. While the action is nothing like that on the offshore sportfishing boats, pier casters regularly do really well at **Oceanside Pier** (periodic barracuda), **Shelter Island Pier** (in San Diego Bay), **Crystal Beach Pier,** and **Ocean Beach Pier.**

Many people are surprised to find out that there's also a world-class freshwater fishery in this area. In fact, there are several spots where trophy bass fishing for lunker descendents of the Florida strain largemouth bass that were long ago stocked in reservoirs around the San Diego area has reached a fevered pitch. Bass fishing here is a scene, with people racing around on $30,000 boats at 60 miles per hour all hoping to latch onto a 10- to 20-pound bigmouth. Stranger things have happened, and some speculate that a new world record could come out of these lakes. Lake Hodges, Lake Miramar, San Vicente Lake, El Capitan Lake, and Lower Otay Lake all have the potential to spit out the big ones.

### HIKING

#### San Clemente to San Onofre

1–8 miles. Easy. Access: There are beach access points at either end, and several in between as well, including Calafia Beach Park and both state campgrounds.

When the tide is low (or outgoing), you can walk the entire sandy stretch from San Clemente State Beach to San Onofre State Beach. The entire hike one-way is roughly 4 miles, and you can choose to do all or part of it. Beginning at San Clemente, walk south along the sand beneath the sandstone bluffs. The roar of the ocean is occasionally interrupted by the sound of the train speeding along the tracks that run parallel to the shore. When you reach the trestles at San Mateo Point, you are at one of the finest surfing beaches on earth. Trestles Beach, named after the construct, was for many years the property of Camp Pendleton Marine base, and surfers in search of the perfect wave were continually trespassing. At San Mateo Point, the official starting point of San Diego County, you'll cross San Mateo Creek, which begins way back in the Santa Ana Mountains and gives the San Mateo Canyon Wilderness its name. Closer to you, however, is the San Mateo Creek Natural Preserve, a nice detour. Heading south, you'll first reach Surf Beach at the northern end of San Onofre State Beach, another primo surfing spot, followed by The Bluffs, at the southern end. You'll know you've reached the final destination by the twin peaks of the nuclear power plant at San Onofre. Return the way you came, or take any one of the trails leading up to the blufftop. Up here, there's a paved bike trail that runs from The Bluffs through Camp Pendleton and all the way to Oceanside, and you can follow sections of it on the return.

## Del Mar to Black's Beach

8 miles round-trip. Easy. Access: Del Mar Beach in Del Mar.

This hike takes you along the beach below the craggy cliffs at Del Mar to Black's Beach, famous for nudists and big, hollow waves. (Be sure to hike on a low or outgoing tide.) Along the way, you can detour through the Highway S21 underpass to Los Peñasquitos Lagoon, a saltwater marsh bird habitat, or take the stairs up to the Torrey Pines State Reserve. About 3 miles into this hike, just past the reserve, you'll see Flat

Rock, a distinctly large, flat rock sticking out into the water, surrounded by some wonderful tide pools. When you start seeing naked people, you're at Black's Beach. Of course clothing is an option, and more often than not, people here are wearing swimsuits. The other identifying characteristic of Black's is the Scripps Pier. If you reach the pier, you're at the southern end of Black's Beach. Return the way you came.

## Los Peñasquitos Canyon

12-mile loop. Easy. Access: Los Peñasquitos County Park, roughly 24 miles north of San Diego proper. I-15 north, exit Mira Mesa Blvd. and head west to Black Mountain Rd. Make a right (north) on Black Mountain Rd. and continue to the park entrance.

Los Peñasquitos means "the little cliffs" and that's what you'll see as you approach this 2,000-acre preserve. The canyon itself is 6 miles long and shaded by sycamore, willows, and live oak. On both ends of the preserve trail lie historic adobes: Ruiz-Alvarado on the west and Johnson-Taylor on the east, which is San Diego's oldest rancho. The hike through the canyon is easy, though popular, so don't go seeking too much solace. I've also listed it as a mountain biking trail.

## Mission Trails Regional Park

The peaceful Mission Trails has over 50 miles of marked trails for every level of ability, ranging from the easy paved paths of Lake Murray and the Father Junipero Serra Trail to the hardcore climbs up Cowles and Fortuna mountains. Stop in at the visitor center to pick up a free trail map, or check out their Web site (206.31.38.177/foundation/foundation.html) for details.

## Bayside Trail

2 miles round-trip. Easy. Access: Cabrillo National Monument.

Beginning at the Old Point Loma Lighthouse, which was built in 1855, a winding paved road takes you past yucca and prickly pear cacti. At the gravel road, go left and head up to Ballast Point. The panoramic views of San Diego Bay are spectacular, and the Point Loma Peninsula offers hands-down some of the best bird, marine, and mammal viewing on the West Coast. (See "Wildlife Viewing" below.)

### MOUNTAIN BIKING

## Lake Hodges

15 miles. Easy. Access: From Escondido, follow Valley Pkwy. southeast until it becomes Del Dios Hwy. Cross Via Rancho Pkwy. and turn right (east) on Date Lane. This ride begins at the intersection of Date Lane and Lake Dr.

Here's an easy dirt road ride along the shore of Lake Hodges in northern San Diego County. From the intersection of Date Lane and Lake Drive, start pedaling along the dirt road that hugs the north shore of Lake Hodges, and follow it as it gently climbs around the base of Bernardo Mountain. When you reach the underpass of I-15, turn around and head back to your starting point. From here, ride due south on the signed Coast to Crest Trail, which begins just west of the parking area at the Hernandez Hideaway Restaurant. (This section of the Coast to Crest Trail is part of a proposed trail that will go from the coastal town of Del Mar to the crest of a mountain pass in Julian.) Follow the Coast to Crest Trail past the dock where the sailboarders launch until you

reach the gate and a sign that says ROAD CLOSED. To keep this ride easy, turn around and head back the way you came.

*Note:* If you're up for more of a challenge, continue on the Coast to Crest Trail to the dam.

## Los Peñasquitos Canyon

12-mile loop. Easy. Access: Los Peñasquitos County Park, roughly 24 miles north of San Diego proper. From the city, take I-15 north. Exit Mira Mesa Blvd. and head west to Black Mountain Rd. Make a right (north) on Black Mountain Rd. and continue to the entrance to Los Peñasquitos Canyon, which will be on the west side of the road.

Los Peñasquitos lives up to its name, "the little cliffs." That's just what you'll see as you approach this 2,000-acre preserve. The 6-mile-long canyon itself is shaded by sycamore, willows, and live oak. On both ends of the preserve trail lie historic adobes: Ruiz-Alvardo on the west and Johnson-Taylor on the east, which is San Diego's oldest rancho. From the beginning of the Los Peñasquitos Canyon Preserve, start riding west on the dirt road, which is in good condition. When you reach the Ruiz-Alvardo adobe, turn around and return the way you came. This trail is busy—hikers, school kids, equestrians use it—so be careful.

## Mission Trails Regional Park

Distance varies. Easy–difficult. Access: Mission Trails Regional Park is located at 1 Father Junipero Serra Trail just a few miles from downtown San Diego. Take I-8 east from San Diego and exit at Mission Gorge Rd. Continue east to FJST, past the visitor center and to the Old Mission Dam Historical Area. Park here.

Originally inhabited by the Kumeya'ay Indians, this 5,800-acre park is also the site of the Old Mission Dam, and it's from this point that most of the rides in the park begin. With so many intersecting and unmarked trails, this park is really the kind of place to explore rather than stick rigidly to one route—it's a slice of wilderness right in the urban sprawl. There are trails for all levels of skill and ability. The Oak Grove, Kumeya'ay Lake, and Grassland Loops are easy and all about 1 mile. Oak Canyon and Rim Trail get trickier, and a climb up to the top of Cowles Mountain Summit is intense. You can pick up a free map at the visitor center.

## Noble Canyon

13.5-mile loop. Difficult. Access: From San Diego, head east on I-8 and exit Pine Valley Rd. Go north and turn left on Hwy 80. In 1 mile, turn right on Pine Creek Rd. and continue up to the Noble Canyon Trailhead parking area on your right.

This very challenging loop has you riding on single track, dirt roads, and some pavement. From the beginning of the Noble Canyon trailhead along Pine Creek Road, follow the signs pointing you in the direction of the Noble Canyon Trail. At 3 miles, go right at the sign pointing you toward Laguna Mountain, and continue up, up, up to the unmarked dirt road, Laguna Meadow Road. Go left. (Up to here, you'll be riding on a rocky, rutted single track and you may have to walk your bike in spots. It's a hard climb, I have to say, and there are bikers riding down the trail.) Laguna Meadow Road takes you to Pine Creek Road, where you'll make a left and head downhill as views of the Cuyamaca Mountains and Laguna Mountain surround you. The road eventually becomes a paved road and takes you back to your car.

## ROAD BIKING

## Camp Pendleton Coast Trail

40 miles round-trip. Moderate. Access: Oceanside Harbor Dr./Camp Pendleton exit off I-5. Turn right on San Rafael Dr. and park in the residential area. Head to the main gate.

The Camp Pendleton route is both the only way for cyclists to ride the 17-mile coastal stretch between Oceanside and San Clemente, and the most beautiful way. Comprised of old military roads, abandoned chunks of old Highway 101, and bike paths, the loop is done south to north so that afternoon winds are at your back. From the main gate, pedal 1.5 miles to Stuart Mesa Road, go left and cross the Santa Margarita River. At Las Pulgas Road, turn left and pedal toward the interstate. Just after the railroad crossing, turn right on the road/bike path that takes you through a tunnel under the freeway and plops you seaside. Follow along through San Onofre State Beach and on to San Clemente. As you make your final approach, turn left onto the bikeway when the road (Basilone Road) veers right to cross I-5. You'll cross San Mateo Creek and pass Trestles, the world-famous surf break; and eventually you'll end up at San Clemente. Return the way you came.

## Rancho Santa Fe

3–15 miles. Moderately easy. Access: Via de la Valle exit off I-5, just north of San Diego.

Rancho Santa Fe, also know as The Ranch, is an extremely wealthy section of northern San Diego County with a historic Spanish land-grant past. The shady rolling hills, avocado and eucalyptus groves, grazing horses, and white picket fences make this a wonderful place to ride—even if you can afford to live here. From the Via de la Valle exit, park your car and start exploring the peaceful roads. Also worth checking out is the Fairbanks Ranch, which is just south of Rancho Santa Fe on Via de Santa Fe. It was built in the 1920s by movie stars Douglas Fairbanks and his wife Mary Pickford.

## Valley Center Tour

15 miles. Moderate. Access: Valley Pkwy. and Bear Valley Pkwy. at the northeastern edge of Escondido.

This scenic ride offers some great climbing practice as you meander through citrus and oak groves under a warm, blue sky. Begin pedaling north on Valley Parkway, turn right at Lake Wohlford Road, and start climbing. When you can see the lake, things level off. The road hugs the lake and takes you into Woods Valley. Turn left on Woods Valley Road and coast downhill. What's that huge mountain to your right, you ask? Palomar Mountain. Woods Valley Road ends at the unfortunately high-traffic Valley Center Road. Go left and whiz back down to Valley Parkway and your car.

## Torrey Pines

17.6 miles out and back. Moderate. Access: Carmel Valley Rd. exit off I-5 in La Jolla. Head west for 1.5 miles and turn south, following North Torrey Pines Rd. past the state reserve and into the visitors' parking lot.

This tour of the San Diego coast takes you through the 2,000-acre Torrey Pines State Reserve (named after the rare Torrey pine tree that only grows here and on Santa Rosa Island), through the posh town of Del Mar, along the border of U.C. San Diego, past the Scripps Institute of Oceanography in La Jolla, and

back. It's a hilly ride with some busy roads but spectacular ocean views. From the parking lot, begin pedaling north on North Torrey Pines Road and head into the reserve. Eventually the road becomes Camino Del Mar and you'll notice the change in your surroundings, too. Coast into the opulent seaside town of Del Mar on 15th Street and go right on Coast Boulevard past the beach and the train station. Oooh and aaaah over the view. Circle back around to Camino Del Mar and begin climbing back up to the reserve. Going south, you can take the car-free road on your right that will bring you back to North Torrey Pines Road. Just below you is Torrey Pines State Beach, and at its southern end lies Black's Beach. Black's is well-known for two things: nudists and surfers on big, hollow waves. (Something to keep in mind for later.) It's a climb up La Jolla Shores Drive, then an easy coast down to Camino Del Oro, where you'll make a quick right, then a left on El Paseo Grande to Frescota, where you'll turn around and retrace your path to your car. Or you may want to walk down the steps and visit the Scripps Institute of Oceanography, their aquarium, and pier. Or perhaps chill on the beach before you head back.

## Mission Beach Bike Path

6 miles. Easy. Access: Mission Beach, along Mission Blvd. between Pacific Beach Dr. and Mission Bay Channel.

You can start riding on the crowded Ocean Front Walk (which does include a bike lane) anywhere along Mission Beach, but I like to begin in the quiet Mariners Bay, which is just east of the ocean, and it's easier to park there. From the bridge at Mariners Way, pick up the bike path that follows along the bay and then swings around to the beginning of Mission Beach. Heading north on this skinny peninsula, you'll pass Belmont Park, which features the Giant Dipper, a recently reopened classic roller coaster, and vintage indoor swimming pool, among other attractions. The path ends just past Crystal Pier, a historic pier dotted with tiny white rental cottages that's also open daily for fishing. Return the way you came. Several places along the way also rent bikes, including **Aquarius Surf 'n Skate** on Pacific Beach Drive (tel. 619/488-9733).

### Coronado Island

15 miles of bike path. Easy. Access: From San Diego, drive across the 2.1-mile Coronado Bridge to the island. Public bus transportation is also available from downtown San Diego, or you can take the San Diego Ferry—both allow you to bring your bicycle. For ferry information call 619/234-4111.

Coronado Island, like San Diego itself, is a very biker-friendly place. The island features 15 miles of dedicated bike and in-line skating paths, and there are even special Bike Bus Stops where you're allowed to take your bike on the bus. Pick up the bike path on the Glorietta Bay side of the island, just behind the landmark Hotel del Coronado. Pedal along Glorietta Boulevard, past the golf course and under the Coronado Bridge to Tidelands Park. Continue up to the Ferry Landing Marketplace, at which point you'll turn around and retrace your path. Or you can continue exploring the bike route. The route crosses the island on 6th Street, and from there you can go your own way.

### Balboa Park

Distance varies. Easy–moderately easy. Access: 6th Ave. and Laurel St. in San Diego.

Balboa Park is an amazing city park. Its 1,400 acres include the world-famous San Diego Zoo, a dozen museums, gardens, historical sites, a golf course, and lots and lots of open space. Beginning at 6th and Laurel, head east on Laurel and make a right on Balboa Drive to explore this one-way loop, which offers some great city views. Back on Laurel, continue east into the park over the Cabrillo Bridge. Now you're on El Prado, the main entrance, which becomes a pedestrian mall. From here, you can choose your own course. Lock up your bike and investigate the museums, or head off on any number of paths.

### MISSION BAY, SAN DIEGO BAY & MORE

San Diego is such a biker-friendly place—it's relatively flat, has lots of bike lanes, and even the city buses have bike racks—that I encourage you to see as much of the city as you can by bike. But instead of giving you a detailed plan of every possible bike path in this town (which would only be a headache for both of us), I'll simply point you in the general direction: **Mission Bay Park, San Diego Bay, Point Loma Peninsula,** and **Mission Hills.** For city maps and the special permit you'll need to take your wheels on public transportation, contact **The Transit Store** at 619/234-1060.

### ROCK CLIMBING

Located just north of San Diego near the town of Poway, **Mount Woodson** offers about 23 climbs, a mix of bouldering and top-rope routes. Famous for its classic cracks, most of Mount Woodson's routes and problems are, however, face climbs. Fall through spring are the best times to climb, as summer heat can take all the fun out of things. To get there, take Highway 67 and exit at Mt. Woodson

Road. Keith Bruckner's *Mount Woodson Bouldering* is recommended reading.

**Mission Gorge** in Mission Trails Regional Park is divided in two areas, Middle Earth and Mission Gorge Crag. The climbs here are lead and top-roped, with some limited bouldering near the streambed below the Junipero Serra Trail. For better bouldering, try **Santee,** just a few miles northeast of Mission Gorge. Follow Mission Gorge Road past the park into the town of Santee, and turn left on Mast Boulevard. A hillside offers medium-size granite boulders with face and mantle problems. Some boulders are 35 feet high, so a short top-rope might be useful. Your other choice is **Crest,** just east of El Cajon. Here, the rock is solid granite with large boulders and pinnacles up to 75 feet high. There are a few crack routes, but most of the climbs are bolted or top-roped face. To get to Crest, take I-8 east past El Cajon and exit at Greenfield Drive. Follow it to La Cresta Road, to La Cresta Boulevard, to Crest Drive. If you're stuck in urban San Diego, try **SolidRock Indoor Rock Climbing** (tel. 619/299-1124), 2704 Hancock St. in Old Town. There are climbs here for all ages and abilities, as well as instruction, rentals, and kids' programs.

## SAILING

San Diego has always been a town that looks toward the sea, and it is today. With not one but two huge natural bays that create some of the finest harbors on earth, San Diego was bound to be a big sailing town. Mission Bay is the place for smaller boat sailing. Large areas are dredged and deep enough for large vessels, but to really rip it up out here it's more fun to be on a catamaran or a small dinghy. There are numerous beach accesses where you can launch your own. If you'd like to rent a catamaran, get in

touch with **Seaforth Boat Rentals** (tel. 619/223-1681).

San Diego Bay to the south is the larger of the two natural harbors, so large, in fact, that the Navy drives aircraft carriers around inside it. You won't need an aircraft carrier to have fun, but certainly look out for them if you're sailing. There are more charter operators here than you can shake a stick at, and as a result prices are fairly good for an urban center. Decide what you want and then let your fingers do the walking. Harbor Sailboats (tel. 619/291-9568), San Diego Sailing Academy (tel. 619/299-9247), Seaforth Boat Rentals (tel. 619/223-1681), San Diego Sailing Club and School (tel. 619/298-6623), Harbor Island Yacht Club (tel. 619/291-7245), and Marina Sailing of San Diego (tel. 619/221-8286) are just some of the charter operators that offer boat rentals and yachting instruction.

## SCUBA DIVING

San Diego County is much like Orange County, in that its northern reaches aren't nearly as good for diving as farther down the coast. Though there are a few unique possibilities, like diving in the glow of San Onofre Nuclear Power Plant at a spot known to locals as **Radiation Bay,** the rest of the northern coastline is dominated by **Camp Pendleton.** However, it's not the kind of place you want to be caught messing around on the beach. A friend recently saw a hovercraft off Pendleton carrying a load of tanks—not scuba tanks, but tanks, the armored variety—at about 60 miles an hour through the surf. Imagine popping up after a dive and seeing that bearing down.

But very few places compare to the quality diving that you can find once you reach the area between **La Jolla and Point Loma.** For an urban area, the diving is simply extraordinary. Though the ocean has suffered from pollution and overharvesting here as well as other places, it is still a rich and vibrant spot.

Dive shops are extremely common in this area. I recommend **Ocean Enterprises** at 7710 Balboa Ave., no. 101 (tel. 619/565-6054), for lessons, gear, and rentals. **Aqua Tech Dive Center** at 1800 Logan Ave. is another good San Diego shop (tel. 619/285-1000), while **Lois Ann Dive Charters** (tel. 619/454-6054) runs boat trips out to the Coronado Islands and to San Clemente Island.

## La Jolla Shores, Canyon Dive

Beginner–advanced. Access: Park at the end of Vallecitos St. near the beach. Bring change for meters.

The submarine canyon that reaches near shore here is a magnet for big sea life and a source of continual upwellings that nourish strong kelp and all the animals that depend on the habitat. A favorite dive is a shore entry near lifeguard tower 20 at La Jolla Shores Park. Within a hundred yards from shore, the bottom drops down to more than 300 feet. The area is an underwater nature preserve, so don't take things, and leave the fish alone.

Obviously you don't want to swim out too far before descending, since you could either lose track and dive too deep or simply stay safe but see nothing. The best drill is to descend slightly inshore of the canyon and follow the sandy bottom until the wall drops away suddenly.

Beginners can enjoy the sensation of watching the ocean drop off into nothingness and can check out the fish that school here. More advanced divers with good buoyancy control should explore down the canyon walls, where lots of holes and caves are filled with sea life. Keep your eyes peeled for large pelagic species, including sharks, that cruise this transitional zone.

## La Jolla Underwater Park, Goldfish Point

Beginner–advanced. Access: Park in the lot near the Curio Shop on Cave St. Carry gear down the stairs.

At the other end of La Jolla Cove, Goldfish Point is almost like diving in a fish tank. It's named for the large schools of California's state fish, the garibaldi, that swarm around divers. The possibilities here are rich. In both directions the coast is rocky, with sheer drop-offs and numerous small caves. Look for moray eels, large lobsters, and fish that seem to believe they rule the world. Here, in fact, they do. It's a protected marine reserve.

Like La Jolla Shores, Goldfish Point is exposed to several swell directions. Use caution before getting in and out of the water here. Even when it's fairly flat, sneaker sets can surprise.

## Casa Pool

Beginner, excellent snorkeling. Access: Parking is plentiful on Coast Blvd.

The Casa Pool is also known as the La Jolla Children's pool, though it's not a pool at all nor an entirely safe place for kids to play alone. What it is great for is getting in and out of the water without having to deal with the pounding surf that can intimidate beginners at other San Diego spots.

A man-made breakwater shelters a sandy beach. You can walk into the water and fuss with your gear all you want without worrying about a wave knocking you down and swallowing your gear. Once ready, kick out to rocky reefs and eel grass beds that lie just outside the protected cove.

It's shallow enough that even snorkelers can enjoy the rocky shelves simply buried in aquatic plants and invertebrate life. Also expect to see numerous schools of fish, ranging from opaleye perch to big yellowtail and halibut.

## Point Loma Kelp Beds

Intermediate–advanced. Access: By boat from San Diego Bay.

Point Loma's massive kelp beds are a short inflatable ride from the marina just inside San Diego Bay, but they are next to impossible to reach from shore. Consequently, they don't see nearly the diving pressure other nearby spots do. Though they've suffered damage both from pollution and from the 1997–98 El Niño, this is still a wonderful spot to cruise looking for big open-water fish like yellowtail, blue sharks, and even the occasional dolphin or whale. On a smaller scale the kelp bed is also home to lobsters, nudibranches, urchins, bat rays, and hundreds of smaller fish. If you are in San Diego with access to a small boat to carry you to this spot, by all means take the time to do it. You won't be disappointed.

### SEA KAYAKING

A rarely paddled stretch of San Diego County coast is the run from **San Onofre** south along the forbidden shoreline of **Camp Pendleton.** It's more than 20 miles of hard paddling, and while the Marines frown upon finding civilians lounging on their beaches, for an ambitious paddler this may be the best challenge of all. Just remember that between San Onofre and Oceanside there's no bailing out except in the case of a severe emergency, when the Marines would probably pardon your intrusion.

All the beaches of San Diego County, from **Oceanside to Del Mar,** are fine for paddling and playing, though high surf

often makes them a little beyond the reach of most beginners.

**Mission Bay** is excellent paddling, especially the more isolated shallow parts of the bay, where you're safely out of reach of the endless catamarans, Jet Skis, sailboats, and water-skiers who whip Mission Bay into a frenzy at times. Head for the smaller bays around Fiesta Isle or the narrow channels around the marsh at the northern edge of the bay. Some are navigable by kayak but keep your eye on the tide; dropping water can leave you high and dry on stinky mud for the next several hours.

**Windsport** on Mission Bay at 844 W. Mission Bay Dr. (tel. 619/488-4642) both rents and sells a nice selection of ocean kayaks. Another favorite San Diego kayaking establishment is **Southwest Sea Kayaks** at 1310 Rosecrans St. (tel. 619/222-3616). Southwest specializes in trips throughout Baja and also runs a wide selection of local clinics, lessons, and trips. They rent all types of kayaking gear and are a great source of information.

### SURFING

Though not as consistently exposed to big winter swells as the central and northern California coast, the coastline of Orange and San Diego counties to the Mexican border is almost entirely wide open to south swells driven up from the southern hemisphere winter and summertime hurricanes off Mexico. As a result, day after day of sunny, playful surf is broken only by short, flat spells and periodic days when it's just HUGE. It's only natural, then, that an enormous culture has grown up around this sport of kings. Following the coast, there are simply too many surf shops to count. New ones open every season, and old ones close. A few trusty legends hang on year after year. Surf clothing, an industry centered largely in Newport Beach and surrounding Orange County towns, is a billion-dollar-a-year industry, selling most of their wares to kids in the heartland who can only dream about getting deeply tubed at the Wedge. And, as mentioned before, the surfing press is almost entirely centered in San Clemente, giving the local scene an influence far beyond its home turf.

And finally, not everyone is born knowing how to rip. Surfing is hard to learn. In fact, it's one of the hardest sports to master simply because there are so many foreign elements. You've got this strange board, waves are crashing on you, and there are people all around you getting every wave. What's a wannabe surfer to do? I recommend surf camp. Surf camps have really taken off in the last few years. The most famous one in the world is probably the **Pascowitz family surf camp.** The Pascowitz family grew up in a converted school bus that drove up and down the coast. All of the family are excellent surfers and teachers. Their surf camp is continually changing in location and contact information. Best bet is to call the Hobie surf shop in Oceanside and ask for the latest number. Despite being tough to find, they're booked more than a year in advance, so plan ahead.

**Surf Diva** is a female-only surf instruction program for girls and women ages 7 and up based in La Jolla. While I personally don't see why a camp that's restricted to women only is seen as some sort of wondrous and liberating symbol of equal rights, while a "Dudes Only" surf camp would be the rightful object of derision and sexual discrimination lawsuits as fast as you can say "surf's up," many women find that they enjoy the 2-day weekend surf clinics by women for women at **La Jolla Shores** (tel. 619-454-8273). Surf Diva also arranges private lessons and multi-day trips into Baja.

Since there are so many fine surf spots in Orange County and San Diego County, I'm not going to even attempt to list them all. That alone would take an entire book. So, I think I'll keep this brief by simply mentioning my favorite picks, a nice variety of everything from the completely white-knuckle to nice, gentle waves perfect for learning. See the introduction at the beginning of this chapter for a discussion of surf etiquette.

From north to south in San Diego County, my favorites are:

## Swami's

In Leucadia, directly in front of the giant yoga ashram on the bluff; you can't miss it.

Not only are the waves here excellent (as is the level of surfing talent), but the beach and surrounding gardens of the ashram are super cool and open to the public. Of course, be respectful of the people here meditating and getting their prana in order.

## Black's

Walk south from Torrey Pines State Beach or north from Scripps Pier in La Jolla. You can also reach the beach via a steep, paved path at the junction of La Jolla Farms Rd. and Blackgold Rd.

As I said earlier, Black's is famous with two different constituencies, for two different reasons. Surfers flock here because Black's consistently gets some of the best waves in California: hollow, large beach break peaks that resemble Puerto Escondido. Nudists flock to Black's because it's one of the few beaches in the area remote enough that you can get nekkid without getting hassled by the cops. It's a hoot to watch surfers, conditioned by years of changing in roadside parking lots, using towels to execute the modest street clothes-to-wetsuit change while just down the beach a raging game of nude volleyball is in full swing.

## Windansea

At the corner of Neptune Place and Bonair St. in La Jolla.

Tom Wolfe wrote about Windansea in his late '60s bestseller *The Pump House Gang.* The book drew its name from the people who hung out every summer at the beach at Windansea, surfing, smoking pot, and hassling outsiders. Those kids have grown up and are now middle-aged, but you can find their latest incarnation here on any given day. It's a great wave and scene if you can deal with the attitude. **Big Rock,** one of the peaks here, is among the gnarliest lefts in the mainland United States.

## Tourmaline Surfing Park

Near the border of La Jolla and Pacific Beach at the end of Tourmaline Street.

Tourmaline is unique in that it's officially a surfing-only beach. Considering how many places in Southern California are closed to surfers ostensibly to protect swimmers, it's nice to see it working the other way for a change. This is one of the classic longboarding scenes, and anyone wanting to surf with some real masters of the sport should make a pilgrimage.

And finally, for those of you who prefer Nutrasweet to sugar and non-dairy creamer to a nice slog of half-and-half, you can also substitute artificial waves for the real thing. **The Wave Waterpark** at 161 Recreation Dr. in Vista (that's slightly southeast of San Diego) is a multimillion-dollar water park with a Flow-Rider. The Flow-Rider is a fake wave, there's no other way to describe it, created by blasting moving water over a sculpted form in the shape of a wave. I've never done it but it looks fun.

## California Surf Museum

308 Pacific St., Oceanside, CA. Tel. 760/721-6876. Thurs–Tues 10am–4pm. Admission free.

Through artifacts, photographs, clothing, and news clippings, this Temple of Surfing pays tribute to both wave-riding legends and today's rippers. Exhibits change regularly, and there are various events to commemorate landmark days in surfing history. (By the time you read this, the museum may have moved to one of the brand-new developments going up behind the Oceanside Pier. Check your local directory.)

## Quail Botanical Gardens

230 Quail Gardens Dr., Encinitas, CA. Tel. 760/436-3036. Open daily. Admission $2.

Encinitas bills itself as the "Flower Capital of the World," in part because it grows a huge number of carnations and dyes them a multitude of colors. To see flowers in their more natural state, wander around the 30-acre Quail Botanical Gardens. It features much native California greenery, as well as exotic botanical life.

## Scripps Institute of Oceanography & Pier/ Stephen Birch Aquarium Museum

8602 La Jolla Shores Dr., La Jolla, CA 92037. Tel. 619/534-3474. Open daily 9am–5pm. Donations accepted.

Founded in 1903, Scripps is one of the oldest and most venerable marine research facilities, continuing to host hundreds of scientific studies. While the heavy-duty science side of the institution isn't for everyone, the 33-tank aquarium is open to the public. The kelp forest display and the artificial tide pools are particularly fascinating. The view from here is extraordinary; you can look out to sea and under the water at virtually the same time.

## San Diego Zoo

Access: Park Blvd. and Zoo Place in Balboa Park. Tel. 619/234-3153. Web Site: www.sandiegozoo.org. Open daily 9am–4pm; extended summer hours 9am–9pm. Adult $16, child $7. Package deals with Wild Animal Park available.

As far as zoos go, this is the finest one in the country. Over 4,000 animals are housed here, including the big attraction: two giant pandas from China. Most of the animals don't live behind bars, but in enclosures that resemble their natural environment. The grounds also include a botanical garden and a petting zoo. Closely allied with the zoo is the Wild Animal Park (tel. 760/747-8702) located 45 minutes north in Escondido. Here, all the animals roam free over 1,800 acres and you view them from your seat on the open-air monorail that winds through the park.

## Torrey Pines State Reserve Trails

0.25 to 0.75 mile. Easy. Access: Torrey Pines State Reserve in La Jolla.

The bluffs that are home to the rare Torrey pine also offer several short, interpretive nature trails. Parry Grove Trail takes you to a grove of Torrey pines and a display of many other native plants. Other trails offer a view of the pines as well as stunning ocean vistas. Stop in at the park museum for a free trail map.

## Ocean Front Walk

3 miles one-way. Easy. Access: Mission Beach, along Mission Blvd. Between Pacific Beach Dive and Mission Bay Channel.

The Ocean Front Walk is a paved 3-mile promenade that runs the entire length of Mission Beach, a peninsula just west of San Diego's Mission Bay. The beach itself is flat, wide, and sandy, and the Walk is generally jammed with bikers, in-line skaters, and joggers. Near the southern end of the boardwalk is Belmont Park (tel. 619/491-2988), a recently restored amusement park that still retains much of its old charm. Attractions include the 70-year-old Giant Dipper Roller Coaster and The Plunge, a vintage indoor swimming pool. Several places along the way also rent bikes, if you'd rather pedal, including Aquarius Surf 'n Skate on Pacific Beach Drive (tel. 619/488-9733).

## WILDLIFE VIEWING

Near La Jolla, **Torrey Pines State Reserve** (tel. 619/755-1275) is not only the place to view the rare Torrey pine itself, but the clifftop preserve serves as a great vista to watch for bottle-nosed dolphins, California sea lions, and—from December to February—the California gray whale. The whales travel from the Bering Sea and Arctic Ocean all the way to Mexico and can often be seen spouting close to shore. Farther south, the **Cabrillo National Monument** (tel. 619/557-5450) on the Point Loma Peninsula offers hands-down some of the best bird, marine, and mammal viewing on the West Coast. The tide pools are teeming with crabs, starfish, anemones, and other sea life. (The pools are best at low tide from April to October.) Offshore, watch for gray whales and dolphins; on the bluffs, look for birds of prey. Gray foxes have been known to hang out near the visitor center in the early mornings and evenings.

# Campgrounds & Other Accommodations

Coastal camping is lovely in this area, though severely limited and dramatically oversubscribed. Several of the parks and beaches in Orange and San Diego counties (including Bolsa Chica State Beach, Huntington City Beach, Harbor Beach in Oceanside, and Silver Strand State Beach) offer what's known as En Route Camping. What that means is that they let people sleep in their cars in the parking lot at night, no campfires, stringing the hammock between a couple of trees, or cooking over the old Coleman stove at a nice picnic table.

To get a real campsite, by which I mean a place you can pitch a tent and sleep on the ground, at any of the popular beachfront state parks, count on calling well ahead of time or visiting in the off-season (which is winter, except for holidays). All camping in this area will be in a state park, and the drill for reserving all state park campgrounds is the same. Decide where you want to go and when you want to go there, then dial **Destinet** at 800/444-7275. Destinet is a new concessionaire; I hope they do the job better than the last one, which involved interminable mazes of voice mail and mechanized voices.

One of the places that allow real camping is **Doheny State Beach,** just south of Dana Point, with 120 sites in a 62-acre wooded campground, a marine interpretive center, and a long sandy beach. **San Clemente State Beach** is just south of the town bearing the same name and also offers surprisingly great

coastal camping. It has 160 sites and access to great surf and diving. **San Onofre State Beach** is beautiful (except the nuclear power plant makes me a bit twitchy) with more than 200 campsites. The sites aren't anything special but the surfing and the relatively uncrowded setting almost make up for the fact that you glow for a week after breaking camp.

Better, perhaps, for people who really don't like to camp next to a potential Three Mile Island, is **South Carlsbad State Beach.** This is a lovely park, with 222 sites located 4 miles south of Carlsbad and the confusingly named Carlsbad State Beach. The campsites are literally a stone's throw from good surf, good fishing, and good beachcombing. For good cause this is among the most popular campgrounds in the state park system. Call well in advance for reservations, like a year in advance.

**San Elijo State Beach** is another score. Its 171 campsites sprawl along the top of a coastal cliff. Some sit right on the edge and look down into the sea. Others back against a busy frontage road. It might pay to call the state park at 619/793-5091 and ask for some campsite recommendations before calling Destinet for that campsite you'd like to reserve next year.

All these state parks charge between $14 and $20 per night for sites, depending on whether it has RV hookups and according to location (beachfront sites are sometimes more expensive, go figure).

## Doryman's Inn Bed & Breakfast

2102 W. Ocean Front, Newport Beach, CA 92663. Tel. 800/634-3303 or 714/675-7300. 8 rms, 2 suites. $135–$230 double. Suites from $185. Includes breakfast. MC, V.

There are very few inns on the crowded Orange County coast that have both charm and location. The Doryman is one. It sits right in the thick of Newport's action on the Newport Beach Pier Promenade. Everything is within walking distance. The interior is nice without being overwhelming, and they fuel you up with a good breakfast before sending you out for a day of adventure.

## Crystal Pier Hotel

4500 Ocean Blvd., San Diego, CA 92109. Tel. 800/748-5894 or 619/483-6983.

26 cottages for up to 4 people. $145–$250. MC, V.

California has lots of oceanfront hotels, but as far as I know this is the only one that's built over the water. Built in 1936 (but updated since) on Mission Beach's Crystal Pier, the cottages have kitchenettes, decks, bedrooms, and living rooms. The management can round up whatever beach gear you need, ranging from umbrellas to boogie boards, and Mission Beach is literally just steps (or a jump) away.

# ANZA-BORREGO STATE PARK & CLEVELAND NATIONAL FOREST

**W**HILE THE MOST FAMOUS OF CALIFORNIA'S DESERT parks—Death Valley and Joshua Tree—are both part of the national parks system, Anza-Borrego State Park gives them both a run for their money. At 600,000 acres, it's one of the biggest state parks in the country and certainly one of the premier places to experience the Colorado Desert at its best. Within the park, you'll find elevations from 6,000 feet on down to sea level and a range of biological diversity from pine mountains to radically desolate desert badlands.

To the west of Anza-Borrego lies the enormous Cleveland National Forest, as well as Palomar Mountain State Park and Cuyamaca Rancho State Park. Situated in the Peninsular Range that separates San Diego and Orange counties from the desert, these parks are a fantastic resource for those looking to get away into pine-forested wilderness just a short drive from the coast.

The range of possible activities is vast. Cyclists of both the road and mountain ilk will find plenty to stay busy. In the summer, when the desert regions are pretty much off-limits because of the intense heat, you can pedal in the high mountains. Conversely, when winter snows cover the roads and trails of the mountains, there's plenty to do down below. The same holds true for hikers. You'll find every kind of terrain under your boots, from sandy desert washes to high country granite. In the winter, Palomar Mountain is often covered with enough snow to entertain cross-country skiers and sledders.

One of the most famous attractions at Anza-Borrego is the blooming of spring wildflowers. Beginning as early as February in the lowlands and lasting through April or May, this explosive bloom of desert flora is one of the most consistent in all of California. Bird watchers and wildlife observers are big fans of the park, too, since it's home to numerous desert oases that support everything from tiny frogs to the dramatic borregos—the desert bighorn sheep from which the park draws its name.

The park and its environs are remarkably accessible for the quality of desert experience they provide. While there are remote corners of Anza-Borrego and the other nearby parks and forests that rarely see visitors, it's also possible to plan a day trip or a short weekend trip from the San Diego area and not feel that you've been cheated by time. Anza-Borrego is only 80 miles east of that city, and the park is also extremely accessible from the Orange County area. A taste, however, will leave you wanting to come back someday for more.

wrung from the sky by these mountains. The western slope is home to some of the rarest and very important southern pine and evergreen forests in the state, literal islands in a sea of desert.

At the eastern edge of the peninsular range, the land quickly drops away toward the **Colorado Desert.** The Colorado, of course, is simply the area of the Sonoran Desert that extends into the United States from Mexico. Don't be confused or surprised to hear people talking about this region as the Sonoran Desert. That's essentially true, though it's more common and accurate to call it the Colorado.

As the land drops away from the evergreen peaks around **Mount Palomar** to the low-lying (in fact, below sea-level) **Imperial Valley,** it passes through extremely diverse and rich transition zones. Anza-Borrego State Park, in particular, exemplifies the wealth of microclimates and environments that occur in a transitional zone like this.

Anza-Borrego is unique among state parks in that it actually contains an entire town within the park boundaries. This town, **Borrego Springs,** offers a reasonable number of hotels, restaurants, and supplies. **Julian,** a small town in the mountains just west of the park, is also a good place for that kind of thing. Larger needs, like having your engine rebuilt or purchasing a case of caviar, might have to wait until you can reach Palm Springs or San Diego.

## The Lay of the Land

This region encompasses two important major geographical features. Just inland from the coast between Laguna Beach and San Diego rise several ranges of mountains that together are considered the **Peninsular Range.** What moisture the Pacific pumps into the air is quickly

## Parks & Other Hot Spots

### Cleveland National Forest

1845 Rancho Bernardo Rd., San Diego, CA 92127-2107. Tel. 619/673-6180.

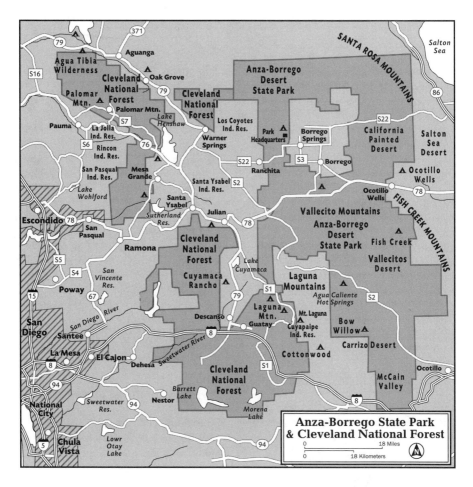

The Cleveland National Forest comprises three segments administered as separate ranger districts. The forest extends from within 5 miles of the Mexican border northward approximately 130 miles to Orange and Riverside counties.

Southernmost of the forest districts is Descanso. This district is noted for the Laguna Mountains, the timbered campsites of the Laguna Mountain Recreation Area, and the southernmost portion of the Pacific Crest Trail across National Forest lands. The Hauser and Pine Creek Wilderness areas provide backcountry experiences in a chaparral/oak woodland ecosystem.

Palomar is the central district, which includes Palomar Mountain. The famed Palomar Observatory, with its 200-inch

Hale telescope, is a state-run facility within the district boundaries. The rugged Agua Tibia Wilderness affords hiking experiences extending from high desert landscapes to Coulter pines and big-cone Douglas fir along its upper reaches. Variety is the trademark of the Palomar District, where wildlife, timber, and recreation values are managed over a wide range of elevations and ecological zones. The district is home to one of the largest stands of rare big-cone Douglas fir in Southern California.

The northern district is Trabuco, where the Santa Ana Mountains thrust up as open space against an urban sea. Use of the hiking trails on this district is heaviest during the cooler fall and spring months. The San Mateo Wilderness provides almost 40,000 acres of rugged Southern California chaparral wildland with steep canyons and arduous foot travel opportunities.

The Cleveland National Forest's western boundary varies in distance along its length from 10 to 30 miles from the Pacific Coast, and its topography rises as a welcome buffer to the eastern heat of the Anza-Borrego Desert. This Mediterranean climate provides a habitat for a variety of wildlife, from the tiny kangaroo rat to the powerful mountain lion. The peregrine falcon, on a managed comeback in the West, is an example of the reintroduction of a species. The Cleveland National Forest has an extensive chaparral environment, but conifers occur on each district at the higher elevations.

### Cuyamaca Rancho State Park

Access: I-8 east to Hwy. 79; head north 9 miles. Tel. 760/765-0755. Horse campsites, picnic areas, nature center, museum, historic sites, rest rooms, showers.

Forty miles east of San Diego, this amazing 25,000-acre park is covered in incense cedar, yellow pine, and oak forests. It's dotted with broad meadows, little streams, and waterfalls, and shoulders up against the man-made Lake Cuyamaca. Much of the park is wilderness. Highlights include the Stonewall Mine Ruins Tour and hikes and mountain biking up to Stonewall Peak (5,730 ft.) and Cuyamaca Peak (6,512 ft.).

### Palomar Mountain State Park

Access: Off Hwy. 76, up Hwy. S6, then left on Hwy. S7 at the junction near the

mountaintop. Tel. 760/765-0755. Historic buildings, picnicking.

Located within the Cleveland National Forest, this mile-high park features spectacular conifer forests much like the ones you'd find in the northern Sierra Nevada, great views of the Pacific, and a prized group of ancient live oaks along the French Valley Trail. The oaks, easily 10 feet in diameter, grow in and around huge clusters of boulders. Doane Pond is stocked year-round with trout. Mount Palomar itself, home of the Palomar Observatory and famous road-biking destination, is actually just outside the park. For information about the observatory, call 760/742-2119.

### Hellhole Canyon Open Space Preserve

19324 Santee Lane, Valley Center, CA. Tel. 619/565-3600 or 619/694-3049. Access: Santee Lane and Kiavo Dr.

Just south of Palomar Mountain State Park and bordering the La Jolla Indian Reservation, the 1,712-acre Hellhole Canyon Preserve contains over 14 miles of trails. Running through the canyon is Hell Creek, which is actually quite heavenly: clear water pouring over granite boulders under a canopy of live oaks and sycamores. No doubt it got its name from the rugged pioneers who tried to cross it in a covered wagon.

### Lake Henshaw

26439 Hwy. 76, Santa Ysabel, CA 92070. Tel. 760/782-3501. Access: I-15 north to Hwy. 76; head east 30 miles to the lake.

Just down Hwy. 76 from Palomar Mountain State Park, this mountain lake is primarily a fishing spot. It makes for a nice picnic spot, too, although there's no swimming. Cabins and boat rentals are available through the Lake Henshaw Resort.

## Lake Cuyamaca

15027 Hwy. 79, Julian, CA 92036. Tel. 760/765-0515. Access: I-8 east to Hwy. 79 north.

Between the town of Julian and Cuyamaca Rancho State Park, this mountain lake is surrounded by oak and pine forests. Nestled in the eastern slopes of the Cuyamaca Mountains at 4,620 feet, it's famous for year-round trout fishing, with 60,000 fish stocked annually.

## Lake Sutherland

Access: Off Hwy. 78 on Sutherland Dam Rd., about 8 miles east of Ramona. For info call San Diego City Lakes at 619/465-3474.

On the lower eastern edge of the Cleveland National Forest's Palomar district sits Lake Sutherland. At 2,058 feet, it was created from the damming of Santa Ysabel and Bloomdale creeks in the nearby foothills. It's a very popular angling spot, open weekends March through October. Nearby Black Canyon Road offers some good biking, too.

## San Vicente Lake

Access: I-8 east to Hwy. 67 north to Morena Dr.; turn left. For info call San Diego City Lakes at 619/465-3474

Just east of the Cleveland National Forest's Descanso district, Lake San Vicente sits at a 659-foot elevation. From November to May, the lake is a bass factory, and from June through October, it's water-skiing central.

## El Capitan Lake

Access: I-8 east to Jennings Park Rd.; head north 2 miles. Turn right on El Monte Rd. to the lake. For information call San Diego City Lakes at 619/465-3474.

In the Descanso district of the Cleveland National Forest, "El Cap" is set in a long canyon at an elevation of 750 feet and is best known for its bass fishing.

## Lake Jennings County Park

Access: I-8 east to Lake Jennings Park Rd.; head north 1 mile. Tel. 619/694-3049 or 619/565-3600.

On the western edge of the Cleveland National Forest near Blossom Valley, Lake Jennings is your backyard fishin' hole. Created in 1964 by the construction of a dam across the mouth of Quail Canyon, the lake is stocked with trout in the winter and catfish in the summer. At an elevation of 700 feet, it also serves up nice views of El Cajon Mountain and the San Diego River Valley. Boats are only allowed on the lake Friday to Sunday.

## Barrett Lake

Access: In the Cleveland National Forest, near the Mexican border. Take I-94 east to Honey Springs Rd. and head east 8 miles to Lyon Valley Rd. Turn right on Lyon Valley Rd. and drive 2 miles until you see the gate. Tel. 619/668-2050. Open Wednesdays and weekends, March–September. Permits required. No private boats; rentals only.

Fishing is the name of the game at Bartlett Lake, but the only way to cast your line is if you win the lottery. Twenty lottery tickets are drawn for each day the lake is open, and only the lucky ones are allowed in. Entering the lottery is free, but the competition is stiff. Fishers from all over the country want to experience the quiet seclusion of this bass-loaded paradise. Closed to the public in 1968, it reopened in 1994. Set on 118 acres in a remote valley, the lake is brimming with crappie, bluegill, bullhead, and bass—although the bass fishing is catch and release. For lottery information, call the San Diego City Lakes at 619/465-3474.

## Lake Morena County Park

Access: In the Cleveland National Forest, near the Mexican border. Take I-8 east, exit at Buckman Springs Rd. (County Rd. S1), and head south 5 miles to Oak Dr. Make a right and follow the signs to the park. Tel. 619/565-3600. Picnicking, wilderness cabins.

Located on the eastern slope of the Laguna Mountains at 3,200 feet, the park features desert, coastal, and mountain geography. The lake itself is loaded with fish, especially bass. Hikers will want to explore the Pacific Crest Trail, which passes through the park on its way to Canada.

## Anza-Borrego Desert State Park

Access: I-8, Hwy. 78, and County Routes S2, S3 and S22 all access the park. Tel. 760/767-5311. Web site: www.anzaborrego.statepark.org. Historical sites and markers, visitor center, jeep trails, showers, rest rooms.

Anza-Borrego Desert State Park is the largest state park in the Lower 48. Named after Spanish explorer Juan Bautista de Anza and the elusive "borrego" or bighorn sheep, this section of the Colorado Desert is roughly 60 miles long and 30 miles wide. Two county parks and the town of Borrego Springs also lie within the park's boundaries. Anza-Borrego is filled with nearly every desert feature you can think of: cacti, canyons, badlands, caves, washes, palm oases, elephant trees, ancient pictographs, stunning wildflowers, hot springs, bighorn sheep, rattlesnakes, desert iguanas, and panoramic vistas. You could spend weeks here and still not see it all. A good place to start is at the underground visitor center, where it's nice and cool and you can pick up free maps and park information. The Desert Garden, just outside the center, makes for a quick introduction to much of the vegetation and also includes a pupfish pond. Despite the park's size, driving tours, like the Erosion Road Tour or the Southern Emigrant Tour, can give you a good overview of the geography, though

# Hunting the Elusive California Wildflower

One of the great rites of spring in Southern California is its profusion of wildflowers. Even the most desolate areas, like Death Valley and the Coachella Valley, can suddenly burst into a wild frenzy of color, the profusion of flowers seeming totally inappropriate to the landscape. The key to it all is rainfall—namely, how much and when it fell.

For an epic wildflower bloom, continuous and generous rains throughout the season are necessary. It's better if the rains are spread out rather than if one giant storm drops 15 inches of rain that simply run off. After a good rainy season, seeds that have laid dormant for years suddenly spring to life. The bloom usually starts first in the low desert; **Anza-Borrego State Park** is one famous location, the low-lying areas of **Death Valley** another. As the season progresses, the display moves upward in altitude as the first blooms wither and die. Joshua Tree, the East Mojave, and the Antelope Valley Poppy Preserve then begin to bloom. Coastal hot spots like Sycamore Canyon and Point Mugu State Park go off on their own schedule, which depends largely on local temperatures.

There's nothing more disappointing than arriving at a wildflower spot after the bloom has faded. Or driving all the way out to the desert only to discover that you're weeks early. Luckily, there are good sources of information that help you decide where and when to plan your wildflower excursion. One of the best is *Florafax*, a weekly publication generated by the Theodore Payne Foundation for Wildflowers and Native Plants. Beginning on March 5 and arriving once a week for the next 13 weeks, the Florafax gives current information on where the best flowers are, along with detailed information about how to get there. The service costs $50 for the entire season or $5 for a single issue. Given the name, you'll need a fax machine to receive it. Call 818/768-1802 to order. Another, cheaper, if somewhat less detailed, service the foundation provides is their **Wildflower Hot Line,** a 24-hour recorded message describing conditions in a variety of Southern California areas. It's updated every Thursday at 7pm, just in time for weekend trips (tel. 818/768-3533).

One of the most popular wildflower spots in the state is the **Antelope Valley Poppy Preserve.** On a weekend day during peak season, you might find thousands of people here standing slack-jawed at incredible carpets of not just poppies but virtually every California wildflower. Of course if you arrive here before or after the bloom, you'll find a lonely parking lot and a bunch of undistinguished grassy hills. To alert people when the flowers are about to go off, the poppy preserve has a postcard notification system. If you mail them a self-addressed, stamped postcard in the fall or winter, they'll mail it to you when the flowers start to pop. (Send cards to 15101 Lancaster Rd., Lancaster, CA 92004; tel. 805/724-1180.)

some of the best sites—Calcite Canyon, Borrego Palms, Elephant Trees, Native American rock art—require a hike. The wildflower bloom, which generally peaks in March, is one of the main attractions.

## Agua Caliente Hot Springs Park

Access: In Anza-Borrego Desert State Park, along Hwy. S2. For info contact San Diego County Parks & Recreation at 619/694-3049. Open September–May. Hot springs, picnicking.

Agua Caliente means "hot water" in Spanish and that's what this park is known for: geothermally heated springs. There are two naturally fed pools: a large outdoor mineral pool is kept at its natural 96°F, while an indoor pool is heated and outfitted with Jacuzzi jets. Spring-fed showers are also available. At 3,100 feet in elevation on the eastern slope of the Tierra Blanca Mountains and surrounded by the desert wilderness of Anza-Borrego, this place is a little piece of heaven. Nearby is **Vallecito Regional Park,** which offers the same amenities as Agua Caliente, but without the hot springs.

## Julian

Access: I-8 east to Hwy. 67 north to Hwy. 78. Julian Chamber of Commerce, P.O. Box 413, Julian, CA 92036. Tel. 760/765-1857. Or call the Julian Information Center at 760/765-0707.

Once a gold rush town, Julian's modern commodity is apples. If you're here in the fall, you can pick the most delicious ones right off the tree during Julian Apple Days, which run from September through the end of November. While the town attracts a high number of tourists—the storefronts and wooden sidewalks are original throwbacks to the Wild West—it is a cool

place with a very active biking community.

## Borrego Springs

Access: In Anza-Borrego Desert State Park, at the intersection of S22 and S3. Borrego Springs Chamber of Commerce, P.O. Box 420, Borrego Springs, CA 92004. Tel. 760/767-5555 or 800/559-5524.

Located within the boundary of Anza-Borrego, the town of Borrego Springs mainly caters to retired folks and those who like to play golf, or both. It's practically deserted in the summer when temperatures soar, but winter packs 'em in. There are several motels, restaurants, and shops, but the centerpiece is La Casa del Zorro (tel. 760/767-5323), a very expensive hotel set on 38 acres that has three swimming pools, a beauty parlor, and fluffy robes in every room.

# What to Do & Where to Do It

### BIRD WATCHING

Despite the Salton Sea's serious pollution problem, caused as agricultural run-off leaches toxic farm chemicals into this below-sea-level basin, the **Salton Sea National Wildlife Refuge** (tel. 619/393-3052) still attracts over 400 bird species, including accidentals like the flamingo, brown booby, and frigatebird, as well as residents such as the great roadrunner and Gambel's quail. Huge flocks of Canada geese winter here, and spring brings many birds of prey. Located east of Anza-Borrego, this area is extremely hot during the summer; best times to visit are fall through spring. Another popular birding spot is **Dos Palmas Preserve** (tel. 619/343-1234). The upper

# Outdoor Resources

## Cleveland National Forest Ranger Districts

**Palomar Ranger District**
1634 Black Canyon Rd.
Ramona, CA 92065
Tel. 760/788-0250

**Trabuco Ranger District**
1147 E. Sixth St.
Corona, CA 91719
Tel. 909/736-1811

**Descanso Ranger District**
3348 Alpine Blvd.
Alpine, CA 91901
Tel. 619/445-6235

**Julian Chamber of Commerce**
P.O. Box 413
Julian, CA 92036
Tel. 760/765-1857

**Julian Information Center**
Tel. 760/765-0707

**Borrego Springs Chamber of Commerce**
P.O. Box 420
Borrego Springs, CA 92004
Tel. 760/767-5555 or 800/559-5524

## On the Web

**USDA Forest Service Recreation Home Page**
http://www.fs.fed.us/recreation

**Southern California Mountain Bike.Com**
http://www.socalmtb.com
This page is a great resource for all sorts of mountain bike info. There are hundreds of mountain bike shops grouped by county and listed alphabetically, too.

**mOthEr rOck: Southern California's Climbing Magazine**
http://members.aol.com/motherrock
This page offers some of the most up-to-date climbing information for the southland.

---

sections of Salt Creek have created a desert oasis for many shorebirds, waterfowl, birds of prey, and songbirds, while artesian water has also filled ponds to create a habitat for the desert pupfish. Several reptiles, like the flat-tailed horned lizard, live in these parts, too. Located east of the Salton Sea, this area gets unbearably hot in the summertime.

## FISHING

Let's begin with the trout fishing in **Doane Pond** in Palomar Mountain State Park and head south. The cattail-rimmed Doane Pond is stocked year-round and makes a nice spot to fish with kids. Nearby **Lake Henshaw** is all about catfish, especially during early summer. Small **Lake Sutherland** is only open for fishing weekends from March through October, but a record 15-pound bass was pulled from its waters, so you never know. **San Vicente Lake,** open weekends from November through May, is also known for its volume of bass, and its rocky shoreline makes a nice home for trout. But if trout is what you're after, then **Lake Cuyamaca** is, by far, the premier trout hole. Because it's at a much higher elevation than the other lakes, the water stays cooler longer (just the way the trout like it) and the Department of Fish & Game stock it consistently. There's also decent bass and crappie fishing in the summer, with bluegill and catfish in the fall. Also in Cuyamaca Rancho State Park is **Sweetwater River,** a little-known rainbow trout spot at Green Valley Falls campground. Now, the fishing here ain't great, but when the stream's flowing in spring, there are a lot of little 7-inchers, and the best part is, you're practically fishing in the desert! If you want fish, lots of fish, head to **El Capitan Lake.** Open weekends from February through September, the lake is a bass factory. Be sure to get on the lake early, though, because wind barreling down the canyon in the afternoon can mess things up. The prime area of El Cap is Conejos Creek arm, but that's no secret. Fishing at **Lake Jennings,** open weekends year-round, is a step above pond fishing because it's quite small, but it's stocked biweekly with channel catfish, and kids like it. In a remote valley near the Mexican border, **Barrett Lake** is a fisher's dream. It's loaded with bass, bluegill, and crappie, but here's the catch: You need to win the lottery to fish here. Twenty lottery tickets are drawn for each day the lake is open, and only the lucky ones are allowed in. Entering the lottery is free, but the competition is stiff. For lottery information, call the **San Diego City Lakes** at 619/465-3474. If you didn't get your chance on Barrett Lake, head east to **Lake Morena.** Because of its high elevation, things at Morena get started a bit later in the year. From April through July, the lake produces huge numbers of bass, as well as catfish, bluegill, and crappie.

## HIKING

### ANZA-BORREGO DESERT STATE PARK

#### Borrego Palm Canyon Trail

3 miles round-trip. Moderately easy. Access: Borrego Palm Canyon Campground.

The palm trees tucked away in the V of Borrego Palm Canyon spring up like a mirage and are a must-see. Beginning

at the pupfish pond, head upcanyon, alongside a seasonal stream. As you hike along this very popular trail, the canyon narrows until you feel as if you're becoming part of a sheer rock wall sandwich. Suddenly the oasis comes into view, and just beyond it, a 10-foot waterfall spills over huge boulders. Return the way you came.

#### Pictograph Trail

3 miles round-trip. Moderately easy. Access: Head 5 miles on the Blair Valley jeep trails, following the signs to Pictograph Trail. Check with a ranger on road conditions.

Over 50 Native American rock art sites exist in the park. This hike takes you to one of them and offers an expansive view of the desert to boot. The trail starts out winding through granite boulders and soon ascends a wash. About 0.75 mile into it, you'll come to a large boulder next to the trail, on which ancient Indians left their mark: geometric streaks of red and yellow pigment. Continue on through Smugglers Canyon. At the end, the canyon closes out and leads to a spectacular 100-foot drop-off, remains of a waterfall. From your seat on a giant boulder, you can see the Vallecito Valley beneath you, and high-desert mountains in the distances. Return the way you came.

#### Calcite Canyon Trail

4 miles round-trip. Moderate. Access: From Christmas Circle in Borrego Springs, follow S-22 west 20 miles to Calcite Jeep Rd., which lies just west of a microwave tower.

Wind and water have shaped Calcite Canyon into pointy and strange formations. The glittering pure calcite crystals attracted miners, and you can still see the deep trenches where the excavations occurred. Follow Calcite Jeep

Road as it drops into the south fork of Palm Wash, then rises, then drops some more on the way to your destination, Calcite Mine. Just beyond the mine is a huge slab of white sandstone called Locomotive Rock. Return the way you came, or take a left about half a mile down from the mine, which leads to the middle fork of Palm Wash. The descent is steep and the sandstone channel soon gets very narrow, but soon you've popped out into another main canyon, which you can follow to Calcite Jeep Road and back to your four-wheel-drive.

## Elephant Trees Nature Trail

1.5 miles round-trip. Easy. Access: From Ocotillo Wells, head south on Split Mountain Rd. and drive 6 miles to the signed turnoff for Elephant Trees.

Elephant trees look like, well, elephants. They're very bulky, with peeling, rough bark that resembles elephant skin, and thick branches that curve and taper like an elephant's trunk. The park has three groves of elephant trees, but this one is the largest, with over 500 trees. Follow the easy nature trail loop or, if you want to see even more trees, leave the trail at signpost no. 10 and hike west about a mile. Return the way you came, heading back to the nature trail loop.

### PALOMAR MOUNTAINS

## Observatory Trail

4 miles round-trip. Moderate. Access: Observatory Campground in the Cleveland National Forest.

Lots of people drive up Highway to the Stars (S6) to reach the Palomar Observatory at the top of Mount Palomar, and the more insane among us actually road bike it. But those of us who fall in between, we take the Observatory Trail.

Pick up the trail, which parallels the road, on the edge of the campground and start hiking up, up, up, stopping at the lookout over Mendenhall Valley. Soon you'll see the observatory in the distance, its famous Hale telescope covered by a silver dome. Once at the top, the panoramic view of Southern California will take your breath away. Return the way you came.

## Scott's Cabin Trail Sampler

3.5-mile loop. Moderate. Access: Silver Crest Picnic Area in Palomar Mountain State Park.

On this any-time-of-year hike, you'll sample four park trails, which include a visit to the historic Scott's Cabin and give you a real sense of the geography. Beginning at Silver Crest Picnic Area, a sign points the way to the ruins of Scott's Cabin, built in the 1880s. Continue past the cabin to the Cedar-Doane Trail. (This trail takes you down a steep, oak-covered slope to Doane Pond, a nice trout fishing and picnic spot.) Go past the Doane Trail junction to the Cedar Grove group campground and pick up the Adams Trail, which leads you through a meadow and eventually up to Nate Harrison Road. Cross the road, and the trail becomes Boucher Trail, which leads up to Boucher Hill summit. Descend on the Oak Ridge Trail and back to your starting point.

## Dripping Springs Trail

7 miles out and back. Moderately difficult. Access: Dripping Springs Campground in the Cleveland National Forest.

This rugged and solitary hike through the Agua Tibia Wilderness takes you up the north face of Agua Tibia Mountain to an area of huge, 100-year-old manzanita. Begin by crossing Arroyo Seco

Creek and switchbacking up the mountainside. Along the way, you'll get views of San Jacinto, San Gorgonio, and Mount Baldy. Be sure to look over your shoulder as you climb, to catch a glimpse of Vail Lake. Technically, manzanita is a shrub, but the ones up here are definitely trees. Pretty amazing. Return the way you came.

## CUYAMACA RANCHO STATE PARK

### Kelly Ditch Trail

5.5 miles one-way. Moderately easy. Access: Trailhead begins near Cuyamaca Reservoir. Car shuttle directions: From Julian, head west 1 mile on Hwy. 78/79. Turn south on Pine Hills Rd. and take it to William Heise Park.

Do this hike during the fall, when the downhill trail from Cuyamaca Reservoir to William Heise Park is blazing with color. The trail begins by dropping you into its namesake ditch. The Kelly Ditch was dug by hundreds of Chinese laborers in order to divert the runoff from the Cuyamaca Mountains to the man-made reservoir. Sometimes you're walking in the ditch itself, and sometimes the trail parallels it, but either way, you're in the cool shade of an oak canopy for the first mile or so. Eventually you'll cross Engineers Road and pick up the trail on the other side. At the junction with an unmarked dirt road, follow the dirt road, bearing right. At the next fork, stay left, and the well-worn road becomes a trail that drops you down into a grassy patch. The final descent into Heise Park is quite steep: 2 miles of switchbacks and a 1,000-foot elevation loss. If you didn't make plans for a car shuttle, good luck hiking back!

### Cuyamaca Peak

6 miles round-trip. Moderate. Access: Paso Picacho Campground.

Even though you're gaining 1,600 feet in elevation here, you're hiking up the Cuyamaca Peak Fire Road, a paved one-laner that's closed to traffic—so it's not too strenuous. And as far as paved roads go, it's quite beautiful, too. All along the way, you're presented with incredible desert views. Summit highlights include the Santa Rosa and Laguna Mountains, the Pacific, and glimpses of Mexico. When you've soaked up all the beauty, head back down the road.

### Stonewall Peak

4 miles round-trip. Moderate. Access: Paso Picacho Campground.

Lower than Cuyamaca Peak by about 1,000 feet, "Old Stony" offers great views of the old Stonewall Mine and Cuyamaca Valley. (Don't go expecting a panoramic vista: nearby mountains block the view.) From the campground, the trail switchbacks up the mountain, through fragrant incense cedar trees. Overall, the hike is fairly easy, but the last 100 yards are tricky. The trail is reduced to steps hacked into the granite, with a guardrail for safety. Going up isn't so bad, but coming down is a bit hair-raising. Return the way you came.

## LAGUNA MOUNTAINS

### Sunset Trail

7 miles round-trip. Moderate. Access: Meadows Information Station in the Cleveland National Forest.

This trail traces the entire western rim of the Laguna Mountain plateau, providing some spectacular views. Pick up the Sunset Trailhead just a few yards north of the Information Station on S1 and begin hiking north to a lovely meadow bordered by pine trees. It's a great place to watch the sky turn to dusk. At the junction with Big Laguna Trail, turn around and retrace your path.

## Oasis Spring

2 miles round-trip. Easy. Access: In the Cleveland National Forest on S1 (Sunrise Highway), approximately 27 miles north of I-8. There's a turnout on the right, marking the Pacific Crest Trail.

Start hiking north on the Pacific Crest Trail, until it joins with a dirt road. At the road's end, a series of switchbacks take you down to Oasis Spring. Here, you'll find a rushing stream in a beautiful shady canyon. Retrace your path on the return.

### HORSEBACK RIDING

Forty miles east of San Diego in Descanso, **Holidays on Horseback** offers half- and full-day trail rides, as well as overnights in the Cuyamaca Rancho State Park. Call your hosts Earl and Liz Hammond at 619/445-3997 for details.

### HOT SPRINGS

If you're on a budget and traveling through Anza-Borrego, head to **Agua Caliente Hot Springs Park.** At an elevation of 3,100 feet, on the eastern slope of the Tierra Blanca Mountains and surrounded by the desert wilderness, this county-run park is a little piece of spa heaven within the state park boundaries.

There are two naturally fed pools: a large outdoor mineral pool kept at its natural 96°F, and an indoor pool that is heated and outfitted with Jacuzzi jets. Spring-fed showers are also available. If you've got some surplus cash and you're in the Palomar Mountains, check out the **Warner Springs Ranch** (tel. 760/782-4200) in Warner Springs. At this turn-of-the-century, members-only mineral springs resort and equestrian ranch, nonmembers can sample the wares by reserving a mid-week spa package, which runs about $325 for two—massage, hot spring privileges, and meals included. Golf, tennis, and equestrian packages are also available.

### MOUNTAIN BIKING

#### ANZA-BORREGO DESERT STATE PARK

##### Jasper Trail/Grapevine Canyon

15 miles. Moderate. Access: Anza-Borrego State Park. This ride begins at the Jasper Trailhead, just east of the town of Ranchita along S22. For the car shuttle, park one car at the Tamarisk Campground, located at the junction of Yaqui Pass Rd. (S3) and Hwy. 78. In the second car, head west on Hwy. 78 and turn right on S2. At the junction with S22, make a right and head through the small town of Ranchita and back into the park. After you've crossed the park boundary, look for the Jasper Trailhead, on your right. It's between mile markers 6 and 7.

From the Jasper Trailhead, it's an easy pedal south for the first 2 miles, then you encounter a hill—and it's a doozy, 600 steep feet, but the only climb on this route. From here, it's all downhill on mostly soft sand/dirt trails. You're surrounded by vertical rock walls now as you head into the canyon. When the Jasper trail ends, go left into Grapevine Canyon, toward Yaqui Well, the Tamarisk Campground, and your car.

## Pinyon Mountain Road

15 miles out and back. Moderately difficult. Access: Anza-Borrego State Park. At the junction with S2, turn right. It's about 5 miles to the sign for Pinyon Mountain Road.

Head east on the right fork of the main trail, also known as Pinyon Mountain Road. There's a bit of intense climbing at the beginning, but once you've reached the Pinyon Mountain Valley Campground, you're done. It's a bit farther to The Squeeze, a section named because the road is so narrow here and bordered by rock walls that four-wheel-drives can barely squeeze through. This is your turnaround point. Cruise downhill. On the way back, you might want to explore that left fork of the trail, which takes you up North Pinyon Mountain. It adds about 2 miles and 500 feet of climb to your trip.

## Fish Creek Wash

28 miles. Moderate. Access: Drive across the park on Hwy. 78 to Ocotillo Wells and head south 10 miles on Split Mountain Rd. to the junction with Fish Creek Wash. Park off-road.

This ride begins at the intersection of Fish Creek Wash and Split Mountain Road, and it's a steady climb the entire way—but that makes for an easy return. From here, pedal south along Fish Creek Wash through some pretty amazing sandstone cliffs to Split Mountain, which really does look like a mountain split in half. (You'll also pass the Wind Caves, which you can't ride to, but

they're worth the short hike.) Follow the trail, lined by near-vertical rock walls. Stay straight on the main road, past the Mud Hills Wash (also worth another short jaunt). About 12.5 miles in, you'll reach Sandstone Canyon, the jewel of this trip: 200-foot-high rock walls and a width of just 9 feet. You'll need to get off your bike to explore this geological wonder. When you're ready, pedal back the way you came.

## Coyote Canyon

30 miles. Difficult. Access: Have a friend drop you off at Coyote Canyon Rd. and pick you up in Borrego Springs. It's a 90-minute drive between the two points, so shuttling isn't much of an option. From San Diego, take Hwy. 67 northeast to Hwy. 78 to Hwy. 79 and head north toward Aguanga in Riverside County. From here, head north on Hwy. 371 and into the town of Anza. Turn south on Kirby Rd. and drive 4.5 miles to the intersection of Terwilliger Rd. and Coyote Canyon Rd.

This ride begins at the intersection of Terwilliger Road and Coyote Canyon Road, just outside the town on Anza in Riverside County. Head east on Coyote Canyon Road, making a right at the first T and heading to the entrance to Anza-Borrego. Now the real fun starts. It's a steep, rocky downhill to Turkey Track, where several canyons converge. Stay straight on the sandy wash to Middle Willows, a palm oasis that appears in the desert like something out of a cartoon. Stay left at Salvador Canyon and again at Sheep Canyon, and eventually you're out on the auto road, which takes you through Lower Willows. You'll cross several streams and then head into the Borrego Valley, through a deliciously scented orange grove. Turn right on Borrego Springs Road and head to Christmas Circle, the center of town. Congrats!

## Granite Mountain

24 miles. Difficult. Access: Just after you enter the park on Hwy. 78, turn right on S2, drive about 4 miles to the Banner Store, and park.

This ride begins near Scissor Crossing, where Highway 78 meets S2. From the small store on S2, begin pedaling south through Shelter Valley toward Blair Valley and head down into Box Canyon (the historic Southern Emigrant Trail and the Butterfield Overland Stage parallels this road in this area) and farther down still into Mason Valley. From Mason Valley, turn right on an unmarked road, where there's a sign for Oriflamme Canyon, and follow the wash through a gated fence at 8 miles. At the next fork, go right on Rodriguez Canyon. (Follow the power line.) What comes next is the steepest part of the ride and you might have to walk your bike at times. Granite Mountain rises on your right as you pedal across a cattle gate at the road summit. The view of the San Felipe Valley and the surrounding mountains is quite dramatic. On the downhill, stay left, passing several old mines and a pasture. There's a bit of a climb before you drop into Chariot Canyon. Stay to the right and descend to Hwy 78. Make a right on 78 and head back to Scissor Crossing.

## CUYAMACA RANCHO STATE PARK

### Green Valley Loop

10 miles. Moderately difficult. Access: Green Valley Campground in the park. Follow the campground entrance road past the first campground, and park in the second day-use parking lot.

On this challenging loop on fire roads and dirt trails, you'll ride through stands of canyon live oak and get some incredible views of the park valley. Be careful of the steep sections and loose rocks. From the second parking area near the Green Valley Campground, pedal north on Arroyo Seco Road. Continue straight past the turnoff to the Arroyo Seco Primitive Campground, and continue along the California Riding and Hiking Trail to the Sweetwater River and Green Valley Falls, a lovely waterfall and several swimming holes, too, during springtime. Continue past the falls to the Green Valley Picnic area and back to camp.

### Upper Green Valley Fire Road

4.5 miles out and back. Easy. Access: Park headquarters.

This easy pedal along a well-graded dirt road is perfect for beginners. From the park headquarters, pedal north. Pass through the gate where Upper Green Valley Road begins. Follow Upper Green Valley Road, which parallels the Sweetwater River. When you reach Soapstone Grade Road, turn around and head back the way you came. Hikers also use these trails, so watch your speed.

### Stonewall Mine

14.5-mile loop. Moderate. Access: Park headquarters.

This trip takes you to the Stonewall Mine, where you can see the old mine shaft and miners' cabins. From the park headquarters, pedal north along a dirt road that begins just behind the headquarters. Pass through a gate that marks the beginning of Upper Green Valley Road, which follows the Sweetwater River. This is an easy pedal along a well-maintained dirt road. When you reach Soapstone Grade Road, turn left. Things can get a bit tricky here: some steep sections, loose rocks, sand. Go right at Stonewall Creek Fire Road and follow the signs to the mine. On the return trip, head back down Stonewall Creek Fire Road, and continue straight through the junction with Soapstone Grade. You'll cross Stonewall Creek and then reach the dirt road that takes you back to the park headquarters.

## Cuyamaca Peak

10-mile loop. Moderately difficult. Access: Paso Picacho Campground and Picnic Area. Park in the day-use lot.

It's a steep ride on fire roads to Cuyamaca Peak at 6,512 feet. First, we pedal to the peak, then we do a loop. From the Paso Picacho day-use parking lot, turn right on Highway 79, pass the Interpretive Center, and then make the first right you can, at the AUTHORIZED VEHICLES ONLY sign. Walk your bike around the locked gate that closes Cuyamaca Peak Fire Road to traffic. It's a very steep 3-mile ride from here to the summit, so brace yourself. On clear days, the view from the summit is extraordinary: San Diego, the Pacific Ocean, the Salton Sea, and across the border into Mexico. Coast 1.5 miles back downhill and turn left on Azalea Springs Road. Follow it to Milk Ranch Road and go right. This takes you out to Lake Cuyamaca and Highway 79. Make a right on Highway 79 and pedal along the highway back to your car.

## Oakzanita Peak

12 miles round-trip. Difficult. Access: Green Valley campground and picnic area.

This is another steep ride on fire roads, this time to Oakzanita Peak at 5,054 feet. From the gate that blocks the fire road at Green Valley Falls parking area, ride down the fire road about a mile to the intersection with South Boundary Fire Road. This stretch of dirt road is in pretty crappy condition, but chin up— the terrain gets better. Stay left, crossing the Sweetwater River and Highway 79. Pick up East Mesa Fire Road directly across the highway and start climbing. It's about 3 miles from here to where you'll turn right on the unmarked spur that will take you to Oakzanita Peak. (Going left takes you to the Granite Springs Primitive Camp.) From here, you could encounter mule deer in the meadow below, and perhaps a red-tailed hawk or golden eagle. Bike back down East Mesa Fire Road to its end at Highway 79 and go right. Pedal along Highway 79 about 0.5 mile and you'll see the Green Valley Campground on your left.

## ROAD BIKING

## Mount Palomar

36 miles. Difficult. Access: From San Diego, take I-15 north to Hwy. 76 and head east to Pauma Village, just outside Palomar Mountain State Park.

Why bike to the summit of Mount Palomar? Because you can. Maybe. Often considered one of the most challenging road rides in the U.S., this one follows the road up to Mount Palomar (6,100 feet) and its eponymous observatory in San Diego County. From the small town of Pauma Village on Highway 76, begin pedaling into Mount Palomar State Park and turn left (north) on S6. This is the road that will take you up to the summit and the Palomar Observatory, home of the legendary Hale telescope. It's 16 miles of unrelenting, steep climb. But just think what a breeze it will be going down.

Here's the cheater's shortcut: If you find the idea of riding *down* Mount Palomar appealing but can't imagine riding up, then contact **Gravity Activated Sports** at 800/985-4427. They'll take you up to the tippy-top in a comfy van, feed you, provide you with all the gear as well as a narrative history of Mount Palomar and the observatory, then follow you in a sag wagon as you whiz 5,000 feet down the mountain. All you need are sunscreen and a camera. It's up to you if you tell anyone how you ascended to the top.

## Mount Laguna

50-mile loop. Moderately difficult. Access: Paso Picacho Campground in Cuyamaca Rancho State Park.

This is a challenging, full-day ride through the Laguna Mountains in the backcountry of San Diego. Initially settled by the Kumeyaay Indians (whose remaining artifacts are on exhibit at the park headquarters) and later founded as a small gold-mining town known as Cuyamaca City, this part of California is still mostly wilderness. Mount Laguna itself peaks at 6,001 feet.

This ride parallels the Pacific Crest Trail, and from here you'll get some amazing desert views. And if you're lucky, you might even spot a mountain lion. Or at least a kangaroo rat. From Paso Picacho camp, ride south on Highway 79. (Ride counterclockwise, so you hit the hottest canyons early in the morning.) It's a fast descent to the first main intersection at Samagatuma Creek—go left on the road to Guatay and Pine Valley. Just after Pine Valley, the road is known as Laguna Mountain Highway, Sunrise Highway, or S1, and on this road you will climb and climb to the Laguna Mountain Trading Post, which borders on the Cuyapaipe Indian Reservation. Just beyond that is the highest point of the ride, Mount Laguna. The desert views are awesome. S1 takes you all the way to the Cuyamaca

Reservoir, over to Highway 79, and back to camp.

## Santa Ysabel–Mesa Grande

23-mile loop. Moderate. Access: Hwy. 79 in Santa Ysabel.

Tucked away at 3,000 feet in northern San Diego County, the small valley town of Santa Ysabel is well-known for two things: Dudley's Bakery's delicious goods and the Santa Ysabel Mission, built in 1818. This ride takes you through its center, on curvaceous Mesa Grande Road and out into the beautiful and rather solitary surrounding countryside. There's one very steep hill, but the rest aren't bad. Start by pedaling north on Highway 79, away from town. After you reach the first summit (total gain on this ride is approximately 2,000 ft.) you'll be able to see Lake Henshaw and the Palomar Observatory straight ahead. Go left at the bottom of the hill, staying on 79. At Mesa Grande Road, go left. This is a big hill and the weak among us may need to walk our bikes. Follow along, around the Mesa Grande Indian Reservation, until you are back at Highway 79. On the return, you'll pass the mission. And don't forget to stop at the bakery for a snack when you're done.

## Black Canyon

16-mile loop. Moderate. Access: Magnolia Ave. and Hwy. 67/78, in the town of Ramona.

From Ramona, begin pedaling north on Magnolia Street, which soon becomes Black Canyon Road and takes you into the Cleveland National Forest. Make a right at Sutherland Dam Road and pedal toward Sutherland Lake. At Highway 78, make a right and loop back to Magnolia Street. Mad cyclists can link this scenic canyon ride to the Mesa

Grande ride above—in which case you'd stay straight on Black Canyon Road until it meets up with Mesa Grande. There are stretches of dirt road on that connection—some smooth, some rough—so a mountain or hybrid bike is necessary, as is a car shuttle.

## Loops of Julian

17 miles. Moderately easy. Access: Main St. in the town of Julian.

Perhaps you're in town for Apple Days, on your way to Anza-Borrego, and want to do a little cycling in Julian to scope out the scene. Here are two relatively easy loops, aside from the steep incline here and there. Do one or both. For the north loop, start pedaling north on Main Street, which becomes Farmers Road. Turn left at Wynola Road and drop down to the roadside town of Wynola. Make a right on Highway 78/79 and head east. From here, you can go back into Julian or do the south loop. For the south loop, make a right on Pine Hills Road and a left at Frisus Road, which takes you down to Heise Park. To return, get back on Frisus and turn right on Deer Lake Road. Turn right on Pine Hills, right on Hwy 78/79, and head back to Julian.

## WALKS & NATURAL ATTRACTIONS

## Green Valley Falls

Here's an easy walk to a lovely waterfall and several swimming holes in Cuyamaca Rancho State Park. From the Green Valley Falls picnic area, it's a quarter-mile walk to the falls themselves. Walk along the Falls Fire Road to the Green Valley Falls Trail and turn left; walk downhill about 100 yards. Several smaller pools above and below the falls can be found along spurs off the fire road.

## Cactus Loop Trail

This easy, 1-mile loop begins across from the Tamarisk Grove Campground in Anza-Borrego Desert State Park. In this cactus gallery, you'll see ocotillo, several kinds of cholla, beavertail, fishhook, hedgehog, and barrel. Go in the spring when the cacti are in bloom for the "Oh-wow!" effect. The desert floor spreads out to the distant mountains where, if you bring your binocs, you just might spot a bighorn.

## Wildflower Bloom

One of the most spectacular displays of wildflowers you'll ever see takes place each spring in Anza-Borrego Desert State Park. Fire-red ocotillo, pink beavertail cactus, yellow brittlebush—you never knew a desert could be so brilliant and lush. The bloom is so popular that the park has developed the Wildflower Notification Program. If you want to be sure to visit Anza-Borrego at the best time for flower viewing, send a stamped, self-addressed postcard to: Anza-Borrego Desert State Park, 200 Palm Canyon Dr., Borrego Springs, CA 92004. They'll return your card a couple of weeks prior to the year's expected bloom peak. Most years, the bloom starts in January and peaks in March. For an up-to-date wildflower recording, call 760/767-4684.

## Palomar Observatory

Located on Palomar Mountain, just outside Palomar Mountain State Park, the observatory is open daily 9am to 4pm for self-guided tours, which include the 200-inch Hale Telescope, gallery exhibits, and museum. Admission is free, and so is the spectacular view. For more information, call the observatory at 760/742-2119.

From badlands to mountain peaks to palm canyons, the vast **Anza-Borrego Desert State Park** (tel. 760/767-4205) is brimming with life of all kinds. The Borrego Palm Canyon is home to the rare desert pupfish, resident hummingbirds, and many other migrants. Rare bighorn sheep balance on steep cliffs, while iguana and other reptiles scurry along the ground. (In the spring, you might get very, very lucky and sight a bighorn lamb.) The spring wildflower bloom is out of this world. All in all, there are over 225 bird species, 60 mammals, and 60 reptiles. Start your trek with a stop at the visitor center, and don't forget your binoculars.

# Camping

There are numerous camping spots in the Cleveland National Forest, which range from buzzing and busy RV parks on the shores of **Lake Henshaw** to the tiny **Bow-Willow Camp** in Anza-Borrego State Park. It's a heavily visited and used area. You can get stuck with a terrible site next to an off-road vehicle rally or find yourself in a lonely corner of desert with no one else around. It's largely a matter of timing and perseverance. For the record, the following are my top picks in the area.

**Yaqui Pass Primitive Camp Area** in Anza-Borrego is set at 1,700 feet about 9 miles south of Borrego Springs. It's a primitive camping area, which means no toilets, no water, no nuthin' except for a really nice spot without too much ac-

tion—but lots of beautiful hiking, mountain biking, and all-around desert action nearby. It's also free and requires no reservation. If that's a little too minimalist for you, **Tamarisk Grove Camp** is only another couple miles down the road and has water, flush toilets, and showers. For that privilege, you'll have to cough up the usual $12 to $14 per night and dial 800/444-PARK if you want to get a reservation, which is highly recommended during high season. Farther south in Anza-Borrego is another minimalist's dream, the **Blair Valley Environmental Camps.** This is the best way to get some seclusion, since all the sites are walk-in only and are at least 100 yards from the parking places. No more being kept up at night by droning motor home generators here. It's also up a little higher (2,500 feet) and consequently cooler, with lots of nearby hiking.

In the mountains to the west of Anza-Borrego you've got a number of nice options. The campground in **Palomar Mountain State Park** is quite nice, with water, showers, and flush toilets. It's on the same reservation system as all the other state parks (tel. 800/444-PARK), and it's open year-round. Since it only has 31 sites, reservations are highly recommended during the summer. Sites will run about $12 to $14. Several other national forest campgrounds lie in this immediate area: **Observatory, Fry Creek, and Crestline Group Camp.** They don't take reservations and cost $7 per site. The County of San Diego also operates a highly developed campground at **Oak Knoll,** which has everything from a swimming pool to laundry to a baseball diamond. Hardly the deepest wilderness experience, but it'll do in a pinch. They don't take reservations, but you can call 619/742-3437 to ask how crowded the park is. The cost is $12 to $14 per night.

# 11

# INTRODUCTION TO BAJA CALIFORNIA

L ONG BEFORE CALIFORNIA WAS SYNONYMOUS WITH DISNEYLAND, the Golden Gate Bridge, Malibu Barbie, and the Beach Boys, the name referred simply to what is now called Baja California, Mexico's 1,000-mile long peninsula. Later, when what we now call California was settled, the two areas were termed Alta (upper) California and Baja (lower) California. Geopolitics led to the two states winding up in separate countries, of course, but if we were sticklers about things, Southern California should really be called Southern Upper California— much like the two Mexican states that make up Baja are called Baja California del Norte and Baja California del Sur (Northern Lower California and Southern Lower California).

A mutineer, Fortún Jiménez, was the first Spaniard to set foot on the Baja peninsula in 1533—but only after murdering his captain. Jiménez and his crew landed in La Paz Bay, where most of them met their own violent deaths at the hands of the region's indigenous inhabitants, the Pericús. A few survivors straggled home with a few black pearls and almost-mythical descriptions of a large landmass, an island across the western sea. Cortés, the conqueror of mainland Mexico, quickly jumped on this opportunity for more glory and mounted his own expedition there.

Etymologists have a field day arguing the exact provenance of the name California, but the favorite explanation centers around a mysterious island of riches and beautiful, but burly, women ruled by a gorgeous Amazon Queen named Calafia in Garcí Ordoñez de Montalvo's 1510 romantic narrative, *The Exploits of Esplandian*. The island, of course, was called California, a harsh and inhospitable land where the Amazons rode on the backs of griffins, wearing suits of gold armor, the only metal they had.

Minus the black and burly Amazons, Baja looked a lot like Calafia's mythical island, and surely the idea of hordes of gold guarded by Amazons had better recruitment potential for explorers than a bunch of cactus and rocks guarded by stone-age Indians. Like an Amazon, the peninsula didn't give itself up to civilization easily. Though Cortés named his first settlement on the peninsula Santa Cruz (near modern-day La Paz), the name California stuck to this desert land when the settlement quickly failed. The myth of Baja California as an island hung around for another hundred years or so, long after Francisco de Ulloa discovered the Colorado River flowing into the northern reaches of the Sea of Cortez. And later, much later, Jesuit missionaries pushed into what's the United States' version of California, necessitating the linguistic breakup of California into Alta California and Baja California.

Prior to the arrival of the Spaniards, Baja was very sparsely populated by indigenous hunter-gatherers, at their peak numbering perhaps 50,000. From north to south, these tribes were broken down into three main groups, the Yumans, the Cochimi, and the Pericú. As the Spaniards discovered, these were tough, no-nonsense people whose lifestyle was as rugged as the landscape they lived in. Living together in loosely defined units numbering from 10 to 200 people, the native people worked the natural economy of Baja's marine and terrestrial landscape for every bit of nutrition they could extract. One can only marvel at how hungry people must have become before they were inspired to devise a successful technique for eating cactus.

One of the great celebrations for the Pericú was the seasonal ripening of the pitaya dulce cactus fruit at the end of the summer. When the pitaya dulce ("dulce" means sweet in Spanish) came ripe, the Pericú would binge until they passed out from exhaustion.

Surprisingly little has changed since then. These days it's not pitaya dulce that provokes the wild binges, but long beaches with great surf, mountains full of hidden canyons and pictograph-decorated caves, oceans full of hard-fighting sportfish, remote islands where you can kayak for weeks, lagoons where gray whales not only tolerate your presence but will come over and rub against the side of your boat. And, of course, there's the extra excitement of being in a foreign country, a foreign culture, where people speak a different language and everything is a little different.

# Baja Realities

## THE WATER

My advice about water: Drink lots of it. Baja is one seriously hot and dry place. You can sweat off a lot of moisture and not even know it until you're dehydrated. Bottled purified water is plentiful and cheap in Mexico. As to whether you should drink the tap water, most people don't, but the municipal water supplies in most towns seem to be fairly well-managed. Given the choice between getting dehydrated on a hot day or drinking from a tap, I'd choose the

# So What About Those Banditos?

Every veteran Baja traveler has heard the question before: You're recounting tales of your last trip—the great fishing, that epic south swell that broke overhead and perfectly for 5 days straight on an isolated point, the beautiful mountain village where you spent the night with a local family, the island where a coyote walked through camp—when your listener looks at you with big eyes and asks, "But weren't you afraid of the banditos?"

"Uh, what banditos?"

"You know, the ones that always rob people down there."

They then launch into a horrific tale. There are several variations, but the gist of it goes like this: The friend of someone I know was down there on his honeymoon (alternately, he's traveling with his pregnant wife). The young couple pulls their Volkswagen van out onto a remote clifftop campsite (it's always a Volkswagen) and goes to sleep. In the middle of the night they're awakened by a bunch of men with guns. Several of the men muscle the horrified husband out of the van while the others line up to rape the wife. With his heels literally hanging over the edge of the cliff and his wife screaming in the van, the husband suddenly develops some superhuman cojones and starts kicking his tormentors' butts. Despite their guns and superior numbers, the cowardly banditos flee into the night from this gringo Jackie Chan, but not before shooting out the tires of the Volkswagen. The couple limps home and vows never to go to Mexico again.

I can't tell you how many times I've heard this tale, almost as many times as I've heard the story about the poodle in the microwave and the lovers who drive home from the makeout spot to find a bloody hook dangling from the door handle. Yet in all my years of traveling in both Baja and mainland Mexico I've never had a single thing stolen, not a ballpoint pen, not a piece of fruit. Once, a guy I was traveling with had his shorts stolen while they hung on a clothesline, but we asked around town and quickly got them back. Usually, in remote parts of Baja I leave my car

latter. Of course, with inexpensive and compact water treatment systems, you should never have to make that choice.

Surface water in Baja should be treated with just as much suspicion as you would treat it in your local forest. While the human population is sparse, there are wild horses, burros, and zillions of range cattle all over Baja. Assume that any creek or pond you find is contaminated with giardia, which causes diarrhea in humans.

## DRIVING

Whether you fly or drive to Baja, if you're planning a lot of outdoor adventures it's almost inevitable that you'll do some driving. Once upon a time a drive down the peninsula was one of the ultimate off-road challenges. Now, it's simply a very long drive on a narrow two-lane highway.

The main road, the Transpeninsular Highway, Mexico 1, is well-maintained and patrolled. The days when a break-

doors unlocked so I can't accidentally get locked out, and so far it's always been there when I got back. Nobody I know has ever been physically threatened, with the exception of a guy who got beaten up for saying something that would have gotten him killed in L.A. or New York.

Which isn't to imply that Mexico is a perfectly safe paradise. It's a poor country with some big problems; the border region in particular is home to a lot of scams and rip-offs (which, for what it's worth, includes the border region on the U.S. side too). And while people no doubt have been robbed at gunpoint, and women raped, those things happen in the United States, too, with probably greater regularity. It's hardly an epidemic. Forced to choose what's safer, Southern California or anywhere in Baja besides the border region, I'd pick Baja without hesitation. Especially in the remote areas, people there depend on each other too much to be ripping each other off. It's a totally unforgiving environment, and the communities are tiny. Anyone who made a habit of crime would quickly be ostracized, which is not an attractive option in a town of 200 people.

The best thing you can do to protect yourself in Baja is the same thing you would do in the U.S.: Don't dangle temptation in front of people; don't flaunt your relative wealth. Leave your valuables at home and keep the ones you can't live without out of sight. And respect the local people; if you treat them with respect, they'll reciprocate. If you don't, well, they may return the favor.

Most of all, don't let your fear get out of hand. Caution is one thing, but if you go down there thinking everyone is looking to prey on you, you'll have a rotten time. It's a terrible mistake in Mexico to assume that just because someone looks like your Hollywood stereotype of a bandito that he really is. Often, that man with the gold tooth, cowboy hat, handlebar mustache, and pistol on his belt is just a kind-hearted family man who is walking into your camp to offer you some fish, or to ask if you can give his son a ride into town to the hospital. Try not to run screaming; it ruins it for the rest of us.

down on the Transpeninsular meant an almost guaranteed near-death experience are long gone. The more pressing danger to travelers on Baja's paved roadways is traffic. While numerous car, bus, and truck skeletons can attest to the dangers of driving too fast while too tired or too drunk on a narrow, precipitous roadway, it's my experience that a little diligence goes a long way. A huge quantity of truck and bus traffic roars along the Transpeninsular every day. My opinion of Mexican truck drivers is that they're really good at what they do and deserve all our respect. A few things you should know: If you see an oncoming truck turn on his left signal or flicking his lights at you, he's telling you he's a wide load and that you should pull to your right. Do it. If you're gaining on a truck and he flicks his left signal, he's telling you the coast is clear to pass. In this situation I live by the credo "trust but verify." I pull out slightly and confirm that he's actually signaling me and hasn't just forgotten to turn off his blinker. Finally, if a big truck is gaining on you and you can see that the coast is clear, give him a left signal to tell him that you are giving him the okay to pass. It's a great system and by the time you reach southern Baja even the most blue-haired gringo motor homers are signaling each other like Mexican truck drivers.

Speed limits in Baja are low but widely ignored. But as you're blasting through the desert at 80 mph instead of 80 km per hour, do take the time to remember that there are range cattle everywhere here, that you might come around a corner and find a goat herder trying to cross the road with a flock of 200, or that you might just come over a rise and find a washed-out bridge ahead. Be very aware and drive within your limits of safety.

Gas in Baja is widely available but you should take just about every chance you get to fill up. It's nerve-wracking when you decide to fill up at the last chance gas station before a long empty section and they tell you they're out of fuel.

Remember that American insurance is very rarely valid in Mexico, and that not having insurance in Mexico is a good way to see the wrong side of the Mexican criminal justice system. While good Mexican insurance can add a couple hundred dollars to a long trip, peace of mind is priceless.

## THE FEDERALES

The other great legend of the Baja traveler is the run-in with the Federales. A bunch of squeaky clean American surfer boys are headed down to their secret surf spot when they come across a police checkpoint. The cops order them out of the car and then, while "searching" for drugs, they plant a bag of dope in the car and arrest the poor gringos for possession, holding them in a dank dark cell until they cough up a couple grand. The one consistent part of this story is that the Americans swear up and down that they didn't have even a stem or a seed in the car, even when you know that they smoke pot like a forest fire in Humboldt County.

Now I'm not saying nobody ever got framed in Mexico, but I've been stopped a lot of times at checkpoints in Mexico and never once have the cops been anything but gracious and polite while they were searching my car, even when I'd been in the desert for weeks and looked like a total dirt bag. The corruption of Mexican law enforcement is legendary, though, but it usually involves taking big bribes to look the other way while a giant cargo plane lands out by the town dump and transfers a bunch of strange-looking white bundles to a waiting speedboat, not nickel and diming a bunch of gringo tourists.

The smart way to avoid these kinds of hassles is to not bring drugs into the country and to not act all uppity when you encounter a checkpoint. I'll be the first to admit that if the California Highway Patrol opened a checkpoint and wanted to search my car, I'd be kicking and screaming about my civil rights and calling my lawyer. But in Mexico, you don't have those civil rights, plain and simple, so don't offend a Mexican cop by telling him that he doesn't have any right to search you. He does. Being cool and cooperative goes a long ways toward speeding things along and can make the difference between a cursory glance through your passenger compartment and a full-blown search.

The biggest hassle in Mexico is dealing with traffic stops. Like small-town America, small-town Mexico is filled with bored cops who have nothing better to do than set up speed traps and hand out tickets. Only a Mexican cop wants you to pay up right then and there, because they know that if you leave they'll never see the money you owe. Very often these things can be resolved with negotiation. If you're guilty, haggle over the fine and then pay up. If you think you've been framed, ask to go to the station and talk to the police chief. Ask them to show you the law you broke and make them explain what you did wrong. If this is too much hassle, just cough up the money, which is rarely more than $10 or $20, and be thankful that you can get all the traffic fines you want in Mexico and your insurance at home will never know about it.

## CAMPING

Camping in Baja can be a truly liberating experience. Federal law in Mexico is explicit that the beaches are public property and that camping is a public right. Forget about spending hours on some miserable 800 number begging a mechanized voice to please, please, give you a campsite. In Mexico, you don't need no stinking campsite. They may have the right to search your car without a warrant, but you have the legal right to camp anywhere on public property, and all beaches are public property. Don't test the limits of this right by trying to camp right in front of some giant resort hotel in Cabo, but if you stop at a place that looks nice to camp and there's nobody around to ask permission of, well, you don't need to ask permission. If you are on what appears to be private property (i.e., adjacent to someone's house), it's generally considerate to ask before setting up camp. Most of the time they'll look at you like you've just asked them if it's okay if you breathe the air. Very rarely will you get turned down, and in those cases I don't get on some high horse about my rights, since I'm not a Mexican citizen; I simply move along and find another spot.

The trick to happy camping in Baja is to follow the Boy Scout motto and be prepared. The number one priority, after the obvious one of enough water, is to provide for some sort of shade. I used to keep an old sail in my Landcruiser that, when tied off the roof rack and staked out to the ground, created a huge area of shade. I can't tell you how many afternoons I lay under that sail with a bucket of wet towels to drape over me and simply waited out the sun. It can be brutal even with shade. Without it, well, forget it.

There are many great campgrounds in Baja where you can rent a little palapa, build your fire, sit at a picnic table, etc. They can seem like a real luxury after spending weeks on some remote wind-blown beach. However, most formal camping setups in Baja are geared toward the recreational vehicle set. To me, there's something disturbing about driving 600 miles into a foreign country only to end up camped with a bunch of other gringos. Not to mention that I don't like the sense of racial entrenchment that sometimes settles over these little colonial outposts of middle America— although many people find them perfect for exactly those reasons.

## PESOS VS. DOLLARS

Many people travel in Baja and never bother to exchange money. Especially in the northern extreme of the state, it's entirely possible to function in a dollar economy. But I recommend that you exchange your dollars for pesos and try to integrate into the Mexican economy more. In the long run it will probably save you money, as paying in dollars immediately tags you as a *turista*. You may also find yourself wanting to buy a meal in some small town where the proprietor simply won't take dollars. A good place to exchange dollars is to buy gas at the local PEMEX in dollars and get change in pesos. They generally give a fair rate and don't hit you with service charges. Hotels are generally the worst. Banks and *cambios* (currency exchange houses) vary widely. And during periods when the peso is devaluing quickly, don't change all your dollars into pesos at once.

# The Lay of the Land

Baja is a wonderful place for a journey. At almost a thousand miles in length, this peninsula is roughly as long as the entire American state of California and varies in width from 26 miles wide near La Paz to 144 miles wide in the middle. Surrounded by the **Pacific** to the west and the **Sea of Cortez** to the east, the Baja Peninsula totals almost 2,000 miles of shoreline. Add in the numerous islands along both coasts and it is significantly more.

Within its interior are seven major mountain ranges (or sierras) ranging up to 10,154 feet tall at Picacho del Diablo (Devil's Peak) in the **Sierra San Pedro Martir** west of San Felipe. Some of these mountains create the spine of the peninsula; others, like **the Sierra La Giganta** near Loreto, tower over the ocean shore like sentinels guarding against seaborne attack. Virtually all the mountains in Baja are extremely steep and cut with rugged canyons. They are difficult places to know; few trails enter their realm and the elements discourage all but the most enthusiastic explorers.

The sierras are separated by vast expanses of flat or rolling desert, the largest segment being the combination of the **Desierto Central** and the **Desierto de Vizcaino,** which span the border between Baja Norte and Baja Sur, the two states that comprise Baja.

Most visitors in Baja look toward the sea. It's understandable, since exploring the inland regions demands so much of you and since both ocean coasts are such fantastic places.

The Pacific and the Sea of Cortez are separated by as much as 150 miles and as little as 25 miles, with an average width of about 70 miles. But despite being as close as the crow flies, the two seas are quite distinct, particularly in their northern coasts.

The Pacific from the U.S. border to the tip of the **Vizcaino Peninsula,** which juts west from the juncture of Baja Norte and Baja Sur near the town of Guerrero Negro, is a cold ocean. The southbound California current keeps a steady flow of water moving down from the north Pacific, and, despite roasting air temperatures, the water stays between 50° and 75°F year-round. In fact, it's entirely possible to travel south from San Diego and find that you need warmer wetsuits in Baja than you did up north.

South of the Vizcaino Peninsula, which juts northwest into the Pacific near Guerrero Negro, the ocean climate changes dramatically. Suddenly, the water warms up and you begin to see more tropical species. In the summer, the water of the southern half of the Pacific coast of Baja can be downright too warm.

Also, as you follow the Pacific coast from north to south, you'll notice that the northern coast tends toward high bluffs and cliffs. As you reach the more southern regions there are more dunes and flat areas. The coast is sculpted with an incredible array of islands, points, bays, and long beaches.

The **Sea of Cortez,** while only a short distance away, is a completely different ball of wax. Shallower and with very little exchange of water with the Pacific, the Sea of Cortez is warmer than the Pacific at almost every given point down the coast. Where the Pacific regularly bears the brunt of huge surf, the Sea of Cortez is often totally placid. At worst it works up a mean storm chop, but nothing like the huge swells that hit the other side. The water on the Cortez side is often startlingly clear, a vibrant turquoise

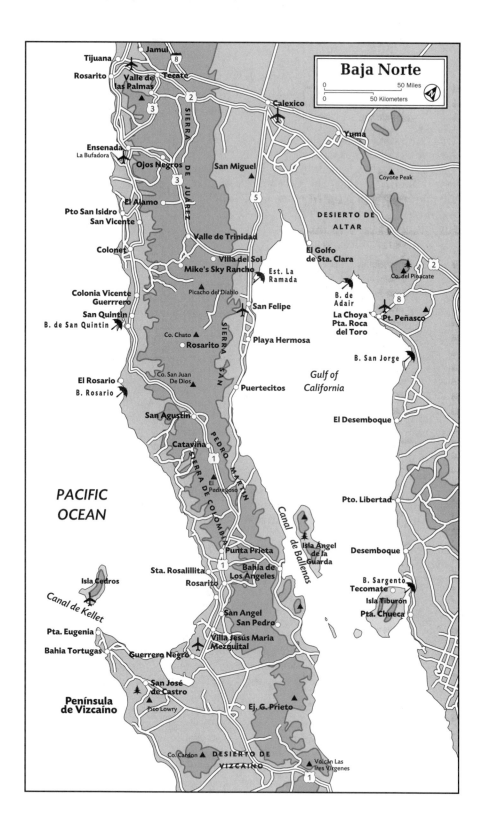

# Baja Norte

0      50 Miles
0      50 Kilometers

Jamul

Tijuana
Rosarito
Valle de
las Palmas
Tecate
8
2
3
Calexico

Yuma

SIERRA DE JUAREZ

Ensenada
La Bufadora
Ojos Negros
3
San Miguel

Coyote Peak

El Alamo
5

Pto San Isidro
San Vicente

DESIERTO DE
ALTAR

Colonet
Valle de Trinidad

El Golfo
de Sta. Clara
2
Co. del Pinacate

Villa del Sol
Mike's Sky Rancho
Est. La
Ramada
Picacho del Diablo

B. de
Adair
8

Colonia Vicente
Guerrrero
San Felipe
La Choya
Pta. Roca
del Toro
Pt. Peñasco

San Quintin
B. de San Quintin
Co. Chato
Rosarito
SIERRA SAN
Playa Hermosa

B. San Jorge

El Rosario
B. Rosario
Co. San Juan
De Dios
Puertecitos

Gulf of
California

El Desemboque

San Agustin

PACIFIC
OCEAN

Cataviña
1
SIERRA DE COLOMBRE
El
Pedregoso
SIERRA MAR

Pto. Libertad

Isla Ángel
de la
Guarda

Canal de Ballenas

Desemboque

Punta Prieta
1
Sta. Rosalillita
Rosarito
Bahía de
Los Angeles

B. Sargento
Tecomate
Isla Tiburón
Pta. Chueca

Isla Cedros
Canal de Kellet

San Angel
San Pedro

Pta. Eugenia
Bahia Tortugas
Guerrero Negro
Villa Jesús Maria
Mezquital

San José
de Castro
Pico Lowry

Península
de Vizcaíno
Ej. G. Prieto

Co. Cardon
DESIERTO DE
VIZCAINO
Volcán Las
Tres Vírgenes
1

color that balances beautifully with the starkness of the Baja landscape. Tides run heavy in the Cortez, particularly in the northern half, where they can vary as much as 25 feet in a day. It's not at all uncommon for unprepared boaters to anchor their vessel and paddle ashore in the dinghy only to return 4 hours later and find both their boat and their dinghy left high and dry, with the nearest ocean a quarter mile away.

For travelers, the most important reality in Baja is the **Transpeninsular Highway,** a.k.a. **Highway 1.** Until completion of the paved road in 1973, driving much farther than Ensenada was the realm of hardened desert rats only. Beyond San Quentin, even the hardened desert rats began to think twice. To drive all the way to Los Cabos took forever, and was a brutal test of your vehicle and your own sanity.

The road opened Baja up to more casual travel. It's still not entirely for the faint of heart. The "highway" is a two-lane road with no shoulder along much of its length, which you share with everything from wild horses to roaring semi-trucks and sun-addled motor homers. In my experience the truck drivers are vastly capable and considerate, but piles of wreckage at the bottom of almost every steep, hairpin turn drop-off attest to the fact that they're not ALL so capable.

The road was pushed through Baja following the path of least resistance. On a patch of land like this, that means it only rarely runs near the coast. Mostly, once you're south of San Quentin, it runs more or less down the middle of the peninsula, winding and swerving to avoid major geological obstacles.

In northern Baja, which has a vastly varied geology ranging from high granite peaks to flat dry lakes and coastal mangrove swamps, you've got a larger population and more cross-peninsular

traffic. Roads like **Mexico highways 2 and 3** make it possible to traverse from one side of the peninsula to the other without it becoming a major production. Below the Ensenada turnoff for Mexico 3, which leads southeast to San Felipe, any crossways traffic from one coast to the other tends to involve difficult dirt road driving.

While I'd encourage anyone with a sense of adventure to drive the length of the Transpeninsular, as tourism has become more developed, we've reached a point where most of the visitors to Baja arrive by plane. Oddly enough, before the road was built, most visitors arrived by plane too, but the construction of the road allowed the kind of infrastructure—hotels, golf courses, condos—that industrial tourism depends upon, therefore drawing more people to fly in.

The busiest airport and destination is **Los Cabos,** meaning San José Del Cabo and Cabo San Lucas. Los Cabos, or more simply, Cabo, is a big destination for fishermen, divers, and tequila drinkers. La Paz, a much bigger city, has less traffic but is a great destination to fly into if you wish to go sailing, diving, or sea kayaking without the spring-break atmosphere of Cabo San Lucas.

The next viable airport is **Loreto,** a city the Mexican tourist development agency has been trying to turn into the next Cancún for about 20 years. They're failing miserably, which is good news. Loreto is so much cooler than Cancún will ever be and is a great place to fly into if you want a sleepy little fishing village on the Sea of Cortez for fishing, sea kayaking, and diving. It's also a good staging point for surfing trips to Scorpion Bay across the peninsula, whale-watching expeditions to Bahia Magdalena, or ambitious treks into the Sierra La Giganta.

The northern half of the state is largely without commercial air service,

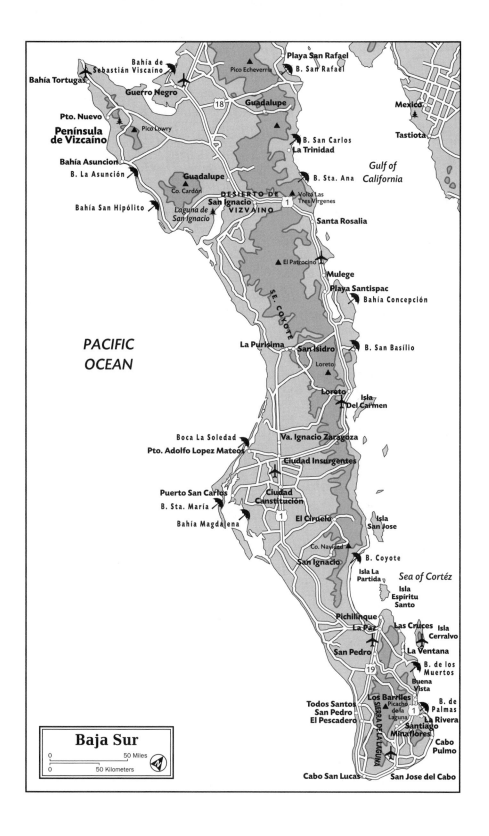

Bahía Tortugas

Bahía de Sebastián Viscaíno

Playa San Rafael
B. San Rafael
Pico Echeverria

Guerro Negro
18
Guadalupe

Mexico

Pto. Nuevo
Península de Vizcaíno
Pico Lowry

Tastiota

B. San Carlos
La Trinidad

Gulf of California

Bahía Asuncion
B. La Asunción

Guadalupe
Co. Cardón

B. Sta. Ana

DESIERTO DE
San Ignacio   VIZCAINO

Volcá Las Tres Virgenes
1

Bahía San Hipólito

Laguna de San Ignacio

Santa Rosalia

El Patrocino
Mulege
Playa Santispac
Bahía Concepción

SE. COYOTE

PACIFIC OCEAN

La Purisima
San Isidro
Loreto

B. San Basílio

Loreto
Isla Del Carmen

Boca La Soledad
Pto. Adolfo Lopez Mateos

Va. Ignacio Zaragoza

Ciudad Insurgentes

Puerto San Carlos
B. Sta. María

Ciudad Constitución

Isla San Jose

Bahía Magdalena

El Ciruelo

Co. Navidad

San Ignacio

B. Coyote

Isla La Partida

Sea of Cortéz

Isla Espíritu Santo

Pichilingue
La Paz

Las Cruces   Isla Cerralvo

San Pedro

La Ventana

19

B. de los Muertos

Buena Vista

Todos Santos
San Pedro
El Pescadero

Los Barriles
Picacho de la Laguna
1

SIERRA DE LA LAGUNA

B. de Palmas
La Rivera
Santiago
Minaflores

Cabo Pulmo

Cabo San Lucas

San Jose del Cabo

## Baja Sur

0        50 Miles
0        50 Kilometers

other than **Tijuana,** which has a huge international airport. But to visit just about anywhere between Tijuana and Loreto, you'd better be prepared for a long drive or have your own airplane. Or, if you're feeling extravagant, you could charter a plane.

The climate of Baja is a mixed bag. Certain places, like Ensenada and San Quentin, lie right on the temperature-regulating waters of the Pacific and rarely vary from a comfortable range of 55°F in the winter to 70°F in the summer. The Sierra San Pedro Martir in the northern part of the peninsula actually receives considerable snowfall in the winter. Get away from the moderating influence of the cold Pacific, however, or the cooling effect of high altitude, and the picture changes dramatically. In the inland desert and along the Sea of Cortez and the southern Pacific coast, I've seen it so hot and humid that there was nothing to do but try to siesta and wait for the afternoon to cool down. Rainfall is generally scarce, coming to the north during the winter and hitting the southern cape during hurricane season of the late summer. Winds can blow up any time and are sometimes so strong they'll knock over tents or send surfboards sliding along the beach; heck, I once

watched a particularly vicious gust blow a fully loaded cast iron skillet full of home fries off a Coleman stove and onto the ground. Winds like this can be unrelenting, particularly in the winter, and can lay even the best-laid plans to waste.

There's no magic formula to determine **when to visit Baja.** However, a good rule of thumb is: You can visit the northern Pacific coast year-round, with summer being the warmest; the inland mountain ranges are best just after the rainy season stops, which means spring for the northern ranges and fall for the Sierra de la Laguna on the cape. The Sea of Cortez coast is pleasant every time of year except during the summer, when it can be unbearably hot (though this is the best time for diving and fishing) and when the worst of the winter winds blow down from Arizona and Utah. The Cape region is again moderated by the fact that it's surrounded by water. Summer is hot but regular afternoon rain showers keep things in control. Occasionally, a *chubasco*, a tropical storm or hurricane, will spin ashore during the late summer and make things very interesting. Winter here is absolutely perfect, with dry, warm days and almost endless sunshine.

# 12

# BAJA NORTE: Tijuana, Rosarito & Ensenada

HE 60-MILE COASTAL CORRIDOR BETWEEN THE AMERICAN BOR-
der and Ensenada has become a major expatriate community of gringos who want beach houses but are unable to
afford the stratospheric prices that coastal property in the
United States costs. For a fraction of the price that it would cost in San
Diego, condos and housing developments along this entire stretch blos-
somed overnight like mushrooms after NAFTA loosened restrictions on
ownership of Mexican property by foreigners.

**Tijuana** itself has also boomed. Once a sleepy little border town, it's now
home to more than a million permanent residents and many more who are
just passing through on their way north or south. It's a sprawling and, by
most standards, dirty city, but as a case study in what happens when the
third world rubs right up against the first world, it's an interesting place.
For the scope of this book, there's very little of interest to the outdoor
adventurer other than getting across the border and getting the heck out
of town.

There are several nice beaches and surf breaks within a few miles of
Tijuana, but before you wax up a board and jump in, take a minute to

304 Baja Norte: Tijuana, Rosarito & Ensenada

consider that Tijuana has 1,000,000 residents and virtually zero effective sewer treatment. Now put that board back on the roof and keep driving south. I can't tell you how many times I've driven past great waves along this stretch of coast chanting to myself, "Hep-a-tit-us, staph-in-fec-tion, perfect-surf, keep-on-driving."

Things start to look up as you leave Tijuana and head toward **Rosarito.** Rosarito has long been a favorite weekend getaway for Southern Californians who just want to scratch the surface of Mexico, drink a little tequila, speak a little Spanish, and head home on Sunday. For many years the main draw to Rosarito was its long, sandy beach and the Rosarito Beach Hotel, which in the '40s and '50s was the glamorous hangout of Lana Turner, Rita Hayworth, Spencer Tracy, Gregory Peck, and numerous other Hollywood glitterati. For decades it looked like Rosarito had seen the last of its movie star days, until James Cameron went looking for a sound stage and water tank where he could film *Titanic.* When he found that there were none that met his criteria, he convinced his studio to build one on the beach just south of Rosarito. During filming, a nearly full-sized replica of the ship was visible along the Rosarito shore and Leonardo DiCaprio sightings were common.

*Titanic,* as we all know, is history, but the movie studio in Rosarito (actually, in the tiny village of Popotla) is going great guns and specializes in water scenes and stunts. The studio is closely guarded and closed to the public, but keep your eyes peeled, you never know who you might bump into in town.

**Ensenada** is the first town south of the border that feels real to me, in the sense that its existence is centered around something other than separating American tourists from their money. There are plenty of people who will separate you from your *dólares* here, don't get me wrong, but there's also a booming economy based on fishing, shipping, and all the other industries of a large port town. The seafood market here is amazing, and the fish tacos from the street stands are some of the best in the world. It's not surprising that there's such great seafood, since Ensenada is the finest harbor on the entire Pacific coast of Baja and the home base of a huge fishing fleet.

There's also a lot more of interest to the outdoors crowd here. North of town there are a few good surf breaks and some nice beaches. The fishing from here is really good, and there's excellent diving and kayaking to be had on Punta Banda, the rocky point of land that anchors the southern end of Todos Santos Bay, the large bay that cradles Ensenada.

# What to Do & Where to Do It

As I mentioned earlier, there are fine beaches in Tijuana, but you wouldn't want to touch the water. The first place south of Tijuana of much merit as a beach is **Rosarito.** Here you'll find a bustling summer scene with lots of vendors, restaurants, and horseback riding on the sand; and rentals of surfboards, boogie boards, beach umbrellas, etc. It, too, is pretty dirty, but the water quality seems to be looking up.

My favorite beach in the area between the border and Ensenada is **La Fonda.** A big creek valley opens up to a wide, sandy beach. Two hotels, a campground, and a couple of restaurants sit on the cliff to the north. Surfing can be pretty good and it's a nice place to spend time on the beach.

Inside Todos Santos Bay, there are a number of long beaches, but once again you'll run into problems with water quality. A few big industrial plants dump effluent into the water near Ensenada, and, like Tijuana, the local sewage treatment isn't all it could be. Toward the southern end of the bay, however, things are cleaner and there are several nice beaches that have been developed into beach clubs. The best is **Playa Punta Banda,** which you can reach by following signs for the La Jolla Beach Camp. It's a very sheltered spot and good for kids.

## CAMPING

Forget about beach camping anywhere between the border and Rosarito. It's just too built up. The first place I can recommend with a clean conscience is **Playa Saldamando,** 10 miles north of Ensenada. It's reached by a short but very steep dirt road that winds down to the beach just past El Mirador on the Tijuana-Ensenada Toll Road. Because the road is so rugged, motor homes and trailers can't make it down to the beach. It's a favorite campsite with surfers and divers. The famous Salsipuedes point break is nearby. Fees are really cheap, and with 100 campsites it doesn't fill up too quickly.

On the other side of Ensenada, the **La Jolla Beach Camp** welcomes tent campers, but it's pretty much a big tourist scene, not a rugged Baja experience. Still, you're near Punta Banda and it's a great, safe place if you just want to feel the sand under your toes.

On the Punta Banda Peninsula, you'll find several official campgrounds that are little more than a cleared space with virtually no supplies. Farther south, numerous side roads lead out to barely developed coastline where you can just find your own spot and camp.

For mountain camping, I suggest that you go to **Parque Nacional Constitución de 1857** (listed in the hiking section, p. 306). There, you'll find wonderful camping in a cool, high-mountain setting with a shallow lake nearby.

## OTHER LODGING

There are tons of large hotels in Rosarito and Tijuana, but the only places in the region that really suit my taste as small coastal inns are **Hotel La Fonda** (no phone; on the free road after you take the La Misión exit from the toll road) and **Hotel la Misión,** which has a U.S. reservation number (tel. 213/420-8500) and sits near the Hotel La Fonda. Both have great ocean views. The restaurant in Hotel La Fonda is one of the best in northern Baja.

## FISHING

**Ensenada Harbor** is the center of all commercial fishing in northern Baja. It's also a great spot for sportfishing. Several different charter operations offer everything from half-day *panga* charters for rockfish to multi-day, long-distance bluewater fishing trips for albacore, bluefin tuna, and other large pelagic gamefish.

You can find a number of operators just by parking at the harbor near the fish market and walking out onto the docks. Gordo's **Sportfishing** (tel. 8-3515 or 8-2377) is a well-respected fleet, as is the **Ensenada Clipper Fleet** (tel. 8-2185).

## HIKING

**Ensenada** is the gateway city to the Parque Nacional Constitución de 1857. Located on the spine of the Sierra de Juárez, the park was once a heavily used mining area. Now, most of the mines are defunct. In contrast to the dry and sometimes desolate surroundings of much of the northern peninsula, the 5,000-hectare preserve averages about 4,000 feet in altitude and is covered in places with pine forests. The most idiosyncratic thing, however, is the sight of a good-sized lake sitting in an alpine setting. The park has no developed trails other than a 6-mile one that circumnavigates the lake, Laguna Hanson, but there are endless opportunities for blazing your own. The lake is named after an early gringo miner who fell victim to his own house guest, another American, who killed him and allegedly ate poor Hanson after boiling his body in a giant cauldron. To get there, take Mexico Highway 3 south from Ensenada and exit at the graded dirt access road at Km 55. The park entrance road is gravel and generally well-maintained, but it can be really rough after a rainy year. It's 35 km (22 miles) to the park entrance. If it's staffed, you'll be asked for a modest entrance fee.

Farther southeast along Mexico 3 (at km 138 to be exact) is the turnoff to **Mike's Sky Rancho.** The Sky Ranch sits directly on the edge of the Parque Nacional Sierra San Pedro Martir at about 4,000 feet. Numerous hiking trails lead into remote canyons with perennial waterfalls and swimming holes. You can camp at the Sky Ranch or stay in the inexpensive lodging. Be forewarned that the Sky Ranch caters largely to an off-road vehicle and motorcycle crowd. If that offends you, it's better to know before you make the long drive.

The **Parque Nacional Sierra San Pedro Martir** is to Baja California what Yosemite is to Alta California. Almost 200,000 acres of the highest mountains on the peninsula have been preserved. The highest peak of all, Picacho del Diablo (Devil's Peak), rises to 10,154 feet. Views from the summit encompass both oceans and an immense stretch of land. Best of all, it's virtually unvisited, something that sets it apart from the normal national park experience in *Los Estados Unidos.*

Farther south on Highway 1 from Ensenada, you'll come to a signed turnoff for the park at km 140 soon after you pass the little town of **Colonet.** The sign also says OBSERVATORIO. Fill up with gas in Colonet, as there is no more to be had until you exit this way again, and reset your odometer at the turnoff. In between it's entirely possible to put on 150 gas-guzzling miles of rugged driving. It's 47 miles to the park entrance.

What you'll find is a high alpine realm of flower-speckled meadows, soaring granite peaks, and year-round creeks. Official trails are few and far between, but anyone who's good with a map and compass or even good at just wandering off and finding their way back can have a great time hiking. Cow trails are numerous (yes, cows in a national park). Four year-round creeks drain the park and make great destinations. **Picacho del Diablo** is a difficult but rewarding overnight hike and long scramble. Always remember that you're in one of the most rugged and remote places in all of Baja, and it's quite likely that if you get lost or hurt nobody is going to come looking for you.

## SEA KAYAKING

The rocky coastline of **Punta la Banda** is a favorite first kayaking trip for beginning ocean kayakers. There are several secluded beaches, sea caves, and terrific scenery. Many kayakers use La Bufadora as a launching point to head out to **Todos Santos Island.** It's about 7 miles from La Bufadora to the southern and largest island of the two Todos Santos Islands. The first 3 miles follow a rocky coast to the tip of Punta Banda. From here it's time to size up the wind, the waves, and the fog. If the coast is clear, take a compass heading and begin the 4-mile open water crossing. Bring water and camping gear to spend a night on the pristine island. **Southwest Sea Kayaks** (tel. 619/222-3616) in San Diego leads weekend trips to the island several times a year.

### SCUBA DIVING & SNORKELING

The little town of **La Bufadora** on the south side of Punta la Banda is the best diving for miles around. La Bufadora means "buffalo snort" in Spanish, but the fishermen who ply these waters have a much more lyrical explanation for this roaring blowhole on the edge of Baja's blue Pacific coast. According to local legend, a mother gray whale and her calf were just beginning their migration from the safety of Baja's San Ignacio Lagoon to Alaska. As they rounded Punta Banda, the curious calf squeezed into a sea cave, only to be trapped. The groan that this 70-foot high blowhole makes every time it erupts is the sound of the stranded calf still crying for his mother, and the tremendous spray is his spout.

La Bufadora is a great dive spot with thick kelp and wonderful sea life. Get underwater and zoom through lovely kelp beds and rugged rock formations covered in strawberry anemones and gypsy shawl nudibranchs. You may also spot spiny lobsters and numerous large fish. It's possible to swim right over to the blowhole, but use extreme caution in this area—you don't want to end up like that mythical whale calf. **La Bufadora Dive Shop** is located right on shore at the best entry point. They'll set you up with fills and advice. But they don't have a phone.

Several dive shops in Ensenada, including **Almar** at 149 Av. Macheros (tel. 8-3013), or **Baja Dive Expeditions** at the Baja Beach and Tennis Club (tel. 3-0220), will arrange boat dives to Todos Santos Island, which sits at the outer edge of Todos Santos Bay. The diving here is similar to the diving at Catalina or the other California Channel Islands—lots of fish, big kelp, urchins, and jagged underwater rock formations. The visibility varies widely depending on the swell.

### SURFING

Undoubtedly the most famous surf spot in all of Mexico is "Killers" at **Todos Santos Island.** Killers reemerged into the global spotlight in the winter of 1997–98, when it was the surprise location of the winning wave in the K2 Challenge, a worldwide contest to ride and photograph the winter's largest wave. Todos Santos had long ago fallen out of favor with the giant wave riding set in favor of places like Maverick's near Half Moon Bay, but you can bank on the fact that it's back in the limelight after dishing up a 30-footer that earned its lucky rider $50,000.

You don't have to be a maniac to ride Todos Santos. Killers is a very makeable wave for confident, competent surfers. Maybe not when it's 30 feet, but you don't have to ride it that big. Anything larger than head high can be great fun. To get there you need a boat. The hardcore Todos Santos regulars bring their own. The rest of us have to settle for hiring the local panga fleet to give us a lift. Generally, it's $100 for a panga for the day. You can ask around but that's pretty much the going rate, and you won't find the tightly knit Ensenada *pangueros* anxious to undercut each other. It's about 10 miles out to the island where you'll anchor and paddle into the lineup. It goes without saying that you must bring everything you'll need: food, water, sunscreen, etc. And ever since a friend of mine spent the most harrowing 3 hours of his life lost in the fog between the island and the harbor because the *panguero* didn't know how to use a compass, I'm a big proponent of carrying a hand-held GPS that will get you back to the harbor in a pinch.

Other less radical and easier-to-reach spots include **Popotla,** just south of Rosarito, where you'll walk to the beach through the Popotla trailer park; and **Calafia,** also just a mile or two south of Rosarito, where there's a reeling right point that can get extremely heavy. **San Miguel** is the point break just south of the final toll booth on the highway into Ensenada. It's an excellent wave but generally crowded, and the scene around the campground there can get really sketchy.

Better surfing lies an hour or more south of Ensenada, where **Puerto Erendrina, Puerto San Isidro, San Antonio Del Mar,** and **Punta San Jacinto** all get good waves during northwest and south swells.

# San Felipe ◆ What to Do & Where to Do It

Little San Felipe (11,000 residents) is the beach town of choice for many Arizona and eastern California residents. A natural headland and an artificial harbor make it the home base of a large commercial shrimping fleet. From the perspective of the traveler, San Felipe is a slightly bedraggled stepsister to towns like Loreto, Mulege, and Los Cabos. Mostly, what recommends it are good fishing and a beach within a couple of hours of the inland deserts of Alta California and Arizona. It's a big favorite with the dune buggy and dirt bike crowd, and during spring break it hops with students from Arizona State, but mostly it's a sleepy little place that's a good stop for

supplies before you head to more remote quarters.

## BEACHES

The beach in San Felipe is heavily influenced by the extreme high and low tides at this end of the Sea of Cortez. A beach that might be a lovely swimming spot at high tide turns into a giant rock garden or mudflat when the tide goes out. The best beaches lie far to the south, but large sand dune fields and long beaches stretch both north and south of town. The beach in town is sandy, suitable for at least sun tanning even if the tide is out.

## CAMPING & LODGING

Numerous fishing camps line the coast in both directions from San Felipe. I have camped for free in the dunes just south of town, but dune buggies woke me up early. For tent campers I recommend driving south toward **Puertecitos.** The first official campground you'll encounter is **Rancho Vista Hermosa.** It's 12 miles from San Felipe, which is actually a good thing. Though it's a trailer park, tenters are welcome and won't feel entirely out of place. **Punta Baja** is another good option that's farther south. The sign on the main road will tip you off to a mile-long spur that takes you down to the beach. Fees here are minimal and the services are, too. There is a campground actually in Puertecitos, a neat little town. You can eat at the little cafe, charter pangas, hike in the hills, and kayak from this base. Once you pass Puertecitos, the options open up. There are still beach camps along most of the road-accessible coastline, but the density is a lot lower. Drive around until you find a suitable spot.

## FISHING

Fishing was one of the first draws to tourists who came down from the United States to San Felipe. This far north in the Sea of Cortez you find an interesting mixture of fish. Some species, like calico bass, would be much more likely found in the kelp forests of Southern California than the rocky shore of San Felipe Bay, but they are here. The big gamefish of choice are white sea bass and yellowtail, which are caught throughout the summer months.

Panga trips can be arranged from several different outfits at the San Felipe Harbor. **Tommy's** (tel. 7-1120) and **Alex's** (tel. 7-1052) are two of the better known.

You may also launch your own boat here at the harbor to explore the Sea of Cortez on your own. Some people use this as a launching point to cruise the entire Sea of Cortez.

## HIKING

The eastern escarpment of the Sierra de San Pedro Martir lies to the west of San Felipe. A dirt road leads west from San Felipe to Rancho Santa Clara. From there it continues another 9 km west to the road's dead end at the mouth of **Cañon el Diablito,** one of the many side canyons that drains El Picacho del Diablo. A trail leads up the canyon where you'll find numerous swimming holes and waterfalls. It's rugged scrambling, and there is one spot where you must use a steel cable bolted in place to help negotiate the slippery granite face of a big waterfall blocking your way. You can actually reach the summit of **Picacho**

**del Diablo** by continuing all the way up this canyon. Count on at least 2 days up and 2 days back. A more comfortable overnight is the trip 7 miles up Cañon el Diablito to **Campo Noche,** a cool and comfortable campsite with plentiful water and swimming holes.

## SCUBA DIVING & SNORKELING

The extreme tides and the bad visibility of this end of the Sea of Cortez make it a bad place for diving. If you decide to strike out on your own, time your excursion so you catch a rising tide and get out before it drops. That's when you'll see the most fish and have the best visibility.

## SEA KAYAKING

The immediate surroundings of San Felipe are boring with a capital B as far as a sea kayaking destination. The first 9 miles south of town are flat, backed by sand dunes, built up with numerous fishing camps and hotels, and subject to incredible tidal variations. Still, many people put in right on the beach in downtown San Felipe to begin their Sea of Cortez journeys.

Given my druthers, I'd put in farther down the coast. **Punta Estrella,** 10 miles south of town, is the beginning of a rocky and more interesting coast. Put in at the fish camp just north for a downwind paddle. The most common destination is long-distance destination **Puertecitos,** which would be a 40-mile, multi-day trip. You can also put in or take out at numerous beach camps along the way for good day paddling.

A much less frequented part of the coast is the 17-mile coast between

Puertecitos and **El Huerfanito.** Rock and gravel beaches framed by high cliffs and bluffs line much of this route. Though the road is not that far inland, you gain a sense of remoteness here. In particular, you'll feel like you're paddling through the land that time forgot as you pass the sheer black face of now dormant **Volcán Prieto** (The Dark Volcano), which cuts the Puertecitos road off from the shoreline and drops straight into the sea. You'll know you're reaching the camp of El Huerfanito when you see and smell the guano-encrusted rocks of tiny Isla Huerfanito. An airstrip and some houses with a few surrounding trees mark the little expatriate fishing colony there, and a nice beach awaits your landing.

# Bahía de Los Angeles ✦ What to Do & Where to Do It

The tiny village of Bahía de Los Angeles would not merit mention were it not the gateway to one of the loveliest spots in Baja Norte. The bay is encircled by 15 distinct islands ranging in size from tiny **Isla Los Gemelitos** to gigantic, 45-mile-long **Isla Ángel de la Guarda,** which rises like a foreign shore from the sea. In and around these islands run some of the richest fishing and diving waters in the entire state. To make it even better, the mainland shore is fronted by perfect sandy beaches. Fishing, diving, swimming, nature watching, and sea kayaking are all fantastic in the area. The numerous islands generate upwellings of nutrient-rich water from the depths of the sea. An entire food chain is supplied by this wealth, including big fish and whales.

There is no phone service and there is only a single road into the Bay of Los Angeles, a 42-mile spur road that separates from the Transpeninsular approximately two-thirds of the way down the peninsula. It's a long day's drive from the border or a comfortable 2-day drive.

## CAMPING & LODGING

You can camp almost anywhere on the entire coast of the Bahía de Los Angeles. Several trailer parks cater to the motor home set. **Campo Gecko** has 10 campsites with palapas and is the best for tent camping. Pitch your tent under the palapa and it'll stay cool and let you sleep in the morning. Fees vary from $3 to $5 per night depending on the season. It's 3.5 miles south of the main village in Bahí de Los Angeles on the beach. There are toilets and showers and a boat ramp, too.

Do-it-yourselfers will like **Punta La Gringa,** which is up on the northern end of the bay, 6 miles north of the main village. It's a narrow spit of land that juts south into the bay and is one of the nearest spots to the offshore islands for those planning on doing some sea kayaking. Though it's named after an American woman who tried to turn this spot into a formal campground, she went out of business, and now it's free and first-come, first-served.

There are several hotels in Bahía de Los Angeles, none of which is a particular standout. They're all functional and cheap. **Motel Vitta Vitta** does have a swimming pool to recommend it during the hot summer months, but it's off the beach. **Guillermo's** has a few large rooms with multiple beds located right on the bay. Finally, **Casa Díaz** has a large bayfront hotel but the rooms are nothing to write home about. Since there are no phones, you just have to take your chances and shop around once you get here. Prices range from $25 to $55 a night and fluctuate wildly depending on demand.

## FISHING

Bahía de Los Angeles is one of those legendary places where the ocean boils with feeding frenzies and fish are actually known to periodically leap into your boat unbidden. Shore casting will produce a lot of smaller fish, but the big action is reached either by launching your own boat at one of the three concrete ramps in the area, or by hiring a panga.

**Guillermo's** is a catchall trailer park, hotel, restaurant, store, and bar that also arranges sportfishing trips. There is no phone number, since there are no phones here, period, but you can find them quite easily along the beachfront in Bahía de Los Ángeles.

## HIKING

The **Sierra de Asamblea** is the backdrop to the Bay of Los Angeles, and there are several good hikes to be had here. Pick any of the numerous canyons behind town and start exploring. While the going can get really rough, you'll have a hard time getting lost if you just turn around and make like water heading downhill. Soon enough you'll come out back at the bay.

A sometimes-resident naturalist divides his time between Bahía de Los Ángeles and Alta California. His name is Raúl Espinosa. In the Bay of Los Angeles, inquire after him at **Campo Turística La Ventana.** In the United States call 818/899-7876. He will lead guided hikes to old mission sites and rock art, and also lead interpretive nature hikes, for $85 a day.

## SCUBA DIVING & SNORKELING

The shoreline underwater terrain of Bahía de Los Angeles is pretty much a giant field of sand. While it seems like a strange thing to snorkel over at first, you can actually find a lot of interesting shells and peculiar fish and eels that live on the sand bottom.

Boat or kayak-based divers will want to head out to the islands inside the bay. Sites here are loaded with invertebrate life and swirling clouds of baitfish. Of particular note is a large sea lion colony at **Calaveras rocks.** Much like the famous **Los Islotes** near La Paz, this is a spot where you can snorkel and scuba with frolicking young sea lions. Keep your distance from the actually haul-out rocks, as you don't want to disturb the sleeping animals, and the giant bulls might just get testy if you invade their turf.

Spearfishing for yellowtail, white sea bass, and grouper can be phenomenal.

At press time the status of any commercial dive operation here was in question. Generally, someone has a working compressor in town. Other than that, bring everything you need. You can hire pangas that will give you a ride to any island destination, but don't expect full dive-master service.

## SEA KAYAKING

This may be the single best place on earth to introduce a beginner to open water crossings. The numerous islands provide no shortage of glamorous destinations, and they're sprinkled a convenient distance apart. No single crossing within the bay should be more than 3 miles if you play your cards right.

Favorite destinations are **Isla la Ventana** and **Cerra y Llave Islands,** where sheltered beaches offer great camping. You can spend days hopping from island to island without much worry about anything except finding the next beautiful cove.

For an excellent guide to kayaking in the bay, go to **Guillermo's** and ask for a copy of the area notes that were put together by a San Diego sea kayaking club. The notes give many excellent tips for navigating the area.

While there are occasional rental kayaks you can hustle up at some of the trailer parks in this spot, it's better to bring your own. One company, **Elakah! Expeditions** of Bellingham, Washington (tel. 206/734-7270), leads 10-day island-hopping trips in the bay.

The ultimate challenge for hardcore sea kayakers here is to do a stepping-stone crossing of the entire Sea of Cortez beginning here and ending up in Bahía Kino on the mainland.

## WILDLIFE VIEWING

Once upon a time Bahía de los Angeles was an important center of the sea turtle meat and egg industry. Fortunately, those days are over and it's now thecenter of sea turtle conservation efforts.

A **conservation center and turtle breeding facility** lie just north of Punta La Gringa. You can visit it; donations for the program are much appreciated. Divers and kayakers frequently have encounters with the lovely green, hawksbill, leatherback, and loggerhead turtles that live in the area.

For guided boat trips to see turtles, whales, dolphins, and basking sharks, contact Raúl Espinosa. In the Bay of Los Angeles inquire after him at **Campo Turística La Ventana.** In the United States, call 818/899-7876. He runs day trips on a super panga to see virtually any species you request.

# 13

# BAJA SUR: Los Cabos, La Paz, Loreto & Mulege

RIOR TO THE OPENING OF THE TRANSPENINSULAR HIGHWAY IN 1973, Baja California Sur was the most geographically isolated region in all of Mexico. Hundreds of miles of hostile desert and roads that at times devolved into little more than donkey tracks kept all but the most hardy from journeying down the peninsula. Baja Sur's capital city, La Paz, thrived through its maritime association with the mainland and traded on the wealth of the Sea of Cortez to sustain hundreds of years of history. San José del Cabo was an important spot for southbound sailing ships to stock up on water, and other towns like Todos Santos and Santa Rosalia sustained themselves through growing sugar cane and copper mining, respectively.

American sportsmen had clued into the great big-game fishing around the cape many years before the highway opened. The famous Hotel Palmilla opened way back in 1956 and attracted the likes of John Wayne and his pals, who would fly down in their private planes to chase the giant marlin and hard-hitting dorado of the cape. But it wasn't until the road connected the border with the tip of Baja that word really leaked out about what a great region this is. Even then it took a long time for things to start changing.

My first visit to southern Baja was in 1987, as a college kid. We flew into San José del Cabo and took a cab to a friend's condo, at the time one of only about 50 in the whole cape. We fished and swam and dove and stumbled around the dirt streets of Cabo San Lucas tipsy on tequila. It was a tiny town you could walk across in 10 minutes. Our favorite *taquería* sat right by the harbor, where twin brothers would greet us nightly and stuff us full of shrimp tacos and homemade bean soup.

One early morning my girlfriend and I were swimming on a remote beach when I noticed two men sitting in a tiny thatched hut scanning the area with binoculars. At first I thought they were just a couple of lechers, but they were way too purposeful about what they were doing. I walked up the hill and asked what they were looking for.

"We're the guards," they said.

I looked around: nothing but cactus, rock, and beach for miles in either direction. "What are you guarding?"

"The land."

"Uh, yeah, I can see that, but what are you guarding it from?"

"So that someone doesn't come here and build on it."

I shook their hands and wished them *buena suerte*. When I told my girlfriend what they'd said we had a good laugh. What a bunch of *locos!* They think someone might come build a hotel on their *jefe*'s land while they're not looking! Hah!

If only I'd known then what I know now, I might have signed on as a guard too.

Fast forward a decade. NAFTA comes, property ownership laws in Mexico become more lenient, Americans in droves hear about the beauty of the cape, the peso plummets to the point

that Americans can practically afford to pay someone to pick the sand grains out of their hair. That beach now is buried under an avalanche of time-share condominiums. The cactus and rock landscape that I gazed out over is now a golf course. Cabo San Lucas is completely unrecognizable—streets paved, cars everywhere, my favorite taquería replaced by a Hard Rock Cafe, and tall hotels block the view of the harbor.

Most of the Mexicans I talk to are happy about this progress. In a country beset by economic troubles, unemployment is virtually unheard of in the cape, and wages are double or triple what they are elsewhere. Those two guys sitting in that shack are probably real estate tycoons by now, and I can't fault them their prosperity. But when I look at the homogeneous industrial tourism that's taken over the corridor between Cabo San Lucas and San José del Cabo, I can't help but mourn for what once was here.

## The Lay of the Land

Baja California Sur is a study in contrasts. The place names say a lot. On the one hand, you've got **Puerto Escondido** (Hidden Port) lying below the **Sierra La Giganta** (Range of the Giants). On the other are places like **El Cien,** a *pueblo* so lacking anything of distinction that it's named after the kilometer sign along the highway. (See "Baja Sur" map on page 301.)

The obvious draw to southern Baja is the ocean; some of the best beaches in the world are here. There's also another world to be found for the hardy few willing to explore the inland regions: hidden painted caves, waterfall-filled canyons, and even a few pine-forested mountaintops. The highest point in Southern Baja is the **Sierra de la Laguna,** the range of peaks that begins just north of Los Cabos and divides the southern peninsula roughly in two. Don't even think about trying to travel north-south through this range, but it is possible to hike east-west along the prevailing drainages.

As far as driving goes, **Highway 1** through Baja Sur spends most of its time inland, with the exception of the area from Santa Rosalia to just south of Mulege and around Loreto, La Paz, and Los Barriles. Mostly, though, it cuts through remote and remarkable desert. The only place at all where Highway 1 comes close to the Pacific in Baja Sur is where it doglegs over to **Ciudad Constitución** between Loreto and La Paz. Even here you're a few miles from **Bahía Magdalena** and separated from the open Pacific by that bay. Dirt roads lead north of this area into remote stretches of coast frequented mostly by surfers.

Recently, the Mexican government paved and "improved" **Highway 19,** which leads down the Pacific side of the Sierra de La Laguna. It's actually a shorter, more direct route between La Paz and Los Cabos now and has increased traffic through the towns of Todos Santos and Pescadero considerably. It has also made it entirely reasonable to get a rental car in either La Paz or Los Cabos and circumnavigate the entire lower peninsula.

Finally, the finest and most endangered unpolished gem of a driving route on the cape is the East Cape Road, which follows the coast from San José del Cabo all the way to La Ribera. It looks short on a map but is a punishing washboard that takes all day to drive. Just when you think you can't take any more shaking and bouncing, you'll see another lovely cove, another perfect swimming spot, and you'll want to stop for a while. Let's keep our fingers crossed that any and all plans to improve

this side of the cape fail miserably. It's perfect the way it is.

# Los Cabos ◆ What to Do & Where to Do It

## BEACHES

It used to be you couldn't throw a stone between San José del Cabo and Cabo San Lucas without hitting a lovely beach. The beaches are still nice, but your rock would probably hit a condo or a luxury hotel now.

Bear in mind that the cape is really exposed to surf. Depending on the time of year, the beaches here can be getting hammered by big grinding waves, the type that make most people take one look and stay on the beach. It's south swells that create these conditions, and they generally arrive between May and October. The other 6 months of the year it can be as placid as a lake. Regardless, you can generally find a sheltered place to swim or snorkel. The following are my favorites:

◆ **Playa del Amor.** With a name like that, you have to love it. This little sand spit is reachable by water taxi from the marina in Cabo San Lucas. Though it's definitely a tourist stop, it's a world apart from the hustle of Cabo San Lucas itself. Bring all the food, water, etc. you'll need for the day, since there's nothing here but sand and perfectly clear water. Bring a mask and snorkel, too, to explore around the rocky outcroppings that make this area famous.

◆ **Playa Santa Maria.** This cove is the Cabo equivalent of Oahu's Hanauma Bay. A circular cove protects a series of coral reefs. Within the reef structure there are zillions of colorful tropical fish. They seem to get larger the farther toward deep water you head. Since it's so well protected, even from summer swells, this is a great place to head year-round. It's 12 km (6.5 miles) east of Cabo San Lucas below the ultra-exclusive Hotel Twin Dolphin. You must walk through the hotel grounds to get to the beach, but since beach access is a guaranteed right in Mexico, there's nothing they can do to stop you. Don't, however, park in the hotel parking lot. Taxi is actually a good way to avoid any parking hassles, or simply park your rental car on the access road to the hotel.

◆ **Playa Palmilla.** The Hotel Palmilla was the first resort built in the cape region way back in the 1950s. It's easy to see why they picked this spot. Punta Mirador protects the beach from wind and swell. Rock and coral reefs abound. A small sport shop will rent you anything from a kayak to a snorkel. Surfers will want to walk or drive down to the east end of this beach, which is where you'll find the surf spots known as The Rock, Old Man's, and Zipper's, respectively. To reach Playa Palmilla, take the turn-off for Hotel Palmilla 5 km southwest of San José del Cabo. Don't drive all the way out to the hotel, but instead park where you see the boat launch and beach rental stand on your left. There's also a bar and snack shack here.

◆ **East Cape Beaches.** From San José del Cabo, Highway 1 heads north, inland, while the rugged East Cape road continues to hug the coast. Anyone with a fetish for lonely, beautiful beaches owes themselves a trip up this way. There are two ways to approach this stretch. One is to simply keep driving east from San José. The other is to take Highway 1 north to Las Cuevas and then head down the East Cape Road. The two most famous spots along this coast are Cabo Pulmo and Bahía Los Frailes. Cabo Pulmo at mile 24.6 (heading south) is now the site of a small town, dive shop, gear rental, restaurants, etc., and still one of the best beaches in all of Baja. It's

most noteworthy for its coral reef, which lies within a few yards of a powdery sand beach. Snorkeling here is wonderful, as is simply walking for miles on the beach. Down the road another 5 miles is Bahía Los Frailes, which sits in the lee of the massive granite headland Cabo Frailes. The hotel here rents kayaks with which you can paddle out to the sheer rock walls of the headland. The beach is nice, but not as alluring as Cabo Pulmo.

## BOARDSAILING

Vacationers on the East Cape used to curse the wintertime north winds that blow from November through March, but a few smart boardsailors figured out that anyplace with all-day 15- to 30-knot winds, warm water, and beautiful beaches can't be half bad. Now, the East Cape towns of **Buena Vista** and **Los Barriles** have become major stops on the global boardsailing circuit.

The days when you could just whip into Buena Vista in your pickup and set up camp on the beach are almost gone. All but a small section of the bay has been developed with vacation homes. But north and south of town you can still find a quiet slice of paradise. Several different windsurfing resorts utilize the hotels here. **Vela High Wind Center** (tel. 800/223-5443) usually sets up camp for the winter at the Hotel Palmas de Cortez, a wonderfully rambling affair with free-standing cottages and simple rooms. **Mr. Bill's Windsurfing** (tel. 800/533-8452) is a smaller operation with its own nice little beachfront inn on the beach in Buena Vista. Accommodations fill up fast for high season in Los Barilles/Buena Vista. Plan as far ahead as possible.

As destinations go, this area is not for beginners. When the winds are going hard, you must either know how to water start or stay home. But for people with solid skills, it's one of the best spots in the world. And for those rare days that the wind doesn't blow, both Vela and Mr. Bill's have loaner mountain bikes and can arrange hikes into the sierra.

## CAMPING & LODGING

It used to be you could pull down onto almost any beach between Cabo San Lucas and San José del Cabo and pitch a tent. While I suppose legally you are still allowed to do that, I've never had much taste for camping in front of a bunch of condominiums.

The one developed campground worth mention in the Corridor between the two Cabos is the **Brisas del Mar** on the beach at Costa Azul, just as you leave San Jose. Many people leave trailers here year-round, but you can pitch a tent out in front of the formal trailer parking for $9 a night. The staff is very cool, and the Brisas del Mar serves as something of a clearing house for good tips on things to do in Baja. They are also the base for a continuously changing cast of adventure excursion operators who can arrange anything from diving to mountain biking to sportfishing. Facilities include full hookups for RVs, pool, showers, and laundry. There's also a restaurant and store here. They accept reservations by mail only (there is no phone). Contact them at: Apartado Postal 45, San José del Cabo, Baja California Sur, Mexico.

An even better option, in my opinion, is the **Delfin Blanco Hotel and Campground** in Pueblo La Playa, on the other side of the Río San José. It's a funny little compound with a communal kitchen, freshwater showers, several cabañas, tent sites, and even tents to rent. Camping for two people is $9. For an extra $5 they'll rent you a tent. Casitas and cabañas vary from $26 per night for one person to $50 for four people. The proprietor is a wonderful Scandinavian woman who is a great source of contacts

and information about the area. It's not fancy, and not for everyone, but if you're looking for a cheap and groovy place to stay in Los Cabos, this is it. The beach is just a few hundred yards away.

On the opposite end of the price spectrum is **La Palmilla Hotel.** La Palmilla was one of the first hotels built on the cape and it's still what I consider the best. Rates vary from $125 to more than $300 per night, but the service is impeccable, the grounds beautiful, and the clientele very discreet. There's great snorkeling right outside your door, and the surf breaks of Old Man's, The Rock, and Zippers are right down the beach. Fishing and diving can be arranged from the hotel. Their U.S. number is 800/637-2226. In Baja, call 2-0583.

On the East Cape, there are several good choices. **Inn at Rancho Leonero** (tel. 800/696-2164) is a very well-run fishing resort and 12-room palapa-style hotel. It sits on top of the best fishing in all of Baja and is situated in a very beautiful spot. They have an in-house dive center and fishing charter. Meals are family style. The **Cabo Pulmo Beach Resort** is a collection of palapa-roofed, solar-powered vacation homes owned by gringos. When the owners aren't in residence, many of the cottages are available as housekeeping units in which you bring everything you need for a few days and have a great time. It's a wonderful setting but the management was beyond terrible when I stayed there, a perfect case study in why nepotism is so rarely a wise business practice. If the developer ever gets around to firing his son and hiring a real manager, the place would be a great resort. To ask if that's happened yet, call 888/997-8566.

Though the area is developing quickly, you can still camp right on the beach north of the little community of Cabo Pulmo. Store your food safely or the cows will eat it. I'm not kidding. There is also a nice and sheltered free camping area at the southern end of the bay that contains Cabo Pulmo. It's an unmarked road that leads into a sheltered cove below the outcropping of Los Frailes.

Just around the corner from Cabo Pulmo is a very well-run and beautiful small hotel on the beach called **Hotel Bahía Los Frailes.** Besides having one of the best restaurants in Baja, the hotel sits in the lee of the towering headland at Los Frailes. The beach is right out front and you're a short paddle or drive from the wonderful snorkeling at Cabo Pulmo. Game fishermen love this spot, too, and you can often hire pangas right off the beach.

On the other side of the peninsula, I recommend that Pacific-bound campers stay near Todos Santos at either **Playa San Pedro,** where you can camp for free, or the San Pedrito RV Park, which also has a number of excellent tent sites right on the beach in front of a great surf break. The prices here are not quite free but still a reasonable $3 per person per night.

My favorite hotel in all of Baja, however, is the **Todos Santos Inn.** Like the setting of a Gabriel García Márquez novel, the brick and adobe walls of the tiny two bedroom (with two more being built) Todos Santos Inn echo with the possibility of something magical happening here. Through heavy wooden doors, the frescoed *zaguán* (arched entry) draws you into a brick interior patio, which overlooks the yard and garden. During the 1910 Mexican revolution, the owner of the building tossed his cash box full of gold coins into the outhouse to stymie looters. It's never been found, despite years of backyard expeditions by Todos Santos kids. French doors off the patio lead to high-ceilinged rooms, which, with their mosquito net–draped beds, period antiques, and cool ceiling fans, tempt you to stay inside for an all day siesta. Don't. Todos

Santos has great beaches, biking, and hiking through the overgrown town arroyo, plus fantastic surf at Playa San Pedrito.

High tourist season is from December to March. Spring and fall, however, are the best times to visit; the weather is still pleasant but the town has returned to its mellow self. Rates are $85 to $120 per night including continental breakfast. For information or reservations, phone or fax 011/52-114-50040.

## FISHING

Fishing is what originally drew tourism to these parts. Both the Pacific and the Sea of Cortez are practically boiling with big gamefish. The most sought-after are marlin, but depending on the season you can catch tuna, sailfish, dorado, wahoo, yellowtail, roosterfish, and just about any other tropical gamefish in huge numbers here. For a long time it seemed the gamefish were endless. Once upon a time it was a badge of honor to be photographed beside your marlin on the dock in Cabo and to send the dead fish to be mounted. Luckily, a conservation ethic has taken hold of the fishing guides here and they generally discourage killing these big fish. Instead, lucky anglers are asked to take pictures and memories and release the fish to fight another day. It seems to be working. Catches are on the rise again and everyone seems happy.

One of the remarkable aspects of this area's gamefishing is that you don't need a big boat to do it. People have actually caught marlin and tuna while shore-casting. Car-top boats regularly boat marlin right off Cabo San Lucas, where the 100-fathom line comes so close to shore that it looks like the boats are going to hit the beach while they're trolling there.

That said, the best way to get into the big fish in a serious way is to sign on with a local guide and boat. This can mean anything from a 16-foot panga, scarcely larger than some of the marlin, to a giant 40-foot sportfisher.

I'm of the opinion that bigger isn't necessarily better when it comes to fishing boats. Sure, it's nice to cruise in the comfort of a 31-footer while heading out to the marlin grounds of Banco San Jaime or Banco Golden Gate, both of which are about 20 miles out to sea, but there's also something to be said for the simplicity of hiring a panga. Your range is limited, but with world-class fishing spots literally right outside the harbor at Cabo San Lucas, sometimes it's better to stay close to home and save yourself the time and expense of all that running around in luxury.

You can hardly walk down the docks in **Cabo San Lucas** without someone offering to take you fishing, and every major hotel also has their favorite guide. Pisces fleet at the corner of Boulevard Marina and Madero is a well-known provider of fishing excursions.

**San José del Cabo** has no harbor, so all sportfishing is done by pangas, which can be beach launched through the surf. Often, the experience of riding out in an 18-foot fiberglass boat through breaking waves is worth the price of admission alone. To find the panga fleet, cross the usually dry Río de San José on Calle Benito Juárez and turn right at the first chance when you reach the wonderful little town of La Playa. At least 20 pangas will be parked on the beach any given afternoon, and you can arrange for the next day's trip. San José del Cabo is near the **Gordo Banks,** a famous fishing and diving spot 10 miles out to sea. Marlin are caught here year-round. Other seasons bring tuna, dorado, wahoo, and roosterfish. And as an added plus, this is one of the best places in the world to spot giant mantas.

Finally, the East Cape has tremendous fishing. **Rancho Leonero** is world-renowned as a destination fishing resort near Punta Colorada that has its own fleet of pangas and cruisers to take guests out. The lodgings here are luxurious and all meals are included. It's a good way for people with fishing in mind to do one-stop shopping. Meanwhile, nonfishing companions have plenty to do, including snorkeling, hiking the nearby mountains, and luxuriating poolside. Call 800/334-2252 in the United States and 114-10216 in Mexico.

Expect to pay about $100 to $150 per day for a panga, including use of their gear. Cruisers go for more, $300 to $400 per day. Prices are by the boat, not per person, and you can bring as many people as you think can comfortably fish together.

## HIKING

There are very few places in Baja where I can unequivocally recommend going for an overnight backpack. The lack of water and unforgiving terrain are simply too hostile. But the **Sierra de La Laguna** that crowns the foot of the Baja Peninsula offers some really tremendous hikes. While the lowlands of Baja Sur swelter, the Sierra is a wonderful place to take refuge in high mountain meadows and steep canyons flowing with streams. The highest point in this range is more than 7,000 feet at **Picacho de la Laguna.** For those who don't speak Spanish, Sierra de la Laguna means "Mountain Range of the Laguna." Sadly, the name amounts to false advertising these days. There was a lake here at one time, in a basin at 5,600 feet, but erosion pulled the plug way back in 1870 and let the water drain down Cañon San Dionisio. Now it's a nice meadow.

There are two chief routes across the Sierra. The northernmost is via Cañon San Dionisio to La Laguna and down the west side to San Juan de Aserradero and eventually Todos Santos. Total hiking distance is about 16 miles, but that sorely underestimates the difficulty involved. There is no actual trail for much of the route and there is much scrambling over boulders. And getting lost here has much more dire prospects than getting lost in Yosemite. There will be no rescue rangers in a helicopter looking to save you here.

Guides can be hired in almost all the towns surrounding the mountain areas; Rancho San Dionisio, Santiago, Miraflores and, if coming at the mountains from the west, Todos Santos. Expect to pay roughly $20 per person per day for guided hikes.

The other favorite route across the Sierra reaches from just outside the little town of Miraflores up and over the range to El Guerigo via Cañon San Bernardo. It's about a mile shorter than the San Dionisio route and stays lower, only reaching 3,000 feet. It's still a difficult hike, though, and getting lost is always a bad idea. For either of these routes you should bank on at least 4 or 5 days. Take all the appropriate topographical maps (which are Mexico F12B23, F12B24, F12B33, and F12B34) and know how to use them.

The best season is fall, with spring coming a close second. Winter can actually be too cold in the high country, but cold is relatively speaking; anyone accustomed to the Sierra Nevada in summer can deal with winter in the Sierra de la Laguna. The summer rainy season is the time to avoid. Not only do rainstorms hit almost every day (this is the wettest part of Baja, getting almost 35 inches of rain per year), sweeping the canyons with flash floods and making things quite dangerous, but the heat can also be totally unbearable in the lower reaches.

Both these canyons are excellent places to head for a day hike, since fine swimming holes can almost always be found within the first few miles of

hiking. To reach any of these trailheads you're going to need a car. While the people of Baja have always been some of the most conscientiously honest I've encountered anywhere, I'd think twice before leaving valuables locked in a car at any of these trailheads. If you must, I suggest you arrange with one of the residents of the nearby ranchos to watch over your stuff.

## MOUNTAIN BIKING

Dirt roads crisscross the Sierra de la Laguna to a number of small ranches and pueblos, leaving the mountain biking possibilities unlimited. There's something about biking in a foreign country, with huge cacti, scorching deserts, dramatic pine-covered peaks, range cattle, and desolate ranches, that just can't be touched by a ride on the local dirt path back home. On the other hand, back home for most people it doesn't get this hot, nor are there tire-devouring cacti at every turn. Carry lots of water and a HUGE patch kit and everything will be just fine.

The road from San José del Cabo to El Salteador 12 miles north and then back to the beach at Punta Palmilla makes a good 25-mile loop. Surprisingly, most of the year you'll find pools of water deep enough to swim in many of the creeks as you climb into the higher sierra. A more ambitious loop leads 20 miles north into the mountains from Cabo San Lucas to the tiny oasis of **Candelaria,** making for a good overnight if you've brought camping gear and aren't superstitious. Candelaria has a reputation among cape residents as a center for black magic, and reputedly several *brujas* (witches) count themselves among the town's citizens. The townspeople are tight-lipped and reserved, but you should be able to bum fresh drinking water here for the ride home or northwest back to Highway 19.

Make camp in a field outside town (ask for permission) or log some more miles and plunk down in any number of sheltered spots along the way, and ride back to Cabo on the paved road with the prevailing wind at your back. Brisa del Mar trailer park in San José del Cabo rents mountain bikes for $15 per day.

## SCUBA DIVING & SNORKELING

This neck of the ocean is legendary for its diving. What makes it so extraordinary is the frequency of encounters with large sea life—mantas, whale sharks, schooling hammerheads, etc.—plus the intensely beautiful underwater geography of Pulmo Reef, the Cabo San Lucas submarine canyon, and some of the remote offshore pinnacle dives.

One of the most unique spots lies right under the nose of party-all-night Cabo San Lucas. Jacques Cousteau first brought films of sandfalls on the edge of Cabo's **submarine canyon** to the general public. Since then, thousands of divers have plunged to see these streams of white sand pouring over the precipice of a 9,000 foot-deep drop-off. The canyon lies just 100 or so feet off Playa Del Amor and the rocks of Lands End. It's an advanced dive, owing to the depths you must contend with to reach the edge of the canyon (between 85 and 130 feet) and the possibility of going too deep if you don't know what you're doing.

Other divers stay shallow and play with the sea lions at the rookery at the end of the point. This is also an excellent area for snorkeling. Despite the easy access and relatively short swim, it's not unheard of for divers to spot mantas, sea turtles, and even whales here. **Amigos del Mar** (tel. 3-0505) in Cabo San Lucas is a good scuba operation.

**Playa Santa María,** 13 km east of Cabo San Lucas below the Twin Dolphin Hotel, is a fine spot for shore div-

ing. The protected cove ranges from 10 to 60 feet deep and is filled with colorful reef fish. It's one of the better dives for beginners and for snorkelers in the area. More advanced divers will want to head out to the deeper waters near the point. Be careful of strong currents in this area.

Longer boat dives head for the **Gorda Banks,** where mantas and schooling hammerheads are common in summer months. The ocean bottom here rises to within 110 feet of the surface and is covered with black coral. Because of the depth, very few divers go all the way to the bottom. Most of the diving is in the middle of the water column, where you'll float hoping to see the big mantas, sharks, and gamefish that make this a famous fishing spot as well. The dive concession at **Hotel Palmilla** (tel. 2-0582) will arrange everything for a trip here. Since there is no large boat harbor in San José, most diving is done from beach-launchable pangas.

On the East Cape, Cabo Pulmo Reef is the largest and most well-preserved coral reef in Baja. Almost every type of dive can be found on these four finger reefs that jut seaward from Pulmo Bay toward the open Sea of Cortez. Groupers lie in big holes, angelfish flutter around coral heads, and puffers are everywhere. Early morning and night divers will see many different varieties of eel and numerous small sharks. Snorkelers will love the reef at **Pulmo,** which breaks the surface in several spots. It's an easy swim through a sheltered lagoon. Be careful crossing the reef. Make sure it's deep enough before you swim over. Periodical waves can leave you high and dry on sharp coral if you're not aware.

Currents along the outer Pulmo reefs can get moving fast, so they're often approached as a drift dive, with one of the local dive masters dropping you upcurrent and following your bubbles

# Doctor Jekyll & Mister Guide

I should have run away the minute he introduced himself. "My name is R," he said, leaning out of a van full of camping gear. "I'm a professional outdoor adventure traveler."

"My name's Andrew," I said, "and this is my wife Lisa."

"Are you guys on vacation? What are you doing in Baja?"

"Well, I'm working. Actually, I guess we've got something in common. I'm writing an adventure travel guide to Baja, and Lisa's just tagging along for the ride."

"An adventure guide." He asked, "Who are you writing that for?"

"For people who want to come down here and go hiking, diving, kayaking," I explained, "you know, the same people who read *Outside Magazine.*"

His head practically spun around and his eyes suddenly brimmed with hostility. "I hate that magazine. I once guided a guy doing a story for them and he was a real ass. And then he didn't pay me. Besides, you guys ruin everywhere you go."

Great, we're staying at Cabo Pulmo on Baja's East Cape, a romantic eco-resort with thatched roofs, solar power, and no locks on the door; and within 2 hours of our arrival, this self-proclaimed "professional outdoor adventure traveler," a muscular guy with crazed eyes, steel-rimmed Nazi prison guard glasses, and, I notice, a machete—perfect for eliminating the scourge of travel writers—strung up on the ceiling of his van is telling me that I'm worse than scum.

We change the subject and six of us go on a lovely hike through the cactus forest to the top of a weathered granite dome, where we can see for miles. Rob, a part-time local resident who'd initially invited us along, tells us all about the ecosystem and local history. Everything seems cool. R is aloof, but civil. Perhaps, I think, he was just a little bent by that other guy stiffing him. Who wouldn't be?

Later that evening, drinking margaritas on Rob's rooftop deck, I'm talking to a filmmaker from Aspen about a photographer we both know, when R gets that crazed look in his eye again. "You people are all the same. You just come here and try to screw people over. Well I'm not going to play that game. You shouldn't have come here." Then he stormed off into the darkness to sleep in his van.

The other guests, a small group of generally well-to-do American expatriates who live in the area, drawn by its excellent fishing, boardsailing, and downstream. **Pepe's Dive Center** in Cabo Pulmo is a great operation that offers full PADI and SSI instruction, rentals, and boat dives. Pepe was instrumental in getting Cabo Pulmo declared a national marine park and knows the area like the back of his hand. He's located right on the only road through Cabo Pulmo, or he can be reached by writing Pepe's Dive Center, P.O. Box 532, Cabo San Lucas, BCS Mexico. Reservations from the United States can be made by calling 208/726-9233.

A short boat ride north of Cabo Pulmo is a seamount known as **El Bajo.** Covered in invertebrate life, El Bajo is a favorite spot for night diving. The pockets in the reef here are home to four different species of lobster, octopuses, eels, and numerous rays. You might also

diving, looked horrified and embarrassed by this hostility. A couple of small jokes and then some more tequila soon smoothed over any awkwardness.

Later that week we decided to go sea kayaking. The resort manager told us we had to talk to R since he was the activities director here, a job description that came as news to me after 3 days at the resort. I found R by his van, The Gray Whale, and asked him if he'd rent us some kayaks. Suddenly, with the prospect of business dangling in front of him, R was a changed man. Nice as could be, he cobbled together a couple of boats and paddles and mapped out a route down coast that would take us past an isolated snorkeling beach, a sea lion rookery, and, finally, to a hotel about 5 miles to the south where he and the Gray Whale would be waiting to give us a ride home. He said it was an easy paddle for us to make by sunset. It sounded great and he wished us bon voyage. And just in case the weather turned or we got tired, we arranged that he'd come back and check the fish camp halfway there if we weren't to the takeout by sunset.

Well, the wind came up, Lisa had trouble with her paddle, we were feeling lazy, and with the sun lying low in the west we headed for the bail-out spot.

A group of campers there invited us to join their fire circle while we waited for our pickup. It got dark, the moon rose, and still no sign of R. Our new friends fed us some grilled fish and we talked about how beautiful the sea was here. I began to worry that something might have happened to R when suddenly, 2 hours late, the gray van came fishtailing into the camp. He leapt from the van and with a noticeable slur said, "God I'm glad to see you. I was worried sick when you didn't show up at the other end."

"Well, I'm glad you made it," I said, "I was getting worried something might have happened to you too. Thanks for coming to pick us up."

We loaded the kayaks onto the van. Lisa climbed into the passenger seat and I slid in behind a milk crate full of empty "Caguamas"—the liter-sized Pacifico beers you drink if you're going for mass consumption. R gunned it up the hill, sand and mud caking the windshield so we could hardly see.

"So what happened?" he asked Lisa. "How come you didn't make it to the finish?"

Lisa explained that we'd gotten tired of fighting a headwind and thought it better to get off the water before dark than to carry on along an unknown coast

encounter mantas here depending on the season.

## SEA KAYAKING

Baja, of course, is legendary for its sea kayaking. The Cape, however, is a little too exposed for most long distance paddles. The general rule is that the farther up the Sea of Cortez you go, the better the paddling. In the direct vicinity of Los Cabos, the best places are **La Palmilla Beach,** which sits inside a sheltered point; **Playa Santa María** below the Twin Dolphin Hotel; and out around the point at **Land's End** in Cabo San Lucas. Rental kayaks are available at all these locations.

If you're looking for a wilderness experience, though, it's much better to

after sundown. That's why we agreed to a bail-out spot.

Suddenly he got that mean look in his eye again, the one from the party. "There was no wind out there. If you think that's wind you should see real wind. And anyway, I thought you said you were a surfer," he spat. "I'd have thought a surfer could make an easy paddle like that without having to drop out. You should try surfing Punta Perfecta, but you probably couldn't hack that either, 'cause that's only for real surfers, not posers from California."

Then he floored it. I would have said something, but watching the speedometer hit 60 on a darkened Baja washboard I was afraid that even a single word might break his concentration and send us to our deaths. He was way over the edge of crazy, running the windshield wipers dry while he squinted to see out the windshield. We four-wheel-drifted through an S-curve, Lisa clinging to the dash, me hugging the Caguamas with all my might. In one of those sudden bouts of religion I get when faced with immediate death, I begged God please, please, please, whatever you've got going elsewhere in the world right now, could you take a few seconds to herd the range cattle off the road ahead of us.

The cows stayed off the road, their eyes glinting red as we hurtled past, and after 10 minutes of white-knuckled terror we came through the gate to Cabo Pulmo. R gunned it at the SLOW sign, and we caught air over a couple of speed bumps, but I knew that even if we crashed here we'd survive. There were doctors vacationing here, and dentists. They could rebuild us. He locked up the brakes rounding the corner to our cabaña, screeched to a halt, and leapt from the car. Without a word he ran off into the darkness and didn't come back.

"Uh, I guess we should get out now," I said to Lisa, prying my fingers from the plastic milk crate. "What was up with that?"

"I don't know," she said, "but I can't believe we didn't die."

I climbed up onto the roof rack and pulled my paddle jacket out of the hatch. In the pocket I felt the rolled-up $50 bill I'd agreed to pay R. I was beginning to understand that there might be more to R's debt collection problems with the first *Outside* writer than the simple fact of somebody stiffing him. Exhausted, we unloaded the rest of our gear and went to bed.

That morning I awoke to a note outside the door.

*Guys, I'm sorry if I was a little short-tempered last night. I'm going to La Paz for the next couple days. If you wish, you can leave your donation with the front office. R.*

I took a mental inventory. Let's see, a guide shows up 2 hours late, drunk, nearly gets us killed driving like a

head up to the **East Cape.** Particularly fine is the region around **Cabo Pulmo.** A short paddle in either direction will lead you to isolated beaches reachable only by boat. An excellent day trip is to paddle from Cabo Pulmo to **Bahía Los Frailes,** stopping on the way to snorkel along the rocky face of Los Frailes. About two-thirds of the way through this trip you'll encounter a California sea lion rookery. Many people snorkel with the juveniles, who are generally resigned to hanging out in the water while the giant bulls occupy the prime sunning spots. If any of the big bulls start giving you attitude, I'd beat a fast retreat away from his rock. You should arrange to have someone meet you at Los Frailes to

lunatic, insults my wife, and then runs away into the darkness without a word. Do I "wish" to leave him a "donation"? Not in this lifetime.

Two days later R strolls up the path to our patio. "I need that money you owe me, Andrew," he said. "I've given you a couple days. It's time for you to pay up."

I told him as bluntly as possible that if he'd wanted to settle up our bill, he probably shouldn't have run off into the darkness when we got home, nor should he have insulted us and put our lives in jeopardy. You can't go around behaving like that, I told him, and expect people to pay you for the privilege.

"But I left you a note the next morning."

"I know you left me a note. And it said if I 'wish' to leave a 'donation' I can. But I don't. You don't deserve to get paid for that, so I'm not going to."

Out of the blue he started crying. For a second I felt bad; maybe I was being too hard on him. Then his face scrunched up into a terrible temper-tantrum and he screamed, "You're just a couple of posers and phonies. This is it. You're leaving Cabo Pulmo tonight. I'm having you thrown out right now. You writers are all the same, coming here and sucking off people." He puffed up in my face like he was going to hit me, glaring right into my eye. Suddenly he was crying again, and ran down the path to the manager's office.

To make a long story a little less long, R now has two stories to tell about *Outside* writers stiffing him, and we weren't thrown out, but our stay at this otherwise paradisical spot was ruined. It's pretty hard to sleep in a screen-sided bungalow with no locks when you know that Dr. Jekyll and Mr. Guide is out there nursing a grudge, slamming down the Caguamas, and sharpening his machete. I'm sure it was just my imagination running wild, but I parked our jeep right next to the house where it would be difficult to sabotage and stacked cans by the door to wake us if he came around. The next morning we woke up early and left.

Never have I been so glad to leave such a beautiful place. The same little village by the sea that seemed so laid-back and perfect a few days earlier now buzzed with a metallic tension, the fear that you could turn a corner and he'd be there.

A friend in Cabo Pulmo told me a few months later that R burned his bridges there and moved on, not saying where he was going. But somewhere in Baja's thousands of miles of wilderness, he's probably sticking out his hand right now and telling someone "Hi, my name's R. I'm a professional outdoor adventure traveler."

My advice? Make a run for it.

shuttle you back to Cabo Pulmo. This is an excellent chance for the shuttle driver to snorkel the reef at Cabo Pulmo, drive to Los Frailes, and enjoy some great margaritas and appetizers in Baja while waiting for the paddlers to round the bend. At the time this book was being prepared, a kayak concession was being created at the hotel on the beach at Los Frailes. **Pepe's Dive Locker** in Cabo Pulmo also had a few kayaks for rent by the hour. There's no phone at Pepe's, but you can contact his U.S. representative at 619/489-7001.

**Lobos Del Mar Kayak Ventures** runs guided trips to the Cabo Pulmo area for $104 per person, including meals, equipment, and transportation to the East

Cape from San José del Cabo. They're based at the Brisas Del Mar RV Park in San José del Cabo, tel. 114-22983.

## SURFING

When summer hurricanes spin off the southern end of the peninsula, they hurl huge surf northward at beaches like **Zippers, Punta Gorda,** and **Old Man's.** People have compared Zippers, which is near the Brisa del Mar trailer park and the Costa Azul surf shop outside San José del Cabo, with places like Pipeline. That may be an exaggeration, but it's a great wave. Sadly, it's become the battle-ground for a grudge match between Mexican locals and visiting gringos. The general rule is that unless you're some-one really special, gringos in the water after 8 am get punched in the face. Luckily, the nearby spots of Old Man's and The Rock aren't quite as uptight.

The **East Cape** is an excellent place to escape the wound-up viciousness of Zippers and experience Baja the way it should be. The road is bad and the waves are fickle, but when a hurricane is pumping, the isolated points up the inside of the Sea of Cortez begin to light up, sometimes as far up as Punta Arena. It's nice because if one is too big, just keep driving north. Eventually, you'll find something to your taste.

Surfboards can be rented by the day at **Costa Azul,** along with surf racks for your rental car, but it's generally better to bring your own.

The Pacific coast is an entirely different story. This coast has yet to face the onslaught of development that's so rapidly changed the cape. An hour-long drive up the coast to the little towns of Pescadero and Todos Santos can be a great surf journey. There are a couple good point breaks near here. **Playa San Pedrito** is reached via the dirt road that begins 7.4 km south of the Todos Santos

town limits. Follow the signs for San Pedrito Campground and you can't go wrong. The point is very rocky and sharp, but it's a wonderful wave on the right swell direction and tide (north-west swell, rising tide). Another stretch down the road will lead you to **Playa los Cerritos** (12.8 km south of Todos Santos), a lovely beach with a surfable point break off a big headland.

Other beach breaks are rideable at various times, but much of the beach around Todos Santos is characterized by a vicious shore break and massive un-dertow. While the unruliness of the ocean has helped keep industrial tour-ism at bay, it also makes you hunt a little harder to find playful waves.

## WILDLIFE VIEWING

The river estuary in San José del Cabo is an important **nesting and resting area** for more than 100 species of birds and other wildlife that depend on a supply of fresh water. Though the *estero* is a declared national ecological reserve, my impression last time I was there was that it's still suffering from people who drive trucks and motorcycles through the surrounding riverbanks and dump illegally here. There is a small dock on the estero next to the Presidente Inter-Continental Hotel, where you can re-portedly sometimes rent canoes. Service is spotty to nonexistent, though. Birders can get some interesting sightings just by walking the foot trail along the west-ern edge of the estuary.

**Whale watching** hasn't quite taken off here, but during the winter months both gray whales and humpbacks can be spotted. Fishermen at La Playa in San José del Cabo or in Cabo San Lucas will arrange special trips to see the whales. **Tourcabos** (tel. 2-1982) runs more formal whale-watching trips for groups of four or more. Expect to pay about $40 per person for a 2-hour trip, about half as long as if you'd arranged it with a fisherman yourself.

The sea lion rookery at Land's End and the pelican nesting area at Pelican Rock are both regular stops on the 45-minute, glass-bottomed **boat cruises** that leave the Dos Mares dock every hour from 8am to 3pm. You can also see these sights from the all-you-can-drink booze cruises that head out to Land's End for sunset, if you haven't fallen overboard by then. Competition for your business on these trips is fierce, so they're often really cheap, usually around $15 per person.

## La Paz ♦ What to Do & Where to Do It

I love La Paz. Tourism may come and tourism may go, but La Paz will be a wonderful city long after Cabo San Lucas has dried up and blown into the sea. La Paz was the first European settlement that actually stuck to the peninsula. It's well-suited by name, which means peace, and many of the families here are descendents of ancestors who fled the political upheaval of the Mexican Revolution on the mainland to find shelter here. The town is built around a fantastic bay, one of the best natural harbors in Mexico. It's an important shipping center, and this is where you catch the ferry to Mazatlán. La Paz is also the epicenter of a big sailing scene. Many people intending to make longer Mexican voyages pull into La Paz and see no reason to go any farther. With offshore islands, a sheltered harbor, and good year-round sailing, there's not much to recommend leaving.

A long sandy beach is the town waterfront, yet it has never been overbuilt with hotels, most likely because at low tide it reveals itself as a giant mudflat. And with close to 200,000 residents, La Paz can soak up gringo tourists without changing the essential nature of the place—an old colonial city on the sea.

Not too long ago La Paz was famous as a center of the pearling industry. Whether overfishing or disease killed the pearl oyster beds is a subject of some debate, but by the 1940s pearl beds that had supported harvesting for 7,000 years were virtually extinct. Today, people flock to La Paz to dive for a different kind of pearl, the priceless interactions with fish and wildlife that characterize the Sea of Cortez. La Paz is encircled by a string of large islands: Espíritu Santo, Isla Partida, and Isla Cerralvo. All are popular sea kayaking and yachting destinations. Fishing is also good, but not as spectacular as down in the Cape Region.

### BEACHES

The town beaches in La Paz turn into big mudflats at low tide, so beach lovers will do well to head east of town along the **Pichilingue Peninsula.** The first beaches you'll encounter are dominated by hotels and private beach clubs, but after the ferry terminal (17 km east of town) the great beaches begin. The first is **Playa Balandra** (23 km), a large, shallow bay with a small coral reef at the south end. A little farther is **Playa El Tecolote.** On weekends it can be noisy here with Jet Skis and Waverunners, but on weekdays you'll have it all to yourself. As you continue down the road a little farther you'll reach a series of isolated but rocky beaches. If you're willing to trade perfect sand for a little solitude, this might be the place for you. The best beaches near La Paz are the ones on the offshore islands, which are written about in the kayaking and sailing sections.

## BOARDSAILING

What is widely reported to be the best boardsailing in all of Baja happens to occur at **La Ventana,** just south of La Paz, reached via Mexico 286 and a short graded road. As the northern zephyrs that blow down the Sea of Cortez blow between Isla Cerralvo and the mainland, they are compressed and accelerated. As a result, this is among the most consistently windy spots in Mexico. It is, in many ways, what Los Barriles and Buena Vista were about 10 years ago.

There is a small fishing village here, but no store or supplies. Most of the boardsailors who flock here during the November to March season camp together under a nice palm grove. The shade is a rare blessing. The nearby farming community of Los Planes has several small stores and a cafe. An alternate place to camp and sail is **Punta Arena de la Ventana,** also reached via a side road off Mexico 286. Pass through the town of Los Planes and look for a major turn to the left. Until a few years ago there was a luxury fishing resort here with an 8,000-foot airstrip. It went out of business and was on the market at last notice. If anyone wants to buy it and hire me to live there as a guard, call my publisher.

## CAMPING & LODGING

I once camped between two pangas on the main town beach in La Paz while waiting overnight to get ferry tickets. It was a great night of sleep and nobody hassled us. Somehow I don't think it would be a good idea if everyone followed this technique, though. The best real camping near La Paz involves getting at least 15 miles out of town. The best, in my opinion, is the camping at **La Ventana.** A cool palm grove shelters enough area to actually make a dramatic difference in the temperature. During winter it's crowded with the hardcore sailboard crowd. In summer, it's ridiculously hot, even considering the shade. The fishing is great in the Cerralvo Channel and small boats can be beach launched here. Another camping spot is **Punta Arena de Ventana.** The boardsailing is still great in winter and the fishing good all year long. South of here the coast is roadless for several miles and makes a good exploration zone.

Closer to La Paz, but much more heavily trafficked, is the beach camping on the **Pichilingue Peninsula** beyond the ferry terminal. I've thought about camping there and always ended up moving on because something seemed a little sketchy. (Of course, I ended up camping on the town beach in La Paz, so don't necessarily take my word for it.)

For real hotel lodging, **Hotel Los Arcos** (tel. 800/347-2252 or 1-5577) is the old standby. You can choose from cabañas and regular hotel rooms. Either way, it's nice in that 1950s way. Ask for one of the original cabañas, which have fireplaces, just for the curiosity of having a fireplace in one of the warmest cities on earth. Luckily, they have AC too. Prices range from $75 to $100. Credit cards are accepted.

Budget travelers have a number of options ranging from the 18th-century convent quarters of **Pension California** (tel. 2-2896; $10 for a room sleeping as many as four) to the **Instituto de la Juventud y Deporte Youth Hostel,** where a bed runs you a startling $6 per night (tel. 2-4615).

## FISHING

Fishing in La Paz is excellent, though it's not quite the hot spot that the cape is. It's a longer run out to the deep water on the other side of Isla Espíritu Santo, where you'll find marlin, tuna, and sailfish; but within the bay you can find incredible fishing for roosterfish, yellowtail, bonito, pompano, and other small and medium-side gamefish.

An old standby in La Paz is **Dorado Velez Fleet,** which is based out of the Hotel Los Arcos. Their number is 2-2744. **Fisherman's Fleet** is another outfit with a reservation desk in the Los Arcos (tel. 2-1313).

It may be cheaper to drive yourself to the fisherman's dock on the east side of the ferry terminal. Though it's a ways out of town, you eliminate any middleman and can often get a cut rate on panga trips. The chief factor is how far you want to go (it's much more expensive to go to the far side of Isla Espíritu Santo) and whether it's high or low season.

## HIKING

There is little hiking directly in the vicinity of La Paz. It's a short drive south to the canyons of the Sierra de la Laguna, though, which are covered in the Los Cabos section.

## SCUBA DIVING & SNORKELING

Initially the lucrative pearl oyster beds drew settlers to La Paz, so diving has a long tradition here. For a look at the early days of La Paz diving, it's worth taking a read of John Steinbeck's *The Pearl.*

Nowadays, thousands of divers flock to La Paz to take advantage of the rich sea life that surrounds the offshore islands. There's very little diving and snorkeling that can be reached from shore. While people do snorkel the shallow coves of the Pichilingue Peninsula, there is not the profusion of marinelife you might expect. Most of the time you have to get on a boat to see the good stuff. But once you do get on a boat, the options are virtually limitless.

The best months for diving in this region are from May to August, when water temperatures are warm enough to dive without a wetsuit and when the visibility reaches more than 100 feet.

Day boats from La Paz head to several excellent destinations. **Los Islotes** is a rock pinnacle with a large colony of several hundred friendly sea lions. Both snorkelers and scuba divers can have a really good time here, since there's plenty to see at the shallower depths too. The young sea lions spiral and swirl around you. Don't be offended if they take a few gentle nips at your flippers; that's how they greet each other too.

**El Bajo,** also known as the Marisla seamount, is a famous schooling ground for hammerhead sharks and the frequent hangout of large pelagic fishes like marlin, mantas, dorado, tiger sharks, and whale sharks—the largest fish on earth. To enjoy most of this spot, which is located in the open ocean east of La Paz with a minimum depth of 60 feet, you must be an experienced and confident scuba diver. During late summer, it is often possible to snorkel with whale sharks, which spend most of their time basking on the surface.

Wreck divers will enjoy diving on the *Salvatierra.* In 1975, one of the La Paz-to-Topolobampo ferries sank on its way out of port. The 300-foot-long wreck, covered with lovely invertebrate life and surrounded by schooling fish, is easily reached in 60 feet of water. Many of the trucks and cars on the ferry were salvaged, but the ship itself is largely intact. It's one of the best reef dives around.

Multi-day overnight dive trips leave from La Paz and head to remote destinations like **Las Ánimas Island** and the other islands north of La Paz.

**Baja Expeditions** runs day trips and overnights on their La Paz–based boats (2625 Garnet Ave., San Diego, CA 92109; tel. 800/843-6967, or 5-3828 in La Paz). Most of their trips are arranged months in advance through the U.S.

office, but periodically you can get on at the last minute.

**Baja Diving and Service** (tel. 2-18-26) is a locally owned dive shop offering trips to many Sea of Cortez destinations, and gear rental and instruction. They're located at Avenida Independencia, 107-B. This is the best place in town to get your gear worked on if the need should arise.

New resorts and dive boats are coming to La Paz all the time, so shop around if you're in town looking for a good deal.

## SEA KAYAKING

La Paz has become the biggest sea kayaking destination in Mexico. It's no mystery why. Only a short paddle or boat ride from this lovely city are some of the most interesting islands in the world. The main destinations for sea kayakers in the La Paz vicinity are **Isla Espíritu Santo** and its neighbor **Isla Partida.**

Self-supported kayakers can make the crossing to Isla Espíritu Santo over the Canal de San Lorenzo, provided they take the winds and currents into account. It's only 4 miles to Punta Lupona, the southern tip of Espíritu Santo, from Playa Tecolote on the Pichilingue Peninsula, but this is no crossing for beginners. It's well worth inquiring about the local tides and winds prior to any crossing. There is no secure place to leave your car at Tecolote Beach. The best bet is to drive out to Tecolote, leave your gear and someone to guard it, then backtrack to the ferry terminal, where there is a guarded parking lot. It's generally not very difficult to thumb a ride back out to Tecolote Beach.

There are several options for trips to Espíritu Santo. Many people opt for the complete circumnavigation of the two islands, which runs about 44 miles if you include the channel crossing. Others prefer to head up the west side of the island, where there are numerous coves and white-sand beaches. Whether you chose a 6-day circumnavigation or just a few days of lounging on the sandy beaches at the southern tip of Espíritu Santo, it's a matter of personal taste.

When the winds are blowing in the channel, the easier way to get to Espíritu Santo is to hire a panga and begin kayaking once you reach the island. You'll be amazed how much stuff can fit into one of these 20-foot fiberglass skiffs. The fisherman's dock at the ferry terminal is a good place to hire a ride. You may also have luck at Playa Tecolote, where some fishermen keep their pangas.

If you're planning your own trip, remember that there is nothing available on the islands. Bring every drop of fresh water you're going to need and plenty of food. The only exception is fish, which you may be able to purchase from local fishermen who have camps on the island. Able-bodied spear fishermen can also do quite well, as can people who troll a line behind their kayak.

The least visited of the La Paz area islands is **Isla Cerralvo,** which lies 6 miles across the Bahía de la Ventana from Punta Arena de la Ventana, the nearest road. It's very windy here. The channel crossing is emphatically not for novices and is best undertaken very early in the morning when the winds are at their most slack.

**Cerralvo** is the southernmost island in the Sea of Cortez, and one of the largest. The fishing and spearfishing are excellent. On shore, scavenge for fossils and look at the unique flora and fauna of this remote island. Reportedly, this island was the last refuge of the *vagabundos del mar,* the final nomadic descendants of the Pericú Indians, who roamed the Sea of Cortez in wooden dugouts leading a subsistence existence until well into the 20th century.

Several professional kayak companies lead guided expeditions to Espíritu

Santo, Isla Partida, and Cerralvo. **Baja Expeditions,** based out of San Diego, is the old standby in this area and has a long history of satisfied customers (2625 Garnet Ave., San Diego, CA 92109; tel. 800/843-6967.) Most of their trips are scheduled between October and June to avoid the hottest time of year and are supported by pangas and larger boats used for making the long open ocean crossings. Their trips usually include a voyage up the coast to Isla San Jose, Isla Santa Cruz, and Isla Santa Catalina, which lie off the virtually uninhabited coast between Loreto and La Paz.

### SURFING

There is no surf on the Sea of Cortez to speak of, but there are several good surfing spots within a reasonable drive of La Paz. The peninsula is at its narrowest here, and you can go coast to coast in less than 2 hours.

Drive north of town on Highway 1 for about 25 km, where you'll see a dirt road turnoff for **Punta Márquez** opposite a microwave tower on the hill. This is a sometimes good point break and there are miles of beach break in either direction. Another 16 km on the Transpeninsular Highway will bring you to the left-hand turnoff for **Punta Conejo,** which is the best left-point break in all of Baja. Many people describe Punta Conejo as Rincon with the photo negative reversed. It's a long, reeling, cobblestone point. The location has little else to recommend it, but the waves can be extraordinary.

# Loreto ✦ What to Do & Where to Do It

Loreto is the town that the Mexican tourist authority badly wants to turn into the next Cabo San Lucas, but reality keeps getting in their way. About 10 years ago a golf course, major resort hotels, huge pleasure craft harbor, and major airport were all in place to handle the hordes of tourists that planners in Fonatur's (the Mexican tourist development agency) had forecast would descend if only the structure was in place.

They never came. Several of the hotels went out of business, the biggest commercial tenant at the harbor moved to La Paz, the golf course just sat there sucking up precious water, and Loreto remained the wonderful and funky fishing town it's always been.

There are two main reasons to come to Loreto—no, make that three. Fishing, sailing, and diving. At times, the sea boils with feeding fish. The first time I saw it I could hardly believe my eyes. **Isla del Carmen** and **Isla Danzante** make for wonderful overnight sailing destinations; though, since The Moorings packed up and consolidated in La Paz, it's much trickier to secure a sailboat here. And the diving around Loreto is great, much like what you find near La Paz; five different islands are within striking distance. It's also a great place to launch kayaks for a trip to the offshore islands or down the remote coast of the Sierra la Giganta all the way to La Paz.

Though tourism hasn't overwhelmed it, you can find plenty of good restaurants, a couple good hotels, and, as I can personally attest, great mechanics and a fantastic salvage yard.

### CAMPING & LODGING

Loreto has a number of RV parks within the city limits, but for real camping you'll need to head out of town a few miles. **Juncalito Beach** is 14 miles south of Loreto at the southern end of Bahía Juncalito. The camping is free and the facilities nonexistent. But if you drive, bike, or walk another 2.5 miles south, you'll reach **Tripui RV Park,** where you can take a shower, buy some supplies, and even eat at the restaurant, so you aren't roughing it entirely. **Tripui Beach** is also a possibility for free camping but is more accessible to the motor homers.

Loreto itself has a number of hotels. The most luxurious is the **Loreto Inn Hotel** on Paseo Costero in the little village of Nopolo. It may be the cheapest high-class motel I've ever stayed in, at about $50 a night (tel. 800/472-3394), but given the choice, I'd rather stay in town where the action is. **Hotel La Pinta** (tel. 5-0025, 800/336-5454) is right on the waterfront and has nice ocean views. Rooms cost $75 per night. **Baja Outpost Bed & Breakfast** (tel. 800/789-5625), on Blvd. Lopez Mateos, is a small inn popular with scuba divers that offers four rooms for $46 per night, including continental breakfast.

## FISHING

The fishing near Loreto is the kind of thing you dream about. Every season has a different sport fish that practically leaps into your boat. In the winter, prepare to land lots of large yellowtail; spring is the time for hot roosterfishing; summer, when the temperatures are hot and the water is warm, is when you can tie into big marlin, sailfish, tuna, dorado, and grouper. Fall, well, that's the weirdest time of them all: Large Humboldt squid pass inshore to spawn between Isla Carmen and Isla Danzante. A lot of people who think they've caught absolutely everything haven't caught a 10-pound, ink-squirting, whopper of a squid. They're hard fighting and good eating.

There are several different sport-fishing operations in town. Most people opt for panga trips, which are cheaper here than at the cape. Try **Alfredo's Sport Fishing** (tel. 5-01-65), on Calle Juárez. Alternately, all the hotels in town can arrange a trip for you. People with

their own boats can launch at the ramp just north of the Malecón in town or at Puerto Loreto (formerly Puerto Escondido), several miles south of town. If you plan on running out to Isla del Carmen, it's better to launch from Puerto Loreto, which cuts 10 km off the crossing. For tackle, head to Deportes Blazer, the catch-all sporting goods store in town.

## HIKING

There are virtually no formal trails in the Sierra de la Giganta, but the locals know their way to many magical spots in these towering mountains. Ask at **Deportes Blazer** at Hidalgo No. 18 for help finding a guide or current trail information.

## SCUBA DIVING & SNORKELING

Much like La Paz, the best diving and snorkeling around Loreto require a boat. There are certainly plenty of places on the mainland shore where you can kick out and see some fish, but the best stuff is out on the five offshore islands: Coronado, Carmen, Danzante, Monserrate, and Catalina. The first three are a short boat ride from Puerto Loreto. The last two involve a larger commitment of time and energy.

The main diving operation in town is **Arturo's Sports Fishing Fleet** (tel. 113-50409). Based on Hidalgo Boulevard in downtown Loreto, they've been doing this a long time. Don't let the name fool you; they're also a fully equipped dive operation with compressors, rental gear, and a fleet of 22-foot super pangas to get you to your destination quickly. Deportes Blazer also has rental tanks and a compressor.

A particularly interesting dive in the area is **Los Candeleros** (the Candlesticks), a trio of granite pinnacles that juts from the water south of Isla

Danzante. Birds nest on the rocks, and it's a pretty stinky spot from all the guano, but the underwater terrain is fabulous. Large fallen boulders make up shallow reefs filled with lobsters and small fish. At the edge of the pinnacles, the ledges drop off into deep water. Large game fish are numerous here and the scenery particularly dramatic.

**Piedra Submarino,** also off the southern end of Danzante, is a shallow rock reef that's suitable for snorkeling as well as scuba. Finally, the western shore of **Isla del Carmen** is a great place to find sheltered coves in the lee of towering cliffs. Both snorkelers and scuba divers can find enough to look at here to keep them happy all day.

## SEA KAYAKING

**Isla del Carmen** is the top destination, as it has several excellent beaches and coves to explore. The crossing from Puerto Loreto is pretty easy, since Isla Danzante sits midway across at the 2-mile mark. The second half is short, too, but winds and stronger currents call for some caution. Once you're at Isla del Carmen, the world is your oyster. Crystal-clear water, secret sea caves, and powdery sand beaches all reveal themselves as you paddle around the island. People who circumnavigate will come across one of the most phantasmagoric sights in all of Baja, a complete ghost town that was abandoned in 1985. There's a large pier, rusting ships, boat parts, and entire buildings on the shore. Wander around the town and you might find a schoolhouse with worm-eaten books still on the shelves. The town chapel is still intact, and a Madonna still watches over it. This was once a company town for the salt evaporation operation on the island. It must not have been profitable because everyone packed up and left. Now, you'll only occasionally find Mexican fisherman

using the old townsite as a camp. About a half mile outside the bay, look for the remains of a 120-foot tuna boat that caught fire and sank. Some of the rusting remains jut above the waterline, and it's an excellent snorkel stop.

Many people don't do the entire circumnavigation, which is a strenuous 50-plus miles if you include the crossing. Instead, they combine a visit to Carmen's southern end with an exploration of little **Danzante,** which seems like a poker chip next to its larger neighbor.

This is also the beginning of one of Baja's ultimate long-distance paddles, the shoreline wilderness stretch between Loreto and La Paz. South of Loreto, just beyond Puerto Escondido, the most romantically named range in Baja, Sierra de La Giganta (Range of the Giant), forces Highway 1 and its thin veneer of civilization away from the coast, leaving miles of barely touched shoreline visited only by Mexican fishermen, adventurous kayakers, and passing yachts.

Sheer cliffs and desolate, soaring peaks are the backdrop for much of the 65-mile paddle from **Bahía Agua Verde** to the takeout at **San Juan de la Costa.** But your more immediate perspective is one of incredible biological riches. The food chain is hardly an abstract concept here, where really big fish chase big fish chasing medium fish who are in turn chasing little fish. Every evening the sea literally boils with all this action, and don't be surprised when some of those little fish literally jump onto your kayak for safety. If you're lucky, you'll get to see one of the graceful and, unfortunately for them, delicious, manta rays winging below you or leaping into the air. Enter the frenzy yourself and snorkel with groupers and reef fish, or stretch your legs after a day's paddle by exploring the side canyon oasis of Rancho Los Dolores, where a short hike takes you to a freshwater waterfall and the ruins of a Jesuit mission.

Below Rancho Dolores you're faced with a choice; either make the 5-mile crossing to **Isla San José** or stay on the mainland shore. Prudence may tell you to cling to mainland security, but the crossing rewards adventurers with one of the most fertile islands in the sea of Cortez. Deer, coyote, and, gasp, scorpions up to 6 inches long live here. Sandy lagoons pay out hearty jackpots of scallops and oysters. On your way back to the mainland, stop at 2-acre **Islote Pardito** just off San Jose's southwest end, home of a prosperous fishing village and colorful diving in the town marine preserve. Traveling under your own power will soon have you living by Baja time, in tune with the pace and rhythm of life in this harsh but stunning environment.

Fall and spring are the best times for this trip, allowing you to avoid the staggering heat of summer and the crippling winds of winter. **Baja Expeditions** runs 10-day trips five or six times a year along this stretch. They're at 2625 Garnet Ave., San Diego, CA 92109; tel. 800/843-6967. **Paddling South,** 4510 Silverado Trail, Calistoga, CA 94515, tel. 707/942-4550, also runs frequent trips in the Loreto area.

To rent a kayak for day use while visiting Loreto, drop by **Deportes Blazer** on Hidalgo in town, the "we have it all" sporting goods store.

## SURFING

Being located as it is on the Sea of Cortez, you're out of luck if you expect to find surf in Loreto. But if you have a car, it's worth the drive across the sierra to the Pacific coast. The main spot in this neck of the woods is Punta Pequeña, better know to surfers as **Scorpion Bay.**

But don't get hung up on racing for waves. It's a long drive over there, and the journey itself is beautiful. Stop off in **La Purísima.** Lots of blue-eyed children tell the history of 1960s and 1970s surfers who came here to escape the turmoil of the Vietnam era and left their mark on the gene pool.

It takes about 3 hours from Loreto to reach Punta Pequeña. First drive about 40 km (24 miles) north to tiny Rosarito, where the road to La Purísima turns off. It's rutted but makeable in a rental car. Once over the sierra and through La Purísima, you'll come to a fork where you can either bear left toward pavement and civilization or right onto an even worse road and good surf. Steer right. In 30 km (18 miles) you'll reach Scorpion Bay, where you'll find a tiny village and, most likely, a bunch of gringo surfers.

## WHALE WATCHING

Loreto is the nearest major airport and city to **Bahía de Magdalena,** the southernmost of the major gray whale calving lagoons on the Pacific coast of Baja. Currently, there are many groups that run expeditions here to see the whales, including **Baja Expeditions** (2625 Garnet Ave., San Diego, CA 92109; tel. 800/843-6967, or 5-38-28 in La Paz). You can also arrange trips yourself by simply driving over to the little towns of Puerto Lopez Mateos or Puerto San Carlos and hiring a panga to show you the whales. The trips arranged through Baja Expeditions and other stateside providers tend to be quite expensive, to the tune of more than a thousand dollars per person, but they provide for your every need. When arranging with local guides for a day trip, expect to pay anywhere from $30 to $45 per person and to tip for good service.

# Mulege ◆ What to Do & Where to Do It

Mulege is one of the garden spots of the peninsula. A large river flows out of the ground and flows for several miles through Mulege and into the sea. Huge date palms tap its generous waters and cast a shady coolness over an otherwise scorching part of the world. It's startling to drive through hundreds of miles of desert only to hear frogs chirping and watch bats devouring the unfortunately plentiful mosquitoes. It is also home to one of the most well-preserved and beautifully situated missions in the peninsula. Even if you're not into churches, it's worth driving or walking up to the mission just to take in the view.

Mulege has great diving, kayaking, and fishing. There are also several well-preserved Indian caves that can be reached by guided hikes into the mountains. There is little in the way of accommodations, but good beach camping is available just south of town in the Bahía de la Concepción.

## BOARDSAILING

Bahía de Concepción south of Mulege gets quite windy in the afternoons and has numerous coves for beginners to practice in. It has never developed the kind of cachet with the hardcore boardsailing crowd of places like Buenavista or La Ventana, but it's a worthy place to stop and rig up on your drive down.

## CAMPING & LODGING

The first time I camped in Mulege, I pulled into town in the evening and paid to sleep in a mosquito-infested RV park campground by the river. I couldn't figure out why there was no one else there. The next morning I drove south a few miles and discovered why: Bahía Concepción. This big bay south of Mulege is scalloped with powdery white beaches, has perfectly clear water, and is framed by plunging cliffs. It is a coastline you might invent in a dream.

Back then you could just pull out onto any of the many beaches and camp. Now, most of them have been developed into more formal camping arrangements and several have turned into motor home colonies, but it's still a stunning place.

The first beach camping is at **Playa Punta Arena,** 10 miles south of Mulege. The beach isn't visible from the road, but it, like all the beaches here, is nice. It's an RV spot, but the rough dirt road keeps it from being overrun. You can rent a palapa right on the sand for about $5 per night. Camping is $3 per night.

A few more miles into the bay will bring you to **Playa Santispac.** Once this was my favorite beach in the area, but it's become very built-up. There are a restaurant and a restaurant/bar here now, and many snowbirds pull their trailers onto the beach in the fall and stay here through spring. Much better for tent campers is **Playa Los Cocos,** 15 miles south of Mulege. The name means Palm Beach, and, indeed, there are some nice palms here. Though it's motor home accessible, it's also very tent friendly. Camping is $4 per night and there are pit toilets and garbage receptacles. **Playa El Coyote** is another nice beach for tent camping, 17 miles south of Mulege. While there are a few palapas, there was, at last notice, no big motor home scene here. Sites are $4 per night.

Hotel-wise, I'd recommend staying at the **Hotel El Moro** (tel. 5-0025) on Resend Robles, right behind the **Hotel La Misión,** a half block from the beach.

Rooms with private bath cost $30 to $40 per night.

## FISHING

All the hotels in town can arrange fishing trips to Punta Chivito, Isla San Marcos, or Punta Concepción, the outermost tip of Bahía de Concepción.

The best fishing in the area is for yellowtail, which run in the winter, and summer catches of dorado, tuna, and billfish like marlin and sailfish.

## HIKING

One of the big attractions to this region is the proliferation of large **cave paintings** in the Sierra de Guadalupe. UNESCO recently declared the cave paintings a World Heritage Site, and the locals take great pride in protecting them. Unlike many typical cave paintings, these are huge and complex murals. You are legally only allowed to visit the caves with a licensed guide.

The most popular series of caves is in **La Trinidad,** a remote rancho 29 km west of Mulege. You'll be driven there by your guide, and then the hiking begins. Count on hiking about 4 miles and getting wet. To reach the caves requires several river crossings in spots deep enough to swim. Rock walls fringe a tight canyon, and there is no way through except swimming. This river in **Cañon La Trinidad** is allegedly the source of the river that flows through Mulege, though it disappears underground for many miles in between.

Among the representations of the cave murals are large deer silhouettes, and a human figure called the "cardón man" because of his resemblance to a cardón cactus.

For about $35 per person, you can arrange for a guide in Mulege at any of the hotels or by asking around, or you can drive yourself out to Rancho La Trinidad and arrange for one there for about half the price. Keep in mind that the drive to the ranch is complicated and unsigned.

Another favorite cave art site is **San Borjitas.** You must first drive a bad four-wheel-drive road to Rancho Las Tinajas, where you'll hire a guide and, depending on your mood, either hike or ride mules into the caves.

## SCUBA DIVING & SNORKELING

Visibility right in Mulege is marred by the freshwater and the, ahem, effluvia that seems to flow into the sea from the numerous septic tanks in this area. But as you head south into Bahía de Concepción, there is excellent snorkeling at the numerous shallow coves and tiny offshore islands. Work the middle of the sandy coves looking for oysters and scallops. For bigger fish and colorful sea life, you'll have to swim out to deeper waters along the edges of each cove.

Boat diving in Mulege tends to head over to **Punta de Concepción** or north of town to **Punta Chivato** and the small offshore islands of Santa Inez and San Marcos. Numerous sites are perfect for both snorkeling and scuba.

**Mulege Divers** is one of the oldest and best-run dive operations in the state. They are located at no. 45 Madero, the main drag through town. Their rates are usually extremely affordable, and they have a great environmental consciousness, too.

# Guerrero Negro/ San Ignacio ◆ What to Do & Where to Do It

San Ignacio and Guerrero Negro couldn't appear more different on the surface. San Ignacio is a sleepy and beautiful old mission town in the middle of a palm oasis. Guerrero Negro is a wind-blasted strip town on a treeless plain. But they're both located next to some of the best whale watching in the world from January through March.

Guerrero Negro is home to two lagoons: Laguna Guerrero Negro and Laguna Ojo de Liebre (a.k.a. Scammon's Lagoon) that are the center of the **Parque Natural de la Ballena Gris** (Gray Whale Natural Park). It says something, and nothing complimentary, I might add, that the Mexican government thinks that an industrial salt facility is an appropriate use of a protected natural reserve, and has their eye on building another one at Laguna San Ignacio. Still, the best **whale-watching** experience in the world is to be had right here.

Local fishermen have conditioned the whales to accept their presence to such a degree that some individual whales approach the tourist-carrying pangas and stick their heads out of the water to be petted. It's an incredible experience. Several storefront travel agencies in Guerrero Negro will make arrangements for these half-day trips.

In San Ignacio, the laguna is more undeveloped than the scene in Guerrero Negro. You can arrange trips either in the town or by driving out to the fish camps surrounding the lagoon and arranging with fishermen there for a guided panga ride.

There is nice camping to be had along the river that flows through San Ignacio. Watch for the signs as you pull into town. For a hotel, the **Hotel La Posada** (tel. 1-1542) is the best, locally owned and operated, inexpensive, and centrally located near the town square. Rooms cost $15 to $25 per night. The **Hotel La Pinta** (tel. 800/336-5454 or 1-1530) chain has one of their branches here, on the main road into San Ignacio, and it's a nicely decorated and well-run place but costs about three times as much as La Posada.

# Index

## ◆ C ◆

**N**

◆  ◆

# FROMMER'S® COMPLETE TRAVEL GUIDES

Alaska
Amsterdam
Arizona
Atlanta
Australia
Austria
Bahamas
Barcelona, Madrid & Seville
Belgium, Holland &
  Luxembourg
Bermuda
Boston
Budapest & the Best of
  Hungary
California
Canada
Cancún, Cozumel &
  the Yucatán
Cape Cod, Nantucket &
  Martha's Vineyard
Caribbean
Caribbean Cruises & Ports
  of Call
Caribbean Ports of Call
Carolinas & Georgia
Chicago
China
Colorado
Costa Rica
Denver, Boulder &
  Colorado Springs
England
Europe
Florida

France
Germany
Greece
Greek Islands
Hawaii
Hong Kong
Honolulu, Waikiki & Oahu
Ireland
Israel
Italy
Jamaica & Barbados
Japan
Las Vegas
London
Los Angeles
Maryland & Delaware
Maui
Mexico
Miami & the Keys
Montana & Wyoming
Montréal & Québec City
Munich & the Bavarian Alps
Nashville & Memphis
Nepal
New England
New Mexico
New Orleans
New York City
Nova Scotia, New Brunswick
  & Prince Edward Island
Oregon
Paris
Philadelphia & the
  Amish Country

Portugal
Prague & the Best of the
  Czech Republic
Provence & the Riviera
Puerto Rico
Rome
San Antonio & Austin
San Diego
San Francisco
Santa Fe, Taos &
  Albuquerque
Scandinavia
Scotland
Seattle & Portland
Singapore & Malaysia
South Pacific
Spain
Switzerland
Thailand
Tokyo
Toronto
Tuscany & Umbria
USA
Utah
Vancouver & Victoria
Vermont, New Hampshire
  & Maine
Vienna & the Danube Valley
Virgin Islands
Virginia
Walt Disney World &
  Orlando
Washington, D.C.
Washington State

# FROMMER'S® DOLLAR-A-DAY GUIDES

Australia from $50 a Day
California from $60 a Day
Caribbean from $60 a Day
England from $60 a Day
Europe from $50 a Day
Florida from $60 a Day

Greece from $50 a Day
Hawaii from $60 a Day
Ireland from $50 a Day
Israel from $45 a Day
Italy from $50 a Day
London from $75 a Day

New York from $75 a Day
New Zealand from $50 a Day
Paris from $70 a Day
San Francisco from $60 a Day
Washington, D.C.,
  from $60 a Day

# FROMMER'S® PORTABLE GUIDES

Acapulco, Ixtapa &
  Zihuatanejo
Alaska Cruises & Ports of Call
Bahamas
California Wine Country
Charleston & Savannah
Chicago

Dublin
Las Vegas
London
Maine Coast
New Orleans
New York City
Paris

Puerto Vallarta, Manzanillo
  & Guadalajara
San Francisco
Sydney
Tampa & St. Petersburg
Venice
Washington, D.C.

## FROMMER'S® NATIONAL PARK GUIDES

Family Vacations in the
National Parks
Grand Canyon

National Parks of the
American West
Yellowstone & Grand Teton

Yosemite & Sequoia/
Kings Canyon
Zion & Bryce Canyon

## FROMMER'S® GREAT OUTDOOR GUIDES

New England
Northern California

Southern California & Baja
Pacific Northwest

## FROMMER'S® MEMORABLE WALKS

Chicago
London

New York
Paris

San Francisco
Washington D.C.

## FROMMER'S® IRREVERENT GUIDES

Amsterdam
Boston
Chicago

London
Manhattan

New Orleans
Paris

San Francisco
Walt Disney World
Washington, D.C.

## FROMMER'S® DRIVING TOURS

America
Britain
California

Florida
France
Germany

Ireland
Italy
New England

Scotland
Spain
Western Europe

## THE COMPLETE IDIOT'S TRAVEL GUIDES

Boston
Cruise Vacations
Planning Your Trip to Europe
Hawaii

Las Vegas
London
Mexico's Beach Resorts
New Orleans

New York City
San Francisco
Walt Disney World
Washington D.C.

## THE UNOFFICIAL GUIDES®

Branson, Missouri
California with Kids
Chicago
Cruises
Disney Companion

Florida with Kids
The Great Smoky &
Blue Ridge
Mountains

Las Vegas
Miami & the Keys
Mini-Mickey
New Orleans

New York City
San Francisco
Skiing in the West
Walt Disney World
Washington, D.C.

## SPECIAL-INTEREST TITLES

Born to Shop: Caribbean Ports of Call
Born to Shop: France
Born to Shop: Hong Kong
Born to Shop: Italy
Born to Shop: New York
Born to Shop: Paris
Frommer's Britain's Best Bike Rides
The Civil War Trust's Official Guide
to the Civil War Discovery Trail
Frommer's Caribbean Hideaways
Frommer's Europe's Greatest Driving Tours
Frommer's Food Lover's Companion to France
Frommer's Food Lover's Companion to Italy
Frommer's Gay & Lesbian Europe

Israel Past & Present
Monks' Guide to California
Monks' Guide to New York City
New York City with Kids
New York Times Weekends
Outside Magazine's Guide
to Family Vacations
Places Rated Almanac
Retirement Places Rated
Washington, D.C., with Kids
Wonderful Weekends from Boston
Wonderful Weekends from New York City
Wonderful Weekends from San Francisco
Wonderful Weekends from Los Angeles